Critical Thinking, Thoughtful Writing:
A Rhetoric with Readings

Critical Thinking, Thoughtful Writing:
A Rhetoric with Readings

John Chaffee, Ph.D.
Director, NY Center for Critical Thinking and Language Learning
LaGuardia College, City University of New York

Christine McMahon
Barbara Stout
English Department, Montgomery College

Houghton Mifflin Company   BOSTON   NEW YORK

For Jessie and Joshua

Senior Sponsoring Editor Suzanne Phelps Weir
Senior Associate Editor Janet Edmonds
Associate Project Editor Gabrielle Stone
Senior Production/Design Coordinator Jill Haber
Senior Manufacturing Coordinator Sally Culler
Senior Marketing Manager Nancy Lyman

Acknowledgments
Cover Designer: Linda Manly Wade
Cover Image: The Discs, 1911–1912 (oil on canvas) by Franz Kupka
(1871–1957). Musee National d'Art Moderne, Paris/Bridgeman Art Library.
Photo by Peter Willi.
Photo Researcher: Linda Sykes
Back Cover Photo: Jessie Chaffee

(Acknowledgments continue on page 533.)

Library of Congress Catalog Number: 98-72008
ISBN: 0-395-73766-4

456789-CS-02 01   00

Contents

CHAPTER 2

Thinking Critically, Writing Thoughtfully   21

Critical Thinking Focus: Thinking about thinking
Writing Focus: Reflecting on experience
Reading Theme: Experiences which affected beliefs
Writing Project: Recalling the impact of experience on a belief

CHAPTER 3

Thinking Creatively, Writing Creatively   54

Critical Thinking Focus: The qualities of a creative thinker
Writing Focus: Generating original ideas
Reading Theme: The creative thinking process
Writing Project: Imagining your life lived more creatively

CHAPTER 4

Thinking Critically About Writing—Revising Purposefully   90

Critical Thinking Focus: Decision making
Writing Focus: Making decisions about drafts
Reading Themes: People making decisions; writers thinking about revision
Writing Project: Analyzing a decision to be made

CHAPTER 5

Language and Thought — Writing Precisely   141

Critical Thinking Focus: Language as a system
Writing Focus: Using language to clarify thinking
Reading Theme: Essays about language
Writing Projects: Experience with language

PART TWO

Thinking and Writing to Show Relationships   205

CHAPTER 6

Exploring Relationships in Space and Time — Writing to Show Observations and Sequences   206

Critical Thinking Focus: Understanding perceptions

CHAPTER 7

Exploring Comparative Relationships — Writing About Perspectives   235

CHAPTER 8

Exploring Causal Relationships — Writing to Analyze Causes   284

Critical Thinking Focus: Causal reasoning

Writing Focus: Presenting causal reasoning

Reading Theme: Ecological relationships

Writing Project: Analyzing causal relationships of a recent event

CHAPTER 9

Forming Concepts — Writing to Classify and Define   321

Critical Thinking Focus: The conceptualizing process
Writing Focus: Defining and applying concepts
Reading Theme: Gender issues
Writing Project: Defining an important concept

PART THREE

Thinking and Writing to Explore Issues and Take Positions 369

CHAPTER 10

Believing and Knowing — Writing to Analyze 370

Critical Thinking Focus: Analyzing beliefs and their accuracy

Writing Focus: Evaluating evidence

Reading Theme: The media: Shaping our thinking

Writing Project: Analyzing influences on beliefs

CHAPTER 11

Solving Problems — Writing to Propose Solutions   430

Critical Thinking Focus: The problem-solving model

Writing Focus: Proposing solutions

Reading Theme: Solving a social problem

Writing Project: Applying the problem-solving model

CHAPTER 12

Constructing Arguments — Writing to Establish Agreement   479

Critical Thinking Focus: Using reasons, evidence, and logic
Writing Focus: Convincing an audience
Reading Theme: Arguments about important issues
Writing Project: Arguing a position on a significant issue

Preface

Critical Thinking, Thoughtful Writing: A Rhetoric with Readings presents an integrated approach to teaching the thinking, writing, and reading skills that first-year composition students need in order to successfully complete academic work. This book's goal is to help students develop complex thinking and writing abilities by having them complete writing assignments and critically evaluate challenging readings drawn from various disciplines and social debate. Thinking↔Writing Activities are carefully integrated with material throughout each chapter and culminate in a Writing Project at the end of each chapter. The Writing Projects combine the thinking and writing skills students have practiced and strengthened throughout the chapter. The Writing Projects also draw upon the components of the Thinking↔Writing Model introduced in Chapter 1 (page 8) and are reinforced throughout the book.

Writers and teachers of writing have long recognized intricate relationships between the extraordinary human processes of thought and language. Leo Tolstoy eloquently observed that *"The relations of word to thought, and the creation of new concepts is a complex, delicate and enigmatic process unfolding in our soul."* To date, this insight has not been clearly translated into a comprehensive approach for beginning college students to become thoughtful writers. Experts in the thinking process (philosophers and psychologists, for example) have not generally concentrated on the complex challenges of teaching writing. Experts in teaching writing have found integrating the critical thinking process into their pedagogy a sometimes problematic endeavor.

Critical Thinking, Thoughtful Writing introduces a comprehensive model of thinking and writing which integrates these processes. As students develop higher-order thinking abilities, they learn to articulate their ideas through writing. And as they develop their abilities in the writing process, they learn to think coherently, precisely, and creatively. This unique approach integrates development of thinking skills with writing skills so that they not only reinforce each other but also become inseparable.

Incorporating Critical Thinking in Composition Instruction

More than one writer has echoed Annie Dillard's observation, "I don't know what I think until I see myself write." *Critical Thinking, Thoughtful Writing* presents writing as a way of thinking and learning by developing critical thinking skills to help writers write clearly and forcefully. It also incorporates critical thinking as a way of teaching composition. An integrated and organic model of thinking, writing, and reading that prepares students for meaningful success in their academic courses, careers, and personal lives rests right at its core. Its approach reflects recent research into the thinking process, as well as contemporary practices in writing pedagogy, including the following areas:

- learning collaboratively
- writing and reading in the disciplines
- appreciating diversity, and
- conducting research

This book stimulates and guides students to think deeply and beyond superficialities, to refuse to be satisfied with the first idea they have, to look objectively at the pros and cons of issues, and to formulate their own informed conclusions. It helps students develop an interest in research and in delving into possibilities rather than into commonplace answers. It encourages students to be independent in their thinking and courageous in their convictions. And it shows them how to organize information, interpret different perspectives, solve challenging problems, analyze complex issues, and communicate their ideas clearly.

Using a Critical Thinking Framework to Teach Writing

Significant advantages to using a critical thinking framework to teach thoughtful writing and informed reading include the following:

- **Critical thinking provides an intellectual and thematic framework that helps writing teachers place structural and grammatical concerns in a meaningful context.** Because students are involved in and concerned about what they are writing, they are motivated to master the technical aspects of writing in order to articulate their thinking with clarity and precision. Critical thinking lends rigor and seriousness to students' writing. *Critical Thinking, Thoughtful Writing* challenges and guides students to think and write about important topics that build on their cognitive activities and critical explorations. This process enables students to improve both the *technical* aspects of their writing (coherence, organization, detail, use of grammatical conventions) as well as the *quality* of their writing (depth, insight, sophistication).

■ **A critical thinking framework permits students to understand the reciprocal relationship between the process of thinking and the process of writing.** Students are stimulated to explore their own composing processes, gradually mastering the forms of thought and critical thinking that are the hallmark of mature and thoughtful writing. Students are challenged to explore, analyze, and evaluate opinions.

■ **The emphasis of critical thinking on actively exploring ideas, listening to others, and carefully evaluating opinions and arguments provides a context for collaborative learning and writing activities.** Students learn to examine their own opinions analytically and relate these opinions to the world at large. They learn to assess alternative points of view in dialogue with others. This approach enables them to use writing as a means of self-discovery, and to learn from the responses of others. The result is a sense of community and mutual support that gives students confidence to learning openly and collaboratively.

■ **The critical thinking framework helps students appreciate that reading is a thinking activity rather than a series of decoding skills.** This understanding results in accelerated and enhanced reading development. Students are better able to understand and develop the interrelated thinking abilities which comprise the reading process. This includes problem-solving, forming and applying concepts, and relating ideas to larger conceptual frameworks.

Distinctive Features of *Thinking Critically, Writing Thoughtfully*

The four-part organization of every chapter integrates thinking, writing and reading. Each chapter focuses on a central critical thinking skill, which is explored through Thinking↔Writing Activities, and readings that embody the thought processes of the kind of writing students should develop. These demonstrate the key point introduced at the beginning of the book: "You can't write better than you think!"

■ **A Comprehensive Thinking↔Writing Model.** The Thinking↔Writing Model introduced in Chapter One (page 8) and reinforced throughout the book provides a clear graphic representation of the writing process and of the connections between critical thinking and thoughtful writing, as well as creative thinking and inventive writing.

- **Thematic Reading Clusters.** Readings in every chapter provide the basis for assignments that initiate students' writing. Engaging themes include creativity, decision making, language discovery, gender issues, ecological relationships, media influences, problem-solving, and arguments on controversial issues.

- **Writing Projects.** Each chapter culminates in a carefully structured Writing Project that builds on the skills developed in the Thinking↔Writing Activities in the chapter. The Writing Projects guide students to use the Thinking↔Writing Model to compose papers with special emphasis on chapter themes. The text moves methodically through each Project, guiding the students through stages toward a finished product.

- **Progression from the Personal to the Social.** The book moves logically from introducing creative and critical thinking to explaining how these tools can be used for the different modes of writing. It helps students understand thinking and writing as ways to show relationships, then moves into more complex modes of expository and argumentative writing. The logical progression evolves from the more personal and spontaneous thrust of creative writing, through attention to language issues, to traditional organizational patterns, and finally to problem-solving and argumentation. Students are encouraged to use external sources in their writing: researching, evaluating, integrating, and referencing. With its emphasis on the interplay of critical thinking and writing, the book provides a productive format for quickly pulling students out of their personal experiences and pushing them to think and write about more challenging issues and concepts. The practical strategies they learn will help students address writing assignments they will face in other academic classes as well as in the workplace.

- **Clear Definition of Critical Thinking.** Critical and creative thinking are often nebulous to many students, but this book introduces them in concrete ways. East chapter contains the following organization: a concept is introduced; a "real world" context for that concept is provided; and then the concept is related to its use in writing and critical thinking (for example, discussing a practical process for making decisions, then applying that process to making decisions about editing and revising drafts).

- **Substantive Treatment of Creative Thinking.** The book discusses creative as well as critical thinking, showing that creative thought can and should be an integral part of academic writing.

- **Emphasis on Collaboration.** The value of collaboration in thinking and writing is emphasized throughout.

- **Cross-disciplinary Approach.** Recognizing that first-year composition courses prepare students to write in all of their courses and after college, this book presents examples, selections, and assignments that apply to a variety of disciplines.

- **Broad Coverage.** In addition to coverage of expository composition themes, the book emphasizes the reasoning process throughout, and includes a chapter on argument. This inclusive coverage and flexible design makes the book suitable for a first or second semester course, as well as a two-semester sequence.

- **Emphasis on the "Whole" Student.** The book views learning to think, write, and read as integral dimensions of an individual's personal growth and transformation. It aims to help students grow. While learning how to think and write, students are encouraged to apply these critical and creative thinking and problem-solving skills to all facets of their lives.

The Authors

Critical Thinking, Thoughtful Writing is the result of collaboration of three authors. John Chaffee, a professor of Philosophy, has been a pioneer in the field of Critical Thinking and Critical Literacy for the last twenty years. His best-selling textbook, *Thinking Critically,* fifth edition, presents a comprehensive, language-based approach to learning to think critically that has helped define the field of Critical Thinking. He has linked Critical Thinking and Composition courses at his college, creating powerful learning communities that accelerate the development of students' thinking, writing, and reading abilities. Barbara Stout and Christine McMahon, both professors of English, have used *Thinking Critically* in their Composition courses for over seven years and have adapted John Chaffee's critical thinking approach to the teaching of writing. Their approaches to teaching writing and their active involvement in the composition field have contributed significantly to a text that is practical, effective, and adaptable to a variety of instructional contexts. This multidisciplinary synthesis has produced a text that provides students with a clear path to becoming literate thinkers, thoughtful writers, and informed readers.

Acknowledgments

John would like to thank Christine McMahon and Barbara Stout for the dedication and expertise they brought to this unique project of extending my work in critical thinking to the field of composition: I would also like to acknowledge my editors at Houghton Mifflin for their outstanding contributions to this book. Janet Edmonds displayed exceptional wisdom and tenacity in nurturing this book through every stage of its development, adamantly refusing to surrender her delightful sense of humor. Suzanne Phelps-Weir brought a creative vision to the book that enabled it to transcend conventional boundaries, and her personal warmth enriched everyone's collaboration on the project. Gabrielle Stone brought her customary high level of professionalism in coordinating the production of the book, as well as a graciousness that made work on it a pleasure. This book has benefited enormously from the keen understanding and marketing savvy of Nancy Lyman, with whom every encounter is a memorable experience. A special acknowledgment goes to Joyce Neff at Old Dominion University for her insightful review of the manuscript and her superb work in writing the Instructor's Resource Guide. I am particularly indebted to the members of the English Department at LaGuardia College for their creative collaboration in linking the Writing and Critical Thinking programs over the last 20 years, which was initially supported with funding from The National Endowment for the Humanities. My children, Jessie and Joshua, and my wife, Heide Lange, have provided ongoing love, support and guidance that have enhanced this book and brought purpose and meaning to my life.

Chris gratefully acknowledges the W. K. Kellogg Foundation whose Beacon College Project supported the Critical Literacy Institute at Oakton College: I acknowledge the faculty at Oakton who obtained the grant and invited Montgomery College to be an Associate College. I came to know John Chaffee's work through them. I am indebted to the administrators at Montgomery College who chose me as Project Coordinator and provided generous resources for Critical Literacy at our three campuses. The students I have taught, some of whose work appears in this book, helped me learn how to teach and motivated me to share what I know. I am in their debt. John and Barbara were wonderful co-authors. Carolyn and Jim Terry solved our computer-related difficulties. My husband, Michael, helped in every way. Finally, I thank my grown-up children, Gregory, Beth, and Chris, for their love and support.

Barbara is very grateful to countless colleagues from many colleges and universities whose scholarship in composition, rhetoric, and writing-across-the-curriculum is the foundation for informed teaching, programs, and textbooks: I am grateful to the Conference on College Composition and Communication, the Two-Year College English Association, and the National Writing Project for providing opportunities for sharing information and ideas. My thanks to the faculty and administrators in Montgomery College's Critical Literacy Project, to the capable staff in the English Department and the Computer Writing Room at the Rockville Campus, to English Department faculty colleagues, and to my students from whom I always learn more than I can teach. Of course, my most heartfelt thanks are to my family: David, Richard, Rebecca, Sally, Lyn, Patrick, Kathleen, and Florence.

We would also like to thank our reviewers, who offered wise insights and suggestions about the manuscript at various stages of development.

Patricia Bizzel	College of the Holy Cross
Paul Bodmer	Bismarck State College
Judith A. Hinman	College of the Redwoods
Frederick T. Janzow	Southeast Missouri State
Shirley Wilson Logan	University of Maryland
Joyce Neff	Old Dominion University
Elizabeth A. Nist	Anoka-Ramsey Community College
Isaiah Smithson	Southern Illinois University
Byron Stay	Mount St. Mary's College
Kay Stokes	Hanover College
Michael Thomas	College of the Redwoods
Elizabeth Wahlquist	Brigham Young University

Understanding the Tools of Thinking and Writing

The chances are that if you stop to think about it, you will notice several ways that thinking and writing are connected. How can you write about a topic unless you have spent time thinking about it? How much better do you understand a topic after you have written about it? Part One of this book sharpens your awareness of the interactive relationships between thinking and writing. It also introduces you to ways of becoming a critical thinker and a thoughtful writer. A **Writing Project** at the end of each chapter asks you to draw from your own experiences and observations as you write about a topic that helps you explore the relationships between thinking and writing.

CHAPTER 1

Thinking Through Writing

Thinking and Writing in College

Thinking and writing exist on many levels, ranging from the simple and basic to the complex and insightful. In the same way that everybody "thinks," most people are able to "write," in that they can put words on paper. In your previous education, "good writing" might have meant mastering the basics of organization, grammar, and spelling. While these are essential, as a college writer you are expected to do more: to write with depth, insight, and analytical understanding. In order to achieve this level of sophistication in writing, you need to develop comparably advanced thinking abilities. (You can't, after all, write better than you think!)

The intimate, interactive relationships among language, thinking, and writing have been remarked on by many professional writers; for example:

The process of transforming all direct experience into imagery or into language has so completely taken possession of the human mind that it is not only a special talent but a dominant, organic need.   SUSANNE K. LANGER

I write to understand as much as to be understood.   ELIE WIESEL

How do I know what I think until I see what I say.   E. M. FORSTER

Words are always with other words, and the other words are almost always in a story of some sort.   LESLIE MARMON SILKO

The mere process of writing is one of the most powerful tools we have for clarifying our own thinking.   JAMES VAN ALLEN

This book is designed to improve your writing abilities as you develop your critical thinking abilities. For example, instead of simply telling you how to write a paper using a problem-solving format, this book is designed to teach you to *think* like a problem solver and then to write like one. Again, rather than providing you with guidelines on how to write an analytical or argumentative essay, the book will help you to *think* through the processes of analyzing complex issues and constructing compelling arguments, and then to *express* your understanding in effective writing.

In order to improve your writing abilities, you also need to write on a regular basis, integrating writing into your life as a vital and natural element. Therefore, this book offers you **Thinking↔Writing Activities.** These can be done in various ways: out of class or in, individually or in pairs or groups, and in whatever format your instructor specifies. He or she might ask you to record your responses in a special journal to be reviewed periodically, or on separate sheets of paper to be handed in. Your writing may also be shared with classmates, or used as a basis for discussion.

Thinking and writing are active processes that all of us learn by engaging in them. By participating in the **Thinking↔Writing Activities,** applying ideas in this book to your own experiences, and completing the **Writing Projects,** you will be sharpening your thinking and writing abilities, and by sharing your ideas with other members of the class, you will expand your own thinking and theirs. Each student has a wealth of experiences and insights to offer the class community.

THINKING ↔ WRITING ACTIVITY 1.1

Recalling a Learning Experience

Recall a memorable learning experience that you have had, either in school or outside. Describe that experience and explain why it had a lasting impact on you. Discuss how the experience contributed to your development as a thinker and writer.

Becoming an effective writer enables you to represent the rich fabric of your experience with clarity and precision. As you may have learned from your writing experiences thus far, the very process of using language serves to generate ideas. As a vehicle for creating and communicating your ideas, writing can be thought of as a catalyst stimulating your personal and intellectual development. Since the writing process also enlarges your understanding of the world, becoming an effective writer is at the heart of your college education.

Reading, Writing, and Thinking

In many ways college is a whole new world. Not only are you expected to do more work in your courses, you also are expected to work at a higher level: to *write more analytically*, to *think more conceptually*, and to *read more critically* than ever before.

Reading, writing, and thinking are, of course, closely connected. Through reading, literate human beings get information to use or to react to in their writing. On the conventional paper pages of books, magazines, and newspapers, on the computer screens of e-mail or the Internet, we read other people's thoughts, reflect on those thoughts ourselves, and deal with them in various ways when we write. Yet in addition to information-gathering, there are at least three other reading/writing/thinking interactions important to understand.

One is critical reading of others' writing. Chapters 2, 10, and 12 will improve your ability to evaluate the ideas that you read about and use them more precisely in your writing. Another is analytical reading. Most people, consciously and unconsciously, emulate as writers what they take in as readers; so one goal of this book is to help you analyze how other writers have put their pieces together. Another goal is to lead you to a third reading/writing/thinking interaction: a more critical, more analytical reading of your own writing, so that you can better revise your drafts into effective papers.

Becoming a Thoughtful Writer

What exactly is "thinking"? Thinking is the cognitive process you use every waking moment to make sense of your world as you work towards your goals, make informed decisions, analyze complex issues, and solve problems. By understanding (and practicing) these thinking abilities, you will be learning to think more effectively. However, in order to become a sophisticated thinker, you need to become an accomplished writer. Writing and thought are intimately related. Writing, with its power to represent our thoughts, feelings, and experiences symbolically, is the most important tool our thinking process has. Working together, thinking and writing enable us to create and communicate meaning, and both processes exhibit the following qualities:

- Thinking and writing are active processes.   Whether you are trying to reach a goal, solve a problem, analyze an issue, or make a decision, you are actively using your thinking and writing abilities to figure something out.

- Thinking and writing are directed toward a purpose.   When you think and write, it is usually for a purpose—to communicate, clarify your understanding, express an idea, or act intelligently.

- Thinking and writing can become organized processes.   When you think and write effectively, these processes usually exhibit an order or organization.

We can put together these conclusions about thinking and writing to form working definitions of the terms.

> **Thinking:**   an active, purposeful cognitive process that we use to make sense of our world.

> **Writing:**   an active, purposeful process that uses a system of
> written symbols for thinking and communicating.

Thinking and writing are processes that develop with use over a lifetime. You can improve your thinking and writing by following these three steps:

- **Becoming aware** of your thinking and writing processes. Have you often taken thinking and writing for granted and paid little attention to them? Developing these abilities means that you really have to "think about" the way you think and write.

- **Carefully examining** your thinking and writing processes (and the thinking and writing of others). By analyzing and understanding these complex processes, you can learn to handle them more effectively.

- **Practicing** your thinking and writing abilities. To improve your thinking, you have to explore and make sense of thinking situations; to improve your writing, you have to write thoughtfully on an ongoing basis. Although it is important to learn how other people think and use language, there is no substitute for engaging in these activities yourself.

The ability to "think about your thinking" by carefully examining the way that you make sense of the world is one of the most satisfying aspects of being a mature, educated human being. We will refer to this ability to think carefully about our thinking as the ability to **think critically**. Using our definition of *thinking* as a starting point, we can define *thinking critically* as follows.

> **Thinking Critically:**   the organized cognitive process we use to
> carefully examine our thinking and the thinking of others, in
> order to clarify and improve our understanding.

Analogously, *writing thoughtfully* involves developing insight into our writing processes so that we can express our ideas effectively.

> **Writing Thoughtfully:**   thinking critically as we move through
> the process of writing.

People are able to think critically and write thoughtfully because of their natural human ability to *reflect*—to think back on what they are thinking, doing, or feeling. By carefully reflecting on your thinking, you are able to see how that thinking operates, so you learn to think more effectively. In the same way, reflecting on your language use, and particularly on the way you write, enables you to improve and refine your writing abilities. In the following chapters, you will be systematically exploring many dimensions of how the human mind works.

Thinking and Writing Creatively

Carefully examining our thinking and writing processes assumes that they have been generating ideas worth examining. Our ability to *think creatively* makes producing such ideas possible. When we think creatively, we discover ideas—and connections among ideas—that are illuminating, useful, often exciting, sometimes original, and usually worthy of elaboration. We can define thinking creatively in this way:

Thinking Creatively: discovering and developing ideas that are unusual and worthy of further elaboration.

Thinking creatively is integrally tied in with thinking critically and writing thoughtfully. In other words, these three dimensions of thinking and language activities are tightly interwoven. Creative thinking and critical thinking work together to bring about effective thinking, which enables us to produce thoughtful writing, which in turn gives form to our ideas and communicates these ideas to others.

The Thinking↔Writing Model

The paradox of acquiring any complex ability is that in the best of all possible worlds, you would learn all the component parts of the activity at the same time. For example, learning to drive a car requires you to master a variety of component skills that operate simultaneously: watching the road ahead, steering, applying the appropriate pressure on the gas pedal, braking, keeping a proper distance from other vehicles, watching for traffic signs and traffic lights, keeping an eye open for pedestrians, and so on. Yet a book on driving, or a video, focuses on one skill at a time, because that is how information is presented most easily. Somehow you have to make the leap from learning all of the skills separately in a linear, step-by-step fashion, to using them all at the same time, in complex relationships with one another. This is very difficult!

One of the authors of this book remembers his first, bewildering, driving lesson with his mother and father: "As I headed directly for a brick wall in the supermarket parking lot, my mother yelled 'Turn right!' while my father screamed 'Turn left!' In my frenzied brain, these contradictory commands canceled each other out, so I continued on my course—with disastrous results."

Learning the complex skills of thinking critically and writing thoughtfully poses a similar dilemma. While it is essential to learn each of the component parts of these processes, what distinguishes critical thinkers and thoughtful writers is that they can use all of these individual skills at the same time.

Our approach to solving this problem will be to introduce a visual **Thinking↔Writing Model** that presents the important parts of these processes. As you work your way through the various chapters and activities in the book, you will become more familiar with the different dimensions of the Thinking↔Writing process as they function in the model we show and as they function for you.

Of course, you already know how to think and write fairly proficiently; otherwise, you wouldn't be in college. This book offers you opportunities to build on the strengths you have and to grow as a critical thinker and thoughtful writer. **Thinking↔Writing Activity 1.2** asks you to reflect on your own Thinking↔Writing process as a starting point.

THINKING↔WRITING ACTIVITY 1.2

Analyzing a Writing Experience

Describe in detail a writing experience you found particularly satisfying: for example, a paper you wrote for school, a market analysis for the company you work for, or a letter that expressed important thoughts and feelings. After completing your description, answer the following questions in your journal or notebook.

- What was your goal or purpose in writing?
- What was the reaction of the people who read it—your audience?
- How did you think up the key ideas you included?
- How did you organize your ideas?
- Did you use other sources (such as readings) to provide support and context for your writing?
- In what ways did you revise your writing?
- How did you feel after completing your writing?

Your analysis of a previous writing experience in this Thinking↔Writing Activity should underscore the fact that you already use many of the abilities that are integral to the Thinking↔Writing process.

Dynamic Relationships

Examine carefully the **Thinking↔Writing Model** on page 8. This model shows the many interactive relationships among its components. The model,

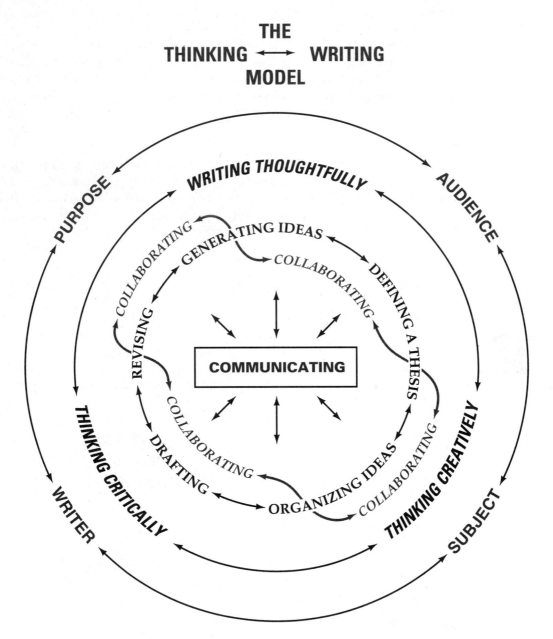

The Thinking↔Writing Model

of course, is only an attempt to make these concepts visible; it would be impossible to draw enough arrows through three dimensions to show how all the components in all the circles connect at various times. Also, people have different writing processes, so they may experience these relationships in different ways and at different times.

Writing occurs in a **context,** a situation within which the act of writing takes place. Countless contextual factors affect a piece of writing: Is the writing done because it has been assigned? Or is it done because the writer wants to do it? How effective does it need to be, and why? Is it done with a pencil or a Braillewriter or a computer? Is it composed in a native language, or a second or third language? Is the writer working under time pressure? Still, whatever else contributes to the context, most writing situations are shaped by consideration of **purpose, audience, subject,** and **writer**. These terms appear in the outermost circle of the model because they provide an immediate context for any act of writing.

The next circle indicates the reciprocal relationships among

- Writing Thoughtfully,
- Thinking Creatively, and
- Thinking Critically.

When you first decide to write something, you *think creatively* to come up with some initial ideas. Simultaneously (or *almost* simultaneously), these beginning ideas find form in language, expressed in writing. Yet the process of *writing thoughtfully* elaborates and shapes the ideas that you are trying to express, especially if you are to bring your *critical thinking* abilities to bear on this evolving process.

This extraordinarily complex process typically takes place in a very natural fashion, in much less time than it takes to describe it. It's like trying to describe a new dance step or a technique in sports; verbal descriptions seem clumsy and unnecessarily complicated, compared with simply helping someone perform the action. Although organized and specific descriptions of a complex activity are important, ultimately the most productive way to learn is to engage in the activity and then have someone coach you in order to refine your performance. It was Ben Franklin who said, *"Tell me, I will forget; teach me, I will remember; involve me, I will learn,"* and the Greek dramatist Sophocles who observed, *"Knowledge must come through action."*

The next circle shows the recursive—the natural tendency to move back and forth among activities—relationships among the activities in which people engage when they write:

- Generating ideas
- Defining a thesis
- Organizing ideas
- Drafting
- Revising

Since collaborating often occurs in all these activities, the line representing collaboration weaves in and out among them in the model.

At the very center of the model is **"communicating,"** the process by which we share our thoughts, feelings, and experiences. Communication creates miraculous moments when our minds touch and engage other minds, and such moments occur throughout the activities in the **Thinking↔Writing Model.**

The model pertains most fully to writing done with enough time for revision. Sometimes you have to write quickly, with little or no time to rethink and rewrite. College examinations often put you in this writing situation. Then the model has to function in a fast-forward mode. *Purpose, subject,* and *audience* are usually very clear (pass the test; discuss the subject well; show your instructor what you know.) *Generating ideas, staying with the focus defined by the question,* and *organizing ideas* are the components most useful to writing that must be quickly done. If you can understand, practice, and improve these abilities in contexts where you have time to draft and revise, you should be able to cope better with writing that must be done quickly.

The model will be explored in the chapters ahead, but the next few pages will introduce you to its components.

The Thinking↔Writing Model: Outer Circle
Purpose

Every act of writing has a purpose. When you are drafting, you are trying to discover what you want to say, what you already know about the topic, and what you have to find out. When you complete a paper for a college course, you hope to show your professor that you can make significant statements about concepts relevant to the class. In a business setting, your aim is to transmit information or requests in a memo or a report; in your social life, you want to communicate with friends through letters or e-mail; in your private life, you write in your journal so that you can recall your activities and feelings. A crucial part of becoming an accomplished writer is maintaining a clear idea of the specific goals of whatever piece you are working on, along with an understanding of the audience for whom you are writing.

Audience

Thoughtful writing is shaped by consideration of its audience, the intended reader or readers. Although there are some instances when you write only for yourself (a diary entry, for example), you probably intend most of your writing to be read by someone else: the person receiving your letter, the coworkers reading your memo, the friend enjoying your poem, the instructor grading your paper. The more you think about your audience, the more concerned you are about making yourself clear, the better your writing will become. The real skill lies in writing so clearly and coherently that your audience will receive exactly the same message that you intend to send.

Effective writers are able to put themselves in their readers' place and view their own writing through of their readers' eyes. This perspective-taking helps them craft their writing so that it will best communicate the ideas and emotions they are seeking to convey. In other words, they think about how much background information their audience will need, or won't need, to understand the intended message. Anticipating possible questions that may come into the audience's minds, they try to answer the questions at appropriate places. Understanding that the audience may have strong feelings about the topic, they take those feelings into consideration when they write.

Effective writers *organize* their expository writing so that the audience can follow it easily. They state their main point, their thesis, in a clear *thesis statement* so that the audience will know what the focus is. They use *examples* so that the audience can "see" what they mean, *transitions* to help the audience make connections among ideas, and standard *grammar, punctuation,* and *spelling* so that the audience will not become distracted and confused. *Errors* cause an audience to stop and reread or, worse yet, they require the audience to guess what the writer means. Errors can create a negative image of you as a writer.

Subject

Obviously, writing has to be about someone or something—a subject. Sometimes the subject originates in your own experience, but often it comes from ideas and information provided by others. Much of college writing involves responding to ideas presented in textbooks, class lectures, or other sources. Your writing task is usually to demonstrate your *understanding* of the ideas presented, and also to *apply, analyze, synthesize,* or *evaluate* the ideas being expressed. The quality of your writing depends on the quality of your thinking as you process ideas and present them in order to communicate your own *informed* perspective on the subject.

Writer

Of course, any writing situation calls for a writer, and the characteristics of the writer affect what is written and how it is produced. Experienced writers usually approach writing with more abilities and confidence than the inexperienced. Someone with considerable knowledge sees a subject differently from someone exploring it for the first time. A writer's identity as a woman or a man or a member of an ethnic or other social group often influences approaches and attitudes. The relationship of the writer to the language or dialect being used makes a difference; whether the writer is tired or energetic, happy or sad, and so forth, makes a difference too.

This book emphasizes the importance of understanding yourself as a writer. You should be aware of what knowledge—and what biases—you bring to the subject, the audience, and the purpose of an assignment. All writers do have at least one thing in common: they want to succeed in their writing tasks by discussing their subjects appropriately, reaching their audiences, and fulfilling their purposes.

The Thinking↔Writing Model: Second Circle
Writing Thoughtfully, Thinking Creatively, Thinking Critically

These three processes work in an integrated way to create meaning and communicate understanding. Effective writers not only use each of these processes, but are also able to integrate them. For example, it is impossible to write thoughtfully without creating ideas that reflect your vision of the world, or without using your critical thinking abilities to evaluate the accuracy and intelligibility of what you are writing about. Unfortunately, these essential abilities are not always taught explicitly. Too often, writing is emphasized as a way of putting words together in conventional forms, not as a dynamic means of personal expression that liberates us to express our creative perspectives—tempered by critical evaluation.

The Thinking↔Writing Model: Third Circle
Activities of People's Writing Processes

Despite the many different writing forms and contexts, the basic elements of the writing process remain relatively constant:

- Generating ideas
- Defining a focus (main idea or "thesis")
- Drafting
- Organizing ideas into various thinking patterns
- Revising, editing, and proofreading
- Collaborating, which can weave through all these activities

The arrows and circular format on the model are designed to emphasize the *recursive* nature of this process. For most writers, these activities rarely take place in a neat, orderly sequence. Instead, writers move in different ways from generating ideas to drafting to more generating to organizing to revising to generating to editing—around and around—as they develop ideas and clarify them.

You have probably discovered that the process of writing does not merely express your thinking; it also *stimulates* your thoughts, bringing to the surface new ideas and ways to explore them. So although you may begin a writing project by *generating* some ideas, you may find yourself returning to generating ideas later on, as you work to *organize* and *draft* your thoughts, developing new or refined concepts to write about. And as you gain more experience with collaboration, you may find yourself turning to others more frequently to benefit from their ideas and perspectives. Writers always need readers.

Generating Ideas

Most writing efforts begin with identifying something to write about. Since ideas are not created in isolation but are almost always related to a particular subject, you expand ideas by exploring that subject. Some writing projects have very specific requirements; others may be more open-ended. In most cases, however, you will be expected to come up with your own ideas. Even when you are responding to an assigned topic or a reading selection, you are typically expected to offer an original insight or viewpoint. At this stage of *generating ideas*, a number of strategies are useful, such as brainstorming, creating mind maps, freewriting, and asking key questions to stimulate your creative thinking. You should return to these pages as you work on the **Writing Projects** at the end of each of the other chapters in this book.

Some Strategies for Generating Ideas

Brainstorming is an activity in which, working individually or with a group of people, you write down all the ideas the group can think of related to a given theme. The goal is to produce as many ideas as possible in a specified period of time. While you are engaged in this idea-generating process, it is important to relax, let your mind run free, build on the ideas of others, and refrain from censoring or evaluating any ideas produced, no matter how marginal they seem at first. Brainstorming stimulates your creative juices, and you will be surprised at how many ideas you are able to come up with. And if you work with other people, you will be exposed to fresh perspectives and the synergy of people working together as a team.

    Mind maps are visual presentations of the various ways ideas can be related to one another. For example, the **Thinking↔Writing Model** is a mind map. Mind maps are also a powerful approach for writing, helping you generate ideas and begin organizing them into various relationships. They are well suited to the writing process for a number of reasons. *First*, the organization grows naturally, reflecting the way your mind naturally makes associations and arranges information. *Second*, the organization can easily be revised on the basis of new information and your developing understanding of how this information should be organized. *Third*, you can express a range

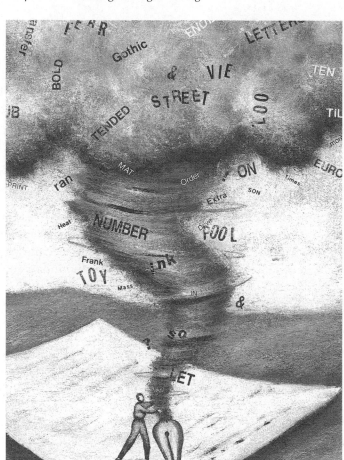

Generating Ideas: A number of strategies like brainstorming, mind maps, and freewriting can be used to generate ideas for writing assignments.

of relationships among the various ideas. Also, instead of being identified once and then forgotten, each idea remains an active part of the overall pattern, suggesting new possible relationships. *Fourth,* you do not have to decide initially on a beginning, subpoints, and so on; you can do this after your pattern is complete, so you save time and avoid frustration.

Freewriting is a sort of written brainstorming in which you write with a minimum of conscious reflection. But rather than simply listing ideas, freewriters usually write in sentences. The goal is to *let* your ideas flow freely, without inhibition, giving your mind the opportunity to develop creative ideas in unique combinations. As with brainstorming, freewriting generally works best in a limited time frame, and you should be unconcerned about spelling, grammar, and evaluation of the ideas you are expressing. Freewriting is an excellent way to "jump-start" your thinking process and prepare you for more thoughtful composing. It also helps you realize what information you already have on a subject, so that you can decide whether to do more research.

Questions that explore a topic provide another strategy for generating ideas. In fact, the ability to ask appropriate and penetrating questions is one of the most powerful thinking/language tools we possess. Asking questions enables us to go beyond the obvious, to think and write in ways that are in-depth, complex, and articulate. Questions come in many different forms and are used for many different purposes. For instance, questions can be classified in terms of the ways people organize and interpret information, and we can identify six such categories of questions:

1. Fact
2. Interpretation
3. Analysis
4. Synthesis
5. Evaluation
6. Application

Thoughtful writers are able to ask appropriate questions from all of these categories in a very natural and flexible way. Listed below is a summary of the six categories of questions, along with sample forms of questions from each category.

1. **Questions of Fact**   Questions of fact seek to determine the basic information of a situation: who, what, when, where, how. These questions seek information that is relatively straightforward and objective:
   Who, what, when, where, how ——————————————— ?
   Describe ————————————————————— .

2. **Questions of Interpretation**   Questions of interpretation seek to select and organize facts and ideas, discovering the relationships between them. Examples of such relationships include the following:
   Chronological relationships, relating things in time sequence
   Process relationships, relating aspects of growth, development, or change
   Comparison/contrast relationships, relating things in terms of their similar or different features
   Causal relationships, relating events in terms of the way some of them are responsible for bringing about others
   These questions can help you discover relationships:
   Retell ———————————————————— in your own words.
   What is the *main idea* of ————————————————— ?
   What is the *time sequence* relating the following events: —————— ?
   What are the steps in the *process of growth* or *development* in ———— ?
   How would you *compare* and *contrast* the features of ——————
   and ————————— ?
   What was/were the *cause(s)* of ————————— ? What was/were the *effect(s)* of ————————— ?

3. **Questions of Analysis**   Questions of analysis seek to separate an entire process or situation into its component parts and understand the relation

of these parts to the whole. These questions attempt to classify various elements, outline component structures, articulate various possibilities, and clarify the reasoning being presented:

What are the *parts* or *features* of _____ ?

Classify _____ according to _____ .

Outline/diagram/web _____ .

What *evidence* can you present to support _____ ?

What are the *possible alternatives* for _____ ?

Explain the *reasons why* you think _____ .

4. **Questions of Synthesis**   Questions of synthesis have as their goal combining ideas to form a new whole or come to a conclusion, making inferences about future events, creating solutions, and designing plans of action:

   What would you *predict/infer* from _____ ?

   What ideas can you *add to* _____ ?

   How would you *create/design* a new _____ ?

   What might happen if you *combined* _____ with _____ ?

   What *solutions/decisions* would you suggest for _____ ?

5. **Questions of Evaluation**   The aim of evaluation questions is to help you make informed judgments and decisions by determining the relative value, truth, or reliability of things. The process of evaluation involves identifying the criteria or standards you are using and then determining to what extent the things being evaluated meet those standards.

   How would you *evaluate* _____ and what *standards* would you use?

   Do you *agree with* _____ ? *Why* or *why not?*

   How would you *decide* about _____ ?

   What *criteria* would you use to *assess* _____ ?

6. **Questions of Application**   The purpose of application questions is to help you take the knowledge or concepts you have gained in one situation and apply them to other situations:

   How is _____ *an example* of _____ ?

   How would you *apply* this rule/principle to _____ ?

THINKING↔WRITING ACTIVITY 1.3

Generating Ideas

To practice the strategies just presented, spend five minutes applying each of them (choose one set of questions) to a specific subject that you are going to write about for this class, for any other class, for your job, or for some organization in which you participate. (If you don't have an assignment, think of a subject that you would like to write about.) Record the ideas you generate. Which technique did you find most effective? Why?

Defining a Focus

After generating a number of possible ideas to write about, academic writers need to define a focus. Academic writing is *expected* to have a focus; classmates, professors, and others interested in your subject expect more than a list of facts. Once selected, your main idea—known as a **thesis**—will organize and direct your thinking. Your thesis will also guide your exploration of the subject and suggest new ideas. Of course, a variety of main ideas can develop out of any particular situation, and your initial working thesis will probably need redefining as you draft your paper.

Sometimes you will need to do some drafting and organizing before you are ready to define your focus. And sometimes you will need to refocus your thesis as you do further drafting. Making decisions about a thesis is highly important.

Organizing Ideas

Once you have a tentative thesis, you can start to plan the organization of your paper. To begin, ask yourself, "What are my main points and how should they be presented to my audience?" You can use a variety of thinking patterns as you organize your writing, such as reporting chronologically, comparing and contrasting, or dividing and classifying. Your choice of thinking pattern will depend on the subject you are exploring, your purpose, and your audience.

It usually helps to have a tentative organization to guide your drafting, but often your organization changes as you draft and revise. This is a natural and productive part of most people's writing processes.

Drafting

Most people have drafting routines of some sort. Some writers must use a pencil; others, a pen; many need to keyboard. Some people need silence; others want background music. Many writers need solitude and comfort in order to draft productively. Effective writers know what they need; they understand their own writing processes and what situation they want as they work.

You need to think about what works for you. If you have not done so previously, you should analyze your drafting practices so that you can accommodate your needs and improve your productivity. Often you will find it useful to draft in sections, according to your plan. Sometimes each section works well as a separate file in your word processor or as an identified group of legal-pad pages.

Always, of course, you need to be aware of *what* you are drafting: a summary, a news story, an essay? Much of your academic writing will be in the form of essays in which you are expected to take a position, analyze a concept, or interpret a subject. The structure normally used to organize ideas in an essay typically reflects the basic questions raised when discussing ideas with others. As you draft, keep in mind the questions posed by Mina Shaughnessey in her book *Errors and Expectations:*

> *What is your point?* (stating the main idea)
>
> *I don't quite get your meaning.* (explaining the main idea)
>
> *Prove it to me.* (providing examples, evidence, and arguments to support the main idea)
>
> *So what?* (drawing a conclusion)

Revising

Because thinking and writing are interactive processes, you are continually revising your thinking and writing as you work on almost any paper. An early draft is usually just a starting point. Some writers need to produce multiple drafts with—they hope—increasing levels of effectiveness; some writers can get things on paper in relatively good shape quickly. However you work, though, once you have expressed your thinking in language, you must be able to go back and "re-see" (the origin of the word *revise*) your drafts as clearly as possible.

Most writers have a hard time looking objectively at their own writing. They know what they mean; they sometimes like certain words or sentences or clever ideas and don't want to change them. But effective writers have acquired the ability to be critical readers of their own work and to face up to the need for making major changes in their drafts.

One way to approach revising is to allow time for drafts to sit; you get away from them so that you can see them with fresh eyes. Another way is to have other readers respond to drafts; be prepared to heed their advice when appropriate.

Revising begins with a rereading of the whole draft and with attention to big questions about it. Does it fulfill its purpose, deal with its subject, address its audience? Does the thesis need to be reformulated? Are ideas supported with sound evidence and explained clearly?

Now might be a good time to create an outline or map of the draft, to identify the main ideas and express their relationships. This, in turn, may suggest ways to clarify your thinking by rearranging different parts, developing certain points further, or deleting whatever is repetitious or irrelevant to the main ideas of the paper. These activities are at the heart of revision. They often bring about a lot of rewriting, maybe a complete redoing of the draft. Fortunately, word processors make revision easier.

Then you need to look at smaller components: paragraph division, topic sentences, sentence variety, connections and transitions. Some writers call this *editing.* Then you need to check spelling and punctuation. Some writers call this *proofreading*. And sometimes while you are editing or proofreading, you will see content and organization problems that require some more revision!

Collaborating

When you work with other people in the writing process, you participate in collaboration. Collaborating with others can occur at every stage of the writing process. People can help one another generate ideas, identify a main idea to pursue, suggest possible approaches and ways of organizing. Some entire pieces of writing, especially in business, are produced collaboratively by a team of writers.

We often appreciate new perspectives when others review drafts of our writing. This is the moment when writers get a sense of how effective their efforts at communication are. No matter how clearly you try to keep your audience in mind as you write, you may not succeed at first. There is no substitute for having your audience (or people like your intended audience) inform you of what you have and have not been able to communicate. With their suggestions, you can improve and refine your writing so that it will better convey what you intended. As a critical thinker and informed writer, you learn to work with others in developing your thinking and writing, welcoming their advice when you are the sole author and contributing well when you are part of a writing team.

The Center

The word *communicating* comes from the Latin word *communicare,* which means "to share, to impart, to make common." As members of a social species, we need to share thoughts and feelings with other human beings. Also, we often need to communicate more clearly with ourselves. Every component in the **Thinking↔Writing Model** helps us reach our external and internal audiences.

As technologies allow very rapid communication throughout the world, **critical thinking** and **thoughtful writing** are ever more vital to the survival and progress of humanity. So, of course, *communicating* is the center.

Thinking and Writing as a Way of Living

Becoming a critical thinker and thoughtful writer does not simply involve mastering certain skills; it affects the entire way that you view the world and live your life. Your development as a critical thinker and thoughtful writer is revealed in many aspects of your life: for example, how you make decisions, how you relate to others, and how you deal with controversial issues. There is no recipe or bag of tricks for becoming a thoughtful writer. Like other achievements, it requires patience and practice. But you can master certain abilities and strategies that will enable you to express your ideas clearly and coherently, and helping you to master them is the explicit purpose of this book and the course you are taking.

By improving your abilities to think critically and write thoughtfully, you will equip yourself to deal with the challenges that life poses: to solve problems, to establish and achieve goals, and to make sense of complex issues. This foundation will be constructed in the chapters ahead, helping to provide you with a basis for success in college and in your career.

CHAPTER 2

Thinking Critically, Writing Thoughtfully

Critical Thinking Focus: Thinking about thinking

Writing Focus: Reflecting on experiences

Reading Theme: Experiences that have affected beliefs

Writing Project: Recalling the impact of experience on a belief

Developing Insight into Thinking and Writing

Traditionally, when people refer to a critical thinker, they mean someone who has developed an understanding of today's complex world, a thoughtful perspective on ideas and issues, the capacity for insight and good judgment, and sophisticated reasoning and language abilities. Critical thinkers are able to articulate their ideas clearly and persuasively in writing, to understand and evaluate the credibility of what they read, and to discuss ideas with others in an informed, productive fashion. These goals of higher education have remained remarkably similar for several thousand years. In ancient Greece, most advanced students studied rhetoric in order to effect persuasion and studied philosophy in order to achieve wisdom. (The Greek word *philosophos* means "lover of wisdom.") In the modern world, many college students do likewise, in order to become informed critical thinkers and capable speakers and writers.

The word *critical* comes from the Greek word *kritikos*, which means "able to perceive, detect, judge, or analyze." By questioning and analyzing, by evaluating and making sense of information, we examine our own thinking and that of others.

These thinking activities aid us in reaching the best possible conclusions and decisions. *Critical* is related to *criticize,* which means "to question and evaluate." Unfortunately, the ability to criticize is often used destructively, to tear down someone else's thinking. Criticism, however, can also be *constructive*—analyzing for the purpose of developing better understanding. To develop your abilities to think critically and write thoughtfully, it is important to offer and receive constructive criticism.

We noted in the last chapter that *thinking* is the way you make sense of the world; *thinking critically* is thinking about your thinking so that you can clarify and improve it. If you can understand the way your mind operates when you work toward your goals, make informed decisions, and solve complex problems, you can learn to think more effectively in these situations. In this chapter, you will explore ways to examine your thinking so that you can develop it to the fullest extent possible. That is, you will develop your ability to think critically.

> **Thinking Critically:**   the organized cognitive process we use to carefully examine our thinking and the thinking of others, in order to clarify and improve our understanding.

Analogously, *writing thoughtfully* involves developing insight into the writing process so that you can express ideas clearly, coherently, and persuasively.

> **Writing Thoughtfully:**   thinking critically as we move through the process of writing.

This chapter explores various qualities that characterize a critical thinker and thoughtful writer, including the following:

- Thinking actively
- Thinking independently
- Viewing a situation from different perspectives
- Supporting a point of view with evidence and reasons

Thinking Actively and Writing

When you think critically, you are *actively* using your intelligence, knowledge, and abilities to deal effectively with life's situations by

- *getting involved* in potentially useful projects and activities instead of remaining disengaged.

- *taking initiative* in making decisions on your own instead of waiting passively to be told what to think or do.
- *following through* on your commitments instead of giving up when you encounter difficulties.
- *taking responsibility* for the consequences of your decisions rather than unjustifiably blaming others or events "beyond your control."

Similarly, when you write thoughtfully, you act in the following ways:

- You *become involved* in the subject you are writing about, and because the writing process stimulates your thinking, you often find ideas that you were unaware of until you started writing. Also, if you keep a journal or notebook and make writing part of your daily life, you find yourself more involved in and more reflective about your world.
- You *take initiative* as you develop confidence in your writer's voice, so you express your perspectives instead of imitating the ideas of others.
- You *follow through* as you revise and edit, in order to produce your best effort.
- You *make yourself responsible* for your work. That is, you begin assignments promptly and budget enough time to complete them. Though your professors will guide you, and your classmates and writing center tutors will make suggestions about your drafts, you are in charge of your writing, and it is up to you to complete it honestly and well.

When you are thinking actively, you are not just waiting for something to happen. You are engaged in the process of achieving goals, making decisions, analyzing issues, and writing thoughtfully.

Imagine, for example, that you are unsure of which career to choose. To make an intelligent decision, you have to work actively to secure information, explore various possibilities, speak with people experienced in your areas of interest, and then critically reflect on all these factors. Thinking critically requires that you think actively—not react passively—to deal effectively with life's situations.

Influences on Your Thinking

As our minds grow and develop, we are exposed to influences that encourage us to think actively. We also, however, have many experiences that encourage us to think passively. For example, some analysts believe that when people, especially children, spend much of their time watching television instead of reading and writing, they are being influenced to think passively, thus inhibiting their intellectual growth. Listed here are some of the influences we all experience in our lives, along with space for you to add others you are aware of. As you read through the list, place an A next to items that you believe influence you to think actively and a P next to items that you feel make you more passive.

Becoming a critical thinker and thoughtful writer transforms you in positive ways by helping you develop your own well-reasoned viewpoints, express yourself clearly, and make informed choices.

ACTIVITIES	PEOPLE
Reading books	Family members
Writing	Friends
Taking drugs	Employers
Drinking alcohol	Advertisers
Drawing and painting	Teachers
Playing video games	Police officers
Playing sports	Religious leaders
Listening to music	Politicians
_____	_____
_____	_____

Of course, certain people or activities can act as either active or passive influences, depending on specific situations and your individual responses. For example, consider employers. If you are performing a routine, repetitive task—such as a summer job in a peanut-butter cracker plant, hand-scooping 2,000 pounds of peanut butter a day—the very nature of the work encourages passive, uncreative thinking (although it might also lead to creative daydreaming!). You are also influenced to think passively if an employer gives you detailed instructions for performing every task, instructions that permit no exception or deviation. On the other hand, when an employer gives you general areas of responsibility within which you are expected to make thoughtful and creative decisions, you are being stimulated to think actively and independently.

These contrasting styles of supervision are mirrored in different approaches to raising children. Some parents encourage children to be active thinkers by teaching them to express themselves clearly, make independent decisions, look at different points of view, and choose what they think is right. Other parents influence their children to be passive thinkers by not letting them do things on their own. These parents give detailed instructions to be followed without question and make the important decisions for their children. Such parents, reluctant to give their children significant responsibilities, unintentionally create dependent thinkers who are not well adapted to making independent decisions and assuming responsibility for their own lives.

Similar experiences occur in college. You will probably find that some of your professors will encourage you to think actively by expecting you to apply, analyze, synthesize, and evaluate the information you are acquiring. These professors may assign independent research projects, give essay exams, and require you to write papers in which you must bring your informed perspective to the course material. Other professors may expect you to represent the information from class lectures and the textbooks, but not ask for your perspective—an approach that may not encourage active thinking.

THINKING ↔ WRITING ACTIVITY 2.1

Active and Passive Influences

Identify one important influence in your life that mainly stimulates you to think actively; then identify one that encourages you to think passively. For each, write an explanation of how it has affected your thinking. Provide at least two specific examples for each influence.

Ways to Approaching Writing

Developing your ability to *think actively*, to use your mind in an initiative-taking way, is crucial for becoming an effective writer. The **Thinking↔ Writing Model** (page 8) shows that active, creative, critical thinking is important throughout the writing process, and each chapter in this book deals with some aspect of the thinking↔writing connection.

To find topics for your writing, you need to think creatively first, to generate a variety of ideas, then think critically to select the ones that you can use. You can ask yourself what you already know about your topics; then you can think about what you need to find out and how to search for the information. As you decide what to include in your writing, you must evaluate your own ideas and those of others. You have to consider what thinking patterns you will use to organize your ideas, so you should compare alternatives before selecting the most appropriate forms.

As you write, you want to remain conscious of both your purpose and your audience, as Chapter 1 points out. When you revise drafts, you will be thinking most actively and critically, deciding what to say and how to organize it. Chapter 4 emphasizes revision.

The questions suggested on pages 15–16 in Chapter 1 are designed to bring about active thinking, as are the suggestions that accompany each Writing Project.

Thinking Independently

Answer the following questions, on the basis of what you believe to be true.

	Yes	No	Not Sure
1. Is the earth flat?			
2. Is there a God?			
3. Is abortion wrong?			
4. Is democracy the best form of government?			
5. Should men be the breadwinners and women the homemakers?			

Your responses to these questions reveal aspects of the way your mind works, beliefs you have developed that you express in your speaking and writing. How did you arrive at these conclusions? Your views on these and many other issues probably had their beginnings with your family, especially your parents or other adults who brought you up. When you were little, you were very dependent on those adults, and you were influenced by the way they saw the world. As you grew up, you learned how to think, feel, and behave in various situations. Very likely your teachers included your brothers and sisters, friends, religious leaders, schoolteachers, books, television, and so on. You absorbed most of what you learned without even being aware of doing so. Many of your ideas about the issues raised in the five questions you just answered probably were shaped by experiences you had while growing up.

As a result of your ongoing experiences, however, your mind—and your thinking—have continued to mature. Instead of simply accepting the views of others, you have gradually developed the ability to examine your earlier thinking and to decide how much of it still makes sense to you and whether you should accept it. Now, when you think through important ideas, use this standard in making a decision: Are there good reasons or evidence that support this thinking? If there are, you can actively decide to adopt these ideas. If the ideas do not make sense, you can modify or reject them.

Of course, you may not *always* examine your own thinking or the thinking of others so carefully. In fact, people often continue to believe in the same ideas they were brought up with, without ever examining and deciding for themselves what to think. Or they may blindly reject the beliefs they were brought up with, without really examining them.

How do you know when you have examined and adopted ideas yourself instead of simply borrowing them from others? One indication of having thought your ideas through is being able to explain why you believe in them, telling the reasons that led you to these conclusions.

Still, not all reasons and evidence are equally strong or accurate. For example, in Europe before the fifteenth century, the common belief that the earth was flat was supported by the following reasons and evidence:

People of Authority: Many educational and religious authorities taught that the earth was flat.

Recorded References: The written opinions of scientific experts supported belief in a flat earth.

Observed Evidence: No person had ever circumnavigated the earth.

Personal Experience: From a normal vantage point, the earth *looks* flat.

THINKING ↔ WRITING ACTIVITY 2.2

Evaluating Beliefs

For each of the five views you expressed at the beginning of this section, explain how you arrived at it and state the reasons and evidence that you believe support it.

1. *Example:* Is the earth flat?
   Belief: I am convinced that the earth is round.
   Reasons/Evidence:
   a. People of Authority: My parents and teachers taught me this.
   b. Recorded References: I read about this in science textbooks and saw films and videos.
   c. Observed Evidence: I have seen a sequence of photographs taken from outer space that show the earth as a globe.
   d. Personal Experience: When I flew across the country, I could see the horizon line changing.

2. Is there a God?

3. Is abortion wrong?

4. Is democracy the best form of government?

5. Should men be the breadwinners and women the homemakers?

To evaluate the strengths and accuracy of the reasons and evidence you identified for holding your beliefs on the five issues, address questions such as the following:

People of Authority: Are the authorities knowledgeable in this area? Are they reliable? Have they ever given inaccurate information? Do other authorities disagree with them?

Recorded References: What are the credentials of the authors? Do other authors disagree with their opinions? On what reasons and evidence do the authors base their opinions?

Observed Evidence: What is the source and foundation of the evidence? Can the evidence be interpreted differently? Does the evidence support the conclusion?

Personal Experience: What were the circumstances under which the experiences took place? Were distortions or mistakes in perception possible? Have other people had either similar or conflicting experiences? Are there other explanations for your experience?

As a college writer, you are going to apply these questions to material you encounter while gathering information for papers or reports. The opposite of thinking for yourself is simply accepting the thinking of others without examining or questioning it.

Learning to become an independent, critical thinker and thoughtful writer is a complex, ongoing process that involves the abilities we have been examining in this chapter to this point:

- Thinking actively
- Thinking independently

Viewing Situations from Different Perspectives

A critical thinker is someone who is willing to listen to other views and new ideas and examine them carefully. No one person has *all* the answers! Your beliefs represent just one perspective on whatever problem you want to solve or situation you are trying to understand. In addition to your own particular viewpoint, there may be others, equally important, that you need to consider if you are to develop a more complete understanding of the problem or situation. Learning to think and write at a high level, in fact, requires this.

Perspective-taking is essential to becoming a thoughtful writer. To begin with, exploring topics from a variety of vantage points is often the best way to present a comprehensive analysis of the subject you are writing about. When you are tied to only one perspective, your writing tends to be one-sided and superficial. Second, effective writing depends on always having a clear sense of your readers, the *audience* for whom you are writing. The ability to keep focus on that audience includes being able to see things from their point of view, to think empathetically within their frame of reference, and to understand their perspective. Finally, in order to produce your most accomplished writing, you need to be open to the informed comments and suggestions of others and flexible enough to use that feedback to refine your written expression.

Consider the following situation:

Imagine that you have been employed at a new job for the past six months. Although you enjoy the challenge of your responsibilities and are performing well, you simply cannot complete all your work during office hours. To keep up, you have to work late, take work home, and occasionally even work on weekends. When you explain this to your employer, she says that although she is sorry that the job interferes with your personal life, it has to be done. She suggests that you view this as an investment in your future and try to work more efficiently. She reminds you that many other people would be happy to have your position.

- What is your initial reaction to your employer's response?
- Describe this situation from the employer's standpoint, identifying reasons that might support her views.
- Describe some different approaches that you and your employer might take toward resolving this situation.

For most of the important issues and problems in your life, one viewpoint is simply not adequate to give a full and satisfactory understanding. To increase and deepen your knowledge, you must seek *other perspectives*. Sometimes you can accomplish this by using your imagination to visualize other viewpoints. Usually, however, you need to seek actively (and *listen to*) other people's viewpoints. It is often very difficult to see things from points of view other than your own; if you are not careful, you can make the serious mistake of assuming that the way you see things is the way they really are. In order to identify with perspectives other than your own, then, you also have to work to grasp the *reasons* for these alternate viewpoints. This approach, which stimulates you to evaluate your beliefs critically, is enhanced by writing: writing about beliefs encourages people to explain their reasons for holding them.

THINKING ↔ WRITING ACTIVITY 2.3

Two Sides of a Belief

Describe in detail a belief of yours that you feel very strongly about. Then explain the reasons or experiences that led you to this belief.

Next, describe a point of view that is different from your belief. Identify some of the reasons for someone's having that point of view. A student example follows.

STUDENT WRITING
A Belief that I Feel Strongly About
by Olavia Heredia

I used to think that we should always try everything in our power to keep a person alive. But now I strongly believe that a person has a right to die in peace and with dignity. I believe this now because of my father's illness and death.

It all started on Christmas Day, December 25, 1987, when my father was admitted to the hospital. The doctors diagnosed his condition as a heart attack. Following this episode, he was readmitted and discharged from several different hospitals. On June 18, 1988, he was hospitalized for what was initially thought to be pneumonia but which turned out to be lung cancer. He began chemotherapy treatments. When complications occurred, he had to be placed on a respirator. At first he couldn't speak or eat. But then they operated on him and placed the tube from the machine in his throat instead of his mouth. He was then able to eat and move his mouth. He underwent radiation therapy when they discovered he had three tumors in his head and that the cancer had spread all over his body. We had to sign a paper which asked us to indicate, if he should stop breathing, whether we would want the hospital to try to revive him or just let him go. We decided to let him go because the doctors couldn't guarantee that he wouldn't become brain-dead. At first they said that there was a forty percent chance that he would get off the machine. But instead of that happening, the percentage went down.

It was hard seeing him like that since I was so close to him. But it was even harder when he didn't want to see me. He said that by seeing me suffer, his suffering was greater. So I had to cut down on seeing him. Everybody that visited him said that he had changed dramatically. They couldn't even recognize him.

The last two days of his life were the worst. I prayed that God would relieve him of his misery. I had come very close to taking him off the machine in order for him not to suffer, but I didn't. Finally he passed away on November 22, 1988, with not the least bit of peace or dignity. The loss was great then and still is, but at least he's not suffering. That's why I believe that when people have terminal diseases with no hope of recovery, they shouldn't place them on machines to prolong their lives of suffering, but instead they should be permitted to die with as much peace and dignity possible.

Somebody else might believe very strongly that we should try everything in our power to keep people alive. It doesn't matter what kind of illness or disease the people have, what's important is that they are kept alive, especially if they are loved ones. Some people want to keep their loved ones alive with them as long as they can, even if it's by a machine. They also believe it is up to God and medical science to determine whether people should live or die. Sometimes doctors give them hope that their loved ones will recover, and many people wish for a miracle to happen. With these hopes and wishes in mind, they wait and try everything in order to prolong a life, even if the doctors tell them that there is nothing that can be done.

Being open to new ideas and different viewpoints means being *flexible* enough to change or modify one's own ideas in the light of new information or better insight. People do have a tendency to cling to the beliefs they were brought up with and the conclusions they have arrived at. If you are going to continue to grow and develop as a thinker, however, you have to be willing to change or modify your beliefs when evidence suggests that you should.

For example, imagine that you have been brought up with certain views concerning an ethnic group—African American, Caucasian, Hispanic, Asian, Native American, or any other. As you mature and your experience increases, you may find that the evidence of your experience conflicts with those earlier views. As a critical thinker, you will become open to receiving new evidence and *flexible* enough to change and modify your ideas.

In contrast to open and flexible thinking, *un*critical thinking tends to be one-sided and closed-minded. People who think uncritically are convinced that they alone see things as they really are and that everyone who disagrees with them is wrong. It is very difficult for them to step outside their own viewpoints and look at issues from other people's perspectives. Words often used to describe this type of person include *dogmatic, subjective,* and *egocentric.*

Supporting Diverse Perspectives with Reasons and Evidence

When you are thinking critically, what you think makes sense and you can offer sound reasons for your views. As a thoughtful writer, you cannot simply take a position on an issue or make a claim; you have to *back up your views,* reinforce them with information that you feel supports your position. There is an important distinction between *what* you believe and *why* you believe it.

If you want to know all sides of an issue, you have to be able to give supporting reasons and evidence not just for your own views, but also for the views of others. Seeing several sides of an issue combines these two critical thinking abilities:

■   Viewing issues from different perspectives and

■   Supporting diverse viewpoints with reasons and evidence.

Consider the issue of whether air bags should be standard equipment for cars. As you try to make sense of this issue, you should attempt to identify not just the reasons for your view, but also the reasons for other views. Following are reasons that support each view of this issue.

ISSUE

Airbags should be standard equipment.	Air bags should not be standard equipment.
Supporting Reasons	*Supporting Reasons*
1. Studies show that air bags save lives in accidents.	1. Air bags sometimes injure and even kill children and small adults.
2. Studies show that airbags reduce injury in accidents.	2. Air bags should not be forced on citizens of a free country.

Now see if you can identify additional supporting reasons for each view on making air bags standard equipment.

For each of the following issues, identify reasons that support each side.

As critical thinkers and thoughtful writers we have an obligation to appreciate diverse perspectives on complex issues and develop informed opinions that are supported by compelling reasons. © Hazel Hankin/Stock Boston.

ISSUE

1. Multiple-choice and true/false exams should be given in college-level courses.

   Multiple-choice and true/false exams should *not* be given in college-level courses.

ISSUE

2. It is better to live in a society in which the government plays a major role in citizens' lives.

   It is better to live in a society that minimizes the role of the government in citizens' lives.

ISSUE

3. The best way to deal with crime is to impose long prison sentences.

   Long prison sentences will not reduce crime.

4. When a couple divorce, the children should choose the parent with whom they wish to live.

When a couple divorce, the court should decide all custody issues regarding the children.

THINKING ↔ WRITING ACTIVITY 2.4

Viewing Different Perspectives

Seeing different perspectives is crucial to getting a more complete understanding of ideas expressed in passages you read. Read the two passages that follow. Then, for each passage, do these four things:

1. Identify the main idea of each passage.
2. List the reasons that support the main idea.
3. Develop another view of the main issue.
4. List the reasons that support the other view.

If we want auto safety but continue to believe in auto profits, sales, styling, and annual obsolescence, there will be no serious accomplishments. The moment we put safety ahead of these other values, something will happen. If we want better municipal hospitals but are unwilling to disturb the level of spending for defense, for highways, for household appliances, hospital service will not improve. If we want peace but still believe that countries with differing ideologies are threats to one another, we will not get peace. What is confusing is that up to now, while we have wanted such things as conservation, auto safety, hospital care, and peace, we have tried wanting them without changing consciousness; that is, while continuing to accept those underlying values that stand in the way of what we want. The machine can be controlled at the "consumer" level only by people who change their whole value system, their whole world view, their whole way of life. One cannot favor saving our wildlife and wear a fur coat.

Most wicked deeds are done because the doer proposes some good to himself. The liar lies to gain some end; the swindler and thief want things which, if honestly got, might be good in themselves. Even the murderer may be removing an impediment to normal desires or gaining possession of something his victim keeps from him. None of these people usually does evil for evil's sake. They are selfish or unscrupulous, but their deeds are not gratuitously evil. The killer for sport has no such comprehensible motive. He prefers death to life, darkness to light. He gets nothing except the satisfaction of saying, "Something which wanted to live is dead. There is that much less vitality, consciousness, and, perhaps, joy in the universe. I am the Spirit that Denies." When a human wantonly destroys one of humankind's own works we call him Vandal. When he wantonly destroys one of the works of God we call him Sportsman.

Readings About Experiences That Affected Beliefs

In the following narratives, four writers reflect on learning experiences that caused them to alter beliefs about themselves, about other people, and about ways to live their lives. Malcolm X describes his odyssey of learning to read and write in prison, Annie Dillard shares the impact of her first scientific observation, N. Scott Momaday describes a loss of childhood innocence, and Peter Rondinone writes on the transforming nature of his college experience.

from The Autobiography of Malcolm X
by Malcolm X with Alex Haley

I became increasingly frustrated at not being able to express what I wanted to convey in letters that I wrote, especially those to Mr. Elijah Muhammad. In the street, I had been the most articulate hustler out there—I had commanded attention when I said something. But now, trying to write simple English, I not only wasn't articulate, I wasn't even functional. How would I sound writing in slang, the way I would *say* it, something such as, "Look, daddy, let me pull your coat about a cat, Elijah Muhammad—"

Many who today hear me somewhere in person, or on television, or those who read something I've said, will think I went to school far beyond the eighth grade. This impression is due entirely to my prison studies.

It had really begun back in the Charlestown Prison, when Bimbi first made me feel envy of his stock of knowledge. Bimbi had always taken charge of any conversation he was in, and I had tried to emulate him. But every book I picked up had few sentences which didn't contain anywhere from one to nearly all of the words that might as well have been in Chinese. When I just skipped those words, of course, I really ended up with little idea of what the book said. So I had come to the Norfolk Prison Colony still going through only book-reading motions. Pretty soon, I would have quit even these motions, unless I had received the motivation that I did.

I saw that the best thing I could do was get hold of a dictionary—to study, to learn some words. I was lucky enough to reason also that I should try to improve my penmanship. It was sad. I couldn't even write in a straight line. It was both ideas together that moved me to request a dictionary along with some tablets and pencils from the Norfolk Prison Colony school.

5   I spent two days just riffling uncertainly through the dictionary's pages. I'd never realized so many words existed! I didn't know *which*

words I needed to learn. Finally, just to start some kind of action, I began copying.

In my slow, painstaking, ragged handwriting, I copied into my tablet everything printed on that first page, down to the punctuation marks.

I believe it took me a day. Then, aloud, I read back, to myself, everything I'd written on the tablet. Over and over, aloud, to myself, I read my own handwriting.

I woke up the next morning, thinking about those words—immensely proud to realize that not only had I written so much at one time, but I'd written words that I never knew were in the world. Moreover, with a little effort, I also could remember what many of these words meant. I reviewed the words whose meaning I didn't remember. Funny thing, from the dictionary's first page right now, that "aardvark" springs to my mind. The dictionary had a picture of it, a long-tailed, long-eared, burrowing African mammal, which lives off termites caught by sticking out its tongue as an anteater does for ants.

I was so fascinated that I went on—I copied the dictionary's next page. And the same experience came when I studied that. With every succeeding page, I also learned of people and places and events from history. Actually the dictionary is like a miniature encyclopedia. Finally the dictionary's A section had filled a whole tablet—and I went on into the B's. That was the way I started copying what eventually became the entire dictionary. It went a lot faster after so much practice helped me to pick up handwriting speed. Between what I wrote in my tablet, and writing letters, during the rest of my time in prison I would guess I wrote a million words.

10   I suppose it was inevitable that as my word-base broadened, I could for the first time pick up a book and read and now begin to understand what the book was saying. Anyone who has read a great deal can imagine the new world that opened. Let me tell you something: from then until I left the prison, in every free moment I had, if I was not reading in the library, I was reading on my bunk. You couldn't have gotten me out of books with a wedge. Between Mr. Muhammad's teachings, my correspondence, my visitors—usually Ella and Reginald—and my reading of books, months passed without my even thinking about being imprisoned. In fact, up to then, I never had been so truly free in my life.

The Norfolk Prison Colony's library was in the school building. A variety of classes was taught there by instructors who came from such places as Harvard and Boston universities. The weekly debates between inmate teams were also held in the school building. You would be astonished to know how worked up convict debaters and audiences would get over subjects like "Should Babies Be Fed Milk?"

Available on the prison library's shelves were books on just about every general subject. Much of the big private collection that Parkhurst had willed to the prison was still in crates and boxes in the back of the library—thousands of old books. Some of them looked ancient: covers faded, old-time parchment-looking binding. Parkhurst, I've mentioned, seemed to have been principally interested in history and religion. He had the money and the special interest to have a lot of books that you wouldn't have in general circulation. Any college library would have been lucky to get that collection.

As you can imagine, especially in a prison where there was heavy emphasis on rehabilitation, an inmate was smiled upon if he demonstrated an unusually intense interest in books. There was a sizable number of well-read inmates, especially the popular debaters. Some were said by many to be practically walking encyclopedias. They were almost celebrities. No university would ask any student to devour literature as I did when this new world opened to me, of being able to read and *understand*.

I read more in my room than in the library itself. An inmate who was known to read a lot could check out more than the permitted maximum number of books. I preferred reading in the total isolation of my own room.

15   When I had progressed to really serious reading, every night at about ten (P.M.) I would be outraged with the "lights out." It always seemed to catch me right in the middle of something engrossing.

Fortunately, right outside my door was a corridor light that cast a glow into my room. The glow was enough to read by, once my eyes adjusted to it. So when "lights out" came, I would sit on the floor where I could continue reading in that glow.

At one-hour intervals the night guards paced past every room. Each time I heard the approaching footsteps, I jumped into bed and feigned sleep. And as soon as the guard passed, I got back out of bed onto the floor area of that light-glow, where I would read for another fifty-eight minutes—until the guard approached again. That went on until three or four every morning. Three or four hours of sleep a night was enough for me. Often in the years in the streets I had slept less than that.

Handed My Own Life

by Annie Dillard

After I read *The Field Book of Ponds and Streams* several times, I longed for a microscope. Everybody needed a microscope. Detectives used microscopes, both for the FBI and at Scotland Yard. Although usually I had to save my tiny allowance for things I wanted, that year for Christmas my parents gave me a microscope kit.

In a dark basement corner, on a white enamel table, I set up the microscope kit. I supplied a chair, a lamp, a batch of jars, a candle, and a pile of library books. The microscope kit supplied a blunt black three-speed microscope, a booklet, a scalpel, a dropper, an ingenious device for cutting thin segments of fragile tissue, a pile of clean slides and cover slips, and a dandy array of corked test tubes.

One of the test tubes contained "hay infusion." Hay infusion was a wee brown chip of grass blade. You added water to it, and after a week it became a jungle in a drop, full of one-celled animals. This did not work for me. All I saw in the microscope after a week was a wet chip of dried grass, much enlarged.

Another test tube contained "diatomaceous earth." This was, I believed, an actual pinch of the white cliffs of Dover. On my palm it was an airy, friable chalk. The booklet said it was composed of the silicaceous bodies of diatoms—one-celled creatures that lived in, as it were, small glass jewelry boxes with fitted lids. Diatoms, I read, come in a variety of transparent geometrical shapes. Broken and dead and dug out of geological deposits, they made chalk, and a fine abrasive used in silver polish and toothpaste. What I saw in the microscope must have been the fine abrasive—grit enlarged. It was years before I saw a recognizable, whole diatom. The kit's diatomaceous earth was a bust.

5   All that winter I played with the microscope. I prepared slides from things at hand, as the books suggested. I looked at the transparent membrane inside an onion's skin and saw the cells. I looked at a section of cork and saw the cells, and at scrapings from the inside of my cheek, ditto. I looked at my blood and saw not much; I looked at my urine and saw long iridescent crystals, for the drop had dried.

All this was very well, but I wanted to see the wildlife I had read about. I wanted especially to see the famous amoeba, who had eluded me. He was supposed to live in the hay infusion, but I hadn't found him there. He lived outside in warm ponds and streams, too, but I lived in Pittsburgh, and it had been a cold winter.

Finally late that spring I saw an amoeba. The week before, I had gathered puddle water from Frick Park, it had been festering in a jar in the basement. This June night after dinner I figured I had waited long enough. In the basement at my microscope table I spread a scummy drop of Frick Park puddle water on a slide, peeked in, and lo, there was the famous amoeba. He was as blobby and grainy as his picture; I would have known him anywhere.

Before I had watched him at all, I ran upstairs. My parents were still at table, drinking coffee. They, too, could see the famous amoeba. I told them, bursting, that he was all set up, that they should hurry before his water dried. It was the chance of a lifetime.

Father had stretched out his long legs and was tilting back in his chair. Mother sat with her knees crossed, in blue slacks, smoking a Chesterfield. The dessert dishes were still on the table. My sisters were nowhere in evidence. It was a warm evening; the big dining-room windows gave onto blooming rhododendrons.

10   Mother regarded me warmly. She gave me to understand that she was glad I had found what I had been looking for, but that she and Father were happy to sit with their coffee, and would not be coming down.

She did not say, but I understood at once, that they had their pursuits (coffee?) and I had mine. She did not say, but I began to understand then, that you do what you do out of your private passion for the thing itself.

I had essentially been handed my own life. In subsequent years my parents would praise my drawings and poems, and supply me with books, art supplies, and sports equipment, and listen to my troubles and enthusiasms, and supervise my hours, and discuss and inform, but they would not get involved with my detective work, nor hear about my reading, nor inquire about my homework or term papers or exams, nor visit the salamanders I caught, nor listen to me play the piano, nor attend my field hockey games, nor fuss over my insect collection with me, or my poetry collection or stamp collection or rock collection. My days and nights were my own to plan and fill.

When I left the dining room that evening and started down the dark basement stairs, I had a life, I sat to my wonderful amoeba, and there he was, rolling his grains more slowly now, extending an arc of his edge for a foot and drawing himself along by that foot, and absorbing it again and rolling on. I have him some more pond water.

I had hit pay dirt. For all I knew, there were paramecia, too, in that pond water, or daphniae, or stentors, or any of the many other creatures I had read about and never seen: volvox, the spherical algal colony; euglena with its one red eye; the elusive glassy diatom; hydra, rotifers, water bears, worms. Anything was possible. The sky was the limit.

The End of My Childhood

by N. Scott Momaday

At Jemez I came to the end of my childhood. There were no schools within easy reach. I had to go nearly thirty miles to school at Bernalillo, and one year I lived away in Albuquerque. My mother and father wanted me to have the benefit of a sound preparation for college, and so we read through many high school catalogues. After long deliberation we decided that I should spend my last year of high school at a military academy in Virginia.

The day before I was to leave I went walking across the river to the red mesa, where many times before I had gone to be alone with my thoughts. And I had climbed several times to the top of the mesa and looked among the old ruins there for pottery. This time I chose to climb the north end, perhaps because I had not gone that way before and wanted to see what it was. It was a difficult climb, and when I got to the top I was spent. I lingered among the ruins for more than an hour, I judge, waiting for my strength to return. From there I could see the whole valley below, the fields, the river, and the village. It was all very beautiful, and the sight of it filled me with longing.

I looked for an easier way to come down, and at length I found a broad, smooth runway of rock, a shallow groove winding out like a stream. It appeared to be safe enough, and I started to follow it. There were steps along the way, a stairway, in effect. But the steps became deeper and deeper, and at last I had to drop down the length of my body and more. Still it seemed convenient to follow in the groove of rock. I was more than halfway down when I came upon a deep, funnel-shaped formation in my path. And there I had to make a decision. The slope on either side was extremely steep and forbidding, and yet I thought that I could work my way down on either side. The formation at my feet was something else. It was perhaps ten or twelve feet deep, wide at the top and narrow at the bottom, where there appeared to be a level ledge. If I could get down through the funnel to the ledge, I should be all right; surely the rest of the way down was negotiable. But I realized that there could be no turning back. Once I was down in that rocky chute I could not get up again, for the round wall which nearly encircled the space there was too high and sheer. I elected to go down into it, to try for the ledge directly below. I eased myself down the smooth, nearly vertical wall on my back, pressing my arms and legs outward against the sides. After what seemed a long time I was trapped in the rock. The ledge was no longer there below me; it had been an optical illusion. Now, in this angle of vision, there was nothing but the ground, far, far below, and jagged boulders set there like teeth. I remember that my arms were scraped and bleeding, stretched out against the walls with all the pressure that I could exert. When once I looked down I saw that my legs, also spread out and pressed hard against the walls, were shaking violently. I was in an impossible situation: I could not move in any direction, save downward in a fall, and I could not stay beyond another minute where I was. I believed then that I would die there, and I saw with a terrible clarity the things of the valley below. They were not the less beautiful to me. It seemed to me that I grew suddenly very calm in view of that beloved world. And I remember nothing else of that moment. I passed out of my mind, and the next thing I knew I was sitting down on the ground, very cold in the shadows, and looking up at the rock where I had been within an eyelash of eternity. That was a strange thing in my life, and I think of it as the end of an age. I should never again see the world as I saw it on the other side of that moment, in the bright reflection of time lost. There are such reflections, and for some of them I have the names.

from Independence and the Inward "I"

by Peter J. Rondinone

The fact is, I didn't learn much in high school. I spent my time on the front steps of the building smoking grass with the dudes from the dean's squad. For kicks we'd grab a freshman, tell him we were undercover cops, handcuff him to a banister, and take his money. Then we'd go to the back of the building, cop some "downs," and nod away the day behind the steps in the lobby. The classrooms were overcrowded anyhow, and the teachers knew it. They also knew where to find me when they wanted to make weird deals: If I agreed to read a book and do an oral report, they'd pass me. So I did it and graduated with a "general" diploma. I was a New York City public school kid.

I hung out on a Bronx streetcorner with a group of guys who called themselves "The Davidson Boys" and sang songs like "Daddy-lo-lo." Everything we did could be summed up with the word "snap." That's a "snap." She's a "snap." We had a "snap." Friday nights we'd paint ourselves green and run through the streets swinging baseball bats. Or we'd get into a little rap in the park. It was all very perilous. Even though I'd seen a friend stabbed for wearing the wrong colors and another blown away for "messin'" with some dude's woman, I was too young to realize that my life too might be headed toward a violent end.

Then one night I swallowed a dozen Tuminols and downed two quarts of beer at a bar in Manhattan. I passed out in the gutter. I puked and rolled under a parked car. Two girlfriends found me and carried me home. My overprotective brother answered the door. When he saw me—eyes rolling toward the back of my skull like rubber—he pushed me down a flight of stairs. My skull hit the edge of a marble step with a thud. The girls screamed. My parents came to the door and there I was: a high school graduate, a failure, curled in a ball in a pool of blood.

The next day I woke up with dried blood on my face. I had no idea what had happened. My sister told my. I couldn't believe it. Crying, my mother confirmed the story. I had almost died! That scared hell out of me. I knew I had to do something. I didn't know what. But pills and violence didn't promise much of a future.

5   I went back to a high school counselor for advice. He suggested I go to college.

On the day I received my letter of acceptance, I waited until dinner to tell my folks. I was proud.

"Check out where I'm going," I said. I passed the letter to my father. He looked at it.

"You jerk!" he said. "You wanna sell ties?" My mother grabbed the letter.

"God," she said. "Why don't you go to work already? Like other people."

10 "Later for that," I said. "You should be proud."

At the time, of course, I didn't understand where my parents were coming from. They were immigrants. They believed college was for rich kids, not the ones who dropped downs and sang songs on streetcorners. . . .

Anyhow, I wasn't about to listen to my parents and go to work; for a dude like me, this was a big deal. So I left the dinner table and went to tell my friends about my decision.

The Davidson Boys hung out in a rented storefront. They were sitting around the pool table on milk boxes and broken pinball machines, spare tires and dead batteries. I made my announcement. They stood up and circled me like I was the star of a cockfight. Sucio stepped to the table with a can of beer in one hand and a pool stick in the other.

"Wha' you think you gonna get out of college?" he said.

15 "I don't know, but I bet it beats this," I said. I shoved one of the pool balls across the table. That was a mistake. The others banged their sticks on the wood floor and chanted, "Oooh-ooh—snap, snap." Sucio put his beer on the table.

"Bull!" he yelled. "I wash dishes with college dudes. You're like us—nuttin', man." He pointed the stick at my nose.

Silence.

I couldn't respond. If I let the crowd know I thought their gig was uncool, that I wanted out of the club, they would have taken it personally. And they would have taken me outside and kicked my ass. So I lowered my head. "Aw, hell, gimme a hit of beer," I said, as if it were all a joke. But I left the corner and didn't go back.

I spent that summer alone, reading books like *How to Succeed in College* and *30 Days to a More Powerful Vocabulary.* My vocabulary was limited to a few choice phrases like "Move over, Rover, and let Petey take over." When my friends did call for me I hid behind the curtains. I knew that if I was going to make it, I'd have to push these guys out of my consciousness as if I were doing the breaststroke in a sea of logs. I had work to do, and people were time consuming. As it happened, all my heavy preparations didn't amount to much.

20 On the day of the placement exams I went paranoid. Somehow I got the idea that my admission to college was some ugly practical joke that I wasn't prepared for. So I copped some downs and took the test nodding. The words floated on the page like flies on a crock of cream.

That made freshman year difficult. The administration had placed me in all three remedial programs: basic writing, college skills, and math. I was shocked. I had always thought of myself as smart. I was the only one in the neighborhood who read books. So I gave up the pills and pushed aside another log.

The night before the first day of school, my brother walked into my room and threw a briefcase on my desk. "Good luck, Joe College," he said. He smacked me in the back of the head. Surprised, I went to bed early.

In Basic Writing I the instructor, Regina Sackmary, chalked her name in bold letters on the blackboard. I sat in the front row and reviewed my *How to Succeed* lessons: Sit in front/don't let eyes wander to cracks on ceilings/take notes on a legal pad/make note of all unfamiliar words and books/listen for key phrases like "remember this," they are a professor's signals. The other students held pens over pads in anticipation. Like me, they didn't know what to expect. We were public school kids from lousy neighborhoods and we knew that some of us didn't have a chance; but we were ready to work hard.

Before class we had rapped about our reasons for going to college. Some said they wanted to be the first in the history of their families to have a college education—they said their parents never went to college because they couldn't afford it, or because their parents' parents were too poor—and they said open admissions and free tuition ($65 per semester) was a chance to change that history. Others said they wanted to be educated so they could return to their neighborhoods to help "the people"; they were the idealists. Some foreigners said they wanted to return to their own countries and start schools. And I said I wanted to escape the boredom and the pain I had known as a kid on the streets. But none of them said they expected a job. Or if they did they were reminded that there were no jobs.

25   In math I was in this remedial program for algebra, geometry, and trigonometry. But unlike high school math, which I thought was devised to boggle the mind for the sake of boggling, in this course I found I could make a connection between different mathematical principles and my life. For instance, there were certain basics I had to learn—call them 1, 2, and 3—and unless they added up to 6 I'd probably be a failure. I also got a sense of how math related to the world at large: Unless the sum of the parts of a society equaled the whole there would be chaos. And these insights jammed my head and made me feel like a kid on a ferris wheel looking at the world for the first time. Everything amazed me!

Like biology. In high school I associated this science with stabbing pins in the hearts of frogs for fun. Or getting high snorting small doses of the chloroform used for experiments on fruit flies. But in college biology I began to learn and appreciate not only how my own life processes functioned but how there were thousands of other life processes I'd never known existed. And this gave me a sense of power, because I could deal with questions like, Why do plants grow? not as I had before, with a simple spill of words: "'Cause of the sun, man." I could actually explain that there was a plant cycle and cycles within the plant cycle. You know how the saying goes—a little knowledge is dangerous. Well, the more I learned the more I ran my mouth off, especially with people who didn't know as much as I did.

I remember the day Ms. Sackmary tossed Sartre's *No Exit* in my lap and said, "Find the existential motif." I didn't know what to look for. What was she talking about? I never studied philosophy. I turned to the table of contents, but there was nothing under E. So I went to the library and after much research I discovered the notion of the absurd. I couldn't believe it. I told as many people as I could. I told them they were absurd, their lives were absurd, everything was absurd. I became obsessed with existentialism. I read Kafka, Camus, Dostoevski, and others in my spare time. Then one day I found a line in a book that I believed summed up my unusual admittance to the college and my determination to work hard. I pasted it to the headboard of my bed. It said: "Everything is possible."

To deal with the heavy workload from all my classes, I needed a study schedule, so I referred to my *How to Succeed* book. I gave myself an hour for lunch and reserved the rest of the time between classes and evenings for homework and research. All this left me very little time for friendships. But I stuck to my schedule and by the middle of the first year I was getting straight A's. Nothing else mattered. Not even my family.

When I entered my second year my family began to ask, "What do you want to do?" And I got one of those cards from the registrar that has to be filled out in a week or you're dropped from classes. It asked me to declare my major. I had to make a quick decision. So I checked off BS degree, dentistry, though I didn't enroll in a single science course.

30   One course I did take that semester was *The Writer and the City*. The professor, Ross Alexander, asked the class to keep a daily journal. He said it should be as creative as possible and reflect some aspect of city life. So I wrote about different experiences I had with my friends. For example, I wrote "Miracle on 183rd Street" about the night "Raunchy" Rick jumped a guy in the park and took his portable radio. When the guy tried to fight back Rick slapped him in the face with the radio; then, using the batteries that spilled out, he pounded this guy in the head until the blood began to puddle on the ground. Those of us on the sidelines dragged Rick away. Ross attached notes to my papers that said things like: "You really have a great hit of talent and ought to take courses in creative writing and sharpen your craft! Hang on to it all for dear life."

In my junior year I forgot dentistry and registered as a creative writing major. I also joined a college newspaper, *The Campus*. Though I knew nothing about journalism, I was advised that writing news was a good way to learn the business. And as Ross once pointed out to me, "As a writer you will need an audience."

I was given my first assignment. I collected piles of quotes and facts and scattered the mess on a desk. I remember typing the story under deadline pressure with one finger while the editors watched me struggle, probably thinking back to their own first stories. When I finished, they passed the copy around. The editor-in-chief looked at it at last and said, "This isn't even English." Yet, they turned it over to a rewrite man and the story appeared with my by-line. Seeing my name in print was like seeing it in lights—flashbulbs popped in my head and I walked into the school cafeteria that day expecting to be recognized by everyone. My mother informed the relatives: "My son is a writer!"

Six months later I quit *The Campus*. A course in New Journalism had made me realize that reporting can be creative. For the first time I read writers like Tom Wolfe and Hunter S. Thompson, and my own news stories began to turn into first-person accounts that read like short stories. *The Campus* refused to publish my stuff, so I joined the *Observation Post*, the only paper on campus that printed first-person material. I wanted to get published.

My first *Post* feature article (a first-person news story on a proposed beer hall at CCNY) was published on the front page. The staff was impressed enough to elect me assistant features editor. However, what they didn't know was that the article had been completely rewritten by the features editor. And the features editor had faith in me, so he never told. He did my share of the work and I kept the title. As he put it: "You'll learn by hanging around and watching. You show talent. You might even get published professionally in 25 years!"

35   God, those early days were painful. Professors would tear up my papers the day they were due and tell me to start over again, with a piece of advice—"Try to say what you really mean." Papers I had spent weeks writing. And I knew I lacked the basic college skills; I was a man reporting to work without his tools. So I smiled when I didn't understand. But sometimes it showed and I paid the price: A professor once told me the only reason I'd pass his course was that I had a nice smile. Yes, those were painful days.

And there were nights I was alone with piles of notebooks and textbooks. I wanted to throw the whole mess out the window; I wanted to give up. Nights the sounds of my friends singing on the corner drifted into my room like fog over a graveyard and I was afraid I would be swept away. And nights I was filled with questions but the answers were like moon shadows on my curtains: I could see them but I could not grasp them.

Yet I had learned a vital lesson from these countless hours of work in isolation: My whole experience from the day I received my letter of acceptance enabled me to understand how in high school my sense of self-importance came from being one of the boys, a member of the pack, while in college the opposite was true. In order to survive, I had to curb my herd instinct.

Nobody, nobody could give me what I needed to overcome my sense of inadequacy. That was a struggle I had to work at on my own. It could never be a group project. In the end, though people could point out what I had to learn and where to learn it, I was always the one who did the work; and what I learned I earned. And that made me feel as good as being one of the boys. In short, college taught me to appreciate the importance of being alone. I found it was the only way I could get any serious work done.

WRITING PROJECT

The **Thinking↔Writing Activities** and the readings in this chapter have encouraged you to become an active thinker, to examine your beliefs, and to observe how some thoughtful people have reflected on their learning experiences. As you work on this project, reread what you wrote for the activities and think about the events and methods of narration in the readings.

WRITING PROJECT   A Formative Experience

Write an essay telling of some experience that had an important impact on a belief that you held or hold. The belief might be about yourself, about another person involved in the experience, or about the issue that the experience illustrates. The experience may have helped form your belief, or it may have changed or strengthened it. You will explain your belief, of course, and describe the experience, reflecting on what happened as you tell of its effects. You will probably want to discuss the sources of the belief (page 28). Follow your instructor's directives as to length, format, and so forth.

Begin by considering the elements in the **Thinking↔Writing Model.**

Purpose

Examining our beliefs is a necessary beginning stage in developing critical thinking abilities. Once we understand and evaluate our own starting points, we can understand and evaluate other people's perspectives. Writing reflective pieces about personal experiences brings insight into the ones that have helped to define us as individuals and have shaped our views of the world. When you reflect on and write about significant experiences, you begin to view them in a new way and relate them to issues in your life. The record that you create allows you to relive the experiences, rethink their significance, share them with others, and profit from others' responses. In the essay you are about to write, you will be explaining your experience and your belief but not trying to convince your readers that they should adopt or reject the belief. You are analyzing the meaning of *your* experience and the impact that it had on *your* life.

Audience

When you write reflectively about your own experiences, you are as important a part of the audience as the people who will read the piece. The noted author and Holocaust survivor Elie Wiesel has stated, "I write to understand as much as to be understood." This form of writing acts a catalyst for self-discovery by encouraging you to reflect on your past experience in a disciplined, analytical way. As you write in this form, your guiding ideas should include these questions:

- How effectively am I *communicating* the richness and reality of this experience?
- How effectively have I *analyzed* the significance of this experience and the lessons I learned from it?

If you believe that your writing is meeting these goals, it is likely that you are moving toward helping other members of your audience share what you are trying to express. However, as a critical thinker, you should still make the extra effort to put yourself in those readers' position and view your writing through their eyes. In doing so, you may find that there are details you have to fill in and assumptions you have to make explicit in order to fully communicate what you intend.

Subject

Autobiographical narratives provide interesting reading. Most of us like to learn about what other people did and what they think their personal stories mean. If the narrator is famous, readers can satisfy their curiosity about an extraordinary life. If the narrator is a more ordinary person, readers often identify with the experiences and can use them as warnings or inspirations for their own lives.

The story must be well told, with thoughtfully selected events, graphic details, and strong verbs. And as you draft and revise, keep your subject and purpose in mind, so that the meaning you attach to your experience becomes clear.

Writer

This Writing Project, like the others in Part One of this book, asks you to use your own experience as the basis of an essay. This puts you in the position of authority on the subject, which should give you confidence. Also, this project invites you to tell a story; most people enjoy doing this. Your challenges are to shape your story and to connect your story to your belief.

The Writing Process

One of this book's main goals is to help you think about your own writing process, to tap its strengths, and to reduce its weaknesses. This project provides a good opportunity for you to reflect on your writing process as you reflect on a significant experience.

Generating Ideas

Brainstorm to find a suitable experience to write about. Look for an experience that had a profound effect on your beliefs and that may have implications for other people's lives. Once you have determined an experience to write about, ask questions and write about your responses. Questions you might ask include these:

- What happened? (Outline the major events of the experience.)
- How did you respond? (What were your thoughts, reactions, feelings?)
- What roles did other people play? Was the place important? (Recall specific details about what people did and said, and about the setting, to make your retelling vivid for your audience.)
- What was the result of the experience? How did it affect your belief?
- As you reflect on it, what was valuable for you about the experience? How has it influenced your life?

You may also refer to the questions for generating ideas in Chapter 1 for other kinds of questions you can ask yourself.

Defining a Focus

In a few sentences, summarize the main point you wish to make in your essay, given your subject, audience, and purpose. Then evaluate your focus: Is it specific, so that you can convey it clearly in an essay? Is it interesting, so that your audience will find it worth reading about? Is it thoughtful, so that it serves the purpose of reflection?

At this point, consider whether or not the experience you have chosen to write about is a good subject. If not, you can begin again by brainstorming for a new experience to write about.

Organizing Ideas

Think about how you can order the elements of your experience. Will you start at the beginning and describe them chronologically? Or will you start at a later point in time and use a flashback to the beginning of the experience? Where will you include your observations and reflections about the experience: at the end, or at various places throughout?

As you are organizing your ideas and drafting, planning, and revising, you need to decide whether your paper will have a visible or an invisible structure. With a *visible structure,* the thesis is stated clearly, most paragraphs contain topic sentences, transitional expressions explicitly point out connections among ideas, and the introductory and concluding sections do their jobs of beginning and ending the piece. Visible structure is sometimes called the "no-fail" method of organization because it usually works and because anybody can learn to use it. Much academic and business writing relies on visible structure.

Invisible structure is, of course, more subtle and demands artistic crafting from the writer. Professional writers often create beautiful pieces with invisible structure. You may want to try it in some of your papers, but first you need to master the visible structure mode so that your expository writing will fulfill its purpose.

Drafting

As you translate your ideas, notes, and early versions into coherent writing, you need to decide how you can draft in ways that will help you revise your work effectively. Because the essay you are about to write has three distinct components—your belief, your experience, and their connections—you may want to draft each component separately and then think about how to connect them. In addition, you should recall the concepts presented in Chapter 1, especially the use of questions as a productive way to begin many forms of writing.

Revising

Once you have completed a draft that you think is close to a final version, you should put it aside for a day or two. If you don't have time to do that, then at least take a break before trying to revise. When you are ready to "re-see" your writing, read it through slowly, preferably aloud.

Consider it in terms of the following questions. (You may also use them when you review and comment on your classmates' drafts.)

- Are the incidents, people, and places involved in the experience related with enough detail to make the experience clear for readers and hold their attention? Where might further specific information or detail be offered?

- Is the effect the experience had on your belief made clear? Does the essay seem focused? If not, where is the focus lost or vague?

- How thoughtful are the reflection on the experience and the process of thinking it through? Is the value of the experience fully expressed?

- Are the opening and the conclusion effective? If not, what might make a better opening to get readers interested? How might the conclusion leave readers with a better understanding?

- Do there seem to be any problems with the use of language or sentence structure, or connections between ideas? Are any parts of the essay difficult to read? How might words and sentences be revised?

Proofreading

After you prepare a final draft, check for standard grammar and punctuation. Proofread carefully for omitted words and punctuation marks. Run your spelling checker program, but be aware of its limitations. Proofread again for the kinds of errors the computer can't catch.

STUDENT WRITING
A Changed Belief
by Agnes Kiragu

I must admit that I have never before paused to think of any belief I have had. Like many people, I just chose to believe or not believe without much of a reason. Now as I stop to think, I see that we have some beliefs that we do not even know we have. I now realize that in my mind I used to hold a belief that life could be a straight and easy, no-struggle routine. People went to school; after school they got employed and then married and they were satisfied. I often wondered why some people worked so hard when they could do this without much effort.

When I was younger most of my needs were catered for by my parents. I went to school and church and that was life for me. I could do the same for my children—I thought—without the pains of working towards a university education. When I was in school, I knew that school was important but I did not see why my parents and my elder brothers and sisters insisted so much on my struggling to get into a university. To me employment was what was important—regardless of what you did.

So after high school I went to a two year secretarial college where I graduated as a bi-lingual secretary (Swahili and English). It was when I was working for the International Committee of the Red Cross that I realized that just working was not enough; I needed more to be satisfied. At the Red Cross I worked on the Great Lakes Region crisis, which covered Rwanda and its neighboring countries. Though I was happy to see the victims of conflict getting the help they so much needed, I knew that I wanted to do more. I wanted to be of greater help to society and at the same time get more satisfaction from what I was doing.

In the real world, I realized, the more qualified, the more chances of rising into the satisfaction I so much desired. One had to work for qualifications. I stopped thinking that life could be effortless and decided to go to a university. In my country it is difficult to get into a university. I began to save up from my salary so that I could be able to study in the United States. I knew I could not save enough from my salary so I discussed it with my family. My parents demonstrated to me that the struggle in life does not end by offering to help me out.

Now I know that I have to work hard for the future because there will be many goals to work for. Now I see life as a stairway without an end. Each time I take a step upward I am relieved, but I realize there are many more steps to be taken. This stairway represents life's struggles. I now believe that life can't be straight and easy if I am to achieve.

STUDENT WRITING

Money Can't Do It
by Michael Persch

Probably only a couple of events in a person's life cause them to completely change their views on a matter. So far, the biggest one for me was when my father and mother lost their business. Several months later, I realized something: that money doesn't bring true happiness but that your family, if given the chance, can and will. This thought was like a light bulb that clicked on in my head. Two experiences caused it to click on, and I am sure glad it did. That light bulb helped me become a more real person.

When I was growing up, and all during high school, I was able to get almost anything that I wanted. For example, at Christmas, everyone in my family always received exactly what they asked for, plus a lot of other stuff. On my birthday and Valentine's day my parents usually sent flowers and balloons to me. Finally, whenever I needed money, all I had to do was ask my mom and dad, and they would give it to me. I used to take money for granted and never really thought about it not being there until it wasn't.

Our home was in the area to live in. During high school I never had to take the bus because I had my own car to drive after I turned sixteen. My friends and I were by far the coolest guys and girls in the school. I was able to live life to the fullest, or at least I thought I was, because I had these important things.

All of this was because my father owned a large variety store in town, and both it and my father were very successful. He was president of the Chamber of Commerce. The biggest reason that the store was so successful is that there was no competition. That is, until Wal-Mart came to town.

Just toward the end of the summer after graduation, my father resigned from the Chamber of Commerce. Then, he called a family meeting and told us that he was going to shut down the store because the new Wal-Mart had put us out of business.

I was grateful that this happened after I graduated from high school because my whole life changed and seemed to be falling apart. I had to sell my car; I felt that I had lost most of my friends, my money, and my self-respect and esteem. To top it off, now I had to get rides to and from work and college.

I couldn't stand it anymore, so I quit my job, dropped out of college and went to work far away as a server at the Grand Canyon North Rim where I didn't know anybody and nobody knew me! It wasn't too long before I had become particularly good buddies with a couple of guys I worked with, and the three of us decided that it would be cool to move to Seattle. So we quit, packed up our stuff, and moved there.

But in Seattle I hit rock bottom. Now there were new stresses, simple things like paying rent and bills. I began looking for an escape and found it in tobacco, alcohol, and drugs.

However, it was also in Seattle that I did a lot of growing up. Although using drugs and alcohol was a bad part of my life, not all of the effects were negative. I found myself talking with people from all walks of life. These were people who before I would never have been caught dead associating with. Now, not only was I talking with them, but I was learning from them. I began to have an open mind and to see that other people were both worse off and better off than I was.

Then a life-changing event happened. I got sick, really sick. I caught Hepatitis A from something, which put me in the hospital. I just knew that I was going to die.

Consequently, I realized how much I needed and missed my family, and it didn't matter how much I had previously thought that they had failed me. I called my mother and she told me that they would be there as soon as possible. When they arrived the next day, I was very happy to see them! When I could leave the hospital, we stayed together in a hotel for a few more days until I was well enough to fly home. Then I realized just how much I was loved.

Now things are going well for my family. Both of my parents went back to school. My mom is the head of the nursing department at Dixie Medical Center, and my father has become a toxic waste manager for the EPA. They are again able to help me financially with school, but I no longer take their help for granted because I now believe that my parents' love is much more valuable than their money.

CHAPTER 3

Thinking Creatively, Writing Creatively

Critical Thinking Focus: The qualities of a creative thinker

Writing Focus: Generating original ideas

Reading Theme: The creative thinking process

Writing Project: Imagining your life lived more creatively

Writing Creatively

Creative writing is often thought of as imaginative fiction, poetry, or drama, for which the author invents characters and situations. So the question naturally arises, what part does creativity have in *expository writing* in which facts, ideas, and concepts are explored, developed, and argued? The answer: a very large part.

You can use your creative thinking in selecting and narrowing your topic (if you are allowed to pick you own topic), in the way you generate and research ideas, in the way you organize your ideas, and in the way you focus on your ideas with your thesis. You can also use creative thinking to help yourself develop your ideas with carefully chosen specific details and examples. You can use creative thinking to develop analogies and metaphors to help your readers grasp your ideas. Finally, you can use creative thinking to write imaginative, inviting introductions that will make your readers anxious to read further, and you can use it to write carefully crafted conclusions that tie in elegantly with your introductions. Of course, your critical thinking abilities too are involved in all these steps, helping you to decide which of your creative ideas to include and which to discard.

Does all this sound like a large amount of work? Well, you're right. It is.

Yet there are good reasons for developing your creativity in writing. Just as "The unexamined life is not worth living," it may be said that "The uncreative piece of writing is not worth reading." If all you do in your expository writing is restate other people's ideas in a dry, formulaic way, you risk boring yourself with your writing—and boring your audience as well.

The challenge to be creative in your writing is a difficult one, and the possibilities for creativity are vast. Focusing on the following four areas for creativity in expository writing will help you further develop the creative writing abilities you may already have.

- Being creative in topic selection
- Being creative in generating ideas, researching, and drafting
- Being creative in using specific details and examples
- Being creative in writing introductions and conclusions

Being Creative in Topic Selection

Some topics are personal and ask you to draw on your own life experiences, others are impersonal and clearly require research, while still others are a blend of the personal and impersonal. Furthermore, some topics are quite precise; for example, "Write about your father's influence on your religious development" or "Write about the causes of the Crimean War." Given such a precise topic, that is exactly what you must write about. Often, though, assigned topics are general enough that they need to be narrowed, to be made more precise. This allows for some creativity on your part: for instance, "Write about how some family member influenced you in an important way," or "Write about some aspect of the Crimean War," or even "Write a paper on some topic related to this course." Given this type of assignment, you may want to allow the creative process to help you in shaping it, a process we will explore later in this chapter in the section Understanding the Creative Process on pages 65–68.

Begin your search for a topic by picking a tentative topic, one that interests you and that you would like to think and learn more about. A good strategy is to state a topic as a question. For example, "What, if any, new military strategies were introduced during the Crimean War?" If it is a topic requiring research, read as much as you can about the general topic area, being on the lookout for ways to modify your tentative topic question or even for a new question altogether. If you are working with a personal topic, begin to make notes that will help you answer your question. Either way, try to gauge whether you have enough information to answer your question, or whether you have too little or too much. You can make your topic question broader or narrow it as you proceed.

Expect false starts! The fact that your original question needs to be modified or even discarded does not mean that you are doing something wrong. Becoming aware of the need to make these changes is a normal development that occurs with almost all writers, so don't become discouraged when it occurs with you. Instead, congratulate yourself for being willing to put to work the time and effort needed for the creative process, as you shape your topic.

Being Creative in Generating Ideas, Researching, and Drafting

Books about writing sometimes speak as though generating ideas, researching, and drafting are three entirely separate stages, and the writer finishes with one stage before beginning the next. This may even be true in some cases, but often writers find themselves getting new ideas while researching, or beginning to draft only to realize the need for more research or brainstorming. Furthermore, writers find that the order of these stages, as well as the time needed to complete them successfully, may vary from one writing project to another.

Since there is often this back-and-forth movement between stages, there are many opportunities for creative thinking. Be sure to review pages 13–17 in Chapter 1 for suggestions on generating and organizing ideas; then experiment with the following strategies to see which of them help you with your writing.

- When brainstorming, don't hesitate to write down every idea, no matter how unusable it may seem at the time.

- When brainstorming, write each idea on a separate post-it note. (This makes it easy to rearrange them into groups later when you need to organize them.)

- Carry a little notebook so that you can jot down ideas whenever they come.

- Phone your own voice mail and leave yourself a message if an idea strikes while away from home.

- Talk into a tape recorder and listen later to what you said.

- Talk to other people about your topic. Knowledgeable people will add to your information; people unfamiliar with the topic will ask useful questions.

- Ask a librarian for research suggestions.

- Hold on to conflicting information or opinions. They are the heart of academic discussion.

- Look in the Yellow Pages for businesses or organizations that can provide information.

- Identify and interview experts on your topic. (Be sure to acknowledge them as sources.)

- Scan the TV schedule, including cable and PBS channels, for related programs.

- Surf the Internet for sources of information.

- When drafting, don't necessarily begin with the introduction. Instead, begin with whatever section is easiest to write.

- Be willing to modify your thesis as you go along, so that you don't lock yourself into a position too early.

- Avoid premature organization; draft sections on separate pages or as separate computer files. Then try arranging them in different orders.

- If you are interrupted while drafting, read what you have already written, to get back into the flow.

In other words, immerse yourself in your writing; live in it and with it long enough for the creative process to work.

Being Creative in Using Specific Details and Examples

Because solid evidence for claims is one of the most important requirements of college writing and one of the essentials in critical thinking, a good thinker will habitually give specific examples for any general statement to show its validity and to make it understandable. However, writers often need to think creatively in order to discover examples and to present them effectively.

A common item of advice to writers is "Don't tell your readers; show them." Good writers show by means of specific details and relevant examples, often searching through levels of specificity to find what is needed. For example:

Telling: Michael Jordan is a great basketball player.

Showing: During the 1995–1996 season, Michael Jordan led the NBA with a scoring average of 30.4 points per game. That same season, he ranked second on the Bulls for rebounding and assists.

     He was chosen for the NBA All-Star Team in his first nine seasons.

     He has won four league MVP awards and two Olympic gold medals.

Often one example will lead to another.

Telling: My brother is an easygoing person.

Showing: My brother lets me borrow his car whenever I want. When I had an accident while driving his car, all he said was, "That's why we have insurance."

In order to come up with abundant examples, you may need to do research and you may need to think creatively, following suggestions given in the section on being creative in generating ideas, researching, and drafting (pp. 56–57).

Writers can also be creative in generating language with which to express the details that most writing needs. While writing must always be as accurate as possible, sometimes metaphorical images can be applied; in other instances, clear descriptors are in order. Think of the differences created by describing someone's hair as *dark,* or *black,* or *like wet pavement,* or *like polished ebony,* or *like a Labrador retriever's.*

Being Creative with Introductions and Conclusions

Another time to think creatively while working on a piece of writing is when you are ready to deal with the beginning and the ending. What is most important to realize is that you need not, and probably should not, try to write these sections in order. Many successful writers work on the beginning or introduction last—or they may draft an introduction at an early stage, but plan to revise it as they complete the paper.

Explore as many different types of introductions and conclusions as you can, if you are writing something for which there can be choices. (Some kinds of writing have expected formats that include types of beginnings and endings: lab reports are an example.)

Following are some types of beginnings.

- Background information or context
- A relevant anecdote
- A quotation or proverb that relates to the topic
- A striking statement (to be contradicted or supported)
- The problem to be addressed in the paper
- Questions connected to the content of the paper
- The who, what, where, when, and why of the paper's focus
- The claim, thesis, or main point
- Combinations of types listed above

You can use creative thinking to come up with more; then use critical thinking and help from your editors, including peers, to decide which beginning your paper should have.

The same approach works for drafting conclusions. Explore the many possibilities for endings, which include these six.

- A summary of the paper's information
- A recommendation or exhortation or call for action
- An apt quotation or proverb
- A telling anecdote
- The thesis or main point stated at the end of an inductively arranged paper
- A suggestion of the need for more discussion of the issue

A conclusion must provide a sense of closure to the piece; readers should recognize it as an ending (you should not have to write "The End"!).

Neither introductions nor conclusions should be apologetic; neither should have a tone different from that of the body of the paper. Both should be carefully revised after being creatively prepared.

THINKING↔WRITING ACTIVITY 3.1

Creative Introductions and Conclusions

Find two or three articles in a publication that you enjoy. Look at the introductions and conclusions. Are they among the types just listed? If not, how would you describe them? For one of the articles, try to write a different introduction or conclusion and evaluate its effectiveness.

Thinking Creatively

Thinking critically and thinking creatively are two essential and tightly interwoven dimensions of the thinking process. Both work together as partners to produce productive, effective thinking, leading to informed decisions and eventually, successful lives. Thinking critically and thinking creatively also work as partners in the writing process, enabling us to find and evaluate new approaches and insights, to discover ways to interest readers in our ideas, and to express our ideas in fresh, striking language. Thinking Creatively involves discovering and developing ideas that are unusual and worthy of further elaboration. Thinking Critically involves carefully examining our thinking and the thinking of others, in order to clarify and improve our understanding.

For example, imagine that you are confronted with a problem to solve. *Thinking critically* enables you to identify and accept the problem. When you generate alternatives for solving the problem, you are using *creative thinking* abilities. When you evaluate the various alternatives and select one or more to pursue, you are *thinking critically*. Developing ideas for implementing alternatives involves *thinking creatively*, while constructing a practical plan of action and evaluating the results depends on *thinking critically*.

Although the first two chapters of this book have emphasized your critical thinking abilities, creative thinking has been involved in every part of our explorations of the mind. In this chapter, we are shifting the emphasis to creative thinking, working to gain insight into this powerful and mysterious dimension of the thinking process, a dimension that can add richness and joy to our lives and to our writing.

THINKING ↔ WRITING ACTIVITY 3.2

Recalling a Creative Experience

1. Write about two different times when you consciously tried to be creative. Answer the following questions for each experience.

   - What was the situation that required your creativity?
   - How did you go about finding a creative idea or solution?
   - What was that creative idea or solution?
   - Was it successful?
   - How do you feel remembering this experience?

2. Select one of your experiences to share with your class or small group.
3. Listen carefully to all the experiences that are shared.
4. On the basis of your own writing and the experiences of others which you've heard, try to make some inferences or general statements about creativity.

Living Creatively

Human beings have a nearly limitless capacity to be creative, our imaginations giving us the power to conceive of new possibilities and put these innovative ideas into action. Using creative resources in this way enriches our lives and brings a special meaning to our activities. While we might not go to the extreme of saying that "The uncreative life is not worth living," it is surely preferable to live a life enriched by the qualities of creativity.

Many people think that being creative is beyond them, that creativity is a mysterious gift bestowed on only a chosen few. One reason for this is that people often confuse being "creative" with being "artistic"—skilled at art, music, poetry, imaginative writing, drama, or dance. Although artistic people are certainly creative, there are an infinite number of ways to be creative that are *not* artistic. Being creative is a state of mind and a way of life. As the writer Eric Gill expresses it: *"The artist is not a different kind of person, but each one of us is a different kind of artist."*

Are you creative? Yes! Think of all the activities that you enjoy: cooking, creating a wardrobe, raising children, playing sports, cutting or braiding hair, dancing, playing music. Whenever you are investing your own personal ideas, putting on your own personal stamp, you are being creative. For example, imagine that you are cooking your favorite dish. To the extent that you are expressing your unique ideas developed through inspiration and experimentation, you are being creative. If, of course, you are simply following someone else's recipe without significant modification, your dish may be tasty—but it is not creative. Similarly, if your moves on the dance floor or the basketball court express your distinctive personality, you are being creative, as you are when you stimulate the original thinking of your children or make your friends laugh with your own brand of humor.

You are an artist, creating your life portrait, and your paints and brush strokes are the choices that you make each day of your life.

Living life creatively means bringing your perspective and creative talents to all of the dimensions of your life. Below are five passages written by students about creative areas in their lives. After reading the passages, complete **Thinking↔Writing Activity 3.3,** which gives you the opportunity to describe a creative area from your own life.

STUDENT WRITING

Cooking

One of the most creative aspects of my life is my diet. I have been a vegetarian for the past five years, while the rest of my family has continued to eat meat. I had to overcome many obstacles to make this lifestyle work for me, including family dissension. The solution was simple: I had to learn how to cook creatively. I have come to realize that my diet is an on-going learning process. The more I learn about and experiment with different foods, the healthier and happier I become. I feel like an explorer setting out on my own to discover new things about food and nutrition. I slowly evolved from a person who could cook food only if it came from a can, into someone who could make bread from scratch and grow yogurt cultures. I find learning new things about nutrition and cooking healthful foods very relaxing and rewarding. I like being alone in my house baking bread; there is something very comforting about the aroma. Most of all I like to experiment with different ways to prepare foods, because the ideas are my own. Even when an effort is less than successful, I find pleasure in the knowledge that I gained from the experience. I discovered recently, for example, that eggplant is terrible in soup! Making mistakes seems to be a natural way to increase creativity, and I now firmly believe that people who say that they do not like vegetables simply have not been properly introduced to them!

Writing

The most creative area in my life is my writing. I love the thrill of inventing a new person or location, and, although I have a host of characters and story lines, there is one character named Pynthe that I am particularly proud of. Pynthe is not only my favorite character, she is also my most creative. When I invented Pynthe, I did more than just arrange a few words on paper. I gave her dimension. I took a daydream, a glimmer of an idea, and turned it into an individual. From my imagination, I created a fantasy world and religion for my character. I also gave her a past with its share of heartaches and happiness, and a future full of hopes and dreams. There is nothing more exhilarating than creating with language. In the extreme, I can destroy my character with two words, or bring her to the other side of the spectrum and let her lead a long and satisfying life. I can best describe this feeling of creation as a euphoric rush. I love letting my imagination roam and I easily lose myself in writing, absorbed in the process.

Raising Children

As any parent knows, children have an abundance of energy to spend, and toys or television do not always meet their needs. In response, I create activities to stimulate their creativity and preserve my sanity. For example, I involve them in the process of cooking, giving them the skin from peeled vegetables and a pot so they make their own "soup." Using catalogs, we cut out pictures of furniture, rugs, and curtains, and they paste them onto cartons to create their own interior decor: vibrant living rooms, plush bedrooms, colorful family rooms. I make beautiful boats from aluminum paper, and my children spend hours in the bathtub playing with them. We "go bowling" with empty soda cans and a ball, and they star in "track meets" by running an obstacle course we set up. When it comes to raising children, creativity is a way of survival!

Carpentry

After quitting the government agency I was working at because of too much bureaucracy, I was hired as a carpenter at a construction site, although I had little knowledge of this profession. I learned to handle a hammer and other tools by watching co-workers, and within a matter of weeks I was skilled enough to organize my own group of workers for projects. Most of my fellow workers used the old-fashioned method of construction carpentry, building panels with inefficient and poorly made bracings. I redesigned the panels in order to save construction time and materials. My supervisor and site engineer were thrilled with my creative ideas, and I was assigned progressively more challenging projects, including the construction of an office building that was completed in record time.

Hair Braiding

My area of creativity is hair braiding, an activity that requires skill, talent, and patience that is difficult for most people to accomplish. Braiding hair in styles that are being worn today consists of braiding small to tiny braids, and it may include adding artificial hair to make the hair look fuller. It takes anywhere from ten to sixteen hours depending on the type of style that is desired: the smaller the braids, the longer it takes. In order to braid, I had to learn how to determine the right hair and color for people that wanted extensions, pick out the right style that would fit perfectly on my customers' faces, learn to cut hair in an asymmetric fashion, put curls in the braids, and know the sequence of activities. Doing hair is a rewarding experience for me because when I am through with my work, my customers think the result is gorgeous!

THINKING ↔ WRITING ACTIVITY 3.3

A Creative Idea

1. Describe a creative area of your life in which you are able to express your personality and talents. Be specific and give examples.
2. Analyze your creative area by answering the following questions:

   - Why do you feel that this activity is creative? Give examples.
   - How would you describe the experience of being engaged in this activity? Where do your creative ideas come from? How do they develop?
   - What strategies do you use to increase your creativity? What obstacles block your creative efforts? How do you try to overcome these blocks?

Becoming More Creative

Although we each have nearly limitless potential to live creatively, most people use only a small percentage of their creative gifts. In fact, there is research to suggest that people typically achieve their highest creative point as young children, after which there is a long, steady decline into uncreativity. Why? Well, to begin with, young children are immersed in the excitement of exploration and discovery. They are eager to try out new things, act on their impulses, and make unusual connections between disparate ideas. They are not afraid to take risks in trying out untested solutions; they do not feel compelled to identify the socially acceptable "correct answer." Children are willing to play with ideas, creating improbable scenarios and imaginative ways of thinking, without fear of being ridiculed.

All of this tends to change as we get older. The weight of "reality" begins to smother our imagination, and we increasingly focus our attention on the nuts and bolts of living, rather than playing with possibilities. The social pressure to conform to group expectations increases dramatically. Whether the group is our friends, schoolmates, or fellow employees, there are clearly defined "rules" for dressing, behaving, speaking, and thinking. When we deviate from these rules, we risk social disapproval, rejection, or ridicule. Most groups have little tolerance for individuals who want to think independently and creatively. As we become older, we also become more reluctant to pursue untested course of action, because we become increasingly afraid of failure. Pursuing creativity inevitably involves failure, because we are trying to break out of established ruts and go beyond traditional methods. For example, going beyond the safety of a proven recipe to create an innovative dish may involve some disasters, yet is the only way to create something genuinely unique. The history of creative discoveries is littered with failures, a fact we tend to forget when we are debating whether to risk an untested idea.

THINKING↔WRITING ACTIVITY 3.4

Inhibitions to Creativity

Reflect on your own creative development and describe some of the fears and pressures that inhibit your own creativity. For example, have you ever been penalized for trying a new idea that didn't work out? Have you ever suffered the wrath of the group for daring to be different and violate the group's unspoken rules? Do you feel that your life is so filled with responsibilities and the demands of reality that you don't have time to be creative?

Understanding the Creative Process

Although the forces that discourage us from being creative are powerful, they can nevertheless be overcome with four productive strategies:

- Understand and trust the creative process.
- Eliminate the "Voice of Judgment."
- Make creativity a priority.
- Establish a creative environment.

Understand and Trust the Creative Process

Discovering your creative talents requires that you understand how the creative process operates, then have confidence in the results it produces. There are no fixed procedures or formulas for generating creative ideas because creative ideas *by definition* go beyond established ways of thinking to the unknown and the innovative. As the ancient Greek philosopher Heraclitus once said, *"You must expect the unexpected, because it cannot be found by search or trail."*

Although there is no fixed path to creative ideas, there are activities we can pursue that make the birth of creative ideas possible. In this respect, generating creative ideas is similar to gardening. We need to prepare the soil; plant the seeds; ensure proper watering, light, and food; and then be patient until the ideas begin to sprout. Here are some steps for cultivating your creative garden:

Absorb yourself in the task: Creative ideas don't occur in a vacuum. They emerge after a great deal of work, study, and practice. For example, if you want to come up with creative ideas in the kitchen, you need to become knowledgeable about the art of cooking. The more knowledgeable you are, the better prepared you are to create valuable and innovative dishes. Similarly, if you are trying to develop a creative perspective for a research paper in college, you need to immerse yourself in the subject, developing an in-depth understanding of the central concepts and issues. Absorbing your-self in the task "prepares the soil" for your creative ideas.

Allow time for ideas to incubate: After absorbing yourself in the task or problem, the next stage in the creative process is to stop working on it. When your conscious mind has stopped actively working on the task, the uncon-scious dimension of your mind continues working—processing, organizing, and ultimately generating innovative ideas and solutions. This process is known as *incubation* because it mirrors the process in which baby chicks grad-ually evolve inside the egg until the moment comes when they break out through the shell. In the same way, your creative mind is at work while you are going about your business until the moment of *illumination*, when the incu-bating idea finally erupts to the surface of your conscious mind. People report that these illuminating moments—when their mental light bulbs go on—often occur when they are engaged in activities completely unrelated to the task.

Seize on the ideas when they emerge and follow them through: Gener-ating creative ideas is of little use unless we recognize them when they ap-pear and then act on them. Too often people don't pay much attention to these ideas when they occur, or they dismiss them as too impractical. Have confidence in your ideas, even if they seem a little strange. Many of the most valuable inventions in our history started as improbable ideas, ridiculed by the popular wisdom. For example, the idea of Velcro started with burrs cov-ering the pants of the inventor as he walked through a field, and Post-It Notes resulted from the accidental invention of an adhesive that was weaker than normal. In other words, thinking effectively means thinking creatively and thinking critically. After we use our *creative thinking* abilities to generate in-novative ideas, we must employ our *critical thinking* abilities to evaluate and refine those ideas and design a practical plan for implementing them.

Eliminate the "Voice of Judgment"

The biggest threat to our creativity lies within ourselves, the negative Voice of Judgment (VOJ). This term was coined by Michael Ray and Rochelle Myers, the authors of *Creativity in Business,* a book based on a Stanford Uni-versity course. The VOJ can undermine your confidence in every area of your life, including your creative activities. For example, when you are drafting a paper, the VOJ may whisper:

"This is a stupid idea and no one will like it."

"Even if I could pull this idea off, it probably won't amount to much."

These statements, and countless others like them, have the ongoing effect of making us doubt ourselves and the quality of our creative thinking. As we lose confidence, we become more timid, reluctant to follow through on ideas and present them to others. After a while our cumulative insecurity discour-ages us from even generating ideas in the first place, and we end up simply conforming to established ways of thinking and the expectations of others. And in so doing, we surrender an important part of ourselves, the vital and dynamic creative core of our personality.

How do we eliminate this unwelcome and destructive inner voice? There are a number of effective strategies to use. Remember, though, that the fight, while worth the effort, will not be easy.

Become aware of the VOJ: You have probably been listening to the negative messages of the VOJ for so long that you may not even consciously be aware of it. To conquer the VOJ, you first need to recognize when it speaks.

Restate the judgment in a more accurate or constructive way: Sometimes there is an element of truth in our self-judgments, but we have blown the reality out of proportion. For example, if you fail a test, your VOJ may translate this as "You're a failure." If you ask someone for a date and get turned down, your VOJ may conclude: "You're a social misfit with emotional bad breath!" In these instances, you need to translate the reality accurately: "I failed this test—I wonder what went wrong and how I can improve my performance in the future." "This person turned me down for a date—I guess we're not compatible, or maybe we just don't know each other well enough."

Get tough with the VOJ: You can't be a wimp if you hope to overcome the VOJ. Instead, you have to be strong and determined, vowing as soon as the VOJ appears, "I'm throwing you out and not letting you back in!" This attack may feel peculiar at first, but it will soon become an automatic response when those negative judgments appear.

Create positive voices and visualizations: The best way to destroy the VOJ for good is to replace it with positive encouragement. As soon as you have stomped on, say, the judgment "You're a jerk," you should replace it with "No, I'm an intelligent, valuable person with many positive qualities and talents." Similarly, you should make extensive use of positive visualization, as you "see" yourself performing well on your examinations; being entertaining and insightful with other people, and succeeding gloriously in the sport or dramatic production in which you are involved.

Use other people for independent confirmation: The negative judgments coming from the VOJ are usually irrational, but until they are dragged out into the light of day for examination, they can be very powerful. Sharing our VOJ with people we trust is an effective strategy because they can provide an objective perspective that reveals to us the irrationality and destructiveness of these negative judgments.

Establish a Creative Environment

An important part of eliminating the negative voices in our mind is to establish environments in which our creative resources can flourish. This means finding or developing physical environments conducive to creative expression as well as supportive social environments. Sometimes, working with other people is stimulating and energizing to our creative juices; at other times, we require a private place where we can work without distraction. One writer says, "I have a specific location in which I do much of my writing: sitting on a comfortable couch, with a calm, pleasing view, music on the stereo, a cold drink, a supply of Tootsie Roll Pops. I'm ready for creativity to strike me, although I sometimes have to wait for some time." Different environments work for different people: you have to find the environment(s) best suited to your own creative process, then make a special effort to do your work there.

The people in our lives who form our social environment play an even more influential role in encouraging or inhibiting our creative process. When we are surrounded by people who are positive and supportive, this increases our confidence and encourages us to take the risk to express our creative vision. They can stimulate our creativity by providing us with fresh ideas and new perspectives. By engaging in *brainstorming* (described on page 13), they can work with us to generate ideas and then, later, help us figure out how to refine and implement the most valuable ones.

Make Creativity a Priority

Having diminished the voice of negative judgment in your mind, established a creative environment, and committed yourself to trusting your creative gifts, you are now in a position to live more creatively. How do you actually do this? Start small. Identify some habitual patterns in your life and break out of them. Choose new experiences whenever possible—for example, ordering unfamiliar items from a menu or getting to know people outside your circle of friends—and strive to develop fresh perspectives on things in your life. Resist falling back into the ruts you were in previously; remember that living things are supposed to be continually growing, changing, and evolving, *not* acting in repetitive patterns like machines.

Examining Creativity

We have defined thinking creatively as the cognitive process we use to discover and develop ideas that are unusual and worthy of further elaboration. But how do we get creative ideas? Where do they come from? The following readings offer us some clues.

from Pizza Tiger
by Tom Monaghan with Robert Anderson

. . . There are some personal approaches in management that I don't think I could have learned from a book. My method of making decisions is one of them. I don't know that it would work for anyone else. But here, for whatever it's worth is how I do it:

I reach decisions by making lists on my yellow legal pads. Down one side of a page, I'll write all the reasons I can think of in favor of a given course of action. On the other side, I list every reason I can think of against it. Thinking of arguments for and against a decision is where my ability to dream comes in handy: I *imagine* the decision has been made. I see in my mind's eye how it affects people and the way they react. If it's a complicated issue, with many reasons for it and a lot of others against, I will break each point down into sublists and assign them a kind of point value so I can weigh them against each other.

Sometimes, as I learned from my experience with the proposal that we change our name to Pizza Dispatch, it's good to consider future situations, too. In that case, my list of the benefits of the name Pizza Dispatch were outweighed by the drawbacks of giving up Domino's. But I concentrated on the immediate situation. I didn't ask myself, Okay, five years from now, when we have more than two thousand stores and are in every state in the Union, what will the pros and cons be then? Had I done so, I would have made a better decision.

I also make lists as a way of brainstorming ideas with myself on paper. This is a written version of what I love to do verbally on the occasions when I can get on the same wavelength with another person. Doing it verbally is more fun because it's exciting to share the exploration of ideas. But the written approach is absorbing, too, and it can be extremely fruitful.

5   At the outset I'm often unable to see a good idea because there's a clutter of other things hiding it. There are roads through the clutter, though, and I have to go down them until I find the one that will take me up mentally above the clutter, to a point where I can see a good idea on the horizon. The roads are propositions that I think up, write down on my list, and follow one by one. A proposition might be stupid or obvious, but I take it anyway because I don't know where it will lead and what it might connect with. I say to myself, Why don't we do this? Well, I see that if we did that, it would allow us to do something else, and I just keep adding to it. If I don't go down those roads, I never get to the good idea, because there's a link, and I find the link by following something that may not work or is impossible.

I sometimes compare my brainstorming on paper to the drilling of oil wells. The only way to strike oil is to drill a lot of wells. My lists are wells, and every once in a while I hit a gusher. I'm working away, making lists, and all of a sudden something pops right out. I'll say, Hey, look at that!

Lots of times I'll be writing lists of things I want to do this year or next year, which I do just for the fun of it, and I'll find one item I want to think about some more. So I'll take a separate page, or sometimes even another pad, and start making lists of ideas about that particular thing. I expand on it, and who knows, maybe I'll find other things in *that* list that I want to expand on. It's like fishing. I never know what kind of idea I might catch.

from Perfecting Our Strategy
by Pauli Murray

My last semester in law school was dizzying, because everything seemed to happen at once. In addition to carrying a heavy course load, as graduation approached I found myself battling simultaneously on three fronts which required constant shifting of intellectual and emotional gears. I was at once a minority voice within the law school in an ongoing debate over civil rights legal strategy, a student leader in the renewed direct action assault upon Washington's segregated restaurants, and a solitary challenger of Harvard Law School's traditional exclusion of women students.

In the early 1940s Howard Law School stood virtually alone in its strong emphasis upon civil rights. Our senior Civil Rights Seminar was easily the most popular course in the curriculum. Presided over by my early supporter, jovial Leon A. Ransom, whose brilliant Supreme Court victories included reversal of the death sentence of one of the famous Scottsboro defendants, the seminar was a forum in which eager students tested their abilities against experienced civil rights lawyers and vied with one another to present the most persuasive arguments for the overthrow of Jim Crow.

Bound together by an overriding passion, we were a tiny band of fighters trying to establish defensible positions from which to launch a massive attack upon the entire system of legally enforced segregation, reinforced as it was by decades of court decisions. We sifted through hundreds of judicial opinions in search of fragments of language to bolster our moral convictions, and although the same ground had been covered many times over, any fresh idea that emerged in the heat of our forensic struggles would be refined through research and developed into a seminar paper. These student efforts added to the law school's reservoir of constitutional theory. In the absence of a law review, our papers remained unpublished, but some of our ideas eventually found their way into briefs presented to the Supreme Court, and in later years we could look back with pride on our performance as anonymous foot soldiers in the early waves of the struggle leading to the great civil rights legal victories of the forties, fifties, and sixties.

Two great roadblocks in our advance toward equality under the law were the Supreme Court's landmark decisions in the *Civil Rights Cases* of 1883 and *Plessy* v. *Ferguson* in 1896. In the 1883 decision, the Court struck down sections of the Civil Rights Act of 1875, which had prohibited denial of equal accommodations in hotels, in theaters, and on railroads and other public conveyances, thus leaving Negroes unprotected against discrimination by private establishments. This decision set the stage for the more far-reaching doctrine of "separate but equal" treatment laid down in the later *Plessy* case, which held that states had the power to enforce separation by race so long as the separate facilities were equal. These two cases, generally presumed to be settled law, locked us into a permanent and visibly inferior status. We needed no sociological data to tell us the decisions were morally wrong and judicially biased—our personal experience contradicted their validity—but our problem was how to overcome an almost impregnable wall of judicial precedent.

5   One day during class discussion, in a flash of poetic insight, I advanced a radical approach that few legal scholars considered viable in 1944—namely, that the time had come to make a frontal assault on the constitutionality of segregation per se instead of continuing to acquiesce in the *Plessy* doctrine while nibbling away at its underpinnings on a case-by-case basis and having to show in each case that the facility in question was in fact *unequal.* In essence I was challenging the traditional NAACP tactic of concentrating on the *equal* side of the *Plessy* equation.

One would have thought I had proposed that we attempt to tear down the Washington Monument or the Statue of Liberty. First astonishment, then hoots of derisive laughter, greeted what seemed to me to be an obvious solution. My approach was considered too visionary, one likely to precipitate an unfavorable decision of the Supreme Court, thus strengthening rather than destroying the force of the *Plessy* case. Spottswood Robinson, the young Bills and Notes professor, who had graduated several years earlier with the highest academic record in the history of the law school and whose encyclopedic knowledge of case law inspired awe among students, not only pooh-poohed my idea but good-naturedly accepted my wager of ten dollars that *Plessy* would be overruled within twenty-five years. None of us dreamed that the Supreme Court would deliver a death blow to the *Plessy* doctrine, in *Brown* v. *Board of Education,* not twenty-five but only ten years later.

Opposition to an idea I cared deeply about always aroused my latent mule-headedness, and I chose for my seminar paper the ambitious topic "Should the *Civil Rights Cases* and *Plessy* v. *Ferguson* Be Overruled?" An inexperienced third-year law student was hardly equipped to deal adequately with an enormously complex constitutional problem which would later tax the best efforts of scores of legal scholars, but Andy Ransom, delighting in what he must have thought of as my naive audacity, egged me on and even extended the deadline for my paper to the end of the summer following graduation.

from Unended Quest
by Karl Popper

. . . What characterizes creative thinking, apart from the intensity of the interest in the problem, seems to me often the ability to break through the limits of the range—or to vary the range—from which a less creative thinker selects his trials. This ability, which clearly is a critical ability, may be described as *critical imagination.* It is often the result of culture clash, that is, a clash between ideas, or frameworks of ideas. Such a clash may help us to break through the ordinary bounds of our imagination.

Remarks like this, however, would hardly satisfy those who seek for a psychological theory of creative thinking, and especially of scientific discovery. For what they are after is a theory of *successful* thinking.

I think that the demand for a theory of successful thinking cannot be satisfied, and that it is not the same as the demand for a theory of creative thinking. Success depends on many things—for example on luck. It may depend on meeting with a promising problem. It depends on not being anticipated. It depends on such things as a fortunate division of one's time between trying to keep up-to-date and concentrating on working out one's own ideas.

But it seems to me that what is essential to "creative" or "inventive" thinking is a combination of intense interest in some problem (and thus a readiness to try again and again) with highly critical thinking, with a readiness to attack even those presuppositions which for less critical thought determine the limits of the range from which trials (conjectures) are selected; with an imaginative freedom that allows us to see so far unsuspected sources of error: possible prejudices in need of critical examination.

(It is my opinion that most investigations into the psychology of creative thoughts are pretty barren—or else more logical than psychological. For critical thought, or error elimination, can be better characterized in logical terms than in psychological terms.)

5   A "trial" or a newly formed "dogma" or a new "expectation" is largely the result of inborn *needs* that give rise to specific *problems.* But it is also the result of the inborn need to form expectations (in certain specific fields, which in their turn are related to some other needs); and it may also be partly the result of disappointed earlier expectations. I do not of course deny that there may also be an element of personal ingenuity present in the formation of trials or dogmas, but I think that ingenuity and imagination play their main part in the *critical process of error elimination.* Most of the great theories which are among the supreme achievements of the human mind are the offspring of earlier dogmas, plus criticism.

What became clear to me first, in connection with dogma-formation, was that children—especially small children—urgently need discoverable regularities around them; there was an inborn need not only for food and for being loved but also for discoverable structural invariants of the environment ("things" are such discoverable invariants), for a settled routine, for settled expectations. This infantile dogmatism has been observed by Jane Austen: "Henry and John were still asking every day for the story of Harriet and the gipsies, and still tenaciously setting [Emma] . . . right if she varied in the slightest particular from the original recital." There was, especially in older children, enjoyment in variation, but mainly within a limited range or framework of expectations. Games, for example, were of this kind; and the rules (the invariants) of the game were often almost impossible to learn by mere observation.

My main point was that the dogmatic way of thinking was due to an inborn need for regularities, and to inborn mechanisms of discovery; mechanisms which make us search for regularities. And one of my theses was that if we speak glibly of "heredity and environment" we are liable to underrate the overwhelming role of heredity—which, among other things, largely determines what aspects of its objective environment (the ecological niche) do or do not belong to an animal's subjective, or biologically significant, environment.

I distinguished three main types of learning process, of which the first was the fundamental one:

(1) Learning in the sense of discovery: (dogmatic) formation of theories or expectations, or regular behaviour, checked by (critical) error elimination.

(2) Learning by imitation. This can be interpreted as a special case of (1).

(3) Learning by "repetition" or "practising," as in learning to play an instrument or to drive a car. Here my thesis is that (a) there is no genuine "repetition" but rather (b) change through error elimination (following theory formation) and (c) a process which helps to make certain actions or reactions automatic, thereby allowing them to sink to a merely physiological level, and to be performed without attention.

The significance of inborn dispositions or needs for discovering regularities and rules may be seen in the child's learning to speak a language, a process that has been much studied. It is, of course, a kind of learning by imitation; and the most astonishing thing is that this very early process is one of trial and critical error elimination, in which the critical error elimination plays a very important role. The power of innate dispositions and needs in this development can best be seen in children who, owing to their deafness, do not participate in the speech situations of their social environment in the normal way. The most convincing cases are perhaps children who are deaf *and* blind like Laura Bridgman—or Helen Keller, of whom I heard only at a later date.

Admittedly, even in these cases we find social contacts—Helen Keller's contact with her teacher—and we also find imitation. But Helen Keller's imitation of her teacher's spelling into her hand is far removed from the ordinary child's imitation of sounds heard over a long period, sounds whose communicative function can be understood, and responded to, even by a dog.

10   The great differences between human languages show that there must be an important environmental component in language learning. Moreover, the child's learning of a language is almost entirely an instance of learning by imitation. Yet reflection on various biological aspects of language shows that the genetic factors are much more important. Thus I agree with the statement of Joseph Church: "While some part of the change that occurs in infancy can be accounted for in terms of physical maturation, we know that maturation stands in a circular, feedback relationship to experience—the things the organism does, feels, and has done to it. This is not to disparage the role of maturation; it is only to insist that we cannot view it as a single blossoming of predestined biological characteristics." Yet I differ from Church in contending that the genetically founded maturation process is much more complex and has much greater influence than the releasing signals and the experiences of receiving them; though no doubt a certain minimum of this is needed to stimulate the "blossoming." Helen Keller's grasping (not mentioned by Church) that the spelled word "water" means the thing which she could feel with her hand and which she knew so well had, I think, some similarity with "imprinting"; but there are also many dissimilarities. The similarity was the ineradicable impression made on her, and the way in which a single experience released pent-up dispositions and needs. An obvious dissimilarity was the tremendous range of variation which the experience opened up for her, and which led in time to her mastery of language.

In the light of this I doubt the aptness of Church's comment: "The baby does not walk because his 'walking mechanisms' have come into flower, but because he has achieved a kind of orientation to space whereby walking becomes a possible mode of action." It seems to me that in Helen Keller's case there was no orientation in linguistic space or, at any rate, extremely little, prior to her discovery that the touch of her teacher's fingers denoted water, and her jumping to the conclusion that certain touches may have denotational or referential significance. What must have been there was a readiness, a disposition, a need, to interpret signals; and a need, a readiness, to learn to use these signals by imitation, by the method of trial and error (by nonrandom trials and the critical elimination of spelling errors).

It appears that there must be inborn dispositions of great variety and complexity which cooperate in this field: the disposition to love, to sympathize, to emulate movements, to control and correct the emulated movements; the disposition to use them, and to communicate with their help; the disposition to react to language; to receive commands, requests, admonitions, warnings; the disposition to interpret descriptive statements, and to produce descriptive statements. In Helen Keller's case (as opposed to that of normal children) most of her information about reality come through language. As a consequence she was unable for a time to distinguish clearly what we might call "hearsay" from experience, and even from her own imagination: all three came to her in terms of the same symbolic code.

The example of language learning showed me that my schema of a natural sequence consisting of a dogmatic phase followed by a critical phase was too simple. In language learning there is clearly an inborn disposition to correct (that is, to be flexible and critical, to eliminate errors) which after a time peters out. When a child, having learned to say "mice" uses "hice" for the plural of "house," then a disposition to find regularities is at work. The child will soon correct himself, perhaps under the influence of adult criticisms. But there seems to be a phase in language learning when the language structure becomes rigid—perhaps under the influence of "automatization," as explained in 3 (c) above.

I have used language learning merely as an example from which we can see that imitation is a special case of the method of trial and error-elimination. It is also an example of the cooperation between phases of dogmatic theory formation, expectation formation, or the formation of behavioural regularities, on the one hand, and phases of criticism on the other.

15   But although the theory of a dogmatic phase followed by a critical phase is too simple, it is true that *there can be no critical phase without a preceding dogmatic phase, a place in which something—an expectation, a regularity of behaviour—is formed, so that error elimination can begin to work on it.*

This view made me reject the psychological theory of learning by induction, a theory to which Hume adhered even after he had rejected induction on logical grounds. (I do not wish to repeat what I have said in *Conjectures and Refutations* about Hume's views on habit.) It also led me to see that there is no such thing as an unprejudiced observation. All observation is an activity with an aim (to find, or to check, some regularity which is *at least* vaguely conjectured); an activity guided by problems, and by the context of expectations (the "horizon of expectations" as I later called it). There is no such thing as passive experience; no passively impressed association of impressed ideas. Experience is the result of active exploration by the organism, of the search for regularities or invariants. There is no such thing as a perception except in the context of interests and expectations, and hence of regularities or "laws."

All this led me to the view that conjecture or hypothesis must have come before observation or perception: we have inborn expectations; we must have latent inborn knowledge, in the form of latent expectations, to be activated by stimuli to which we react as a rule while engaged in active exploration. All learning is a modification (it may be a refutation) of some prior knowledge and thus, in the last analysis, of some inborn knowledge.

It was this psychological theory which I elaborated, tentatively and in a clumsy terminology, between 1921 and 1926. It was this theory of the formation of our knowledge which engaged and distracted me during my apprenticeship as a cabinetmaker.

One of the strange things about my intellectual history is this. Although I was at the time interested in the contrast between dogmatic and critical thinking, and although I looked upon dogmatic thinking as prescientific (and, where it pretends to be scientific, as "unscientific"), and although I realized the link with the falsifiability criterion of demarcation between science and pseudoscience, I did not appreciate that there was a connection between all this and the problem of induction. For years these two problems lived in different (and it appears almost watertight) compartments of my mind, even though I believed that I had solved the problem of induction by the simple discovery that induction by repetition did not exist (any more than did learning something new by repetition): the alleged inductive method of science had to be replaced by the method of (dogmatic) trial and (critical) error elimination, which was the mode of discovery of all organisms from the amoeba to Einstein.

20   Of course I was aware that my solutions to both these problems—the problem of demarcation, the problem of induction—made use of the same idea: that of the separation of dogmatic and critical thinking. Nevertheless the two problems seemed to me quite different; demarcation had no similarity with Darwinian selection. Only after some years did I realize that there was a close link, and that the problem of induction arose essentially from a solution of the problem of demarcation—from the mistaken (positivist) belief that what elevated science over pseudoscience was the "scientific method" of finding true, secure, and justifiable knowledge, and that this method was the method of induction: a belief that erred in more ways than one.

from Original Spin

by Lesley Dormen and Peter Edidin

Creativity, somebody once wrote, is the search for the elusive "Aha," that moment of insight when one sees the world, or a problem, or an idea, in a new way. Traditionally, whether the discovery results in a cubist painting or an improved carburetor, we have viewed the creative instant as serendipitous and rare—the product of genius, the property of the elect.

Unfortunately, this attitude has had a number of adverse consequences. It encourages us to accept the myth that the creative energy society requires to address its own problems will never be present in sufficient supply. Beyond that, we have come to believe that "ordinary" people like ourselves can never be truly creative. As John Briggs, author of *Fire in the Crucible: The Alchemy of Creative Genius,* said, "The way we talk about creativity tends to reinforce the notion that it is some kind of arbitrary gift. It's amazing the way 'not having it' becomes wedded to people's self-image. They invariably work up a whole series of rationalizations about why they 'aren't creative,' as if they were damaged goods of some kind." Today, however, researchers are looking at creativity, not as an advantage of the human elite, but as a basic human endowment. As Ruth Richards, a psychiatrist and creativity researcher at McLean Hospital in Belmont, MA, says, "You were being creative when you learned how to walk. And if you are looking for something in the fridge, you're being creative because you have to figure out for yourself where it is." Creativity, in Richards' view, is simply fundamental to getting about in the world. It is "our ability to adapt to change. It is the very essence of human survival."

In an age of rampant social and technological change, such an adaptive capability becomes yet more crucial to the individual's effort to maintain balance in a constantly shifting environment. "People need to recognize that what Alvin Toffler called future shock is our daily reality," says Ellen McGrath, a clinical psychologist who teaches creativity courses at New York University. "Instability is an intrinsic part of our lives, and to deal with it every one of us will need to find new, creative solutions to the challenges of everyday life. I think creativity will be the survival skill of the '90s."

But can you really become more creative? If the word *creative* smacks too much of Picasso at his canvas, then rephrase the question in a less intimidating way: Do you believe you could deal with the challenges of life in a more effective, inventive and fulfilling manner? If the answer is yes, then the question becomes, "What's stopping you?"

Defining Yourself as a Creative Person

5   People often hesitate to recognize the breakthroughs in their own lives as creative. But who has not felt the elation and surprise that come with the sudden, seemingly inexplicable discovery of a solution to a stubborn problem? In that instant, in "going beyond the information given," as psychologist Jerome Bruner has said, to a solution that was the product of your own mind, you were expressing your creativity.

This impulse to "go beyond" to a new idea is not the preserve of a genius, stresses David Henry Feldman, a developmental psychologist at Tufts University and the author of *Nature's Gambit,* a study of child prodigies. "Not everybody can be Beethoven," he says, "but it is true that all humans, by virtue of being dreamers and fantasizers, have a tendency to take liberties with the world as it exists. Humans are always transforming their inner and outer worlds. It's what I call the 'transformational imperative.'"

The desire to play with reality, however, is highly responsive to social control, and many of us are taught early on to repress the impulse. As Mark Runco, associate professor of psychology at California State University at Fullerton and the founder of the new *Creativity Research Journal,* says, "We put children in groups and make them sit in desks and raise their hands before they talk. We put all the emphasis on conformity and order, then we wonder why they aren't being spontaneous and creative."

Adults too are expected to conform in any number of ways and in a variety of settings. Conformity, after all, creates a sense of order and offers the reassurance of the familiar. But to free one's natural creative impulses, it is necessary, to some extent, to resist the pressure to march in step with the world. Begin small, suggests Richards. "Virtually nothing you do can't be done in a slightly different, slightly better way. This has nothing to do with so-called creative pursuits but simply with breaking with your own mindsets and trying an original way of doing some habitual task. Simply defer judgment on yourself for a little while and try something new. Remember, the essence of life is not getting things right, but taking risks, making mistakes, getting things *wrong.*"

But it also must be recognized that the creative life is to some degree, and on some occasions, a solitary one. Psycholinguist Vera John-Steiner, author of *Notebooks of the Mind: Explorations of Thinking,* is one of many creativity researchers who believe that a prerequisite for creative success is "intensity of preoccupation, being pulled into your activity to such an extent that you forget it's dinnertime." Such concentration, John-Steiner believes, is part of our "natural creative bent," but we learn to ignore it because of a fear that it will isolate us from others. To John-Steiner, however, this fear is misplaced. Creative thought, she has written, is a "search for meaning," a way to connect our inner sense of being with some aspect of the world that preoccupies us. And she believes that only by linking these two aspects of reality—the inner and the outer—can we gain "some sense of being in control of life."

Avoiding the Myths

10   David Perkins, co-director of Project Zero at the Harvard Graduate School of Education, asks in *The Mind's Best Work,* "When you have it—

creativity, that is—what do you have?" The very impalpability of the subject means that often creativity can be known only by its products. Indeed, the most common way the researchers define creativity is by saying it is whatever produces something that is: a. original; b. adaptive (i.e., useful); c. meaningful to others. But because we don't understand its genesis, we're often blocked or intimidated by the myths that surround and distort this mercurial subject.

One of these myths is, in Perkins's words, that creativity is "a kind of 'stuff' that the creative person has and uses to do creative things, never mind other factors." This bit of folk wisdom, that creativity is a sort of intangible psychic organ—happily present in some and absent in others—so annoys Perkins that he would like to abolish the word itself.

Another prevalent myth about creativity is that it is restricted to those who are "geniuses"—that is, people with inordinately high IQs. Ironically, this has been discredited by a study begun by Stanford psychologist Lewis Terman, the man who adapted the original French IQ test for America. In the early 1920s, Terman had California schoolteachers choose 1,528 "genius" schoolchildren (those with an IQ above 135), whose lives were then tracked year after year. After six decades, researchers found that the putative geniuses, by and large, did well in life. They entered the professions in large numbers and led stable, prosperous lives. But very few made notable creative contributions to society, and none did extraordinary creative work.

According to Dean Simonton, professor of psychology at the University of California at Davis and the author of *Genius, Creativity and Leadership* and *Scientific Genius,* "There just isn't any correlation between creativity and IQ. The average college graduate has an IQ of about 120, and this is high enough to write novels, do scientific research, or any other kind of creative work."

A third myth, voiced eons ago by Socrates, lifts creativity out of our own lives altogether into a mystical realm that makes it all but unapproachable. In this view, the creative individual is a kind of oracle, the passive conduit or channel chosen by God, or the tribal ancestors, or the muse, to communicate sacred knowledge.

15   Although there *are* extraordinary examples of creativity, for which the only explanation seems to be supernatural intervention (Mozart, the story goes, wrote the overture to *Don Giovanni* in only a few hours, after a virtually sleepless night and without revision), by and large, creativity begins with a long and intensive apprenticeship.

Psychologist Howard Gruber believes that it takes at least 10 years of immersion in a given domain before an eminent creator is likely to be able to make a distinctive mark. Einstein, for example, who is popularly thought to have doodled out the theory of relativity at age 26 in his spare time, was in fact compulsively engaged in thinking about the problem at least from the age of 16.

Finally, many who despair of ever being creative do so because they tried once and failed, as though the truly creative always succeed. In fact, just the opposite is true, says Dean Simonton. He sees genius, in a sense, as inseparable from failure. "Great geniuses make tons of mistakes," he says. "They generate lots of ideas and they accept being wrong. They have a kind of internal fortress that allows them to fail and just keep going. Look at Edison. He held over 1,000 patents, but most of them are not only forgotten, they weren't worth much to begin with."

Mindlessness vs. Mindfulness

"Each of us desires to share with others our vision of the world, only most of us have been taught that it's wrong to do things differently or look at things differently," says John Briggs. "We lose confidence in ourselves and begin to look at reality only in terms of the categories by which society orders it."

This is the state of routinized conformity and passive learning that Harvard professor of psychology Ellen Langer calls, appropriately enough, mindlessness. For it is the state of denying the perceptions and promptings of our own minds, our individual selves. Langer and her colleagues' extensive research over the past 15 years has shown that when we act mindlessly, we behave automatically and limit our capacity for creative response. Mired down in a numbing daily routine, we may virtually relinquish our capacity for independent thought and action.

20   By contrast, Langer refers to a life in which we use our affective, responsive, perceptive faculties as "mindful." When we are mindful, her research has shown, we avoid rigid, reflexive behavior in favor of a more improvisational and intuitive response to life. We notice and feel the world around us and then act in accordance with our feelings. "Many, if not all, of the qualities that make up a mindful attitude are characteristic of creative people," Langer writes in her new book, *Mindfulness*. "Those who can free themselves of mindsets, open themselves to new information and surprise, play with perspective and context, and focus on process rather than outcome are likely to be creative, whether they are scientists, artists, or cooks."

Much of Langer's research has demonstrated the vital relationship between creativity and uncertainty, or conditionality. For instance, in one experiment, Langer and Alison Piper introduced a collection of objects to one group of people by saying, "This is a hair dryer," and "This is a dog's chew toy," and so on. Another group was told "This *could* be a hair dryer," and "This *could* be a dog's chew toy." Later, the experimenters for both groups invented a need for an eraser, but only those people who had been conditionally introduced to the objects thought to use the dog's toy in this new way.

The intuitive understanding that a single thing is, or could be, many things, depending on how you look at it, is at the heart of the attitude Langer calls mindfulness. But can such an amorphous state be cultivated? Langer believes that it can, by consciously discarding the idea that any given moment of your day is fixed in its form. "I teach people to 'componentize' their lives into smaller pieces," she says. "In the morning, instead of mindlessly downing your orange juice, *taste it*. Is it what you want? Try something else if it isn't. When you walk to work, turn left instead of right. You'll notice the street you're on, the buildings and the weather. Mindfulness, like creativity, is nothing more than a return to who you are. By minding your responses to the world, you will come to know yourself again. How you feel. What you want. What you want to do."

Creating the Right Atmosphere

Understanding the genesis of creativity, going beyond the myths to understand your creative potential, and recognizing your ability to break free of old ways of thinking are the three initial steps to a more creative life. The fourth is finding ways to work that encourage personal commitment and expressiveness.

Letting employees learn what they want to do has never been a very high priority in the workplace. There, the dominant regulation has always been, "Do what you are told."

25   Today, however, economic realities are providing a new impetus for change. The pressure on American businesses to become more productive and innovative has made creative thinking a hot commodity in the business community. But innovation, business is now learning, is likely to be found wherever bright and eager people *think* they can find it. And some people are looking in curious places.

Financier Wayne Silby, for example, founded the Calvert Group of funds, which today manages billions of dollars in assets. Silby, whose business card at one point read Chief Daydreamer, occasionally retreats for inspiration to a sensory deprivation tank, where he floats in warm water sealed off from light and sound. "I went into the tank during a time when the government was changing money-market deposit regulations, and I needed to think how to compete with banks. Floating in the tank I got the idea of joining them instead. We would up creating an $800-million program. Often we already have answers to our problems, but we don't quiet ourselves enough to see the solutions bubbling just below the surface." Those solutions will stay submerged, he says, "unless you create a culture that encourages creative approaches, where it's OK to have bad ideas."

Toward this goal, many companies have turned to creativity consultants, like Synectics, Inc., in Cambridge, MA. Half the battle, according to Synectics facilitator Jeff Mauzy, is to get the clients to relax and accept that they are in a safe place where the cutthroat rules of the workplace don't apply, so they can allow themselves to exercise their creative potential in group idea sessions.

Pamela Webb Moore, director of naming services (she helps companies figure out good names for their products) at Synectics, agrees. One technique she uses to limber up the minds of tightly focused corporate managers is "sleight of head." While working on a particular problem, she'll ask clients to pretend to work on something else. In one real-life example, a Synectics-trained facilitator took a group of product-development and marketing managers from the Etonic shoe corporation on an "excursion," a conscious walk away from the problem—in this case, to come up with a new kind of tennis shoe.

The facilitator asked the Etonic people to imagine they were at their favorite vacation spot. "One guy," Moore says, "was on a tropical island, walking on the beach in his bare feet. He described how wonderful the water and sand felt on his feet, and he said, 'I wish we could play tennis barefoot.' The whole thing would have stopped right there if somebody had complained that while his colleague was wandering around barefoot, they were supposed to come up with a *shoe*. Instead, one of the marketing people there was intrigued, and the whole group decided to go off to play tennis barefoot on a rented court at 10 at night."

30   While the Etonic people played tennis, the facilitator listed everything they said about how it felt. The next morning, the group looked at her assembled list of comments, and they realized that what they liked about playing barefoot was the lightness of being without shoes, and the ability to pivot easily on both the ball of the foot and the heel. Nine months later, the company produced an extremely light shoe called the Catalyst, which featured an innovative two-piece sole that made it easier for players to pivot.

The Payoff

In *The Courage to Create,* Rollo May wrote that for much of this century, researchers had avoided the subject of creativity because they perceived it as "unscientific, mysterious, disturbing and too corruptive of the scientific training of graduate students." But today researchers are coming to see that creativity, at once fugitive and ubiquitous, is the mark of human nature itself.

Whether in business or the arts, politics or personal relationships, creativity involves "going beyond the information given" to create or reveal something new in the world. And almost invariably, when the mind exercises its creative muscle, it also generates a sense of pleasure. The feeling may be powerfully mystical, as it is for New York artist Rhonda Zwillinger, whose embellished artwork appeared in the film

Slaves of New York. Zwillinger reports, "There are times when I'm working and it is almost as though I'm a vessel and there is a force operating through me. It is the closest I come to having a religious experience." The creative experience may also be quiet and full of wonder, as it was for Isaac Newton, who compared his lifetime of creative effort to "a boy playing on the seashore and diverting himself and then finding a smoother pebble or prettier shell than ordinary, while the greater ocean of truth lay all undiscovered before me."

But whatever the specific sensation, creativity always carries with it a powerful sense of the mind working at the peak of its ability. Creativity truly is, as David Perkins calls it, the mind's best work, its finest effort. We may never know exactly how the brain does it, but we can feel that it is exactly what the brain was meant to do.

Aha!

WRITING PROJECT

This chapter has included a number of **Thinking↔Writing Activities** and readings that encouraged you to reflect on the nature of creativity and on your own creativity—past, present, and future. Be sure to reread what you wrote for those activities: you may be able to use it to help yourself complete this project. You may also want to include material from the chapter readings in your essay; if so, be sure to document them correctly by introducing the authors and acknowledging their ideas. And, of course, use quotation marks or set off the quote by indenting if you decide to use their words.

WRITING PROJECT   Imagining Your Life More Creatively

Think creatively to imagine how some part of your life could be (or could have been) more satisfying or exciting. You need to focus on one or more specific areas of your life, such as an important relationship, your college work, or a job that would be ideal for you. You could write about the past and how things might have been different with a more creative approach, or you could describe a plan for the present, or you might look to the future in a creative way. Then write an essay in which you put forth your vision. Follow directions given by your instructor as to length, format, and so forth.

Begin by considering the key elements of the **Thinking↔Writing Model.**

Purpose

Your primary purpose here is to employ the strategies for thinking, living, and writing creatively that have been presented in this chapter, to create a new vision of your own life. Doing this will require you, to some extent, to step back from your life, to become an observer of how you have lived, are living, or might be living, and then to become a creator of a potentially different vision.

Another purpose will be to show, not tell, what the creative changes in your life would be by giving enough examples to let your readers picture what you mean.

Audience

You have an interesting and varied audience for this Writing Project. In a real sense, you are your own most important audience, for who else could be more involved with or interested in the subject? Beyond yourself, you may choose to show your writing to key people in your life, especially if any of them would be affected by the creative changes you propose. Their reactions to early drafts could be very helpful as you revise your writing.

At another level, your classmates may be part of your audience, especially if your writing is going to be shared with them or reviewed by them. All the readers mentioned so far—yourself, key people in your life, and your classmates—will be interested in what you say, and especially in the changes you propose, so be sure to include enough background information about how your life was, or is, for them to readily understand the impact of what you are proposing.

Finally, your instructor is also part of your audience, and his or her judgment of your work will matter to you. Therefore, carefully consider both your instructor's directions and the points that have been emphasized in class. Be aware that as a writing teacher, your instructor is interested not only in what you say, but also in how you say it; edit your final draft with great care so that no errors remain to detract from your ideas.

Subject

Thinking and writing about our own lives can be both exciting and challenging. Often we get so busy just living our lives that we don't take time to actually think about them and about how they might be different. We begin to think that whatever *is* has to be.

For this Writing Project, you should try to use as many of the suggestions in the chapter as you can to help yourself generate ideas. This will take time, so begin as soon as possible. You may think of changes you aren't sure you want to make in your life, and your critical thinking abilities will help you sort these out.

A potential problem with this subject is that you may believe that there is little in your life that can be changed; if this is the case, think carefully and honestly about how true this really is. If some areas cannot be changed, think creativity to discover other areas to write about. Note that you are not necessarily being asked to propose major changes. What you end up writing about could be a very different life or simply a richer, more fully realized version of what your life is now. For instance, you might envision an ideal job situation in which you would like to find yourself after you have completed your education.

Writer

As the expert on your own life, you can feel comfortable as you work on this project. If you are the creative type, you should welcome the chance to let your imagination go! If you consider yourself unimaginative, take this opportunity to develop your creative side. (We are all creative, as this chapter reminds us.)

The Writing Process

The following sections will guide you through the stages of generating, planning, drafting, and revising as you work on an essay about more creativity in some aspect of your life. Try to be particularly conscious of how creative thinking can help you discover and connect ideas.

Generating Ideas

You have already written about your creativity if you've done the **Thinking↔Writing Activities** in this chapter. Review what you wrote. You will probably see that you noted a number of ideas that can pertain to this project. Then, to discover more ideas and a possible focus, follow these suggestions and jot down your responses.

- Think about two or three things you do that are particularly important to you. How might they become more satisfying if you became more creative in your approach.

- Think about a difficult or tedious situation in the past that you now realize could have been improved by a more creative approach.

- Envision your life five years from now. What activities do you hope to be involved in? How do you believe they could be shaped by creative thinking? What would be your ideal job situation?

- Ask yourself which of the three suggestions above intrigues you most. Do you want to think more creatively about the present, the past, or the future—or a combination of time frames?

- Choose a situation and brainstorm or ask questions (see page 13 in Chapter 1 and page 56 in this chapter).

- Talk to friends or family members about your brainstorming, to find out if they have some suggestions.

- Ask yourself if you have enough ideas to begin to draft your paper. If not, you may want to try again, with some other aspect of your life.

Defining a Focus

Write a few sentences in which you explore the question of whether you want to focus on one area of change or several. If several, do they have a common thread or are they quite different? Your sentences might be like these:

I think that I would like to be a more creative cook. Why? How? So that my housemates and I can have more enjoyable meals when it's my turn in the kitchen; so that I can really enjoy cooking. . . . Some ways that I can do this is to take a cooking course, get some really different cookbooks out of the library—like from other countries or other regions, or vegan, or barbecue; I should spend some time with my uncle who makes such good one-dish meals, find some tasty Web sites, watch some of those cooking shows instead of surfing away.

Some things in my life that I want to make better are my relationship with my girlfriend, the way my rooms looks, and my boring job. There's not much in common here except that I'm not very excited by any of them right now. I wonder how I would like these three parts of my life to be different within the next six months. I wonder what my ideal job would be.

Can you see how these focus sentences provide a good start on the paper?

Organizing Ideas

Once you have decided whether you will focus on one area or on two or three, and after having done some drafting, you can

- describe your current or past situation,
- describe some changes you would like to make or wish you had made,
- describe the improved situation.

Does this thinking suggest a method of organization? Is that organization effective or is it too stodgy for a paper about creative thinking? If something other than a regular essay structure seems right for this project, how about narrating the events at a time in the future when you have made some changes? How about imagining your new (or old) situation from your boyfriend's or mother's or boss's point of view? How about some graphics? or a poem or a song as part of the paper?

Map out an organization or plan that you think might work.

Drafting

As you translate your ideas, notes, and early versions into coherent writing, you need to decide how you can draft in ways that will help you revise your work effectively. Because the essay you are about to write has three distinct components—your belief, your experience, and their connections—you may want to draft each component separately and then think about how to connect them. In addition, you should recall the concepts presented in Chapter 1, especially the use of questions as a productive way to begin many forms of writing.

Revising

Once you have completed a draft that you think is close to a final version, you should put it aside for a day or two. If you don't have time to do that, then at least take a break before trying to revise. When you are ready to "re-see" your writing, read it through slowly, preferably aloud.

Consider it in terms of the following questions. (You may also use these questions when you review and comment on your classmates' drafts.)

- Are the incidents, people, and places involved in the experience related with enough detail to make the experience clear for readers and hold their attention? Where might further specific information or detail be offered?

- Is the effect the experience had on your belief made clear? Does the essay seem focused? If not, where is the focus lost or vague?

- How thoughtful are the reflection on the experience and the process of thinking it through? Is the value of the experience fully expressed?

- Are the opening and the conclusion effective? If not, what might make a better opening to get readers interested? How might the conclusion leave readers with a better understanding?

- Do there seem to be any problems with the use of language or sentence structure, or connections between ideas? Are any parts of the essay difficult to read? How might words and sentences be revised?

Proofreading

After you prepare a final draft, check for standard grammar and punctuation. Proofread carefully for omitted words and punctuation marks. Run your spelling checker program, but be aware of its limitations. Proofread again for the kinds of errors the computer can't catch.

STUDENT WRITING
Discovering Creativity by Not Looking For It
by Jessie Lange

There have been numerous times when I have sat in front of a blank computer screen, a writing assignment in hand, feeling completely uninspired and uncreative. Without having even begun I think, "Now what?" There have been numerous times when I've just started filling up that screen with meaningless, dry words that really have no effect on me or anyone else. Yes, I'm getting the job done, but not the job I'd like—not my best work, not anywhere near it. One thing that I've found in my life is that in your most uncreative ruts sometimes you can't pull yourself out all on your own. You can't always, sitting in an idea-less vacuum, turn on the creativity. Sometimes you will save yourself time and produce a much more fulfilling piece of work if you take the time out to go *out* of the world of your blank screen. For me this has always meant literally getting outdoors, because somehow it always seems that I find *outside* what I've been looking for *inside*.

It was the first English assignment of my senior year of high school—an interpretation of a Buddhist legend—and I was struggling with its meaning. The legend is about a set of stairs leading to the top of the tower from where you can see the "whole horizon" and the "loveliest landscape"—a symbol of attaining nirvana. The paradox in the legend is that you can only reach the top if you do not believe in the legend itself. How would those who believe, then, ever reach the top? How can you even start the climb without making the conscious decision to do so?

Being in the country on weekends has many benefits, one of them being that I could go outside to clear my head. I lit my Williams Sonoma oil lamp and walked out into the night that offered the occasional drizzle and a strong breeze that ruffled the leaves of the tree I lay down under. I was there for an hour, feeling the drops on my face and the dampness settling into my body, before it happened. I rolled over and looked out into the field, because I sensed something the way that you can and will when you're listening with your entire body. Farther out, right before the lawn becomes high grass and eventually woods, were four white shapes moving across my line of vision. The same deer I casually glance at during the day, were like ghosts grazing out there at night. Just faint, light vaporous figures against the pitch black. That moment was like seeing the "whole horizon." Those animals, moving with such grace, were unaware of my presence. For all they knew, I was another tree silently overseeing their nightly ritual. Watching these beasts—becuase that's what they are, wonderfully wild animals—I was witnessing a scene that could have taken place in this same spot on this same night hundreds or thousand of years before. I reached for my lantern and turned up the flame, holding it in front of me for a better view. This light, however, obstructed my vision rather than illuminating it. It was only when I put the flame aside and cupped my hands around my eyes, creating a deeper darkness, that I could really see the deer. And then I realized that perhaps that was why only those who do not believe the legend ever climb the stairs of the tower—because when you actively search for things, like holding the light, perhaps you prevent yourself from seeing them. Had I not put my writing aside and taken that walk I would never have found this answer, the answer I was looking for. I wrote my English essay and I also learned something about creativity in my own life. Some of your most creative moments happen when you're not looking. In the journey up the steps of the tower toward creativity, sometimes it is not those who are keenly searching for a victory of sorts, but those who are instead turning down the light, that begin the climb.

CHAPTER 4

Thinking Critically About Writing— Revising Purposefully

Critical Thinking Focus: Decision making

Writing Focus: Making decisions about drafts

Reading Themes: People making decisions; writers thinking about revision

Writing Project: Analyzing a decision to be made

Thinking Critically and Revising

After professional writers have used creative thinking to generate ideas and early drafts, they bring their critical thinking abilities into play to revise their writing—to "see it again." As writers revise, they keep purpose and audience in mind and make decisions about what to keep and what to change in their drafts. In other words, revision involves identifying possible changes and then deciding whether these changes will help to accomplish the writer's purpose with an audience.

Revision is often the key to the success of a piece of writing. Effective writers have the ability to reread drafts critically, to rethink what those drafts are saying, and to rewrite—or revise—when necessary.

Decision making, an important application of critical thinking, plays a key role in life as well. This chapter presents an organized method for making decisions, one that can even lead to the best possible life decisions. The chapter then applies this method to revising drafts and to a **Writing Project.**

Making Decisions

In order to reach various goals in life, we try to make the best decisions for ourselves or our community. Even so, we don't always make the most *informed* or *intelligent* decisions possible. In fact, most of us regularly have the experience of mentally kicking ourselves because of having made a poor decision. (Can you remember any recent decision you made that you would correct, if you had an opportunity to do so?)

Many faulty or regrettable decisions involve relatively minor issues, such as selecting an unappealing dish in a restaurant, hastily agreeing to go on a blind date, taking a course that does not meet our expectations. Although these decisions may result in unpleasant consequences, the discomfort is neither life threatening nor long-lasting (although a disappointing course may *seem* to last forever!). However, there also are a great number of significant decisions in which poor choices can result in considerably more damaging and far-reaching consequences. For example, one reason the current divorce rate in the United States stands at 50 percent is poor decisions people make before or after the vows "till death do us part." Similarly, the fact that many employed adults wake up in the morning unhappy about going to their jobs, anxiously waiting for the end of the day and the conclusion of the week (TGIF!) when they will be free to do what they really want to, suggests that somewhere along the line, they have made poor decisions or felt trapped by circumstances beyond their control.

THINKING ↔ WRITING ACTIVITY 4.1

Analyzing a Previous Decision

1. Think back to an important decision you made that turned out well and describe the experience as specifically as possible.
2. Reconstruct the reasoning process you used in making your decision. Did you do any or all of the following things?

- Clearly define the decision to be made and the related issues?
- Consider various choices and anticipate their consequences?
- Gather additional information to help in your analysis?
- Evaluate the various pros and cons of different courses of action?
- Use a chart or diagram to aid in your deliberations?
- Create a specific plan of action to implement your ideas?
- Periodically review your decision to make any necessary adjustments?

An Organized Approach to Making Decisions

As you were reflecting on the successful decision you wrote about in **Thinking↔Writing Activity 4.1,** you probably noticed your mind working in a systematic way as you thought your way through the decision situation. Of course, we often make important decisions with less thoughtful analysis by acting impulsively and we are forced to cope with the consequences of these mistaken choices. Our "intuitions" can be a useful guide to success when the intuitions are **informed intuitions**—based on lessons learned from past experience and thoughtful reflection. Naturally, there are no guarantees that a careful analysis will lead to a successful result—there are often too many unknown elements and factors beyond our control. But we can certainly improve our success rate as well as our speed by becoming more knowledgeable about the decision-making process.

This approach consists of five steps. As you master these steps, they will become integrated into your way of thinking, and you will be able to apply them in a natural and flexible way.

Step 1: Define the Decision Clearly

This seems like an obvious step, but very frequently, decision making goes wrong at the starting point. For example, imagine that you decide you want to have a "more active social life" (or perhaps a "less active social life"). The problem with characterizing your decision this way is that it defines the situation too generally and doesn't provide any clear direction for your analysis. Do you mean that you want to develop an intimate, romantic relationship? Do you want to cultivate more close friendships? Do you want to engage in more social activities? Do you want to meet new people? In short, there are many ways to define more clearly the decision to have a "more active social life." The more specific your definition of the decision to be made, the clearer will be your analysis and the greater the likelihood of success.

Strategy: Write a one-page analysis that describes your decision-making situation as clearly and specifically as possible.

Step 2: Consider All Possible Choices

Successful decision makers explore all possible choices in their situation, not simply the obvious ones. In fact, the less obvious choices often turn out to be the most effective. For instance, one student couldn't decide whether to major in accounting or in business management. In discussing his situation with other members of the class, he revealed that his real interest was in the area of graphic design and illustration. Although he was very talented, he considered this area only a hobby, not a possible career choice. Class members pointed out to him that design and illustration could prove to be his best career opportunity, but he needed first to see it as a possibility.

People who approach decision situations thoughtfully are more successful decision makers in every area of their lives, including their writing.

Strategy: *List as many possible choices for your situation as you can, both obvious and not obvious. Ask other people for additional suggestions and don't censor
or prejudge any ideas.*

Step 3: Gather All Relevant Information and Evaluate the Pros and Cons of Each Possible Choice

In many cases, you may lack sufficient information to make an informed
choice. Unfortunately, this doesn't prevent people from plunging ahead anyway, making a decision that is more a gamble than an informed choice. In
contrast to this questionable approach, it makes much more sense to seek out
the information you need in order to determine which of the choices you

have identified has the best chance of success. In the case of the student mentioned in Step 2, he would need to secure certain crucial information in order to determine whether to consider a career in graphic design and illustration: What are the specific careers within this general field? What sort of academic preparation and experience is required for the various careers? What are the prospects for employment in these areas, and how well do they pay?

Strategy: For each possible choice that you identified, create questions regarding information you need; then obtain that information.

In addition to obtaining all relevant information, each of the possible choices you identified has certain advantages and disadvantages, and it is essential that you analyze these pros and cons in an organized fashion. In the case of the student in Step 2, the choice of a career in accounting might on the one hand offer advantages like ready employment opportunities, the flexibility of working in many different situations and geographical locations, moderate-to-high income expectations, and job security. On the other hand, disadvantages might be that accounting does not reflect a deep and abiding interest of the student, that he might lose interest in it over time, and that the career might not result in a personal challenge and fulfillment that he needs.

Strategy: Using a format similar to the one presented below, analyze the pros and cons of each of your possible choices.

Possible Choices	Information Needed	Pros	Cons
1.			
2.			

Step 4: Select the Choice That Seems Best Suited to the Situation

The first three steps of this organized approach to making decisions are designed to help you analyze your decision situation: to clearly define the decision, to generate possible choices, to gather relevant information, and to evaluate the pros and cons of the choices you have identified. In the fourth step, you must attempt to synthesize what you have learned, weaving together all the various threads into a conclusion that you consider your "best" choice. How do you do this? There is no one simple way to identify your "best" choice, but there are some useful strategies for guiding your deliberations.

Strategy: Identify and prioritize the goal(s) of your decision situation and determine which of your choices best meets these goals. This process will probably involve reviewing and perhaps refining your definition of the decision situation. For example, in the case of the student we have been considering, some goals might include choosing a career that will (a) provide financial security, (b) provide personal fulfillment, (c) make use of special talents, and (d) offer plentiful opportunities along with job security.

Once identified, the goals can be ranked in order of priority, which will then suggest what the "best" choice will be. If the student ranks goals (a) and (d) at the top of the list, a choice of accounting or business administration may make sense. However, if the student ranks goals (b) and (c) at the top, pursuing a career in graphic design and illustration may be the best selection.

   Strategy: Anticipate the consequences of each choice by "preliving" the choices. This is another helpful strategy for deciding on the best choice. Project yourself into the future, imagining as realistically as you can the consequences of each possible choice. As with previous strategies, this process is aided by writing your thoughts down and discussing them with others.

Step 5: Implement a Plan of Action and Monitor the Results, Making Necessary Adjustments

Once you have made your best choice, you need to develop and implement a specific, concrete plan of action. The more specific and concrete your plan of action, the greater the likelihood of success. If, for instance, the student in the case we have been considering decides to pursue a career in graphic design and illustration, his plan should include reviewing the major that best meets his needs, discussing his situation with students and faculty in that department, planning what courses to take, and perhaps speaking with people working in the field.

   Strategy: Create a schedule that details the steps you will be taking to implement your decision, along with a time line for taking these steps. Naturally, your plan is merely a starting point. As you actually begin taking the steps in your plan, you will likely discover that changes and adjustments need to be made. You may find new information in the light of which the choice you made appears to be wrong. For example, as the student we have been discussing takes courses in graphic design and illustration, he may realize that his interest in the field is not as serious as he once thought and that although he liked this area as a hobby, he does not want it to be his life work. In this case, he should return to considering his other choices, perhaps adding some choices that he did not consider before.

   Strategy: After implementing your choice, evaluate its success by identifying what is working and what is not; then make the necessary adjustments to improve the situation.

Method for Making Decisions

Step 1: Define the decision clearly.

Step 2: Consider all possible choices.

Step 3: Gather all relevant information and evaluate the pros and cons of each possible choice.

Step 4: Select the choice that seems best suited to the situation.

Step 5: Implement a plan of action and monitor the results, making necessary adjustments.

Applying the Method for Making Decisions

Achieving objectivity about the lives and decisions of others is sometimes easier than attaining objectivity about our own lives. To familiarize yourself with applying the five steps just presented, read the following excerpt from Amy Tan's book of short stories *The Joy Luck Club*. "The Red Candle" is one of Tan's short stories complete in itself. Then work through **Thinking↔Writing Activity 4.2.**

from The Joy Luck Club
The Red Candle
by Amy Tan

Lindo Jong

I once sacrificed my life to keep my parents' promise. This means nothing to you, because to you promises mean nothing. A daughter can promise to come to dinner, but if she has a headache, if she has a traffic jam, if she wants to watch a favorite movie on TV, she no longer has a promise.

I watched this same movie when you did not come. The American soldier promises to come back and marry the girl. She is crying with a genuine feeling and he says, "Promise! Promise! Honey-sweetheart, my promise is as good as gold." Then he pushes her onto the bed. But he doesn't come back. His gold is like yours, it is only fourteen carats.

To Chinese people, fourteen carats isn't real gold. Feel my bracelets. They must be twenty-four carats, pure inside and out.

It's too late to change you, but I'm telling you this because I worry about your baby. I worry that someday she will say, "Thank you, Grandmother, for the gold bracelet. I'll never forget you." But later, she will forget her promise. She will forget she had a grandmother.

* * *

5   In this same war movie, the American soldier goes home and he falls to his knees asking another girl to marry him. And the girl's eyes run back and forth, so shy, as if she had never considered this before. And suddenly!—her eyes look straight down and she knows now she loves him, so much she wants to cry. "Yes," she says at last, and they marry forever.

This was not my case. Instead, the village matchmaker came to my family when I was just two years old. No, nobody told me this, I remember it all. It was summertime, very hot and dusty outside, and I could hear cicadas crying in the yard. We were under some trees in our orchard. The servants and my brothers were picking pears high above me. And I was sitting in my mother's hot sticky arms. I was waving my hand this way and that, because in front of me floated a small bird with horns and colorful paper-thin wings. And then the paper bird flew away and in front of me were two ladies. I remember them because one lady made watery "shrrhh, shrrhh" sounds. When I was older, I came to recognize this as a Peking accent, which sounds quite strange to Taiyuan people's ears.

The two ladies were looking at my face without talking. The lady with the watery voice had a painted face that was melting. The other lady had the dry face of an old tree trunk. She looked first at me, then at the painted lady.

Of course, now I know the tree-trunk lady was the old village matchmaker, and the other was Huang Taitai, the mother of the boy I would be forced to marry. No, it's not true what some Chinese say about girl babies being worthless. It depends on what kind of girl baby you are. In my case, people could see my value. I looked and smelled like a precious buncake, sweet with a good clean color.

The matchmaker bragged about me: "An earth horse for an earth sheep. This is the best marriage combination." She patted my arm and I pushed her hand away. Huang Taitai whispered in her shrrhh-shrrhh voice that perhaps I had an unusually bad *pichi*, a bad temper. But the matchmaker laughed and said, "Not so, not so. She is a strong horse. She will grow up to be a hard worker who serves you well in your old age."

10 And this is when Huang Taitai looked down at me with a cloudy face as though she could penetrate my thoughts and see my future intentions. I will never forget her look. Her eyes opened wide, she searched my face carefully and then she smiled. I could see a large gold tooth staring at me like the blinding sun and then the rest of her teeth opened wide as if she were going to swallow me down in one piece.

This is how I became betrothed to Huang Taitai's son, who I later discovered was just a baby, one year younger than I. His name was Tyan-yu—*tyan* for "sky," because he was so important, and *yu*, meaning "leftovers," because when he was born his father was very sick and his family thought he might die. Tyan-yu would be the leftover of his father's spirit. But his father lived and his grandmother was scared the ghosts would turn their attention to this baby boy and take him instead. So they watched him carefully, made all his decisions, and he became very spoiled.

But even if I had known I was getting such a bad husband, I had no choice, now or later. That was how backward families in the country were. We were always the last to give up stupid old-fashioned customs. In other cities already, a man could choose his own wife, with his parents' permission of course. But we were cut off from this type of new thought. You never heard if ideas were better in another city, only if they were worse. We were told stories of sons who were so influenced by bad wives that they threw their old, crying parents out into the street. So,

Taiyuanese mothers continued to choose their daughters-in-law, ones who would raise proper sons, care for the old people, and faithfully sweep the family burial grounds long after the old ladies had gone to their graves.

Because I was promised to the Huangs' son for marriage, my own family began treating me as if I belonged to somebody else. My mother would say to me when the rice bowl went up to my face too many times, "Look how much Huang Taitai's daughter can eat."

My mother did not treat me this way because she didn't love me. She would say this biting back her tongue, so she wouldn't wish for something that was no longer hers.

15   I was actually a very obedient child, but sometimes I had a sour look on my face—only because I was hot or tired or very ill. This is when my mother would say, "Such an ugly face. The Huangs won't want you and our whole family will be disgraced." And I would cry more to make my face uglier.

"It's no use," my mother would say. "We have made a contract. It cannot be broken." And I would cry even harder.

I didn't see my future husband until I was eight or nine. The world that I knew was our family compound in the village outside of Taiyuan. My family lived in a modest two-story house with a smaller house in the same compound, which was really just two side-by-side rooms for our cook, an everyday servant, and their families. Our house sat on a little hill. We called this hill Three Steps to Heaven, but it was really just centuries of hardened layers of mud washed up by the Fen River. On the east wall of our compound was the river, which my father said liked to swallow little children. He said it had once swallowed the whole town of Taiyuan. The river ran brown in the summer. In the winter, the river was blue-green in the narrow fast-moving spots. In the wider places, it was frozen still, white with cold.

Oh, I can remember the new year when my family went to the river and caught many fish—giant slippery creatures plucked while they were still sleeping in their frozen riverbeds—so fresh that even after they were gutted they would dance on their tails when thrown into the hot pan.

That was also the year I first saw my husband as a little boy. When the firecrackers went off, he cried loud—wah!—with a big open mouth even though he was not a baby.

20   Later I would see him at red-egg ceremonies when one-month-old boy babies were given their real names. He would sit on his grandmother's old knees, almost cracking them with his weight. And he would refuse to eat everything offered to him, always turning his nose away as though someone were offering him a stinky pickle and not a sweet cake.

So I didn't have instant love for my future husband the way you see on television today. I thought of this boy more like a troublesome cousin. I learned to be polite to the Huangs and especially to Huang Taitai. My mother would push me toward Huang Taitai and say, "What do you say to your mother?" And I would be confused, not knowing which mother she meant. So I would turn to my real mother and say, "Excuse me, Ma," and then I would turn to Huang Taitai and present her with a little goodie to eat, saying, "For you, Mother." I remember it was once a lump of *syaumei,* a little dumpling I loved to eat. My mother told Huang Taitai I had made this dumpling especially for her, even though I had only poked its steamy sides with my finger when the cook poured it onto the serving plate.

My life changed completely when I was twelve, the summer the heavy rains came. The Fen River which ran through the middle of my family's land flooded the plains. It destroyed all the wheat my family had planted that year and made the land useless for years to come. Even our house on top of the little hill became unlivable. When we came down from the second story, we saw the floors and furniture were covered with sticky mud. The courtyards were littered with uprooted trees, broken bits of walls, and dead chickens. We were so poor in all this mess.

You couldn't go to an insurance company back then and say, Somebody did this damage, pay me a million dollars. In those days, you were unlucky if you had exhausted your own possibilities. My father said we had no choice but to move the family to Wushi, to the south near Shanghai, where my mother's brother owned a small flour mill. My father explained that the whole family, except for me, would leave immediately. I was twelve years old, old enough to separate from my family and live with the Huangs.

The roads were so muddy and filled with giant potholes that no truck was willing to come to the house. All the heavy furniture and bedding had to be left behind, and these were promised to the Huangs as my dowry. In this way, my family was quite practical. The dowry was enough, more than enough, said my father. But he could not stop my mother from giving me her *chang,* a necklace made out of a tablet of red jade. When she put it around my neck, she acted very stern, so I knew she was very sad. "Obey your family. Do not disgrace us," she said. "Act happy when you arrive. Really, you're very lucky.

* * *

25   The Huangs' house also sat next to the river. While our house had been flooded, their house was untouched. This is because their house sat higher up in the valley. And this was the first time I realized the Huangs had a much better position than my family. They looked down on us, which made me understand why Huang Taitai and Tyan-yu had such long noses.

When I passed under the Huangs' stone-and-wood gateway arch, I saw a large courtyard with three or four rows of small, low buildings.

Some were for storing supplies, others for servants and their families. Behind these modest buildings stood the main house.

I walked closer and stared at the house that would be my home for the rest of my life. The house had been in the family for many generations. It was not really so old or remarkable, but I could see it had grown up along with the family. There were four stories, one for each generation: great-grandparents, grandparents, parents, and children. The house had a confused look. It had been hastily built and then rooms and floors and wings and decorations had been added on in every which manner, reflecting too many opinions. The first level was built of river rocks held together by straw-filled mud. The second and third levels were made of smooth bricks with an exposed walkway to give it the look of a palace tower. And the top level had gray slab walls topped with a red tile roof. To make the house seem important, there were two large round pillars holding up a veranda entrance to the front door. These pillars were painted red, as were the wooden window borders. Someone, probably Huang Taitai, had added imperial dragon heads at the corners of the roof.

Inside the house held a different kind of pretense. The only nice room was a parlor on the first floor, which the Huangs used to receive guests. This room contained tables and chairs carved out of red lacquer, fine pillows embroidered with the Huang family name in the ancient style, and many precious things that gave the look of wealth and old prestige. The rest of the house was plain and uncomfortable and noisy with the complaints of twenty relatives. I think with each generation the house had grown smaller inside, more crowded. Each room had been cut in half to make two.

No big celebration was held when I arrived. Huang Taitai didn't have red banners greeting me in the fancy room on the first floor. Tyanyu was not there to greet me. Instead, Huang Taitai hurried me upstairs to the second floor and into the kitchen, which was a place where family children didn't usually go. This was a place for cooks and servants. So I knew my standing.

30   That first day, I stood in my best padded dress at the low wooden table and began to chop vegetables. I could not keep my hands steady. I missed my family and my stomach felt bad, knowing I had finally arrived where my life said I belonged. But I was also determined to honor my parents' words, so Huang Taitai could never accuse my mother of losing face. She would not win that from our family.

As I was thinking this I saw an old servant woman stooping over the same low table gutting a fish, looking at me from the corner of her eye. I was crying and I was afraid she would tell Huang Taitai. So I gave a big smile and shouted, "What a lucky girl I am. I'm going to have the best life." And in this quick-thinking way I must have waved my knife too close to her nose because she cried angrily, *Shemma bende ren!*—

What kind of fool are you? And I knew right away this was a warning, because when I shouted that declaration of happiness, I almost tricked myself into thinking it might come true.

I saw Tyan-yu at the evening meal. I was still a few inches taller than he, but he acted like a big warlord. I knew what kind of husband he would be, because he made special efforts to make me cry. He complained the soup was not hot enough and then spilled the bowl as if it were an accident. He waited until I had sat down to eat and then would demand another bowl of rice. He asked why I had such an unpleasant face when looking at him.

Over the next few years, Huang Taitai instructed the other servants to teach me how to sew sharp corners on pillowcases and to embroider my future family's name. How can a wife keep her husband's household in order if she has never dirtied her own hands, Huang Taitai used to say as she introduced me to a new task. I don't think Huang Taitai ever soiled her hands, but she was very good at calling out orders and criticism.

"Teach her to wash rice properly so that the water runs clear. Her husband cannot eat muddy rice," she'd say to a cook servant.

35 Another time, she told a servant to show me how to clean a chamber pot: "Make her put her own nose to the barrel to make sure it's clean." That was how I learned to be an obedient wife. I learned to cook so well that I could smell if the meat stuffing was too salty before I even tasted it. I could sew such small stitches it looked as if the embroidery had been painted on. And even Huang Taitai complained in a pretend manner that she could scarcely throw a dirty blouse on the floor before it was cleaned and on her back once again, causing her to wear the same clothes every day.

After a while I didn't think it was a terrible life, no, not really. After a while, I hurt so much I didn't feel any difference. What was happier than seeing everybody gobble down the shiny mushrooms and bamboo shoots I had helped to prepare that day? What was more satisfying than having Huang Taitai nod and pat my head when I had finished combing her hair one hundred strokes? How much happier could I be after seeing Tyan-yu eat a whole bowl of noodles without once complaining about its taste or my looks? It's like those ladies you see on American TV these days, the ones who are so happy they have washed out a stain so the clothes look better than new.

Can you see how the Huangs almost washed their thinking into my skin? I came to think of Tyan-yu as a god, someone whose opinions were worth much more than my own life. I came to think of Huang Taitai as my real mother, someone I wanted to please, someone I should follow and obey without question.

When I turned sixteen on the lunar new year, Huang Taitai told me she was ready to welcome a grandson by next spring. Even if I had not wanted to marry, where would I go live instead? Even though I was strong as a horse, how could I run away? The Japanese were in every corner of China.

* * *

"The Japanese showed up as uninvited guests," said Tyan-yu's grandmother, "and that's why nobody else came." Huang Taitai had made elaborate plans, but our wedding was very small.

40 She had asked the entire village and friends and family from other cities as well. In those days, you didn't do RSVP. It was not polite not to come. Huang Taitai didn't think the war would change people's good manners. So the cook and her helpers prepared hundreds of dishes. My family's old furniture had been shined up into an impressive dowry and placed in the front parlor. Huang Taitai had taken care to remove all the water and mud marks. She had even commissioned someone to write felicitous messages on red banners, as if my parents themselves had draped these decorations to congratulate me on my good luck. And she had arranged to rent a red palanquin to carry me from her neighbor's house to the wedding ceremony.

A lot of bad luck fell on our wedding day, even though the matchmaker had chosen a lucky day, the fifteenth day of the eighth moon, when the moon is perfectly round and bigger than any other time of the year. But the week before the moon arrived, the Japanese came. They invaded Shansi province, as well as the provinces bordering us. People were nervous. And the morning of the fifteenth, on the day of the wedding celebration, it began to rain, a very bad sign. When the thunder and lightning began, people confused it with Japanese bombs and would not leave their houses.

I heard later that poor Huang Taitai waited many hours for more people to come, and finally, when she could not wring any more guests out of her hands, she decided to start the ceremony. What could she do? She could not change the war.

I was at the neighbor's house. When they called me to come down and ride the red palanquin, I was sitting at a small dressing table by an open window. I began to cry and thought bitterly about my parents' promise. I wondered why my destiny had been decided, why I should have an unhappy life so someone else could have a happy one. From my seat by the window I could see the Fen River with its muddy brown waters. I thought about throwing my body into this river that had destroyed my family's happiness. A person has very strange thoughts when it seems that life is about to end.

It started to rain again, just a light rain. The people from downstairs called up to me once again to hurry. And my thoughts became more urgent, more strange.

45 I asked myself, What is true about a person? Would I change in the same way the river changes color but still be the same person? And then

I saw the curtains blowing wildly, and outside rain was falling harder, causing everyone to scurry and shout. I smiled. And then I realized it was the first time I could see the power of the wind. I couldn't see the wind itself, but I could see it carried the water that filled the rivers and shaped the countryside. It caused men to yelp and dance.

I wiped my eyes and looked in the mirror. I was surprised at what I saw. I had on a beautiful red dress, but what I saw was even more valuable. I was strong. I was pure. I had genuine thoughts inside that no one could see, that no one could ever take away from me. I was like the wind.

I threw my head back and smiled proudly to myself. And then I draped the large embroidered red scarf over my face and covered these thoughts up. But underneath the scarf I still knew who I was. I made a promise to myself: I would always remember my parents' wishes, but I would never forget myself.

When I arrived at the wedding, I had the red scarf over my face and couldn't see anything in front of me. But when I bent my head forward, I could see out the sides. Very few people had come. I saw the Huangs, the same old complaining relatives now embarrassed by this poor showing, the entertainers with their violins and flutes. And there were a few village people who had been brave enough to come out for a free meal. I even saw servants and their children, who must have been added to make the party look bigger.

50 Someone took my hands and guided me down a path. I was like a blind person walking to my fate. But I was no longer scared. I could see what was inside me.

A high official conducted the ceremony and he talked too long about philosophers and models of virtue. Then I heard the matchmaker speak about our birthdates and harmony and fertility. I tipped my veiled head forward and I could see her hands unfolding a red silk scarf and holding up a red candle for everyone to see.

The candle had two ends for lighting. One length had carved gold characters with Tyan-yu's name, the other with mine. The matchmaker lighted both ends and announced, "The marriage has begun." Tyan-yu yanked the scarf off my face and smiled at his friends and family, never even looking at me. He reminded me of a young peacock I once saw that acted as if he had just claimed the entire courtyard by fanning his still-short tail.

I saw the matchmaker place the lighted red candle in a gold holder and then hand it to a nervous-looking servant. This servant was supposed to watch the candle during the banquet and all night to make sure neither end went out. In the morning the matchmaker was supposed to show the result, a little piece of black ash, and then declare, "This candle burned continuously at both ends without going out. This is a marriage that can never be broken."

I still can remember. That candle was a marriage bond that was worth more than a Catholic promise not to divorce. It meant I couldn't divorce and I couldn't ever remarry, even if Tyan-yu died. That red candle was supposed to seal me forever with my husband and his family, no excuses afterward.

55 And sure enough, the matchmaker made her declaration the next morning and showed she had done her job. But I know what really happened, because I stayed up all night crying about my marriage.

* * *

After the banquet, our small wedding party pushed us and half carried us up to the third floor to our small bedroom. People were shouting jokes and pulling boys from underneath the bed. The matchmaker helped small children pull red eggs that had been hidden between the blankets. The boys who were about Tyan-yu's age made us sit on the bed side by side and everybody made us kiss so our faces would turn red with passion. Firecrackers exploded on the walkway outside our open window and someone said that this was a good excuse for me to jump into my husband's arms.

After everyone left, we sat there side by side without words for many minutes, still listening to the laughing outside. When it grew quiet, Tyan-yu said, "This is my bed. You sleep on the sofa." He threw a pillow and a thin blanket to me. I was so glad! I waited until he fell asleep and then I got up quietly and went outside, down the stairs and into the dark courtyard.

Outside it smelled as if it would soon rain again. I was crying, walking in my bare feet and feeling the wet heat still inside the bricks. Across the courtyard I could see the matchmaker's servant through a yellow-lit open window. She was sitting at a table, looking very sleepy as the red candle burned in its special gold holder. I sat down by a tree to watch my fate being decided for me.

I must have fallen asleep because I remember being startled awake by the sound of loud cracking thunder. That's when I saw the matchmaker's servant running from the room, scared as a chicken about to lose its head. Oh, she was asleep too, I thought, and now she thinks it's the Japanese. I laughed. The whole sky became light and then more thunder came, and she ran out of the courtyard and down the road, going so fast and hard I could see pebbles kicking up behind her. Where does she think she's running to, I wondered, still laughing. And then I saw the red candle flickering just a little with the breeze.

60 I was not thinking when my legs lifted me up and my feet ran me across the courtyard to the yellow-lit room. But I was hoping—I was praying to Buddha, the goddess of mercy, and the full moon—to make that candle go out. It fluttered a little and the flame bent down low, but still both ends burned strong. My throat filled with so much hope that it finally burst and blew out my husband's end of the candle.

I immediately shivered with fear. I thought a knife would appear and cut me down dead. Or the sky would open up and blow me away. But nothing happened, and when my senses came back, I walked back to my room with fast guilty steps.

The next morning the matchmaker made her proud declaration in front of Tyan-yu, his parents, and myself. "My job is done," she announced, pouring the remaining black ash onto the red cloth. I saw her servant's shame-faced, mournful look.

* * *

I learned to love Tyan-yu, but it is not how you think. From the beginning, I would always become sick thinking he would someday climb on top of me and do his business. Every time I went into our bedroom, my hair would already be standing up. But during the first months, he never touched me. He slept in his bed, I slept on my sofa.

In front of his parents, I was an obedient wife, just as they taught me. I instructed the cook to kill a fresh young chicken every morning and cook it until pure juice came out. I would strain this juice myself into a bowl, never adding any water. I gave this to him for breakfast, murmuring good wishes about his health. And every night I would cook a special tonic soup called *tounau*, which was not only very delicious but has eight ingredients that guarantee long life for mothers. This pleased my mother-in-law very much.

65   But it was not enough to keep her happy. One morning, Huang Taitai and I were sitting in the same room, working on our embroidery. I was dreaming about my childhood, about a pet frog I once kept named Big Wind. Huang Taitai seemed restless, as if she had an itch in the bottom of her shoe. I heard her huffing and then all of a sudden she stood up from her chair, walked over to me, and slapped my face.

"Bad wife!" she cried. "If you refuse to sleep with my son, I refuse to feed you or clothe you." So that's how I knew what my husband had said to avoid his mother's anger. I was also boiling with anger, but I said nothing, remembering my promise to my parents to be an obedient wife.

That night I sat on Tyan-yu's bed and waited for him to touch me. But he didn't. I was relieved. The next night, I lay straight down on the bed next to him. And still he didn't touch me. So the next night, I took off my gown.

That's when I could see what was underneath Tyan-yu. He was scared and turned his face. He had no desire for me, but it was his fear that made me think he had no desire for any woman. He was like a little boy who had never grown up. After a while I was no longer afraid. I even began to think differently toward Tyan-yu. It was not like the way a wife loves a husband, but more like the way a sister protects a younger brother. I put my gown back on and lay down next to him and rubbed his back. I knew I no longer had to be afraid. I was sleeping with Tyan-yu. He would never touch me and I had a comfortable bed to sleep on.

After more months had passed and my stomach and breasts remained small and flat, Huang Taitai flew into another kind of rage. "My son says he's planted enough seeds for thousands of grandchildren. Where are they? It must be you are doing something wrong." And after that she confined me to the bed so that her grandchildren's seeds would not spill out so easily.

70   Oh, you think it is so much fun to lie in bed all day, never getting up. But I tell you it was worse than a prison. I think Huang Taitai became a little crazy.

She told the servants to take all sharp things out of the room, thinking scissors and knives were cutting off her next generation. She forbade me from sewing. She said I must concentrate and think of nothing but having babies. And four times a day, a very nice servant girl would come into my room, apologizing the whole time while making me drink a terrible-tasting medicine.

I envied this girl, the way she could walk out the door. Sometimes as I watched her from my window, I would imagine I was that girl, standing in the courtyard, bargaining with the traveling shoe mender, gossiping with other servant girls, scolding a handsome delivery man in her high teasing voice.

One day, after two months had gone by without any results, Huang Taitai called the old matchmaker to the house. The matchmaker examined me closely, looked up my birthdate and the hour of my birth, and then asked Huang Taitai about my nature. Finally, the matchmaker gave her conclusions: "It's clear what has happened. A woman can have sons only if she is deficient in one of the elements. Your daughter-inlaw was born with enough wood, fire, water, and earth, and she was deficient in metal, which was a good sign. But when she was married, you loaded her down with gold bracelets and decorations and now she has all the elements, including metal. She's too balanced to have babies."

This turned out to be joyous news for Huang Taitai, for she liked nothing better than to reclaim all her gold and jewelry to help me become fertile. And it was good news for me too. Because after the gold was removed from my body, I felt lighter, more free. They say this is what happens if you lack metal. You begin to think as an independent person. That day I started to think about how I would escape this marriage without breaking my promise to my family.

75   It was really quite simple. I made the Huangs think it was their idea to get rid of me, that they would be the ones to say the marriage contract was not valid.

I thought about my plan for many days. I observed everyone around me, the thoughts they showed in their faces, and then I was ready. I chose an auspicious day, the third day of the third month. That's the day of the Festival of Pure Brightness. On this day, your thoughts must be clear as you prepare to think about your ancestors. That's the day when everyone goes to the family graves. They bring hoes to clear the weeds and brooms to sweep the stones and they offer dumplings and oranges as spiritual food. Oh, it's not a somber day, more like a picnic, but it has special meaning to someone looking for grandsons.

On the morning of that day, I woke up Tyan-yu and the entire house with my wailing. It took Huang Taitai a long time to come into my room. "What's wrong with her now," she cried from her room. "Go make her be quiet." But finally, after my wailing didn't stop, she rushed into my room, scolding me at the top of her voice.

I was clutching my mouth with one hand and my eyes with another. My body was writhing as if I were seized by a terrible pain. I was quite convincing, because Huang Taitai drew back and grew small like a scared animal.

"What's wrong, little daughter? Tell me quickly," she cried.

80   "Oh, it's too terrible to think, too terrible to say," I said between gasps and more wailing.

After enough wailing, I said what was so unthinkable. "I had a dream," I reported. "Our ancestors came to me and said they wanted to see our wedding. So Tyan-yu and I held the same ceremony for our ancestors. We saw the matchmaker light the candle and give it to the servant to watch. Our ancestors were so pleased, so pleased . . ."

Huang Taitai looked impatient as I began to cry softly again. "But then the servant left the room with our candle and a big wind came and blew the candle out. And our ancestors became very angry. They shouted that the marriage was doomed! They said that Tyan-yu's end of the candle had blown out! Our ancestors said Tyan-yu would die if he stayed in this marriage!"

Tyan-yu's face turned white. But Huang Taitai only frowned. "What a stupid girl to have such bad dreams!" And then she scolded everybody to go back to bed.

"Mother," I called to her in a hoarse whisper. "Please don't leave me! I am afraid! Our ancestors said if the matter is not settled, they would begin the cycle of destruction."

85   "What is this nonsense!" cried Huang Taitai, turning back toward me. Tyan-yu followed her, wearing his mother's same frowning face. And I knew they were almost caught, two ducks leaning into the pot.

"They knew you would not believe me," I said in a remorseful tone, "because they know I do not want to leave the comforts of my marriage. So our ancestors said they would plant the signs, to show our marriage is now rotting."

"What nonsense from your stupid head," said Huang Taitai, sighing. But she could not resist. "What signs?"

"In my dream, I saw a man with a long beard and a mole on his cheek."

"Tyan-yu's grandfather?" asked Huang Taitai. I nodded, remembering the painting I had observed on the wall.

90 "He said there are three signs. First, he has drawn a black spot on Tyan-yu's back, and this spot will grow and eat away Tyan-yu's flesh just as it ate away our ancestor's face before he died."

Huang Taitai quickly turned to Tyan-yu and pulled his shirt up. "Ai-ya!" She cried, because there it was, the same black mole, the size of a fingertip, just as I had always seen in these past five months of sleeping as sister and brother.

"And then our ancestor touched my mouth," and I patted my cheek as if it already hurt. "He said my teeth would start to fall out one by one, until I could no longer protest leaving this marriage."

Huang Taitai pried open my mouth and gasped upon seeing the open spot in the back of my mouth where a rotted tooth fell out four years ago.

"And finally, I saw him plant a seed in a servant girl's womb. He said this girl only pretends to come from a bad family. But she is really from imperial blood, and . . ."

95 I lay my head down on the pillow as if too tired to go on. Huang Taitai pushed my shoulder, "What does he say?"

"He said the servant girl is Tyan-yu's true spiritual wife. And the seed he has planted will grow into Tyan-yu's child."

By mid-morning they had dragged the matchmaker's servant over to our house and extracted her terrible confession.

And after much searching they found the servant girl I liked so much, the one I had watched from my window every day. I had seen her eyes grow bigger and her teasing voice become smaller whenever the handsome delivery man arrived. And later, I had watched her stomach grow rounder and her face become longer with fear and worry.

So you can imagine how happy she was when they forced her to tell the truth about her imperial ancestry. I heard later she was so struck with this miracle of marrying Tyan-yu she became a very religious person who ordered servants to sweep the ancestors' graves not just once a year, but once a day.

* * *

100 There's no more to the story. They didn't blame me so much. Huang Taitai got her grandson. I got my clothes, a rail ticket to Peking, and enough money to go to America. The Huangs asked only that I never tell anybody of any importance about the story of my doomed marriage.

It's a true story, how I kept my promise, how I sacrificed my life. See the gold metal I can now wear. I gave birth to your brothers and then your father gave me these two bracelets. Then I had you. And every few years, when I have a little extra money, I buy another bracelet. I know what I'm worth. They're always twenty-four carats, all genuine.

But I'll never forget. On the day of the Festival of Pure Brightness, I take off all my bracelets. I remember when I finally knew a genuine thought and could follow it where it went. It was the day I was a young girl with my face under a red marriage scarf. I promised not to forget myself.

How nice it is to be that girl again, to take off my scarf, to see what is underneath and feel the lightness come back into my body!

THINKING ↔ WRITING ACTIVITY 4.2

Analyzing Lindo Jong's Decision

Using the five steps for decision making, write an analysis of Lindo Jong's decision concerning the solution to her unhappy marriage. Do you think she has been satisfied with the results of her decision?

Now try to apply these same steps to a decision in your own life.

THINKING ↔ WRITING ACTIVITY 4.3

Analyzing a Future Decision

1. Make a list of whatever important decisions in your academic or personal life you have to make now or will have to make in the near future.
2. Use the format given on page 95 to begin analyzing one of the decisions you have just listed.

There are no guarantees in life. Our decisions may or may not turn out well. Still, following an organized method for making decisions can at least assure us of having used our creative thinking ability to generate many possible choices and our critical thinking ability to evaluate the choices and choose one that seemed to best meet our needs. In other words, we will know that we made the best decision that we could have, at the time. And we can be reasonably hopeful that in years to come, we will look back with the same attitude expressed by Robert Frost in the following poem.

The Road Not Taken
by Robert Frost

Two roads diverged in a yellow wood,
And sorry I could not travel both
And be one traveler, long I stood
And looked down as far as I could
5   To where it bent in the undergrowth;

Then took the other, as just as fair,
And having perhaps the better claim,
Because it was grassy and wanted wear;
Though as for that the passing there
10 Had worn them really about the same,

And both that morning equally lay
In leaves no step had trodden black.
Oh, I kept the first for another day!
Yet knowing how way leads on to way,
15 I doubted if I should ever come back.

I shall be telling this with a sigh
Somewhere ages and ages hence:
Two roads diverged in a wood, and I—
I took the one less traveled by,
20 And that has made all the difference.

Making Decisions When Revising Drafts

Revising your writing is the key to producing your best possible work. It is very rare for a first draft to represent the most effective writing of which a writer is capable. Most accomplished writers expect their work to undergo a number of revisions, based on their own re-evaluation of it and on feedback from others. The difference between outstanding and mediocre writing often depends on revision.

Revising your writing involves making a series of decisions in response to questions that you might want to picture as a revision template—a template that you place over your work for help with refining it. Notice how some of the concepts in the **Method for Making Decisions,** page 95, can be applied to revising your drafts.

- You *define the decision* by identifying what in a draft needs to be revised and what should be left as it is.

- You *consider possible choices* for improving a draft, especially with major components such as composing and placing the thesis statement, presenting evidence, and arranging material in sequences or sections or paragraphs. You also often have several possible choices among sentence patterns and words when you work at the editing level of revision.

- You *gather relevant information* and *evaluate* the different choices so that you can *select* what best meets the need of the writing situation. Sometimes you may actually write down the different possibilities; in other instances, you may just try them out in your mind.

- After *implementing* your choices by revising a draft, you *evaluate* your writing by *reading it again,* slowly and completely, to be sure that the whole piece is as good as you can make it.

- *Collaborating* with classmates or other trusted readers in all these decisions about your drafts will usually be very helpful. Other readers can see your drafts more objectively and help you "re-see" and revise them.

Specific Choices at Several Levels

While effective writers revise all kinds of drafts, much of what is said in Chapter 1, in this chapter, and in the Writing Projects pertains to drafts that are in a close-to-finished stage, that have moved beyond discovery writing to an organized version. Such drafts may not need many changes, or they may require major reworking. The following suggestions should help you improve your almost-finished drafts.

Read your entire draft slowly and carefully. You may find, as many writers do, that reading out loud helps you to locate parts that don't sound right. Also, ask someone whose judgment you trust to read the draft and help you to decide what improvement is needed. If your class allows peer review, be prepared for this opportunity by having a completed draft ready.

If you decide that improvement is required, the need for a decision immediately presents itself. At what level should you begin in make changes? Some people think that revision means making corrections in grammar, punctuation, and spelling. Revision can indeed include those corrections, but it usually means much more. In fact, those corrections are often identified separately, as editing and proofreading, to distinguish them from larger aspects of revision.

A helpful way to decide where to begin revising is to move through the following hierarchy of concerns and questions about your draft. If you find yourself answering any of the questions in a way that suggests ways to improve your writing, stop and try to make changes or additions to your draft before you move on to the next level. There is no point in worrying about punctuation if your draft lacks focus or good examples.

However, you must remember that revision, like all activities in a writing process, is recursive. You may see content, organization, or wording problems while you are checking punctuation; you may fix a typo while you're rewording the thesis statement. The hierarchy that follows emphasizes the importance of looking first at major concerns, but you should be prepared to move around among the levels of attention as you make your decisions about a draft.

1. **Think big.** Look at your draft as a whole.
- Does it fulfill the assignment in terms of topic and length?
- Does it have a focus?
- Have you stated the thesis clearly?
- Do all parts of the draft relate to the thesis?
- How about organization and logical order of ideas?
- Do you provide enough evidence to accomplish your purpose?

- Is your point of view consistent?
- Is there a discernible flow between your paragraphs and throughout the whole piece?

2. **Think medium.** Look at your draft paragraph by paragraph.
- Will your *introduction* make your audience want to read on?
- Is it appropriate for the rest of the draft—that is, does the tone of the introduction match the tone of the rest of the draft?
- Is your focus stated clearly if you are working with a "visible" structure?
- If you are working with an "invisible structure," is your focus clearly implied?
     Then look at each of your *body paragraphs.*
- Does each support the thesis?
- Does each present relevant, specific evidence not presented elsewhere?
- Should any paragraphs be combined or eliminated?
- Are topic sentences used effectively?
- Do paragraphs without topic sentences need them?
- Are there transitions between paragraphs and within them?
     Look at your conclusion. It is your last chance to accomplish your purpose.
- Does your *conclusion* provide a satisfying ending?
- Is it appropriate in tone?
- Is there any way that you can make it more effective?

3. **Think small.** Look at your draft sentence by sentence.
- Are any sentences difficult to understand?
- Are any so long that your audience could get lost in them?
- Are there several short, choppy sentences that can be combined?
- Do any sentences strike you as vague?
- Do any sentences have errors in standard English grammar or usage?

4. **Think "picky."** Look at your draft as your fussiest critic might.
- Are any words not clear or not quite right for your meaning?
- Are any words spelled incorrectly?
- Are there any punctuation errors?
- Is your format correct?
- Are the pages numbered consecutively?
- Will the finished paper make a good impression by being neat?
- Is there anything else you can do to improve your draft?

THINKING↔WRITING ACTIVITY 4.4

Previous Revision Experiences

Write about your past experiences with revision. Use the preceding four-level hierarchy of concerns and questions for help. Which of these questions have you regularly been concerned about? Which, if any, are new to you? Which strike you as especially important, and why?

Beyond considering your own earlier experiences, you can deepen your understanding of revision by reading the following selections by three expert writers. After thinking about their ideas, answer the questions in **Thinking↔Writing Activity 4.5.**

from The Maker's Eye: Revising Your Own Manuscripts
by Donald M. Murray

When students complete a first draft, they consider the job of writing done—and their teachers too often agree. When professional writers complete a first draft, they usually feel that they are at the start of the writing process. When a draft is completed, the job of writing can begin.

That difference in attitude is the difference between amateur and professional, inexperience and experience, journeyman and craftsman. Peter F. Drucker, the prolific business writer, calls his first draft "the zero draft"—after that he can start counting. Most writers share the feeling that the first draft, and all of those which follow, are opportunities to discover what they have to say and how best they can say it.

To produce a progression of drafts, each of which says more and says it more clearly, the writer has to develop a special kind of reading skill. In school we are taught to decode what appears on the page as finished writing. Writers, however, face a different category of possibility and responsibility when they read their own drafts. To them the words on the page are never finished. Each can be changed and rearranged, can set off a chain reaction of confusion or clarified meaning. This is a different kind of reading, which is possibly more difficult and certainly more exciting.

Writers must learn to be their own best enemy. They must accept the criticism of others and be suspicious of it; they must accept the praise of others and be even more suspicious of it. Writers cannot depend on others. They must detach themselves from their own pages so that they can apply both their caring and their craft to their own work.

5   Such detachment is not easy. Science fiction writer Ray Bradbury supposedly puts each manuscript away for a year to the day and then rereads it as a stranger. Not many writers have the discipline or the time

to do this. We must read when our judgment may be at its worst, when we are close to the euphoric moment of creation.

Then the writer, counsels novelist Nancy Hale, "should be critical of everything that seems to him most delightful in his style. He should excise what he most admires, because he wouldn't thus admire it if he weren't . . . in a sense protecting it from criticism." John Ciardi, the poet, adds, "The last act of writing must be to become one's own reader. It is, I suppose, a schizophrenic process, to begin passionately and to end critically, to begin hot and to end cold; and, more important, to be passion-hot and critic-cold at the same time."

Most people think that the principal problem is that writers are too proud of what they have written. Actually, a greater problem for most professional writers is one shared by the majority of students. They are overly critical, think everything is dreadful, tear up page after page, never complete a draft, see the task as hopeless.

The writer must learn to read critically but constructively, to cut what is bad, to reveal what is good. Eleanor Estes, the children's book author, explains: "The writer must survey his work critically, coolly, as though he were a stranger to it. He must be willing to prune, expertly and hard-heartedly. At the end of each revision, a manuscript may look . . . worked over, torn apart, pinned together, added to, deleted from, words changed and words changed back. Yet the book must maintain its original freshness and spontaneity."

Most readers underestimate the amount of rewriting it usually takes to produce spontaneous reading. This is a great disadvantage to the student writer, who sees only a finished product and never watches the craftsman who takes the necessary steps back, studies the work carefully, returns to the task, steps back, returns, steps back, again and again. Anthony Burgess, one of the most prolific writers in the English-speaking world, admits, "I might revise a page twenty times." Roald Dahl, the popular children's writer, states, "By the time I'm nearing the end of a story, the first part will have been reread and altered and corrected at least 150 times. . . . Good writing is essentially rewriting. I am positive of this."

10   Rewriting isn't virtuous. It isn't something that ought to be done. It is simply something that most writers find they have to do to discover what they have to say and how to say it. It is a condition of the writer's life.

There are, however, a few writers who do little formal rewriting, primarily because they have the capacity and experience to create and review a large number of invisible drafts in their minds before they approach the page. And some writers slowly produce finished pages, performing all the tasks of revision simultaneously, page by page, rather than draft by draft. But it is still possible to see the sequence followed by most writers most of the time in rereading their own work.

Most writers scan their drafts first, reading as quickly as possible to catch the larger problems of subject and form, then move in closer and closer as they read and write, reread and rewrite.

The first thing writers look for in their drafts is *information.* They know that a good piece of writing is built from specific, accurate, and interesting information. The writer must have an abundance of information from which to construct a readable piece of writing.

Next, writers look for meaning in the information. The specifics must build a pattern of significance. Each piece of specific information must carry the reader toward meaning.

15

Writers reading their own drafts are aware of *audience.* They put themselves in the reader's situation and make sure that they deliver information which a reader wants to know or needs to know in a manner which is easily digested. Writers try to be sure that they anticipate and answer the questions a critical reader will ask when reading the piece of writing.

Writers make sure that the *form* is appropriate to the subject and the audience. Form, or genre, is the vehicle which carries meaning to the reader, but form cannot be selected until the writer has adequate information to discover its significance and an audience which needs or wants that meaning.

Once writers are sure the form is appropriate, they must then look at the *structure,* the order of what they have written. Good writing is built on a solid framework of logic, argument, narrative, or motivation which runs through the entire piece of writing and holds it together. This is the time when many writers find it most effective to outline as a way of visualizing the hidden spine by which the piece of writing is supported.

The element on which writers may spend a majority of their time is *development.* Each section of a piece of writing must be adequately developed. It must give readers enough information so that they are satisfied. How much information is enough? That's as difficult as asking how much garlic belongs in a salad. It must be done to taste, but most beginning writers underdevelop, underestimating the reader's hunger for information.

As writers solve development problems, they often have to consider questions of *dimension.* There must be a pleasing and effective proportion among all the parts of the piece of writing. There is a continual process of subtracting and adding to keep the piece of writing in balance.

20

Finally, writers have to listen to their own voices. *Voice* is the force which drives a piece of writing forward. It is an expression of the writer's authority and concern. It is what is between the words on the page, what glues the piece of writing together. A good piece of writing is always marked by a consistent, individual voice.

As writers read and reread, write and rewrite, they move closer and closer to the page until they are doing line-by-line editing. Writers read their own pages with infinite care. Each sentence, each line, each clause, each phrase, each word, each mark of punctuation, each section of white space between the type has to contribute to the clarification of meaning.

Slowly the writer moves from word to word, looking through language to see the subject. As a word is changed, cut, or added, as a construction is rearranged, all the words used before that moment and all those that follow that moment must be considered and reconsidered.

Writers often read aloud at this stage of the editing process, muttering or whispering to themselves, calling on the ear's experience with language. Does this sound right—or that? Writers edit, shifting back and forth from eye to page to ear to page. I find I must do this careful editing in short runs, no more than fifteen or twenty minutes at a stretch, or I become too kind with myself. I begin to see what I hope is on the page, not what actually is on the page.

This sounds tedious if you haven't done it, but actually it is fun. Making something right is immensely satisfying, for writers begin to learn what they are writing about by writing. Language leads them to meaning, and there is the joy of discovery, of understanding, of making meaning clear as the writer employs the technical skills of language.

25 Words have double meaning, even triple and quadruple meanings. Each word has its own potential for connotation and denotation. And when writers rub one word against the other, they are often rewarded with a sudden insight, an unexpected clarification.

The maker's eye moves back and forth from word to phrase to sentence to paragraph to sentence to phrase to word. The maker's eye sees the need for variety and balance, for a firmer structure, for a more appropriate form. It peers into the interior of the paragraph, looking for coherence, unity, and emphasis, which make meaning clear.

I learned something about this process when my first bifocals were prescribed. I had ordered a large section of the reading portion of the glass because of my work, but even so, I could not contain my eyes within this new limit of vision. And I still find myself taking off my glasses and bending my nose towards the page, for my eyes unconsciously flick back and forth across the page, back to another page, forward to still another, as I try to see each evolving line in relation to every other line.

When does this process end? Most writers agree with the great Russian writer Tolstoy, who said, "I scarcely ever reread my published writings, if by chance I come across a page, it always strikes me: all this must be rewritten; this is how I should have written it."

The maker's eye is never satisfied, for each word has the potential to ignite new meaning. This article has been twice written all the way through the writing process, and it was published four years ago. Now it is to be republished in a book. The editors make a few small suggestions, and then I read it with my maker's eye. Now it has been re-edited, re-vised, re-read, re-re-edited, for each piece of writing to the writer is full of potential and alternatives.

30 A piece of writing is never finished. It is delivered to a deadline, torn out of the typewriter on demand, sent off with a sense of accomplish-

ment and shame and pride and frustration. If only there were a couple more days, time for just another run at it, perhaps then . . .

from Writing with a Word Processor
by William Zinsser

Writing is a deeply personal process, full of mystery and surprise. No two people go about it in exactly the same way. We all have little devices to get us started, or to keep us going, or to remind us of what we think we want to say, and what works for one person may not work for anyone else. The main thing is to get something written—to get the words out of our heads. There is no "right" method. Any method that will do the job is the right method for you.

It helps to remember that writing is hard. Most non-writers don't know this; they think that writing is a natural function, like breathing, that ought to come easy, and they're puzzled when it doesn't. If you find that writing is hard, it's because it *is* hard. It's one of the hardest things that people do. Among other reasons, it's hard because it requires thinking. You won't write clearly unless you keep forcing yourself to think clearly. There's no escaping the question that has to be constantly asked: What do I want to say next?

So painful is this task that writers go to remarkable lengths to postpone their daily labor. They sharpen their pencils and change their typewriter ribbon and go out to the store to buy more paper. Now these sacred rituals, as IBM would say, have been obsoleted.

When I began writing this article on my word processor I didn't have any idea what would happen. Would I be able to write anything at all? Would it be any good? I was bringing to the machine what I assumed were wholly different ways of thinking about writing. The units massed in front of me looked cold and sterile. Their steady hum reminded me that they were waiting. They seemed to be waiting for information, not for writing. Maybe what I wrote would also be cold and sterile.

5   I was particularly worried about the absence of paper. I knew that I would only be able to see as many lines as the screen would hold—twenty lines. How could I review what I had already written? How could I get a sense of continuity and flow? With paper it was always possible to flick through the preceding pages to see where I was coming from—and where I ought to be going. Without paper I would have no such periodic fix. Would this be a major hardship?

The only way to find out was to find out. I took a last look at my unsharpened pencils and went to work.

My particular hang-up as a writer is that I have to get every paragraph as nearly right as possible before I go on to the next paragraph. I'm somewhat like a bricklayer: I build very slowly, not adding a new row until I feel that the foundation is solid enough to hold up the house. I'm the exact opposite of the writer who dashes off his entire first draft, not caring how sloppy it looks or how badly it's written. His only objective at this early stage is to let his creative motor run the full course at full speed; repairs can always be made later. I envy this writer and would like to have his metabolism. But I'm stuck with the one I've got.

I also care how my writing looks while I'm writing it. The visual arrangement is important to me: the shape of the words, of the sentences, of the paragraphs, of the page. I don't like sentences that are dense with long words, or paragraphs that never end. As I write I want to see the design that my piece will have when the readers see it in type, and I want that design to have a rhythm and a pace that will invite the reader to keep reading. O.K., so I'm a nut. But I'm not alone; the visual component is important to a large number of people who write.

One hang-up we visual people share is that our copy must be neat. My lifelong writing method, for instance, has gone like this. I put a piece of paper in the typewriter and write the first paragraph. Then I take the paper out and edit what I've written. I mark it up horribly, crossing words out and scribbling new ones in the space between the lines. By this time the paragraph has lost its nature and shape for me as a piece of writing. It's a mishmash of typing and handwriting and arrows and balloons and other directional symbols. So I type a clean copy, incorporating the changes, and then I take that piece of paper out of the typewriter and edit it. It's better, but not much better. I go over it with my pencil again, making more changes, which again make it too messy for me to read critically, so I go back to the typewriter for round three. And round four. Not until I'm reasonably satisfied do I proceed to the next paragraph.

10 This can get pretty tedious, and I have often thought that there must be a better way. Now there is. The word processor is God's gift, or at least science's gift, to the tinkerers and the refiners and the neatness freaks. For me it was obviously the perfect new toy. I began playing on page 1—editing, cutting and revising—and have been on a rewriting high ever since. The burden of the years has been lifted.

Mostly I've been cutting. I would guess that I've cut at least as many words out of this article as the number that remain. Probably half of those words were eliminated because I saw that they were unnecessary—the sentence worked fine without them. This is where the word processor can improve your writing to an extent that you will hardly believe. Learn to recognize what is clutter and to use the DELETE key to prune it out.

How will you know clutter when you see it? Here's a device I used when I was teaching writing at Yale that my students found helpful; it may be a help here. I would put brackets around every component in a student's paper that I didn't think was doing some kind of work. Often it was only one word—for example, the useless preposition that gets appended to so many verbs (order up, free up), or the adverb whose meaning is already in the verb (blare loudly, clench tightly), or the adjective that tells us what we already know (smooth marble, green grass). The brackets might surround the little qualifiers that dilute a writer's authority (a bit, sort of, in a sense), or the countless phrases in which the writer explains what he is about to explain (it might be pointed out, I'm tempted to say). Often my brackets would surround an entire sentence—the sentence that essentially repeats what the previous sentence has said, or tells the reader something that is implicit, or adds a detail that is irrelevant. Most people's writing is littered with phrases that do no new work whatever. Most first drafts, in fact, can be cut by fifty percent without losing anything organic. (Try it; it's a good exercise.)

By bracketing these extra words, instead of crossing them out, I was saying to the student: "I may be wrong, but I think this can go and the meaning of the sentence won't be affected in any way. But *you* decide: Read the sentence without the bracketed material and see if it works." In the first half of the term, the students' papers were festooned with my brackets. Whole paragraphs got bracketed. But gradually the students learned to put mental brackets around their many different kinds of clutter, and by the end of the term I was returning papers to them that had hardly any brackets, or none. It was always a satisfying moment. Today many of those students are professional writers. "I still see your brackets," they tell me. "They're following me through life."

You can develop the same eye. Writing is clear and strong to the extent that it has no superfluous parts. (So is art and music and dance and typography and design.) You will really enjoy writing on a word processor when you see your sentences growing in strength, literally before your eyes, as you get rid of the fat. Be thankful for everything that you can throw away.

15   I was struck by how many phrases and sentences I wrote in this article that I later found I didn't need. Many of them hammered home a point that didn't need hammering because it had already been made. This kind of overwriting happens in almost everybody's first draft, and it's perfectly natural—the act of putting down our thoughts makes us garrulous. Luckily, the act of editing follows the act of writing, and this is where the word processor will bail you out. It intercedes at the point where the game can be won or lost. With its help I cut hundreds of unnecessary words and didn't replace them.

Hundreds of others were discarded because I later thought of a better word—one that caught more precisely or more vividly what I was trying to express. Here, again, a word processor encourages you to play. The English language is rich in words that convey an exact shade of meaning. Don't get stuck with a word that's merely good if you can find one that takes the reader by surprise with its color or aptness or quirkiness. Root around in your dictionary of synonyms and find words that are fresh. Throw them up on the screen and see how they look.

Also learn to play with whole sentences. If a sentence strikes you as awkward or ponderous, move your cursor to the space after the period and write a new sentence that you think is better. Maybe you can make it shorter. Or clearer. Maybe you can make it livelier by turning it into a question or otherwise altering its rhythm. Change the passive verbs into active verbs. (Passive verbs are the death of clarity and vigor.) Try writing two or three new versions of the awkward sentence and then compare them, or write a fourth version that combines the best elements of all three. Sentences come in an infinite variety of shapes and sizes. Find one that pleases you. If it's clear, and if it pleases you and expresses who you are, trust it to please other people. Then delete all the versions that aren't as good. Your shiny new sentence will jump into position, and the rest of the paragraph will rearrange itself as quickly and neatly as if you had never pulled it apart.

Another goal that the word processor will help you to achieve is unity. No matter how carefully you write each sentence as you assemble a piece of writing, the final product is bound to have some ragged edges. Is the tone consistent throughout? And the point of view? And the pronoun? And the tense? How about the transitions? Do they pull the reader along, or is the piece jerky and disjointed? A good piece of writing should be harmonious from beginning to end in the voice of the writer and the flow of its logic. But the harmony usually requires some last-minute patching.

I've been writing a book by the bricklayer method, slowly and carefully. That's all very well as far as it goes—at the end of every chapter the individual bricks may look fine. But what about the wall? The only way to check your piece for unity is to go over it one more time from start to finish, preferably reading it aloud. See if you have executed all the decisions that you made before you started writing.

20   One such decision is in the area of tone. I decided, for instance, that I didn't want my book to be a technical manual. I'm not a technician; I'm a writer and an editor. The book wouldn't work if I expected the reader to identify with the process of mastering a new technology. He would have to identify with me. The book would be first of all a personal journey and only parenthetically a manual. I knew that this was a hybrid form and that its unities would never be wholly intact. Still, in going over each finished chapter I found places where the balance could be improved—where instructional detail smothered the writer and his narrative, or, conversely, where the writer intruded on the procedures he was trying to explain. With a word processor it was easy to make small repairs—perhaps just a change of pronoun and verb—that made the balance less uneven.

The instructional portions of the book posed a problem of their own—one that I had never faced before. My hope was to try to explain a technical process without the help of any diagrams or drawings. Would this be possible? It would be possible only if I kept remembering one fundamental fact: (published) Writing is linear and sequential. This may seem so obvious as to be insulting: Everybody knows that (published) writing is linear and sequential. Actually everybody doesn't know. Most people under thirty don't know. They have been reared since early childhood on television—a kaleidoscope of visual images flashed onto their brain—and it doesn't occur to them that sentence B must follow sentence A, and that sentence C must follow sentence B, or all the elegant sentences in the world won't add up to anything but confusion.

I mention this because word processors are going to be widely used by people who need to impart technical information: matters of operating procedure in business and banking, science and technology, medicine and health, education and government, and dozens of other specialized fields. The information will only be helpful if readers can grasp it quickly and easily. If it's muddy they will get discouraged or angry, or both, and will stop reading.

You can avoid this dreaded fate for your message, whatever it is, by making sure that every sentence is a logical sequel to the one that preceded it. One way to approach this goal is to keep your sentences short. A major reason why technical prose becomes so tangled is that the writer tries to make one sentence do too many jobs. It's a natural hazard of the first draft. But the solution is simple: See that every sentence contains only one thought. The reader can accommodate only one idea at a time. Help him by giving him only one idea at a time. Let him understand A before you proceed to B.

In writing this article, I was eager to explain the procedures that I had learned, and I would frequently lump several points together in one sentence. Later, editing what I had written, I asked myself if the procedure would be clear to someone who was puzzling through it for the first time—someone who hadn't struggled to figure the procedure out. Often I felt that it wouldn't be clear. I was giving the reader too much. He was being asked to picture himself taking various steps that were single and sequential, and that's how he deserved to get them.

25   I therefore divided all troublesome long sentences into two short sentences, or even three. It always gave me great pleasure. Not only is it the fastest way for a writer to get out of a quagmire that there seems to be no getting out of; I also like short sentences for their own sake. There's almost no more beautiful sight than a simple declarative sentence. This article is full of simple declarative sentences that have no punctuation and that carry one simple thought. Without a word processor I wouldn't have chopped as many of them down to their proper size, or done it with so little effort. This is one of the main clarifying jobs that your machine can help you to perform, especially if your writing requires you to guide the reader into territory that is new and bewildering.

Not all my experiences, of course, were rosy. The machine had disadvantages as well as blessings. Often, for instance, I missed not being able to see more than twenty lines at a time—to review what I had written earlier. If I wanted to see more lines I had to "scroll" them back into view.

But even this wasn't as painful as I had thought it would be. I found that I could hold in my head the gist of what I had written and didn't need to keep looking at it. Was this need, in fact, still another writer's hang-up that I could shed? To some extent it was. I discovered, as I had at so many other points in this journey, that various crutches I had always assumed I needed were really not necessary. I made a decision to just throw them away and found that I could still function. The only real hardship occurred when a paragraph broke at the bottom of the screen. This meant that the first lines of the paragraph were on one page and the rest were on the next page, and I had to keep flicking the two pages back and forth to read what I was writing. But again, it wasn't fatal. I learned to live with it and soon took it for granted as an occupational hazard.

from How to Say Nothing in Five Hundred Words
by Paul Roberts

It's Friday afternoon, and you have almost survived another week of classes. You are just looking forward dreamily to the weekend when the English instructor says: "For Monday you will turn in a five-hundred-word composition on college football."

Well, that puts a good big hole in the weekend. You don't have any strong views on college football one way or the other. You get rather excited during the season and go to all the home games and find it rather more fun than not. On the other hand, the class has been reading Robert Hutchins in the anthology and perhaps Shaw's "Eighty-Yard Run," and from the class discussion you have got the idea that the instructor thinks college football is for the birds. You are no fool. You can figure out what side to take.

You might as well get it over with and enjoy Saturday and Sunday. Five hundred words is about two double-spaced pages with normal margins. You put in a sheet of paper, think up a title, and you're off:

WHY COLLEGE FOOTBALL SHOULD BE ABOLISHED

College football should be abolished because it's bad for the school and also bad for the players. The players are so busy practicing that they don't have any time for their studies.

This, you feel, is a mighty good start. The only trouble is that it's only thirty-two words. You still have four hundred and sixty-eight to go, and you've pretty well exhausted the subject. It comes to you that you do your best thinking in the morning, so you put away the typewriter and go to the movies. But the next morning you have to do your washing and some math problems, and in the afternoon you go to the game. The English instructor turns up too, and you wonder if you've taken the right side after all. Saturday night you have a date, and Sunday morn-

ing you have to go to church. (You can't let English assignments interfere with your religion.) What with one thing and another, it's ten o'-
clock Sunday night before you get out the typewriter again. You make
a pot of coffee and start to fill out your views on college football. Put a
little meat on the bones.

WHY COLLEGE FOOTBALL SHOULD BE ABOLISHED

5   In my opinion, it seems to me that college football should be abolished. The reason why I think this is to be true is because I feel that
football is bad for the colleges in nearly every aspect. As Robert
Hutchins says in his article in our anthology in which he discusses
college football, it would be better if the colleges had race horses and
had races with one another, because then the horses would not have
to attend classes. I firmly agree with Mr. Hutchins on this point, and
I am sure that many other students would agree too.

One reason why it seems to me that college football is bad is that
it has become too commercial. In the olden times when people
played football just for the fun of it, maybe college football was all
right, but they do not play football just for the fun of it now as they
used to in the old days. Nowadays college football is what you might
call a big business. Maybe this is not true at all schools, and I don't
think it is especially true here at State, but certainly this is the case at
most colleges and universities in America nowadays, as Mr.
Hutchins points out in his very interesting article. Actually the
coaches and alumni go around to the high schools and offer the high
school stars large salaries to come to their colleges and play football
for them. There was one case where a high school star was offered a
convertible if he would play football for a certain college.

Another reason for abolishing college football is that it is bad for
the players. They do not have time to get a college education, because they are so busy playing football. A football player has to practice every afternoon from three to six and then he is so tired that he
can't concentrate on his studies. He just feels like dropping off to
sleep after dinner, and then the next day he goes to his classes without having studied and maybe he fails the test.

(Good ripe stuff, so far, but you're still a hundred and fifty-one words
from home. One more push.)

Also I think college football is bad for the colleges and the universities because not very many students get to participate in it. Out of
a college of ten thousand males only seventy-five or a hundred play
football, if that many. Football is what you might call a spectator
sport. That means that most people go to watch it but do not play it
themselves.

(Four hundred and fifteen. Well, you still have the conclusion, and when you retype it, you can make the margins a little wider.)

These are the reasons why I agree with Mr. Hutchins that college football should be abolished in American colleges and universities.

10 On Monday you turn it in, moderately hopeful, and on Friday it comes back marked "weak in content" and sporting a big "D."

This essay is exaggerated a little, not much. The English instructor will recognize it as reasonably typical of what an assignment on college football will bring in. He knows that nearly half of the class will contrive in five hundred words to say that college football is too commercial and bad for the players. Most of the other half will inform him that college football builds character and prepares one for life and brings prestige to the school. As he reads paper after paper all saying the same thing in almost the same words, all bloodless, five hundred words dripping out of nothing, he wonders how he allowed himself to get trapped into teaching English when he might have had a happy and interesting life as an electrician or a confidence man.

Well, you may ask, what can you do about it? The subject is one on which you have few convictions and little information. Can you be expected to make a dull subject interesting? As a matter of fact, that is precisely what you are expected to do. This is the writer's essential task. All subjects, except sex, are dull until somebody makes them interesting. The writer's job is to find the argument, the approach, the angle, the wording that will take the reader with him. This is seldom easy, and it is particularly hard in subjects that have been much discussed: College Football, Fraternities, Popular Music, Is Chivalry Dead?, and the like. You will feel that there is nothing you can do with such subjects except repeat the old bromides. But there are some things you can do which will make your papers, if not throbbingly alive, at least less insufferably tedious than they might otherwise be.

Avoid the Obvious Content

Say the assignment is college football. Say that you've decided to be against it. Begin by putting down the arguments that come to your mind: It is too commercial, it takes the students' minds off their studies, it is hard on the players, it makes the university a kind of circus instead of an intellectual center, for most schools it is financially ruinous. Can you think of any more arguments, just off hand? All right. Now when you write your paper, *make sure that you don't use any of the material on this list.* If these are the points that leap to your mind they will leap to everyone else's too, and whether you get a "C" or a "D" may depend on whether the instructor reads your paper early when he is fresh and tolerant or late, when the sentence "In my opinion, college football has become too commercial," inexorably repeated, has brought him to the brink of lunacy.

Be against college football for some reason or reasons of your own. If they are keen and perceptive ones, that's splendid. But even if they are trivial or foolish or indefensible, you are still ahead so long as they are not everybody else's reasons too. Be against it because the colleges don't spend enough money on it to make it worthwhile, because it is bad for the characters of the spectators, because the players are forced to attend classes, because the football stars hog all the beautiful women, because it competes with baseball and is therefore un-American and possibly Communist inspired. There are lots of more or less unused reasons for being against college football.

15   Sometimes it is a good idea to sum up and dispose of the trite and conventional points before going on to your own. This has the advantage of indicating to the reader that you are going to be neither trite nor conventional. Something like this:

> We are often told that college football should be abolished because it has become too commercial or because it is bad for the players. These arguments are no doubt very cogent, but they don't go to the heart of the matter.

Then you go to the heart of the matter.

Take the Less Usual Side

One rather simple way of getting into your paper is to take the side of the argument that most of the citizens will want to avoid. If the assignment is an essay on dogs, you can, if you choose, explain that dogs are faithful and lovable companions, intelligent, useful as guardians of the house and protectors of children, indispensable in police work—in short, when all is said and done, man's best friends. Or you can suggest that those big brown eyes conceal, more often than not, a vacuity of mind and an inconstancy of purpose; that the dogs you have known most intimately have been mangy, ill-tempered brutes, incapable of instruction; and that only your nobility of mind and fear of arrest prevent you from kicking the flea-ridden animals when you pass them on the street.

Naturally personal convictions will sometimes dictate your approach. If the assigned subject is "Is Methodism Rewarding to the Individual?" and you are a pious Methodist, you have really no choice. But few assigned subjects, if any, will fall into this category. Most of them will lie in broad areas of discussion with much to be said on both sides. They are intellectual exercises, and it is legitimate to argue now one way and now another, as debaters do in similar circumstances. Always take the side that looks to you hardest, least defensible. It will almost always turn out to be easier to write interestingly on that side.

This general advice applies where you have a choice of subjects. If you are to choose among "The Value of Fraternities" and "My Favorite

High School Teacher" and "What I Think About Beetles," by all means plump for the beetles. By the time the instructor gets to your paper, he will be up to his ears in tedious tales about the French teacher at Bloombury High and assertions about how fraternities build character and prepare one for life. Your views on beetles, whatever they are, are bound to be a refreshing change.

Don't worry too much about figuring out what the instructor thinks about the subject so that you can cuddle up with him. Chances are his views are no stronger than yours. If he does have convictions and you oppose him, his problem is to keep from grading you higher than you deserve in order to show he is not biased. This doesn't mean that you should always cantankerously dissent from what the instructor says; that gets tiresome too. And if the subject assigned is "My Pet Peeve," do not begin, "My pet peeve is the English instructor who assigns papers on 'my pet peeve.'" This was still funny during the War of 1812, but it has sort of lost its edge since then. It is in general good manners to avoid personalities.

Slip Out of Abstraction

20 If you will study the essay on college football [near the beginning of this essay], you will perceive that one reason for its appalling dullness is that it never gets down to particulars. It is just a series of not very glittering generalities: "Football is bad for the colleges," "it has become too commercial," "football is a big business," "it is bad for the players," and so on. Such round phrases thudding against the reader's brain are unlikely to convince him, though they may well render him unconscious.

If you want the reader to believe that college football is bad for the players, you have to do more than say so. You have to display the evil. Take your roommate, Alfred Simkins, the second-string center. Picture poor old Alfy coming home from football practice every evening, bruised and aching, agonizingly tired, scarcely able to shovel the mashed potatoes into his mouth. Let us see him staggering up to the room, getting out his econ textbook, peering desperately at it with his good eye, falling asleep and failing the test in the morning. Let us share his unbearable tension as Saturday draws near. Will he fail, be demoted, lose his monthly allowance, be forced to return to the coal mines? And if he succeeds, what will be his reward? Perhaps a slight ripple of applause when the third-string center replaces him, a moment of elation in the locker room if the team wins, of despair if it loses. What will he look back on when he graduates from college? Toil and torn ligaments. And what will be his future? He is not good enough for pro football, and he is too obscure and weak in econ to succeed in stocks and bonds. College football is tearing the heart from Alfy Simkins and, when it finishes with him, will callously toss aside the shattered hulk.

This is no doubt a weak enough argument for the abolition of college football, but it is a sight better than saying, in three or four variations, that college football (in your opinion) is bad for players.

Look at the work of any professional writer and notice how constantly he is moving from the generality, the abstract statement, to the concrete example, the facts and figures, the illustration. If he is writing on juvenile delinquency, he does not just tell you that juveniles are (it seems to him) delinquent and that (in his opinion) something should be done about it. He shows you juveniles being delinquent, tearing up movie theaters in Buffalo, stabbing high school principals in Dallas, smoking marijuana in Palo Alto. And more than likely he is moving toward some specific remedy, not just a general wringing of the hands.

It is no doubt possible to be *too* concrete, too illustrative or anecdotal, but few inexperienced writers err this way. For most the soundest advice is to be seeking always for the picture, to be always turning general remarks into seeable examples. Don't say, "Sororities teach girls the social graces." Say, "Sorority life teaches a girl how to carry on a conversation while pouring tea, without sloshing the tea into the saucer." Don't say, "I like certain kinds of popular music very much." Say, "Whenever I hear Gerber Sprinklittle play 'Mississippi Man' on the trombone, my socks creep up my ankles."

Get Rid of Obvious Padding

25   The student toiling away at his weekly English theme is too often tormented by a figure: five hundred words. How, he asks himself, is he to achieve this staggering total? Obviously by never using one word when he can somehow work in ten.

He is therefore seldom content with a plain statement like "Fast driving is dangerous." This has only four words in it. He takes thought, and the sentence becomes:

> In my opinion, fast driving is dangerous.

Better, but he can do better still:

> In my opinion, fast driving would seem to be rather dangerous.

If he is really adept, it may come out:

> In my humble opinion, though I do not claim to be an expert on this complicated subject, fast driving, in most circumstances, would seem to be rather dangerous in many aspects, or at least so it would seem to me.

Thus four words have turned into forty, and not an iota of content has been added.

Now this is a way to go about reaching five hundred words, and if you are content with a "D" grade, it is as good a way as any. But if you aim higher, you must work differently. Instead of stuffing your sentences with straw, you must try steadily to get rid of the padding, to make your sentences lean and tough. If you are really working at it, your first draft will greatly exceed the required total, and then you will work it down, thus:

> It is thought in some quarters that fraternities do not contribute as much as might be expected to campus life.

> Some people think that fraternities contribute little to campus life.

> The average doctor who practices in small towns or in the country must toil night and day to heal the sick.

> Most country doctors work long hours.

> When I was a little girl, I suffered from shyness and embarrassment in the presence of others.

> I was a shy little girl.

> It is absolutely necessary for the person employed as a marine fireman to give the matter of steam pressure his undivided attention at all times.

> The fireman has to keep his eye on the steam gauge.

You may ask how you can arrive at five hundred words at this rate. Simple. You dig up more real content. Instead of taking a couple of obvious points off the surface of the topic and then circling warily around them for six paragraphs, you work in and explore, figure out the details. You illustrate. You say that fast driving is dangerous, and then you prove it. How long does it take to stop a car at forty and eighty? How far can you see at night? What happens when a tire blows? What happens in a head-on collision at fifty miles an hour? Pretty soon your paper will be full of broken glass and blood and headless torsos, and reaching five hundred words will not really be a problem.

Call a Fool a Fool

Some of the padding in freshman themes is to be blamed not on anxiety about the word minimum but on excessive timidity. The student writes, "In my opinion, the principal of my high school acted in ways that I believe every unbiased person would have to call foolish." This isn't exactly what he means. What he means is, "My high school principal was a fool." If he was a fool, call him a fool. Hedging the thing about with "in-my-opinion's" and "it-seems-to-me's" and "as-I-see-it's" and "at-least-from-my-point-of-view's" gains you nothing. Delete these phrases whenever they creep into your paper.

30   The student's tendency to hedge stems from a modesty that in other circumstances would be commendable. He is, he realizes, young and inexperienced, and he half suspects that he is dopey and fuzzy-minded beyond the average. Probably only too true. But it doesn't help to an-

nounce your incompetence six times in every paragraph. Decide what you want to say and say it as vigorously as possible, without apology and in plain words.

Linguistic diffidence can take various forms. One is what we call *euphemism*. This is the tendency to call a spade "a certain garden implement" or women's underwear "unmentionables." It is stronger in some eras than others and in some people than others but it always operates more or less in subjects that are touchy or taboo: death, sex, madness, and so on. Thus we shrink from saying "He died last night" but say instead "passed away," "left us," "joined his Maker," "went to his reward." Or we try to take off the tension with a lighter cliché: "kicked the bucket," "cashed in his chips," "handed in his dinner pail." We have found all sorts of ways to avoid saying *mad*: "mentally ill," "touched," "not quite right upstairs," "off his trolley," "not in his right mind." Even such a now plain word as *insane* began as a euphemism with the meaning "not healthy."

Modern science, particularly psychology, contributes many polysyllables in which we can wrap our thoughts and blunt their force. To many writers there is no such thing as a bad schoolboy. Schoolboys are maladjusted or unoriented or misunderstood or in the need of guidance or lacking in continued success toward satisfactory integration of the personality as a social unit, but they are never bad. Psychology no doubt, makes us better men and women, more sympathetic and tolerant, but it doesn't make writing any easier. Had Shakespeare been confronted with psychology, "To be or not to be" might have come out, "To continue as a social unit or not to do so. That is the personality problem. Whether 'tis a better sign of integration at the conscious level to display a psychic tolerance toward the maladjustments and repressions induced by one's lack of orientation in one's environment or—" But Hamlet would never have finished the soliloquy.

Writing in the modern world, you cannot altogether avoid modern jargon. Nor, in an effort to get away from euphemism, should you salt your paper with four-letter words. But you can do much if you will mount guard against those roundabout phrases, those echoing polysyllables that tend to slip into your writing to rob it of its crispness and force.

Beware of Pat Expressions

Other things being equal, avoid phrases like "other things being equal." Those sentences that come to you whole, or in two or three doughy lumps, are sure to be bad sentences. They are no creation of yours but pieces of common thought floating in the community soup.

35 Pat expressions are hard, often impossible, to avoid, because they come too easily to be noticed and seem too necessary to be dispensed with. No writer avoids them altogether, but good writers avoid them more often than poor writers.

By "pat expressions" we mean such tags as "to all practical intents and purposes," "the pure and simple truth," "from where I sit," "the time of his life," "to the ends of the earth," "in the twinkling of an eye," "as sure as you're born," "over my dead body," "under cover of darkness," "took the easy way out," "when all is said and done," "told him time and time again," "parted the best of friends," "stand up and be counted, "gave him the best years of her life," "worked her fingers to the bone." Like other clichés, these expressions were once forceful. Now we should use them only when we can't possibly think of anything else.

Some pat expressions stand like a wall between the writer and thought. Such a one is "the American way of life." Many student writers feel that when they have said that something accords with the American way of life or does not they have exhausted the subject. Actually, they have stopped at the highest level of abstraction. The American way of life is the complicated set of bonds between a hundred and eighty million ways. All of us know this when we think about it, but the tag phrase too often keeps us from thinking about it.

So with many another phrase dear to the politician: "this great land of ours," "the man in the street," "our national heritage." These may prove our patriotism or give a clue to our political beliefs, but otherwise they add nothing to the paper except words.

Colorful Words

The writer builds with words, and no builder uses a raw material more slippery and elusive and treacherous. A writer's work is a constant struggle to get the right word in the right place, to find that particular word that will convey his meaning exactly, that will persuade the reader or soothe him or startle or amuse him. He never succeeds altogether—sometimes he feels that he scarcely succeeds at all—but such successes as he has are what make the thing worth doing.

40   There is no book of rules for this game. One progresses through everlasting experiment on the basis of ever-widening experience. There are few useful generalizations that one can make about words as words, but there are perhaps a few.

Some words are what we call "colorful." By this we mean that they are calculated to produce a picture or induce an emotion. They are dressy instead of plain, specific instead of general, loud instead of soft. Thus, in place of "Her heart beat," we may write, "Her heart *pounded, throbbed, fluttered, danced.*" Instead of "He sat in his chair," we may say, "He *lounged, sprawled, coiled.*" Instead of "It was hot," we may say, "It was *blistering, sultry, muggy, suffocating, steamy, wilting.*"

However, it should not be supposed that the fancy word is always better. Often it is as well to write "Her heart beat" or "It was hot" if that is all it did or all it was. Ages differ in how they like their prose. The nineteenth century liked it rich and smoky. The twentieth has usually preferred it lean and cool. The twentieth century writer, like all writers, is forever seeking the exact word, but he is wary of sounding feverish. He tends to pitch it low, to understate it, to throw it away. He knows that if he gets too colorful, the audience is likely to giggle.

See how this strikes you: "As the rich, golden glow of the sunset died away along the eternal western hills, Angela's limpid blue eyes looked softly and trustingly into Montague's flashing brown ones, and her heart pounded like a drum in time with the joyous song surging in her soul." Some people like that sort of thing, but most modern readers would say, "Good grief," and turn on the television.

Colored Words

Some words we call not so much colorful as colored—that is, loaded with associations, good or bad. All words—except perhaps structure words—have associations of some sort. We have said that the meaning of a word is the sum of the contexts in which it occurs. When we hear a word, we hear with it an echo of all the situations in which we have heard it before.

45   In some words, these echoes are obvious and discussible. The word *mother*, for example, has for most people, agreeable associations. When you hear *mother* you probably think of home, safety, love, food, and various other pleasant things. If one writes, "She was like a mother to me," he gets an effect which he would not get in "She was like an aunt to me." The advertiser makes use of the associations of *mother* by working it in when he talks about his product. The politician works it in when he talks about himself.

So also with such words as *home, liberty, fireside, contentment, patriot, tenderness, sacrifice, childlike, manly, bluff, limpid.* All of these words are loaded with associations that would be rather hard to indicate in a straightforward definition. There is more than a literal difference between "They sat around the fireside" and "They sat around the stove." They might have been equally warm and happy around the stove, but *fireside* suggests leisure, grace, quiet tradition, congenial company, and *stove* does not.

Conversely, some words have bad associations. *Mother* suggests pleasant things, but *mother-in-law* does not. Many mothers-in-law are heroically lovable and some mothers drink gin all day and beat their children insensible, but these facts of life are beside the point. The point is that *mother* sounds good and *mother-in-law* does not.

Or consider the word *intellectual.* This would seem to be a complimentary term, but in point of fact it is not, for it has picked up associations of impracticality and ineffectuality and general dopiness. So also such words as *liberal, reactionary, Communist, socialist, capitalist, radical, schoolteacher, truck driver, undertaker, operator, salesman, huckster, speculator.* These convey meaning on the literal level, but beyond that—sometimes, in some places—they convey contempt on the part of the speaker.

The question of whether to use loaded words or not depends on what is being written. The scientist, the scholar, try to avoid them; for the poet, the advertising writer, the public speaker, they are standard equipment. But every writer should take care that they do not substitute for thought. If you write, "Anyone who thinks that is nothing but a Socialist (or Communist or capitalist)," you have said nothing except that you don't like people who think that, and such remarks are effective only with the most naive readers. It is always a bad mistake to think your readers more naive then they really are.

Colorless Words

50   But probably most student writers come to grief not with words that are colorful or those that are colored but with those that have no color at all. A pet example is *nice,* a word we would find it hard to dispense with in casual conversation but which is no longer capable of adding much to a description. Colorless words are those of such general meaning that in a particular sentence they mean nothing. Slang adjectives like *cool* ("That's real cool") tend to explode all over the language. They are applied to everything, lose their original force, and quickly die.

Beware also of nouns of very general meaning, like *circumstances, cases, instances, aspects, factors, relationships, attitudes, eventualities,* etc. In most circumstances you will find that those cases of writing which contain too many instances of words like these will in this and other aspects have factors leading to unsatisfactory relationships with the reader resulting in unfavorable attitudes on his part and perhaps other eventualities, like a grade of "D." Notice also what "etc." means. It means "I'd like to make this list longer, but I can't think of any more examples."

THINKING ↔ WRITING ACTIVITY 4.5

Analyzing Writers' Ideas on Writing

What points about revision does each writer—Murray, Zinsser, and Roberts—emphasize? What do these readings tell you about how different writers work through their writing processes? What points of revision do you want to become more concerned with?

WRITING PROJECT

This chapter has included both readings and **Thinking↔Writing Activities** that encouraged you to reflect on decision making and on revision. Be sure to reread what you wrote for those activities; you may be able to use it to help yourself complete this project.

WRITING PROJECT Analyzing a Decision to be Made

Write an essay in which you analyze a decision you must make now or in the near future. Be sure to select a decision for which you already have considerable information or want to obtain more. (If you are not facing an immediate decision, you may write about one you made recently.) If you can, include all five steps in the decision-making method. After you have drafted your essay, revise it to the best of your ability. Follow directions given by your instructor as to length, format, and so forth.

Begin by considering the key elements in the **Thinking↔Writing Model.**

Purpose

You have a variety of purposes here. First, you can use this opportunity to work through an important real-life decision so as to obtain the best possible outcome. If others will be involved in or affected by this decision, your paper can help them to see your best thinking about it and thus be more likely to agree with your decision. Also, in writing this paper, you can practice the creative and critical thinking involved in the five-step method for making decisions. You can hone your revision skills both by carefully working through the revision questions presented on pages 111–112 and by using ideas about revision you acquired from Chapter 1, as well as from this chapter and its readings. Finally, of course, you want to receive a satisfactory grade for completing the assignment well.

Audience

Just as you did in the Writing Project for Chapter 3, you have a range of readers within your audience. You yourself are an important audience, for in working through the possible choices, you may find yourself actually making the decision you face. If the decision involves other people in your life, they would make an excellent audience for both early drafts and final copy because they could provide ideas about the choices, possibly suggest choices you haven't thought of, and offer their reactions to your decision. Your classmates can be valuable peer reviewers of a draft, reacting as intelligent readers who are not involved in the decision and therefore able to be objective about both the clarity of your writing and the logic of your decision. Finally, your instructor remains an audience who will judge how well you have planned, drafted, and revised. As a writing teacher, your instructor cares about a clear focus, logical organization, specific examples, and correctness; keep these requirements in mind as you revise, edit, and proofread.

Subject

Decisions are often challenging to think about and difficult to make. Sometimes we haven't enough information to make an intelligent choice; sometimes we *think* we know what the right decision is, yet are reluctant to actually make the decision. Therefore, we often tend to put off making a decision for as long as possible. It may be helpful to consider that not making a decision is, in a way, making a decision to do nothing. And doing nothing is one choice that can be included in the five-step method. Actually evaluating the pros and cons of doing nothing can help us to see whether or not we need to make some other decision—one that would change the situation we are considering.

Writer

You approach this Writing Project as the expert on the subject, since you are analyzing one of your own decisions. If you have done the projects in Chapter 2 or Chapter 3, you may have felt the confidence that such expertise brings and the satisfaction of sharing your experiences with the audience to whom you have directed your writing. One challenge here is to distinguish between your own expertise about the decision-making situation and the needs of your audience for enough background and information. Another challenge is to focus on the material provided earlier in this chapter, because this assignment moves away from recollecting experience and asks you to apply the decision-making process.

The Writing Process

The following sections will guide you through the stages of generating, planning, drafting, and revising as you work on an essay about making a decision. Try to be particularly conscious of both the creative and critical thinking you do in making your decision, and the critical thinking and decision-making you do when you revise.

Generating Ideas

Refer back to the list you made in **Thinking↔Writing Activity 4.3** for possible subject choices. You may want to develop the writing you did there on one decision, or you may see that another decision would work better for this writing project.

- Think about when each of the decisions must be made. Is there one you must make in the near future? If so, this is a good opportunity for you to accomplish two things at one time: writing your paper and making your decision.

- Think about how much additional information you would need to evaluate possible choices for each of the decisions on your list. Do you have time to locate and absorb all that information?

- Think about which decision you are most interested in making, or which you are most worried about making.

- Decide on a tentative topic: that is, which decision you will work on.

- Describe the decision-making situation as clearly as you can.

- Brainstorm as many possible choices as you can. Ask others involved in the decision to help.

- Eliminate choices that you know are impractical or morally repugnant to you.

- Determine what information you need to find for each choice. Locate that information.

- Write each choice on a separate sheet of paper. Divide the paper into two columns: Pros and Cons. Write as much as you can in each column.

- Freewrite for five minutes on what would happen and how you would feel following each possible choice.

- Freewrite for five minutes on how you would know if any given choice were the right one.

Defining a Focus

Write a tentative thesis statement making clear to your audience that you are going to explore a decision-making situation. You might write something like "After thinking about the situation carefully, I realize that I have only two possible choices." Or you might name the possible choices: "My choices for housing next year come down to these three: living with my aunt, sharing an apartment with my friend, or looking for a live-in job situation." You may even decide to announce your decision in your thesis statement: "After carefully weighing my options, I have decided to major in business administration."

Organizing Ideas

The five-step method for making decisions fits well with essay structure. Your description of the decision-making situation might be the beginning of an introduction, to be completed by your thesis statement. Each of the possible choices, explained in as much detail as possible, along with the pros and cons of that choice, could provide a body paragraph. Your decision on the best choice and your plan for monitoring it could provide a conclusion to the essay.

Drafting

Begin with the easiest part to draft. True, the description you wrote of the decision-making situation could begin the introduction, but consider what, if any, additional information your audience will need in order to understand the situation. The introduction can end with your tentative thesis statement.

A clear way to begin each body paragraph is with a topic sentence that names the possible choice being discussed. Then provide the audience with sufficient information to help them understand what that choice would mean. Use the sheets you prepared on the advantages and disadvantages of each choice for help.

Once you have drafted your body paragraphs, you will be ready to decide on the best order for them. Try arranging them in different orders until you discover the one most likely to be helpful to your audience.

In your conclusion or in your thesis statement, name the choice you have decided on. You may want to explain why, if you think your reason may not be obvious to your audience. Remember to explain how you will monitor the results of your decision.

Revising

Ideally, at this point, you should put your draft aside for a day or two. If deadlines won't permit you to do that, then at least take a break before you try to revise. When you are ready to "re-see" your writing, begin by reading it through slowly, preferably aloud. If possible, have someone whose opinion you respect read it; ask for feedback. Then work through the hierarchy of revision concerns that follows. Remember that you have two decisions to make for each question: (1) Where is improvement needed? and (2) Where improvement is needed, how exactly, can I make my draft better?

1. **Think big.** Look at your draft as a whole.
   - Does it fulfill the assignment in terms of topic and length?
   - Have you stated the thesis clearly?
   - Do all parts of the draft relate to the thesis?
   - Is the organization logical?
   - Do you provide enough evidence?
   - Is your point of view consistent?
   - Is there a discernible flow between your paragraphs?
   - Have you documented information from your sources accurately?
   - Have you used quotation marks around direct quotes or set the quotes off by indenting?

2. **Think medium.** Look at your draft paragraph by paragraph.
   - Will your introduction make your audience want to read on?

- Is the introduction appropriate for the rest of the draft?
- Is your focus stated clearly if you are working with a "visible" structure?
- If you are working with an "invisible" structure, is your focus clearly implied?
- Are topic sentences used effectively?
- Does each body paragraph develop a different idea?
- Should any paragraphs be combined or eliminated?
- Is your conclusion effective?

3. **Think small.** Look at your draft sentence by sentence.
- Are any sentences difficult to understand?
- Are any so long that your audience could get lost in them?
- Are sentences with blended quotations (that is, quotations that are integrated into the syntax of the sentence instead of introduced with "He said . . ." or "She said . . .") complete and easy to read?
- Are quotations shortened with ellipsis marks accurate and readable?
- Are there several choppy sentences that can be combined?
- Are any sentences vague?
- Do any sentences need to be corrected for standard English grammar and usage?

4. **Think "picky."** Look at your draft as your fussiest critic might.
- Are any words not clear or not quite right for your meaning?
- Are any words misspelled?
- Are there any punctuation errors?
- Is your format correct?
- Are the pages numbered consecutively?
- Does your paper make a good impression by being neat?
- Is there anything else you could do to improve your draft?

Proofreading

After you prepare a final draft, check for standard grammar and punctuation. Proofread carefully for omitted words and punctuation marks. Run your spelling checker program, but be aware of its limitations. Proofread again for the kinds of errors the computer can't catch.

Student Essay

The following essays show how two students responded to this assignment.

STUDENT WRITING
Deciding What to Do About My Hearing Problem
by Bao-Toan Le

I work in the Computer Writing Center at my college. Every day I listen and reply to many students' questions. But six months ago, when students asked me questions, I noticed that I could not hear them very clearly. I had to ask them to repeat three or four times. From that day forward, my hearing kept getting worse. I realized that I had to do something about it. I thought I had two alternative solutions to consider and choose from: using the traditional Chinese treatments or following the advice of my otolaryngologists. Fortunately, I discovered that there was a third alternative, which combined the best features of the other two.

The first alternate solution was to use the traditional treatments, such as the therapy of point acupuncture and Chinese medicinal herbs. Point acupuncture is a very effective method to cure various kinds of diseases, especially earache, by massaging the thumb and index fingers right on the fourteen pressure points of the head. Chinese medical herbs, which are refined from roots, stalks, and leaves of many different trees, are also good medicines. The advantage of this solution was that I could restore my hearing and gain more confidence. For instance, massaging eight particular vital points around my head and neck with my thumb, I could alleviate the headache which accompanies my deafness in just a few minutes. Therefore, I would not be scared of getting sick anymore. Another advantage was that I would not have to pay anything for this treatment because my uncle who is a traditional pharmacist would teach me at no charge. Nevertheless, these remedies require much time and precision. I would have to spend at least three months to memorize the pressure points, and of course I would stay "deaf" for five or six months more. Also, I would have to find the right kinds of herbs and to prepare the combination of these herbs. For instance, first I would need to find three different herbs: A, B, and C. Then I would have to blend 25 percent of the A leaves, 30 percent of the B radicles, 45 percent of the stalks of the vegetable C herbs, and salt, and then pour in the water and boil until the water equals one-third of the original amount. Another minor disadvantage is that most of the Chinese herbs are very bitter and have unpleasant smells.

Another alternative was to follow the advice of my otolaryngologists: have some tests done, take medicine, and have surgery if necessary. The doctors carefully did the tests, including graphing tests, beeping tests, listening and speaking tests, and examining the throat, the nose and both ears. Therefore, their opinions were reliable, and the remedy would be quick and effective. After the tests, they told me that my eardrums did not have enough air flow into them. They decided to give me medicine. If the medicine did not cure me, they would do surgery to rearrange the ear bones. The surgery would stop the problem forever. And because I have health insurance, the fees for the doctors were not expensive: only ten dollars per visit. But there were some disadvantages to their treatments: suffering from lack of appetite and sleeplessness from the medication as well as suffering from the ringing in my ears which I thought it caused. The operation, if I needed it, might hurt and leave a scar on my face.

After considering the advantages and disadvantages of each solution, I decided to use the point acupuncture therapy and to ask the otolaryngologists to give me a lighter dose of the medicine to reduce the side effects. I also stopped taking the Chinese herbs with my medicine, and this helped with the ear ringing. After three weeks of taking the lighter drugs and massaging the fourteen vital points, my hearing now is much better than it was before. My decision was the right one, and I am very happy with my progress.

STUDENT WRITING
A Space Problem
by Jon Cohen

My rock and roll band, "The Love Machine," needed a place to practice. We had practiced at my parents' spacious home in Bethesda, which had worked out very well. We had made noise until 10:00 P.M. without any problems, we had practiced in a location central to the members of the band, we had easy parking, we had not caused any tension in a user-lender relationship as my parents were supportive of us, our practice space had been comfortable, and we had been able to store our equipment with confidence that it would be safe. Unfortunately, my parents sold their home and moved into a condominium where loud noise was not allowed. We had to find a different place to practice; we didn't have many choices, and deciding what to do wasn't easy.

One place I was interested in was a large apartment in Georgetown. In this apartment were people I did not know who had their own rock band that practiced in a loft located in the apartment. They wanted someone else to use their practice space at an arranged time for a small fee. I actually looked at the place. The tenants claimed we could make noise because they were located in the business district of Georgetown where noise was allowed in the evenings. The location was close to all of us. The fee was small, at less than $200 a month, and the tenants said we could store equipment in the space.

There were problems with this apartment, however. Parking in Georgetown was very difficult. Also, the practice space, although big, could only be reached by way of a ladder and that I felt was an uncomfortable prospect. Finally, we did not know the people who were renting the space at all, and I was a little nervous about leaving our equipment with them.

Another place in which I was interested was a group house in Arlington, Virginia. The people who were living in the group house I knew a little bit as they had seen "The Love Machine" perform. The people in the group house were planning to have a space in their basement available for music. They were going to use it for their own projects but felt we could use it also. Their location in Arlington was close to everyone in the band. The rent they asked was very low at less than $100 a month. Parking was readily available in front of the house, and I felt that the band's relationship with these people would be strengthened by our association because they truly believed in the band.

There were some problems with the house in Virginia. The houses in the residential neighborhood were very close together, and there was a possibility that the neighbors would be bothered by the noise and would not tolerate it. Also, there was sometimes flooding in the basement where the practice space was. The people in the house wanted to build a stage over the space to protect it from water; also, they wanted to insulate the space so that sound would not escape.

Another choice I had was to pass these places up and keep waiting. My band and I were looking for opportunities and people were aware that we had a problem. However, while waiting, the band would not be practicing. When a band does not stay active, band members start to set aside their time for other things. Getting the band started again might have been impossible.

The decision we made was to practice at the group house in Virginia. Our equipment did stay safe, and our relationship with the people in the house became better. However, we were still a little uncomfortable using the place of people we did not know really well. Also, the neighbors did start to complain about the noise.

Fortunately, my drummer recently moved into a house in Washington, D.C., that happened to have space for a band to practice. We are practicing there now, and we will see how it goes.

Language and Thought—Writing Precisely

Critical Thinking Focus: Language as a system

Writing Focus: Using language to clarify thinking

Reading Theme: Essays about language

Writing Projects: Experience with language

Understanding and Using Language

The first four chapters of this book have focused on the **Thinking↔Writing Model** (introduced in Chapter 1, page 8) and on how it illustrates the interactive relationships among critical thinking, creative thinking, and thoughtful writing. Language is the instrument that makes all these activities possible. With its power to represent thoughts, feelings, and experiences symbolically, language is the most important tool the thinking process has.

Every time we use language, we send a message about our thinking. When we speak or write, we are not simply making sounds or writing symbols; we are using language to communicate our thinking by conveying ideas, sharing feelings, and describing experiences. At the same time, the process of using language generates ideas, and language itself shapes and influences thinking. When use of language is sloppy—vague, general, indistinct, imprecise, foolish, inaccurate, and so on—it leads to thinking of the same sort. The reverse is also true: clear, precise language leads to clear, precise thinking, speaking, and writing.

Thus, using language with clarity and precision is a vital requirement if other people are to understand the thoughts we are trying to communicate. And to use language effectively, we need to view language as a system, with agreed-upon sets of rules and expectations.

To grasp this essential tool more fully and use it more powerfully, we will begin by considering both the development of languages and the symbolic nature of language. We will then consider strategies for using language effectively and for using language to clarify thinking. Finally, we will consider the social uses of language: how language is used in different social contexts and how it can be used to influence thinking and behavior.

THINKING ↔ WRITING ACTIVITY 5.1

A World Without Language

Imagine a world without language. Imagine that you suddenly lose your ability to speak, to write, to read. Imagine that your only means of expression is grunts, shrieks, and gestures. And finally, imagine that you soon discover that everyone else in the world has also lost the ability to use language. Write a one-page description of what such a world would be like. Be prepared to share your response with your class.

The Development of Language

Language forms the bedrock of human relations. Sharing thoughts, feelings, and experiences draws people together and leads to forming relationships.

Consider the social groups in your school, your neighborhood, or your community. Have you ever thought about how language plays a central role in bringing people together into groups and in maintaining these groups? A loss of language would both limit the complexity of your individual relationships with others and drastically affect the way you live in society.

Speculation on the origin of language has excited the human imagination for ages. Herodotus, the ancient Greek "father of history," told of an Egyptian king who wanted to find out which language might have been the parent of all other languages. In order to solve this problem, the king arranged to have two newborn infants raised away from all hearing of human speech, so that he would find out the first words of humans not influenced by others' speech. After two years, the children were heard to say *bekos*. The king asked in which language this word had meaning and learned that in Phrygian, one of the dialects spoken in Asia Minor, *bekos* meant "bread." After that time Phrygian was regarded as the parent language of all the languages of the world.

Today we know more than either the Egyptian king or Herodotus about the development of languages. We know that no single language was the parent of all others. Rather, like people, languages belong to families. Languages in the same family share some characteristics with other members of their family, but they also demonstrate individual characteristics. We know that languages, like the human beings of whom they are a natural part, live, change, and die. Phrygian is no longer a living language; neither is the ancient Indian language Sanskrit, nor is Latin.

English, like Spanish, French, Chinese, Urdu, or any of the other languages that you may speak, is a living language—and it has changed over hundreds of years. The English language has gone through four major evolutionary stages: Old English, A.D. 460–1050; Middle English, A.D. 1050–1450; Early Modern English, A.D. 1450–1700; and Modern English, A.D. 1700 to the present. Because languages are systems based on sound, these stages of English reflect variations in how the language has sounded. It is difficult to represent these sounds accurately for the older periods of English because of the absence of tapes or phonograph recordings. For example, the following different versions of the Lord's Prayer, sacred to Christians, present written symbols that are approximations based on the consensus of linguistic scholars.

The Lord's Prayer

Old English

Faeder ure
Thu the eart on heofonum,
Si thin name gehalgod.
Tobecume thin rice.
Gewurthe thin willa on eorthan swa swa on heofonum.
Urne gedaeghwamlican hlaf syle you to daeg.
And forgyf you urne gyltas, swa swa you forgytath urum gyltendum.
And ne gelaed thu you on costnunge, ac alys you of yfele. Sothlice.

Middle English

Oure fadur
that art in hauenes
halewid be thi name;
thi kyngdoom come to;
be thi wile don in erthe as in heuene;
zyue to vs this dai oure breed ouer othir substaunce;
and forzyue to vs oure dettis, as you forzyuen to oure dettouris;
and lede vs not in to temptacioun,
but delyuere vs from yeul. Amen.

Early Modern English

Our Father
which art in heaven,
hallowed be thy name.
Thy kingdom come.

Thy will be done, in earth, as it is in heaven.
Give us this day our daily bread.
And forgive us our debts, as we forgive our debtors.
And lead us not into temptation,
but deliver us from evil:
for Thine is the kingdome, and the power, and the glory for ever, Amen.

Modern English

Our Father in heaven
may your name be held holy.
Your kingdom come,
your will be done, on earth as in heaven.
Give us today our daily bread.
And forgive us our debts as we have forgiven those who are in debt to us.
And do not put us to the test,
but save us from evil.

As you read these versions of the Lord's Prayer, think about the variations in sounds, words, and sentences. With the other members of your class, discuss variations in the language(s) you speak.

The Symbolic Nature of Language

As human beings, we are able to share our thoughts and feelings with one another because of our ability to *symbolize,* or let one thing represent something else. Words are the most common symbols we use in our daily life. Although words are only sounds or written marks that have no meaning in and of themselves, they stand for objects, ideas, and other aspects of human experience. For example, the word *sailboat* is a symbol that represents a watergoing vessel with sails that is propelled by the wind. When you speak or write *sailboat,* you are able to communicate the sort of thing you are thinking about. Of course, if other people are to understand what you are referring to when you use this symbol, they must first agree that this symbol *(sailboat)* does in fact represent that wind-propelled vessel that floats on the water. Naturally, you could always take others to the object you have in mind and point it out to them, but using a symbol is much more convenient.

Language symbols (or words) can take two forms; they can be spoken sounds or written markings. The symbol *sailboat* can be either written down or spoken aloud. Either way, it can communicate the sort of thing you are referring to. Since using language is so natural to us, we rarely stop to realize that our language is really a system of spoken sounds and written markings that we use to represent various aspects of our experience.

> **Language:**   a system of symbols for thinking and communicating.

Sounds

In certain respects, language is like a set of symbolic building blocks. The basic blocks are sounds, which may be symbolized by letters:

Letters—such as A T C Q Y N, and so on—symbolize sounds

Sounds form the phonetic foundation of a language, and this explains why different languages have such distinctly different "sounds." Try having members of the class speak a word or a few sentences in other languages they know. Listen to how the overall sound of each language differs from the others.

When human beings are infants, they possess the ability to make all the sounds of all languages. As they are continually exposed to the specific group of sounds of their own society's language, they gradually concentrate on making only those sounds, while discarding or never developing others.

Words

Sounds combine to form larger sets of blocks called words. Words are used to represent the various aspects of our experience—they symbolize objects, thoughts, feelings, actions, and concepts. When you read, hear, or think about a word, it usually elicits in you a variety of ideas and feelings. Describe, for instance, the ideas or feelings that the following words arouse in you: *college education, happiness, freedom, creativity, love.*

The combination of all the ideas and feelings that a word arouses in your mind comprises the "meaning" of that word to you. The ideas and feelings that you just described reflect the meaning that each of those words has for you as an individual. And although the meanings that these words have for you is probably similar in many respects to the meanings they have for other people, there are also many differences. Consider the different meanings those same words have for the two people in the following dialogue:

*A: For me, a **college education** represents the most direct path to my dreams. It's the only way I can develop the knowledge and abilities required for my career.*

*B: I can't agree with you. I pursued a **college education** for a while, but it didn't work out. I found that most of my courses consisted of large classes with professors lecturing about subjects that had little relation to my life. The value of a college education is overblown. I know many people with college degrees who have not been able to find rewarding careers.*

*A: Don't you see? An important part of achieving **happiness** is learning about things you aren't familiar with, expanding your horizons about the world, developing new interests. That's what college can give you.*

B: *I have enough interests. As far as I'm concerned,* **happiness** *consists of having the opportunity to do the things that I enjoy doing with the people I enjoy doing them with. For me, happiness is* **freedom!**

A: **Freedom** *to do what? Freedom is meaningful only when you have worthwhile options and the wisdom to select the right ones. A college education can help provide both!*

B: *That sounds very idealistic, but it's also naive. Many of the college graduates I have met are neither wise nor happy. In order to be truly happy, you have to be involved in creative activities. Every day should be a surprise, something different to look forward to. Many careers pay well, but they don't provide creative opportunities.*

A: *Being* **creative** *means doing things you* **love.** *When you really love something you're doing, you are naturally creative. For example, I love to draw and paint, and this provides a creative outlet for me. I don't need to be creative at work—I have enough creative opportunities outside work.*

B: *You're wrong!* **Creativity** *doesn't mean simply being artistic. We should strive to be creative in every part of our lives, keep looking for new possibilities and unique experiences. And I think that you are misusing the word* love. *You can really love only things that are alive, like people and pets.*

A: *That's a very weird idea of* **love** *you have. As far as I'm concerned,* love *is a word that expresses a strong positive emotion that can be directed toward objects ("I love my car"), activities ("I love to dance"), or people. I don't see what's so complicated about that.*

B: *To be able to* **love** *in any meaningful sense, the object of your love has to be able to respond to you, so that the two of you can develop a relationship together. When was the last time that your car responded to your love for it?*

A: *Very funny. I guess that we just have different ideas about the word* **love**—*as well as the words* **happiness, freedom,** *and* **creativity.**

As this dialogue suggests, words are not simple entities with one clear meaning that everyone agrees on. Instead, most words are complex, multidimensional carriers of meaning; their exact meaning often varies from person to person. These differences in meaning can lead to disagreements and confusion, as the foregoing dialogue illustrates. To clarify your understanding about the way words function in your language and your thinking, you have to examine the way words serve as vehicles to express meaning.

Words arouse in each of us a variety of ideas, feelings, and experiences. Taken together, these ideas, feelings and experiences express the total meaning of the words for the individual person. Linguists believe that this total meaning is actually composed of four different types of meaning:

- Semantic meaning
- Perceptual meaning
- Syntactic meaning
- Pragmatic meaning

Let us examine each of them in turn.

Semantic Meaning

The semantic meaning of a word expresses the relationship between a linguistic event (speaking or writing) and a nonlinguistic event (an object, idea, or feeling). For example, saying "Chair" relates to an object you sit in, while saying "College education" relates to the experience of earning an academic degree through postsecondary study. What events (ideas, feelings, objects) relate to happiness? to freedom? to creativity? to love?

The semantic meaning of a word, also referred to as its *denotative meaning,* expresses the general properties of the word, and these properties determine how the word is used within its language system. How do you discover the general properties that determine word usage? Besides examining your own knowledge of the meaning and use of words, you can check dictionary definitions. They tend to focus on the general properties that determine word usage. For example, a dictionary definition of *chair* might be "a piece of furniture consisting of a seat, legs, and back, and often arms, designed to accommodate one person."

However, to understand fully the semantic meaning of a word, you often need to go beyond defining its general properties to identifying examples of the word that embody those properties. If you are sitting in a chair or can see one from where you are, examine its design. Does it embody all the properties identified in the definition? (Sometimes unusual examples embody most, but not all, the properties of a dictionary definition—for example, a beanbag chair lacks legs and arms.) If you are trying to communicate the semantic meaning of a word to someone, it is generally useful to provide both the general properties of the word and examples that embody those general properties. Try identifying the general properties and examples for the following words: *happiness, freedom, creativity, love.*

Perceptual Meaning

The total meaning of a word also includes its perceptual meaning, which expresses the relationship between a linguistic event and an individual's consciousness. For each of us, words elicit unique and personal thoughts and feelings based on previous experiences and past associations. A person might relate saying "chair" to his favorite chair in his living room or the small chair that he built for his daughter. Perceptual meaning also includes an individual's positive and negative responses to the word. When you read or hear the word *book,* what positive or negative feelings does it arouse in you? What about *textbook? mystery book? comic book? cookbook?* In each case, the word probably elicited distinct feelings in your mind, and these feelings contribute to the meaning each word has for you. For this reason, perceptual meaning is also sometimes called *connotative meaning,* the literal or basic meaning of a word plus all it suggests or connotes to you.

Think about the words you considered earlier and describe what personal perceptions, experiences, associations, and feelings they evoke in your mind: *college education, happiness, freedom, creativity, love.*

Syntactic Meaning

A third component of a word's total meaning is its syntactic meaning, which defines its relation to other words in a sentence. The syntactic meaning defines three relationships among words:

- Content: words that express the major message of the sentence
- Description: words that elaborate or modify the major message of the sentence
- Connection: words that join the major message of the sentence

For example, in the sentence "The two novice hikers crossed the ledge cautiously," *hikers* and *crossed* represent the content, or major message, of the sentence. *Two* and *novice* define a descriptive relationship to *hikers,* and *cautiously* defines a descriptive relationship to *crossed.*

At first, you may think that this sort of relationship among words involves nothing more than semantic meaning. The following sentence, however, clearly demonstrates the importance of syntactic meaning in language: "Invisible fog rumbles in on lizard legs." At first this sentence seems to make sense. Although *fog* does not *rumble,* and it is not *invisible,* and the concept of moving on *lizard legs* seems incompatible with *rumbling,* the sentence does "make sense" at some level of meaning—namely, at the syntactic level. One reason it does is that in this sentence, there are three basic content words—*fog, rumbles,* and *legs*—and two descriptive words—namely, *invisible* and *lizard.*

The third major syntactic relationship is that of connection. You use connective words to join ideas, thoughts, or feelings being expressed. For example, you could connect content meaning to either of your two sentences in the following fashion:

- The two novice hikers crossed the ledge cautiously *after* one of them slipped.
- Invisible fog rumbles in on lizard legs, *but* acid rain doesn't.

When you add content words such as *one slipped* and *rain doesn't,* you join the ideas, thoughts, and feelings they represent to the earlier expressed ideas, thoughts, or feelings (*hikers crossed* and *fog rumbles*), using connective words like *after* and *but,* as in the preceding sentences.

The second reason that "Invisible fog rumbles in on lizard legs" makes sense at the syntactic level of meaning is that the words of that sentence obey the syntax, or order, of English. Most speakers of English would have trouble making sense of "Invisible rumbles legs lizard on fog in"—or of "Barks big endlessly dog brown the," for that matter. Because of syntactic meaning, each word in the sentence derives part of its total meaning from its combination with the other words in that sentence in order to express and join ideas, thoughts, and feelings. Look at the following sentences and explain the difference in meaning between the two in each pair.

1.a.　The process of achieving an *education at college* changes a person's future possibilities.
 b.　The process of achieving a *college education* changes a person's future possibilities.

2.a.　She felt *happiness* for her long-lost brother.
 b.　She felt the *happiness* of her long-lost brother.

3.a.　The most important thing to me is *freedom from* the things that restrict my choices.
 b.　The most important thing to me is *freedom to* make my choices without restrictions.

4.a.　Michelangelo's painting of the Sistine Chapel ceiling represents his *creative* genius.
 b.　The Sistine Chapel ceiling represents the *creative* genius of Michelangelo's greatest painting.

5.a.　I *love* the person I have been involved with for the past year.
 b.　I am *in love* with the person I have been involved with for the past year.

Pragmatic Meaning

The fourth element that contributes to the total meaning of a word is its pragmatic meaning. The pragmatic meaning of a word involves the person who is speaking and the situation in which the word is spoken. For example, the statement "That student likes to borrow books from the library" allows a number of pragmatic interpretations:

1. Was the speaker outside looking at *that student* carrying books out of the library?
2. Did the speaker have this information because of being a classmate of *that student*, but not see him or her carrying books?
3. Was the speaker in the library watching *that student* check the books out?

The correct interpretation or meaning of the sentence depends on what was actually taking place in the situation—in other words, its pragmatic meaning, which could also be called its *situational meaning*. For each of the following sentences, try describing a pragmatic context that identifies the person speaking and the situation in which it is being spoken.

1. A *college education* is currently necessary for many careers that formerly required high school preparation.
2. The utilitarian ethical system is based on the principle that the right course of action is that which brings the greatest *happiness* to the greatest number of people.

3. The laws of this country attempt to balance the *freedom* of the individual with the rights of society as a whole.
4. "You are all part of things, you are all part of *creation*, all kings, all poets, all musicians, you have only to open up, to discover what is already there."—Henry Miller
5. "If music be the food of *love*, play on."—Shakespeare

Having completed the activity, compare your answers with those of your classmates. In what ways are the answers similar or different? Analyze the way different pragmatic contexts (persons speaking and situations) affect the meanings of the italicized words.

The four meanings you just examined—**semantic, perceptual, syntactic, pragmatic**—create the total meaning of a word. That is to say, all the dimensions of any word—all the relationships that connect linguistic events with nonlinguistic events, with your consciousness, with other linguistic events, and with situations in the world—make up the meaning you assign to a word. *Chapter 9, Forming Concepts—Writing to Classify and Define*, will build on the ideas of this section.

Using Language Effectively

To develop your ability to use language effectively in communicating your thoughts, feelings, and experiences, you have to understand how language functions when it is used well. One way to develop your writing ability is to understand and use the relationships between sentence structure and meaning; that is, to craft sentences in which the grammar actually supports your intended meaning.

Another way of improving your writing is to read widely. By reading as much good writing as possible, you get a "feel" for how language can be used well. You can get more specific ideas by analyzing the work of highly regarded writers who use semantic and syntactical meanings accurately. They also often use many action verbs, concrete nouns, and vivid adjectives to communicate effectively. And of course a way to become a better writer is by writing and by seeking feedback from readers. In this section, you will be working with all these strategies.

Using Sentence Structure to Support Meaning

The word is the basic element of thought and language, and we have just examined the importance of word meaning to language, to our ability to organize experience and express concepts. However, we rarely use single words alone. The exclamations "Oh!" or "Help!" may be exceptions, but when we use even those words alone, the pragmatic meaning (or situation) is usually unmistakable. That is why we could argue that the sentence, not the word, is the basic unit of speech and writing. Therefore it is essential for a writer to create effective sentences, which brings us to grammar.

In your past education, you may have thought of grammar as one part of English and of composition as another part (and, quite possibly, of literature as yet another). Grammar may have seemed merely a set of rules, and tricky rules at that, to memorize and be quizzed on. It is true that grammar and composition are often taught separately, but good writers understand that they can use grammar to support their meaning. Grammar is the agreed-upon set of principles about how to arrange and use words within sentences.

Good readers, especially good readers in college, know and respond to the rules of grammar. As they read, they are constantly looking for the subject (What is this sentence about?) and the predicate (What is the subject doing?) of each sentence. Good writers are careful to use the two "power positions" of the sentence, the subject and the predicate, to convey main ideas. For example, consider these three sentences:

> *Cal Ripkin slammed the baseball over the fence for a home run.*
> *The baseball was hit far enough for a home run.*
> *There was a baseball hit far enough for a home run.*

The first sentence uses the power positions to tell us *who did what*. It places the doer of the action in the subject position and uses a vigorous verb as its predicate. The second sentence places the receiver of the action (the *baseball*) in the subject position, leaving us to wonder *who did what*, and it uses a less interesting verb *(was hit)* in its predicate position. The third sentence wastes both power positions by using *was* in the predicate position and making the reader wait until after the verb to find out what the subject is. Yet all three sentences are grammatically correct.

Most people would agree, however, that the first of the three sentences is the most interesting and has that somewhat mysterious quality writing teachers talk about, "good style." That sentence sketches a scene for us and conveys some of the excitement of the moment. What we really are talking about in this section is not grammatical correctness but about the logic of a sentence and about using that logic to help your readers. And the way to master that logic is to understand basic sentence structures and ways that basic sentence structures can be combined.

Sentence Structure: The Basics

English sentences must have at least a subject and a verb. A group of words that contains a subject and a verb is called a *clause*. A clause that can stand on its own and make sense is called an *independent clause*. A clause that needs to be attached to another clause because it does not express a complete idea is called a *dependent clause*. These terms are never difficult to understand or remember if you relate them to yourself: at the point where you are able to be on your own, you are independent. At any point where you need the support of others, you are dependent.

Every clause is made up of two basic structural units: the subject and the verb. Because these are so basic, every reader looks for them to learn what is going on in the sentence. That is why the subject and the verb are considered the power positions in any given clause and why, as a writer, you want to use these positions with great care.

Within many clauses, the subject and the verb have other words that logically connect to them. The subject position is occupied by a noun, a pronoun, or a noun clause (a clause used as a noun). Nouns, the representatives of people, objects, and ideas, can be modified, or described, by adjectives, prepositional phrases, or clauses. The *complete subject* of a clause or sentence is the noun (or pronoun or noun clause) and all the words that describe or add to the meaning of the noun. In the simple sentence unit "I swim," the complete subject includes only *I.* The same is true for the simple sentence "I swim in the summer." If we add the group of words *My friend and* to make the simple sentence "My friend and I swim in the summer," the complete subject becomes *My friend and I.* (It also is a compound subject; here, a noun and a pronoun joined by a conjunction, *and.*)

The predicate position of the sentence must be occupied by a verb. The verb, the representative of action or existence, may have a direct object or a predicate adjective or predicate noun following it. The verb may be modified by prepositional phrases or by adverbs. The verb with all its complements and modifiers, the words that help describe or clarify its meaning, is called the *complete predicate.* For example, the verb in the simple sentence unit "I swim" is *swim.* In the simple sentence unit "I swim in the summer," the complete predicate includes the group of words *in the summer* along with the verb *swim.* In the sentence "Cal Ripkin slammed the ball over the fence for a home run," the complete predicate is *slammed the ball over the fence for a home run.*

Clauses, made up of their complete subjects and verbs, can be arranged in a variety of patterns. The clauses may do any of the following things:

- Stand alone (in *simple* sentences)
- Be combined by coordination, showing equal importance for both clauses (in *compound* sentences)
- Be combined hierarchically by the use of subordination, showing that one clause is more important than the other (in *complex* sentences)

Simple Sentences

The sentence patterns we use when we speak or write reflect the connections of our thoughts, and these connections are influenced by the context in which they occur. These sentence patterns also influence the thought connections of our listeners and readers. So as writers, we need to be conscious of the sentence forms we use.

As an illustration, in the course of our discussion, the following situation narrated by a traveler will be explained from three perspectives. These perspectives illustrate the varying relationships of simple, coordinate, and subordinate sentence forms with patterns of thinking. Here is the first version:

It was Memorial Day 1993 and a lovely time to take a leisurely trip up the coast. I looked forward to the relaxing prospect of browsing around the lazy town and maybe catching an old-time parade. As I drove along the scenic route, dividing my attention between the gentle curves of the road and the spectacular view to my right, I came upon a police car blocking the road. The officer standing outside his vehicle flagged me off the road.

"Stop right here. No traffic's goin' through," he told me.

"I just want to get into town."

"Then park yer car over there." (He pointed.) "Walk down that street. Take yer first right. Then take a left. You'll be standing in Dock Square."

"Okay."

"Wait a minute, ma'am. Let me see yer handbag."

"What?"

"Well, he's givin' a speech in the square in just about an hour. We've got to check everything." (He smiled.) "Hurry up now. You'll miss the whole thing."

In this account, the officer's "explanation" consists of *simple* sentences, which are perfect stylistically to reflect the officer's brisk personality and to account for some of the tourist's confusion, because each idea that the officer expresses is separate. The officer's statements are not connected or related.

Notice that each simple sentence contains only one independent clause; that is, one complete subject and one complete predicate. Remember that both the complete subject and the complete predicate may contain a number of words (and phrases) that enhance the meaning of the noun (as in *your first right*) or the verb (as in *givin' a speech in the square*).

Coordinate and Subordinate Sentences

Language is rich and complex. Usually, sophisticated thinkers don't speak or write only in simple sentences; they use more involved types of sentences as well. Complexity of language goes hand in hand with complexity of thought. Combining sentences in varied ways encourages thinking that joins and juxtaposes thoughts and ideas from various perspectives. It also helps readers to see the connections the writer wishes them to make.

Coordinate (compound) sentences and *subordinate (complex) sentences* are two types of sentence structure that the English language uses, and they are common in both speech and writing. Coordinate sentences and subordinate sentences both include more than one clause; each clause is composed of a complete subject and a complete predicate. The difference between these two major sentence types is the way in which the sentence units are connected to each other.

In *coordinate sentences*, neither clause is more important or carries more weight in terms of the meaning of the whole sentence. Here are some examples:

Our dog's name is Harry, but we didn't name him.

Harry loves dog biscuits, and he eats them daily.

Let's see how coordinate sentence construction works in the continuing narrative of our traveler's situation.

It was only a couple of minutes before I reached the center of town and spied an appealing little restaurant, a sign proclaiming "Allison's" over it—a perfect place for a much-needed cup of coffee. As I made myself comfortable at a small window table, I began to absorb the conversations going on around me.

"I heard Hillary put 'im up to it, and Barbara's mad as a wet hen."

"Well, you know George. He's generous with his invitations, but he never thought he'd hafta honor this one."

"Well, they're gonna be heah now, and George will hafta play second fiddle this weekend."

"Ayuh. Same as he did last Novemba, and he can just like it or lump it!"

The conversation between local residents that our traveler overheard was composed largely of coordinate sentences such as "Well, they're gonna be heah now, and George will hafta play second fiddle this weekend" and "I heard Hillary put 'im up to it, and Barbara's mad as a wet hen." Just as in the case of the simple sentence, the degree of description in the noun or verb phrase has nothing to do with making a sentence coordinate. A sentence is a coordinate sentence if it contains two or more clauses that carry the same weight in the meaning of the entire sentence.

Coordinate sentence construction is often used to express a number of important thinking patterns, which will be examined in Chapters 6–8 of this book:

- *Chronological* thinking patterns: relating events in time sequence
- *Process* thinking patterns: relating aspects of the growth, development, or change of an act, event, or object
- *Comparative* thinking patterns: relating things in the same general category in terms of their similarities and dissimilarities
- *Causal* thinking patterns: relating events not just in terms of chronology but in terms of causes and effects

The following chart describes some of the language-thinking links between these syntactic patterns and thinking patterns.

LANGUAGE-THINKING LINKS

Syntactic Patterns	*(Connectors)*	*Thinking Patterns*
Sentence coordination	and, or, but, nor, either, neither, like, as, -er, more, similar to	Chronological, process, comparative, causal

In *subordinate sentences,* two or more clauses are joined in hierarchical relationships; that is, one clause is considered more important than the other(s) to the meaning being expressed. One of the clauses always carries the main idea or meaning of the sentence; the other clause or clauses add to or modify that meaning.

When *we got our dog,* his name was Harry.
Harry is happy if *we give him dog biscuits daily.*

When we *subordinate* clauses, we are relating ideas so closely that they rely on each other to express the full meaning of the sentence—the entire meaning that the speaker or writer wants to convey. When we use subordinate sentences, we reveal the relationships of our thoughts to each other in a specific way, just as we do with simple and coordinate sentences. In other words, the syntax reflects and influences our thinking processes.

Let's examine the final explanation of the roadblock situation faced by our traveler—this time in *subordinate sentence* form.

—*Hillary? Barbara? George? Then it clicked. This was Kennebunkport, the location of the former president's summer house. He must have come Down East and invited the new White House residents as his guests. Although as I left Allison's I could catch only a glimpse of a black limousine winding through Dock Square, I could recognize my situation in the article in the next day's local newspaper.*

Residents and Tourists Cram K'Port for Memorial

When media hype hit Kennebunkport during George Bush's first presidential summer at Walker's Point, it drew even more vacationers than usual to a town that has catered to tourists since the turn of the century. When George Bush lost the presidential election to Bill Clinton, the town resigned itself to a return to normalcy. This weekend will undoubtedly stand out as its "Last Hurrah." Kennebunkport police officer William Redman noted that traffic this weekend suggests the Clintons' visit marks a historic event.

Monday morning, authorities blocked off roads so that no one would know which route President Clinton was taking to Dock Square, where he was scheduled to deliver the annual Memorial Day address. Increased concern with security required all those who wanted to observe the holiday in town to have their handbags and packages examined after parking their cars outside the commercial area. Despite minor inconvenience, all went smoothly, and townsfolk and visitors alike seemed to appreciate presidential participation in a long-standing local tradition.

A sentence like "When media hype hit Kennebunkport during George Bush's first presidential summer at Walker's Point, it drew even more vacationers than usual to a town that has catered to tourists since the turn of the century" uses subordination because it is composed of clauses that, although they all contribute to the full meaning of the sentence, are unequal in importance. By placing the idea of *it* (media hype) *drew even more vacationers than usual to a town* in the independent clause, the reporter made that idea the most important one in the sentence. By placing the idea *that has catered to tourists since the turn of the century* in a subordinate clause, the reporter indicated that this idea was less important, as was the idea *when media hype hit Kennebunkport during George Bush's first presidential summer at Walker's Point.* By understanding sentence logic, the writer placed a spotlight on the most important idea of the sentence.

Connections among sentence units in subordinate sentences often reflect a number of important thinking concepts, such as the following:

- *Time* concepts: relating things in time sequence
- *Condition* concepts: relating events when the occurrence of one event depends on the occurrence of another event
- *Causal* concepts: relating events in terms of the way they are responsible for bringing abou'others

In the sentence we have been examining, for example, the clause *When media hype hit Kennebunkport during George Bush's first presidential summer at Walker's Point* reflects an element of *time.* If the clause had read *because media hype hit Kennebunkport during George Bush's first presidential summer at Walker's Point,* it would have reflected an element of *cause.* The following chart demonstrates the language-thinking links between subordinate linguistic forms and thinking patterns.

LANGUAGE-THINKING LINKS

Syntactic Patterns	*(Connectors)*	*Thinking Patterns*
S Subordination *Time*	when, until, after, before, since	Chronological, process
S Subordination *Condition*	when, until, unless, if	Comparative
S Subordination *Cause*	because, so, so that, since	Causal

Sentence subordination is particularly significant because whenever we change a *connector* (language-thinking link) or change the order of a sentence, the focus of meaning and thinking expressed by the sentence also changes. Review the three accounts of the Kennebunkport traveler and analyze them by answering these questions:

- How do the various syntactic forms influence the thoughts and actions expressed?
- What thinking patterns are linked to each of the different accounts?

We have just examined some of the relationships between sentence structures and thinking patterns. These relationships are abstract and require careful attention on the part of writers. The writer must first figure out what the relationship is between ideas, then decide which sentence structure and connector word will best convey that relationship to the reader. The revision stage of the writing process is a good time to pay attention to these relationships. Some of the relationships may have been made explicit in the draft, but if not, the writer can combine and revise sentences to make the relationships easier for the reader to see and understand.

THINKING ↔ WRITING ACTIVITY 5.2

Creating Complex Sentences

Combine the following simple sentences into no more than four by using coordination and subordination. You may delete words or change them if necessary for sentence sense, and you may change the order of the ideas presented, for clarity, but you should not omit any ideas or change the sense of the sentences. Try to figure out the relationships between ideas and make those relationships explicit with your sentence structure.

1. Two oil tankers were sighted in the Persian Gulf.
2. The UN declared a boycott of Iraqi oil.
3. The oil tankers were registered in Iraq.
4. Shots were fired across the bow.
5. The ships were told to stop for a search.
6. The ships continued on course.
7. A U.S. Navy frigate patrolled the Persian Gulf.
8. The U.S. frigate pursued the tankers until they reversed their course.

Effective Writing: Effective writing paints a picture in the mind of the reader.

THINKING ↔ WRITING ACTIVITY 5.3

Thinking Critically About Writing

Reread the writing you did for **Thinking↔Writing Activity 5.1,** the description of a world without language. Identify sentences where you used coordination and sentences where you used subordination to show relationships. Then decide whether you used the best sentence structure and connector words to show these relationships. Also, identify places where you could have used subordination or coordination. Rewrite at least three of your sentences, adjusting and improving the sentence structure to support your meaning.

Reading and Analyzing the Work of Others

The following selection is from *Blue Highways,* a book written by a young man of Native American heritage. After losing his teaching job at a university and separating from his wife, he decided to explore America. He outfitted his van (named "Ghost Dancing") and drove around the country using back roads (represented on maps by blue lines) rather than superhighways. During his travels, he saw fascinating sights, met intriguing people, and developed some significant insights about himself. Read the passage carefully; then do **Thinking↔Writing Activity 5.4.**

from Blue Highways
by William Least Heat-Moon

Back at Ghost Dancing, I saw a camper had pulled up. On the rear end, by the strapped-on aluminum chairs, was something like "The Wandering Watkins." Time to go. I kneeled to check a tire. A smelly furry white thing darted from behind the wheel, and I flinched. Because of it, the journey would change.

"Harmless as a stuffed toy." The voice came from the other end of the leash the dog was on. "He's nearly blind and can't hear much better. Down just to the nose now." The man, with polished cowboy boots and a part measured out in the white hair, had a face so gullied even the Soil Conservation Commission couldn't have reclaimed it. But his eyes seemed lighted from within.

"Are you Mr. Watkins?" I asked.

"What's left of him. The pup's what's left of Bill. He's a Pekingese. Chinese dog. In dog years, he's even older than I am, and I respect him for that. We're two old men. What's your name?"

5   "Same as the dog's."

"I wanted to give him a Chinese name, but old what's-her-face over there in the camper wouldn't have it. Claimed she couldn't pronounce Chinese names. I says, 'You can't say Lee?' She says, 'You going to name a dog Lee?' 'No,' I says, 'but what do you think about White Fong?' Now, she's not a reader unless it's a beauty parlor magazine with a Kennedy or Hepburn woman on the cover, so she never understood the name. You've read your Jack London, I hope. She says, 'When I was a girl we had a horse called William, but that name's too big for that itty-bitty dog. Just call him Bill.' That was that. She's a woman of German descent and a decided person. But when old Bill and I are out on our own, I call him White Fong."

Watkins had worked in a sawmill for thirty years, then retired to Redding; now he spent time in his camper, sometimes in the company of Mrs. Watkins.

"I'd stay on the road, but what's-her-face won't have it."

As we talked, Mrs. What's-her-face periodically thrust her head from the camper to call instructions to Watkins or White Fong. A finger-wagging woman, full of injunctions for man and beast. Whenever she called, I watched her, Watkins watched me, and the dog watched him. Each time he would say, "Well, boys, there you have it. Straight from the back of the horse."

10   "You mind if I swear?" I said I didn't. "The old biddy's in there with her Morning Special—sugar doughnut, boysenberry jam, and a shot of Canadian Club in her coffee. In this beauty she sits inside with her letters.

"What kind of work you in?" he asked.

That question again. "I'm out of work," I said to simplify.

"A man's never out of work if he's worth a damn. It's just sometimes he doesn't get paid. I've gone unpaid my share and I've pulled my share of pay. But that's got nothing to do with working. A man's work is doing what he's supposed to do, and that's why he needs a catastrophe now and again to show him a bad turn isn't the end, because a bad stroke never stops a good man's work. Let me show you my philosophy of life." From his pressed Levi's he took a billfold and handed me a limp business card. "Easy. It's very old."

The card advertised a cafe in Merced when telephone numbers were four digits. In quotation marks was a motto: "Good Home Cooked Meals."

15   "'Good Home Cooked Meals' is your philosophy?"

"Turn it over, peckerwood."

Imprinted on the back in tiny, faded letters was this:

I've been bawled out, balled up, held up, held down, hung up, bulldozed, black-jacked, walked on, cheated, squeezed and mooched; stuck for war tax, excess profits tax, sales tax, dog tax, and syntax, Liberty Bonds, baby bonds, and the bonds of matrimony, Red Cross, Blue Cross, and the double cross; I've worked like hell, worked others like hell, have got drunk and got others drunk, lost all I had, and now because I won't spend or lend what little I earn, beg, borrow or steal, I've been cussed, discussed, boycotted, talked to, talked about, lied to, lied about, worked over, pushed under, robbed, and damned near ruined. The only reason I'm sticking around now is to see WHAT THE HELL IS NEXT.

"I like it," I said.

"Any man's true work is to get his boots on each morning. Curiosity gets it done about as well as anything else."

20

THINKING ↔ WRITING ACTIVITY 5.4

Analyzing a Writing Passage

After reading the passage from *Blue Highways*, analyze the language Least Heat Moon used. Make three columns on a page in your journal. Head them as follows: Action Verbs, Concrete Nouns, and Vivid Adjectives. List at least six examples of each from the reading.

THINKING ↔ WRITING ACTIVITY 5.5

Writing and Asking for the Response of Others

Create your own description of an experience you have had while traveling. Use language as effectively as possible to communicate the thoughts, feelings, and impressions you are trying to share. Be conscious of your use of action verbs, concrete nouns, and vivid adjectives. Ask other students to read your description and identify examples of these. Then ask them for feedback on ways to improve your description.

Using Language to Clarify Thinking

Language reflects thinking, and thinking is shaped by language. Previous sections of this chapter have examined the creature we call *language,* which is composed of small cells, or units, pieces of sound that combine to form larger units called *words.* When words are combined into groups allowed by the rules of the language to form sentences, the creature grows by leaps and bounds. Various types of sentence structure not only provide multiple ways of expressing the same ideas, thoughts, and feelings, but also help to structure those thoughts, weaving into them nuances of focus. In turn, patterns of thinking breathe life into language, giving both processes power.

The relationship between thinking and language is *interactive;* both processes are continually influencing each other in many ways. This is particularly true in the case of language, as the writer George Orwell points out in the following passage from his classic essay "Politics and the English Language":

> A man may take a drink because he feels himself to be a failure, and then fail all the more completely because he drinks. It is rather the same thing that is happening to the English language. It becomes ugly and inaccurate because our thoughts are foolish, but the slovenliness of our language makes it easier for us to have foolish thoughts. The point is that the process is reversible. Modern English, especially written English, is full of bad habits which spread by imitation and which can be avoided if one is willing to take the necessary trouble. If one gets rid of these habits one can think more clearly.

Just as a drinker can fall into a cycle that keeps getting worse, so too can language and thinking. When the use of language is sloppy—that is, vague, general, indistinct, imprecise, foolish, inaccurate, and so on—it leads to thinking of the same sort. And the reverse is also true. Clear and precise language leads to clear and precise thinking:

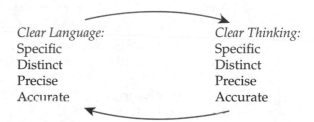

Clear Language:
Specific
Distinct
Precise
Accurate

Clear Thinking:
Specific
Distinct
Precise
Accurate

The opposite of clear, effective language is language that fails to help the reader picture or understand what we mean because it is vague or ambiguous. Most of us are guilty of using such ineffective language in speech ("It was a great party!"), but for our college and work writing we need to be as precise as possible. And our writing can gain clarity and power by our using creative thinking skills to develop fresh, striking figures of speech to illuminate our ideas for readers.

Improving Vague Language

Although our ability to name and identify gives us the power to describe the world in a precise way, we often tend to describe the world in words that are imprecise and general. Such nonspecific words are rightly *vague* words. Consider the following sentences:

- I had a *nice* time yesterday.
- That is an *interesting* book.
- She is an *old* person.

In each of these cases, the italicized word does not give a precise description of the thought, feeling, or experience that the writer or speaker is trying to communicate. Its meaning is not clear and distinct. Vagueness occurs whenever a word is used to represent an area of experience in such a way that the area is not clearly defined.

Vague Word: a word that lacks a clear and distinct meaning.

Most words of general measurement—*short, tall, big, small, heavy, light,* and so on—are vague. The exact meanings of these words depend on the specific situation in which they are used and on the particular perspective of the person using them. For example, give specific definitions for the following words in italics by filling in the blanks. Then compare your responses with those of other members of the class. Can you account for the differences in meaning?

1. A *middle-aged* person is one who is ____ years old.
2. A *tall* person is one who is over ____ feet ____ inches tall.
3. It's *cold* when the temperature is ____ degrees.
4. A person is *wealthy* when he or she is worth ____ dollars.

Although the vagueness of general measurement terms can lead to confusion, other forms of vagueness are more widespread and often more problematic. Terms such as *good* and *enjoyable*, for example, are imprecise and unclear. Vagueness of this sort permeates every level of human discourse, undermines clear thinking, and is extremely difficult to combat. To use language clearly and precisely, you must develop an understanding of the way language functions and commit yourself to breaking the entrenched habits of vague expression.

For example, read the following opinion of a movie and circle all the vague, general words that do not express a clear meaning.

> *Pulp Fiction* is a really funny movie about some really unusual characters in California. The movie consists of several different stories that connect up at different points. Some of the stories are nerve-wracking and others are hilarious, but all of them are very well done. The plots are very interesting, and the main characters are excellent. I liked this movie a lot.

Because of the vague language in this passage, it expresses only general approval—it does not explain in exact or precise terms what the experience of seeing the movie was like. Thus, the writer of the passage is not successful in communicating the experience.

Strong language-users have the gift of symbolizing their experiences so clearly that you can actually relive those experiences with them. You can identify with them, sharing the same thoughts, feelings, and perceptions that they had when they underwent (or imagined) the experience. Consider how effectively the passage written by William Least Heat Moon on pages 158–160 communicates the writer's thoughts, feelings, and experiences.

One useful strategy that journalists often use for clarifying vague language is to ask and try to answer the questions Who? What? Where? When? How? Why? Let's see how this strategy applies to the vague movie review you have just read.

- *Who* were the people involved in the movie? (actors, director, producer, characters portrayed)
- *What* took place in the movie? (setting, events, plot development)
- *Where* does the movie take place? (physical location, cultural setting)
- *When* do the events in the movie take place? (historical situation)
- *How* does the film portray its events? (How do the actors create their characters? How does the director use film techniques to accomplish his or her goals?)
- *Why* do I have this opinion of the film? (For what reasons have I formed the opinion?)

Even if we don't give an elaborate version of our thinking, we can still communicate effectively by using language clearly and precisely. For example, examine this review summary of *Pulp Fiction* by the professional film critic David Denby. Compare and contrast it with the earlier review.

> An ecstatically entertaining piece of suave mockery by Quentin Tarantino that revels in every manner of pulp flagrancy—murder and betrayal, drugs, sex, and episodes of sardonically distanced sadomasochism—all told in three overlapping tales. It's a very funky, American sort of pop masterpiece: improbable, uproarious, with bright colors and danger and blood right on the surface.

THINKING ↔ WRITING ACTIVITY 5.6

Writing a Movie Review

Write a review of a movie that you saw recently, concentrating on expressing your ideas clearly and precisely. Use the following questions to guide your analysis.

1. Who were the people involved with the movie?
2. What took place in the movie?
3. Where does the movie take place?
4. When do the events in the movie take place?
5. How does the film portray its events?
6. Why did you form this particular opinion about the film?

Virtually all of us use vague language extensively in our day-to-day conversations. In many cases, it is natural that your immediate reaction to an experience would be fairly general ("That's nice," "She's interesting," etc.). If you are truly concerned with sharp thinking and meaningful communication, however, you should follow up these initial general reactions with a more precise clarification of what you really mean.

- I think that she is a nice person **because** . . .
- I think that he is a good teacher **because** . . .
- I think that this is an interesting class **because** . . .

Vagueness is always a matter of degree. In fact, you can think of your descriptive/informative use of language as falling somewhere on a scale between extreme generality and extreme specificity. For example, the following statements move from the general to the specific.

General

> She is really smart.
> She does well in school.
> She gets straight A's.
> She earned an A+ in physics

Specific

Although different situations require various degrees of specificity, you should work at becoming increasingly precise in your use of language. For example, examine the following response to the assignment "Describe what you think about the school you are attending." Circle the vague words.

> I really like it a lot. It's a very good school. The people are nice and the teachers are interesting. There are a lot of different things to do, and students have a good time doing them. Some of the courses are pretty hard, but if you study enough, you should do all right.

Notice how general the passage is. The writer says, for example, that "the people are nice," but gives no concrete and specific descriptions of why he thinks the people are nice. The writer would have been more specific if he had used statements such as the following:

- Everyone says hello.
- The students introduced themselves to me in class.
- I always feel welcome in the student lounge.
- The teachers take a special interest in each student.

Although these statements are more precise than saying, "The people are nice," they can also be made more specific. To illustrate this, create more specific descriptions for each of these statements.

Improving Ambiguous Language

Ambiguity is another obstacle to clear expression of your thoughts and feelings. We have noted that words are used to represent various areas of experience. We sometimes make the mistake of thinking that each word stands for one distinct area of experience—an object, thought, or feeling. In fact, a word may represent various areas of experience and so have a number of different meanings. When a word has more than one distinct meaning and we are not sure which meaning is being intended, we say that the word is *ambiguous*. For example, the word *rich* can mean having a large amount of money (like a millionaire), or it can mean having lots of sugar and calories (like chocolate cream pie). Thus, *rich* is a potentially ambiguous word.

> **Ambiguous Word:**   a word having more than one meaning and therefore open to different interpretations.

How do you know which of its multiple meanings an ambiguous word is intended to convey? Usually you can tell by *how* the word is used—by the situation, or context, in which it is employed. When someone asks if you are "rich," you can be fairly certain that the person is not asking if you are full of sugar and calories. As an example, give at least two meanings for the following potentially ambiguous words.

exercise   *critical*   *major*   *bar*   *cool*

Groups of words, also, can be ambiguous. If someone tells you, "I hope you get what you deserve!" you may not be sure whether the speaker is wishing you well, or ill, unless the context of the remark makes his or her intention clear.

THINKING ↔ WRITING ACTIVITY 5.7

Analyzing Ambiguity

Think of two meanings for each of the following sentences. Then rewrite each sentence twice in ways which will eliminate any ambiguity.

- He fed her dog biscuits.
- The duck is ready to eat.
- Flying planes can be dangerous.
- The shooting of the hunter disturbed him.

Thinking Passage: The Crash of Avianca Flight 52

Using language imprecisely can lead to miscommunication, sometimes with disastrous results. For example, on January 29, 1990, an Avianca Airlines flight from Colombia, South America, to New York City crashed, killing seventy-three persons. After circling Kennedy Airport for 45 minutes, the plane ran out of fuel before it could land, apparently the result of imprecise communication between the pilot and the air traffic controllers. Read the following excerpts from the *New York Times* account of the incident on January 30, 1990; then answer the questions that follow.

An Account of Avianca Flight 52

The Federal Aviation Administration today defended the controllers who guided a Colombian jetliner toward Kennedy International Airport, releasing the first verbatim transcripts of communication in the hour before the jet crashed. The officials suggested that the plane's pilot should have used more precise language, such as the word "emergency," in telling controllers how seriously they were short of fuel. They made the statements a day after Federal investigators said that regional controllers never told local controllers the plane was short of fuel and had asked for priority clearance to land.

The transcripts show that the crew of Avianca Flight 52 told regional controllers about 45 minutes before the plane crashed that "we would run out of fuel" if the plane was redirected to Boston instead of being given priority to land at Kennedy. The crew said it would be willing to continue in its holding pattern 40 miles south of Kennedy for "about five minutes—that's all we can do" before the plane would have to move onward to Kennedy. But the regional controllers who gave that message to the local controllers who were to guide the plane on its final descent to Kennedy did not tell them that there was a problem with fuel supplies on the jet or that the plane had requested priority handling, the transcripts recorded by the FAA confirmed.

Taken by itself, the information that the plane could circle for just five more minutes would not make the immediate danger of the plane clear to the local controllers. Without being told that the plane did not have enough fuel to reach Boston or that its crew had asked for priority clearance, the local controllers might have assumed that it had reached a point where it could still land with adequate reserves of fuel still on board.

Despite the apparent lapse in communications among controllers, an FAA spokesman said they acted properly because the plane's crew had not explicitly declared a fuel emergency. An emergency would require immediate clearance to land.

5   R. Steve Bell, president of the National Air Traffic Controllers Association, called the safety board's statement during its inquiry "highly

misleading and premature." Mr. Bell, in a statement issued today, said the pilots of the plane should have made known to controllers the extent of their problem in order to obtain immediate clearance to land the plane. "The Avianca pilot never declared a 'fuel emergency' or 'minimum fuel,' both of which would have triggered an emergency response by controllers," he said. "Stating that you are low on fuel does not imply an immediate problem. In addition, this information would not necessarily be transmitted when one controller hands off to another."

Chronology of final minutes of Flight 52:

> 8:00 P.M.: Forty miles south of Kennedy, Avianca Flight 52 is delayed for 46 minutes, after earlier delays of 16 minutes over Norfolk, Va., and 27 minutes farther north.
>
> 8:46 P.M.: The plane's crew tells regional air controllers in Islip, L.I., that they have a low-fuel problem. Regional controllers immediately release the plane from its holding pattern, passing it to local controllers in Garden City, L.I.
>
> 9:24 P.M.: First landing attempt at Kennedy is aborted and jet circles. Pilot twice tells Kennedy tower that he is low on fuel.
>
> 9:32 P.M.: Pilot tells tower while circling: "Two engines lost"; he also says that he is very short on fuel.
>
> 9:35 P.M.: The plane crashes.

THINKING ↔ WRITING ACTIVITY 5.8

Analyzing the Crash of Avianca Flight 52

Write the answers to the following questions in your journal.

1. If the pilot of the airplane were alive (all crew died in the crash), how do you think he would analyze the cause of the crash?
2. How did the air traffic controllers and the FAA analyze the cause of the crash?
3. What do you consider the cause of the crash? What are the reasons for your conclusion?
4. Describe a situation that you were involved in, or that you heard about, in which a serious misunderstanding resulted from an ambiguous use of language.

Using Figurative Language

Thus far in this section, we have been concerned with saying and writing exactly what we mean, in as precise a way as possible. There is another, different way to use language to express our thinking: to say something we do not literally mean. When we do this effectively, our readers understand that we do not mean to be taken literally, but that we are speaking *figuratively*, using a *figure of speech*. There are many different figures of speech; some literary experts have identified as many as 250. Here, though, we will focus on two with which you may already be familiar: *simile* and *metaphor*.

Both simile and metaphor are based on a special kind of comparative thinking called *analogy*. Analogy involves a limited comparison between two essentially unlike things. Analogies are different from the more common comparisons that involve examining the similarities and differences of two items in the same general category, such as two items on a menu or two methods of birth control. Similes and metaphors focus on unexpected likenesses between items from different categories. Thus, when we compare a baby's mouth to a rose, we may be calling attention to the color or softness of the mouth, but we are not suggesting that the mouth has thorns or that it attracts bees. *Chapter 7, Exploring Comparative Relationships—Writing About Perspectives*, will have more to say about analogies.

The goal of figures of speech based on analogy is to clarify or illuminate a concept from one category by saying that in one or more limited ways, it is the same as a concept from a very different category. Consider the following example:

> *Life's but a walking shadow, a poor player*
> *That struts and frets his hour upon the stage,*
> *And then is heard no more. . . .*

> —Shakespeare, *Macbeth*

In this famous metaphor, Shakespeare is comparing two things that at first seem to have nothing in common: life and an actor. Yet a close look shows that even though they are unlike in many ways, there are some undeniable similarities between them. (What are some of the similarities?)

We ourselves often create and use similes and metaphors to make a point. Using them appropriately can help you communicate better. That is particularly important when you have trouble finding the right words to represent your experiences. Powerful or complex emotions can make you speechless or make you say things like "Words cannot describe what I feel." Imagine that you are trying to describe your feelings of love and caring for another person. You might compare your emotions to "the first rose of spring," noting the following similarities:

- Like the first rose, this is the first great love of my life.
- Like the fragile yet supple petals of the rose, my feelings are tender and sensitive.

Remember, however, that you are dealing with a limited comparison. You would not want anyone to think, "Like the rose, that love will die after a week"! Readers who are familiar with similes and metaphors will not make that mistake.

Another favorite subject for similes and metaphors is the idea of the meaning or purpose of life, which the simple use of the word *life* does not communicate. You have just seen Shakespeare's comparison of life to an actor. Here are some other popular metaphors involving life. What are some points of similarity in each?

- Life is just a bowl of cherries.
- Life is a football game.
- Life is like a box of chocolates.
- "[Life] is a tale / Told by an idiot, full of sound and fury, / Signifying nothing."—Shakespeare

Create a metaphor for life representing some of your feelings, and explain the points of similarity.

- Life is . . .

Distinguishing Similes and Metaphors

From the examples discussed so far, you can see that these figures of speech have two parts: an *original subject* and a *compared subject* (what the original is being likened to). In comparing your love to the first rose of spring, the *original subject* is your feelings of love and caring for someone; the *compared subject* is what you are comparing those feelings to in order to describe them—namely, the first rose of spring.

The connection between the original subject and the compared subject can be either obvious (explicit) or implied (implicit). For example, you can echo the lament of the great pool hustler Minnesota Fats and say, "A pool player in a tuxedo is like a hotdog with whipped cream on it." This is a *simile* because it explicitly notes the connection between the original subject (man in tuxedo) and the compared subject (hotdog with whipped cream) by using the comparative term *like*.

> **Simile:** an explicit, effective comparison between basically dissimilar things.

You can also use other forms of obvious comparison, such as *is similar to, reminds me of,* or *makes me think of.* Or you could say, "A pool player in a tuxedo *is* a hotdog with whipped cream on it." In this case, you are creating a metaphor because you have not included any words that point out that you are making a comparison. Instead, you are stating that the original subject *is* the compared subject. (Most people will understand that you are making a limited comparison between two different things, not describing a biological transformation.)

> **Metaphor:** an implied, effective comparison between basically dissimilar things.

Use your creative thinking skills to create a simile for a subject of your own choosing, noting at least two points of comparison.

Subject

1.

2.

Now use your creative thinking skills to create a metaphor (implied analogy) for a subject of your own choosing, noting at least two points of comparison.

Subject

1.

2.

A final point about figurative language is that it does need to be fresh. "He runs like a deer" and "I slept like a baby" were wonderful similes the first time they were used, but they have become old and tired: clichés. Use your creative thinking skills to write fresh, striking figures of speech.

THINKING ↔ WRITING ACTIVITY 5.9

Analyzing "I Have a Dream"

Very skillful speakers and writers are able to weave similes and metaphors together into a striking tapestry. Read the following selection by Martin Luther King, Jr. Then respond to these questions in your journal.

1. List at least four different similes or metaphors that King uses.
2. Pick one of these similes or metaphors and trace it throughout the speech; that is, list each time it occurs.
3. Why, do you think, did King use these figures of speech? What effect do they have on you? Do you think they had the same effect on his listeners?

from I Have a Dream

by **Martin Luther King, Jr.**

Five score years ago, a great American, in whose symbolic shadow we stand, signed the Emancipation Proclamation. This momentous decree came as a great beacon light of hope to millions of Negro slaves who had been seared in the flames of withering injustice. It came as a joyous daybreak to end the long night of captivity.

But one hundred years later, we must face the tragic fact that the Negro is still not free. One hundred years later, the life of the Negro is still sadly crippled by the manacles of segregation and the chains of discrimination. One hundred years later, the Negro lives on a lonely island of poverty in the midst of a vast ocean of material prosperity. One hundred years later, the Negro is still languishing in the corners of American society and finds himself an exile in his own land. So we have come here today to dramatize an appalling condition.

In a sense we have come to our nation's capital to cash a check. When the architects in our republic wrote the magnificent words of the Constitution and the Declaration of Independence, they were signing a promissory note to which every American was to fall heir. This note was a promise that all men would be guaranteed the unalienable rights of life, liberty, and the pursuit of happiness.

It is obvious today that America has defaulted on this promissory note insofar as her citizens of color are concerned. Instead of honoring this sacred obligation, America has given the Negro people a bad check; a check which has come back marked "insufficient funds." But we refuse to believe that the bank of justice is bankrupt. We refuse to believe that there are insufficient funds in the great vaults of opportunity of this nation. So we have come to cash this check—a check that will give us upon demand the riches of freedom and the security of justice. We have also come to this hallowed spot to remind America of the fierce urgency of *now*. This is no time to engage in the luxury of cooling off or to take the tranquilizing drugs of gradualism. *Now* is the time to make real the promises of Democracy. *Now* is the time to rise from the dark and desolate valley of segregation to the sunlit path of racial justice. *Now* is the time to open the doors of opportunity to all of God's children. *Now* is the time to lift our nation from the quicksands of racial injustice to the solid rock of brotherhood.

5   It would be fatal for the nation to overlook the urgency of the moment and to underestimate the determination of the Negro. This sweltering summer of the Negro's legitimate discontent will not pass until there is an invigorating autumn of freedom and equality. 1963 is not an end, but a beginning. Those who hope that the Negro needed to blow off steam and will now be content will have a rude awakening if the nation returns to business as usual. There will be neither rest nor tranquillity in America until the Negro is granted his citizenship rights. The whirlwinds of revolt will continue to shake the foundations of our nation until the bright day of justice emerges.

But there is something that I must say to my people who stand on the warm threshold which leads into the palace of justice. In the process of gaining our rightful place we must not be guilty of wrongful deeds. Let us not seek to satisfy our thirst for freedom by drinking from the cup of bitterness and hatred. We must forever conduct our struggle on the high plane of dignity and discipline. We must not allow our creative protest to degenerate into physical violence. Again and again we must rise to the majestic heights of meeting physical force with soul force. The marvelous new militancy which has engulfed the Negro community must not lead us to a distrust of all white people, for many of our white brothers, as evidenced by their presence here today, have come to realize that their destiny is tied up with our destiny and their freedom is inextricably bound to our freedom. We cannot walk alone.

And as we walk, we must make the pledge that we shall march ahead. We cannot turn back. There are those who are asking the devotees of civil rights, "When will you be satisfied?" We can never be satisfied as long as the Negro is the victim of the unspeakable horrors of police brutality. We can never be satisfied as long as our bodies, heavy with the fatigue of travel, cannot gain lodging in the motels of the highways and the hotels of the cities. We cannot be satisfied as long as the Negro's basic mobility is from a smaller ghetto to a larger one. We can never be satisfied as long as a Negro in Mississippi cannot vote and a Negro in New York believes he has nothing for which to vote. No, no, we are not satisfied, and we will not be satisfied until justice rolls down like waters and righteousness like a mighty stream.

I am not unmindful that some of you have come here out of great trials and tribulations. Some of you have come fresh from narrow jail cells. Some of you have come from areas where your quest for freedom left you battered by the storms of persecution and staggered by the winds of police brutality. You have been the veterans of creative suffering. Continue to work with the faith that unearned suffering is redemptive.

Go back to Mississippi, go back to Alabama, go back to South Carolina, go back to Georgia, go back to Louisiana, go back to the slums and ghettos of our northern cities, knowing that somehow this situation can and will be changed. Let us not wallow in the valley of despair.

10   I say to you today, my friends, that in spite of the difficulties and frustrations of the moment I still have a dream. It is a dream deeply rooted in the American dream.

I have a dream that one day this nation will rise up and live out the true meaning of its creed: "We hold these truths to be self-evident; that all men are created equal."

I have a dream that one day on the red hills of Georgia the sons of former slaves and the sons of former slaveowners will be able to sit down together at the table of brotherhoood.

I have a dream that one day even the state of Mississippi, a desert state sweltering with the heat of injustice and oppression, will be transformed into an oasis of freedom and justice.

I have a dream that my four little children will one day live in a nation where they will not be judged by the color of their skin but by the content of their character.

15   I have a dream today.

I have a dream that one day the state of Alabama, whose governor's lips are presently dripping with the words of interposition and nullification, will be transformed into a situation where little black boys and black girls will be able to join hands with little white boys and white girls and walk together as sisters and brothers.

I have a dream today.

I have a dream that one day every valley shall be exalted, every hill and mountain shall be made low, the rough places will be made plain, and the crooked places will be made straight, and the glory of the Lord shall be revealed, and all flesh shall see it together.

This is our hope. This is the faith with which I return to the South. With this faith we will be able to hew out of the mountain of despair a stone of hope. With this faith we will be able to transform the jangling discords of our nation into a beautiful symphony of brotherhood. With this faith we will be able to work together, to pray together, to struggle together, to go to jail together, to stand up for freedom together, knowing that we will be free one day.

20   This will be the day when all of God's children will be able to sing with new meaning:

My country, 'tis of thee, Sweet land of liberty, Of thee I sing: Land where my fathers died, Land of the pilgrims' pride, From every mountain-side Let freedom ring.

And if America is to be a great nation this must become true. So let freedom ring from the prodigious hilltops of New Hampshire. Let freedom ring from the mighty mountains of New York. Let freedom ring from the heightening Alleghenies of Pennsylvania!

Let freedom ring from the snowcapped Rockies of Colorado!

Let freedom ring from the curvaceous peaks of California!

25   But not only that; let freedom ring from Stone Mountain of Georgia!

Let freedom ring from Lookout Mountain of Tennessee!

Let freedom ring from every hill and molehill of Mississippi. From every mountainside, let freedom ring.

When we let freedom ring, when we let it ring from every village and every hamlet, from every state and every city, we will be able to speed up that day when all of God's children, black men and white men, Jews and Gentiles, Protestants and Catholics, will be able to join hands and sing in the words of the old Negro spiritual, "Free at last! free at last! thank God almighty, we are free at last!"

Using Language in Social Contexts

Language Styles

Language is always used in a context. We always speak or write with a person or a group of people in mind. The person may be only oneself; the group may be made up of friends, coworkers, or strangers. Moreover, we always use language in a particular situation. We converse with friends, meet with the boss, or carry out a business transaction with the bank or supermarket. In each situation, we use the appropriate language style. For example, describe how you usually greet the following people when you see them:

A teacher

A parent

An employer

A good friend

A waiter/waitress

When greeting a friend, you are likely to say something like "Hey, Richard, how's it going?" "Hi, Sue, good to see ya." When greeting your employer, however, or even a coworker, something more like "Good morning, Mrs. Jones," or "Hello, Dan, how are you this morning?" is in order. The two different contexts, personal friendship and the workplace, call for different language responses. In a working environment, no matter how frequently we interact with coworkers or employers, our language style tends to be more formal and less abbreviated than it is with personal friends. Conversely, the more familiar we are with someone, the better we know him or her, the more abbreviated the *style* of language will be in that context, for you share a variety of ideas, opinions, and experiences with that person. The language style identifies this shared thinking and consequently restricts the group of people who can communicate within this context.

All of us belong to social groups in which we use styles that separate "insiders" from "outsiders." When you use an abbreviated style of language with a friend, you are identifying that person as a friend and sending a social message that says, "I know you very well; I can assume many common perspectives between us." When you speak to someone at the office in a more elaborate language style, you send a different social message: "I know you within a particular context (this workplace), and I can assume only certain common perspectives between us."

In this way we use language to identify the social context and to define the relationship between the people communicating. Language styles vary from *informal,* in which we abbreviate not only sentence structure but also the sounds that form words—as in *ya* in the example—to increasingly *formal,* in which we use more complex sentence structure as well as complete words in terms of sound patterns.

The language style called for in academic and most workplace writing is called *Standard American English (SAE)*. SAE follows the rules and conventions given in handbooks and taught in school. The ability to use SAE marks a person as part of an educated group who understands how and when to use it.

Slang

Read the following dialogue; then rewrite it in your own style.

Girl 1: "Hey, did you see that new guy? He's a dime. I mean, really diesel."

Girl 2: "All the guys in my class are busted. They are tore up from the floor up. Punks, crackheads, lowlifes. Let's exit. There's a jam tonight that is going to be the bomb, really fierce. I've got to hit the books so that I'll still have time to chill."

How would you describe the style of the original dialogue? How would you describe the style of your version of the dialogue? The linguist Shoshana Hoose writes:

> As any teen will tell you, keeping up with the latest slang takes a lot of work. New phrases sweep into town faster than greased lightning, and they are gone just as quickly. Last year's "hoser" is this year's "dweeb" (both meaning somewhat of a "nerd"). Some slang consists of everyday words that have taken a new, hip meaning. "Mega" for instance, was used mainly by astronomers and mathematicians until teens adopted it as a way of describing anything great, cool, and unbelievable. Others are words such as gag that seem to have naturally evolved from one meaning (to throw up) to another (a person or thing that is gross to the point of making one want to throw up). And then there are words that come from movies, popular music, and the media. "Rambo," the macho movie character who singlehandedly defeats whole armies, has come to mean a muscular, tough, adventurous boy who wears combat boots and fatigues.

> As linguists have long known, cultures create the most words for the things that preoccupy them the most. For example, Eskimos have been reported to have more than seventy-six words for *ice* and *snow,* and Hawaiians can choose from scores of variations on the word *water.* Most teenage slang falls into one or two categories: words meaning "cool" and words meaning "out of it." Persons considered really out of it have been described as nerds, goobers, geeks, fades, or pinheads, to name just a few possibilities.

THINKING ↔ WRITING ACTIVITY 5.10

Analyzing Slang

Review the slang terms and definitions in the following glossary. How do your terms match up? For each term, list a word that you use, or have heard of, to mean the same thing.

Word:	Your Word:	Meaning:
dime, buff, diesel		good-looking guy
phat, shorty, fly, all that		good-looking (girl)
busted		gross, disgusting
punk		someone who hangs out
hip, fierce		cool, awesome
the bomb		really cool
trifling		showoff
played		stupid, out-of-date
exit, be out, step off		leave

If your meanings did not match those in the glossary, or if you did not recognize some of the words in the glossary, what do you think was the main reason?

Slang, while creative and entertaining, is a restrictive style of language in that it limits its users to a particular group. As Hoose points out, age is usually the determining factor in using slang. But there are special forms of slang that are not determined by age; rather, they are determined by profession or interest group. Let's look at this other type of language style.

Jargon

Jargon is made up of words, expressions, and technical terms that are intelligible to professional circles or interest groups but not to the general public. Consider the following interchanges:

1. A: Breaker 1–9. Com'on, Little Frog.
   B: Roger and back to you, Charley.
   A: You got to back down, you got a Smokey ahead.
   B: I can't afford to feed the bears this week. Better stay at 5–5 now.
   A: That's a big 10–4.
   B: I'm gonna cut the coax now.
2. OK Al, number six takes two eggs, wreck 'em, with a whiskey down and an Adam and Eve on a raft. Don't forget the Jack Tommy, express to California.
3. Please take further notice, that pursuant to and in accordance with Article II, Paragraphs Second and Fifteenth of the aforesaid Proprietary Lease Agreement, you are obligated to reimburse Lessor for any expense Lessor incurs including legal fees in instituting any action or proceeding due to a default of your obligations as contained in the Proprietary Lease Agreement.

Word meaning in the three items is shared by (1) CB radio operators, (2) restaurant and diner cooks, and (3) attorneys.

Dialects

Within the boundaries of geographical regions and ethnic groups, the form of a language used may be so different from the usual (or standard) in terms of its sound patterns, vocabulary, and sentence structure that it cannot be understood by people outside the specific regional or ethnic group. Here, we are no longer referring to variations in language *style;* we are referring to distinct *dialects.* Consider these sentences from three different dialects of English:

Dialect A: Dats allabunch of byoks at de license bureau. He fell out de rig and broke his leg boon.

Dialect B: My teacher she said I passed on the skin of my teeth. My sisters and them up there talkin' 'bout I should stayed back.

Dialect C: I went out to the garden to pick the last of them Kentucky Wonder pole beans of mine, and do you know, there on the grass was just a little mite of frost.

Though you can recognize these sentences as English, you may not recognize all the words, sentence structures, and sound patterns that the speakers used. Dialects differ from language styles not only in being restricted to geographical or ethnic groups, but also in varying from the standard language to a greater degree than language styles do. Dialects vary not only in words but also in sound patterns and in syntax. In the following three examples of dialect, how do the sound patterns, vocabulary, and sentence structure differ from that of standard English?

1. *Ah don lak to fly in dem big jet arrowpleen. Dey had a bad wreck on de hairline. Tie loose de boat!*
2. *I can skate better than Lois and I be only eight. If you be goin' real fast, hold it. You be goin, too fast, well, you don't be in the ring. You be outside if you be goin, too fast. That man he a clip you up. I think they call him Sonny.*
3. *A: Mornin' Alf, ow're yer goin?*
   B: Not bad, me ol' mate, not bad. Ow's yerself?
   A: Oh, same as usual, can't complain.
   B: 'Ow much are yer Herberts then?
   A: To you me ol' son, an Alan Whicker for a bag.
   B: Gawdelpus! An Alan Whicker! Yer goin' orf yer head. That's too dear. I'll give yer ten bob, not a penny more.
   A: Alrigh, mate—let's not have a bull and cow gimme the bees and honey and take yer bag of Herberts.
   B: Cheers! An give me regards to yer carving knife.

Can you interpret the meaning conveyed by each passage? What words or syntactic forms contributed to any difficulty you may have had in interpreting meaning? If you speak a dialect, write one or two sentences in that dialect and share them with your classmates. How does your dialect vary from the standard in terms of words and syntactic forms?

Of course, many people are not limited to one form of English. They are "bilingual" in that they can switch from using a dialect fluently to using Standard American English fluently. Such speakers often report, in fact, that their ability to use several forms of the language gives them great pleasure and an enhanced perspective on experience.

So far in this section, we have noted that almost all of us have different language styles that we use on different occasions, and that some of us even have a variety of dialects which are expressed in our speech and writing. It is important to consider that the language you use and the way you use it serve as important clues to your social identity. For example, dialect identifies your geographical area or group; slang marks your age group and subculture; and jargon often identifies your occupation or other areas of interest.

The connection between language and thought, in both speech and writing, turns language into a powerful social force that separates us as well as binds us together. Social dimensions of language are important influences in shaping our responses to others. Sometimes the social dimensions of language can trigger stereotypes we hold about someone's interests, social class, intelligence, personal attributes, and so on. When we fall into stereotyping, we are not thinking critically. The ability to think critically gives us the insight and the intellectual ability to distinguish people's language use from their individual qualities, to correct inaccurate beliefs about people, and to avoid stereotypical responses in the future. These insights contribute to enlightened relationships with others, and provide guidance for our spoken and written use of language.

THINKING ↔ WRITING ACTIVITY 5.11

Thinking About Language Styles and Dialects

Write responses to the following questions in your journal.

1. Describe examples, drawn from individuals in your personal experience, of each of the following: dialect, jargon, and slang.
2. Describe your immediate responses to the examples you just provided. For example, what is your immediate response to someone speaking in each of the dialects on pages 176–177? to someone with a British accent? someone speaking "computerese"? to someone speaking a slang that you don't understand?
3. Analyze the responses you just described. How did they get formed? Does each represent an accurate understanding of a person, or a stereotyped belief?
4. Identify strategies for using critical thinking abilities to overcome inaccurate and inappropriate responses to others based on their language usage.

Thinking Passage: Gender Differences in Language

Recently gender differences in language use have reached the forefront of social research, even though variation in language use between the sexes has been observed for centuries. Proverbs such as "A woman's tongue wags like a lamb's tail" historically attest to supposed differences—usually, alleged inferiorities—in women's speech and, by implication, in their thinking, as opposed to men's. Vocabulary, swearing and taboo language, pronunciation, and verbosity have all been pointed to as contexts that illustrate gender differences in language. Only within the last two decades, however, have scholars of the social use of language paid serious attention to variation between men's and women's language and to social factors that contribute to these differences. The following excerpt from the work of Deborah Tannen reflects current interest in sociolinguistic variations between women and men. After reading the selection, respond to **Thinking↔Writing Activity 5.12** on page 183.

from Sex, Lies and Conversation
Why Is It So Hard for Men and Women
to Talk to Each Other?

by Deborah Tannen

I was addressing a small gathering in a suburban Virginia living room—a women's group that had invited men to join them. Throughout the evening, one man had been particularly talkative, frequently offering ideas and anecdotes, while his wife sat silently beside him on the couch. Toward the end of the evening, I commented that women frequently complain that their husbands don't talk to them. This man quickly concurred. He gestured toward his wife and said, "She's the talker in our family." The room burst into laughter; the man looked puzzled and hurt. "It's true," he explained. "When I come home from work I have nothing to say. If she didn't keep the conversation going, we'd spend the whole evening in silence."

This episode crystallizes the irony that although American men tend to talk more than women in public situations, they often talk less at home. And this pattern is wreaking havoc with marriage.

The pattern was observed by political scientist Andrew Hacker in the late '70s. Sociologist Catherine Kohler Riessman reports in her new book *Divorce Talk* that most of the women she interviewed—but only a few of the men—gave lack of communication as the reason for their divorces. Given the current divorce rate of nearly 50 percent, that amounts to millions of cases in the United States every year—a virtual epidemic of failed conversation.

In my own research, complaints from women about their husbands most often focused not on tangible inequities such as having given up the chance for a career to accompany a husband to his, or doing far more than their share of daily life-support work like cleaning, cooking, social arrangements and errands. Instead, they focused on communication: "He doesn't listen to me," "He doesn't talk to me." I found, as Hacker observed years before, that most wives want their husbands to be, first and foremost, conversational partners, but few husbands share this expectation of their wives.

5   In short, the image that best represents the current crisis is the stereotypical cartoon scene of a man sitting at the breakfast table with a newspaper held up in front of his face, while a woman glares at the back of it, wanting to talk.

Linguistic Battle of Sexes

How can women and men have such different impressions of communication in marriage? Why the widespread imbalance in their interests and expectations?

In the April issue of *American Psychologist,* Stanford University's Eleanor Maccoby reports the results of her own and others' research showing that children's development is most influenced by the social structure of peer interactions. Boys and girls tend to play with children of their own gender, and their sex-separate groups have different organizational structures and interactive norms.

I believe these systematic differences in childhood socialization make talk between women and men like cross-cultural communication, heir to all the attraction and pitfalls of that enticing but difficult enterprise. My research on men's and women's conversations uncovered patterns similar to those described for children's groups.

For women, as for girls, intimacy is the fabric of relationships, and talk is the thread from which it is woven. Little girls create and maintain friendships by exchanging secrets; similarly, women regard conversation as the cornerstone of friendship. So a woman expects her husband to be a new and improved version of a best friend. What is important is not the individual subjects that are discussed but the sense of closeness, a life shared, that emerges when people tell their thoughts, feelings, and impressions.

10   Bonds between boys can be as intense as girls', but they are based less on talking, more on doing things together. Since they don't assume talk is the cement that binds a relationship, men don't know what kind of talk women want, and they don't miss it when it isn't there.

Boys' groups are larger, more inclusive, and more hierarchical, so boys must struggle to avoid the subordinate position in the group. This may play a role in women's complaints that men don't listen to them. Some men really don't like to listen, because being the listener makes them feel one-down, like a child listening to adults or an employee to a boss.

But often when women tell men, "You aren't listening," and the men protest, "I am," the men are right. The impression of not listening results from misalignments in the mechanics of conversation. The misalignment begins as soon as a man and a woman take physical positions. This became clear when I studied videotapes made by psychologist Bruce Dorval of children and adults talking to their same-sex best friends. I found that at every age, the girls and women faced each other directly, their eyes anchored on each other's faces. At every age, the boys and men sat at angles to each other and looked elsewhere in the room, periodically glancing at each other. They were obviously attuned to each other, often mirroring each other's movements. But the tendency of men to face away can give women the impression they aren't listening even when they are. A young woman in college was frustrated: Whenever she told her boyfriend she wanted to talk to him, he would lie down on the floor, close his eyes, and put his arm over his face. This signaled to her, "He's taking a nap." But he insisted he was listening extra hard. Normally, he looks around the room, so he is easily distracted. Lying down and covering his eyes helped him concentrate on what she was saying.

Analogous to the physical alignment that women and men take in conversation is their topical alignment. The girls in my study tended to talk at length about one topic, but the boys tended to jump from topic to topic. Girls exchanged stories about people they knew. The second-grade boys teased, told jokes, noticed things in the room and talked about finding games to play. The sixth-grade girls talked about problems with a mutual friend. The sixth-grade boys talked about 55 different topics, none of which extended over more than a few turns.

Listening to Body Language

Switching topics is another habit that gives women the impression men aren't listening, especially if they switch to a topic about themselves. But the evidence of the 10th-grade boys in my study indicates otherwise. The 10th-grade boys sprawled across their chairs with bodies parallel and eyes straight ahead, rarely looking at each other. They looked as if they were riding in a car, staring out the windshield. But they were talking about their feelings. One boy was upset because a girl had told him he had a drinking problem, and the other was feeling alienated from all his friends.

15   Now, when a girl told a friend about a problem, the friend responded by asking probing questions and expressing agreement and understanding. But the boys dismissed each other's problems. Todd assured Richard that his drinking was "no big problem" because "sometimes you're funny when you're off your butt." And when Todd said he felt left out, Richard responded, "Why should you? You know more people than me."

Women perceive such responses as belittling and unsupportive. But the boys seemed satisfied with them. Whereas women reassure each other by implying, "You shouldn't feel bad because I've had similar experiences," men do so by implying, "You shouldn't feel bad because your problems aren't so bad."

There are even simpler reasons for women's impression that men don't listen. Linguist Lynette Hirschman found that women make more listener-noise, such as "mhm," "uhuh," and "yeah," to show "I'm with you." Men, she found, more often give silent attention. Women who expect a stream of listener-noise interpret silent attention as no attention at all.

Women's conversational habits are as frustrating to men as men's are to women. Men who expect silent attention interpret a stream of listener-noise as overreaction or impatience. Also, when women talk to each other in a close, comfortable setting, they often overlap, finish each other's sentences and anticipate what the other is about to say. This practice, which I call "participatory listenership," is often perceived by men as interruption, intrusion and lack of attention.

A parallel difference caused a man to complain about his wife, "She just wants to talk about her own point of view. If I show her another view, she gets mad at me." When most women talk to each other, they assume a conversationalist's job is to express agreement and support. But many men see their conversational duty as pointing out the other side of an argument. This is heard as disloyalty by women, and refusal to offer the requisite support. It is not that women don't want to see other points of view, but that they prefer them phrased as suggestions and inquiries rather than as direct challenges.

20   In his book *Fighting for Life,* Walter Ong points out that men use "agonistic," or warlike, oppositional formats to do almost anything; thus discussion becomes debate, and conversation a competitive sport. In contrast, women see conversation as a ritual means of establishing rapport. If Jane tells a problem and June says she has a similar one, they walk away feeling closer to each other. But this attempt at establishing rapport can backfire when used with men. Men take too literally women's ritual "trouble talk," just as women mistake men's ritual challenges for real attack.

The Sounds of Silence

These differences begin to clarify why women and men have such different expectations about communication in marriage. For women, talk creates intimacy. Marriage is an orgy of closeness: you can tell your feelings and thoughts, and still be loved. Their greatest fear is being pushed away. But men live in a hierarchical world, where talk maintains independence and status. They are on guard to protect themselves from being put down and pushed around.

This explains the paradox of the talkative man who said of his silent wife, "She's the talker." In the public setting of a guest lecture, he felt challenged to show his intelligence and display his understanding of the lecture. But at home, where he has nothing to prove and no one to defend against, he is free to remain silent. For his wife, being home means she is free from the worry that something she says might offend someone, or spark disagreement, or appear to be showing off; at home she is free to talk.

The communication problems that endanger marriage can't be fixed by mechanical engineering. They require a new conceptual framework about the role of talk in human relationships. Many of the psychological explanations that have become second nature may not be helpful, because they tend to blame either women (for not being assertive enough) or men (for not being in touch with their feelings). A sociolinguistic approach by which male-female conversation is seen as cross-cultural communication allows us to understand the problem and forge solutions without blaming either party.

Once the problem is understood, improvement comes naturally, as it did to the young woman and her boyfriend who seemed to go to sleep when she wanted to talk. Previously, she had accused him of not listening, and he had refused to change his behavior, since that would be admitting fault. But then she learned about and explained to him the differences in women's and men's habitual ways of aligning themselves in conversation. The next time she told him she wanted to talk, he began, as usual, by lying down and covering his eyes. When the familiar negative reaction bubbled up, she reassured herself that he really was listening. But then he sat up and looked at her. Thrilled, she asked why. He said, "You like me to look at you when you talk, so I'll try to do it." Once he saw their differences as cross-cultural rather than right and wrong, he independently altered his behavior.

25 Women who feel abandoned and deprived when their husbands won't listen to or report daily news may be happy to discover their husbands trying to adapt once they understand the place of small talk in women's relationships. But if their husbands don't adapt, the women may still be comforted that for men, this is not a failure of intimacy. Accepting the difference, the wives may look to their friends or family for that kind of talk. And husbands who can't provide it shouldn't feel their wives have made unreasonable demands. Some couples will still decide to divorce, but at least their decisions will be based on realistic expectations.

In these times of resurgent ethnic conflicts, the world desperately needs cross-cultural understanding. Like charity, successful cross-cultural communication should begin at home.

THINKING ↔ WRITING ACTIVITY 5.12

Thinking About Gender-Related Communication Styles

Choose one of the following questions and write a one-page response in your journal.

1. Identify the distinctive differences between the communication styles of men and women, as described by Deborah Tannen, and explain how these differences can lead to miscommunication and misunderstanding.
2. On the basis of your own experience, explain whether or not you believe Tannen's analysis of these different communication styles is accurate. Provide specific examples to support your viewpoint.
3. Describe a situation in which you have a miscommunication with a person of the opposite sex. Analyze this situation on the basis of what you read in the Tannen article.
4. Identify strategies that both men and women can use to avoid the miscommunication that can result from their contrasting styles.

Using Language to Influence

Because of the intimate relationship between language and thinking, people naturally use language to influence the thinking of others. We noted earlier that within the boundaries of social groups, people use a given language style or dialect to emphasize shared information and experience. Not only does this sharing identify the members of the group socially; it also provides a base for them to influence one another's thinking. The expression "Now you're speaking my language" illustrates this point.

Some people actually make a profession of using language to influence others' thinking. In fact, many individuals and groups are interested in influencing—and sometimes in controlling—your thoughts, your feelings, and your behavior. To avoid being unconsciously manipulated by these efforts, you must have an understanding and awareness of how language functions. Such an understanding will help you distinguish actual arguments, information, and reasons from techniques of persuasion that others use to get you to accept their views without critical thinking. Two types of language often used to promote the uncritical acceptance of views are *euphemistic language* and *emotive language.* By developing insight into these language strategies, you will strengthen your abilities to function as a critical thinker.

Euphemistic Language

The term *euphemism* derives from a Greek word meaning "to speak with good words," and using a euphemism involves substituting a more pleasant, less objectionable expression for a blunt or more direct one. For example, an entire collection of euphemisms exists to disguise the unpleasantness of death: *passed away, went to her reward, departed this life,* and *blew out the candle.*

Why do people use euphemisms? Probably to help smooth out the "rough edges" of life, to make the unbearable bearable and the offensive, inoffensive. Sometimes people use them to make their occupations seem more dignified (a garbage collector, for instance, might be called a "sanitation engineer").

Euphemisms can become dangerous, though, when they are used to evade or create misperceptions of serious issues. An alcoholic may describe himself as a "social drinker," thus denying the problem and the need for help. A politician may indicate that one of his statements was "somewhat at variance with the truth"—meaning that he lied. Even more serious examples would include describing rotting slums as "substandard housing," making deplorable conditions appear reasonable and the need for action less important. One of the most devastating examples of the destructive power of euphemisms was Nazi Germany's characterizing the slaughter of millions of men, women, and children as "the final solution" and "the purification of the race." The 1990s' "ethnic cleansing" in Bosnia is a similar example.

In the following passage from his classic essay "Politics and the English Language," George Orwell describes how governments often employ euphemisms to disguise and justify wrongful policies.

In our time, political speech and writing are largely the defense of the indefensible. Things like the continuance of British rule in India, the Russian purges and deportations, the dropping of the atom bombs on Japan, can indeed be defended, but only by arguments which are too brutal for most people to face, and which do not square with the professed aims of political parties. Thus political language has to consist largely of euphemism, question-begging and sheer cloudy vagueness. Defenseless villages are bombarded from the air, the inhabitants driven out into the countryside, the cattle machine-gunned, the huts set on fire with incendiary bullets: this is called pacification. Millions of peasants are robbed of their farms and sent trudging along the roads with no more than they can carry: this is called transfer of population or rectification of frontiers. People are imprisoned for years without trial, or shot in the back of the neck or sent to die of scurvy in Arctic lumber camps: this is called elimination of unreliable elements. Such phraseology is needed if one wants to name things without calling up mental pictures of them.

THINKING ↔ WRITING ACTIVITY 5.13

Thinking Critically About Euphemisms

Read the following passage by *New York Times* columnist Bob Herbert, dealing with euphemisms for "getting fired." Then answer these questions in your journal.

1. Why, do you think, are these bureaucratic euphemisms so prevalent?
2. Select an important social problem, such as drug use, crime, poverty, juvenile delinquency, support for wars in other countries, racism, unethical or illegal behavior in government, and so on. List several euphemisms used to describe the problem; then explain how the euphemisms can lead to dangerous misperceptions and serious consequences.

from "Separation Anxiety"
by Bob Herbert

The euphemism of choice for the corporate chopping block is downsizing, but variations abound. John Thomas, a 59-year-old AT&T employee, was told on Tuesday that his job was "not going forward." One thinks of a car with transmission trouble, or the New York Jets offense, not the demise of a lengthy career.

Other workers are discontinued, involuntarily severed, surplussed. There are men and women at AT&T who actually talk about living in a "surplus universe."

There are special leaves, separations, rebalances, bumpings and, one of my favorites, cascade bumpings. A cascade bumping actually sounds like a joyful experience.

In the old days some snarling ogre would call you into the office and say, "Jack, you're fired." It would be better if they still did it that way because that might make the downsized, discontinued, surplussed or severed employee mad as hell. And if enough employees got mad they might get together and decide to do something about the ever-increasing waves of corporate greed and irresponsibility that have capsized their lives and will soon overwhelm many more.

5   Instead, with the niceties scrupulously observed, and with employment alternatives in extremely short supply, the fired workers remain fearful, frustrated, confused, intimidated and far too docile. . . . The staggering job losses, even at companies that are thriving, are rationalized as necessary sacrifices to the great gods of international competition. Little is said about the corrosive effect of rampant corporate greed, and even less about peculiar notions like corporate responsibility and accountability—not just to stockholders, but to employees and their families, to the local community, to the social and economic well-being of the country as a whole.

New York Times, January 19, 1996

Emotive Language

What is your immediate reaction to the following words?

sexy	*peaceful*	*disgusting*	*God*	*filthy*
mouthwatering	*bloodthirsty*	*whore*	*Nazi*	

Most of these words probably stimulate strong feelings in you. In fact, this ability to evoke feelings accounts for the extraordinary power of language.

Making sense of the way that language can influence your thinking and behavior means understanding the emotional dimension of language. Special words (like those just listed) are used to stand for the emotive areas of your experience. These emotive words symbolize the whole range of human feelings, from powerful emotions ("I adore you!") to the subtlest of feeling, as revealed in this passage spoken by Chief Seattle in 1855, responding to a U.S. government proposal to buy his tribe's land and place the tribe on a reservation:

> Every part of this soil is sacred in the estimation of my people. Every hillside, every valley, every plain and grove, has been hallowed by some sad or happy event in days long vanished. . . . The very dust upon which you now stand responds more lovingly to their footsteps than to yours, because it is rich with the blood of our ancestors and our bare feet are conscious of the sympathetic touch. . . . And when the last red man shall have perished, and the memory of my tribe shall have become a myth among the white men, these shores will swarm with the invisible dead of my tribe. . . . At night when the streets of your cities and villages are silent and you think them deserted, they will throng with the returning hosts that once filled and still love this beautiful land. The white man will never be alone. Let him be just and deal kindly with my people, for the dead are not powerless. Dead, did I say? There is no death, only a change of worlds.

Emotive language often plays a double role: it not only symbolizes and expresses our feelings but also arouses or *evokes* feelings in others. When you tell someone, "I love you," you usually are not simply expressing your feelings toward the person; you also hope to inspire similar feelings in that person toward you. Even when communicating factual information, we make use of the emotive influence of language to interest other people in what we are saying. For example, compare the more objective, factual account by *The New York Times* (page 242) of Malcolm X's assassination with the more emotive/action account by *Life* magazine (page 242). Which account do you find more engaging? Why?

Although an emotive statement may be an accurate description of feelings, it is not the same as a factual statement, because it is true only for the speaker—not for others. For instance, even though you may feel that a movie is tasteless and repulsive, someone else may find it exciting and hilarious. By describing your feelings about the movie, you are giving your personal evaluation, which often differs from the personal evaluations of others (it is not unusual to see conflicting reviews of the same movie). A factual statement, on the other hand, is a statement with which all "rational" people will agree, providing that suitable evidence for its truth is available (for example, the fact that mass transit uses less energy than automobiles).

In some ways, symbolizing emotions is more difficult than representing factual information about the world. Expressing feelings toward a person often seems considerably more challenging than describing facts about him or her.

When emotive words are used in larger groups (such as sentences, paragraphs, compositions, poems, plays, novels, and so on), they become even more powerful. The pamphlets of Thomas Paine helped inspire American patriots in the Revolutionary War, and Abraham Lincoln's Gettysburg Address has endured as an expression of Americans' most cherished values. In horrifying contrast were the vehement speeches of Adolf Hitler that influenced German people before and during World War II.

One way to think about the meaning and power of emotive words is to see them on a scale or continuum, from mild to strong. For example:

overweight/plump
fat
obese

The thinker Bertrand Russell used this feature of emotive words to show how we perceive the same trait in various people:

- I am firm.
- You are stubborn.
- He/she is pigheaded.

We usually tend to perceive ourselves favorably ("I am firm"). I am speaking to you face to face, so I view you only somewhat less favorably ("You are stubborn"). But since a third person is not present, you can use stronger emotive language ("He/she is pigheaded"). Try this technique with two other emotive words:

1. I am . . .   You are . . .   He/she is . . .
2. I am . . .   You are . . .   He/she is . . .

Finally, emotive words can be used to confuse opinions with facts, a situation that commonly occurs when we combine emotive uses of language with informative uses. Although people may appear to be giving factual information, they actually may be adding personal evaluations that are not factual. These opinions are often emotional, biased, unfounded, or inflammatory. Consider the following statement: "New York City is filthy and dangerous; only idiots would want to live there." Although the speaker appears at first to be giving factual information, he or she is really using emotive language to advance an opinion. Yet emotive uses of language are not always negative. The statement "She's the most generous, wise, honest, and warm friend anyone could have" also illustrates the potential confusion of the emotive and the informative uses of language, except that in this case the feelings are positive.

Emotive words usually signal that a personal opinion or evaluation, rather than a fact, is being stated. Speakers occasionally do identify their opinions as opinions, with phrases like "In my opinion . . ." or "I feel that. . . ." Often, however, speakers do not identify their opinions as such because they want you to treat their judgments as facts. In these cases, the combination of the informative use of language with the emotive use can be misleading and even dangerous.

THINKING ↔ WRITING ACTIVITY 5.14

Evaluating Emotive Language

Identify examples of emotive language in the following passages and explain how the writer is using it to influence people's thoughts and feelings.

I draw the line in the dust and toss the gauntlet before the heel of tyranny, and I say segregation now, segregation tomorrow, segregation forever.   —Governor George C. Wallace, 1963

We dare not forget today that we are heirs of that first revolution. Let the word go forth from this time and place, to friend and foe alike, that the torch has been passed to a new generation of Americans—born in this century, tempered by war, disciplined by a hard and bitter peace, proud of our ancient heritage—and unwilling to witness or permit the slow undoing of those human rights to which this nation has always been committed, and to which we are committed today at home and around the world.   —President John F. Kennedy, Inaugural Address, 1961

Every criminal, every gambler, every thug, every libertine, every girl ruiner, every home wrecker, every wife beater, every dope peddler, every moonshiner, every crooked politician, every pagan Papist priest, every shyster lawyer, every white slaver, every brothel madam, every Rome-controlled newspaper, every black spider—is fighting the Klan. Think it over. Which side are you on?   —From a Ku Klux Klan circular

We need another and a wiser and perhaps a more mystical concept of animals. Remote from universal nature, and living by complicated artifice, man in civilization surveys the creature through the glass of his knowledge and sees thereby a feather magnified and the whole image in distortion. We patronize them for the incompleteness, for their tragic fate of having taken form so far below ourselves. And therein we err, and greatly err. For the animal shall not be measured by man. In a world older and more complete than ours they move finished and complete, gifted with extensions of the senses you have lost or never attained, living by voices you shall never hear. They are not brethren, they are not underlings; they are other nations, caught with ourselves in the net of life and time, fellow prisoners of the splendor and travail of the earth.   —Henry Beston, *The Outermost House*

THINKING ↔ WRITING ACTIVITY 5.15

Thinking Critically About Racist Speech

One arena where the power and influence of language has become an issue of controversy is that of whether to prohibit racist, sexist, and otherwise offensive speech on college campuses. In the following article, "On Racist Speech," Stanford University law professor Charles R. Lawrence III contends that racial insults do not deserve the First Amendment's protection of free speech because the intention of the speaker "is not to discover truth or initiate dialogue but to injure the victim." Therefore, he believes it is reasonable for colleges to enact rules that punish people who use this sort of speech. In contrast, the next article, "Free Speech on the Campus," by Nat Hentoff, contends that these attempts to restrict free expression pose a grave threat to our freedom of speech. As a writer and as a champion of First Amendment rights, Hentoff believes that such prohibitions not only violate the Constitution but are counterproductive: "After all, if students are to be 'protected' from bad ideas, how are they going to learn to identify and cope with them? Sending such ideas underground simply makes them stronger and more dangerous." After carefully reading the two articles, write answers to these questions in your journal.

1. Summarize the main reasons and arguments that each author uses to support his position.
2. Describe an experience in which you witnessed an example of racist, sexist, or other offensive speech on your campus. What was your reaction to the incident? What are some destructive consequences of behavior like this?
3. Adopt the perspective of Charles R. Lawrence and analyze the incident you witnessed, explaining what the college ought to do in response to this sort of behavior.
4. Now adopt the perspective of Nat Hentoff and analyze the incident, explaining why the college should do nothing in response to this type of behavior.
5. Identify approaches, other than enacting campus rules, that can discourage and prevent racist, sexist, and offensive speech.

from On Racist Speech
by Charles R. Lawrence III

I have spent the better part of my life as a dissenter. As a high-school student, I was threatened with suspension for my refusal to participate in a civil-defense drill, and I have been a conspicuous consumer of my First Amendment liberties ever since. There are very strong reasons for protecting even racist speech. Perhaps the most important of these is that such protection reinforces our society's commitment to tolerance as a value, and that by protecting bad speech from government regulation, we will be forced to combat it as a community.

But I also have a deeply felt apprehension about the resurgence of racial violence and the corresponding rise in the incidence of verbal and symbolic assault and harassment to which blacks and other traditionally subjugated and excluded groups are subjected. I am troubled by the way the debate has been framed in response to the recent surge of racist incidents on college and university campuses and in response to some universities' attempts to regulate harassing speech. The problem has been framed as one in which the liberty of free speech is in conflict with the elimination of racism. I believe this has placed the bigot on the moral high ground and fanned the rising flames of racism.

Above all, I am troubled that we have not listened to the real victims, that we have shown so little understanding of their injury, and that we have abandoned those whose race, gender, or sexual preference continues to make them second-class citizens. It seems to me a very sad irony that the first instinct of civil libertarians has been to challenge even the smallest, most narrowly framed efforts by universities to provide black and other minority students with the protection the Constitution guarantees them.

The landmark case of *Brown v. Board of Education* is not a case that we normally think of as a case about speech. But *Brown* can be broadly read as articulating the principle of equal citizenship. *Brown* held that segregated schools were inherently unequal because of the *message* that segregation conveyed—that black children were an untouchable caste, unfit to go to school with white children. If we understand the necessity of eliminating the system of signs and symbols that signal the inferiority of blacks, then we should hesitate before proclaiming that all racist speech that stops short of physical violence must be defended.

5   University officials who have formulated policies to respond to incidents of racial harassment have been characterized in the press as "thought police," but such policies generally do nothing more than impose sanctions against intentional face-to-face insults. When racist speech takes the form of face-to-face insults, catcalls, or other assaultive speech aimed at an individual or small group of persons, it falls directly within the "fighting words" exception to First Amendment protection. The Supreme Court has held that words which "by their very utterance inflict injury or tend to incite an immediate breach of the peace" are not protected by the First Amendment.

If the purpose of the First Amendment is to foster the greatest amount of speech, racial insults disserve that purpose. Assaultive racist speech functions as a preemptive strike. The invective is experienced as a blow, not as a proffered idea, and once the blow is struck, it is unlikely that a dialogue will follow. Racial insults are particularly undeserving of First Amendment protection because the perpetrator's intention is not to discover truth or initiate dialogue but to injure the victim. In most situations, members of minority groups realize that they are likely to lose if they respond to epithets by fighting and are forced to remain silent and submissive.

Courts have held that offensive speech may not be regulated in public forums such as streets where the listener may avoid the speech by moving on, but the regulation of otherwise protected speech has been permitted when the speech invades the privacy of the unwilling listener's home or when the unwilling listener cannot avoid the speech. Racist posters, fliers, and graffiti in dormitories, bathrooms, and other common living spaces would seem to clearly fall within the reasoning of these cases. Minority students should not be required to remain in their rooms in order to avoid racial assault. Minimally, they should find a safe haven in their dorms and in all other common rooms that are a part of their daily routine.

I would also argue that the university's responsibility for insuring that these students receive an equal educational opportunity provides a compelling justification for regulations that insure them safe passage in all common areas. A minority student should not have to risk becoming the target of racially assaulting speech every time he or she chooses to walk across campus. Regulating vilifying speech that cannot be anticipated or avoided would not preclude announced speeches and rallies—situations that would give minority-group members and their allies the chance to organize counter-demonstrations or avoid the speech altogether

The most commonly advanced argument against the regulation of racist speech proceeds something like this: we recognize that minority groups suffer pain and injury as the result of racist speech, but we must allow this hate mongering for the benefit of society as a whole. Freedom of speech is the lifeblood of our democratic system. It is especially important for minorities because often it is their only vehicle for rallying support for the redress of their grievances. It will be impossible to formulate a prohibition so precise that it will prevent the racist speech we want to suppress without catching in the same net all kinds of speech that it would be unconscionable for a democratic society to suppress.

10   Whenever we make such arguments, we are striking a balance on the one hand between our concern for the continued free flow of ideas and the democratic process dependent on that flow, and, on the other, our desire to further the cause of equality. There can be no meaningful discussion of how we should reconcile our commitment to equality and our commitment to free speech until it is acknowledged that there is real harm inflicted by racist speech and that this harm is far from trivial.

To engage in a debate about the First Amendment and racist speech without a full understanding of the nature and extent of that harm is to risk making the First Amendment an instrument of domination rather than a vehicle of liberation. We have not known the experience of victimization by racist, misogynist, and homophobic speech, nor do we equally share the burden of the societal harm it inflicts. We are often quick to say that we have heard the cry of the victims when we have not.

The *Brown* case is again instructive because it speaks directly to the psychic injury inflicted by racist speech by noting that the symbolic message of segregation affected "the hearts and minds" of Negro children "in a way unlikely ever to be undone." Racial epithets and harassment often cause deep emotional scarring and feelings of anxiety and fear that pervade every aspect of a victim's life.

Brown also recognized that black children did not have an equal opportunity to learn and participate in the school community if they bore the additional burden of being subjected to the humiliation and psychic assault contained in the message of segregation. University students bear an analogous burden when they are forced to live and work in an environment where at any moment they may be subjected to denigrating verbal harassment and assault. The same injury was addressed by the Supreme Court when it held that sexual harassment that creates a hostile or abusive work environment violates the ban on sex discrimination in employment of Title VII of the Civil Rights Act of 1964.

Carefully drafted university regulations would bar the use of words as assault weapons and leave unregulated even the most heinous of ideas when those ideas are presented at times and places and in manners that provide an opportunity for reasoned rebuttal or escape from immediate injury. The history of the development of the right to free speech has been one of carefully evaluating the importance of free expression and its effects on other important societal interests. We have drawn the line between protected and unprotected speech before without dire results. (Courts have, for example, exempted from the protection of the First Amendment obscene speech and speech that disseminates official secrets, that defames or libels another person, or that is used to form a conspiracy or monopoly.)

15   Blacks and other people of color are skeptical about the argument that even the most injurious speech must remain unregulated because, in an unregulated marketplace of ideas, the best ones will rise to the top and gain acceptance. Our experience tells us quite the opposite. We have seen too many good liberal politicians shy away from the issues that might brand them as being too closely allied with us.

Whenever we decide that racist speech must be tolerated because of the importance of maintaining societal tolerance for all unpopular speech, we are asking blacks and other subordinated groups to bear the burden for the good of all. We must be careful that the ease with which we strike the balance against the regulation of racist speech is in no way influenced by the fact that the cost will be borne by others. We must be certain that those who will pay that price are fairly represented in our deliberations and that they are heard.

At the core of the argument that we should resist all government regulation of speech is the ideal that the best cure for bad speech is good, that ideas that affirm equality and the worth of all individuals will ultimately prevail. This is an empty ideal unless those of us who would fight racism are vigilant and unequivocal in that fight. We must look for ways to offer assistance and support to students whose speech and political participation are chilled in a climate of racial harassment.

Civil rights lawyers might consider suing on behalf of blacks whose right to an equal education is denied by a university's failure to insure a nondiscriminatory educational climate or conditions of employment. We must embark upon the development of a First Amendment jurisprudence grounded in the reality of our history and our contemporary experience. We must think hard about how best to launch legal attacks against the most indefensible forms of hate speech. Good lawyers can create exceptions and narrow interpretations that limit the harm of hate speech without opening the floodgates of censorship.

Everyone concerned with these issues must find ways to engage actively in actions that resist and counter the racist ideas that we would have the First Amendment protect. If we fail in this, the victims of hate speech must rightly assume that we are on the oppressors' side.

from Free Speech on the Campus
by Nat Hentoff

A flier distributed at the University of Michigan some months ago proclaimed that blacks "don't belong in classrooms, they belong hanging from trees."

At other campuses around the country, manifestations of racism are becoming commonplace. At Yale, a swastika and the words WHITE POWER! were painted on the building housing the University's Afro-American Cultural Center. At Temple University, a White Students Union has been formed with some 130 members.

Swastikas are not directed only at black students. The Nazi symbol has been spray-painted on the Jewish Student Union at Memphis State University. And on a number of campuses, women have been singled out as targets of wounding and sometimes frightening speech. At the law school of the State University of New York at Buffalo, several women students have received anonymous letters characterized by one professor as venomously sexist.

These and many more such signs of the resurgence of bigotry and know-nothingism throughout the society—as well as on campus—have to do solely with speech, including symbolic speech. There have also been physical assaults on black students and on black, white, and Asian women students, but the way to deal with physical attacks is clear: call the police and file a criminal complaint. What is to be done, however, about speech alone—however disgusting, inflammatory, and rawly divisive that speech may be?

5   At more and more colleges, administrators—with the enthusiastic support of black students, women students, and liberal students—have been answering that question by preventing or punishing speech. In public universities, this is a clear violation of the First Amendment. In private colleges and universities, suppression of speech mocks the secular religion of academic freedom and free inquiry.

The Student Press Law Center in Washington, D.C.—a vital source of legal support for student editors around the country—reports, for example, that at the University of Kansas, the student host and producer of a radio news program was forbidden by school officials from interviewing a leader of the Ku Klux Klan. So much for free inquiry on that campus.

In Madison, Wisconsin, the *Capital Times* ran a story in January about Chancellor Sheila Kaplan of the University of Wisconsin branch at Parkside, who ordered her campus to be scoured of "some anonymously placed white supremacist hate literature." Sounding like the legendary Mayor Frank ("I am the law") Hague of Jersey City, who booted "bad speech" out of town, Chancellor Kaplan said, "This institution is not a lamppost standing on the street corner. It doesn't belong to everyone."

Who decides what speech can be heard or read by everyone? Why, the Chancellor, of course. That's what George III used to say, too.

University of Wisconsin political science professor Carol Tebben thinks otherwise. She believes university administrators "are getting confused when they are acting as censors and trying to protect students from bad ideas. I don't think students need to be protected from bad ideas. I think they can determine for themselves what ideas are bad."

After all, if students are to be "protected" from bad ideas, how are they going to learn to identify and cope with them? Sending such ideas underground simply makes them stronger and more dangerous.

10   Professor Tebben's conviction that free speech means just that has become a decidedly minority view on many campuses. At the University of Buffalo Law School, the faculty unanimously adopted a "Statement Regarding Intellectual Freedom, Tolerance, and Political Harassment." Its title implies support of intellectual freedom, but the statement warned students that once they enter "this legal community," their right to free speech must become tempered "by the responsibility to promote equality and justice."

Accordingly, swift condemnation will befall anyone who engages in "remarks directed at another's race, sex, religion, national origin, age, or sex preference." Also forbidden are "other remarks based on prejudice and group stereotype."

This ukase is so broad that enforcement has to be alarmingly subjective. Yet the University of Buffalo Law School provides no due process procedures for a student booked for making any of these prohibited remarks. Conceivably, a student caught playing a Lenny Bruce, Richard Pryor, or Sam Kinison album in his room could be tried for aggravated insensitivity by association.

When I looked into this wholesale cleansing of bad speech at Buffalo, I found it had encountered scant opposition. One protester was David Gerald Jay, a graduate of the law school and a cooperating attorney for the New York Civil Liberties Union. Said the appalled graduate: "Content-based prohibitions constitute prior restraint and should not be tolerated."

You would think that the law professors and administration at this public university might have known that. But hardly any professors dissented, and among the students only members of the conservative Federalist Society spoke up for free speech. The fifty-strong chapter of the National Lawyers Guild was on the other side. After all, it was more important to go on record as vigorously opposing racism and sexism than to expose oneself to charges of insensitivity to these malignancies.

15   The pressures to have the "right" attitude—as proved by having the "right" language in and out of class—can be stifling. A student who opposes affirmative action, for instance, can be branded a racist.

At the University of California at Los Angeles, the student newspaper ran an editorial cartoon satirizing affirmative action. (A student stops a rooster on campus and asks how the rooster got into UCLA. "Affirmative action," is the answer.) After outraged complaints from various minority groups, the editor was suspended for violating a publication policy against running "articles that perpetuate derogatory or cultural stereotypes." The art director was also suspended.

When the opinion editor of the student newspaper at California State University at Northridge wrote an article asserting that the sanctions against the editor and art director at UCLA amounted to censorship, he was suspended too.

At New York University Law School, a student was so disturbed by the pall of orthodoxy at that prestigious institution that he wrote to the school newspaper even though, as he said, he expected his letter to make him a pariah among his fellow students.

Barry Endick described the atmosphere at NYU created by "a host of watchdog committees and a generally hostile classroom reception regarding any student comment right of center." This "can be arguably viewed as symptomatic of a prevailing spirit of academic and social intolerance of . . . any idea which is not 'politically correct.'"

20   He went on to say something that might well be posted on campus bulletin boards around the country, though it would probably be torn down at many of them: "You ought to examine why students, so anxious to wield the Fourteenth Amendment, give short shrift to the First. Yes, Virginia, there are racist assholes. And you know what, the Constitution protects them, too."

Not when they engage in violence or vandalism. But when they speak or write, racist assholes fall right into this Oliver Wendell Holmes definition—highly unpopular among bigots, liberals, radicals, feminists, sexists, and college administrators: "If there is any principle of the Constitution that more imperatively calls for attachment than any other, it is the principle of free thought—not free only for those who agree with you, but freedom for the thought you hate."

The language sounds like a pietistic Sunday sermon, but if it ever falls wholly into disuse, neither this publication nor any other journal of opinion—right of left—will survive.

WRITING PROJECT

This chapter on language explores the essential role of language in developing sophisticated thinking abilities. The goal of clear, effective thinking and communication—avoiding ambiguity and vagueness—is accomplished through the joint efforts of thought and language. Learning to use the appropriate language style, depending on the social context in which you are operating, requires both critical judgment and flexible expertise with various language forms. Critically evaluating the pervasive attempts of advertisers and others to bypass your critical faculties and influence your thinking involves insight into the way language and thought create and express meaning. We will be examining these relationships between language and thought further in the ensuing chapters, especially in *Chapter 12, Constructing Arguments—Writing to Bring Agreement.*

The following **Writing Project** provides an opportunity for you to apply what you have learned in this chapter to your own writing.

WRITING PROJECT   Language and You

Write a paper in which you discuss some specific aspect of your experience with language. You will analyze some way or ways in which words have affected you. You may want to write about a poem or a song lyric that you love, or how the language in a religious ceremony or political statement influenced you, or about advertisements that made you want or reject the product. You might tell of the impact of statements or remarks from your parents, grandparents, teachers, or friends. You might recount one event or several situations; you can discuss positive or negative effects. When possible, connect your experience with concepts explained in this chapter. After you have drafted your paper, revise it to the best of your ability. Follow directions given by your instructor as to topic limitations, length, format, and so forth.

Because this paper may either focus on one experience or pull several situations together, the principles you need to think about are those involved in writing any paper that connects your personal experience with a complex issue.

1. Make clear that you know that your experience is illustrative, not conclusive, evidence.
2. Present your experience as vividly as you think effective. Use specific details.
3. State clearly your point or thesis about the effect(s) on you. Think about where to do this.

4. Be explicit about the connections you see between your experience and the concepts about language that they illustrate. Perhaps you will quote from the chapter. If you do, cite as directed by your instructor.

Begin by considering the key elements in the **Thinking↔Writing Model** (illustrated in Chapter 1, page 8).

Purpose

You have several purposes for this piece of writing. One is to connect abstract ideas about language with real-life experiences so that you and your readers can understand the concepts better. Another is to deal with the challenge of connecting ideas, a thinking activity that is central to your college studies. As with any writing project, a major purpose is to make your points clear and convincing to your audience.

Audience

Whenever you draw on your own experiences, you are an important member of your own audience because you can clarify your thinking about something that has happened to you. Other people involved in your experiences would probably also be a good audience. As always, consider who would benefit from reading your paper.

Your classmates are an important audience since they share this reading and writing experience and should enjoy learning from your paper. They are a particularly good audience for your drafts. If your instructor encourages or requires peer review sessions, be sure to take advantage of this opportunity to work with knowledgeable readers.

Your instructor is the audience who will judge how well you have planned, drafted, and revised. As a writing teacher, your instructor cares about a clear focus, logical organization, sound evidence, and correctness in finished versions.

Subject

Because, as this chapter has pointed out, language is essential to our definition as human beings, the subject of your paper is tremendously important. Also, because language is a huge subject, one about which fairly simple and very complex ideas abound, writing about some real-life experience can clarify—and test—the ideas you decide to write about.

Writer

Because this project draws on your own experience, you are in a position of authority. However, the project asks you to focus on an aspect of your experience that you might not have thought about before, and it requires an analytical approach rather than a narrative one, even though you may decide to tell of an event. Therefore, you will need a sort of double consciousness as a writer: you want to recall your experience as directly as you can, but then you will have to distance yourself as you analyze what language did or does in the experience that you are writing about.

The Writing Process

The following sections will guide you through the stages of generating, planning, drafting, and revising as you work on this writing assignment.

Generating Ideas

1. Think of times when what you heard, read, or even said had some impact on you. Did someone use harsh language that upset you, or comforting language? Did you say something funny, helpful, embarrassing, or astute? Have you read something over and over? Why?
2. Do you find any common denominator among several experiences? Or does one experience stand out and ask to be told as a single story?
3. Have your significant language experiences involved spoken words more than written ones?
4. Have any of your experiences involved more than one language or more than one dialect or level of usage?
5. Freewrite for five minutes about the ideas that have come to you. Do any of them seem to be developing into a focus for your essay?
6. Look at the questions for generating ideas on pages 13–16 in Chapter 1. Can any of them help you with this project?

Defining a Focus

Draft a thesis statement that makes a point about your experience. If you haven't selected one experience or a cluster of several, draft several possible thesis statements. Share your tentative statement with classmates; do they consider your idea worthwhile? Then list things you might say to develop your thesis.

Organizing Ideas

The organization of this paper will depend on whether you are telling about one or two events or noting a number of experiences. However you approach it, you will need to consider what arrangement will help your audience understand the effects that you are describing. If you are using specific concepts from the chapter, you will have to think about how and where to present them so that their relevance is clear. Maybe a mind map or a web would help.

Drafting

Start with the part that will be easiest to write. Look at your freewriting and your possible thesis statement and your list or map of ideas. Now, work those early-stage writings into a coherent draft. Remember that shaping ideas is your biggest concern at this stage. Trust yourself to speak about your own experiences and to explain what they mean to you.

After you have drafted enough material, give attention to paragraphs.

Where does your material cluster into divisions? Which paragraphs need topic sentences? Where in the paragraphs should topic sentences be placed?

Draft an opening paragraph and a conclusion. What connections exist between them? How can they create an effective beginning and a good ending for your essay?

Revising

Ideally, at this point, you should put your draft aside for a day or two. If deadlines won't permit you to do that, then at least take a break before you try to revise. When you are ready to "re-see" your writing, begin by reading it through slowly, preferably aloud. If possible, have someone whose opinion you respect read it; ask for feedback. Then work through the hierarchy of revision concerns that follows. Remember that you have at least one and possibly two decisions to make for each question: (1) Is improvement needed? and (2) If improvement is needed, how, exactly, can I make my draft better?

1. **Think big.** Look at your draft as a whole.
   - Does it fulfill the assignment in terms of topic and length?
   - Have you stated the thesis clearly?
   - Do all parts of the draft relate to the thesis?
   - Is the organization logical?
   - Do you provide enough evidence?
   - Is your point of view consistent?
   - Is there a discernible flow between your paragraphs?
   - Have you documented information from your sources accurately?
   - Have you used quotation marks around direct quotes or set the quotes off by indenting?

2. **Think medium.** Look at your draft paragraph by paragraph.
   - Will your introduction make your audience want to read on?
   - Is the introduction appropriate for the rest of the draft?
   - Is your focus stated clearly if you are working with a "visible" structure?
   - If you are working with an "invisible" structure, is your focus clearly implied?
   - Are topic sentences used effectively?
   - Does each body paragraph develop a different idea?
   - Should any paragraphs be combined or eliminated?
   - Is your conclusion effective?

3. **Think small.** Look at your draft sentence by sentence.
   - Are any sentences difficult to understand?
   - Are any so long that your audience could get lost in them?

- Are sentences with blended quotations (that is, quotations that are integrated into the syntax of the sentence instead of introduced with "He said . . ." or "She said . . .") complete and easy to read?

- Are quotations shortened with ellipsis marks accurate and readable?

- Are there several choppy sentences that can be combined?

- Are any sentences vague?

- Do any sentences need to be corrected for standard English grammar and usage?

4. **Think "picky."** Look at your draft as your fussiest critic might.

- Are any words not clear or not quite right for your meaning?

- Are any words misspelled?

- Are there any punctuation errors?

- Is your format correct?

- Are the pages numbered consecutively?

- Does your paper make a good impression by being neat?

- Is there anything else you could do to improve your draft?

Editing and Proofreading

After you prepare a final draft, check again for correct grammar and punctuation. Proofread carefully for omitted words or punctuation marks. Run your spelling checker program, but be aware of its limitations. Proofread again for the kinds of errors the computer can't catch.

Student Essay

The following essay shows how one student responded to this assignment. Concluding the chapter is a poem by Roberto Obregon.

STUDENT WRITING
The Power of Language
by Jessie Lange

Language is indeed one of the most powerful things we possess. It is how we communicate our ideas, how we put out abstract feelings for others into words, and it is what we use to describe and evaluate our human experience. Being a "good speaker" in public is something we value highly as we do effective communication in our personal lives. One of the most incredible things about language is the power that just a phrase or even a single word can have. In fact, just a few words often have more of an impact than long speeches and run-on sentences. How does it happen that a small combination of letters can have such a tremendous effect on us?

In the play *Kiss of the Spider Woman* by Manuel Puig, one of the characters, Molina, comments on the power of language. Molina, a gentle soul and an expert storyteller, is desperately in love with the man with whom he is sharing a prison cell. "How does it happen that sometimes someone says something and wins someone else over forever?" he wonders. If only he knew, he could win the love of his cell-mate, Valentin. What Molina is acknowledging is that it doesn't take an infinite number of words to say something powerful. It can be a phrase or even a single word that has the most profound impact on others. In this case, it is the "one thing" uttered that causes another to fall in love with you. In the everyday, there are particular words and phrases that stay with us, that we roll over in our minds, repeating them to ourselves again and again. There are certain words that have such an impact that they stay with us eternally longer than the time it took to utter them. I recently had a personal experience with the effects of this.

After my first four months of college, I returned home for the winter break. After four months of reading inspirational writers, attending the lectures of powerful speakers, learning about language itself in my linguistics course, speaking French, and having discussions with intelligent professors who are at the top of their field, I returned home to be more affected by one word uttered by my twelve-year-old brother than I had been by any of the speaking or listening I'd engaged in first semester. My brother and I have always been extremely close. We do not have the "sibling rivalry" I so often hear about from others. And so, being apart had been a struggle. The fact that we had been apart so long and the impending separation just a few weeks away were probably much of the reason his words had such an effect on me. We were saying goodnight one night and my brother who, in many ways, is a miniature me, was holding my hand. I'd just finished assuring him that he was the "bomb" and he was smiling at me. Somewhere out of his slim twelve-year-old frame a thought emerged in the form of speech: "I wish I could take you with me," he said. "Where?" I asked, thoroughly confused. His smile broadened. "Everywhere," he said matter-of-factly. Such a simple word but, to me, so profoundly meaningful, causing a complete overflow of emotion. I had visions of never letting go of his hand. Of bringing him to college with me, of going to school with him, of bringing him all through my life and never missing a day or a second of his getting older. Just one word: *Everywhere*. If I've learned anything about language it's that the cliché "quality, not quantity" definitely applies. It took one utterance from my brother to almost bring me to tears. With one word, I could imagine myself holding his fingers in mine wherever I went, wherever we went.

Equal to a Pebble
by Roberto Obregon
Translated by Zoe Anglesey

Words, when exposed to air
grow like calves.
Over the years they mature and increase in value
or they may be stillborn.
5   Either one.

The word reveals to us
what constitutes the spirit.
It's a very delicate thing.

In the mouth of a liar
10   it exposes to the bone
a thankless soul.

The word, equal to nuclear power
in good hands can save lives
if not, it amounts to doomsday
15   in a darkened conscience.

By impact of a.word alone
a Hollywood star can fall from grace.
Tyrants fear it
and the guilty prefer not to use it.

20   Like coins we drop words
into the mind of a child
so that with time
the thinking will be a storehouse of riches.

The word is the most precious of gems
25   we give to our loved ones
so they believe and confide in us.
If love falls apart it's proof we lie.

A moist word, vital like earth
whispers in the hush of silence
30   and true it can soothe, be lusty
or instrumental to a plan that urges on a nation.

Sure. People live not by bread alone.
The word also offers sustenance
being what it is:
35   product of my hands, and yours.
And no such things!

Thinking and Writing to Show Relationships

All of us actively shape, as well as discover, the world of our experience in which we live. Our world does not exist as a finished product waiting for us to perceive it, think about it, and describe it with words and pictures. Instead, we are active participants in composing our world— selecting, organizing, and interpreting sensations into a coherent whole. Many times, our shaping of this world will reflect basic thinking patterns that we rely on constantly whenever we think, act, speak, or write.

Part Two explores four basic ways of relating and organizing: relationships in space and time, relationships of comparison, relationships of cause, and relationships of classification and definition. **The Writing Projects** at the end of each chapter ask you to integrate ideas from one, two, or three other sources into your essays as you explore these relationships.

CHAPTER 6

Exploring Relationships in Space and Time—Writing to Show Observations and Sequences

Critical Thinking Focus: Understanding perceptions

Writing Focus: Detail and order in descriptions and chronologies

Reading Theme: Depicting objects and experiences

Writing Project: Narrative that illuminates an issue in society

Experiencing, Perceiving, and Thinking Critically

The way we make sense of the world is through thinking, but our first experiences of the world come to us by means of our senses: sight, hearing, smell, touch, and taste. These senses are our bridges to the world, making us aware of what occurs outside us, and the process of becoming aware of the world through our senses is known as perceiving.

This chapter and Chapter 7 will explore the way the perceiving process operates and how it relates to the ability to think, read, and write effectively. In particular, these chapters examine the way each of us shapes personal experience by actively selecting from, organizing, and interpreting the information provided by the senses. In a way, we each view the world through a pair of individual "contact lenses" that reflect our past experiences and our unique personalities. As critical thinkers, we want to become aware of the nature of our own "lenses," so as to offset any bias or distortion they may be causing. We also want to become aware of the "lenses" of others, so that we can better understand why they view things the way they do.

Some of the most basic patterns of thinking and of presenting ideas seem to draw directly on perceptions, and this chapter will focus on two such patterns of description: **chronological** and **process.** Those two patterns are used in some way in almost every kind of writing and often are starting points for other patterns, as you will see in Chapters 7, 8, and 9. You will also consider the strengths and weaknesses of narratives as examples and evidence. **The Writing Project** offers you an opportunity to integrate material from a published article with a narrative of your own that illuminates an important societal issue.

Thinking Critically About Perceptions

At almost every waking moment of life, our senses are being bombarded by a tremendous number of stimuli: images to see, noises to hear, odors to smell, textures to feel, and flavors to taste. Experiencing all such sensations at once could create what the nineteenth-century American philosopher William James called "a bloomin' buzzin' confusion." Yet to us, the world usually seems much more orderly and understandable. Why is this so?

In the first place, our sense equipment can receive sensations only within certain limited ranges. For example, there are many sounds and smells that animals can detect but we cannot; animals' sense organs have broader ranges in these areas than ours do. A second reason we can handle sensory bombardment is that from the stimulation available, we select only a small amount on which to focus our attention.

To demonstrate this, try the following exercise. Concentrate on what you can see, ignoring your other senses for the moment. Focus on sensations that you were not previously aware of; then answer the first of the following five questions. Concentrate on each of your other senses in turn, following the same procedure.

1. What can you *see?* (for example, the shape of the letters on the page, the design of the clothing on your arm)
2. What can you *hear?* (for example, the hum of the air circulator, the rustling of a page)
3. What can you *feel?* (for example, the pressure of the clothes against your skin, the texture of the page on your fingers)
4. What can you *smell?* (for example, the perfume or cologne someone is wearing, the odor of stale cigarette smoke)
5. What can you *taste?* (for example, the aftereffects of your last meal)

Compare your responses with those of other students in the class. Did your classmates perceive sensations different from the ones you perceived? If so, how do you explain these differences?

By practicing this simple exercise, it should be clear that for every sensation you focus on, there are countless other sensations you are simply ignoring. If you were aware of everything that was happening at every moment, you would be completely overwhelmed. By selecting particular sensations, you are able to make sense of your world in a relatively orderly way. That is, you are *perceiving.*

> **Perceiving**   actively selecting, organizing, and interpreting what is experienced by the senses.

It is tempting to think that our senses simply record what is happening out in the world, as if we were human camcorders. We are not, however, passive receivers of information, "containers" into which sense experience is poured. Instead, we are *active participants* who are always trying to understand the sensations we are encountering. As we perceive the world, our experiences are the result of combining the sensations we are having with the way we understand these sensations. For instance, examine the collection of markings in Figure 6.1. What do you see? If all you see is a collection of black spots, try turning the illustration sideways; you will probably perceive a familiar animal.

Figure 6.1

From this example you can grasp how, when you perceive the world, you are doing more than simply recording what your senses experience: you are actively making sense of these sensations. This collection of black spots suddenly became the figure of an animal because you were able to actively organize the spots into a pattern you recognized. Or think about times when you were able to look up at the white, billowy clouds in the sky and see different figures and designs. The figures you were perceiving were not actually in the clouds but were the result of your giving a meaningful form to shapes you were experiencing.

The same is true for virtually everything we experience. Our perceptions of the world result from combining the information provided by our senses with the way we actively make sense of this information. And since making sense of information is what we are doing when we are thinking, perceiving the world involves using our minds in an active way. Of course, we are usually not aware that we are using our minds to interpret the sensations we are

Your world, and your perception of it, is created by your ongoing experiences and your reflections on these events.

experiencing. We simply see the animal or the figures in the clouds as if they were really there.

Actively Selecting, Organizing, and Interpreting Sensations

When we actively perceive the sensations we are experiencing, we are usually engaged in three distinct activities:

- *Selecting* certain sensations to pay attention to
- *Organizing* these sensations into a design or pattern
- *Interpreting* what this design or pattern means

In the case of Figure 6.1, you were able to perceive an animal because you selected certain of the markings to concentrate on, organized these markings into a pattern, and interpreted this pattern as representing a dog.

Of course, when we perceive, the three operations of selecting, organizing, and interpreting are usually performed quickly, automatically, and often simultaneously. Also, because they are so rapid and automatic, we are normally unaware that we are performing these operations.

Take a few moments to explore more examples that illustrate how you actively select, organize, and interpret your perceptions of the world. Carefully examine Figure 6.2. Do you see both the young woman and the old woman? If you do, try switching back and forth between the two images. As you switch back and forth, notice how for each image, you are doing the following things:

- *Selecting* certain lines, shapes, and shadings on which to focus your attention
- *Organizing* these lines, shapes, and shadings into different patterns
- *Interpreting* these patterns as representing things you can recognize—a hat, a nose, a chin

Figure 6.2

Another way for you to become aware of your active participation in perceiving your world is to consider how you see objects. Examine Figure 6.3. Do you perceive different-sized people, or same-sized people at different distances?

Figure 6.3

When we see someone who is far away, we usually do not perceive a tiny person. Instead, we receive a normal-sized person who is far away. Our experience in the world has enabled us to discover that the farther things are, the smaller they look. The moon in the night sky appears about the size of a quarter, yet we perceive it as considerably larger. As we look down a long stretch of railroad tracks or gaze up at a tall building, the boundary lines seem to come together. Even though these images are what our eyes "see," we do not usually perceive the tracks meeting or the building coming to a point. Instead, our minds actively organize and interpret a world composed of constant shapes and sizes, even though the images seen usually vary, depending on how far away they are and the angle from which they are perceived.

So far, we have been exploring how the mind actively participates in the ways we perceive the world. By combining the sensations we are receiving with the way our minds select, organize, and interpret these sensations, we perceive a world that is stable and familiar. Thus, each of us develops a perspective on the world, a perspective that usually makes sense to us.

The process of perceiving takes place at a variety of different levels. At the most basic level, the concept of "perceiving" refers to the selection, organization, and interpretation of sensations: for example, being able to perceive various objects such as a basketball. However, we also perceive larger patterns of meaning at more complex levels, as in watching the action of a group of people engaged in a basketball game. Although these are very different contexts, both engage us in the process of actively selecting, organizing, and interpreting what is experienced by our senses—in other words, perceiving.

Differences in People's Perceptions

We have noted that our active participation in perceiving the world is something we are not usually aware of. We normally assume that what we are perceiving is what is actually taking place. Only when we find that our perception of the same event differs from the perceptions of others are we forced to examine the manner in which we are selecting, organizing, and interpreting the event.

THINKING ↔ WRITING ACTIVITY 6.1

Interpreting Your Perceptions

Carefully examine the picture of the boy presented in Figure 6.4. What do you think is happening in this picture? Write the answers to questions 1–3 in your journal; then, after you hear the perceptions of other students, add the answers to question 4.

Figure 6.4

1. Describe as specifically as possible what you perceive is taking place in the picture.
2. Describe what you think will take place next.
3. Identify which details of the picture led you to your perceptions.
4. Compare your perceptions with those of other students in the class. List several perceptions that differ from yours.

In most cases, people in a group will have a variety of perceptions about what is taking place in Figure 6.4. Some will see the boy as frustrated because the work is too difficult. Others will see him concentrating on what has to be done. Still others may see him as annoyed because he is being forced to do something he doesn't want to do. In each case, the perception depends on how the person is actively using his or her mind to organize and interpret what is taking place.

Writing Thoughtfully About Sensory Perceptions

While the verb *describe* can be used to mean the giving of any detailed account, it more precisely indicates the reporting of sensory impressions: what one sees, hears, feels, smells, or tastes—one's perceptions. Look back at the questions on page 207 to be reminded of how your five senses responded;

also, reflect on what you have been reading about selecting, organizing, and interpreting sensations. This material should help you understand the two types of descriptions that you will be asked to write in the following **Thinking↔Writing Activity,** descriptions that you might write in other college courses or in work situations.

Descriptions can be broadly divided into two categories: *objective,* with as little judgment as possible, or *subjective,* with whatever personal judgment is appropriate to a writer's purpose. Objective descriptions are often expected in scientific, medical, engineering, and law enforcement writing. An art history course might require an objective description of a painting or a piece of sculpture. The purpose of an objective description is to help the audience sense the item as it "is." Later, judgments and implications can be drawn from objective descriptions, but the cleanest possible rendering is needed as a starting point. Of course, the selection and presentation of *any* ideas or information involves conscious and unconscious judgments; but when objectivity is the purpose, you should try to perceive with as little bias as you can and to describe in language that is as neutral as possible.

In other writing situations, descriptions are intended to be more subjective. Then the explicit purpose is to shape the audience's opinion of the object under scrutiny. Subjective descriptions occur in literary texts of all kinds: stories, poems, personal essays, and biographies; in argumentative pieces; and in personal writing, such as letters to friends and journal entries. Think of how a novelist describes characters or settings; think of how an attorney might reword the police report's objective description of a victim in order to influence a jury; think of how you would describe your new special person to a close friend! When writing a subjective description, you will be selecting details purposefully and using language that creates the effect that you are aiming for.

THINKING↔WRITING ACTIVITY 6.2

Contrasting Objective and Subjective Writing

Read "Woodworking Joints" and the paragraphs from *The Way to Rainy Mountain.* Then write answers to these questions in your journal.

1. Which of these selections is more *objective?* Is it completely so? Identify some objective sentences; identify some that seem subjective.
2. Could you have pictured the joints without the drawings (Fig. 6.5)? If so, what in the description helps you see? If not, rewrite one paragraph, using more graphic language. What effect does your experience with carpentry have on your understanding of this piece?
3. Which of these selections is more *subjective?* Identify some words and sentences that you believe the author is using to influence your thinking. What impressions do you get from these words and sentences?

4. In each selection, identify one or two sentences that you think contribute well to the description. Which senses are involved? What details are effective?

Woodworking Joints

At the heart of woodworking is a question: How do you join two pieces of wood together? In fact, this is the reason why cabinetmaking was traditionally known as the art of "joinery" (see Figure 6.5).

The simplest way to attach two pieces of wood is simply to nail or screw the edge of one board to another. This is known as a butt joint, from the word *abut*. Though this is a simple joint, it is not a very strong joint because it depends entirely on the nail or screw to hold the two pieces together.

The *miter joint,* used in most picture frames, is like a butt joint except that the two edges which are to be joined are cut at an angle (usually 45 degrees) and together form a 90-degree corner.

Although it sounds like a cartoon character, the *dado joint* is in reality a strong, effective joint found in many bookshelves. It is formed by cutting a channel across one of the pieces to be joined, into which the other board fits snugly.

5 To understand the *tongue and groove joint,* imagine sticking your tongue into a small opening—and then having it glued in place! Because of its unusual strength, this joint is used extensively in the construction of furniture (particularly chairs) that will receive considerable active use over its lifetime.

The *dovetail joint,* cut in the shape of a dove's tail, is formed by fitting together two interlocking sets of "tails" in the same way that you interlock your fingers together. It is one of the strongest edge joints and is used in making desk and bureau drawers because of the constant pulling and pushing these joints will receive.

In summary, joining two pieces of wood is not simply a matter of nailing them together—it is an art that has been developed over the last seven thousand years. In each case, the particular wood joint selected should reflect the specific purposes for which the joint will be used.

from The Way to Rainy Mountain

by N. Scott Momaday

A single knoll rises out of the plain in Oklahoma, north and west of the Wichita range. For my people, the Kiowas, it is an old landmark, and they gave it the name Rainy Mountain. The hardest weather in the world is there. Winter brings blizzards, hot tornadic winds arise in the

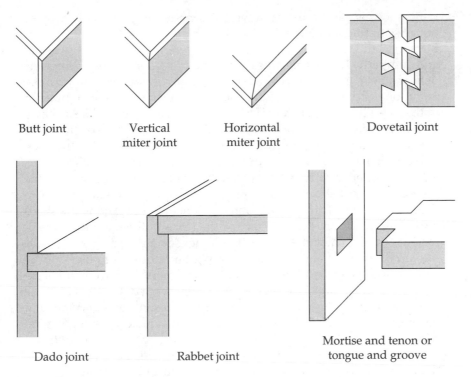

Butt joint Vertical Horizontal   Dovetail joint
miter joint miter joint

Dado joint   Rabbet joint   Mortise and tenon or
tongue and groove

Figure 6.5

spring, and in summer the prairie is an anvil's edge. The grass turns brittle and brown, and it cracks beneath your feet. There are green belts along the rivers and creeks, linear groves of hickory and pecan, willow and witch hazel. At a distance in July or August the steaming foliage seems almost to writhe in fire. Great green and yellow grasshoppers are everywhere in the tall grass, popping up like corn to sting the flesh, and tortoises crawl about on the red earth, going nowhere in the plenty of time. Loneliness is an aspect of the land. All things in the plain are isolate; there is no confusion of objects in the eye, but *one* hill or *one* tree or *one* man. To look upon that landscape in the early morning, with the sun at your back, is to lose the sense of proportion. Your imagination comes to life, and this, you think, is where Creation was begun.

I returned to Rainy Mountain in July. My grandmother had died in the spring, and I wanted to be at her grave. Now that I can have her only in memory, I see my grandmother in the several postures that were peculiar to her: standing at the wood stove on a winter morning and turning meat in a great iron skillet; sitting at the south window, bent above her beadwork, and afterwards, when her vision failed, looking down for a long time into the fold of her hands; going out upon a cane, very slowly as she did when the weight of age came upon her; praying. I remember her most often at prayer. She made long, rambling prayers out of suffering and hope, having seen many things. I was never sure that I had the right to hear, so exclusive were they of all mere custom and company. The last time I saw her she prayed standing by the side of her bed at night, naked to the waist, the light of a kerosene lamp moving upon her dark skin. Her long black hair, always drawn and braided in the day, lay upon her shoulders and against her breasts like a shawl. I do not speak Kiowa, and I never understood her prayers, but there was something inherently sad in the sound, some merest hesitation upon the syllables of sorrow. She began in a high and descending pitch, exhausting her breath to silence; then again and again—and always the same intensity of effort, of something that is, and is not, like urgency in the human voice. Transported so in the dancing light among the shadows of her room, she seemed beyond the reach of time. But that was illusion; I think I knew then that I should not see her again.

Once there was a lot of sound in my grandmother's house, a lot of coming and going, feasting and talk. The summers there were full of excitement and reunion. The Kiowas are a summer people; they abide the cold and keep to themselves, but when the season turns and the land becomes warm and vital they cannot hold still; an old love of going returns upon them. The aged visitors who came to my grandmother's house when I was a child were made of lean and leather, and they bore themselves upright. They wore great black hats and bright ample shirts that shook in the wind. They rubbed fat upon their hair and wound their braids with strips of colored cloth. Some of them painted their faces and carried the scars of old and cherished enmities. They were an old council of warlords, come to remind and be reminded *of* who they were. Their wives and daughters served them well. The women might indulge themselves; gossip was at once the mark and compensation of their servitude. They made loud and elaborate talk among themselves, full of jest and gesture, fright and false alarm. They went abroad in fringed and flowered shawls, bright beadwork and German silver. They were at home in the kitchen, and they prepared meals that were banquets.

Now there is a funereal silence in the rooms, the endless wake of some final word. The walls have closed in upon my grandmother's house. When I returned to it in mourning, I saw for the first time in my life how small it was. It was late at night, and there was a white moon, nearly full. I sat for a long time on the stone steps by the kitchen door. From there I could see out *across* the land; I could see the long row of trees by the creek, the low light upon the rolling plains, and the stars of the Big Dipper. Once I looked at the moon and caught sight of a strange thing. A cricket had perched upon the handrail, only a few inches away. My line of vision was such that the creature filled the moon like a fossil. It had gone there, I thought, to live and die, for there, of all places, was its small definition made whole and eternal. A warm wind rose up and purled like the longing within me.

THINKING ↔ WRITING ACTIVITY 6.3

Creating Objective and Subjective Descriptions

Write two separate paragraphs in which you describe the same person or object in the two ways discussed above. That is, one paragraph will be as objective as possible; the other, mainly subjective in order to create the impression that you want your readers to have. Each paragraph should be of about six to eight sentences.

Which of these paragraphs will have a strong topic sentence? Why? Which will not have a topic sentence or will have one that makes no claim? Why? (If you need a review, see your handbook about topic sentences.)

Writing Thoughtfully About Perceptions of Sequences

Chronological patterns and **process patterns** of thinking organize events or ideas in terms of their occurrence in time, though the two patterns tend to differ in focus. The chronological pattern of thinking organizes something into a series of events in the sequence in which they occurred. Many chronologies are narratives or stories. For example, when we relate a personal experience in the order in which the events occurred, we are presenting it chronologically. The process mode of thinking organizes an activity into a series of steps necessary for reaching a certain end. Here the focus is on describing aspects of growth, development, or change, as we might do when explaining how to prepare a favorite dish or perform a new dance. Processes involve causally connected steps, whereas many chronologies are ordered by time alone.

Chronological Relationships

The simplest examples of time-ordered patterns are chronological descriptions such as logs or diaries, in which people record events that occurred at given points in time. Perhaps the oldest and most universal form of chronological expression is the narrative, a way of thinking and communicating in which someone tells a story about real or fictional experiences. Many people who study communication believe that narrative is a starting point for other patterns of presentation because we often process our perceptions to ourselves in storylike (or filmlike) ways. Then, if we wish to shape what we write or say into exposition, or argument, or poetry, we move away from "simple" narrative and emphasize claims and evidence or images.

Another basic aspect of narration is that every human culture has used narratives to pass on values and traditions from one generation to the next, as is exemplified by such enduring works as the *Odyssey,* the Bible, and the Koran. One of America's great storytellers, Mark Twain, once said that a good story has to accomplish something and arrive somewhere. In other words, if a story is to be effective in engaging the interest of the audience, it has to have a purpose. The purpose may be to provide more information on a subject, to illustrate an idea, to lead the audience to a particular way of thinking, or to entertain. An effective narrative does not merely record the complex, random, and often unrelated events of life. Instead, it has focus, an ordered structure, and a meaningful point of view.

Writers and speakers often use narratives as examples of the points that they are trying to make. In previous **Writing Projects,** you did so in order to examine some of your own thinking experiences. In the **Writing Project** at the end of this chapter, you will again write a narrative, but this time you will connect it to a social issue, rather than to a personal concern. Effective thinkers and writers understand the weakness, as well as the strength, of this kind of support, usually called anecdotal evidence. A story can illustrate a point, often very effectively; but such evidence cannot really prove anything. Anecdotal evidence provides a good starting point for more rigorous thinking.

THINKING ↔ WRITING ACTIVITY 6.4

Analyzing a Chronological Narrative

Read the following chronologically presented narrative by Maria Muniz; then write answers to these questions in your journal.

1. What point is Muniz making with her narrative? Where does she state it? Are her statements well placed? Why?
2. If you or other members of your family have recently come to the United States, draft a similar narrative. What point do you want to make? If your family has been here for generations, draft a fictional narrative in the voice of one of the first arrivals. What point do you want to make?

from Back, But Not Home

by Maria Muniz

With all the talk about resuming diplomatic relations with Cuba, and with the increasing number of Cuban exiles returning to visit friends and relatives, I am constantly being asked, "Would you ever go back?" In turn, I have asked myself, "Is there any reason for me to go?" I have had to think long and hard before finding my answer. *Yes.*

I came to the United States with my parents when I was almost five years old. We left behind grandparents, aunts, uncles and several cousins. I grew up in a very middle-class neighborhood in Brooklyn. With one exception, all my friends were Americans. Outside of my family, I do not know many Cubans. I often feel awkward visiting relatives in Miami because it is such a different world. The way of life in Cuban Miami seems very strange to me and I am accused of being too "Americanized." Yet, although I am now an American citizen, whenever anyone has asked me my nationality, I have always and unhesitatingly replied, "Cuban."

Outside American, inside Cuban.

I recently had a conversation with a man who generally sympathizes with the Castro regime. We talked of Cuban politics and although the discussion was very casual, I felt an old anger welling inside. After 16 years of living an "American" life, I am still unable to view the revolution with detachment or objectivity. I cannot interpret its results in social, political or economic terms. Too many memories stand in my way.

5   And as I listened to this man talk of the Cuban situation, I began to remember how as a little girl I would wake up crying because I had dreamed of my aunts and grandmothers and I missed them. I remembered my mother's trembling voice and the sad look on her face whenever she spoke to her mother over the phone. I thought of the many letters and photographs that somehow were always lost in transit. And as the conversation continued, I began to remember how difficult it often was to grow up Latina in an American world.

It meant going to kindergarten knowing little English. I'd been in this country only a few months and although I understood a good deal of what was said to me, I could not express myself very well. On the first day of school I remember one little girl's saying to the teacher: "But how can we play with her? She's so stupid she can't even talk!" I felt so helpless because inside I was crying, "Don't you know I can understand everything you're saying?" But I did not have words for my thoughts and my inability to communicate terrified me.

As I grew a little older, Latina meant being automatically relegated to the slowest reading classes in school. By now my English was fluent, but the teachers would always assume I was somewhat illiterate or slow. I recall one teacher's amazement at discovering I could read and write just as well as her American pupils. Her incredulity astounded me. As a child, I began to realize that being Latina would always mean proving I was as good as the others. As I grew older, it became a matter of pride to prove I was better than the others.

As an adult I have come to terms with these memories and they don't hurt as much. I don't look or sound very Cuban. I don't speak with an accent and my English is far better than my Spanish. I am beginning my career and look forward to the many possibilities ahead of me.

But a persistent little voice is constantly saying, "There's something missing. It's not enough." And this is why when I am now asked, "Do you want to go back?" I say "yes" with conviction.

10 I do not say to Cubans, "It is time to lay aside the hurt and forgive and forget." It is impossible to forget an event that has altered and scarred all our lives so profoundly.

But I find I am beginning to care less and less about politics. And I am beginning to remember and care more about the child (and how many others like her) who left her grandma behind. I have to return to Cuba one day because I want to know that little girl better.

When I try to review my life during the past 16 years, I almost feel as if I've walked into a theater right in the middle of a movie. And I'm afraid I won't fully understand or enjoy the rest of the movie unless I can see and understand the beginning. And for me, the beginning is Cuba. I don't want to go "home" again; the life and home we all left behind are long gone. My home is here and I am happy. But I need to talk to my family still in Cuba.

Like all immigrants, my family and I have had to build a new life from almost nothing. It was often difficult, but I believe the struggle made us strong. Most of my memories are good ones.

But I want to preserve and renew my cultural heritage. I want to keep "la Cubana" within me alive. I want to return because the journey back will also mean a journey within. Only then will I see the missing piece.

Process Relationships

A second type of time-ordered thinking pattern is the process relationship, which focuses on relating aspects of the growth and development of an event or an experience. From birth, we are involved with processes in every facet of life. They can be classified in various ways: *natural* (such as growing physically), *mechanical* (such as assembling a bicycle), *physical* (such as learning a sport), *mental* (such as developing our thinking), and *creative* (such as writing a poem).

Performing a *process analysis* involves two basic tasks. The first is to divide the process being analyzed into parts or stages. The second is to explain the movement of the process through these parts or stages from beginning to end. The stages identified should be separate and distinct and should involve no repetition or significant omissions.

A process analysis attempts to achieve either of two goals. One goal is to give step-by-step instruction on how to perform an activity, such as taking a photograph or changing a tire. The other goal is to give information about a process, not to teach someone how to perform it. For example, a biology teacher would explain the process of photosynthesis to help students understand how green plants function, not to teach them how to transform sunlight into chlorophyll. Instructions use the pronoun *you*; explanations do not. (This is a good time to ask your professor and consult your handbook as to when to use *you* in college writing—and when not to use it.)

THINKING ↔ WRITING ACTIVITY 6.5

Analyzing Process Writing

After you read the two passages that follow, write answers to these questions in your journal.

1. What is the goal of each paragraph? How can you tell?
2. What are some words in each paragraph that indicate process?

Jacketing was a sleight-of-hand I watched with wonder each time, and I have discovered that my father was admired among sheepmen up and down the valley for his skill at it: He was just pretty catty at that, the way he could get that ewe to take on a new lamb every time. Put simply, jacketing was a ruse played on a ewe whose lamb had died. A substitute lamb quickly would be singled out, most likely from a set of twins. Sizing up the tottering newcomer, Dad would skin the dead lamb, and into the tiny pelt carefully snip four leg holes and a head hole. Then the stand-in lamb would have the skin fitted onto it like a snug jacket on a poodle. The next step of disguise was to cut out the dead lamb's liver and smear it several times across the jacket of pelt. In its borrowed and bedaubed skin, the new baby lamb then was presented to the ewe. She would sniff the baby impostor endlessly, distrustful but pulled by the blood-smell of her own. When in a few days she made up her dim sheep's mind to accept the lamb, Dad snipped away the jacket and recited his victory: Mother him like hell now, don't ye? See what a hellava dandy lamb I got for ye, old sister? Who says I couldn't jacket day onto night if I wanted to, now-I-ask-ye?   —Ivan Doig, *This House of Sky*

If you are inexperienced in relaxation techniques, begin by sitting in a comfortable chair with your feet on the floor and your hands resting easily in your lap. Close your eyes and breathe evenly, deeply, and gently. As you exhale each breath let your body become more relaxed. Starting with one hand direct your attention to one part of your body at a time. Close your fist and tighten the muscles of your forearm. Feel the sensation of tension in your muscles. Relax your hand and let your forearm and hand become completely limp. Direct all your attention to the sensation of relaxation as you continue to let all tension leave your hand and arm. Continue this practice once or several times each day, relaxing your other hand and arm, your legs, back, abdomen, chest, neck, face, and scalp. When you have this mastered and can relax completely, turn your thoughts to scenes of natural tranquillity from your past. Stay with your inner self as long as you wish, whether thinking of nothing or visualizing only the loveliest of images. Often you will become completely unaware of your surroundings. When you open your eyes you will find yourself refreshed in mind and body.   —Laurence J. Peter, *The Peter Prescription*

THINKING ↔ WRITING ACTIVITY 6.6

Writing Process Descriptions

Write two paragraphs about two processes that you understand very well. In one, give instructions to a specific audience who would profit from learning how to perform this activity. In the other, explain—but do not give instructions. (What pronoun should not appear in the second paragraph?)

THINKING ↔ WRITING ACTIVITY 6.7

Analyzing the Process of Dying

Read "We Are Breaking the Silence About Death" and write answers to these questions in your journal.

1. Where in this essay is the process explained? Identify the steps that are given.
2. Obviously, the process discussed in this piece is not a mechanical one, but a complex emotional and psychological sequence. Think of another such human process, perhaps one that you have experienced. What is it, and what are its stages?
3. Write your personal reaction to the ideas in this essay. If someone close to you has died recently, you may have strong reactions. If you have not experienced a loved one's death, you might respond with less emotion. Do you want to share this writing? Why or why not?
4. This article was first published in 1976. Are the concepts in it still relevant? What connections do you see with current questions about the "right to die"?

---

from We Are Breaking the Silence About Death
by Daniel Goleman

Psychiatrist Elisabeth Kübler-Ross and I were to meet and fly together to Colorado Springs, where she was to give a workshop for nurses, doctors and volunteers who work with dying patients. Our flight was soon to board, but there was no sign of Kübler-Ross. Then she appeared, bustling down the corridor, a small, wiry woman carrying two huge shoulder-bags. After the briefest exchange of amenities, she explained that she was concerned that one of her patients might be late *for* the flight. The patient was to be one of 12 dying people at the seminar. They would teach those who work with the dying by sharing their private fears and hopes.

At the last minute her patient, an emaciated but smiling woman, showed up at the gate. Kübler-Ross and I had planned to talk on the plane, but instead she spent the entire flight giving her patient emergency oxygen. Later I learned that Kübler-Ross had met her patient the week before. She saw that the woman had only a few more weeks or months to live, and learned that she had never traveled far from her hometown. So, on the spur of the moment, Kübler-Ross invited her to come along as her guest. She should, the doctor felt, live her remaining days fully.

Kübler-Ross began her work with the dying in the mid '60s when she decided to interview a dying patient for a medical-school seminar she was teaching. She searched the school's 600-bed hospital, asking the staff on each ward if there were any dying patients. On every ward she got the same answer: No. Yet on any given day in a hospital that size, many patients are near death. When she then went back and asked about specific patients, their doctors reluctantly admitted that they were terminally ill.

Medical schools in those days avoided the topic of death and dying. Medical staffs treated the physical problems of their dying patients but, more often than not, ignored the fact of approaching death. Virtually no one, the doctor included, was comfortable with the fact of death. It was taboo, best kept out of sight and out of mind.

5   Once a patient died, he vanished. One of Kübler-Ross's students realized that in all her months as a hospital resident she could hardly recall seeing a dead person. In part she chose to avoid them, but there was also "the remarkable disappearing act that occurs as the body is cleverly whisked out of sight . . ."

In the decade since Kübler-Ross first gave her seminar on dying, the taboo has weakened. Death is in vogue as a topic of books, seminars, scholarly articles, and classes at every level from college down to elementary school. There are two professional journals devoted to the study of death, dozens of volunteer groups working with the dying, and one or two medical facilities geared solely to helping people die with dignity.

There is no single cause for this change, but Elisabeth Kübler-Ross has done more to further it than any other person. Through her 1969 best seller *On Death and Dying,* her seminars for physicians, clergy, and others who work with dying people, and her public talks, Kübler-Ross has alerted us to a new way of handling dying.

Kübler-Ross is Chairman of the National Advisory Council to Hospice in New Haven, Connecticut, which leads the way in humane care of the dying. Modeled on a similar center in London, New Haven Hospice puts Kübler-Ross's advice into practice with a team on call around-the-clock to help people die in their own homes rather than in a strange hospital. Hospice has plans for building a center for dying patients. In contrast to policy at most hospitals, family members will be encouraged to join the medical staff in caring for their dying relatives. Visiting hours will be unlimited, and patients, children and even pets will be free to visit.

Kübler-Ross's natural openness toward the dying reflects her experience as a child in rural Switzerland. In her community, she saw death confronted with honesty and dignity. She also has the authority of one whose medical practice has been limited for the last decade to dying patients and their families; lately, her practice has been restricted to dying children. Her public life as an author and a lecturer allows her a rare luxury in her medical work; she charges no one for her services.

10   Kübler-Ross's career has been unusually humanitarian from the start. Before entering medical school in Switzerland, she worked at the close of the Second World War in eastern Europe, helping the survivors of bombed-out cities and death camps. After becoming a psychiatrist, she gravitated to treating chronic schizophrenics, and then to work with retarded children, whose mental slowness was compounded by being deaf, dumb or blind.

From the thousands of hours she has spent with patients facing death, Kübler-Ross has charted the psychological stages people typically go through once they know they are soon to die. Though any single person need not go through the entire progression, most everyone facing death experiences at least one of these stages. The usual progression is from denial of death through rage, bargaining, depression, and finally, acceptance.

These reactions are not restricted to dying, but can occur with a loss of any kind. We all experience them to some degree in the ordinary course of life changes. Every change is a loss, every beginning an end. In the words of the Tibetan poet Milarepa, "All worldly pursuits end in sorrow, acquisition in dispersion, buildings in destruction, meetings in separation, birth in death."

A person's first reaction to the news that he has a terminal disease is most often denial. The refusal to accept the fact that one is soon to die cushions death's impact. It gives a person time to come to grips with the loss of everything that has mattered to him.

Psychoanalysts recognize that at the unconscious level, a person does not believe he will die. From this refusal to believe in one's own death springs the hope that, despite a life-threatening illness, one will not die. This hope can take many forms: that the diagnosis is wrong, that the illness is curable, that a miracle treatment will turn up. As denial fades into a partial acceptance, the person's concern shifts from the hope of longer life to the wish that his or her family will be well and his affairs taken care of after his death.

15   Denial too often typifies the hospital staff's reaction to a patient who faces death. Doctors and nurses see themselves as healers; a dying

patient threatens this role. Further, a person who cannot contemplate his own death, even if he is a physician, feels discomfort with someone who is dying. For this reason hospital staff often enclose the dying patient in a cocoon of medical details that keeps death under wraps.

Sociologists Barney Glaser and Anselm Strauss studied the mutual pretense that often exists when patient and staff know the patient is dying. A staff member and a terminal patient might safely talk about his disease, they found, so long as they skirt its fatal significance. But they were most comfortable when they stuck to safe topics like movies and fashions—anything, in short, that signifies life going on as usual.

This is a fragile pretense, but not one that either party can easily break. Glaser and Strauss found that a patient would sometimes send cues to the staff that he wanted to talk about dying, but the nurses and doctors would decide not to talk openly with him because they feared he would go to pieces. The patient would openly make a remark acknowledging his death, but the doctor or nurse would ignore him. Then, out of tact or empathy for the embarrassment or distress he caused, the patient would resume his silence. In this case, it is the staff's uneasiness that maintains the pretense, not the patient's.

In the reverse instance, a doctor may give the patient an opening to talk about dying, and have the patient ignore it. Kübler-Ross urges hospital staff members to let the patient know that they are available to talk about dying, but not to force the subject on the patient. When he no longer needs to deny his death, the patient will seek out a staff member and open the topic.

When the family knows a patient is dying and keeps the secret from him, they create a barrier that prevents both patient and family from preparing for the death. The dying patient usually sees through a make-believe, smiling mask. Genuine emotions are much easier on the patient, allowing relatives to share his feelings. When his family can be open about the seriousness of the illness, there is time to talk and cry together and to take care of important matters under less emotional pressure.

20   A student nurse hospitalized for a fatal illness wrote to her professional colleagues in a nursing journal: "You slip in and out of my room, give me medications and check my blood pressure. Is it because I am a student nurse myself that I sense your fright? If only we could be honest, both admit our fears, touch one another. Then it might not be so hard to die—in a hospital—with friends close by."

Denial becomes increasingly hard as the patient's health deteriorates. Although mutual pretense avoids embarrassment and emotional strains, it sacrifices valuable time in which the dying patient and his family could take care of unfinished emotional and practical matters, like unsettled arguments or unwritten wills, that death will forestall forever.

Kübler-Ross feels that a period of denial is useful if it gives the patient and his family time to find a way to deal with the stark truth of death. But when denial persists until the person dies, the survivors' grief is needlessly prolonged by the guilt and regrets. Often patients near death say they wished they had been told they were dying sooner so that they could have prepared themselves and their families.

A few rare patients, though, need to cling to denial because the reality is too much to bear. When those closest to the person offer no love or comfort, as when children of the dying patient blame the parent for deserting them, the patient may deny the inevitable to the very end. But this is rare; of 500 patients, Kübler-Ross found only four who refused to the last to admit that they were dying.

Once a dying patient accepts the invitation to talk about his death, Kübler-Ross tries to help him recognize any unfinished business that needs his attention. Straightforward truth helps the dying person fully live the time left. She tries to elicit their hidden hopes and needs, then find someone who can fulfill these needs.

25   Physical pain sometimes prevents a dying patient from making the best use of his remaining days. When his pain is overwhelming, he either becomes preoccupied with it or dependent on painkillers that leave him groggy. Kübler-Ross controls pain with Brompton's mixture. This old-time formula of morphine, cocaine, alcohol, syrup, and chloroform water dulls the patient's pain without dimming his alertness.

When a patient stops denying his impending death, the feelings that most often well up are rage and anger. The question, "Why me?" is asked with bitterness. The patient aims his resentment at whoever is handy, be it staff, friends or family. Healthy people remind the patient that he will die while they live. The unfairness of it all arouses his rage. He may be rude, uncooperative, or downright hostile. For example, when a nurse was late with his pain medication, the patient snapped "Why are you late? You don't care if I suffer. Your coffee break is more important to you than my pain."

As the rage abates the patient may start to bargain with God or fate, trying to arrange a temporary truce. The question switches from "Why me?" to "Why now?" He hopes for more time to finish things, to put his house in order, to arrange for his family's future needs, to make a will. The bargain with God takes the form of the patient promising to be good or to do something in exchange for another week, month, or year of life.

With full acceptance of his approaching death, a person often becomes depressed. Dying brings him a sense of hopelessness, helplessness and isolation. He mourns past losses, and regrets things left undone or wrongs he's committed. One of Kübler-Ross's patients, for example, regretted that when his daughter was small and needed him, he was on the road making money to provide a good home. Now that he was dying, he wanted to spend every moment he could with her, but she was grown and had her own friends. He felt it was too late. At this stage the dying person starts to mourn his own death, the loss of all the people and things he has found meaningful, the plans and hopes never to be fulfilled. Kübler-Ross calls this kind of depression a "preparatory grief." It allows a person to get ready for his death by letting go of his attachments to life.

During this preparatory grief, the patient may stop seeing family and friends, and become withdrawn and silent. His outer detachment matches the inner renouncement of what once mattered to him. Family members sometimes misinterpret his detachment as a rejection. Kübler-Ross helps them to see that the patient is beginning to accept his death. Hence, he needs much less contact with family and friends.

30   After this preparatory mourning, the dying person can reach a peaceful acceptance. He is no longer concerned with the prolongation of his life. He has made peace with those he loves, settled his affairs, relinquished his unfinished dreams. He may feel an inner calm, and become mellow in outlook. He can take things as they come, including the progress of his illness. People bring him pleasure, but he no longer speaks of plans for the future. His focus becomes the simple joys of everyday life; he enjoys today without waiting for tomorrow. At this stage, the person is ready to live his remaining days fully and die well. The story of a modern Zen master's death shows this frame of mind. As the master lay dying, one of his students brought him a special cake, of which he had always been fond. With a wan smile the master slowly ate a piece of the cake. As he grew weaker still, his students leaned close and asked if he had any final words for them. "Yes," he said, as they leaned forward eagerly. "My, but this cake is delicious."

What the dying teach us, says Kübler-Ross, is how to live. In summing up what she has learned from her dying patients, she likes to recite a poem by Richard Allen that goes:

. . . as you face your death, it is only the love you have given and received which will count . . . if you have loved well then it will have been worth it . . . but if you have not death will always come too soon and be too terrible to face.

WRITING PROJECT

The readings and **Thinking↔Writing Activities** in this chapter encouraged you to think about describing and narrating in ways appropriate to the purpose of a particular piece of writing. Be sure to reread what you wrote for those activities because you may be able to use some of it to help yourself complete this project.

WRITING PROJECT	Narrative That Illuminates an Issue in Society

Write an essay telling about an experience that either you or someone you know had that threw some light on an issue in society. The issue may perhaps involve race, ethnicity, gender, education, housing, or employment. Be sure to choose an issue you are concerned about. Find a magazine or newspaper article dealing with the issue and quote from it at least once in your essay. Document the quoted material according to your professor's instructions. If she or he requires an academic documentation format, such as Modern Language Association (MLA) or American Psychological Association (APA), be sure to conform exactly to the models in your handbook. After drafting your essay, revise it to the best of your ability. Follow instructions given by your professor as to topic limitations, length, format, and so on.

The following principles for writing illustrative narratives are not fixed rules; you may have good reason for not following some of them. In general, though, they should help you to write an effective, responsibly handled essay.

1. Make clear that the story you tell is an example or illustration, not an item of conclusive evidence.
2. Identify the relevant issue fully so that the narrative has a meaningful context.
3. State your thesis well; place it effectively in your paper.
4. Use description to introduce your readers to the people involved; to let your readers visualize the place; to invoke several of their senses. Consider whether subjective or objective description, or a combination of the two, will serve your purpose better.
5. Tell the story as fully as seems appropriate, without either running on and on or leaving out important details or events.
6. Be sure to begin and end effectively. The conclusion is likely to be especially important in this essay, since you may want to reiterate your main point there.

Begin by considering the key elements in the **Thinking↔Writing Model.**

Purpose

You have a variety of purposes here. You have the opportunity to recall and relate a significant experience. You also can think about a social issue that concerns you and learn more about it by finding the required article. In addition, you will be improving your ability to connect what you read with your own ideas, something you must do regularly as a college student. Most important, you can inform your classmates, your professor, and your other readers about the issue of concern to you. Finally, by connecting the issue with what the author of the article has written and with an actual experience, you will increase its meaning to your audience. As a student in a college writing class, you have the additional purpose of completing your assignment well.

Audience

As always, you are a member of your own audience and perhaps the person who will enjoy the narrative most, since it is connected with your life. If you are telling someone else's story, that person, of course, will be a most interested reader. Your classmates will be a good audience, both to learn from your narrative and to share your experience; in addition, they are a valuable audience as peer reviewers of your draft, reacting as intelligent readers who are also immersed in the assignment. Of course, anyone else involved with the issue would also benefit from your essay. Finally, your professor remains the audience who will judge how well you have planned, drafted, and revised. As a writing teacher, he or she cares about a clear focus, logical organization, specific details, and correctness. Keep these in mind as you revise, edit, and proofread.

Subject

Although you and your readers are doubtless concerned about many social issues, both you and they may need to be reminded of how one such issue affects your life or that of someone you know. People do at times forget how connected they may be to situations the media present. In addition, it is valuable to reflect on the validity of anecdotal evidence: To what extent does your narrative illuminate a widespread situation in society?

Writer

You are in a dual position here. You are, of course, the expert on your own story. This is both an advantage and a disadvantage: no one can argue with you about your story, but you need to remember that your audience was not there. You must provide them with sufficient background and description to make them feel as if they did share the experience with you, but you don't want to overwhelm them with details. Therefore, you will need to be selective as you decide what to include and what to omit. Yet you are not the expert on the article from which you plan to quote, so do think carefully about what it says and where to refer to it in your own work.

The Writing Process

The following sections will guide you through the stages of generating, planning, drafting, and revising as you work on an illustrative and descriptive narrative.

Generating Ideas

1. You may have had (or witnessed or heard about) such a meaningful experience that you know immediately what you want to narrate. If not, think about events that were worrisome, or frightening, or amusing, or exciting and then think again about the context of the event.
2. You may be deeply involved in some social issue because of who you are or where you live or which organizations you support. If so, you should have no problem identifying the concern you want to address. If not, look around, talk with friends and family members, read newspapers and magazines, and watch the news.
3. Think locally. Look at problems in your community or at issues connected with your college or your job. Then try to recall any personal experiences related to these concerns.
4. Think of how a local issue may be part of a national or a worldwide one. Here, you will need to consult and acknowledge sources if you have not had direct experience with such situations.

Defining a Focus

Draft a thesis sentence that connects your experience with the issue you plan to write about. You may want to emphasize the directness of the connection, or you may need to show that what is not obvious is indeed related. You may want to emphasize a time element: "I didn't understand at the time, but now I see that . . ." or "I knew at that moment that . . ." Perhaps you will want to focus on the impact of this issue on your life and on the lives of others.

Organizing Ideas

This essay is likely to be organized somewhat like Maria Muniz's essay on pages 218–220, with introductory and concluding paragraphs that state the point, and the narration in between. Or statements about the issue might be made regularly throughout the narration, as different events show various aspects of the situation. Some writers might tell the story first and then connect it with the issue. You need to consider what arrangements will best help your audience see the connection that you want to make. Be sure to select carefully and place carefully the material quoted from your source, and to connect that material smoothly with your writing by introducing it and commenting on it.

Drafting

Begin with the easiest part to write, possibly the experience itself. Tell it fully; then plan to increase its effectiveness by including sharp details and a tight sequence of events at the revision stage. The paragraphs within the narrative may or may not have topic sentences. This is one of the differences between narration and exposition. Since your purpose is to connect the experience with an issue, you may want to have topic sentences for the paragraphs which do that.

After you have drafted the narrative, draft the paragraphs that state the thesis and make the connection between the experience and the issue. Then establish and write any needed transitions between and among the sections of your draft.

Revising

Ideally, at this point, you should put your draft aside for a day or two. If deadlines won't permit that, then at least take a break before you try to revise. When you are ready to "re-see" your writing, begin by reading it through slowly, preferably aloud. If possible, have someone whose opinion you respect read it; if you are fortunate enough to have peer review in class, ask for feedback and consider it carefully. Then work through the hierarchy of revision concerns that follow.

1. **Think big.** Look at your draft as a whole.
- Does it fulfill the assignment in terms of topic and length?
- Have you stated the thesis clearly?
- Do all parts of the draft relate to the thesis?
- Is the organization logical?
- Do you provide enough evidence?
- Is your point of view consistent?
- Is there a discernible flow between your paragraphs?
- Have you documented information from your sources accurately?
- Have you used quotation marks with direct quotes or set them off by indenting them?
2. **Think medium.** Look at your draft paragraph by paragraph.
- Will your introduction make your audience want to read on?
- Is the introduction appropriate for the rest of the draft?
- Is your focus stated clearly if you are working with a "visible" structure?
- If you are working with an "invisible" structure, is your focus clearly implied?
- Are topic sentences used effectively?

- Does each body paragraph develop a different idea?
- Should any paragraphs be combined or eliminated?
- Is your conclusion effective?

3. **Think small.** Look at your draft sentence by sentence.
- Are any sentences difficult to understand?
- Are any so long that your audience could get lost in them?
- Are sentences with blended quotations (that is, quotations that are integrated into the syntax of the sentence instead of introduced with "He said . . ." or "She said . . .") complete and easy to read?
- Are quotations shortened with ellipsis marks accurate and readable?
- Are there several choppy sentences that can be combined?
- Are any sentences vague?
- Do any sentences need to be corrected for standard English grammar and usage?

4. **Think "picky."** Look at your draft as your fussiest critic might.
- Are any words not clear or not quite right for your meaning?
- Are any words misspelled?
- Are there any punctuation errors?
- Is your format correct?
- Are the pages numbered consecutively?
- Does your paper make a good impression by being neat?
- Is there anything else you could do to improve your draft?

Proofreading

After you prepare a final draft, check for standard grammar and punctuation. Proofread carefully for omitted words or punctuation marks. Run your spelling checker program, but be aware of its limitations. Proofread carefully for the kinds of errors the computer can't catch.

Student Essay

The following essay shows how one student responded to this assignment.

STUDENT WRITING
Unfair Expectations
by Angelica Willey

The most influential people in a child's world are her or his parents. Parents, therefore, should try to be aware of their biases based on traditions inherited from their upbringings that are not appropriate for a younger generation. If they are not careful, parents can limit the potential of their children by not recognizing that some preconceived notions that they carry over from their childhoods are not helpful to their children. This situation happened in my life when my father couldn't reconcile his generation's version of gender roles with a more modern version for the raising of his children.

My father is a born and bred southern gentleman. Being raised on the eastern shore (across the Bay), he connects with the old southern way of doing things. He plants Crepe Myrtles, refuses to walk ahead of a lady through a doorway, and speaks with a slight accent if you catch him off guard. However, he also has a tendency towards admiring "southern" ladies who carry parasols to shield the sun and act out an overplayed shyness to attract "gentleman callers." Somehow he envisioned me as fitting into that mold, and he took it upon himself to make sure that I lived up to those standards which he admired.

The earliest incident which I can recall of my father acting on these notions occurred when my best childhood friend from across the road took off his shirt to relieve the heat of a summer day. Watching this, through my five year old eyes, I decided to also cool down by removing my shirt. Upon seeing this, my father flew out of the house and herded me inside, all the while trying to explain why I could not do the same thing as a boy. These tendencies became most apparent after the birth of my brother.

Though I was five years his senior, my brother was treated as if, solely due to his gender, he was entitled to special privileges in some areas. For example, he was allowed to get his driver's license at the minimum age of sixteen because he had to take girls out on dates. I was told that I would not be allowed to have my license until I turned eighteen because it was not a necessity—my dates could pick me up. Never mind that I had a job, internship, and a school career to maintain. While I'm sure that he sent my brother back to wash his face when we were going out, his nudges at me to go back and put on some make-up and change to a dress had a negative effect on my attitude and my self-esteem.

Today I know that my father was not trying to inhibit me. He was simply acting on the way he was raised. He probably wanted me to become the kind of woman that one article calls "The Princess, the most desirable woman in patriarchal culture and fantasy," a woman who "waits for a man to make her life meaningful" (Gilbert and Webster 47). However, I don't want to be a helpless, flirtatious "princess." I want to be an independent, capable person who has good relationships with men, and with women. I like to look nice, but I don't want to worry very much about make-up and dresses. Most of my fellow, female students feel the same way that I do.

I suppose that there will always be generation gaps. However, parents need to think about their hand-me-down ideals and try to have fair expectations that fit with their children's generation's ideas.

Work Cited

Gilbert, Lucy, and Paula Webster. "The Dangers of Feminity," *The Gender Reader*, ed. Evelyn Ashton Jones and Gary Olson. Boston: Allyn and Bacon, 1991.

CHAPTER 7

Exploring Comparative Relationships—
Writing About Perspectives

Critical Thinking Focus: Critically evaluating perceptions

Writing Focus: Comparing and contrasting

Reading Theme: Recognizing differing perspectives

Writing Project: Critically evaluating different perspectives on an issue or an event

Thinking Critically About Differing Perceptions

Chapter 6 introduced the concept of perceptions and showed how writers use their perceptions when they describe, narrate, and explain processes. Chapter 7 emphasizes critical evaluation of perceptions. It will help you think about the differing perspectives people bring to what they say and write. Because so many life situations and college assignments involve comparing and contrasting perspectives in an organized way, we will be considering some steps and strategies involved in thinking critically and writing thoughtfully about differing perspectives. The **Writing Project** asks you to analyze different perspectives on one issue or event.

To understand how various people can be exposed to the same stimuli or events and yet have different perceptions, it helps to imagine that each of us views the world through a personal pair of "contact lenses," an analogy we introduced in the previous chapter. We aren't usually aware that we are wearing these lenses. Instead, without our realizing it, our lenses act as filters that select and shape what we perceive. When members of your class had different perceptions of the boy at the desk in **Thinking↔Writing Activity 6.1,** those different perceptions were caused by the different lenses through which each of you views the world.

To understand the way people perceive the world, we have to understand their individual lenses, which influence how they actively select, organize, and interpret the events in their experience. A diagram of the process might look like Figure 7.1:

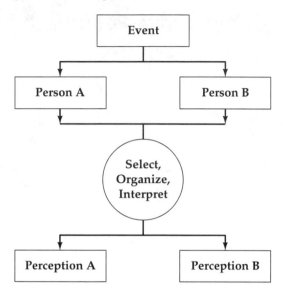

Figure 7.1

Consider the following pairs of statements. In each pair, two people are being exposed to the same basic stimulus or event, yet each has a very different perception of the experience. Explain how the various perceptions might have developed.

1. a. That chili was much too spicy to eat.
      Explanation:
   b. That chili needed more hot peppers and chili powder to spice it up a little.
      Explanation:
2. a. People who wear lots of make-up and jewelry are very sophisticated.
      Explanation:
   b. People who wear lots of make-up and jewelry are ostentatious and overdressed.
      Explanation:
3. a. The music young people enjoy listening to is a highly creative cultural expression.
      Explanation:
   b. The music young people enjoy listening to is obnoxious noise.
      Explanation:

Effective critical thinkers are aware of the lenses that they—and others—are wearing. People unaware of the nature of their own lenses can often mistake their own perceptions for objective truth, not having examined either the facts or others' perceptions of a given issue.

In Figure 7.2, "The Investigation," each witness is giving what he or she (or it!) believes is an accurate description of the man in the center, and all the witnesses are unaware that their descriptions are being influenced by who they are and the way that they perceive things.

Figure 7.2

Selecting Perceptions

We tend to *select* perceptions about subjects that have been called to our attention. For instance, at the age of three, one child suddenly became aware of beards. On entering a subway car, she would ask in a penetrating voice, "Any beards here?" and proceed to count them out loud. In so doing, she naturally focused her parents' attention—as well as that of other passengers—on beards.

Another aspect of our "perceiving" lenses is our tendency to notice what we need, desire, or otherwise find of interest. When we go shopping, we focus on whatever items we are looking for. Walking down the street, we tend to notice certain kinds of people or events while completely ignoring others. Even while watching a movie or reading a book, we tend to concentrate on and remember the elements we find of interest. Another person can perform *exactly* the same actions—shop at the same store, walk down the same street, read the same book, or go to the same movie—and yet see and remember entirely different things. What we do or do not see does indeed depend largely on our personal interests, needs, and desires.

Feelings—moods or emotional states—can also affect the perceptions we select. When in a bad mood, we often are ready to focus on every potential insult or criticism by others—and ready to respond the same way.

Although we tend to focus on what is familiar, normally we are not aware of doing so. In fact, we often take for granted what is familiar to us—the taste of chili or eggs, the street that we live on, our family or friends—and normally don't think about our perception of it. When something happens that makes the familiar seem strange and unfamiliar, though, we become aware of our perceptions and start to evaluate them.

To sum up, we actively select our perceptions on the basis of

■   what has been called to our attention,

■   what our needs or interests are,

■   what our moods or feelings are, and

■   what seems familiar or unfamiliar.

The way we select perceptions is a paramount factor in shaping the lenses through which we view the world.

Organizing Perceptions

Not only do you actively select certain perceptions; you also actively *organize* them into meaningful relationships and patterns. Consider the series of lines in Figure 7.3.

Figure 7.3

Did you perceive them as individual lines, or did you group them into pairs? We naturally try to order and organize what we are experiencing into patterns and relationships that make sense to us. When we succeed in doing so, the completed whole means more than the sum of the individual parts.

We are continually organizing the world in this way at virtually every waking moment. We do not live in a world of isolated sounds, patches of color, random odors, and individual textures. Instead, we live in a world of objects and people, language and music—a world in which all these individual stimuli are woven together. We are able to perceive this world of complex experiences because we can organize the individual stimuli we are receiving into relationships that have meaning to us.

Interpreting Perceptions

Besides selecting and organizing perceptions, we also actively *interpret* what we perceive: we are figuring out what something means. One of the elements that influences interpretations is the *context*, or overall situation, within which the perception is occurring. For example, imagine that you see a man running down the street. Your interpretation of his action will depend on the specific context. For example, is there a bus waiting at the corner? Is a police officer running behind him? Is the man wearing a jogging suit?

We are continually trying to interpret what we perceive, whether it is a design, someone else's behavior, or a social situation. As in the example of someone running down the street, many perceptions can be interpreted in more than one way. When a situation has more than one possible interpretation, it is ambiguous. The more ambiguous a situation is, the greater its possible meanings or interpretations.

Our perceptions reveal the lenses through which we are viewing each event. Watching our team play baseball, for example, we may really believe that the opposing runner was "out by a mile"—even though the replay may show otherwise.

Similarly, feelings can influence our interpretations of experience. When we feel happy and optimistic, the world often seems friendly and the future full of possibilities, and we interpret problems as challenges to be overcome. When we are depressed or unhappy, we may perceive the world entirely differently. The future can appear full of problems that are trying to overcome us. In both cases the outer circumstances may be very similar; it is our own interpretations of the world through our lenses that varies so completely.

Perceptions of the world are also influenced by the way we were brought up by our training and education. Consider two people watching a football game. One of them, who has very little understanding of football, sees merely a bunch of grown men hitting each other for no apparent reason. The other person, who loves football, sees complex play patterns, daring coaching strategies, effective blocking and tackling techniques, and zone defenses with seams that the receivers are trying to split. Both spectators have their eyes focused on the same event, but they are perceiving two entirely different situations. Their perceptions differ because each person is actively selecting, organizing, and interpreting the available stimuli in different ways.

The same is true of any situation in which we are perceiving something about which we have special knowledge or expertise. The following are examples.

- A builder examining the construction of a new house
- A music lover attending a concert
- A naturalist experiencing the outdoors
- A cook tasting a dish just prepared
- A lawyer examining a contract
- An art lover visiting a museum

Think about a special area of interest or expertise that you have and how your perceptions of that area differ from those of people who don't share your knowledge. Ask other class members about their areas of expertise. Notice how their perceptions of those areas differ from your own because of these classmates' greater knowledge and experience.

In all the cases just discussed, the perceptions of the knowledgeable person differ substantially from those of a person who lacks the same specialized knowledge. The following reading illuminates this point.

from Two Ways of Viewing the River
by Mark Twain

Now when I had mastered the language of this water and had come to know every trifling feature that bordered the great river as familiarly as I knew the letters of the alphabet, I had made a valuable acquisition. But I had lost something, too. I had lost something which could never be restored to me while I lived. All the grace, the beauty, the poetry, had gone out of the majestic river! I still kept in mind a certain wonderful sunset which I witnessed when steamboating was new to me. A broad expanse of the river was turned to blood; in the middle distance the red hue brightened into gold, through which a solitary log came floating, black and conspicuous; in one place a long, slanting mark lay sparkling upon the water; in another the surface was broken by boiling, tumbling rings, that were as many-tinted as an opal; where the ruddy flush was faintest, was a smooth spot that was covered with graceful circles and radiating lines, ever so delicately traced; the shore on our left was densely wooded and the somber shadow that fell from this forest was broken in one place by a long, ruffled trail that shone like silver; and high above the forest wall a clean-stemmed dead tree waved a single leafy bough that glowed like a flame in the unobstructed splendor that was flowing from the sun. There were graceful curves, reflected images, woody heights, soft distances, and over the whole scene, far and near, the dissolving lights drifted steadily, enriching it every passing moment with new marvels of coloring.

I stood like one bewitched. I drank it in, in a speechless rapture. The world was new to me and I had never seen anything like this at home. But as I have said, a day came when I began to cease from noting the glories and the charms which the moon and the sun and the twilight wrought upon the river's face; another day came when I ceased altogether to note them. Then, if that sunset scene had been repeated, I should have looked upon it without rapture, and should have commented upon it inwardly after this fashion: "This sun means that we are going to have wind tomorrow; that floating log means that the river is rising, small thanks to it; that slanting mark on the water refers to a bluff reef which is going to kill somebody's steamboat one of these nights, if it keeps on stretching out like that; those tumbling 'boils' show a dissolving bar and a changing channel there; the lines and circles in the slick water over yonder are a warning that the troublesome place is shoaling up dangerously; that silver streak in the shadow of the forest is the 'break' from a new snag and he has located himself in the very best place he could have found to fish for steamboats; that tall dead tree, with a single living branch, is not going to last long, and then how is a body ever going to get through this blind place at night without the friendly old landmark?"

No, the romance and beauty were all gone from the river. All the value any feature of it had for me now was the amount of usefulness it could furnish toward compassing the safe piloting of a steamboat. Since those days, I have pitied doctors from my heart. What does the lovely flush in a beauty's cheek mean to a doctor but a "break" that ripples above some deadly disease? Are not all her visible charms sown thick with what are to him the signs and symbols of hidden decay? Does he ever see her beauty at all, or doesn't he simply view her professionally and comment upon her unwholesome condition all to himself? And doesn't he sometimes wonder whether he has gained most or lost most by learning his trade?

THINKING ↔ WRITING ACTIVITY 7.1

Five Accounts of the Assassination of Malcolm X

Let's examine a situation in which a number of different people had somewhat different perceptions about an event they were describing. The second chapter of this book contains a passage by Malcolm X (pages 35–37), written when he was just beginning his life's work. A few years later, this work came to a tragic end with his assassination at a meeting in Harlem. As you read through the various accounts, pay particular attention to the perceptions each presents. After reading the accounts, analyze some of the differences in these perceptions by writing answers in your journal to the questions that follow. You may decide to limit your answer to two or three of the accounts.

1. What details of the events has each writer *selected* to focus on?
2. How has each writer *organized* the details selected? Remember that most newspapers present what they consider the most important information first and the least important last.
3. How does each writer interpret Malcolm X, his followers, the gunmen, and the significance of the assassination?
4. How has each author used language to express his or her perspective and to influence the reader's thinking?

The New York Times (February 22, 1965)

Malcolm X, the 39-year-old leader of a militant Black Nationalist movement, was shot to death yesterday afternoon at a rally of his followers in a ballroom in Washington Heights. The bearded Negro extremist had said only a few words of greeting when a fusillade rang out. The bullets knocked him over backwards.

A 22-year-old Negro, Thomas Hagan, was charged with the killing. The police rescued him from the ballroom crowd after he had been shot and beaten.

Pandemonium broke out among the 400 Negroes in the Audubon Ballroom at 160th Street and Broadway. As men, women and children ducked under tables and flattened themselves on the floor, more shots were fired. The police said seven bullets struck Malcolm. Three other Negroes were shot. Witnesses reported that as many as 30 shots had been fired. About two hours later the police said the shooting had apparently been a result of a feud between followers of Malcolm and members of the extremist group he broke with last year, the Black Muslims. . . .

Life (March 5, 1965)

His life oozing out through a half dozen or more gunshot wounds in his chest, Malcolm X, once the shrillest voice of black supremacy, lay dying on the stage of a Manhattan auditorium. Moments before, he had stepped up to the lectern and 400 of the faithful had settled down expectantly to hear the sort of speech for which he was famous—flaying the hated white man. Then a scuffle broke out in the hall and Malcolm's bodyguards bolted from his side to break it up—only to discover that they had been faked out. At least two men with pistols rose from the audience and pumped bullets into the speaker, while a third cut loose at close range with both barrels of a sawed-off shotgun. In the confusion the pistol man got away. The shotgunner lunged through the crowd and out the door, but not before the guards came to their wits and shot him in the leg. Outside he was swiftly overtaken by other supporters of Malcolm and very likely would have been stomped to death if the police hadn't saved him. Most shocking of all to the residents of Harlem was the fact that Malcolm had been killed not by "whitey" but by members of his own race.

The *New York Post* (February 22, 1965)

They came early to the Audubon Ballroom, perhaps drawn by the expectation that Malcolm X would name the men who firebombed his home last Sunday. . . . I sat at the left in the 12th row and, as we waited, the man next to me spoke of Malcolm and his followers: "Malcolm is our only hope. You can depend on him to tell it like it is and to give Whitey hell."

There was a prolonged ovation as Malcolm walked to the rostrum. Malcolm looked up and said "A salaam aleikum (Peace be unto you)" and the audience replied "We aleikum salaam (And unto you, peace)."

Bespectacled and dapper in a dark suit, sandy hair glinting in the light, Malcolm said: "Brothers and sisters . . ." He was interrupted by two men in the center of the ballroom, who rose and, arguing with each other, moved forward. Then there was a scuffle at the back of the room. I heard Malcolm X say his last words: "Now, brothers, break it up," he said softly. "Be cool, be calm."

Then all hell broke loose. There was a muffled sound of shots and Malcolm, blood on his face and chest, fell limply back over the chairs behind him. The two men who had approached him ran to the exit on my side of the room, shooting wildly behind them as they ran. I heard people screaming, "Don't let them kill him." "Kill those bastards." At an exit I saw some of Malcolm's men beating with all their strength on two men. I saw a half dozen of Malcolm's followers bending over his inert body on the stage. Their clothes stained with their leader's blood.

Four policemen took the stretcher and carried Malcolm through the crowd and some of the women came out of their shock and one said: "I hope he doesn't die, but I don't think he's going to make it."

Associated Press (February 22, 1965)

A week after being bombed out of his Queens home, Black Nationalist leader Malcolm X was shot to death shortly after 3 (P.M.) yesterday at a Washington Heights rally of 400 of his devoted followers. Early today, police brass ordered a homicide charge placed against a 22-year-old man they rescued from a savage beating by Malcolm X supporters after the shooting. The suspect, Thomas Hagan, had been shot in the left leg by one of Malcolm's bodyguards as, police said, Hagan and another assassin fled when pandemonium erupted. Two other men were wounded in the wild burst of firing from at least three weapons. The firearms were a .38, a .45 automatic and a sawed-off shotgun. Hagan allegedly shot Malcolm X with the shotgun, a double-barrelled sawed-off weapon on which the stock also had been shortened, possibly to facilitate concealment. Cops charged Reuben Frances, of 871 E. 179th St., Bronx, with felonious assault in the shooting of Hagan, and with Sullivan Law violation—possession of the .45. Police recovered the shotgun and the .45.

The *Amsterdam News* (February 27, 1965)

"We interrupt this program to bring you a special newscast . . . ," the announcer said as the Sunday afternoon movie on the TV set was halted temporarily. "Malcolm X was shot four times while addressing a crowd at the Audubon Ballroom on 166th Street." "Oh no!" That was my first reaction to the shocking event that followed one week after the slender, articulate leader of the Afro-American Unity was routed from his East Elmhurst home by a bomb explosion. Minutes later we alighted from a cab at the corner of Broadway and 166th St. just a short 15 blocks from where I live on Broadway. About 200 men and women, neatly dressed, were milling around, some with expressions of awe and disbelief. Others were in small clusters talking loudly and with deep emotion in their voices. Mostly they were screaming for vengeance. One woman, small, dressed in a light gray coat and her eyes flaming with indignation, argued with a cop at the St. Nicholas corner of the block. "This is not the end of it. What they were going to do to the Statue of Liberty will be small in comparison. We black people are tired of being shoved around." Standing across the street near the memorial park one of Malcolm's close associates commented: "It's a shame." Later he added that "if it's war they want, they'll get it." He would not say whether Elijah Muhammed's followers had anything to do with the assassination. About 3:30 P.M. Malcolm X's wife, Betty, was escorted by three men and a woman from the Columbia Presbyterian Hospital. Tears streamed down her face. She was screaming, "They killed him!" Malcolm X had no last words. . . . The bombing and burning of the No. 7 Mosque early Tuesday morning was the first blow by those who are seeking revenge for the cold-blooded murder of a man who at 39 might have grown to the stature of respectable leadership.

THINKING ↔ WRITING ACTIVITY 7.2

Analyzing and Contrasting Perspectives of an Event

Locate three different newspaper or magazine accounts of a significant event—a court decision, a compromise between heads of state, and a political demonstration are possible topics. Analyze the perceptual "lenses" of each of the writers by answering the questions in **Thinking↔Writing Activity 7.1.**

THINKING ↔ WRITING ACTIVITY 7.3

Seven Accounts of Events at Tiananmen Square, 1989

In the spring of 1989, a vigorous pro-democracy movement erupted in Beijing, the capital of China. Protesting the authoritarian control of the Communist regime, thousands of students staged demonstrations, engaged in hunger strikes, and organized marches involving hundreds of thousands of people. The geographical heart of these activities was the historic Tiananmen Square, taken over by the demonstrators who had erected a symbolic "Statue of Liberty." On June 4, 1989, the fledgling pro-democracy movement came to a bloody end when the Chinese army entered Tiananmen Square and seized control of it. The following are various accounts of this event from different sources. After analyzing these accounts, construct your own version of what you believe took place on that day. Use these questions to guide your analysis of the varying accounts:

- Does the account provide a convincing description of what took place?
- What reasons and evidence support the account?
- How reliable is the source? What are the author's perceiving lenses, which might influence his or her account?
- Is the account consistent with other reliable descriptions of this event?

The New York Times (June 4, 1989)

Tens of thousands of Chinese troops retook the center of the capital from pro-democracy protesters early this morning, killing scores of students and workers and wounding hundreds more as they fired submachine guns at crowds of people who tried to resist. Troops marched along the main roads surrounding central Tiananmen Square, sometimes firing in the air and sometimes firing directly at crowds who refused to move. Reports on the number of dead were sketchy. Students said, however, that at least 500 people may have been killed in the crackdown. Most of the dead had been shot, but some had been run over by personnel carriers that forced their way through the protesters' barricades.

A report on the state-run radio put the death toll in the thousands and denounced the Government for the violence, the Associated Press reported. But the station later changed announcers and broadcast another report supporting the governing Communist party. The official news programs this morning reported that the People's Liberation Army had crushed a "counter-revolutionary rebellion." They said that more than 1,000 police officers and troops had been injured and some killed, and that civilians had been killed, but did not give details.

Deng Xiaoping, Chairman of the Central Military Commission, as reported in *Beijing Review* (July 10–16, 1989)

The main difficulty in handling this matter lay in that we had never experienced such a situation before, in which a small minority of bad people mixed with so many young students and onlookers. Actually, what we faced was not just some ordinary people who were misguided, but also a rebellious clique and a large number of the dregs of society. The key point is that they wanted to overthrow our state and the Party. They had two main slogans: to overthrow the Communist Party and topple the socialist system. Their goal was to establish a bourgeois republic entirely dependent on the West.

During the course of quelling the rebellion, many comrades of ours were injured or even sacrificed their lives. Some of their weapons were also taken from them by the rioters. Why? Because bad people mingled with the good, which made it difficult for us to take the firm measures that were necessary. Handling this matter amounted to a severe political test for our army, and what happened shows that our People's Liberation Army passed muster. If tanks were used to roll over people, this would have created a confusion between right and wrong among the people nationwide. That is why I have to thank the PLA officers and men for using this approach to handle the rebellion. The PLA losses were great, but this enabled us to win the support of the people and made those who can't tell right from wrong change their viewpoint. They can see what kind of people the PLA are, whether there was bloodshed at Tiananmen, and who were those that shed blood.

This shows that the people's army is truly a Great Wall of iron and steel of the Party and country. This shows that no matter how heavy the losses we suffer and no matter how generations change, this army of ours is forever an army under the leadership of the Party, forever the defender of the country, forever the defender of socialism, forever the defender of the public interest, and they are the most beloved of the people. At the same time, we should never forget how cruel our enemies are. For them we should not have an iota of forgiveness.

Reporter (*eyewitness account*), reported in *The New York Times* (June 4, 1989)

Changan Avenue, or the Avenue of Eternal Peace, Beijing's main east-west thoroughfare, echoed with screams this morning as young people carried the bodies of their friends away from the front lines. The dead or seriously wounded were heaped on the backs of bicycles or tricycle rickshaws and supported by friends who rushed through the crowds, sometimes sobbing as they ran.

The avenue was lit by the glow of several trucks and two armed personnel carriers that students and workers set afire, and bullets

Aftermath of the bloody clash between a prodemocracy student movement and the Chinese army on June 4, 1989. © Patrick Durand/SYGMA

swooshed overhead or glanced off buildings. The air crackled almost constantly with gunfire and tear gas grenades.

Students and workers tried to resist the crackdown, and destroyed at least sixteen trucks and two armored personnel carriers. Scores of students and workers ran alongside the personnel carriers, hurling concrete blocks and wooden staves into the treads until they ground to a halt. They then threw firebombs at one until it caught fire, and set the other alight after first covering it with blankets soaked in gasoline. The drivers escaped the flames, but were beaten by students. A young American man, who could not be immediately identified, was also beaten by the crowd after he tried to intervene and protect one of the drivers.

Clutching iron pipes and stones, groups of students periodically advanced toward the soldiers. Some threw bricks and firebombs at the lines of soldiers, apparently wounding many of them. Many of those killed were throwing bricks at the soldiers, but others were simply watching passively or standing at barricades when soldiers fired directly at them.

5   It was unclear whether the violence would mark the extinction of the seven-week-old democracy movement, or would prompt a new phase in the uprising, like a general strike. The violence in the capital ended a period of remarkable restraint by both sides, and seemed certain to arouse

new bitterness and antagonism among both ordinary people and Communist Party officials for the Government of Prime Minister Li Peng.

"Our Government is already done with," said a young worker who held a rock in his hand, as he gazed at the army forces across Tiananmen Square. "Nothing can show more clearly that it does not represent the people." Another young man, an art student, was nearly incoherent with grief and anger as he watched the body of a student being carted away, his head blown away by bullets. "Maybe we'll fail today," he said. "Maybe we'll fail tomorrow. But someday we'll succeed. It's a historical inevitability."

Official Chinese Government Accounts

"Comrades, thanks for your hard work. We hope you will continue with your fine efforts to safeguard security in the capital."
—Prime Minister Li Peng (addressing a group of soldiers after the Tiananmen Square event)

"It never happened that soldiers fired directly at the people."
—General Li Zhiyun

"The People's Liberation Army crushed a counter-revolutionary rebellion. More than 1,000 police officers and troops were injured and killed, and some civilians were killed."
—Official Chinese news program

"At most 300 people were killed in the operation, many of them soldiers."
—Yuan Mu, official government spokesman

"Not a single student was killed in Tiananmen Square."
—Chinese army commander

"My government has stated that a mob led by a small number of people prevented the normal conduct of the affairs of state. There was, I regret to say, loss of life on both sides. I wonder whether any other government confronting such an unprecedented challenge would have handled the situation any better than mine did."
—Han Xu, Chinese ambassador to the United States

The New York Times (June 5, 1989)

It was clear that at least 300 people had been killed since the troops first opened fire shortly after midnight on Sunday morning but the toll may be much higher. Word-of-mouth estimates continued to soar, some reaching far into the thousands. . . . The student organization that coordinated the long protests continued to function and announced today that 2,600 students were believed to have been killed. Several doctors said that, based on their discussions with ambulance drivers and colleagues who had been on Tiananmen Square, they estimated that at least 2,000 had died. Soldiers also beat and bayoneted students and workers after daybreak on Sunday, witnesses said, usually after some provocation but sometimes entirely at random. "I saw a young woman tell the soldiers that they are the people's army, and that they mustn't hurt the people," a young doctor said after returning from one clash Sunday. "Then the soldier shot her, and ran up and bayoneted her."

Xiao Bin (*eyewitness account immediately after the event*)

Tanks and armored personnel carriers rolled over students, squashing them into jam, and the soldiers shot at them and hit them with clubs. When students fainted, the troops killed them. After they died, the troops fired one more bullet into them. They also used bayonets. They were too cruel. I never saw such things before.

Xiao Bin (*account after being taken into custody by Chinese authorities*)

I never saw anything. I apologize for bringing great harm to the party and the country.

Shaping and Changing Perceptions

Just as Mark Twain changed his perceptions of the river with increased knowledge, your ways of viewing the world are developed over a long period of time through the experiences you have, the knowledge you acquire, and your thinking about, or reflecting on, these experiences and your new knowledge. As you think critically about your perceptions, you learn more from your experiences and more about how you make sense of the world. This understanding may strengthen your perceptions, or it may change them. Read the following student passage and consider the way the writer's experiences—and her reflection on these experiences—contributed to shaping her perspective on the world.

STUDENT WRITING

Acquired Knowledge

Anonymous

When news of the Acquired Immune Deficiency Syndrome first began to spread, it was just another one of those issues on the news that I felt did not really concern me. Along with cancer, leukemia, and kidney failure, I knew these diseases ran rampant across the country, but they didn't affect me.

Once the AIDS crisis became a prevalent problem in society, I began to take a little notice of it, but my interest only extended as far as taking precautions to insure that I would not contract the disease. Sure, I felt sorry for all the people who were dying from it, but again, it was not my problem.

My father was an intravenous drug user for as long as I can remember. This was a fact of life when I was growing up. I knew that what he was doing was wrong, and that eventually he would die from it, but I also knew that he would never change.

On July 27th, my father died. An autopsy showed his cause of death as pneumonia and tuberculosis, seemingly natural causes. However, I was later informed that these were two very common symptoms related to carriers of the HIV virus. My father's years of drug abuse had finally caught up with him. He had died from AIDS.

My father's death changed my life. Prior to that, I had always felt that as long as a situation did not directly affect me, it was really no concern of mine. I felt that somewhere, someone would take care of it. Having a crisis strike so close to me made me wake up to reality. Suddenly I became acutely aware of all the things that are wrong in the world. I began to see the problems of AIDS, famine, homelessness, unemployment, and others from a personal point of view, and I began to feel that I had an obligation to join the crusade to do something about these problems.

I organized a youth coalition called UPLIFT INC. In this group, we meet and talk about the problems in society, as well as the everyday problems that any of our members may have in their lives. We organize shows (talent shows, fashion shows) and give a large portion of our proceeds to the American Foundation for AIDS Research, the Coalition for the Homeless, and many other worthy organizations.

Now I feel that I am doing my duty as a human being by trying to help those who are less fortunate than myself. My father's death gave me insight into my own mortality. Now I know that life is too short not to only try to enjoy it, but to really achieve something worthwhile out of it. Material gains matter only if you are willing to take your good fortune and spread it around to those who could use it.

Thinking Critically About Perceptions

So far, we have emphasized the great extent to which, by selecting, organizing, and interpreting, we actively participate in what we perceive. We have suggested that each of us views the world through his or her own unique lenses, that no two of us perceive the world in exactly the same way.

Because we actively participate in selecting, organizing, and interpreting the sensations we experience, however, our perceptions are often incomplete, inaccurate, or subjective. To complicate the situation even more, our own limitations in perceiving are not the only ones that can cause us problems. Other people often purposefully create perceptions and misperceptions. An advertiser who wants to sell a product may try to create the impression that our lives will be changed if we use it. Or a person who wants to discredit someone else may spread untrue rumors about her.

The only way of correcting the mistakes, distortions, and incompleteness of our perceptions is to *become aware of* the ordinarily unconscious process by which we perceive and make sense of the world. By becoming aware of this process, we can think critically about what is going on and correct our mistakes and distortions. In other words, we can use our critical thinking abilities to create a clearer and more informed idea of what is taking place. We cannot rely on perception alone, and if we remain unaware of how it operates and unaware of our active role, we will be unable to control it. We will be convinced that the way we see the world is the way the world is, even when our perceptions are mistaken, distorted, or incomplete.

The first step in critically examining perceptions is to be willing to *ask questions* about them. As long as we believe that the way we see things is the only way to see them, we will be unable to recognize when our perceptions are distorted or inaccurate.

For instance, if you are certain that your interpretation of the boy shown at the computer in *Thinking↔Writing Activity 6.1* is the only correct one, you will not be likely to try and see other possible interpretations. But if you are willing to question your perception ("What are some other possible interpretations?"), you will open the way to more fully developing your perception of what is taking place.

Besides asking questions, we have to make ourselves aware of the personal factors our lenses bring to our perceptions. Each of us brings to every situation a whole collection of expectations, interests, fears, and hopes that can influence what we are perceiving.

Consider the following situations:

- You've been fishing all day without a nibble. Suddenly you get a strike! You reel it in, but just as you're about to pull the fish into the boat, it frees itself from the hook and swims away. When you get home later, your friends ask you, "How large was the fish that got away?"

- The teacher asks you to evaluate the performance of a classmate who is giving a report to the class. You don't like this other student because he acts as if he's superior to all the other students in the class. How do you evaluate his report?

- You are asked to estimate the size of an audience attending an event that your organization has sponsored. How many people are there?

In each of these cases, your perceptions might be influenced by whatever hopes, fears, or prejudices you brought to the situation, causing your observations to become distorted or inaccurate. Although usually you cannot eliminate the personal feelings that influence your perceptions, you can become aware of these feelings and try to control them.

As was explained in Chapter 2, critical thinkers strive to see things from different perspectives. One of the best ways to do so is by communicating with others and engaging in *dialogue* with them. This means exchanging and critically examining ideas in an open and organized way. Similarly, dialogue is one of the main ways to check out perceptions—by asking others what their perceptions are and comparing and contrasting these with one's own.

This is exactly what you did when you discussed the different possible interpretations of the boy at the computer. By exchanging your perceptions with those of other members of the class, you developed a more complete sense of how differently events can be viewed, as well as an appreciation of the reasons supporting the different perspectives. Looking for reasons to support perceptions involves trying to discover independent proof or evidence regarding the perception, and it is possible to evaluate the accuracy of perceptions when evidence is available in the form of records, photographs, videotapes, or the results of experiments. What independent forms of evidence could verify perceptions about the boy at the computer?

Thinking critically about perceptions means trying to avoid developing impulsive or superficial ones that we are unwilling to change. As has been explained in Chapter 2, a critical thinker is *thoughtful* in approaching the world and open to modifying his or her views in the light of new information or better insight. Consider the following perceptions:

- Women are very emotional.
- Politicians are corrupt.

- Teenagers are wild and irresponsible.
- People who are good athletes are usually poor students.
- Men are thoughtless and insensitive.

These types of general perceptions are known as *stereotypes* because they express a belief about an entire group of people without recognizing the individual differences among members of the group. For instance, it is probably accurate to say that there are some politicians who are corrupt, but this is not the same as saying that all, or even most, politicians are corrupt. Stereotypes affect our perceptions of the world because they encourage us to form an inaccurate and superficial idea of a whole group of people ("Teenagers are reckless drivers"). When we meet someone who falls into this group, we automatically perceive that person as having these stereotyped qualities ("This person is a teenager, so he is a reckless driver"). Even if we find that the person does not fit our stereotyped perceptions ("This teenager is not a reckless driver"), this sort of superficial and thoughtless labeling does not encourage us to change our perceptions of the group as a whole. Instead, it encourages us to overlook the conflicting information in favor of our stereotyped perceptions ("All teenagers are reckless drivers—except for this one"). In contrast, when we are perceiving in a thoughtful fashion, we try to see what a person is like as an individual, instead of trying to fit him or her into a preexisting category.

THINKING ↔ WRITING ACTIVITY 7.4

Stereotyping

1. In your journal, describe an incident in which you were perceived as a stereotype because of your age, ethnic or religious background, employment, accent, or place of residence.
2. Describe how it felt to be stereotyped in this way.
3. Conclude by explaining what you think are the best ways to overcome stereotypes.

Sometimes stereotypes are so built into a culture that it is difficult to be aware of them until they are brought to one's attention. The *perspective,* or view of the world, that the culture presents may not even acknowledge the possibility of other perspectives, so it can be very difficult for an individual to become aware of any and then to "switch lenses" to try those viewpoints. True critical thinkers can and do switch lenses and in their writing, help others to do so as well. The following readings, one by a man born in the eighteenth century, one by a man born in the nineteenth century, and two by women born in the twentieth century, all attempt this difficult task.

from Remarks Concerning the Savages of North America
by Benjamin Franklin

Savages we call them, because their Manners differ from ours, which we think the Perfection of Civility; they think the same of theirs.

Perhaps, if we could examine the Manners of different Nations with Impartiality, we should find no People so rude, as to be without any Rules of Politeness; nor any so polite, as not to have some Remains of Rudeness.

The Indian Men, when young, are Hunters and Warriors; when old, Counsellors; for all their Government is by Counsel of the Sages; there is no Force, there are no Prisons, no Officers to compel Obedience, or inflict Punishment. Hence they generally study Oratory, the best Speaker having the most Influence. The Indian Women till the Ground, dress the Food, nurse and bring up the Children, and preserve and hand down to Posterity the Memory of public Transactions. These Employments of Men and Women are accounted natural and honourable. Having few artificial Wants, they have abundance of Leisure for Improvement by Conversation. Our laborious Manner of Life, compared with theirs, they esteem slavish and base; and the Learning, on which we value ourselves, they regard as frivolous and useless. An Instance of this occurred at the Treaty of Lancaster, in Pennsylvania, *anno* 1744, between the Government of Virginia and the Six Nations. After the principal Business was settled, the Commissioners from Virginia acquainted the Indians by a Speech, that there was at Williamsburg a College, with a Fund for Educating Indian youth; and that, if the Six Nations would send down half a dozen of their young Lads to that College, the Government would take care that they should be well provided for, and instructed in all the Learning of the White People. It is one of the Indian Rules of Politeness not to answer a public Proposition the same day that it is made; they think it would be treating it as a light matter, and that they show it Respect by taking time to consider it, as of a Matter important. They therefore deferr'd their Answer till the Day following; when their Speaker began, by expressing their deep Sense of the kindness of the Virginia Government, in making them that Offer; "for we know," says he, "that you highly esteem the kind of Learning taught in those Colleges, and that the Maintenance of our young Men, while with you, would be very expensive to you. We are convinc'd, therefore, that you mean to do us Good by your Proposal; and we thank you heartily. But you, who are wise, must know that different Nations have different Conceptions of things; and you will therefore not take it amiss, if our Ideas of this kind of Education happen not to be the same with yours. We have had some Experience of it; Several of our young People were formerly brought up at the Colleges of the Northern Provinces; they were instructed in all your Sciences; but, when they came back to us, they were bad Runners, ignorant of every means of living in the Woods, unable to bear either Cold or Hunger, knew neither how to build a Cabin, take a Deer, or kill an Enemy, spoke our Language imperfectly, were therefore neither fit for Hunters, Warriors, nor Counsellors; they were totally good for nothing. We are however not the less oblig'd by your kind Offer, tho' we decline accepting it; and, to show our grateful Sense of it, if the Gentlemen of Virginia will send us a Dozen of their Sons, we will take great Care of their Education, instruct them in all we know, and make *Men* of them."

Having frequent Occasions to hold public Councils, they have acquired great Order and Decency in conducting them. The old Men sit in the foremost Ranks, the Warriors in the next, and the Women and Children in the hindmost. The Business of the Women is to take exact Notice of what passes, imprint it in their Memories (for they have no Writing), and communicate it to their Children. They are the Records of the Council, and they preserve Traditions of the Stipulations in Treaties 100 Years back; which, when we compare with our Writings, we always find exact. He that would speak, rises. The rest observe a profound Silence. When he has finish'd and sits down, they leave him 5 to 6 Minutes to recollect, that, if he has omitted anything he intended to say, or has any thing to add, he may rise again and deliver it. To interrupt another, even in common Conversation, is reckon'd highly indecent. How different this is from the conduct of a polite British House of Commons, where scarce a day passes without some Confusion, that makes the Speaker hoarse in calling *to Order;* and how different from the Mode of Conversation in many polite Companies of Europe, where, if you do not deliver your Sentence with great Rapidity, you are cut off in the middle of it by the Impatient Loquacity of those you converse with, and never suffer'd to finish it!

5   The Politeness of these Savages in Conversation is indeed carried to Excess, since it does not permit them to contradict or deny the Truth of what is asserted in their Presence. By this means they indeed avoid Disputes; but then it becomes difficult to know their Minds, or what Impression you make upon them. The Missionaries who have attempted to convert them to Christianity, all complain of this as one of the great Difficulties of their Mission. The Indians hear with Patience the Truths of the Gospel explain'd to them, and give their usual Tokens of Assent and Approbation; you would think they were convinc'd. No such matter. It is mere Civility.

A Swedish Minister, having assembled the chiefs of the Susquehanah Indians, made a Sermon to them, acquainting them with the principal historical Facts on which our Religion is founded; such as the Fall of our first Parents by eating an Apple, the coming of Christ to repair the Mischief, his Miracles and Suffering, &c. When he had finished, an Indian Orator stood up to thank him. "What you have told us," says he, "is all very good. It is indeed bad to eat Apples. It is better to make them all into Cyder. We are much oblig'd by your kindness in coming so far, to tell us these Things which you have heard from your Mothers. In return, I will tell you some of those we had heard from ours. In the Beginning, our Fathers had only the Flesh of Animals to subsist on; and if their Hunting was unsuccessful, they were starving. Two of our young Hunters, having kill'd a Deer, made a Fire in the Woods to broil some Part of it. When they were about to satisfy their Hunger, they beheld a beautiful young Woman descend from the Clouds, and seat herself on that Hill, which you see yonder among the blue Mountains. They said to each other, it is a Spirit that has smelt our broiling Venison, and wishes to eat of it; let us offer some to her. They presented her with the Tongue; she was pleas'd with the Taste of it, and said, 'Your kindness shall be rewarded; come to this Place after thirteen Moons, and you shall find something that will be of great Benefit in nourishing you and your Children to the latest Generations.' They did so, and, to their Surprise, found Plants they had never seen before; but which, from that ancient time, have been constantly cultivated among us, to our great Advantage. Where her right Hand had touched the Ground, they found Maize; where her left hand had touch'd it, they found Kidney-Beans; and where her Backside had sat on it, they found Tobacco." The good Missionary, disgusted with this idle Tale, said, "What I delivered to you were sacred Truths; but what you tell me is mere Fable, Fiction, and Falshood." The Indian, offended, reply'd, "My brother, it seems your Friends have not done you Justice in your Education; they have not well instructed you in the Rules of common Civility. You saw that we, who understand and practise those Rules, believ'd all your stories; why do you refuse to believe ours?"

When any of them come into our Towns, our People are apt to crowd round them, gaze upon them, and incommode them, where they desire to be private; this they esteem great Rudeness, and the Effect of the Want of Instruction in the Rules of Civility and good Manners. "We have," say they, "as much Curiosity as you, and when you come into our Towns, we wish for Opportunities of looking at you; but for this purpose we hide ourselves behind Bushes, where you are to pass, and never intrude ourselves into your Company."

Their Manner of entering one another's village has likewise its Rules. It is reckon'd uncivil in travelling Strangers to enter a Village abruptly, without giving Notice of their Approach. Therefore, as soon as they arrive within hearing, they stop and hollow, remaining there till invited to enter. Two old Men usually come out to them, and lead them in. There is in every Village a vacant Dwelling, called *the Strangers' House.*

Here they are plac'd, while the old Men go round from Hut to Hut, acquainting the Inhabitants, that Strangers are arriv'd, who are probably hungry and weary; and every one sends them what he can spare of Victuals, and Skins to repose on. When the Strangers are refresh'd, Pipes and Tobacco are brought; and then, but not before, Conversation begins, with Enquiries who they are, whither bound, what News, &c.; and it usually ends with offers of Service, if the Strangers have occasion of Guides, or any Necessaries for continuing their Journey; and nothing is exacted for the Entertainment.

The same Hospitality, esteem'd among them as a principal Virtue, is practis'd by private Persons; of which Conrad Weiser, our Interpreter, gave me the following Instance. He had been naturaliz'd among the Six Nations, and spoke well the Mohock Language. In going thro' the Indian Country, to carry a Message from our Governor to the Council at Onondaga, he call'd at the Habitation of Canassatego, an old Acquaintance, who embrac'd him, spread Furs for him to sit on, plac'd before him some boil'd Beans and Venison, and mix'd some Rum and Water for his Drink. When he was well refresh'd, and had lit his Pipe, Canassatego began to converse with him; ask'd how he had far'd the many Years since they had seen each other; whence he then came; what occasion'd the Journey, &c. Conrad answered all his Questions; and when the Discourse began to flag, the Indian, to continue it, said, "Conrad, you have lived long among the white People, and know something of their Customs; I have been sometimes at Albany, and have observed, that once in Seven Days they shut up their Shops, and assemble all in the great House; tell me what it is for? What do they do there?" "They meet there," says Conrad, "to hear and learn *good Things.*" "I do not doubt," says the Indian, "that they tell you so; they have told me the same; but I doubt the Truth of what they say, and I will tell you my Reasons. I went lately to Albany to sell my Skins and buy Blankets, Knives, Powder, Rum, &c. You know I us'd generally to deal with Hans Hanson; but I was a little inclin'd this time to try some other Merchant. However, I call'd first upon Hans, and asked him what he would give for Beaver. He said he could not give any more than four Shillings a Pound; 'but,' says he, 'I cannot talk on Business now; this is the Day when we meet together to learn *Good Things,* and I am going to the Meeting.' So I thought to myself, 'Since we cannot do any Business to-day, I may as well go to the meeting too,' and I went with him. There stood up a Man in Black, and began to talk to the People very angrily. I did not understand what he said; but, perceiving that he look'd much at me and at Hanson, I imagin'd he was angry at seeing me there; so I went out, sat down near the House, struck Fire, and lit my Pipe, waiting till the Meeting should break up. I thought too, that the Man had mention'd something of Beaver, and I suspected it might be the Subject of their Meeting. So, when they came out, I accosted my Merchant.

'Well, Hans,' says I, 'I hope you have agreed to give more than four Shillings a Pound.' 'No,' says he, 'I cannot give so much; I cannot give more than three shillings and sixpence.' I then spoke to several other Dealers, but they all sung the same song,—Three and sixpence,—Three and sixpence. This made it clear to me, that my Suspicion was right; and, that whatever they pretended of meeting to learn *good Things,* the real purpose was to consult how to cheat Indians in the Price of Beaver. Consider but little, Conrad, and you must be of my Opinion. If they met so often to learn *good Things,* they would certainly have learnt some before this time. But they are still ignorant. You know our Practice. If a white Man, in travelling thro' our Country, enters one of our Cabins, we all treat him as I treat you; we dry him if he is wet, we warm him if he is cold, we give him Meat and Drink, that he may allay his Thirst and Hunger; and we spread soft Furs for him to rest and sleep on; we demand nothing in return. But, if I go into a white Man's House at Albany, and ask for Victuals and Drink, they say, 'Where is your Money?' and if I have none, they say, 'Get out, you Indian Dog.' You see they have not yet learned those little *Good Things,* that we need no Meetings to be instructed in, because our Mothers taught them to us when we were Children; and therefore it is impossible their Meetings should be, as they say, for any such purpose, or have any such Effect; they are only to contrive *the Cheating of Indians in the Price of Beaver."*

from The Soul of the Indian
The Great Mystery

by Charles Alexander Eastman

The original attitude of the American Indian toward the Eternal, the "Great Mystery" that surrounds and embraces us, was as simple as it was exalted. To him it was the supreme conception, bringing with it the fullest measure of joy and satisfaction possible in this life.

The worship of the "Great Mystery" was silent, solitary, free from all self-seeking. It was silent, because all speech is of necessity feeble and imperfect; therefore the souls of my ancestors ascended to God in wordless adoration. It was solitary, because they believed that He is nearer to us in solitude, and there were no priests authorized to come between a man and his Maker. None might exhort or confess or in any way meddle with the religious experience of another. Among us all men were created sons of God and stood erect, as conscious of their divinity. Our faith might not be formulated in creeds, nor forced upon any who were unwilling to receive it; hence there was no preaching, proselyting, nor persecution, neither were there any scoffers or atheists.

There were no temples or shrines among us save those of nature. Being a natural man, the Indian was intensely poetical. He would deem it sacrilege to build a house for Him who may be met face to face in the mysterious, shadowy aisles of the primeval forest, or on the sunlit bosom of virgin prairies, upon dizzy spires and pinnacles of naked rock, and yonder in the jeweled vault of the night sky! He who enrobes Himself in filmy veils of cloud, there on the rim of the visible world where our Great-Grandfather Sun kindles his evening camp-fire, He who rides upon the rigorous wind of the north, or breathes forth His spirit upon aromatic southern airs, whose warcanoe is launched upon majestic rivers and inland seas—He needs no lesser cathedral!

That solitary communion with the Unseen which was the highest expression of our religious life is partly described in the word *hambeday,* literally "mysterious feeling," which has been variously translated "fasting" and "dreaming." It may better be interpreted as "consciousness of the divine."

5   The first *hambeday,* or religious retreat, marked an epoch in the life of the youth, which may be compared to that of confirmation or conversion in Christian experience. Having first prepared himself by means of the purifying vapor-bath, and cast off as far as possible all human or fleshly influences, the young man sought out the noblest height, the most commanding summit in all the surrounding region. Knowing that God sets no value upon material things, he took with him no offerings or sacrifices other than symbolic objects, such as paints and tobacco. Wishing to appear before Him in all humility, he wore no clothing save his moccasins and breech-clout. At the solemn hour of sunrise or sunset he took up his position, overlooking the glories of earth and facing the "Great Mystery," and there he remained, naked, erect, silent, and motionless, exposed to the elements and forces of His arming, for a night and a day to two days and nights, but rarely longer. Sometimes he would chant a hymn without words, or offer the ceremonial "filled pipe." In this holy trance or ecstasy the Indian mystic found his highest happiness and the motive power of his existence.

When he returned to the camp, he must remain at a distance until he had again entered the vapor-bath and prepared himself for intercourse with his fellows. Of the vision or sign vouchsafed to him he did not speak, unless it had included some commission which must be publicly fulfilled. Sometimes an old man, standing upon the brink of eternity, might reveal to a chosen few the oracle of his long-past youth.

The native American has been generally despised by his white conquerors for his poverty and simplicity. They forget, perhaps, that his religion forbade the accumulation of wealth and the enjoyment of luxury. To him, as to other single-minded men in every age and race, from Diogenes to the brothers of Saint Francis, from the Montanists to the Shakers, the love of possessions has appeared a snare, and the burdens of a complex society a source of needless peril and temptation. Furthermore, it was the rule of his life to share the fruits of his skill and success with his less fortunate brothers. Thus he kept his spirit free from the clog of pride, cupidity, and envy, and carried out, as he believed, the divine decree—a matter profoundly important to him.

It was not, then, wholly from ignorance or improvidence that he failed to establish permanent towns and to develop a material civilization. To the untutored sage, the concentration of population was the prolific mother of all evils, moral no less than physical. He argued that food is good, while surfeit kills; that love is good, but lust destroys; and not less dreaded than the pestilence following upon crowded and unsanitary dwellings was the loss of spiritual power inseparable from too close contact with one's fellow-men. All who have lived much out of doors know that there is a magnetic and nervous force that accumulates in solitude and that is quickly dissipated by life in a crowd; and even his enemies have recognized the fact that for a certain innate power and self-poise, wholly independent of circumstances, the American Indian is unsurpassed among men.

The red man divided mind into two parts—the spiritual mind and the physical mind. The first is pure spirit, concerned only with the essence of things, and it was this he sought to strengthen by spiritual prayer, during which the body is subdued by fasting and hardship. In this type of prayer there was no beseeching of favor or help. All matters of personal or selfish concern, as success in hunting or warfare, relief from sickness, or the sparing of a beloved life, were definitely relegated to the plane of the lower or material mind, and all ceremonies, charms, or incantations designed to secure a benefit or to avert a danger, were recognized as emanating from the physical self.

10   The rites of this physical worship, again, were wholly symbolic, and the Indian no more worshiped the Sun than the Christian adores the Cross. The Sun and the Earth, by an obvious parable, holding scarcely more of poetic metaphor than of scientific truth, were in his view the parents of all organic life. From the Sun, as the universal father, proceeds the quickening principle in nature, and in the patient and fruitful womb of our mother, the Earth, are hidden embryos of plants and men. Therefore our reverence and love for them was really an imaginative extension of our love for our immediate parents, and with this sentiment of filial piety was joined a willingness to appeal to them, as to a father, for such good gifts as we may desire. This is the material or physical prayer.

The elements and majestic forces in nature, Lightning, Wind, Water, Fire, and Frost, were regarded with awe as spiritual powers, but always secondary and intermediate in character. We believed that the spirit pervades all creation and that every creature possesses a soul in some degree, though not necessarily a soul conscious of itself. The tree, the waterfall, the grizzly bear, each is an embodied Force, and as such an object of reverence.

The Indian loved to come into sympathy and spiritual communion with his brothers of the animal kingdom, whose inarticulate souls had for him something of the sinless purity that we attribute to the innocent and irresponsible child. He had faith in their instincts, as in a mysterious wisdom given from above; and while he humbly accepted the supposedly voluntary sacrifice of their bodies to preserve his own, he paid homage to their spirits in prescribed prayers and offerings.

In every religion there is an element of the supernatural, varying with the influence of pure reason over its devotees. The Indian was a logical and clear thinker upon matters within the scope of his understanding, but he had not yet charted the vast field of nature or expressed her wonders in terms of science. With his limited knowledge of cause and effect, he saw miracles on every hand,—the miracle of life in seed and egg, the miracle of death in lightning flash and in the swelling deep! Nothing of the marvelous could astonish him; as that a beast should speak, or the sun stand still. The virgin birth would appear scarcely more miraculous than is the birth of every child that comes into the world, or the miracle of the loaves and fishes excite more wonder than the harvest that springs from a single ear of corn.

Who may condemn his superstition? Surely not the devout Catholic, or even Protestant missionary, who teaches Bible miracles as literal fact! The logical man must either deny all miracles or none, and our American Indian myths and hero stories are perhaps, in themselves, quite as credible as those of the Hebrews of old. If we are of the modern type of mind, that sees in natural law a majesty and grandeur far more impressive than any solitary infraction of it could possibly be, let us not forget that, after all, science has not explained everything. We have still to face the ultimate miracle,—the origin and principle of life! Here is the supreme mystery that is the essence of worship, without which there can be no religion, and in the presence of this mystery our attitude cannot be very unlike that of the natural philosopher, who beholds with awe the Divine in all creation.

15   It is simple truth that the Indian did not, so long as his native philosophy held sway over his mind, either envy or desire to imitate the splendid achievements of the white man. In his own thought he rose superior to them! He scorned them, even as a lofty spirit absorbed in its stern task rejects the soft beds, the luxurious food, the pleasure-worshiping dalliance of a rich neighbor. It was clear to him that virtue and happiness are independent of these things, if not incompatible with them.

There was undoubtedly much in primitive Christianity to appeal to this man, and Jesus' hard sayings to the rich and about the rich would have been entirely comprehensible to him. Yet the religion that is preached in our churches and practiced by our congregations, with its element of display and self-aggrandizement, its active proselytism, and its open contempt of all religions but its own, was for a long time extremely repellent. To his simple mind, the professionalism of the pulpit, the paid exhorter, the moneyed church, was an unspiritual and unedifying thing, and it was not until his spirit was broken and his moral and physical constitution undermined by trade, conquest, and strong drink, that Christian missionaries obtained any real hold upon him. Strange as it may seem, it is true that the proud pagan in his secret soul despised the good men who came to convert and to enlighten him!

Nor were its publicity and its Phariseeism the only elements in the alien religion that offended the red man. To him, it appeared shocking and almost incredible that there were among this people who claimed superiority many irreligious, who did not even pretend to profess the national faith. Not only did they not profess it, but they stooped so low as to insult their God with profane and sacrilegious speech! In our own tongue His name was not spoken aloud, even with utmost reverence, much less lightly or irreverently.

More than this, even in those white men who professed religion we found much inconsistency of conduct. They spoke much of spiritual things, while seeking only the material. They bought and sold everything: time, labor, personal independence, the love of woman, and even the ministrations of their holy faith! The lust for money, power, and conquest so characteristic of the Anglo-Saxon race did not escape moral condemnation at the hands of his untutored judge, nor did he fail to contrast this conspicuous trait of the dominant race with the spirit of the meek and lowly Jesus.

He might in time come to recognize that the drunkards and licentious among white men, with whom he too frequently came in contact, were condemned by the white man's religion as well, and must not be held to discredit it. But it was not so easy to overlook or to excuse national bad faith. When distinguished emissaries from the Father at Washington, some of them ministers of the gospel and even bishops, came to the Indian nations, and pledged to them in solemn treaty the national honor, with prayer and mention of their God; and when such treaties, so made, were promptly and shamelessly broken, is it strange that the action should arouse not only anger, but contempt? The historians of the white race admit that the Indian was never the first to repudiate his oath.

20   It is my personal belief, after thirty-five years' experience of it, that there is no such thing as "Christian civilization." I believe that Christianity and modern civilization are opposed and irreconcilable, and that the spirit of Christianity and of our ancient religion is essentially the same.

from Women's Reality: An Emerging Female System in a White Male Society

by Anne Wilson Schaef

Let me explain what I mean by the White Male System. It is the system in which we live, and in it, the power and influence are held by white males. This system did not happen overnight, nor was it the result of the machinations of only a few individuals; we all not only let it occur but participated in its development. Nevertheless, the White Male System is just that: a system. We all live in it, but it is not reality. It is not the way the world is. Unfortunately, some of us do not recognize that it is a system and think it *is* reality or the way the world is.

The White Male System—and it is important to keep in mind that I am referring to a *system* here and not pointing a finger at specific individuals within it—controls almost every aspect of our culture. It makes our laws, runs our economy, sets our salaries, and decides when and if we will go to war or remain at home. It decides what *is* knowledge and how it is to be taught. Like any other system, it has both positive and negative qualities. But because it is only a system, it can be clarified, examined, and changed, both from within and without.

There are other systems within our culture. The Black System, the Chicano System, the Asian-American System, and the Native American System are completely enveloped in and frequently overshadowed by the White Male System. As, of course, is the Female System, which includes women from the other ethnic systems as well as white women.

There are a few white men who do not fit into the White Male System. They form a small but growing group which is frequently perceived as a sanctuary by white men who do not want to acknowledge their sexism. Whenever I mention the existence of this group during a lecture, I can almost see the men in the room rushing to crowd into it. If they can just get into that circle, they can be "different" and not have to face themselves. I wait until they are comfortably crowded in before saying, "Of course, at this point in history that group is largely homosexual." They then quickly rush right out again! I use this statement for effect, and while it is not necessarily accurate, it *does* encourage men to realize that there is more to sexism than meets the eye. This keeps the focus where it should be and is also an amusing process to observe.

5   Saying that you are not sexist—or that you do not want to be, or would rather not admit that you are—is not the same as doing something about your sexism. To give a parallel example, this is much like what many of us white liberals did during the civil rights movement. We needed our Black friends to tell us that we were different. We needed to hear that we were not like everyone else, that we were not discriminatory and racist. Once we heard that, we could avoid having

to deal with our racism, which was real no matter how hard we tried to ignore it or cover it up.

I had two Black colleagues who simply refused to tell me what I wanted to hear. I finally learned that the issue was not one of *whether* I was racist, but of *how* I was racist. As soon as I was able to acknowledge this—with my friends' help—then and only then could I begin to work on my own racist attitudes and behaviors. Similarly, because we all live in a white male culture, the question is not one of *whether* we are sexist, but of *how* we are sexist. (This is true for women as well as men, by the way.)

Before we can deal with our sexism, we must learn to distance ourselves from the White Male System. We must learn to step back, take a long look at it, and see it for what it really is.

Clearing the Air: Pollution vs. Non-Pollution

I like to think of the White Male System as analogous to pollution. When you are in the middle of pollution, you are usually unaware of it (unless it is especially bad). You eat in it, sleep in it, work in it, and sooner or later start believing that that is just the way the air is. You are unaware of the fact that pollution is *not* natural until you remove yourself from it and experience non-pollution.

I live in the Colorado mountains where the air is very clear. Whenever I go to the East Coast, I almost immediately start coughing and fighting a postnasal drip. As I choke and sputter, I comment to local residents, "My, the pollution is bad today!" They in turn look startled and ask, "What pollution?" What they are really saying, of course, is this: "Isn't the air always a little thick and yellowish-gray?"

10   When flying into New York—or Los Angeles, for that matter—it is easy enough to look down and say, "Now, that's pollution!" Once you are in it for a while, though, you simply forget all about it and accept polluted air as a given.

Native Americans have always recognized the White Male System as pollution. The Blacks were the next group to challenge the system. The Blacks went off by themselves and said, "We have a system of our own—the Black system. It isn't always right, but it isn't always wrong. Black is beautiful and our system is just fine." Until then, very few groups had stepped away from the White Male System, reflected on it, and declared their own alternatives.

It is very difficult to stand back from the White Male System because it is everywhere in our culture. You can get away from pollution by leaving New York City and going to the mountains, but you can not get away from the White Male System as easily as that. It *is* our culture. We all live in it. We have been educationally, politically, economically, philosophically, and theologically trained in it, and our emotional, psychological, physical, and spiritual survival have depended on our knowing and supporting the system. White women believe that they get their identity externally from the White Male System and that the White Male System is necessary to validate that identity. Therefore, challenging the system becomes almost impossible.

There is a direct correlation between buying into the White Male System and surviving in our culture. Since white women have bought into the system the most, they have survived better than other groups both economically and physically although they do get battered and raped and mutilated (for example, through unnecessary surgery). They have had to hide and/or unlearn their own system and accept the stereotypes that the White Male System has set up for them.

Blacks have accepted the White Male System less wholeheartedly than white women and have not done as well within it. (Of course, white men have not exactly been enthusiastic about welcoming Blacks into their system.) Chicanos and Asian Americans are even further removed. Finally, most Native Americans have generally refused to have anything at all to do with it. When one looks at how Native Americans have fared within this culture, one sees graphic evidence of what happens to those who try to escape or ignore the White Male System. They are either exterminated outright or have to fight every step of the way. Economic and physical survival have been directly related to accepting and incorporating the White Male System.

15   There is also an *inverse* relationship between accepting and incorporating the White Male System and personal survival. The stress of having to be innately superior at all times is more than the human organism can tolerate. Those persons who buy into the system the most and work the hardest to become shining examples of what it means tend to drop dead ahead of their time from heart attacks, strokes, high blood pressure, ulcers, and other physical after effects of unrelenting tension and stress.

One unforeseen consequence of the civil rights movement is that more Black males are dying of heart attacks these days. As they move into the White Male System and become part of it, they inherit the unfortunate legacy of stress and early death. The same appears to be true for women who are "making it" in the White Male System. It seems as if high blood pressure goes hand in hand with three-piece suits and attaché cases.

This does not have to be so, however. One big problem with the White Male System is that stress is assumed to be an integral part of the system. If one tries to live up to the myths of the system, then one naturally undergoes a great deal of strain. One can choose *not* to live up to these myths. One can choose to remove the causes of stress rather than merely learning how to cope with them. The only really effective way to go about doing this is to challenge the myths of the White Male

System and eventually to change the system itself. It can be done; in some cases, it *is* already being done.

I am not talking here about women's liberation, or Black liberation, or the liberation of any other single group within our culture. Instead, I am looking forward to a time when we can all become the persons we really are. Blacks and women are learning to tell the difference between pollution and non-pollution. They are showing us that it is possible to stand back and say, "The White Male System is only a system. It is not reality. It is not the way the world is." Blacks have defined their own system, and some of them have tried to communicate this to the rest of us. Unfortunately, many of us have been very slow learners. It is difficult to teach a new concept to someone who already "knows it all" (one of the myths of the White Male System). Some Blacks have not bothered trying to tell others about their system. They have just focused on getting into the White Male System because they know they must in order to survive.

I have described the White Male System as it is perceived by Female System women. Similarly, there is a Female System. It is not good or bad. It just is. It is not necessary to choose one system over the other. As the Female System is described, we will see and understand another system. The more systems we know about, the more choices we have. Over time, perhaps, more new—and better—systems, models, and alternatives will emerge.

Sometimes a powerful part of a culture decides that it is time to change perspectives and proceeds to do so. An example is a tremendous change that has taken place in American history textbooks. Anyone who went to school in the 1950s or before may be surprised to hear what current textbooks are like. If you went to school in the 1960s or later, you may be surprised to hear what they used to be like!

from America Revised
by Frances FitzGerald

Those of us who grew up in the fifties believed in the permanence of our American-history textbooks. To us as children, those texts were the truth of things: they were American history. It was not just that we read them before we understood that not everything that is printed is the truth, or the whole truth. It was that they, much more than other books, had the demeanor and trappings of authority. They were weighty volumes. They spoke in measured cadences: imperturbable, humorless, and as distant as Chinese emperors. Our teachers treated them with respect, and we paid them abject homage by memorizing a chapter a week. But now the textbook histories have changed, some of them to such an extent that an adult would find them unrecognizable.

One current junior-high-school American history begins with a story about a Negro cowboy called George McJunkin. It appears that when McJunkin was riding down a lonely trail in New Mexico one cold spring morning in 1925 he discovered a mound containing bones and stone implements, which scientists later proved belonged to an Indian civilization ten thousand years old. The book goes on to say that scientists now believe there were people in the Americas at least twenty thousand years ago. It discusses the Aztec, Mayan, and Incan civilizations and the meaning of the word "culture" before introducing the European explorers.

Another history text—this one for the fifth grade—begins with the story of how Henry B. Gonzalez, who is a member of Congress from Texas, learned about his own nationality. When he was ten years old, his teacher told him he was an American because he was born in the United States. His grandmother, however, said, "The cat was born in the oven. Does that make him bread?" After reporting that Mr. Gonzalez eventually went to college and law school, the book explains that "the melting pot idea hasn't worked out as some thought it would," and that now "some people say that the people of the United States are more like a salad bowl than a melting pot."

Poor Columbus! He is a minor character now, a walk-on in the middle of American history. Even those books that have not replaced his picture with a Mayan temple or an Iroquois mask do not credit him with discovering America—even for the Europeans. The Vikings, they say, preceded him to the New World, and after that the Europeans, having lost or forgotten their maps, simply neglected to cross the ocean again for five hundred years. Columbus is far from being the only personage to have suffered from time and revision. Captain John Smith, Daniel Boone, and Wild Bill Hickok—the great self-promoters of American history—have all but disappeared, taking with them a good deal of the romance of the American frontier. General Custer has given way to Chief Crazy Horse; General Eisenhower no longer liberates Europe single-handed; and, indeed, most generals, even to Washington and Lee, have faded away, as old soldiers do, giving place to social reformers such as William Lloyd Garrison and Jacob Riis. A number of black Americans have risen to prominence: not only George Washington Carver but Frederick Douglass and Martin Luther King, Jr. W. E. B. Du Bois now invariably accompanies Booker T. Washington. In addition, there is a mystery man called Crispus Attucks, a fugitive slave about whom nothing seems to be known for certain except that he was a victim of the Boston Massacre and thus became one of the first casualties of the American Revolution. Thaddeus Stevens has been reconstructed—his character changed, as it were, from black to white, from cruel and vindictive to persistent and sincere. As for Teddy Roosevelt, he now champions the issue of conservation instead of charging up San Juan Hill. No single President really stands out as a hero, but all Presidents—except certain unmentionables in the second half of the nineteenth century—seem to have done as well as could be expected, given difficult circumstances.

5   Of course, when one thinks about it, it is hardly surprising that modern scholarship and modern perspectives have found their way into children's books. Yet the changes remain shocking. Those who in the sixties complained of the bland optimism, the chauvinism, and the materialism of their old civics texts did so in the belief that, for all their protests, the texts would never change. The thought must have had something reassuring about it, for that generation never noticed when its complaints began to take effect and the songs about radioactive rainfall and houses made of ticky-tacky began to appear in the textbooks. But this is what happened.

The history texts now hint at a certain level of unpleasantness in American history. Several books, for instance, tell the story of Ishi, the last "wild" Indian in the continental United States, who, captured in 1911 after the massacre of his tribe, spent the final four and a half years of his life in the University of California's museum of anthropology, in San Francisco. At least three books show the same stunning picture of the breaker boys, the child coal miners of Pennsylvania— ancient children with deformed bodies and blackened faces who stare stupidly out from the entrance to a mine. One book quotes a soldier on the use of torture in the American campaign to pacify the Philippines at the beginning of the century. A number of books say that during the American Revolution the patriots tarred and feathered those who did not support them, and drove many of the loyalists from the country. Almost all the present-day history books note that the United States interned Japanese-Americans in detention camps during the Second World War.

Ideologically speaking, the histories of the fifties were implacable, seamless. Inside their covers, America was perfect: the greatest nation in the world, and the embodiment of democracy, freedom, and technological progress. For them, the country never changed in any important way: its values and its political institutions remained constant from the time of the American Revolution. To my generation—the children of the fifties—these texts appeared permanent just because they were so self-contained. Their orthodoxy, it seemed, left no handholds for attack, no lodging for decay. Who, after all, would dispute the wonders of technology or the superiority of the English colonists over the Spanish? Who would find fault with the pastorale of the West or the Old South? Who would question the anti-Communist crusade? There was, it seemed, no point in comparing these visions with reality, since they were the public truth and were thus quite irrelevant to what existed and to what anyone privately believed. They were—or so it seemed—the permanent expression of mass culture in America.

But now the texts have changed, and with them the country that American children are growing up into. The society that was once uniform is now a patchwork of rich and poor, old and young, men and women, blacks, whites, Hispanics, and Indians. The system that ran so smoothly by means of the Constitution under the guidance of benevolent conductor Presidents is now a rattletrap affair. The past is no highway to the present; it is a collection of issues and events that do not fit together and that lead in no single direction. The word "progress" has been replaced by the word "change": children, the modern texts insist, should learn history so that they can adapt to the rapid changes taking place around them. History is proceeding in spite of us. The present, which was once portrayed in the concluding chapters as a peaceful haven of scientific advances and Presidential inaugurations, is now a tangle of problems: race problems, urban problems, foreign-policy problems, problems of pollution, poverty, energy depletion, youthful rebellion, assassination, and drugs. Some books illustrate these problems dramatically. One, for instance, contains a picture of a doll half buried in a mass of untreated sewage; the caption reads, "Are we in danger of being overwhelmed by the products of our society and wastage created by their production? Would you agree with this photographer's interpretation?" Two books show the same picture of an old black woman sitting in a straight chair in a dingy room, her hands folded in graceful resignation; the surrounding text discussed the problems faced by the urban poor and by the aged who depend on Social Security. . . .

Writing Thoughtfully About Perspectives

Whenever we place two or more perspectives, or two or more other things, together and examine them for likenesses and differences, we are engaging in the powerful thinking pattern called **comparison and contrast.** To be precise, when we *compare,* we are focusing on similarities or areas of agreement; when we *contrast,* we are focusing on differences or areas of disagreement. Generally, the items examined are from the same category, such as two perspectives. We will discuss writing about items from the same category in the following section, Comparative Relationships. Sometimes, in order to make a point or explain something we cannot explain otherwise, we compare items from different categories. We will discuss these unusual comparisons in the next section, Analogical Relationships (pp. 272–274).

Comparative Relationships

We use comparison and contrast informally in our daily lives to help ourselves make decisions about what to buy or which TV programs to watch—or to note, for instance, how much one of our relatives does or doesn't resemble another. When we use comparison and contrast in a formal way, by following certain established principles, we are using it to think critically toward a significant conclusion. That is, we use it not just to list areas of similarity or difference, but for help with achieving clearer understanding or new insight. When we use comparison and contrast to examine different perspectives, we do so in order to understand each perspective, to see if one is superior to the other, to see if we ourselves have yet another perspective, and so on.

The principles for using comparison and contrast to think critically are not difficult to understand or remember:

1. *Compare or contrast two or more things with something essential in common; that is, from the same category.* Thus, it makes sense to compare two accounts of the same event or two essays on affirmative action. (This principle is violated, for good reason, when we use analogical relationships.)
2. *Establish important bases or points for comparison and contrast.* In everyday situations, it is fairly easy to determine which points are important. In deciding between two cars, the important points may be price, model, and safety features; exterior color or exact trunk capacity may not be important. But when you are working with written texts, finding points for comparison and contrast and deciding which of them are important require careful thought. In comparing or contrasting two accounts of the same event, important points might include the actual presence of the writers at the event or the writers' reliance on the accounts of others; the language the writers use to describe the participants or actions; and which details the writers have included or omitted. The gender of a writer or the length of an account might or might not be significant.
3. *Develop or locate relevant, specific evidence for each point.* True, you are entitled to your opinion. However, opinions valued by critical thinkers are those supported by evidence. In everyday situations, the evidence usually means facts: the prices of two different cars, the presence or absence of air bags, and so on. With written texts, the evidence comes from the texts themselves, in the form of either accurate paraphrases or direct quotations.
4. *Determine the significance of the comparison and contrast: What can be learned from it?* What should be done as a result? In everyday situations, this significance is often a determination that this car is superior to that one and is therefore the one to purchase. When you are working with written texts, the significance may be that the texts disagree on important points, and therefore, at least one is more persuasive than the other; or that one or both

texts are biased; or that an important truth has emerged from the comparison and contrast, and so forth.

When we are ready to present the results of our critical thinking in writing for others to read and consider, we need to become concerned about presenting our thinking in such a way that readers will be able to follow it and, we hope, agree with its conclusion. Therefore, for writing, we need to add these principles:

5. *Early and accurately, introduce the things to be compared and contrasted.* When you work with written texts, this means identifying what the texts are (personal essays, poems, newspaper accounts, excerpts from books, etc.) and naming the titles and authors early, probably in the introductory paragraph.

6. *Develop a thesis which indicates that likenesses and/or differences will be examined.* Because two or more things are being discussed and points about each will be introduced, the audience will be confronting a difficult reading task. A clear statement of what is to come can offer that audience a framework to follow.

7. *Organize the comparison and contrast in the way that will be easiest for the audience to follow.* Basically, there are three ways to organize a comparison and contrast: block, point-by-point, and some combination of block and point-by-point. *Block* means that after the introduction, all the material about the first subject is presented; then, all the material about the second. The selection from Mark Twain on pages 240–241 of this chapter uses block organization. *Point-by-point* means that for each key point or basis of comparison, information is given first about one of the things being compared and contrasted, then about the other. Thus, the writer moves back and forth between the two things being compared and contrasted. The selection by Benjamin Franklin on pages 254–258 of this chapter uses point-by-point organization. A combination of these two organizational patterns is sometimes used, as when there are a few points of similarity that can easily be dealt with in block, followed by several points of difference that the writer wishes to address one at a time.

8. *Bring up the same bases or points of comparison or contrast for each subject, and in the same order.* An incomplete comparison results when, for instance, the language used in one text is addressed but the language used in another text is not discussed. If an important point appears in one text but not in the other, it is reasonable to simply tell the audience this. For example, "No mention is made of a doctor in this account."

9. *Assist the audience by using transitional words, phrases, or sentences to show relationships and shifts.* Logical connections that exist in the writer's head are not necessarily apparent to the audience, but they can be made visible by the use of appropriate transitions.

10. *State the significance of your comparison and contrast at the place in the essay where it will be most effective.* Sometimes writers use the significance

as the opening lead, sometimes they incorporate it into the thesis statement, and sometimes they save it for the conclusion. In deciding where to place it, ask yourself where it will have the greatest impact on the audience.

Analogical Relationships

We noted earlier that comparative relationships involve examining the similarities and differences of two items in the same general category, such as two perspectives or two items on a menu or two methods of birth control. There is another kind of comparison, however, one that does not focus on things in the same category. Such comparisons are known as analogies, and their goal is to clarify or illuminate a concept from one category by saying that in some ways, it is the same as a concept from a very different category.

The purpose of an analogy is not the same as the purpose of the comparison considered in the last section. There, we noted that the goal of comparing similar things is usually to make a choice and that the process of comparing can provide us with information on which we can base an intelligent decision. The main goal of analogies, however, is not to choose or decide; it is to illuminate our understanding. Identifying similarities between very different things can often stimulate us to see these things in a new light, from a fresh perspective.

> **Analogy:**   a comparison between things that are basically
> dissimilar, made for the purpose of illuminating our
> understanding of the things being compared.

We ourselves often create and use analogies to put a point across. Used appropriately, analogies can help to illustrate what we are trying to communicate. This is particularly useful when we have difficulty in finding the right words to represent our experiences. Similes and metaphors, two figures of speech based on analogy that help us to "say things for which we have not words," are discussed on pages 167–170 of Chapter 5 of this book.

In addition to communicating experiences that resist simple characterization, analogies are useful when a writer is explaining a complicated concept. For instance, you might compare the eye to a camera lens, or the immunological system of the body to the National Guard (corpuscles are called to active duty and rush to the scene of danger when undesirable elements threaten the well-being of the organism).

Analogies are often used to describe shape or size. Thus, even those of us who don't know what an S-hook or an I-beam are can envision their shapes because of our familiarity with the shapes of letters. In the same way, it helps

Analogical thinking and writing patterns clarify or illuminate a concept from one category by relating it to a concept from a very different category.

our readers to understand size if we describe an object as "about the size of a dollar bill" or a piece of property as "roughly the size of two football fields."

Analogies enliven human discourse by evoking images that illuminate the points of comparison. Consider the following analogies and explain the points of comparison.

> "Laws are like cobwebs, which may catch small flies, but let wasps and
> hornets break through."—Jonathan Swift
> "I am as pure as the driven slush."—Tallulah Bankhead
> "He has all the qualities of a dog, except its devotion."—Gore Vidal

A word of caution about analogies is in order here. Since they are based on items from different categories and have only limited points of similarity, be very careful when writing or reading arguments based on analogies. The failed United States policy in Vietnam was based on the "domino theory," which held that since the countries in Southeast Asia had common borders, if one country became Communist the other countries would also "fall" to Communism, just as a row of dominoes would all fall if one were knocked down. However, the countries were separate entities, places with people, history, cultures, and policies of their own. They were not small game pieces like dominoes, and the theory proved false. Analogies do have value for describing and explaining, but by their very nature they have a limited value in argument.

THINKING ↔ WRITING ACTIVITY 7.5

Extended Analogies

Read the following passage, which uses an analogical pattern of thinking. Identify the major ideas being compared and describe their points of similarity. Explain how the analogy helps illuminate the subject being discussed.

The mountain guide, like the true teacher, has a quiet authority. He or she engenders trust and confidence so that one is willing to join the endeavor. The guide accepts his leadership role, yet recognizes that success (measured by the heights that are scaled) depends upon the close cooperation and active participation of each member of the group. He has crossed the terrain before and is familiar with the landmarks, but each trip is new and generates its own anxiety and excitement. Essential skills must be mastered; if they are lacking, disaster looms. The situation demands keen focus and rapt attention; slackness, misjudgment, or laziness can abort the venture. The teacher is not a pleader, not a performer, not a huckster, but a confident, exuberant guide on expeditions of shared responsibility into the most exciting and least-understood terrain on earth—the mind itself. —Nancy K. Hill, *Scaling the Heights: The Teacher as Mountaineer*

WRITING PROJECT

This chapter has included both readings and Thinking↔Writing Activities that encouraged you to reflect on the nature of perception and on comparing and contrasting different perspectives. Be sure to reread what you wrote for those activities; you may be able to use it for help in completing this project.

> **WRITING PROJECT**   Critically Evaluating Different Perspectives on an Issue or Event
>
> Write an essay comparing and contrasting two or more written texts that present different perspectives. Your goal is to arrive at a significant insight about the texts. After you have drafted the essay, revise it to the best of your ability. Follow instructions given by your professor as to which texts to choose, the length and format of the essay, and so forth.

Begin by considering the key elements in the **Thinking↔Writing Model** on page 8.

Purpose
You are being asked to demonstrate your ability to think and write critically while applying the principles for using comparison and contrast. The essay-writing assignment includes establishing the significance of your comparison and contrast. You will be developing your critical thinking skills by comparing and contrasting in a formal way and by discovering what you can learn about the texts you choose. Finally, you will be sharing your insights about the texts with your audience.

Audience
Although your introduction may include a very brief summary of the texts, your audience is not interested in everything the texts include, but rather in your analysis of the areas of likeness and difference in the texts. Therefore, you may prefer not to mention some large areas of the texts at all, if they are not relevant to the points you wish to discuss. However, you will need to include enough evidence from the texts about those points to help your audience to understand and agree with your conclusions. Remember that you should not merely *tell* your audience that a likeness or difference exists; you must *show* the evidence of that likeness or difference, so that the audience can "see" it for themselves.

Your classmates can be valuable peer reviewers of a draft, reacting as intelligent readers who are able to comment on the logic and clarity of your writing. Ultimately, your professor remains the audience who will judge how well you have applied the principles in this chapter and how well you have planned, drafted, and revised. As a writing teacher, he or she cares about a clear focus, logical organization, specific details and examples, and correctness. Keep these in mind as you revise, edit, and proofread.

Subject

If your professor specifies which texts you should compare and contrast, consider why he or she may have chosen them. Another question to ask yourself is what those texts have in common. If your professor has left the choice to you, remember that you must use texts that do have something essential in common. It helps a great deal to pick texts that genuinely interest you, either because of their subject matter or because of their style. Or you may decide to pick an issue or event that interests you and use your research skills to locate texts about that issue or event. In that case, it may be necessary to provide copies of the texts for your audience.

Writer

This project asks you to bring your critical reading and thinking to other writers' works and to analyze their perspectives. Your position of authority and your comfort level may well depend on how much you know about the subject of the pieces that you are analyzing. However, neither your personal opinions nor your experiences are the focus in this project. You must be as objective as possible as you write and as thoughtful as possible as you establish the significance of your analysis.

The Writing Process

The following sections will guide you through the stages of generating, planning, drafting, and revising as you work on your essay. Try to be particularly conscious of applying the principles discussed in this chapter, and of the critical thinking you do when you revise.

Generating Ideas

Once you have decided which texts you will work on, reread each of them several times. Likenesses and differences may not be immediately apparent, nor may any significance strike you at the start. Some preliminary writing may help.

- Make a list of the ideas in each text.
- Make a list of *what you notice about each text.* Are you struck by the opening, the choice of words, the author's bias or objectivity, the presence or absence of specific details, or any other elements or characteristics?

- After you have made these lists, begin to look for bases or points of likeness or difference. This requires abstract thinking on your part, but patience yields results.

- Collaboration can be productive. Talk with others about the texts.

- Read the student papers at the end of this chapter. They may help you to see what needs to be done.

- Read carefully any other models your professor provides.

- Try five minutes of freewriting on what the texts have in common, then five minutes on how they differ.

- Once you have some bases for comparison or contrast, go back to the texts themselves and look for passages you could quote to illustrate your ideas.

- If you own the book or books in which the texts appear, use a highlighting pen to mark areas you may wish to quote. If you don't own the book, copy the quotations or make photocopies of the entire text and use highlighting.

- Now begin to think about significance. What are you beginning to see about the texts? What are you beginning to feel about them?

- Try freewriting for five minutes on any or all of these questions:

  Does one text do a better job than the other? If so, in what way or ways?

  Do you agree with either or both texts? If not, what is your perspective?

  Do either or both texts cause you to re-evaluate or change your own ideas or perspectives?

Defining a Focus

Write a thesis statement that will clearly inform your audience that you are going to explore likenesses, differences, or both. You might decide to write something like "After studying both these accounts carefully, I saw two distinct differences." Or you might decide to name the areas of likeness or difference: "The authors are alike in their recognition of the need for more education and their determination in pursuing that education." You may even decide to announce your significance in your thesis statement: "Seeing the biased way in which one of the texts presented this event made me wary of accepting any printed material at face value."

Organizing Ideas

This assignment fits well with what you have already learned about essay structure, but requires you to move a few steps beyond what you have accomplished previously. Your description of the issue or event and of the texts that describe it will give you a "working" introduction that will end with your thesis statement. The actual discussion of likenesses and/or differences will take place in the body paragraphs, and the significance of your analysis can be introduced or enlarged upon in the conclusion. The major decision you will have to make is whether to use block or point-by-point organization, or some combination of the two.

Drafting

Begin with the easiest paragraph to draft. If you are using point-by-point, remember to begin each body paragraph with a topic sentence indicating that this point will be discussed for both (or all) texts: for example, "Both accounts agree on the cause of the contamination." Then provide the audience with as much information as is needed to help them see what you mean. Use the quotations you highlighted to support your points and let the audience see that the texts really do say very similar—or very different—things. You will, of course, have to decide on the most logical order for the body paragraphs: which point to present first, which second, and so on.

Generally, readers have an easier time with point-by-point organization, but some writing situations call for block. Fortunately, word processors make it easy to move sentences around, so try it both ways to see which will be easier for your audience to follow.

In your conclusion, name or enlarge on the significance of your analysis, but be careful not to make too broad a statement. Consideration of two or three texts does not prove, for instance, that all texts are racist or sexist, but discovering racism or sexism in some texts should encourage you and your readers to be aware that these characteristics may be present in others.

Revising

Ideally, at this point, you should put your draft aside for a day or two. If deadlines won't permit you to do that, then at least take a break before you try to revise. When you are ready to "re-see" your writing, begin by reading it through slowly, preferably aloud. If possible, have someone whose opinion you respect read it; ask for feedback. Then work through the hierarchy of revision concerns that follows. Remember that you have at least one and possibly two decisions to make for each question: (1) Is improvement needed? and (2) If improvement is needed, how, exactly, can I make my draft better?

1. **Think big.** Look at your draft as a whole.
- Does it fulfill the assignment in terms of topic and length?
- Have you stated the thesis clearly?
- Do all parts of the draft relate to the thesis?
- Is the organization logical?
- Do you provide enough evidence?
- Is your point of view consistent?
- Is there a discernible flow between your paragraphs?

- Have you documented information from your sources accurately?
- Have you used quotation marks with direct quotes or set them off by indenting them?
2. **Think medium.** Look at your draft paragraph by paragraph.
- Will your introduction make your audience want to read on?
- Is the introduction appropriate for the rest of the draft?
- Is your focus stated clearly if you are working with a "visible" structure?
- If you are working with an "invisible" structure, is your focus clearly implied?
- Are topic sentences used effectively?
- Does each body paragraph develop a different idea?
- Should any paragraphs be combined or eliminated?
- Is your conclusion effective?
3. **Think small.** Look at your draft sentence by sentence.
- Are any sentences difficult to understand?
- Are any so long that your audience could get lost in them?
- Are sentences with blended quotations (that is, quotations that are integrated into the syntax of the sentence instead of introduced with "He said . . ." or "She said . . .") complete and easy to read?
- Are quotations shortened with ellipsis marks accurate and readable?
- Are there several choppy sentences that can be combined?
- Are any sentences vague?
- Do any sentences need to be corrected for standard English grammar and usage?
4. **Think "picky."** Look at your draft as your fussiest critic might.
- Are any words not clear or not quite right for your meaning?
- Are any words misspelled?
- Are there any punctuation errors?
- Is your format correct?
- Are the pages numbered consecutively?
- Does your paper make a good impression by being used?
- Is there anything else you could do to improve your draft?

Proofreading

After you prepare a final draft, check again for correct grammar and punctuation. Proofread carefully for omitted words or punctuation marks. Run your spelling checker program, but be aware of its limitations. Proofread carefully for the kinds of errors the computer can't catch.

Student Essay

The following essays show how students responded to this assignment. The first is organized by block, and the second by point-by-point.

STUDENT WRITING

Different Perspectives

by Jesse Chen

I can never forget what happened to my people at Tiananmen Square in Beijing, China, on the morning of June 4, 1989. My parents and I stayed up all night in our home in Hong Kong watching the news on television. It was broadcasting the quelling of the demonstrators in Tiananmen Square, and it was abhorrent and unbelievable. The Chinese Army entered Tiananmen Square and shot the students who were protesting for the pro-democracy movement. It came to a bloody end in that many innocent students were killed on that blood red morning. I remember that my parents were both crying when they saw their own people being killed by the "People's Army." When I read the accounts in my textbook from *The New York Times* (June 4, 1989) and the Official Chinese Government Accounts which include quotations from six Chinese persons, I found it incredible that they turned out to be two completely different stories even though they were about the same event. *The New York Times* tends to focus on reporting the facts of the slaughter while the Official Chinese Government Accounts tend to glorify the People's Liberation Army and the sacrifices made by its members. Because of different backgrounds and perspectives, *The New York Times* and the Official Chinese Government Accounts have come to two different stories about the slaughter; therefore, we need to think critically and analyze carefully before we can recognize a reliable source.

As a public medium, *The New York Times* plays a neutral role which only reports the fact of the slaughter without adding any biased opinion. It describes the students as "students," a factual title. Moreover, when describing the scene of the slaughter, it reports that the troops "fired submachine guns at the crowd of people who tried to resist." It states, "Troops marched along the roads surrounding central Tiananmen Square, sometimes firing in the air and sometimes firing directly at crowds who refused to move." It reports, "Most of the dead had been shot, but some had been run over by personnel carriers that forced their way through the protestors' barricades." Those descriptions of the scene are very close to the news which I saw and heard broadcast on TV, so the reliability is high. Moreover, in reporting the death toll, *The Times* does not give a very accurate number because it is impossible to be estimated or proved. Therefore, it merely gives a sketchy death toll: "Students said, however, that at least 500 people may have been killed in the crackdown." Furthermore, *The Times* does not render a judgment; it neither praises nor criticizes one side or the other since its responsibility is to report the facts only.

On the contrary, the Official Chinese Government Accounts give a different report, mainly glorifying the People's Liberation Army and sympathizing with the sacrifices made by its soldiers. Unlike *The Times,* these accounts do not name the students as "students." Han Xu, the Chinese ambassador to the United States, criticized them as "a mob led by a small number of people" who were trying to prevent "the normal conduct of the affairs of state." Also, General Lie Zgiyun said, "It never happened that soldiers fired directly at the people." Moreover, the Official Accounts even deny the death of the students: "Not a single student was killed at Tiananmen Square," said a Chinese army commander. However, the Official Chinese news program reported, "More than 1,000 police officers and troops were injured and killed, and some civilians were killed." Yuan Mu, an official government spokesman, said, "At most 300 people were killed in the operation, many of them soldiers." Finally, Prime Minister Li Peng offered his appreciation to the army: "Comrades, thanks for your hard work. We hope you will continue your fine efforts to safeguard security in the capital."

In conclusion, people's perspectives vary according to their backgrounds and status. Because of the differences in the backgrounds and status, *The Times* and the Chinese Government came to two opposed stories. We can measure their reliability by analyzing their backgrounds and status. Being a public medium, *The Times* tends to be neutral, not biased toward either side. However, in order to evade responsibility and cover up the faults, the Official Chinese Government Accounts tend to by-pass the sacrifices of the students and glorify the "hard work" of the army. Even until now, the Chinese Government still denies that they killed any students. Therefore, before we can trust or believe a source, we need to think critically about its perspective before we accept its reliability.

STUDENT WRITING
The Tiananmen Square Event:
An Analysis of Several Different Accounts
by Rissa Miller

To depict an event truthfully is a task reporters hold sacred in this country, but to report a story free of bias and perception is almost an impossibility. As Americans we accept this and realize as long as uncovering truth is the ultimate goal, sifting through bias is up to the reader. However, through bias a story may take a politically or personally motivated angle, and without several different views, there is no way for a reader to decipher this perception. This is seen in seven accounts given in our textbook of the Tiananmen Square event.

In an eye-witness account published in *The New York Times* on June 4, 1989, the opening scene was set on a main road in Beijing which ". . . echoed with screams . . . as young people carried the bodies of their friends . . . sobbing. . . ." The depiction of violence was detailed, and took up over half the article. The students were said to be fighting with iron pipes, stones, and other crude and ineffective objects against the army's more advanced weapons. "Many of those killed were throwing bricks at the soldiers . . . students and workers ran alongside the personnel carriers, hurling concrete blocks and wooden staves into the treads. . . ." Any description of action taken by the People's Liberation Army was entirely left out. The best sense the reader gets of it is from a student who says, "Nothing can show more clearly that it does not represent the people." The students' political stand was described as a "democracy movement" and an " uprising."

Another article in *The New York Times,* published on June 5, 1989, focused on the number of student deaths. It began, ". . . 300 people had been killed since the troops first opened fire. . . ." The report continued to state that, through word of mouth, estimates were between 2,000 and 2,600 casualties. Also, its only depictions of soldiers were of beating and bayoneting students, workers, and young women, ". . . after daybreak . . . sometimes entirely at random." This article is absent of any explanation of the political motivation on the students' part or that of the army. The language used was extremely neutral. "The student organization" was how the protesters were named, as opposed to calling them "rebels" or "democrats."

According to Deng Xiaoping as reported in the *Bejing Review,* the protesters were ". . . bad people mixed with students and onlookers . . . a rebellious clique and the dregs of society." They were not described as part of a movement or uprising but as wanting to "overthrow our state. . . ." Their stated goal was to establish a system dependent on the Western world. The only statement that addressed any student death was, "*If* tanks were used to roll over people. . . ." The soldiers, however, were named ". . . comrades [who] were injured or even sacrificed their lives." Xiaoping alluded to the army's victimization when they ". . . had their weapons taken by the rioters." However, their strength overcame and they were congratulated as ". . . truly a Great Wall of iron and steel." This article finished with exclamations of the army as forever the defender of socialism, public interest, and the country, with a quick and final reminder of the cruelty of the "enemies."

The first two articles were written for a pro-Democracy public that had been intensely steered against Communism in the previous decade. Knowing this, it seems fitting that no motivation on the soldiers' part was taken into account. Also that the student death tolls and the violence against them was of great importance, rather than the underlying causes and effects of the incident. However, trying to attain a factual account was the main goal in the American articles. This is shown best by the quoting of protesters and eyewitnesses, as well as the impartial language found in the second *Times* article. We see the blatant opposition to this approach in the third article, and can assume some effects it might have on an unenlightened audience. It is possible to conclude that the American articles give a more accurate account. However, we must remember that no writer is free from bias and personal perspective. He/she will inevitably state, or just as importantly not state, things that will leave the reader lacking a complete perspective.

CHAPTER 8

Exploring Causal Relationships— Writing to Analyze Causes

Critical Thinking Focus: Causal reasoning

Rhetorical Focus: Presenting causal reasoning

Reading Theme: Ecological relationships

Writing Project: Analyzing causal relationships of a recent event

---

Determining Causal Relationships

The last two chapters have examined thinking and writing patterns that help us to understand and control our perceptions as we make sense of the world. Yet even as we perceive and make sense of the world, we experience the human tendency to ask why things are as they are: Why do some marriages endure for years and others end in divorce? Why does a northern area of the country have relatively mild winters for several years, then a record-breaking blizzard? Why do certain political ideas take hold during particular periods of history?

When we contemplate such questions, we are asking about (1) **causes,** factors that contribute to events and bring them about, and (2) **effects,** events that result directly or indirectly from other events. Much thinking about causes and effects occurs in an impromptu way as we attempt to guess why things happened the way they did. For example, in the case of a divorce, we might say, "I think the marriage failed because of money problems." Though that might in fact be the reason, it is important to realize that it is only a guess. Determining causes is a complicated business, since

■ an event can have more than one cause,

■ an event can have various types of causes, and

■ determining causes with certainty is often impossible.

Nevertheless, because we want to "know why," and because it may be important to know why, we do try to determine causes and effects. When we think about causal relationships in an organized way, ever conscious of the difficulty and uncertainty of the task, we are taking part in the important critical thinking pattern called **causal analysis.** And when we use causal analysis in writing, there are important considerations to be aware of and serious problems to avoid.

Thinking Critically About Causal Relationships

> **Causality:**   relating events in terms of the way some of them are responsible for bringing about others.

Causal patterns of thinking involve relating events in terms of the influence or effect they have on one another. For example, if right now you were to pinch yourself hard enough to feel it, you would be demonstrating a cause-and-effect relationship. Stated very simply, a *cause* is anything responsible for bringing about something else—usually termed the *effect.* The cause (the pinch) brings about the effect (the feeling of pain). When you make a **causal statement,** you are simply stating that a causal relationship exists between two or more things: "The pinch *caused* the pain in my arm."

Of course, when you make (or think) causal statements, you do not always use the word *cause.* For example, the following statements are all causal statements. In each case, underline the cause and circle the effect.

■ Since I was the last to leave, I turned off the lights.

■ Taking plenty of vitamin C really cured that terrible cold I had.

■ I accidentally toasted my hand along with the marshmallows by getting too near the campfire.

In these statements, the words *turned off, cured,* and *getting* all point to the fact that something has caused something else to take place. Our language contains thousands of these causal "cousins." Now, try composing three statements of your own that express a causal relationship without using the word *cause.*

You are doubtless realizing that you make causal statements all the time, and that you are constantly thinking in terms of causal relationships. In fact, the goal of much of your thinking is to figure out why something happened or how something came about, since if you can figure out how and why things occur, you may be able to predict what will happen in the future.

Predictions of anticipated results form the basis of many of your decisions. For example, the experience of toasting your hand along with the marshmallows might lead you to choose a longer stick for toasting—simply because you are able to figure out the causal relationships involved and make predictions based on your understanding (namely, a longer stick will keep your hand well away from the fire).

Consider the following activities, which you probably performed today. Each activity assumes that certain causal relationships exist, which influenced your decision to perform them. Explain one such causal relationship for each activity.

- Brushing your teeth
  Causal relationship:

- Locking the door
  Causal relationship:

- Studying for an exam
  Causal relationship:

Causal Chains

Although you may think of causes and effects in isolation—A caused B—in reality, causes and effects rarely appear by themselves. They generally appear as parts of more complex patterns, including three that are about to be examined here: *causal chains, contributory causes,* and *interactive causes.* Consider the following scenario:

Your paper on the topic "life after death" is due on Monday morning. You have reserved the whole weekend to work on it and are just getting started when the phone rings: a favorite childhood friend is in town and wants to stay with you for the weekend. You say yes. By Sunday night, you've had a great weekend but have made little progress on your paper. You brew a pot of coffee and get started. At 3:00 A.M. you are too exhausted to continue. Deciding to get a few hours' sleep, you set the alarm clock for 6:00 A.M., giving yourself plenty of time to finish up. When you wake up, it's nine o'clock; the alarm failed to go off. Your class starts in forty minutes. You have no chance of getting the paper done on time. On your way to class, you mentally review the causes of this disaster. No longer concerned about life after death, you are very worried about life after this class!

- What causes in this situation are responsible for your paper's being late?
- What do you think is the single most important cause?
- What do you think your instructor will identify as the most important cause? Why?

Causal thinking and writing patterns relate events in terms of the influence or effect they have on one another.

A **causal chain,** as you have gathered from the preceding examples, is a situation in which one thing leads to another, which then leads to another, and so on. There is not just one cause for the resulting effect; there is a whole string of causes. Which cause in the string is the "real" cause? Your answer often depends on your perspective on the situation. In the example of the unfinished paper on the topic of life after death, you might see the cause as a defective alarm clock. The instructor, though, might see the cause of the problem as overall lack of planning. Proper planning, he or she might say, does not leave things until the last minute, when unexpected problems can prevent you from reaching your goal. You can illustrate this causal structure with Figure 8.1.

CAUSAL CHAIN

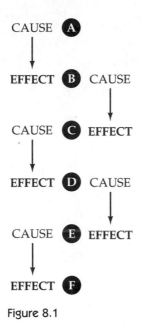

Figure 8.1

THINKING ↔ WRITING ACTIVITY 8.1

Creating a Causal Chain

1. Create a similar scenario of your own, detailing a chain of causes that results in being late for class, meeting the "right" person, saving someone's life, or an effect of your own choosing.
2. Review the scenario you have just created. Explain how the "real" cause of the final effect could vary, depending on your perspective on the situation.

Contributory Causes

In addition to operating in causal chains over a period of time (A leads to B, which leads to C, which leads to D, etc.), causes can serve simultaneously to produce an effect. When this happens (as it often does), you have a situation in which a number of different **contributory causes** are instrumental in bringing something about. Instead of working in isolation, each cause *contributes to* bringing about the final effect. When this situation occurs, each cause serves to support and reinforce the action of the other causes, a structure illustrated in Figure 8.2.

Consider the following situation:

CONTRIBUTORY CAUSES

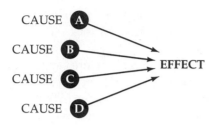

Figure 8.2

It is the end of the term, and you have been working incredibly hard at school—writing papers, preparing for exams, finishing up course projects. You haven't been getting enough sleep, and you haven't been eating regular, well-balanced meals. To make matters worse, you have been under intense pressure in your personal life, having serious arguments with the person you have been dating, and this is constantly on your mind. It is the middle of the flu season and many people you know have been sick with various respiratory infections. Walking home one evening, you get soaked by an unexpected downpour. By the time you get home, you are shivering. You soon find yourself in bed with a thermometer in your mouth—you are sick!

What was the "cause" of your illness? In this situation, you can see that evidently, a combination of factors led to your physical breakdown: low resistance, getting wet and chilled, being exposed to various germs and viruses, physical exhaustion, lack of proper eating, and so on. Taken by itself, no one factor might have been enough to cause your illness. Together, they all contributed to the final outcome.

THINKING ↔ WRITING ACTIVITY 8.2

Creating a Contributory Cause Scenario

Create a similar scenario of your own, detailing the contributory causes that led to asking someone for a date, choosing a major, losing or winning a game you played in, or an effect of your own choosing.

Interactive Causes

Our examination of causal relationships has revealed that causes rarely operate in isolation but instead often influence (and are influenced by) other factors. Imagine that you are scheduled to give a speech to a large group of people. As your moment in the spotlight approaches, you become anxious, which results in a dry mouth and throat, making your voice sound more like a croak. The prospect of sounding like a bullfrog increases your anxiety, which in turn dries your mouth and constricts your throat further, reducing your croak to something much worse—silence.

This not uncommon scenario reveals the way different factors can relate to one another through reciprocal influences that flow back and forth from one to the other. This type of **interactive** causal relationship is an extremely important way of organizing and making sense of your experiences. For instance, to understand social relationships, such as families, teams, groups of friends, and so on, you have to understand the complex ways each individual influences—and is influenced by—all the other members of the group. Understanding biological systems and other systems is similar to understanding social systems. To understand and explain how an organ such as your heart, liver, or brain functions, you have to describe its complex, interactive relationships with all the other parts of your biological system. Figure 8.3 illustrates these dynamic causal relationships.

INTERACTIVE CAUSES

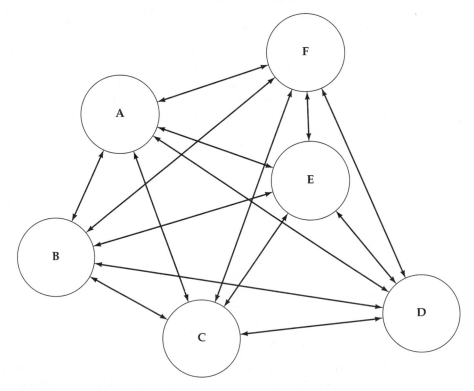

Figure 8.3

THINKING ↔ WRITING ACTIVITY 8.3

Analyzing Causal Patterns

Read the following passages, which illustrate causal patterns of thinking. For each passage:

1. Create mind maps that illustrate cause-and-effect relationships.
2. Identify the kind of causal relationship (direct, chain, contributory, or interactive).

Nothing posed a more serious threat to the bald eagle's survival than a modern chemical compound called DDT. Around 1940, a retired Canadian banker named Charles L. Broley began keeping track of eagles nesting in Florida. Each breeding season, he climbed into more than 50 nests, counted the eaglets and put metal bands on their legs. In the late 1940's, a sudden drop-off in the number of young produced led him to conclude that 80 percent of his birds were sterile. Broley blamed DDT. Scientists later discovered that DDE, a breakdown product of DDT, causes not sterility, but a fatal thinning of eggshell among birds of prey. Applied on cropland all over the United States, the pesticide was running off into waterways where it concentrated in fish. The bald eagles ate the fish and the DDT impaired their ability to reproduce. They were not alone, of course. Ospreys and pelicans suffered similar setbacks.
—Jim Doherty, *"The Bald Eagle and DDT"*

It is popularly accepted that Hitler was the major cause of World War II, but the ultimate causes go much deeper than one personality. First, there were long-standing German grievances against reparations levied on the nation following its defeat in World War I. Second, there were severe economic strains that caused resentment among the German people. Third, there were French and English reluctance to work out a sound disarmament policy and American noninvolvement in the matter. Finally, there was the European fear that communism was a much greater danger than National Socialism. These factors contributed to the outbreak of World War II. —Gilbert Muller, *The American College Handbook*

You crunch and chew your way through vast quantities of snacks and confectioneries and relieve your thirst with multicolored, flavored soft drinks, with and without calories, for two basic reasons. The first is simple; the food tastes good, and you enjoy the sensation of eating it. Second, you associate these foods, often without being aware of it, with the highly pleasurable experiences depicted in the advertisements used to promote their sale. Current television advertisements demonstrate this point: people turn from grumpiness to euphoria after crunching a corn chip. Others water ski into the sunset with their loved ones while drinking a popular soft drink. People entertain on the patio with friends, cook over campfires without mosquitoes, or go to carnivals with granddad munching away at the latest candy or snack food. The people portrayed in these scenarios are all healthy, vigorous, and good looking; one wonders how popular the food they convince you to eat would be if they would crunch or drink away while complaining about low back pain or clogged sinuses.—Judith Wurtman, *Eating Your Way Through Life*

Sufficient Cause and Necessary Condition

In addition to the three patterns of causality we have just examined, we need to consider sufficient cause and necessary condition. **Sufficient cause** is a factor that of itself is always sufficient for bringing about a certain result. In an example given earlier in this chapter, a pinch on the arm is a sufficient cause for pain. Of course, even with a sufficient cause, there may be a **necessary condition,** or several necessary conditions, for a result to occur. Having healthy nerves in the arm and being conscious are two necessary conditions for someone's feeling pain when pinched on the arm. Another example of sufficient cause is flipping a light switch to turn on an electric light. An obvious necessary condition is a sufficient supply of electricity. (Most of us have experienced that moment of bewilderment when we flip on a light during a power failure—and nothing happens!)

Immediate and Remote Causes

Yet another way to think critically about causes is to classify them by how close in time the cause is to its result. Something that happens just before an event that it causes is called an **immediate cause.** A factor that also helped to bring about this same event but that occurred further back in time is called a **remote cause.** For example, a last-minute touchdown could be the immediate cause of a football championship, but wise trades made for key players before the season began might be remote causes.

To give a more personal example, getting an A on a college history exam is a happy outcome that may result from the following different types of causes and conditions. The immediate cause could be the fact that you spent an entire weekend studying, carefully reviewing your notes and rehearsing answers to possible questions. More remote causes could include your faithful attendance throughout the semester and your having asked questions in class to clear up any areas of misunderstanding. An even more remote cause might be a grade school trip to a museum, which sparked your interest in history. Necessary conditions for your success include having sufficient intelligence to understand the material and being in good health on the day of the exam.

THINKING ↔ WRITING ACTIVITY 8.4

Analyzing Causal Relationships

Read the following essay by Joan Didion, "Holy Water." Then write the answers to the questions in your journal.

1. Why does Didion think so much about water?
2. What are the effects on her of thinking so much about water?
3. List the three reasons (causes) she gives for authorities' deciding to alter the water delivery schedule.
4. Identify all the causes that led to Sam Peckinpah's film company's having to wait out the weekend idly in Needles.

from Holy Water
by Joan Didion

Some of us who live in arid parts of the world think about water with a reverence others might find excessive. The water I will draw tomorrow from my tap in Malibu is today crossing the Mojave Desert from the Colorado River, and I like to think about exactly where that water is. The water I will drink tonight in a restaurant in Hollywood is by now well down the Los Angeles Aqueduct from the Owens River, and I also think about exactly where that water is: I particularly like to imagine it as it cascades down the 45-degree stone steps that aerate Owens water after its airless passage through the mountain pipes and siphons. As it happens my own reverence for water has always taken the form of this constant meditation upon where the water is, of an obsessive interest not in the politics of water but in the waterworks themselves, in the movement of water through aqueducts and siphons and pumps and forebays and afterbays and weirs and drains, in plumbing on the grand scale. I know the data on water projects I will never see. I know the difficulty Kaiser had closing the last two sluiceway gates on the Guri Dam in Venezuela. I keep watch on evaporation behind the Aswan in Egypt. I can put myself to sleep imagining the water dropping a thousand feet into the turbines at Churchill Falls in Labrador. If the Churchill Falls Project fails to materialize, I fall back on waterworks closer at hand—the tailrace at Hoover on the Colorado, the surge tank in the Tehachapi Mountains that receives California Aqueduct water pumped higher than water has ever been pumped before—and finally I replay a morning when I was seventeen years old and caught, in a military-surplus life raft, in the construction of the Nimbus Afterbay Dam on the American River near Sacramento. I remember that at the moment it happened I was trying to open a tin of anchovies with capers. I recall the raft spinning into the narrow chute through which the river had been temporarily diverted. I recall being deliriously happy.

I suppose it was partly the memory of that delirium that led me to visit, one summer morning in Sacramento, the Operations Control Center for the California State Water Project. Actually so much water is moved around California by so many different agencies that maybe only the movers themselves know on any given day whose water is where, but to get a general picture it is necessary only to remember that Los Angeles moves some of it, San Francisco moves some of it, the Bureau of Reclamation's Central Valley Project moves some of it and the California State Water Project moves most of the rest of it, moves a vast amount of it, moves more water farther than has ever been moved anywhere. They collect this water up in the granite keeps of the Sierra Nevada and they store roughly a trillion gallons of it behind the Oroville Dam and every morning, down at the Project's headquarters in Sacramento, they decide how much of their water they want to move the next day. They make this morning decision according to supply and demand, which is simple in theory but rather more complicated in practice. In theory each of the Project's five field divisions—the Oroville, the Delta, the San Luis, the San Joaquin and the Southern divisions—places a call to headquarters before nine A.M. and tells the dispatchers how much water is needed by its local water contractors, who have in turn based their morning estimates on orders from growers and other big users. A schedule is made. The gates open and close according to schedule. The water flows south and the deliveries are made.

In practice this requires prodigious coordination, precision, and the best efforts of several human minds and that of a Univac 418. In practice it might be necessary to hold large flows of water for power production, or to flush out encroaching salinity in the Sacramento-San Joaquin Delta, the most ecologically sensitive point on the system. In practice a sudden rain might obviate the need for a delivery when that delivery is already on its way. In practice what is being delivered here is an enormous volume of water, not quarts of milk or spools of thread, and it takes two days to move such a delivery down through Oroville into the Delta, which is the great pooling place for California water and has been for some years alive with electronic sensors and telemetering equipment and men blocking channels and diverting flows and shoveling fish away from the pumps. It takes perhaps another six days to move this same water down the California Aqueduct from the Delta to the Tehachapi and put it over the hill to Southern California. "Putting some over the hill" is what they say around the Project Operations Control Center when they want to indicate that they are pumping Aqueduct water from the floor of the San Joaquin Valley up and over the Tehachapi Mountains. "Pulling it down" is what they say when they want to indicate that they are lowering a water level somewhere in the system. They can put some over the hill by remote control from this room in Sacramento with its Univac and its big board and its flashing lights. They can pull down a pool in the San Joaquin by remote control from this room in Sacramento with its locked doors and its ringing alarms and its constant print-outs of data from sensors out there in the water itself. From this room in Sacramento the whole system takes on the aspect of a perfect three-billion-dollar hydraulic toy, and in certain ways it is. "LET'S START DRAINING QUAIL AT 12:00" was the 10:51 A.M. entry on the electronically recorded communications log the day I visited the Operations Control Center. "Quail" is a reservoir in Los Angeles County with a gross capacity of 1,636,018,000 gallons. "OK" was the response recorded in the log. I knew at that moment that I had missed the only vocation for which I had any instinctive affinity: I wanted to drain Quail myself.

Not many people I know carry their end of the conversation when I want to talk about water deliveries, even when I stress that these deliveries affect their lives, indirectly, every day. "Indirectly" is not quite enough for most people I know. This morning, however, several people I know were affected not "indirectly" but "directly" by the way the water moves. They had been in New Mexico shooting a picture, one sequence of which required a river deep enough to sink a truck, the kind with a cab and a trailer and fifty or sixty wheels. It so happened that no river near the New Mexico location was running that deep this year. The production was therefore moved today to Needles, California, where the Colorado River normally runs, depending upon releases from Davis Dam, eighteen to twenty-five feet deep. Now. Follow this closely: yesterday we had a freak tropical storm in Southern California, two inches of rain in a normally dry month, and because this rain flooded the fields and provided more irrigation than any grower could possibly want for several days, no water was ordered from Davis Dam.

5   No order, no releases.

Supply and demand.

As a result the Colorado was running only seven feet deep past Needles today, Sam Peckinpah's desire for eighteen feet of water in which to sink a truck not being the kind of demand anyone at Davis Dam is geared to meet. The production closed down for the weekend. Shooting will resume Tuesday, providing some grower orders water and the agencies controlling the Colorado release it. Meanwhile many gaffers, best boys, cameramen, assistant directors, script supervisors, stunt drivers and maybe even Sam Peckinpah are waiting out the weekend in Needles, where it is often 110 degrees at five P.M. and hard to get dinner after eight. This is a California parable, but a true one.

I have always wanted a swimming pool, and never had one. When it became generally known a year or so ago that California was suffering severe drought, many people in water-rich parts of the country seemed obscurely gratified, and made frequent reference to Californians having to brick up their swimming pools. In fact a swimming pool requires, once it has been filled and the filter has begun its process of cleaning and recirculating the water, virtually no water, but the symbolic content of swimming pools has always been interesting: a pool is misapprehended as a trapping of affluence, real or pretended, and of a kind of hedonistic attention to the body. Actually a pool is, for many of us in the West, a symbol not of affluence but of order, of control over the uncontrollable. A pool is water, made available and useful, and is, as such, infinitely soothing to the western eye.

It is easy to forget that the only natural force over which we have any control out here is water, and that only recently. In my memory California summers were characterized by the coughing in the pipes that meant the well was dry, and California winters by all-night watches on rivers about to crest, by sandbagging, by dynamite on the levees and flooding on the first floor. Even now the place is not all that hospitable to extensive settlement. As I write a fire has been burning out of control for two weeks in the ranges behind the Big Sur coast. Flash floods last night wiped out all major roads into Imperial County. I noticed this morning a hairline crack in a living-room tile from last week's earthquake, a 4.4 I never felt. In the part of California where I now live aridity is the single most prominent feature of the climate, and I am not pleased to see, this year, cactus spreading wild to the sea. There will be days this winter when the humidity will drop to ten, seven, four. Tumbleweed will blow against my house and the sound of the rattlesnake will be duplicated a hundred times a day by dried bougainvillea drifting in my driveway. The apparent ease of California life is an illusion, and those who believe the illusion real live here in only the most temporary way. I know as well as the next person that there is considerable transcendent value in a river running wild and undammed, a river running free over granite, but I have also lived beneath such a river when it was running in flood, and gone without showers when it was running dry.

10   "The West begins," Bernard DeVoto wrote, "where the average annual rainfall drops below twenty inches." This is maybe the best definition of the West I have ever read, and it goes a long way toward explaining my own passion for seeing the water under control, but many people I know persist in looking for psychoanalytical implications in this passion. As a matter of fact I have explored, in an amateur way, the more obvious of these implications, and come up with nothing interesting. A certain external reality remains, and resists interpretation. The West begins where the average annual rainfall drops below twenty inches. Water is important to people who do not have it, and the same is true of control. Some fifteen years ago I tore a poem by Karl Shapiro from a magazine and pinned it on my kitchen wall. This fragment of paper is now on the wall of a sixth kitchen, and crumbles a little whenever I touch it, but I keep it there for the last stanza, which has for me the power of a prayer:

It is raining in California, a straight rain
Cleaning the heavy oranges on the bush,
Filling the gardens till the gardens flow,
Shining the olives, tiling the gleaming tile,
Waxing the dark camellia leaves more green,
Flooding the daylong valleys like the Nile.

I thought of those lines almost constantly on the morning in Sacramento when I went to visit the California State Water Project Operations Control Center. If I had wanted to drain Quail at 10:51 that morning, I wanted, by early afternoon, to do a great deal more. I wanted to open and close the Clifton Court Forebay intake gate. I wanted to produce some power down at the San Luis Dam. I wanted to pick a pool at random on the Aqueduct and pull it down and then refill it, watching for the hydraulic jump. I wanted to put some water over the hill and I wanted to shut down all flow from the Aqueduct into the Bureau of Reclamation's Cross Valley Canal, just to see how long it would take somebody over at Reclamation to call up and complain. I stayed as long as I could and watched the system work on the big board with the lighted checkpoints. The Delta salinity report was coming in on one of the teletypes behind me. The Delta tidal report was coming in on another. The earthquake board, which has been desensitized to sound its alarm (a beeping tone for Southern California, a high-pitched one for the north) only for those earthquakes which register at least 3.0 on the Richter Scale, was silent. I had no further business in this room and yet I wanted to stay the day. I wanted to be the one, that day, who was shining the olives, filling the gardens, and flooding the daylong valleys like the Nile. I want it still.

THINKING ↔ WRITING ACTIVITY 8.5

Analyzing Causal Relationships

Read the following excerpt from Carl Hiaasen's article "The Last Days of Florida Bay," originally published in *Sports Illustrated*. Then write the answers to the questions in your journal.

1. List the causes Hiassen identifies as having brought about the present condition of the bay.
2. What is the immediate cause?
3. Do any of these causes make up a causal chain?
4. Are any of the causes contributory?
5. Are any of the causes interactive? If so, how?

from The Last Days of Florida Bay
by Carl Hiaasen

On a gum-gray June afternoon, between thundershowers, my son and I are running a 17-foot skiff through the backcountry of Florida Bay. The wind has lain down, the water is silk. Suddenly, a glorious eruption: bottle-nosed dolphins, an acre of them, in a spree of feeding, play and rambunctious lust. From a hundred yards we can hear the slap of flukes and the hiss of blowholes. We can see the misty geysers, the slash of black dorsals, the occasional detonation as a luckless bait fish gets gobbled.

No matter how often I witness the sight, I'm always dazzled. A stranger to these waters could only assume he was traveling in authentic wilderness, pure and thriving. If only it were so.

It's easy, when surrounded by dolphins, to forget that the bay is fatefully situated downstream from the ulcerous sprawl of Florida's Gold Coast. Four-and-a-half million people live only a morning's drive away.

The river that feeds the backcountry is the Everglades, sometimes parched and sometimes flooded. Water that once ran untainted and bountiful is now intercepted and pumped extravagantly to sugarcane fields, swimming pools, golf courses, city reservoirs—and even the Atlantic. What's left is dispensed toward the bay in a criminally negligent fraction of its natural flow. The water isn't as clean as it once was, and it doesn't always arrive in the right season.

5   That the bay is sick is hardly a surprise. The wonder is that it has survived so long and the dolphins haven't fled to sea forever. . . .

That's why it is imperative that a natural flow be restored as soon as possible, while the political will and funds exist to do it. The engineering isn't as daunting as the politics. Powerful special-interest groups are demanding a say in where the lifeblood of the Everglades goes, how much they get to keep and what they're allowed to dump in the water on its way downstream.

The battle begins up at Lake Okeechobee, where Big Sugar finally (and reluctantly) has agreed to filter phosphates from the runoff of the cane fields. Farther south, the cities siphon heavily from the diked "conservation areas"—cheap, accessible reservoirs that help fuel the breakneck westward growth in Palm Beach, Broward and Dade counties. Even below Miami, on Florida's still rural southern tip, water policy is disproportionately influenced by private interests. In the dry months what would otherwise trickle through the glades to the bay is diverted instead to a small cluster of tomato and avocado farms. Conversely, in the wet season the surplus water is pumped off the fields to protect the crops. The canal network was absurdly designed to flush millions of gallons not into the Everglades (which were made to absorb them) but into Manatee Bay and Barnes Sound, which are saltwater bodies. The effect of such a copious, sudden injection of freshwater is an overdose—lethal on an impressive scale to fish, corals and other marine life.

But it's all for a good cause. Upstream the avocados are plump and safe.

THINKING ↔ WRITING ACTIVITY 8.6

Analyzing Causal Relationships

Read the following excerpt from *Coastal Alert,* by Dwight Holing; then write the answers to the questions in your journal.

1. What causes for oil spills does Holing discuss? List them.
2. Identify each cause as sufficient, contributory, interactive, or part of a causal chain.

---

from Coastal Alert

by Dwight Holing

The environmental impacts of oil and gas production on the outer continental shelf (OCS) have been debated for many years. The issues arise from the complexity of coastal and offshore marine processes and ecosystems, human socioeconomic systems, and interactions with OCS oil and gas development activities. . . . Mounting scientific evidence reveals that each step of offshore energy development—from exploration to drilling, from transport to refining—exposes land, air, and water to a host of pollutants. Hazardous wastes and air toxics are just a few of the harmful by-products that can affect marine life as well as the quality of life onshore.

The Department of the Interior's call to open the nation's coast to offshore drilling raises many questions: What are the effects of toxic and other waste generated by drilling? What are the risks of oil spills fouling the nation's coast? What will the impact be on marine wildlife and the commercial fishery? How will the tourist industry be affected? Will the coast become industrialized? Are there alternatives to offshore oil drilling? Each of these issues is addressed in the following pages.

Oil Spills

Offshore drilling causes oil spills. Between 1964 and 1985, twenty-one major spills involving one thousand barrels or more occurred as a result of drilling and production operations on the OCS. Those numbers are sure to increase if more sites are opened to drilling. The DOI estimated that twenty-two to forty-six major spills would occur as a result of the 1987–92 five-year program. New oil drilling off the coast of Southern California, for example, would increase the chance of a large oil spill in the region appreciably and make a major spill almost certain within the next thirty-one years, according to a DOI assessment. The study found one chance in seven of a "large" spill of one thousand barrels. The probability of one or more major spills occurring from all OCS activities off Southern California is 99+ percent.

Those risk estimates don't even take into consideration spills under one thousand barrels, even though such spills make up 97 percent of all spills. The DOI does not input data of spills of this size into its Oil Spill Risk Analysis (OSRA), a computer model used to estimate risk. This means that official risk estimates contained in environmental impact statements—key documents prepared before deciding whether or not to drill in specific areas—can underestimate the likelihood of an oil spill by a factor of as much as 260.

5   According to a 1989 report issued by the National Academy of Sciences, the DOI's OSRA is fatally flawed. The NAS found that the DOI lacks important scientific information about physical oceanography on which oil spill risk estimates are based. The NAS report concluded that "[m]odel studies need to be supplemented with observations. Trajectory predictions or estimations of trajectory statistics realistic for use in risk analysis or in accident management cannot be obtained without new fieldwork. . . ."

The report also faulted DOI for relying "too heavily upon the OSRA model for prediction of impacts. This has resulted in an emphasis on the probability of an oil spill instead of on the effects of a spill."

Spill Sources

A variety of sources during offshore development and production can trigger an oil spill, including tanker accidents, well blowouts, pipeline leaks, and routine operations.

Tankers.   Tanker mishaps are the leading cause of spills. Take the six-month period between December 1988 and June 1989, for example. Six major oil spills off the U.S. coast were caused by ships. On December 22 a collision between two vessels caused 230,000 gallons of oil to spill off Washington's Olympic Peninsula. On March 3 the oil tanker *Exxon Houston* struck a coral reef near Honolulu and spilled 117,000 gallons of fuel. Three weeks later its sister ship, the *Exxon Valdez*, ran aground in Prince William Sound, flooding the pristine waters with nearly 11 million gallons of Alaskan crude. On June 23, about one million gallons of fuel began washing ashore in Newport, Rhode Island, from a grounded Greek tanker. That same day, 250,000 gallons of heavy crude oil were spilled in the Houston Ship Channel near Galveston, Texas, when a tug-driven barge collided with a cargo vessel. And the next day, an Uruguayan oil tanker spilled 800,000 gallons of fuel into the Delaware River.

According to the U.S. Coast Guard, there were 981 accidents involving tankers registered in the United States from 1981 through 1988, including 175 collisions. During the same time 413 foreign-registered tankers were involved in accidents in U.S. waters.

10 Millions of gallons of oil are dumped into U.S. waters each year as a result. In 1988, there were five thousand to six thousand spills involving oil and other toxic substances along our coasts and in other navigable waters, says the Coast Guard. Of those spills, twelve were classified as major because they involved 100,000 gallons or more. An additional ten spilled 10,000 to 100,000 gallons, and the rest involved less than 10,000 gallons. Data from the Coast Guard's Pollution Incident Reporting System reveal that 91 million gallons of oil and 36 million gallons of other toxic substances were spilled into U.S. waters from 1980 through 1986. Of the spilled oil, two-thirds came from oil tankers and barges, usually because of ruptures in accidents. The rest came from offshore drilling platforms, refineries, and other sources such as runoff and tank ballast washings.

Human error, according to the Coast Guard, is responsible for most of the accidents. Though spills do result from negligence by intoxicated crew members, most accidents are made by well-trained seamen and have nothing to do with drugs or alcohol or incompetence.

Tankers are vulnerable to all kinds of accidents caused by human error. On February 7, 1990, for example, the *American Trader* spilled about 400,000 gallons of Alaskan crude off the Southern California coast when it apparently struck its own anchor. The tanker punctured its hull while trying to hook up with a mooring buoy and unload its cargo via an underwater pipeline that feeds refineries and tank farms along the coast.

Drilling platforms. Offshore rigs contribute significantly to the total amount of oil spilled in U.S. waters. During drilling there is a risk of a blowout, an uncontrolled discharge of oil from the drill hole. A blowout can occur when, because of equipment failure, human error, or unpredicted geological conditions, the pressure in the underground oil reservoir cannot be contained.

The most famous U.S. blowout took place in California's Santa Barbara Channel in 1969. It happened when Union Oil was drilling nearly one mile below the ocean's floor. The protective casing used to line the 5,000-foot deep well was only 240 feet long—too short to control the pressure of surging oil. The drill's bit went through a fracture in the rock and the pressurized oil shot out through the fissures. The pressure was so great that it blasted a hole in the seabed 200 yards away from the well. For twelve days oil gushed unchecked into the ocean. Some 50,000 to 70,000 barrels of oil spread over 660 square miles, fouling 150 miles of coastline and leaving thousands of dead birds, mammals, and fish in its wake.

15   Oil can also leak from holding tanks on board the drilling platforms. Earthquakes, vessel collisions, structural failures, human and operational errors, and mechanical defects can rupture storage tanks.

Oil is also discharged into the sea from the produced water—water in the formation that is produced along with oil. Produced water often contains large amounts of dissolved or emulsified oil and grease, as much as thousands of barrels a year.

Pipelines.   The pipelines used to transfer the oil from the platform to either offshore or onshore processing plants are also vulnerable to leaks and ruptures. Corrosion, being struck by a ship's anchor, and mechanical defects are the leading causes for the majority of all pipeline failures. Pipeline leaks can also be triggered by earthquakes, internal corrosion, and human error.

THINKING ↔ WRITING ACTIVITY 8.7

Analyzing Causal Relationships

Read the following excerpt from *This Land Is Your Land,* by Jon Naar and Alex J. Naar, then write the answers to the questions in your journal.

1. List the causes of the degradation of the ocean environment that the excerpt discusses.
2. Identify each cause as sufficient, contributory, interactive, or part of a causal chain.

---

from This Land Is Your Land

by John Naar and Alex J. Naar

Until relatively recently it was assumed that, because of their size and the huge quantities of water they contain, oceans had an infinite capacity to absorb wastes by dilution and the natural process of regeneration. However, in the 1950s and '60s Rachel Carson's writings and Jacques Cousteau's films and books alerted the public to a growing threat to the ocean's ecosystems. The thinning of seabirds' eggshells by DDT, described by Carson, was the first of a long series of reports on degradation of the marine environment. In 1970 the newly formed U.S. Council on Environmental Quality (CEQ) issued a major warning: Pollution had already closed one-fifth of the nation's commercial shellfish beds; increasing levels of ocean dumping had created serious environmental damage; and there was a vast new threat from municipalities using the oceans "as a convenient sink for their wastes."

Overfishing; dumping of garbage, human sewage, and industrial wastes; oil spills, runoff of chemicals from agriculture and transportation; heating of rivers and bays from nuclear reactors and conventional power plants; acid rain; dredging; channelization; and sandblasting of ships: These are some of the ways in which aquatic ecosystems are now subjected to damage and destruction comparable with that of Superfund toxic-waste sites and air pollution from carbon and sulfur dioxides, CFCs, ozone, and other substances.

Overfishing

Overfishing is a global problem threatening many species of marine life and the systems of which they are part. Since the 1980s the world's yearly catch of fish has exceeded what the United Nations considers to be a maximum sustainable yield. This is the result of a sharply increased world demand for fish, the development of new factory-fishing technologies, and government encouragement for building ever bigger fishing boats and using nets with smaller mesh sizes that trap fish too young and small to be eaten.

Catch as Catch Can

In the late 1980s the fishing of capelin, a tiny sardine used in animal feed and commercial fats, was banned because of an interrelated chain of events. The catching of capelin off the shores of Norway deprived cod of their natural food and forced them to eat their own young. With the disappearance of capelin and cod, the seals were deprived of *their* main source of food. Then hundreds of thousands of starving seals invaded the Norwegian coast in search of food, depleting coastal fish stocks and destroying salmon hatcheries in the fjords. At the same time, sixty thousand seals were accidentally caught and drowned in Norwegian fishing nets.

Natural Causes

5 Natural causes can also contribute to a decline in marine life. A recently identified climatic phenomenon that recurs every three to eight years, known as *El Niño*, prevents the upwelling of cold water to the ocean's surface in the Eastern Equatorial Pacific, depriving it of nutrients, causing thousands of seabirds to starve and destroying huge numbers of fish and other marine organisms. Along with overfishing, *El Niño* is believed to have contributed to the failure of the anchovetta catch off

Ecuador and the collapse of the California sardine fisheries in the mid-1960s and early 1970s.

Ocean Dumping

Dumping of sludge, dredged and radioactive materials and burning of wastes at sea represent serious threats to marine ecosystems. Sludge, a mudlike semiliquid end product of sewage treatment, often contains lead, mercury, zinc, chromium, cadmium, copper, pesticides, and disease-causing microorganisms and pathogens. These harmful substances can kill marine organisms and reduce species' vitality and growth. Nutrients contained in the sludge, while useful on land, can overfertilize ocean waters, resulting in eutrophication. The high organic content of sludge can drastically change the kinds of organisms that can live on the bottom of the ocean.

In 1976 a huge fish kill was discovered off the New Jersey shore just south of a sewage sludge dump located within a few miles of New York Harbor. "I went out to a shipwreck and it was completely dead—starfish, eels, lobsters, all sizes of crab—everything was dead," said Pat Yanaton, a microbiologist and environmental committeeman for the Eastern Diveboat Association. In 1991, by order of Congress and its own state legislature, New Jersey ceased dumping treated sewage sludge into the Atlantic Ocean. New York City and its neighboring Westchester and Nassau counties were given a June 1992 deadline to stop dumping their annual 8 million tons of sewage sludge into the Atlantic 106 miles east of Cape May, New Jersey, where the marine environment and the ecological balance of the ocean might already have been impacted.

Unfortunately, even when an ocean dump is phased out, it continues to endanger marine ecosystems for decades because, as in New York's case, it leaves behind millions of tons of solid wastes, industrial residue, and other contaminants accumulated over long periods of time. In addition to polluting the area where they are dumped, many of the toxic materials are carried by currents to threaten vital plant and animal habitats hundreds and sometimes thousands of miles away.

The alternatives to dumping cost money. New Jersey invested more than $200 million on new processing equipment and another $26 million a year for shipping the sludge by truck and train to a short-term landfill 1,450 miles away in Texas. On a longer-term basis, different disposal methods must be found because there is growing nationwide resistance against trucking waste to out-of-state landfills. There is also increased opposition to incineration of waste because of air pollution, building costs, and disposal of the toxic ash. At an international meeting held in January 1991 at the Woods Hole Oceanographic Institution in Woods Hole, Massachusetts, a number of proposals for delivering sewage sludge to the deep-sea bottom without contaminating the upper levels of seawater were discussed. In one of them an 18-inch hose several miles long with a 40-ton nozzle at its lower end would be lowered from a sludge ship to dump its load close to the bottom. Another idea was to link 55-gallon drums of waste into "trains" with a heavy nose cone that would sink at 50 miles per hour, penetrating deep into the bottom ooze, which in some regions is thousands of feet deep. Concerns were raised, however, that too little is known about the long-term fate of such sludge and its effects on marine life, especially deep-dwelling organisms.

10   The most environmentally sound solution is to reclaim the sludge by removing the heavy metals and other contaminants and use it as a fertilizer rather than dumping it in the ocean or in a landfill. However, even this option can be difficult to implement on a large scale. In March 1992 New York City announced that it was proceeding with a billion-dollar plan to build eight plants to convert the 13,000 tons of sludge it produces daily into fertilizer, soil conditioner, or landfill cover that the city could use in parks and housing-project grounds. Residents and business people in the boroughs where the plants would be built expressed opposition to the plan because they feared noxious odors and greatly increased truck traffic. At least one of the sites was reported to have heavily contaminated soil. However, according to Albert Appleton, New York City's commissioner of environmental protection, the plants would be "completely odor-controlled." The volume of trucks would be reduced by the use of barges; as for the contaminated site, "We can clean it up and bring it back into the city's land-use inventory," he promised.

In June 1992, one year after a Congressional deadline, New York City ceased dumping sewage sludge in the Atlantic, but there are more than one hundred licensed ocean dump sites in the Gulf of Mexico, the Atlantic, and the Pacific that receive materials dredged primarily from harbor and river channels. These materials are a mix of water and sediments often containing heavy metals, PCBs, oil, grease, and other pollutants. However, even "clean" dredged materials can harm marine life, because they bury marine organisms and increase the level of suspended sediments. The bulk of this dredging is carried out by the U.S. Army Corps of Engineers, whose task it is to maintain free passage for ports and harbors. If the corps' dredging program continues, there will be an even greater threat to marine ecosystems in coastal and ocean waters.

Radioactive Waste

The Ocean Dumping Act expressly bars high-level radioactive waste dumping at sea. But between 1946 and 1970 the United States was allowed to dump more than 110,000 packages of plutonium and cesium into its waters, most of it close to major metropolitan areas—the Farallon Islands 30 miles west of San Francisco, Massachusetts Bay just outside of Boston, and two dump sites within 3 miles of Newark, New Jersey. According to a 1990 NOAA study, about a quarter of the 47,500 barrels of the atomic waste dumped in the Gulf of the Farallones National Marine Sanctuary have ruptured, threatening Pacific herring, Dover sole, rockfish, sablefish, and Dungeness crab commercially fished in the area. Plutonium, which can remain toxic for hundreds of thousands of years, and cesium have been found at levels "possibly more than 1,000 times the level expected to occur naturally." The Farallon Islands have the largest population of seabirds south of Alaska and an abundance of fish, invertebrates, and marine mammals. In January 1991 NOAA began a $900,000 study to determine the extent of the damage from the radioactive material to the richest marine habitat in the West.

Ocean Incineration

Burning wastes aboard ships is also regulated by the Ocean Dumping Act, because it releases waste and toxic by-products into the marine environment.

The law permits burning only liquid wastes of a certain composition, representing roughly 8 percent of the 250 million metric tons of hazardous wastes produced every year in the United States. Yet even this "small" percentage (some 2 million metric tons) of concentrated toxic and carcinogenic material is lethal to marine life immediately or through long-term contamination; it also can affect humans who eat the poisoned fish and seafood. Another problem is spills and leaks during the transportation of the wastes to the incinerator ship or during the actual burning at sea, which in turn causes additional problems of water pollution and ecosystem damage.

Thinking Critically About Causal Fallacies

Because causality plays such a dominant role in the way we make sense of the world, it is not surprising that people make many mistakes and many errors in judgment in trying to determine causal relationships. These mistakes and errors can lead to unsound arguments, or **fallacies.** The following are some of the most common fallacies associated with causality.

- Questionable cause
- Misidentification of the cause
- *Post hoc ergo propter hoc*
- Slippery slope

Questionable Cause

The fallacy of questionable cause occurs when someone presents a causal relationship for which no real evidence exists. Superstitious beliefs, such as "If you break a mirror, you will have seven years of bad luck," usually fall into this category. Some people feel that astrology, a system of beliefs tying one's personality and fortunes in life to the position of the planets at the moment of birth, also falls into this category.

Consider the following passage from the *Confessions* of St. Augustine. Does it seem to support the causal assertions of astrology, or deny them? Why?

> Firminus had heard from his father that when his mother had been pregnant with him, a slave belonging to a friend of his father's was also about to bear. It happened that since the two women had their babies at the same instant, the men were forced to cast exactly the same horoscope for each newborn child down to the last detail, one for his son, the other for the little slave. Yet Firminus, born to wealth in his parents' house, had one of the more illustrious careers in life whereas the slave had no alleviation of his life's burden.

Other examples of this fallacy include explanations like those given by fourteenth-century sufferers of the bubonic plague who claimed that the Jews were poisoning the Christians' wells. This charge was nonsensical. An equal percentage of Jews were dying of the plague. No evidence supported the allegation.

Misidentification of the Cause

In causal situations, we are not always certain about what is causing what—in other words, about what is the cause and what is the effect. For example, in the following pairs of items, which are the causes and which are the effects? Why?

- Headaches and tension
- Failure in school and personal problems
- Shyness and lack of confidence
- Substance abuse and emotional difficulties

Sometimes a third factor is responsible for two effects we are examining. Headaches and tension may both be the result of a third element—such as some new medication we are taking. When we fail to recognize the third element, we commit the fallacy of *ignoring a common cause*. There also exists the fallacy of *assuming a common cause*—such as assuming that one's sore toe and earache both stem from the same cause.

Post Hoc Ergo Propter Hoc

The translation of the Latin phrase *post hoc ergo propter hoc* is "After that, therefore because of that." It refers to situations in which, because two things occur close together in time, we assume that one has caused the other. Suppose your team wins the game each time you wear your favorite shirt; you just may be tempted to conclude that the one event (wearing your favorite shirt) has some influence on the other event (winning the game). As a result, you may continue to wear this shirt "for good luck." It is easy to see how this sort of mistaken thinking can lead to all sorts of superstitious beliefs. Consider the following causal conclusion arrived at by Mark Twain's fictional character Huckleberry Finn in the following passage. How would you analyze the conclusion that he comes to?

> I've always reckoned that looking at the new moon over your left shoulder is one of the carelessest and foolishest things a body can do. Old Hank Bunker done it once, and bragged about it; and in less than two years he got drunk and fell off a shot tower and spread himself out so that he was just a kind of layer. . . . But anyway, it all came of looking at the moon that way, like a fool.

Can you identify any superstitious beliefs or practices of your own that may have resulted from *post hoc* thinking?

Slippery Slope

The causal fallacy of slippery slope is illustrated in the following advice:

> Don't miss that first deadline, because if you do, it won't be long before you're missing all your deadlines. This will spread to the rest of your life, as you will be late for every appointment. This terminal procrastination will ruin your career, and friends and relatives will abandon you. You will end up a lonely failure who is unable to ever do anything on time.

Slippery slope thinking asserts that one undesirable action will inevitably lead to a worse action, which will necessarily lead to still a worse one, all the way down the "slippery slope" to some terrible disaster at the bottom. Although this progression may indeed occur, there certainly is no causal guarantee that it will. Create slippery slope scenarios for one of the following warnings:

- If you get behind on one credit card payment . . .
- If you fail that first test . . .
- If you eat that first fudge square . . .

THINKING ↔ WRITING ACTIVITY 8.8

Analyzing Causal Fallacies

Review the four causal fallacies just described; then identify and explain the reasoning pitfalls illustrated in the following examples:

1. The person who won the lottery says she dreamed the winning numbers. I'm going to start writing down the numbers in my dreams.
2. Yesterday I forgot to take my vitamins and I immediately got sick. That mistake won't occur again!
3. I'm warning you: if you start missing classes, it won't be long before you flunk out of school and ruin your future.
4. I always take the first seat in the bus. Today I took another seat, and the bus broke down.
5. I think the reason I'm not doing well in school is that I'm just not interested. Also, I simply don't have enough time to study.

Causal Claims

Many people want us to see the cause-and-effect relationships that they believe exist, and they sometimes utilize questionable or outright fallacious reasoning. Consider the following examples:

1. Politicians assure us that a vote for them will result in "a chicken in every pot and a car in every garage."
2. Advertisers tell us that using this detergent will leave our wash "cleaner than clean, whiter than white."
3. Doctors tell us that eating a balanced diet will result in better health.
4. Educators tell us that a college degree is worth an average of $830,000 additional income over an individual's lifetime.
5. Scientists inform us that nuclear energy will result in a better life for all of us.

In each of these examples, certain **causal claims** are being made about how the world operates, in an effort to persuade us to adopt a certain point of view. As critical thinkers, it is our duty to evaluate these various causal claims as to whether they are sensible.

THINKING ↔ WRITING ACTIVITY 8.9

Evaluating Causal Claims

Explain how you might go about evaluating whether each of the following causal claims makes sense.

- *Example:* Taking the right vitamins will improve health.
- *Evaluation:* Review the medical research that examines the effect of taking vitamins on health; speak to a nutritionist; speak to a doctor.

1. Sweet Smell deodorant will keep you drier all day long.
2. Allure perfume will cause men to be attracted to you.
3. Natural childbirth will result in a more fulfilling birth experience.
4. Aspirin Plus will give you faster, longer-lasting relief from headaches.
5. Radial tires will improve the gas mileage of your car.

Writing Thoughtfully About Causal Relationships

Clearly, because of the complexity of determining cause and effect, writing a causal analysis requires special care. Causal analyses range all the way from rigorous scientific studies that can establish causes with some degree of certainty to theorizing about events in our personal lives. The causal analysis assignments you encounter in college are likely to be of two types: those for which you conduct some kind of study to determine causality and then report your results, and those for which you research what others have said about the causes of an event and report what they have said.

For the *first* type, you are likely to be given a format, such as for a lab report or an experimental design. It will be important for you to follow directions as you plan and conduct your study, and important for you to observe the conventions of the discipline in which you are writing as you prepare your report. Models are extremely helpful, so study them carefully if your professor provides them. If not, ask a librarian for guidance.

The *second* type, in which you report what others have said about the causes of an event, can be structured in the traditional essay format. Though you may worry that a paper for which research is required will be more difficult to write, you may be pleasantly surprised to discover that the sources discovered in research became "assistant writers"; the authors of the sources help you complete the paper by providing information for you to include. Of course, the information from sources must be properly documented, but correctly documenting information not only is required for honesty but also shows your audience that you have "done your homework."

The principles for presenting causal analysis in writing are not rules set in stone; at times you may have good reason for varying or ignoring them. In general, though, it makes sense for you to follow them.

1. Be cautious. Causal relationships are difficult to prove. You may have to use language such as possible cause or may have affected.
2. Name the event, and perhaps describe it and/or people's reactions to it, in your introduction.

3. In your thesis statement, indicate that you will be analyzing the causes of this event or that you will be reporting what others have said about its causes.
4. Discuss each cause in a separate section (at least one body paragraph for each cause).
5. Amplify on how or why each cause brought about the event. Simply naming the cause is not enough.
6. Whenever possible, focus on immediate rather than remote causes.
7. Use correct vocabulary to identify causes (contributory, causal chain, interactive, sufficient, etc.).
8. Represent accurately any sources you use and document them honestly and correctly.
9. Avoid logical fallacies, such as post hoc ergo propter hoc.
10. In your conclusion, name the causes and discuss the level of certainty about them. You may, of course, wish to do more than this in your conclusion.

WRITING PROJECT

This chapter has included both readings and **Thinking↔Writing Activities** that encouraged you to think about causal relationships in your own life and in the environment. Be sure to reread what you wrote for those activities; you may be able to use some of it for help in completing this project.

WRITING PROJECT   Analyzing Causal Relationships
of a Recent Event

Write an essay in which you report and discuss causes of a specific event that occurred within the last three years. Include material from at least three sources. After you have drafted your essay, revise it to the best of your ability. Follow instructions given by your professor as to topic limits and specifications, length, format, and so forth.

Begin by considering the key elements in the **Thinking↔Writing Model.**

Purpose

You have a variety of purposes here. You can satisfy your own curiosity about why an event occurred and explain the causes to others. You can improve your ability to think critically about causal relationships. You can hone your revision skills by working through the revision questions that follow. Of course, you also want to receive a satisfactory grade by completing the assignment well.

Audience

You have a range of readers within your audience. *You* are an important audience, for in researching and analyzing causes, you can become a better thinker and possibly a more concerned citizen. Your classmates can be a valuable audience for review of a draft, reacting as intelligent readers who are not as knowledgeable as you about the causes of this event. Others interested in the event may find your paper enlightening, so you might find a way to share it. Finally, your instructor remains the audience who will judge how well you have planned, drafted, and revised. As a writing teacher, he or she cares about a clear focus, logical organization, specific details and examples, accurate documentation of sources, and correctness. Keep these in mind as you revise, edit, and proofread.

Subject

You should think seriously about the event, in terms of its causes and of its effects on society. For example, if you decide to write about an event affecting the environment, consider that all of us need to be concerned about both positive and negative environmental changes. Not only our future, but our children's and their children's futures depend on our careful stewardship of the earth. At the same time, there are competing economic and political pressures that can act against a strict conservationist view. By researching and analyzing even one specific event, we can add to our own knowledge and that of our audience, thereby preparing for responsible future action.

Writer

You will be using sources for this essay, but you should not feel intimidated by them; rather, you should view your sources as "assistant writers" for you. Or think of yourself as the host of a talk show with your sources as the guests; others will speak, but you will be in control, so your paper should be in your own voice (it should sound like you). You will report and document the published writers' words and ideas and comment upon them as you think appropriate. If you find disagreement among your sources, don't discard any of them: the lack of agreement gives you a variety of views to report.

The Writing Process

The following sections will guide you through the stages of generating, planning, drafting, and revising as you work on your essay. Try to be particularly conscious of both the critical thinking you find in your sources and the critical thinking you do about it.

Generating Ideas

- Within whatever confines your instructor may have set, begin by finding an event that interests you and that you have wondered about. If one comes to mind immediately, you can begin to research it. If not, begin by brainstorming a list of all the local and national events you can remember from the last few years. Other good sources for events are encyclopedia yearbooks and December ("The Year in Review") issues of magazines. Then make a tentative choice.

- Once you have chosen an event to research, you can use a variety of research techniques, depending on which are available and on your own proficiency. Most libraries have computer indexes for newspapers and periodicals as well as for books, which will enable you to generate a list of articles related to your event. The Internet, if you know how to navigate it, offers you a world of information. Check any list of titles or sites carefully, especially if it's long, for words indicating that articles deal with the causes of the event: "causes, factors, results in, underlie, etc."

- Locate or print the sources you identify, and read them carefully. First, check to see that they do indeed discuss the causes of the event, not just the event itself. Then see what causes they identify and how they label them (contributory, interactive, etc.). If they do not label them, try to do that yourself. Also, look for language that indicates the level of certainty about these causes ("has been definitely identified as a cause," or "may be partially responsible").

■ Mark sections of the source you will include (of course, you can do this only if you own the source or have made a photocopy). If you are required to do so, make notecards based on the marked sections.

■ Think about how much information you have. Do you need more? If so, continue researching, reading, and marking until you have enough to answer the question "Why did this event take place?"

Defining a Focus

Write a thesis statement that will make clear to your audience that you are going to analyze *why* the event occurred. There are at least two possible ways to frame this type of thesis. The first is simply to report what your sources say. If your sources are in agreement and present some degree of certainty, you can simply state this. If your sources disagree, you can state that as your thesis; if your sources were less than certain about the causes, you can include that as well. A second type of thesis involves one more level of thinking on your part: if you want or are required to take a position on the causal relationships involved, this position should be included in your thesis statement; for example, "Having read four sources dealing with the causes of this event, I agree with three of them but reject a theory proposed in the fourth." Your instructor should be able to offer you additional advice about what focus to take.

Organizing Ideas

If you made notecards, read through them two or three times. Then spread them all out on a table or desk so that you can see all of them at once. Begin to group them into stacks: one stack to describe the event and one for each cause mentioned. Ideally, this will help you to integrate material from your different sources into various parts of your essay. You may find that you have a few notecards that you decide not to use; this often happens and indicates that you have done a good job in finding sufficient information. If you discover that you don't have enough information, you can do more research.

If you didn't make notecards, spread your marked sources out and try to plan how you will use information from each.

Review the principles for writing an essay of causal analysis on pages 312–313 of this chapter. In addition, you will need to decide on the order of your body paragraphs. For a causal chain, you will probably want chronological order. For contributory causes, you may want to use climactic (least to most important) order. For interactive causes, you may want to try different orders until you discover which will make the interaction of the causes easiest for your audience to understand.

Drafting

If you have notecards in stacks, you can draft one section from each stack. A highly specific description of the event whose causes you are about to analyze could become the introduction. Quotations from eyewitnesses or participants in the event can help to interest the reader. The introduction can conclude with the tentative focus sentence (thesis statement) you have written.

Clearly introduce each cause. If you have several causes and are devoting one paragraph to each, begin each body paragraph with a topic sentence that names the cause or possible cause being discussed. Then provide the audience with as much information as necessary to help them understand how that cause actually brought about the event. Remember to document all quotations and paraphrases from your sources.

In your conclusion, you can summarize the causes and discuss the level of certainty, or uncertainty, about them. If you found considerable disagreement among your sources, you can comment on that. If research is still ongoing about the causes, you can say so. You can, of course, do more than this in your conclusion, depending on your content. A well-chosen quotation from a source is often an effective last sentence.

On a separate page, draft a list of Works Cited, using the format specified by your instructor.

Revising

Ideally, at this point, you should put your draft aside for a day or two. If deadlines won't permit you to do that, then at least take a break before you try to revise. When you are ready to "re-see" your writing, begin by reading it through slowly, preferably aloud. If possible, have someone whose opinion you respect read it; ask for feedback. Then work through the hierarchy of revision concerns that follows. Remember that you have two decisions to make for each question: (1) Where is improvement needed? and (2) If improvement is needed, how, exactly, can I make my draft better?

1. **Think big.** Look at your draft as a whole.
- Does it fulfill the assignment in terms of topic and length?
- Have you stated the thesis clearly?
- Do all parts of the draft relate to the thesis?
- Is the organization logical?
- Do you provide enough evidence?

- Is your point of view consistent?
- Is there a discernible flow between your paragraphs?
- Have you documented information from your sources accurately?
- Have you used quotation marks around direct quotes or set the quotes off by indenting?

2. **Think medium.** Look at your draft paragraph by paragraph.

- Will your introduction make your audience want to read on?
- Is the introduction appropriate for the rest of the draft?
- Is your focus stated clearly if you are working with a "visible" structure?
- If you are working with an "invisible" structure, is your focus clearly implied?
- Are topic sentences used effectively?
- Does each body paragraph develop a different idea?
- Should any paragraphs be combined or eliminated?
- Is your conclusion effective?

3. **Think small.** Look at your draft sentence by sentence.

- Are any sentences difficult to understand?
- Are any so long that your audience could get lost in them?
- Are sentences with blended quotations (that is, quotations that are integrated into the syntax of the sentence instead of introduced with "He said . . ." or "She said . . .") complete and easy to read?
- Are quotations shortened with ellipsis marks accurate and readable?
- Are there several choppy sentences that can be combined?
- Are any sentences vague?
- Do any sentences need to be corrected for standard English grammar and usage?

4. **Think "picky."** Look at your draft as your fussiest critic might.

- Are any words not clear or not quite right for your meaning?
- Are any words misspelled?
- Are there any punctuation errors?
- Is your format correct?
- Are the pages numbered consecutively?
- Does your paper make a good impression by being neat?
- Is there anything else you could do to improve your draft?

Proofreading

After you prepare a final draft, check again for correct grammar and punctuation. Proofread carefully for omitted words or punctuation marks. Run your spelling checker program, but be aware of its limitations. Proofread carefully for the kinds of errors the computer can't catch.

Check your list of Works Cited against your model once more, paying special attention to indentation, use of underlining and quotation marks for titles, and special use of punctuation.

Student Essays

The following essays show how two students responded to this assignment.

STUDENT WRITING
Crows at the Mall
by Ly Truc Hoang

I am a newcomer to the United States. Amazingly, a bird which I saw on my first day in this country was a crow. I wondered if in America crows are common birds. Now I know that there are thousands of crows which live around my city. Recently, some of these crows have caused concern because they have moved into the trees at White Flint Mall, a large, upscale shopping center.

In *The Washington Post,* an article by reporter Alona Wartofsky has a photo of crows with this caption: "Ruling the roost: Crows are making their presence known and felt at White Flint Mall" (D1). Because people are upset about too many crows at the mall, Wartofsky reports the people tend "to use words like 'eradicate' and 'terminate'" (D8). Why have the crows appeared at White Flint Mall? After reading some articles, I think I can answer this question. Missing the trees in Rockville, seeking spaces to live, and looking for food are some causes that many experts discuss about the crows' taking up residence in the mall parking lot.

First of all, missing the trees in Rockville is a cause for the crows to immigrate to White Flint. Wartofsky believes, "As many as 200,000 crows spent fall and winter around the intersection of Montrose Road and East Jefferson Drive in Rockville. But last November, developers cut down many of the trees there, and most of the birds have moved on" (D1). This is consistent with a national trend. Crows "[have] suffered huge losses in recent decades from disease, predation, logging, and development" (Kelly 107). Since the traditional habitats of crows are being destroyed by development, the birds are increasingly finding new homes. Moreover, Miller observes that "they must rapidly search for new habitat and shelter when critical habitats are disturbed" (32).

Thus, seeking a new place to live is a cause for the crows' coming to White Flint. In "Birds Need Open Space," Miller indicates, "Birds have tried to adapt and seek new shelters and places . . . as our human encroachment continues to grow" (32). They choose places that provide an appropriate habitat for nesting and for spending the winter. Some species, such as crows, prefer to spend the winter in large colonies. "Colonial roosts afford individual crows several advantages, primarily greater awareness of predators, such as owls and hawks" (Wartofsky D8). The same article quotes Audubon Naturalist Society's Mark Garland, who told Wartofsky that "many birds packed together can actually raise the ambient temperature of a particular area" (D8). In the case of White Flint, the displaced crows did not have to go far from their old location; White Flint was only a few blocks away from their old trees.

A good food supply was another cause for the crows' choice of White Flint. Many experts agree that birds' movements are typically motivated by food. In *National Wildlife*, Les Line states, "Migration is the avian solution to the problem of a disappearing food supply" (54). Crows are among the most intelligent and adaptable of birds. "The crow is a flexible omnivore," says Pete Budo, a reporter for *The New York Times* (8:9). Therefore, their food includes garbage as well as eggs and nestlings, small animals, vegetables, and carrion. And, like parking lots in malls all across the country, the lot at White Flint has food dropped by shoppers, trash receptacles, and the small animal life which trash attracts.

For all these reasons, thousands of crows enjoy spending the winter in the White Flint parking lot; that has become a serious problem for this mall. The crows are noisy, and their droppings fall on cars, sidewalks, bushes, benches, and sometimes shoppers.

Human beings intervene in natural environments, perhaps only slightly and with good intentions. However, the results are unforeseen and unwanted effects, like the crows at the mall.

Works Cited

Bodo, Pete. "The Cunning, Resourceful Crow Doesn't Deserve Its Bad Rap." *The New York Times,* 21 Jan. 1996: 8:9.

Kelly, Mary Sidney. "A Crow's Last Stand." *Audubon,* Sept. 1996: 107.

Line, Les. "Staying the Winter." *National Wildlife,* Feb. 1995: 52–59.

Miller, David. "Birds Need Open Space." *New York State Conservationist,* Aug. 1996: 32.

Wartofsky, Alona. "Caws for Concern at White Flint." *The Washington Post* 2 Apr. 1997: D1+.

STUDENT WRITING
What Caused the Flood at Yosemite National Park
by Elmon L. Burton IV

"Heavy snowpack in the high Sierras was melted on New Year's Eve by the arrival of the 'Pineapple Express,' a warm moist storm that blew

onto the mountains from Hawaii, dropping rain and raising temperatures above 37 degrees at 10,000 feet" (Booth A1). The result: a
record breaking flood which swept through Yosemite National Park
destroying everything in its path. Newspaper accounts say that park
officials had no choice but to close access to most of the park for
several months (Brooke 5:3). When all was done "the New Year's flood
caused an estimated $178 million in damage" (Booth A1). The amount
of snowfall that was present at Yosemite and the arrival of the Pineapple Express are the two contributory causes of this flood that I will
discuss.

The first contributory cause of the flood was the massive amount
of snow which laid upon the mountains within Yosemite National Park.
This is nothing out of the ordinary, however. The book *Floods* says that
each year the western mountain regions receive over 60 inches of pre-
cipitation in the form of snow, and sometimes snowfall accumulates
to over 200 inches (Hoyt and Langbein 28). In fact, says *Floods,* each
spring the Merced River rises above its average height as a result of
the enormous amount of snowmelt; and " . . . many northern and high
mountainous areas have deep snow every year without floods because the thaw begins slowly with the onset of spring, and snow
cover is fairly depleted before high temperatures occur" (Hoyt and
Langbein 28). However, the 1997 flood took place January 1, at the
early part of winter. This was obviously a rare occurrence, leaving the
residents in a complete state of bewilderment. According to William
G. Hoyt and Walter B. Langbein, the authors of *Floods:*

> It's important to note that snowmelt is only a contributor to winter
> floods, . . . which are primarily caused by heavy rains. Snow sets the
> stage, but seldom causes serious floods by itself. Even the most rapid
> rate of snowmelt is only equal to a moderate rain. (29)

Also, scientists point out that the amount of snow and the rate at
which it melts are important factors contributing to the severity of
snowmelt floods (Ward 28). Further, when rain is added to the equation, it magnifies the rate of snowmelt which could increase the river
by ten times its usual size (Flood 236). The result: total devastation to
everything in its path. Such was the case when the Merced River,
within Yosemite National Park, flooded.

The Pineapple Express, the second contributory cause of the
flood, was a warm tropical storm when it originated off the Pacific
Ocean, hundreds of miles away near the Hawaiian Islands. *The Washington Post* reported that the storm followed the atmosphere's jet
stream which carried it east towards the coast of California. Then,
upon the storm's arrival, California experienced a period of heavy
rains and extremely mild temperatures. Although the Yosemite region
was not hit directly by this unusual storm, it definitely felt the effects.

The result was an incredible rate of snowmelt along the Sierra mountain range. The most cataclysmic results took place near and along the rising Merced River within Yosemite. Park officials are calling it "the cruelest winter on record" (Booth A1).

The abundant amount of snowfall in the high Sierras, the heavy amount of rain that fell, and the extended period of mild temperatures supported and reinforced the actions of one another, creating a synergistic effect. While no one contributor would have caused such a devastating outcome, when working in conjunction with each other they created a force greater than the sum of their individual effects, thus creating a rare, yet horrific natural disaster.

Works Cited

Booth, William. "Floods Brought Yosemite the Break of the Century." *The Washington Post,* 7 Mar. 1997, sec. A1+.

Brooke, James. "Flood Damage Closes Much of Yosemite Valley." *The New York Times,* 2 Feb. 1997, sec. 5:3.

"Flood." The World Book Encyclopedia, 1992.

Hoyt, William G., and Walter B. Langbein. *Floods.* Princeton: Princeton University Press, 1955.

Ward, Roy. *Floods: A Geographical Perspective.* New York: Roy Ward, 1978.

CHAPTER 9

Forming Concepts—Writing to Classify and Define

Critical Thinking Focus: The conceptualizing process

Writing Focus: Defining and applying concepts

Reading Theme: Gender issues

Writing Project: Defining an important concept

Thinking Critically About Concepts

Music video, person, education, computer, sport, situation comedy, and *thinking* are only a few examples of concepts in a world filled with them. As you represent and describe your experience, you refer to concepts you have formed. Your academic study involves learning new concepts as well, and being successful in college and in your career requires understanding the conceptualizing process. For example, when you read textbooks or listen to lectures and take notes, you have to grasp key concepts and follow them as they are developed and supported. Many course examinations involve applying the key concepts you have learned to new sets of circumstances. When you write papers, you are usually expected to focus on certain concepts, develop a thesis around them, present the thesis (itself a concept) with carefully argued points, and back it up with specific evidence.

Your college writing will often require the defining of terms or concepts. Chapter 5 briefly discussed the fact that words are complex carriers of meaning—with meanings varying from person to person—and stated that people arrive at *semantic meanings, perceptual meanings, syntactic meanings,* and *pragmatic meanings* through different experiences with a word. This chapter will explore further implications of these vital communication issues. In addition, you will see that definition usually involves using all the patterns of thinking that the previous chapters in Part Two have discussed.

Definition involves a very important thinking and writing pattern. The analytical activity of classifying, which underlies defining, also is essential to good thinking. Defining and classifying rely on comparative relationships in order to establish categories by means of similarities and in order to distinguish among concepts within categories by identifying differences. Definitions usually include descriptions and sometimes employ causal, chronological, or process analyses to make distinctions or show the development of a concept. Understanding the common patterns that you have already worked with and being able to use them effectively can ease the difficult task of defining concepts.

To help you define significant concepts, this chapter will explain the conceptualizing process, present readings that involve definitions, and give you opportunities to define some terms that are significant in various aspects of your life.

What Are Concepts?

Concepts are general ideas you use to organize your experience and, in so doing, bring order to your life. In the same way that words are the vocabulary of language, concepts are the vocabulary of thought. As organizers of your experience, concepts work in conjunction with language to identify, describe, distinguish, and relate all the various aspects of your world.

> **Concepts:**   general ideas that people use to identify and organize experience.

To become a sophisticated thinker, you must develop expertise in the conceptualizing process, thereby improving your ability to form, apply, and relate concepts. This complex conceptualizing process is going on all the time in your mind, enabling you to think in a distinctly human way. When you form opinions or make judgments, you are applying and relating concepts.

How do you use concepts to organize and make sense of experience? Think back to the first day of the semester. For most students, this is a time to evaluate their courses by trying to determine which concepts apply.

- Will this course be interesting? useful? challenging?
- Is the instructor stimulating? demanding? understanding?
- Are the other students friendly? intelligent? conscientious?

Each of these descriptive words or phrases represents a concept you are attempting to apply so that you can understand what is occurring at the moment and also anticipate what will occur. As the course progresses, you gather further information from experiences in class. This information may support your initial concepts, or it may conflict with them. If it supports them, you tend to maintain them ("Yes, I can see that this is going to be a difficult course"). When the information you receive conflicts with your initial concepts, you tend to find new concepts to explain the situation ("No, I can see that I was wrong—this course isn't going to be as difficult as I thought at first"). A diagram of this process might look something like the one in Figure 9.1.

Throughout this thinking process, as you can see, you are making judgments that establish classifications of kinds or types: What *kind* of course— difficult? easy? What *kind* of teacher? What *kind* of reading? What *kind* of student am I in relation to this course? And you are consciously or unconsciously using definitions that you have formulated: When I say difficult

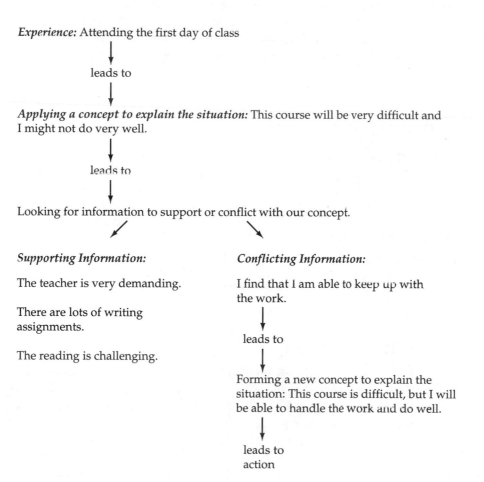

Experience: Attending the first day of class

leads to

Applying a concept to explain the situation: This course will be very difficult and I might not do very well.

leads to

Looking for information to support or conflict with our concept.

Supporting Information:

The teacher is very demanding.

There are lots of writing assignments.

The reading is challenging.

Conflicting Information:

I find that I am able to keep up with the work.

leads to

Forming a new concept to explain the situation: This course is difficult, but I will be able to handle the work and do well.

leads to
action

Figure 9.1

course, I *mean* one that . . . When I say demanding teacher, I *mean* one who . . . And so on.

For another example, imagine that you are a physician and one of your patients comes to you complaining of shortness of breath and occasional pain in his left arm. After he describes his symptoms, you will ask a number of questions, examine him, and perhaps order some tests. Your ability to diagnose the underlying problem depends on your knowledge of various human diseases. Each disease is identified and described by a different concept. Identifying these various diseases means that you can distinguish different concepts and that you know in which situations to apply a given concept correctly. In addition, when the patient asks, "What's wrong with me, doctor?" you are able to describe the overall concept (for example, heart disease) and explain how it is revealed by his symptoms. Fortunately, modern medicine has developed (and is continuing to develop) remarkably precise concepts to describe and explain diseases. In the patient's case, you may conclude that the problem is heart disease. Of course, there are different kinds of heart disease, represented by different concepts, and success in treating the patient will depend on figuring out exactly which type of disease is involved.

THINKING ↔ WRITING ACTIVITY 9.1

Changing Concepts

Identify an initial concept you had about an event in your life (a new job, attending college, getting married, etc.). After identifying your initial concept, describe in your journal the experiences that led you to change or modify the concept; then explain the new concept you formed to explain the situation. Your response should include the following elements.

- Initial concept
- New information provided by additional experiences
- New concept formed to explain the situation

The Importance of Concepts

Learning to understand concepts will help you in every area of your life: academic, career, and personal. In college study, each academic discipline or subject is composed of many different concepts that are used to organize experience, give explanations, and solve problems. Here is a sampling of college-level concepts: *entropy, subtext, Gemeinschaft, cell, metaphysics, relativity, unconscious, transformational grammar, aesthetic, minor key, interface, health, quantum mechanics, schizophrenia.* To make sense of how disciplines function, you need to understand what the concepts of that discipline mean, how to define them, how to apply them, and how they relate to other concepts. You also need to learn the methods of investigation, patterns of thought, and forms of reasoning that various disciplines use to form larger conceptual theories and methods.

Regardless of their specific knowledge content, all careers require conceptual abilities, whether you are trying to apply a legal principle, develop a promotional theme, or devise a new computer program. Similarly, expertise in forming and applying concepts helps you to make sense of your personal life, understand others, and make informed decisions. It was the Greek philosopher Aristotle who said that the intelligent person is a "master of concepts."

The Structure of Concepts

Concepts, in addition to being general ideas you use to identify and organize your experience, are useful for distinguishing and relating the various aspects of experience. Concepts allow you to organize your world into patterns that make sense to you. This is the process by which you discover and create meaning in your life.

In their role of organizers of experience, concepts act to group aspects of your experience on the basis of those aspects' similarity. Consider the item that you usually write with: a pen. The concept *pen* represents a type of object that you use for writing. Now look around the classroom at other instruments people are using to write. You use the concept *pen* to identify these as well, even though they may look very different from the one you are using. Thus, the concept *pen* not only helps you to make distinctions in your experience by indicating how pens differ from pencils, crayons, or markers; it also helps you to determine which items are similar enough to one another to be called pens. When you put items into a group with a single description—such as "pen"—you are focusing on their similarities:

- They use ink.
- They are used for writing.
- They are held in one hand.

Being able to see and name the similarities between certain things in your experience is the way you form concepts and is crucial for making sense of your world. If you were not able to do this, everything in the world would be different, with its own individual name.

The Process of Classifying

The process by which you group things on the basis of their similarities is known as *classifying.* Classifying is a natural human activity that goes on all the time. In most cases, however, you are not conscious that you are classifying something in a particular sort of way; you do so automatically. The process of classifying is one of the main ways that you order, organize, and make sense of your world. Because no two things or experiences are exactly alike, your ability to classify things into various groups is what enables you to recognize things in your experience. When you perceive a pen, you recognize it as a *kind* of object you have seen before. Even though you may not have seen this particular pen, you recognize that it belongs to a group of things that you are familiar with.

The best way to understand the structure of concepts is to visualize them by means of a model. Examine Figure 9.2. The *sign* is the word or symbol used to name or designate the concept; for example, the word *triangle* is a sign. The *referents* represent all the various examples of the concept; the three-sided figure we are using as our model is an example of the concept *triangle*. The *properties* of the concept are the features that all things named by the word or sign share in common; all examples of the concept *triangle* share the characteristics of being a polygon and having three sides. These are the *properties* that we refer to when we *define* concepts; thus, "A triangle is a three-sided polygon."

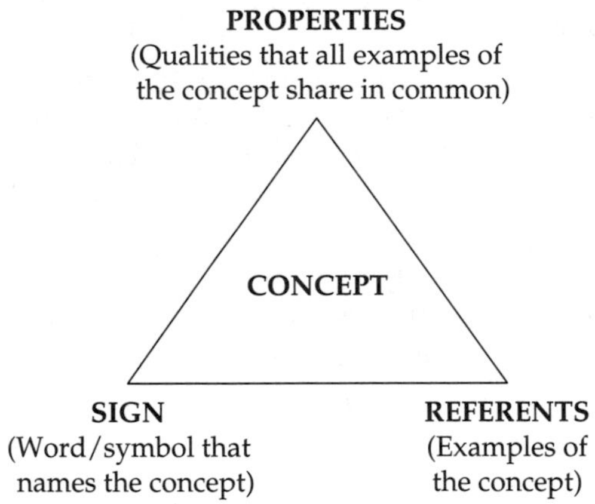

PROPERTIES
(Qualities that all examples of
the concept share in common)

CONCEPT

SIGN   **REFERENTS**
(Word/symbol that   (Examples of
names the concept)   the concept)

Figure 9.2

Let's take another example. Suppose you wanted to explore the structure of the concept *automobile*. The *sign* that names the concept is the word *automobile* or the symbol 🚗 . *Referents* of the concept include the 1954 MG "TF" currently residing in the garage, as well as the Ford Explorer parked in front of the house. The *properties* that all things named by the sign automobile include are wheels, a chassis, an engine, seats for passengers, and so on. Figure 9.3 shows a conceptual model of the concept *automobile*.

PROPERTIES
Wheels, Chassis, Engine,
Seats for passengers

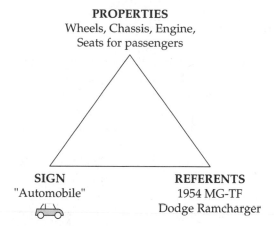

SIGN	**REFERENTS**
"Automobile"	1954 MG-TF
	Dodge Ramcharger

Figure 9.3

THINKING‹›WRITING ACTIVITY 9.2

Diagramming Concepts

Using the model we have developed, diagram the structure of the following concepts, as well as those of two concepts of your own choosing: *dance, successful, student, religion, music, friend.*

Forming Concepts

Throughout your life you are engaged in the process of forming—and applying—concepts to organize your experience, make sense of what is happening at the moment, and anticipate what may happen in the future. You form concepts by the interactive processes of *generalizing* (focusing on the common properties shared by a group of things) and *interpreting* (finding examples of the concept). The common properties form the necessary requirements that must be met in order for you to be able to apply the concept to your experience. If you examine the diagrams of concepts in the last section, you can see that the process of forming concepts involves moving back and forth between the *referents* (examples) of the concept and the *properties* (common features) shared by all examples of the concept. Let's explore further the way this interactive process of forming concepts operates.

Consider the following sample conversation between two people trying to form and clarify the concept *philosophy.*

A: What is your idea of what philosophy *means?*

B: Well, I think philosophy involves expressing important beliefs that you have—like discussing the meaning of life, assuming that there is a meaning.

A: Is explaining my belief about who's going to win the Super Bowl engaging in philosophy? After all, this is a belief that is very important to me—I've got a lot of money riding on the outcome!

B: I don't think so. A philosophical belief is usually a belief about something that is important to everyone—like what standards we should use to guide our moral choices .

A: What about the message that was in my fortune cookie last night: "Eat, drink, and be merry, for tomorrow we diet!"? This is certainly a belief that most people can relate to, especially during a holiday season! Is this philosophy?

B: I think that's what my grandmother used to call "foolosophy"! Philosophical beliefs are usually deeply felt views that we have given a great deal of thought to—not something plucked out of a cookie.

A: What about my belief in the Golden Rule: "Do unto others as you would have them do unto you," because if you don't, "What goes around comes around." Doesn't that have all of the qualities that you mentioned?

B: Now you've got it!

As we review this dialogue, we can see that *forming* the concept *philosophical belief* works hand in hand with *applying* the concept to different examples. When two or more things work together in this way, we say that they *interact.* In this case, there are two parts of this interactive process.

We form concepts by *generalizing,* by focusing on the similar features among different things. In the dialogue just given, the things from which generalizations are being made are types of beliefs—beliefs about the meaning of life or about standards we use to guide our moral choices. By focusing on the similar features among these beliefs, the two participants in the dialogue develop a list of properties philosophical beliefs share, including (1) beliefs dealing with important issues in life that everyone is concerned about and (2) beliefs reflecting deeply felt views—views to which we have given a great deal of thought. These common properties act as the requirements an area must meet to be considered a philosophical belief.

We apply concepts by *interpreting,* by looking for different examples of a concept and seeing if they meet the requirements of the concept we are developing. In the preceding dialogue, one participant attempts to apply the concept *philosophical belief* to the following examples:

> a belief about the outcome of the Super Bowl
>
> a fortune cookie message: "Eat, drink, and be merry, for tomorrow we diet."

Each of the proposed examples in the dialogue suggests the development of new requirements for the concept to help clarify how the concept can be applied. Applying a concept to different possible examples thus becomes the way we develop and gradually sharpen our idea of it. Even when a proposed example turns out not to be a valid one, our understanding of that concept is often clarified. For instance, although the proposed example of a belief about the outcome of the Super Bowl turned out *not* to be an example of the concept *philosophical belief,* examining it helped to clarify the concept and suggest other examples.

The process of developing concepts involves a constant back-and-forth movement between these two activities:

Generalizing: Focusing on certain similar features among things to develop the requirements for the concept.

Interpreting: Looking for different things to apply the concept to, in order to determine whether they "meet the requirements" of the concept one is developing.

As the back-and-forth movement progresses, we gradually develop a list of specific requirements for an example of the concept; at the same time, we give ourselves a clearer idea of how the concept is defined. We are also developing a collection of examples that embody the qualities of the concept and demonstrate situations in which the concept applies. This interactive process is illustrated in Figure 9.4.

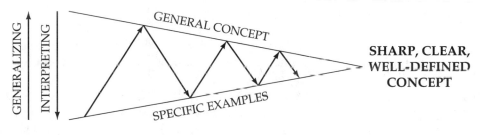

Figure 9.4

THINKING ↔ WRITING ACTIVITY 9.3

Forming a Concept

Select a type of music with which you are familiar (e.g., jazz) and write a dialogue similar to the one just examined. In the course of the dialogue, be sure to include the following:

1. Examples from which you are generalizing (such as big band).
2. General properties shared by various types of this music (e.g., the jazz audience spans many generations).
3. Examples to which you are trying to apply the developing concept (such as the music of Marian McPartland, Miles Davis, or Thelonius Monk).

Forming concepts involves performing the operations of generalizing and interpreting together, for two reasons.

1. You cannot form a concept unless you know how it might apply. If you have absolutely no idea what *jazz* or *philosophy* might exemplify, you cannot begin to form the concept, even in vague or general terms.
2. You cannot gather examples of the concept unless you know what they might be examples of. Until you begin to develop some idea of what the concepts, *jazz* or *philosophy* might be (based on certain similarities between various things) you won't know where to look for examples of the concept (or how to evaluate them).

This interactive process is the way that you usually form all concepts, particularly the complicated ones. In school, much of your education is focused on carefully forming and exploring key concepts such as *democracy, dynamic equilibrium,* and *personality.* This book, too, has focused on key concepts, such as *thinking critically, writing effectively, solving problems, revising drafts, perceiving, thinking creatively,* and *language.* In each case, you have carefully explored these concepts through the interactive process of *generalizing* the properties or requirements of the concept and *interpreting* the concept by examining examples to which the concept applies.

Applying Concepts

Making sense of our experience means finding the right concept to explain what is going on. To determine whether the concept we have selected fits a situation, we have to determine whether the requirements that form the concept are being met. For example, episodes of the original radio series "Superman" used to begin with the words "Faster than a speeding bullet—more powerful than a locomotive. Look—up in the sky! It's a bird! It's a plane! It's Superman!"

To figure out which concept applies to the situation (so that we can figure out what is going on), we must do the following:

1. Be aware of the properties that form the boundaries of the concept.
2. Determine whether the experience meets those requirements, for only if it does can we apply the concept to it.

In the opening lines from "Superman," what are some of the requirements for using the concepts being identified?

- Bird:
- Plane:
- Superman:

If we have the requirements of the concept clearly in mind, we can proceed to figure out which of these requirements are met by the experience—

whether it is a bird, a plane, or the "man of steel" himself. This is the way we apply concepts, which is one of the most important ways we figure out what is taking place in our experience.

Determining the Requirements of a Concept

In determining exactly what the requirements of the concept are, we can ask ourselves: *Would something still be an example of this concept if that thing did not meet this requirement?* If the answer to this question is no—that something would *not* be an example of this concept if it did not meet this requirement—we can say the requirement is a necessary part of the concept.

Consider the concept *dog.* Which of the following descriptions are requirements that must be met by an example of this concept?

1. Is an animal
2. Normally has four legs and a tail
3. Bites the mail carrier

It is clear that descriptions 1 and 2 are requirements that must be met to apply the concept *dog,* because if we apply our test question—"Would something be an example of this concept if that thing did not meet this requirement?"—we can say that something would not be an example of the concept *dog* if it did not fit the first two descriptions: if it was not an animal and did not normally have four legs and a tail.

This does not seem to be the case, however, with description 3. If we ask ourselves the same test question, we can see that something might still be an example of the concept *dog* even if it did not bite the mail carrier. Even though some dogs do in fact bite mail carriers, this is not a requirement for being a dog.

Of course, there may be other things that meet these requirements but are not dogs. For example, a cat is an animal (description 1) that normally has four legs and a tail (description 2). What this means is that the requirements of a concept tell us only what something must have, to be an example of the concept. As a result, we often have to identify additional requirements that will define the concept more sharply. This point is clearly illustrated as children form concepts. Not identifying a sufficient number of the concept's requirements leads to such misconceptions as "All four-legged animals are doggies" or "All yellow-colored metal is gold."

This is why it is so important for us to have a very clear idea of the greatest possible number of specific requirements of each concept. These requirements determine when the concept can be applied and indicate those things that qualify as examples of it. When we are able to identify all the requirements of the concept, we say these requirements are both necessary and sufficient for applying the concept.

Analyzing Complex Concepts

Although dealing with concepts like *dog* and *cat* may seem straightforward, matters become somewhat confusing when you start analyzing the more complex concepts you encounter in your academic study. For example, consider the concepts of *masculinity* and *femininity*, two of the more emotionally charged and politically contentious concepts in our culture. There are many different perspectives on what these concepts mean, what they should mean, or whether we should be using them at all. Identify what you consider the essential properties (specific requirements that must be met to apply the concept) for each of these concepts, as well as examples of people or behavior that illustrates these properties. For example, you might identify physical strength as a property of the concept *masculinity*, and identify Arnold Swartzenegger as a person who illustrates this quality. Or you might identify intuition as a property of the concept *femininity*, illustrating this with the behavior "knowing without the conscious use of rational processes."

General Properties   *Specific Examples*
Femininity

1. _____   1. _____
2. _____   2. _____
3. _____   3. _____

Masculinity

1. _____   1. _____
2. _____   2. _____
3. _____   3. _____

Compare your responses with those of other students in the class. What similarities and differences do you discover? What factors might account for these similarities and differences? Look back at your responses after you read the following selections.

THINKING ↔ WRITING ACTIVITY 9.4

Exploring the Concept *Femininity*

Read the following passage by Susan Brownmiller. Then write answers to the questions in your journal.

1. According to Brownmiller, what are some of the properties of *femininity*? What are some examples that she gives of the properties that she identifies?
2. Do you agree with the conceptual properties that Brownmiller has identified? Explain why or why not? Do you think that she has defined *femininity*? Explain how she has achieved a definition.

3. What thinking-writing patterns has Brownmiller used? Identify specific examples.

---

from Femininity

by Susan Brownmiller

We had a game in our house called "setting the table" and I was Mother's helper. Forks to the left of the plate, knives and spoons to the right. Placing the cutlery neatly, as I recall, was one of my first duties, and the event was alive with meaning. When a knife or a fork dropped on the floor, that meant a man was unexpectedly coming to dinner. A falling spoon announced the surprise arrival of a female guest. No matter that these visitors never arrived on cue, I had learned a rule of gender identification. Men were straight-edged, sharply pronged and formidable; women were softly curved and held the food in a rounded well. It made perfect sense, like the division of pink and blue that I saw in babies, an orderly way of viewing the world . Daddy, who was gone all day at work and who loved to putter at home with his pipe, tobacco and tool chest was knife and fork. Mommy and Grandma, with their ample proportions and pots and pans, were grownup soup spoons, large and capacious. And I was a teaspoon, small and slender, easy to hold and just right for pudding, my favorite dessert.

Being good at what was expected of me was one of my earliest projects, for not only was I rewarded, as most children are, for doing things right, but excellence gave pride and stability to my childhood existence. Girls were different from boys, and the expression of that difference seemed mine to make clear. Did my loving, anxious mother, who dressed me in white organdy pinafores and Mary Janes and who cried hot tears when I got them dirty, give me my first instruction? Of course. Did my doting aunts and uncles with their gifts of pretty dolls and miniature tea sets add to my education? Of course. But even without the appropriate toys and clothes, lessons in the art of being feminine lay all around me and I absorbed them all: the fairy tales that were read to me at night, the brightly colored advertisements I pored over in magazines before I learned to decipher the words, the movies I saw, the comic books I hoarded, the radio soap operas I happily followed whenever I had to stay in bed with a cold. I loved being a little girl, or rather I loved being a fairy princess, for that was who I thought I was.

As I passed through a stormy adolescence to a stormy maturity, femininity increasingly became an exasperation, a brilliant, subtle esthetic that was bafflingly inconsistent at the same time that it was minutely, demandingly concrete, a rigid code of appearance and behavior defined by do's and don't-do's that went against my rebellious grain. Femininity was a challenge thrown down to the female sex, a challenge no proud, self-respecting young woman could afford to ignore, particularly one with enormous ambition that she nursed in secret, alternately feeding or starving its inchoate life in tremendous confusion.

"Don't lose your femininity" and "Isn't it remarkable how she manages to retain her femininity?" had terrifying implications. They spoke of a bottom-line failure so irreversible that nothing else mattered. The pinball machine had registered "tilt," the game had been called. Disqualification was marked on the forehead of a woman whose femininity was lost. No records would be entered in her name, for she had destroyed her birthright in her wretched, ungainly effort to imitate a man. She walked in limbo, this hapless creature, and it occurred to me that one day I might see her when I looked in the mirror. If the danger was so palpable that warning notices were freely posted, wasn't it possible that the small bundle of resentments I carried around in secret might spill out and place the mark on my own forehead? Whatever quarrels with femininity I had I kept to myself; whatever handicaps femininity imposed, they were mine to deal with alone, for there was no women's movement to ask the tough questions, or to brazenly disregard the rules.

5   Femininity, in essence, is a romantic sentiment, a nostalgic tradition of imposed limitations. Even as it hurries forward in the 1980s, putting on lipstick and high heels to appear well dressed, it trips on the ruffled petticoats and hoopskirts of an era gone by. Invariably and necessarily, femininity is something that women had more of in the past, not only in the historic past of prior generations, but in each woman's personal past as well—in the virginal innocence that is replaced by knowledge, in the dewy cheek that is coarsened by age, in the "inherent nature" that a woman seems to misplace so forgetfully whenever she steps out of bounds. Why should this be so? The XX chromosomal message has not been scrambled, the estrogen-dominated hormonal balance is generally as biology intended, the reproductive organs, whatever use one has made of them, are usually in place, the breasts of whatever size are most often where they should be. But clearly, biological femaleness is not enough.

Femininity always demands more. It must constantly reassure its audience by a willing demonstration of difference, even when one does not exist in nature, or it must seize and embrace a natural variation and compose a rhapsodic symphony upon the notes. Suppose one doesn't care to, has other things on her mind, is clumsy or tone-deaf despite the best instruction and training? To fail at the feminine difference is to appear not to care about men, and to risk the loss of their attention and approval. To be insufficiently feminine is viewed as a failure in core sexual identity, or as a failure to care sufficiently about oneself, for a woman found wanting will be appraised (and will appraise herself) as mannish or neutered or simply unattractive, as men have defined these terms.

We are talking, admittedly, about an exquisite esthetic. Enormous pleasure can be extracted from feminine pursuits as a creative outlet or purely as relaxation; indeed, indulgence for the sake of fun, or art, or attention, is among femininity's great joys. But the chief attraction (and the central paradox, as well) is the competitive edge that femininity seems to promise in the unending struggle to survive, and perhaps to triumph. The world smiles favorably on the feminine woman: it extends little courtesies and minor privilege. Yet the nature of this competitive edge is ironic, at best, for one works at femininity by accepting restrictions, by limiting one's sights, by choosing an indirect route, by scattering concentration and not giving one's all as a man would to his own, certifiably masculine, interests. It does not require a great leap of imagination for a woman to understand the feminine principle as a grand collection of compromises, large and small, that she simply must make in order to render herself a successful woman. If she has difficulty in satisfying femininity's demands, if its illusions go against her grain, or if she is criticized for her shortcomings and imperfections, the more she will see femininity as a desperate strategy of appeasement, a strategy she may not have the wish or the courage to abandon, for failure looms in either direction.

It is fashionable in some quarters to describe the feminine and masculine principles as polar ends of the human continuum, and to sagely profess that both polarities exist in all people. Sun and moon, yin and yang, soft and hard, active and passive, etcetera, may indeed be opposites, but a linear continuum does not illuminate the problem. (Femininity, in all its contrivances, is a very active endeavor.) What, then, is the basic distinction? The masculine principle is better understood as a driving ethos of superiority designed to inspire straightforward, confident success, while the feminine principle is composed of vulnerability, the need for protection, the formalities of compliance and the avoidance of conflict—in short, an appeal of dependence and good will that gives the masculine principle its romantic validity and its admiring applause.

Femininity pleases men because it makes them appear more masculine by contrast; and, in truth, conferring an extra portion of unearned gender distinction on men, an unchallenged space in which to breathe freely and feel stronger, wiser, more competent, is femininity's special gift. One could say that masculinity is often an effort to please women, but masculinity is known to please by displays of mastery and competence while femininity pleases by suggesting that these concerns, except in small matters, are beyond its intent. Whimsy, unpredictability and patterns of thinking and behavior that are dominated by emotion, such as tearful expressions of sentiment and fear, are thought to be feminine precisely because they lie outside the established route to success.

10   If in the beginnings of history the feminine woman was defined by her physical dependency, her inability for reasons of reproductive biology to triumph over the forces of nature that were the tests of masculine strength and power, today she reflects both an economic and emotional dependency that is still considered "natural," romantic and attractive. After an unsettling fifteen years in which many basic assumptions about the sexes were challenged, the economic disparity did not disappear. Large numbers of women—those with small children, those left high and dry after a mid-life divorce—need financial support. But even those who earn their own living share a universal need for connectedness (call it love, if you wish). As unprecedented numbers of men abandon their sexual interest in women, others, sensing opportunity, choose to demonstrate their interest through variety and a change in partners. A sociological fact of the 1980s is that female competition for two scarce resources—men and jobs—is especially fierce.

So it is not surprising that we are currently witnessing a renewed interest in femininity and an unabashed indulgence in feminine pursuits. Femininity serves to reassure men that women need them and care about them enormously. By incorporating the decorative and the frivolous into its definition of style, femininity functions as an effective antidote to the unrelieved seriousness, the pressure of making one's way in a harsh, difficult world. In its mandate to avoid direct confrontation and to smooth over the fissures of conflict, femininity operates as a value system of niceness, a code of thoughtfulness and sensitivity that in modern society is sadly in short supply.

There is no reason to deny that indulgence in the art of feminine illusion can be reassuring to a woman, if she happens to be good at it. As sexuality undergoes some dizzying revisions, evidence that one is a woman "at heart" (the inquisitor's question) is not without worth. Since an answer of sorts may he furnished by piling on additional documentation, affirmation can arise from such identifiable but trivial feminine activities as buying a new eyeliner, experimenting with the latest shade of nail color, or bursting into tears at the outcome of a popular romance novel. Is there anything destructive in this? Time and cost factors, a deflection of energy and an absorption in fakery spring quickly to mind, and they need to be balanced, as in a ledger book, against the affirming advantage.

THINKING ↔ WRITING ACTIVITY 9.5

Exploring the Concept *Masculinity*

Read the following passage by Michael Norman and write answers to the questions in your journal.

1. According to Michael Norman, what are the properties of the concept *masculinity*? What are some examples he gives of the properties that he has identified?
2. Do you agree with the properties that Norman has identified? Explain why or why not. Does Norman achieve a definition of *masculinity,* or a partial definition? What thinking-writing patterns has he used?
3. Some people believe that the concepts of *masculinity* and *femininity* were formed by earlier cultures, are outdated in our current culture, and should be revised. Other people believe that these concepts reflect essential qualities of the human species and should not be excessively tampered with. Where do you stand on this issue?
4. Do you see connections with the concepts *feminism/feminist* and *masculism/masculinist* and the concepts of *femininity* and *masculinity*? What are some differences among these related concepts? Where does *macho* fit in?

from Standing His Ground

by Michael Norman

I have bruised a knuckle and bloodied another man's nose, but I am not, by most measures, a fighter. The last time I broke the peace was more than a decade ago in a small restaurant on the west slope of the Rocky Mountains in Colorado. My stepfather had encountered an old nemesis. Words were exchanged and the distance between the two narrowed. I stepped in to play the peacemaker and ended up throwing the first punch. For the record, my target, a towering 230-pound horseman, easily absorbed the blow and then dispatched the gnat in front of him.

The years since have been filled with discretion—I preach it, embrace it and hide behind it. I am now the careful watchman who keeps his eye on the red line and reroutes pressure before it has a chance to blow. Sometimes, I backslide and turn a domestic misdemeanor into a capital case or toss the cat out of the house without bothering to see where he lands. But I do not punch holes in the plaster or call my antagonists to the woodshed. The Furies may gather, but the storm always stays safely out to sea. And yet, lately, I have been struggling with this forced equanimity. The messenger of reason, the advocate of accord, once again has the urge to throw the first punch—in spirit at least.

All of this began rather quietly, a deep stirring that would come and go and never take form, an old instinct, perhaps, trying to reassert itself. I was angry, restless, combative, but I could not say why. It was a mystery of sorts. I was what I was expected to be, the very model of a modern man, a partner instead of a husband, a proponent of peace over action, thin-skinned rather than thick, a willow instead of a stone. And yet there was something about this posture that did not fit my frame.

Then, an acquaintance, a gentle man who spent his Peace Corps days among the villagers of Nepal, suddenly acted out of character. He got into an argument with a local brute in a neighborhood tavern and instead of walking away from trouble, stood his ground. It was, he said, a senseless confrontation, but he had no regrets, and it made me think of Joey.

Joey, the bully of the sixth grade, used to roam the hallways picking victims at random and slugging them on the arm. When he rounded a corner, we scattered or practiced a crude form of mysticism and tried to think ourselves invisible in the face of the beast. Since I was slow and an inept mystic, my mother kept on hand an adequate supply of Ben Gay to ease the bruises and swelling.

5   One day, a boy named Tony told the marauder that he had had enough and an epic duel was scheduled in the playground after school. Tony had been taking boxing lessons on the sly. He had developed a stinging left jab and when the appointed hour arrived, he delivered it in the name of every bruised shoulder in the school.

The meek pack of which Tony was once a part took courage from his example and several weeks later when a boy at my bus stop sent me sprawling, I returned the favor.

There were only a few challenges after that. On the way up, a Joey would occasionally round the corner. But in the circles I traveled, he was the exception rather than the rule. In the Marine Corps in Vietnam, we were consumed by a much larger kind of warfare. In college, faculty infighting and bullying aside, violence was considered anti-intellectual. And in the newsrooms where I have practiced my trade, reporters generally have been satisfied with pounding a keyboard instead of their editors.

And then came Colorado and the battle of the west slope. For years, I was embarrassed by the affair. I could have walked away and dragged my stepfather with me. As it was, we almost ended up in jail. I had provoked a common brawl, a pointless, self-destructive exercise. The rationalist had committed the most irrational of acts. It was not a matter of family or honor, hollow excuses. I had simply succumbed to instinct, and I deeply regretted it. But not any longer. Now I see virtue in that vulgar display of macho. It disqualifies me from the most popular male club—the brotherhood of nurturers, fraternity sensitivus.

From analyst's couch to tavern booth, their message is the same: The male animus is out of fashion. The man of the hour is supposed to be gentle, thoughtful, endearing and compassionate, a wife to his woman, a mother to his son, an androgynous figure with the self-knowledge of a hermaphrodite. He takes his lumps on the psyche, not the chin, and bleeds with emotion. Yes, in the morning, he still puts on a three-piece suit, but his foulard, the finishing touch, is a crying towel.

10   He is so ridden with guilt, so pained about the sexist sins of his kind,

he bites at his own flanks. Not only does he say that he dislikes being a man, but broadly proclaims that the whole idea of manhood in America is pitiful.

He wants to free himself from the social conditioning of the past, to cast off the yoke of traditional male roles and rise above the banality of rituals learned at boot camp or on the practice field. If science could provide it, he would swallow an antidote of testosterone, something to stop all this antediluvian thumping and bashing.

And he has gone too far. Yes, the male code needs reform. Our rules and our proscriptions have trapped us in a kind of perpetual adolescence. Why else would a full-grown rationalist think he could get even with Joey by taking a poke at another bully 25 years later in a bar in Colorado? No doubt there is something pitiful about that.

But the fashion for reform, the drive to emasculate macho, has produced a kind of numbing androgyny and has so blurred the lines of gender that I often find myself wanting to emulate some of the women I know—bold, aggressive, vigorous role models.

It sometimes seems that the only exclusively male trait left is the impulse to throw a punch, the last male watermark, so to speak, that is clear and readable. Perhaps that is why the former Peace Corps volunteer jumped into a brawl and why I suspect that the new man—the model of sensitivity, the nurturer—goes quietly through the day with a clenched fist behind his back.

THINKING ↔ WRITING ACTIVITY 9.6

Exploring the Concept *Woman*

Read the following speech by Sojourner Truth, "Ain't I a Woman?" Then write the answers to the questions in your journal.

1. Understanding that Sojourner Truth was a famous black speaker in the nineteenth-century abolitionist and women's suffrage movements, can you identify passages in her speech that pertain to those political issues?
2. Some people claim that some of the concerns addressed by present-day gender studies are middle-class issues and are not relevant to less affluent groups. Can you connect Sojourner Truth's speech to this issue? Can you identify some gender questions that seem specific to social classes?

from Ain't I a Woman?

by Sojourner Truth

Well, children, where there is so much racket there must be something out of kilter. I think that 'twixt the negroes of the South and the women at the North, all talking about rights, the white men will be in a fix pretty soon. But what's all this here talking about?

That man over there says that women need to be helped into carriages, and lifted over ditches, and to have the best place everywhere. Nobody ever helps me into carriages, or over mud-puddles, or gives me any best place! And ain't I a woman? Look at me! Look at my arm! I have ploughed and planted, and gathered into barns, and no man could head me! And ain't I a woman? I could work as much and eat as much as a man—when I could get it—and bear the lash as well! And ain't I a woman? I have borne thirteen children, and seen them most all sold off to slavery, and when I cried out with my mother's grief, none but Jesus heard me! And ain't I a woman?

Then they talk about this thing in the head: what's this they call it? [Intellect, someone whispers.] That's it, honey. What's that got to do with women's rights or negro's rights? If my cup won't hold but a pint, and yours holds a quart, wouldn't you be mean not to let me have my little half-measure full?

Then that little man in black there, he says women can't have as much rights as men, 'cause Christ wasn't a woman! Where did your Christ come from? Where did your Christ come from? From God and a woman! Man had nothing to do with Him.

5   If the first woman God ever made was strong enough to turn the world upside down all alone, these women together ought to be able to turn it back, and get it right side up again! And now they is asking to do it, the men better let them.

Obliged to you for hearing me, and now old Sojourner ain't got nothing more to say.

THINKING ↔ WRITING ACTIVITY 9.7

Exploring the Concept of *Friendship*

Read the essay "Men and Their Hidden Feelings," by Richard Cohen. Then write the answers to the questions in your journal.

1. According to Cohen, what are the properties of men's relationships? Why does he think that these properties do not fit a definition of friendship?
2. Do you believe that talking about feelings is a good idea? If so, talking with whom? under what circumstances? How important is such talk to friendship?

from Men and Their Hidden Feelings

by Richard Cohen

My friends have no friends. They are men. They think they have friends, and if you ask them whether they have friends they will say yes, but they don't really. They think, for instance, that I'm their friend, but I'm not. It's OK. They're not my friends either.

The reason for that is that we are all men—and men, I have come to believe, cannot or will not have real friends. They have something else—companions, buddies, pals, chums, someone to drink with and someone to wench with and someone to lunch with, but no one when it comes to saying how they feel—especially how they hurt.

Women know this. They talk about it among themselves. I heard one woman describe men as the true Third World people—still not yet emerged. To women, this inability of men to say what they feel is a source of amazement and then anguish and then, finally, betrayal. Women will tell you all the time that they don't know the men they live with. They talk of long silences and drifting off and of keeping feelings hidden and never letting on that they are troubled or bothered or whatever.

If it's any comfort to women, they should know that it's nothing personal. Men treat other men the same way.

5   For instance, I know men who have suffered brutal professional setbacks and never mentioned it to their friends. I know of a guy who never told his best friend that his own son had a rare childhood disease. And I know others who never have sex with their wives, but talk to their friends as though they're living in the Playboy Mansion, either pretending otherwise or saying nothing.

This is something men learn early. It is something I learned from my father, who taught me, the way fathers teach sons, to keep my emotions to myself. I watched him and learned from him. One day we went to the baseball game, cheered and ate and drank, and the next day he was taken to the hospital with yet another ulcer attack. He had several of them. My mother said he worried a lot, but I saw none of this.

Legend has it that men talk a lot about sex. They don't. They talk about it only in the sense that it is treated like sports. They joke about it and rate women from 1 to 10. But they almost never talk about it in a way that matters—the quality of it. They almost never talk in real terms, in terms other than a cartoon, in terms that apply to them and the woman or women with whom they have a relationship.

Women do talk that way. Women talk about fulfillment, and they admit—maybe complain is the better word—to nonexistent sex lives. No man would admit to having virtually no sex life, yet there are plenty who do.

When I was a kid, I believed that it was men who had real friendships and women who did not. This seemed to be the universal belief, and boys would talk about this. We wondered about girls, about what made them so catty that they could not have friendships, and we really thought we were lucky to be men and have real friends.

10   We thought our friendships would last forever; we talked about them in some sort of Three Musketeer fashion—all for one and one for all. If one of us needed help, all of us would come running. We are still good friends, some of us, anyway, and I still feel that I will fight for them, but I don't think I could confide in them. No—not that.

Sometimes I think that men are walking relics—outmoded and outdated, programmed for some other age. We have all the essential qualities for survival in the wild and for success in battle, but we run like hell from talking about our feelings. We are, as the poet said in a different context, truly a thing of wonder.

Some women say that they have always had this ability to confide in one another—to talk freely. Others say that this is something relatively new—yet another benefit of the women's movement. I don't know. All I know is that they have it, and most men don't, and even the men who do—the ones who can talk about how they feel—talk to women. Have we been raised to think of feelings and sentiment as feminine? Can a man talk intimately with another man and not wonder about his masculinity? I don't know. I do know it sometimes makes the other men feel uncomfortable.

I know this is a subject that concerns me, and yet I find myself bottling it all up—keeping it all in. I've been on automatic pilot for years now.

It would be nice to break out of it. It would be nice to join the rest of the human race, connect with others in a way that makes sense, in a way that's meaningful—in a way that's more than a dirty joke and a slap on the back. I wonder whether it can be done.

15   If it can, it will happen because women will insist on it, because they themselves have shown the way, come out of the closet as women, talked about it, organized, defined an agenda, set their goals and admitted that as women—just as women—they have problems in common. So do men. It's time to talk about them.

THINKING ↔ WRITING ACTIVITY 9.8

Exploring the Concept *Friendship*

Read the following essay by Carol Tavris; then answer the questions in your journal.

1. What perspectives does Tavris present that are different from those of Cohen? What ideas in her essay are similar to those in Cohen's?

2. How do you respond to reading these two essays together? Do you see connections with Chapter 7?
3. How do Cohen's and Tavris's essays relate to your definition of friendship?

---

from How Friendship Was "Feminized"
by Carol Tavris

Once upon a time and not so very long ago, everyone thought that men had the great and true-blue friendships. The cultural references stretched through time and art: Damon and Pythias, Hamlet and Horatio, Butch Cassidy and the Sundance Kid. The Lone Ranger never rode off with anyone but Tonto, and Laurel never once abandoned Hardy in whatever fine mess he got them into.

Male friendships were said to grow from the deep roots of shared experience and faithful camaraderie, whereas women's friendships were portrayed as shallow, trivial and competitive, like Scarlett O'Hara's with her sisters. Women, it was commonly claimed, would sell each other out for the right guy, and even for a good time with the wrong one.

Some social scientists told us that this difference was hard wired, a result of our evolutionary history. In the early 1970's, for example, the anthropologist Lionel Tiger argued in "Men in Groups" that "male bonding" originated in prehistoric male hunting groups and was carried on today in equivalent pack-like activities: sports, politics, business and war.

Apparently, women's evolutionary task of rummaging around in the garden to gather the odd yam or kumquat was a solo effort, so females do not bond in the same way. Women prattle on about their feelings, went the stereotype, but men act.

5   My, how times have changed. Today, we are deluged in the wave of best-selling books that celebrate female friendships—"Girlfriends," "Sisters," "Mothers and Daughters" and its clever clone, "Daughters and Mothers." The success of this genre is partly because the book market is so oriented to female readers these days.

But it is also a likely result of two trends that began in the 1970's and 1980's: Female scholars began to dispel the men-are-better stereotype in all domains and women became the majority of psychotherapists. The result was a positive reassessment of the qualities associated with women, including a "feminizing" of definitions of intimacy and friendship.

Accordingly, female friendships are now celebrated as the deep and abiding ones, based as they are on shared feelings and confidences.

Male friendships are scorned as superficial, based as they are on shared interests in, say, the Mets and Michelle Pfeiffer.

In our psychologized culture, "intimacy" is defined as what many women like to do with their friends: talk, express feelings and disclose worries. Psychologists, most of whom are good talkers, validate this definition as the true measure of intimacy. For example, in a study of "intimacy maturity" in marriage, published in the Journal of Personality and Social Psychology, researchers equated "most mature" with "most verbally expressive." As a woman, I naturally think this is a perfectly sensible equation, but I also know it is an incomplete one. To label people mature or immature, you also have to know how they actually behave toward others.

What about all the men and women who support their families, put the wishes of other family members ahead of their own or act in moral and considerate ways when conflicts arise? They are surely mature, even if they are inarticulate or do not express their feelings easily. Indeed, what about all the men and women who define intimacy in terms of deeds rather than words: sharing activities, helping one another or enjoying companionable silence? Too bad for them. That's a "male" definition, and out of favor in these talky times.

10   Years ago, my husband had to have some worrisome medical tests, and the night before he was to go to the hospital we went to dinner with one of his best friends who was visiting from England. I watched, fascinated, as male stoicism combined with English reserve produced a decidedly unfemale-like encounter. They laughed, they told stories, they argued about movies, they reminisced. Neither mentioned the hospital, their worries or their affection for each other. They didn't need to.

It is true that women's style of intimacy has many benefits. A large body of research in health psychology and social psychology finds that women's greater willingness to talk about feelings improves their mental and physical health and makes it easier to ask for help.

But as psychologists like Susan Nolen-Hoeksema of Stanford University have shown, women's fondness for ruminating about feelings can also prolong depression, anxiety and anger. And it can keep women stuck in bad jobs or relationships, instead of getting out of them or doing what is necessary to make them better.

Books and movies that validate women's friendships are overdue, and welcome as long as they don't simply invert the stereotype. Playing the women-are-better game is fun, but it blinds us to the universal need for intimacy and the many forms that friendship takes. Maybe men could learn a thing or two about friendship from women. But who is to say that women couldn't learn a thing or two from them in exchange?

Using Concepts to Classify

Previous sections of this chapter briefly stated that the thinking pattern of classification is essential to dealing with concepts and definitions. This section will provide a more thorough discussion.

When you apply a concept to an object, idea, or experience, you are in effect *classifying* the object, idea, or experience by placing it in a group of things that are defined by the properties or requirements of the concept. In fact, the same things can often be classified in many different ways. For example, if someone handed you a tomato and asked, "Which category does this tomato belong in, fruit or vegetable?" how would you respond? The fact is, a tomato can be classified as both a fruit and as a vegetable, because its botanical definition does not seem consistent with its uses as a food.

Let's consider another example. Imagine that you are walking on undeveloped land with some other people when you come across an area of soggy ground with long grass and rotting trees. One person in your group surveys the parcel and announces, "That's a smelly marsh. All it does is

THE TREE, as seen by...

the planner...   the parks department...   the publisher...

the highways department...   the developer...   the landscape architect.

From PULP! *Used by permission of Louis Hellman.*

breed mosquitoes. It ought to be covered with landfill and built on, so that we can use it productively." Another member of your group disagrees with the classification "smelly marsh," stating, "This is a wetland of great ecological value. There are many plants and animals that need this area and other areas like it to survive. Wetland areas also help to prevent the rivers from flooding, by absorbing excess water during heavy rains." Which person is right? Should the wet area be classified as a "smelly marsh" or as a "valuable wetland"? Actually, the wet area can be classified both ways. The classification that you select depends on your needs and your interests. Someone active in construction and land development may tend to view the parcel through perceptual lenses that reflect his or her interests and experience and classify it accordingly. On the other hand, someone involved in preserving natural resources will tend to view the same parcel through different lenses and place it in a different category. The diagram on page 348 illustrates how a tree might be "seen" from a variety of perspectives, depending on the interest and experience of those involved.

These examples illustrate how the way you classify reflects and influences the way you see the world, the way you think about the world, and the way you behave in the world. This is true for virtually all the classifications you make. Consider the racehorse Secretariat, who won the Triple Crown in 1973 and was one of the most famous racehorses that ever lived. Which category should Secretariat be placed in?

- A magnificent thoroughbred
- A substantial investment
- An animal ill-equipped for farming
- A descendant of Bold Ruler
- A candidate for the glue factory

You classify many of the things in your experience differently than others do because of your individual needs, interests, and values. For instance, smoking marijuana might be classified by some as "use of a dangerous drug" and by others as a "harmless good time." Some view large cars as "gas guzzlers"; others see the same cars as "safer, more comfortable vehicles." Some people categorize body piercing as "perverse abuse," while others think of it as "creative fashion." The way you classify aspects of your experience reflects the kind of individual you are and the way you think and feel about the world.

You also place people in various categories. The specific categories you select depend on who you are and how you see the world. Similarly, each of us is placed in a variety of classifications by different people. Here, for instance, are some of the categories in which certain people have placed me:

Classification	People Who Classify Me
First-born son	My parents
Taxpayer	Internal Revenue Service
Tickler	My son/daughter
Bagel with cream cheese	Restaurant where I pick up my breakfast

List some of the different ways that you can be classified, and identify the people who would classify you that way.

Not only do you continually classify things and people, place them in various groups on the basis of common properties you choose to focus on; you also classify ideas, feelings, actions, and experiences. Explain, for instance, why the killing of another person might be classified in different ways, depending on the circumstances.

Classification	Circumstance	Example
1. Manslaughter	Killing someone accidentally	Driving while intoxicated
2. Self-defense		
3. Premeditated		
4. Mercy killing		
5. Diminished capacity		

Each of these classifications represents a separate legal concept, with its own properties and referents (examples). Of course, even when you understand clearly what the concept means, the complexity of the circumstances often makes it difficult to determine which concept applies. Court cases raise complex and disturbing issues. During a trial, trying first to identify the appropriate concepts, and then to determine which of the further concepts "guilty" or "not guilty" also applies, is a challenging process. This is true of many of life's other complex situations: you must work hard at identifying appropriate concepts to apply to the circumstances you are trying to make sense of, then be prepared to change or modify these concepts on the basis of new information or better insight.

Defining Concepts

When you define a concept, you usually identify the necessary properties or requirements that determine when the concept can be applied. In fact, the word *definition* is derived from a Latin word meaning "boundary," and a definition gives the boundaries of whatever territory in your experience can be described by the concept.

Definitions also often make strategic use of examples of the concept being defined. Consider the following definition by Ambrose Bierce:

An edible: Good to eat and wholesome to digest, as a worm to a toad, a toad to a snake, a snake to a pig, a pig to a man, and a man to a worm.

Contrast this definition with the one illustrated in the following passage from Charles Dickens's *Hard Times:*

> "Bitzer," said Thomas Gradgrind. "Your definition of a horse." "Quadruped. Graminivorous. Forty teeth, namely twenty-four grinders, four eye teeth, and twelve incisive. Sheds coat in the spring; in marshy countries shed hoofs, too. Hoofs hard, but requiring to be shod with iron. Age known by marks in mouth." That (and much more) Bitzer. "Now girl number twenty," said Mr. Gradgrind, "you know what a horse is."

Although Bitzer has certainly done an admirable job of listing some of the necessary properties or requirements of the concept *horse,* it is unlikely that "girl number twenty" has any better idea of what a horse is than she had before, since the definition relies exclusively on a technical listing of the properties characterizing the concept *horse* without giving any examples that might illustrate the concept more completely. Definitions like this, relying exclusively on a technical description of the concept's properties, are not very helpful unless you already know what the concept means. A more concrete way of communicating the concept *horse* would be to point out various animals that qualify as horses and other animals that do not. You could also explain why they do not. (For example, "That can't be a horse because it has two humps and its legs are far too long.")

Although examples do not take the place of a clearly understood definition, they are often very useful in clarifying, supplementing, and expanding such a definition. If someone asked you, "What is a horse?" and you replied by giving examples of different kinds of horses (thoroughbred racing horses, plow horses for farming, quarter horses for cowhands, circus horses), you certainly would be communicating a good portion of the meaning of *horse.* Giving examples of a concept complements and clarifies the necessary requirements for the correct use of that concept.

Defining a Concept

Giving an effective definition of a concept requires:

- Identifying the general qualities of the concept, which determine when it can be correctly applied.
- Classifying it, which means identifying its category, type, or "family."
- Using appropriate examples to demonstrate actual applications of the concept—that is, examples that embody its general qualities.
- Differentiating it from other items in its classification.

The process of providing definitions of concepts is basically the same process that you use to develop concepts. Of course, this process is often difficult and complex, and people don't always agree on how concepts should be defined.

THINKING ↔ WRITING ACTIVITY 9.9

Defining the Concept *Responsibility*

Review the ideas we have explored in this chapter by analyzing the concept *responsibility*, a complex idea that has an entire network of meaning. The word comes from the Latin word *respondere*, which means "to pledge or promise." Write your responses to the instructions below in your journal.

Generalizing

1. Describe two important responsibilities you have in your life and identify the qualities they embody that lead you to think of them as "responsibilities."

2. Describe a person in your life who you think is responsible and describe one you think is irresponsible. In reflecting on these individuals, identify the qualities they embody that lead you to think of them as "responsible" and "irresponsible."

Interpreting

3. In each of the following situations, describe what you consider examples of responsible behavior and irresponsible behavior.
   a. You are a member of a group of three students who are assigned the task of writing a report on a certain topic. Your life is very hectic; in addition, you find the topic dull. What is your response? Why?
   b. You are employed at a job in which you observe your supervisor and other employees engaged in activities that break the company rules. You are afraid that if you "blow the whistle," you may lose your job. What is your response? Why?

Defining

4. Using these activities of generalizing and interpreting as a foundation, define the concepts *responsible* and *irresponsible* by listing the qualities that make up the boundaries of each concept and identifying the key examples that embody and illustrate its qualities.

THINKING ↔ WRITING ACTIVITY 9.10

Defining the Concept *Religion*

There are few concepts more complex and emotionally charged than that of *religion*. The following passage is taken from the book *Ways of Being Religious* and presents a provocative introduction to the concepts *religion* and *religious experience*. After reading the selection, write answers to these questions in your journal.

1. Where in this excerpt is the definition of *religion* given? Do you find that placement effective? If so, why?

2. What do you find helpful about the questions at the beginning of many of the paragraphs?
3. Apply one of those questions to a different concept and write a paragraph modeled after the one following the question, substituting this other concept for *religion.*

---

from What Is Religion?

by Frederick J. Strong, Charles L. Lloyd, and Jay T. Allen

An African proverb, from the Ganda tribe in central Uganda, states, "He who never visits thinks his mother is the only cook." As with most proverbs, its meaning is larger than the explicit subjects referred to—in this case food and visiting. It suggests that a person is much the poorer for not having had exposure to and acquaintance with the ways of other people.

All of us have had some acquaintance with religious people, just as we have tasted our mother's food. But do we really understand very well what it means to be religious? The "Father of the Scientific Study of Religion," Max Mueller, once said: "He who knows one religion understands none." That is perhaps too extreme a statement as it stands, and yet it says about the study of religion what the African proverb says about the knowledge of life in general—that we sacrifice much if we confine ourselves to the familiar.

If a visit is to be fruitful, the "traveler" must do more than just move from place to place. He must respond to what he sees. But what is it that shapes the way we respond to new experiences? Our perception of things is often colored by our previous attitudes toward them. In this case, what do you, the reader, expect from an exposure to various expressions of religion? What sorts of things do you expect to see? How do you think you will respond to them? If you were asked to define, illustrate, or to characterize religious behavior, how would you do so? The answers to these questions, of course, reflect your pre-conceptions. To become conscious of your pre-conceptions, ask yourself the following four questions:

Does your definition *reduce* **religion to what you happen to be acquainted with by accident of birth and socialization?** Perhaps that goes without saying. It may be true of anyone's "off-the cuff" definition of religion. However, we ask this question to encourage you to consider whether your definition has sufficient *scope.* Is it broad enough to include the religious activities of human beings throughout the world? In surveying university students we have commonly gotten responses to the question, "What is religion?" as follows: "Being Christian, I would define it [religion] as personal relationship with Christ." "Religion [is]: God, Christ, and Holy Ghost and their meaning to each individual." Other students think of worship rather than belief. In this vein, one edition of Webster's dictionary, in the first of its definitions, describes religion as "the service and adoration of God or a god as expressed in forms of worship." If we were to accept any of the above definitions, many people in the world would be excluded—people who regard some of their most important activities as religious, but who do not focus upon a deity. That is to say, not all religions are theistic. It remains to be seen, of course, whether and to what extent this is true. But let us all be warned of taking our habits or our dictionary as the sole resource for defining religion. In some areas, the main lines of significant understanding are already well established. Therefore we have no serious quarrel with Webster's definition of food as "nutritive material taken into an organism for growth, work, or repair and for maintaining the vital processes." But in religion, interpretive concepts are more problematical. Therefore we are suspicious of the adequacy of the dictionary's definition of religion.

5   Another common way to define religion is to regard it as "morality plus stories," or "morality plus emotion." These are ways of asserting that religion has to do mainly with ethics, or that its myths merely support the particular views of a people. There are, of course, persons for whom religion has been reduced to ethics, as when Thomas Paine stated (in *The Rights of Man*): "My country is the world, and my religion is to do good." But we should be cautious in assuming that this testimony would do for all religious people.

A final example of a definition that begins with personal experience is one that claims: "Religion is a feeling of security"; or, as one student put it: "Religion is an aid in coping with that part of life which man does not understand, or in some cases a philosophy of life enabling man to live more deeply." In locating the basis of religion in man's need for a sense of security, this approach suggests that the deepest study of religion is through psychology. It has been dramatically expressed by the psychiatrist and writer C. G. Jung when he wrote: "Religion is a relationship to the highest or strongest value . . . the value by which you are possessed unconsciously. That psychological fact which is the greatest power in your system is the god, since it is always the overwhelming psychic factor which is called 'god.'" Although this understanding of religion expresses a very important point, many theologians and religious philosophers point out that an interpretation that reduces all of religious experience to psychological, biological, or social factors omits the central reality exposed in that experience—the Sacred or Ultimate Reality. Thus, a student of religion should keep open the question of whether a familiar interpretation of religious life that fits into a conventional, social science perspective of man is adequate for interpreting the data.

Does your definition reflect a *bias* on your part—positive or negative—toward religion as a whole, or toward a particular religion? There are many examples of biased definitions that could be cited. Some equate religion with superstition, thus reflecting a negative evaluation. One man defined religion as "the sum of the scruples which impede the free exercise of the human faculties." Another hostile view of religion is to see religion as a device of priests to keep the masses in subjection and themselves in comfort. Similarly, Karl Marx, while not actually attempting to define religion, called it "the opiate of the people," again reflecting a bias against (all) religion.

Still others, in defining religion, are stating their concept of *true* religion as opposed to what they regard as false or pagan faiths. Henry Fielding, in his novel *Tom Jones*, has the provincial parson Mr. Thwackum saying, "When I mention religion I mean the Christian religion; and not only the Christian religion, but the Protestant religion; and not only the Protestant religion; but the Church of England." Some Christians assume that their personal conviction comprises a definition of religion, so the religion is regarded as "the worship of God through his Son Jesus Christ," or "a personal relationship with Christ." A Muslim can point out that the essence of religion is to make peace with God through complete submission to God's will, a submission that he will insist is brought to fulfillment in Islam. (In Arabic the word "Islam" means "submission," "peace," "safety," and "salvation.")

Therefore the student interested in reflecting on religious experience that includes more than a single institutional or cultural expression should remember the distinction between descriptive (neutral) and evaluative definitions. A descriptive definition attempts to be as inclusive as possible about a class of items, such as religious forms. An evaluative definition, on the other hand, reflects one's own criteria for truth or falsity, for reality or illusion. In "visiting" religious people, we suggest that you delay making an evaluation until you have understood why their expressions and processes have profound meaning for them—however strange those expressions may seem to you. In the final analysis, each person must evaluate different religious alternatives; but one of our goals in bringing together the material in this volume is to provide you with a variety of options—a variety that is reduced if you limit religion to any single historical expression.

10   Obviously the believer who advocates one religion to the exclusion of all others differs sharply from one who rejects all. Nevertheless, if either accepts his own convictions about what is best or worst in religion as a description of what religion in fact is everywhere and for everyone, he exhibits a common indifference to unfamiliar, and therefore poten-

tially surprising, religious patterns. As a believer (or skeptic), you have a right to declare your own understanding of what is most important, most real, in religion. This declaration is, in fact, essential, for it guides you in your quest for whatever is most real in life. As a student, on the other hand, you have an obligation to carry your studies as far as necessary to include relevant data. In this role, your obligation is not only to your own perception of value but also to a common world of understanding in which men of many religious persuasions can converse with each other.

Does your definition *limit* religion to what it has been in the past, and nothing else, or does your definition make it possible to speak of emerging forms of religion?   In asking this question, we should observe two striking facts of the history of religion: there was a time when some present religions did not exist, and some of the religions which once emerged no longer exist (for example, the Egyptian and Babylonian religions). Human history, then, has witnessed the emergence and abandonment of several religions.

Even religious traditions that have maintained a sense of continuity over vast stretches of time (Hinduism, Buddhism, Judaism, Christianity, for example) have undergone important changes. Is it really as obvious as we tend to think that they are essentially the same now as they were at their origins? Do the terms naming these traditions even today point to a single entity, however complex? You are familiar with at least some instances of religious warfare *within* the Christian tradition. Roman Catholics have persecuted and killed Lutherans; Lutherans have persecuted and killed Calvinists; Calvinists, Anglicans; Anglicans, Quakers; and most have returned the act with interest. Are all of these groups expressions of "the one true church"? Are some more Christian than others? Is there only one form of Christianity? Are new movements violations of the tradition? Or is the one who speaks to his own time the one who is most faithful to the genius of his tradition? These questions can be asked of all religious traditions. All have experienced change and diversity. Furthermore, it seems likely that this will continue, and that new religious traditions will emerge. Therefore, the conventions of the past cannot be regarded as the limits of future religious forms.

In part because history has witnessed the emergence and internal changes of many religions, anthropologists and cultural historians commonly suggest that religion (and human culture in general) has attained only its adolescence. Likewise, philosophers and religious thinkers in both East and West point to the anxiety and tensions today that are expressed in political, social, economic, and intellectual upheaval. They raise a question of whether or not man's moral, psychic, and evaluative resources can catch up with his self-destructive potential seen in technologically advanced weapons and psychological-chemical techniques for social control. The most hopeful of these philosophers perceive the present turmoil as a lack of "maturity" in human consciousness, and express the hope that it is not too late (quite) to change the direction of man from self-destruction to self-fulfillment.

From this perspective most of mankind's experience is still in the future. The history of religious life to the present is only a beginning. But the basis of these projections is the recognition that man's survival requires him to recognize religious dynamics and processes for evaluations as major forces in human life. Should not a definition of religion aid us in looking at contemporary phenomena to see if any new ways of being religious are emerging? At least it should not inhibit persons with an interest in this matter, and we think an introduction to religion should encourage such reflection.

15   **Does your definition have sufficient** *precision?*   Are there any limits to the scope of religion, or are the limits so vague that they fail to mark out an object of study? In an attempt to be as broadminded as possible, many definitions are like a student's statement that religion is "the means man has of coping with his world." Or they are similar to the claim that religion is "believing in a way of life which involves understanding and caring for others," or "religion is love." Such definitions tell us a good deal, but without some qualification they might refer to many other expressions of human life than specifically religious ones. In order to find a focus and a set of limitations at the outer circumference of that focus, we need to designate what are those essential elements of religion that will expose the *religious* meaning of the evidence we look at.

When one has "visited" (seen) a wide range of religious life, from all parts of the world and throughout human history, it becomes apparent that religion is a way of life that involves many processes—all of which, in different ways, are directed toward a common end. The goal is to reach a state of being that is conceived to be the highest possible state or condition. Religion is the general term for the various ways by which people seek to become changed into that highest state. We understand *religion as a means toward ultimate transformation.* By this we are not claiming that every activity you think of as religious will in fact transform you ultimately. It might, but that is not our point. We mean that *any* reasonably specific means that *any* persons adopts with the serious hope and intention of moving toward ultimate transformation should be termed "religious." We think it possible to speak of all religious activity (Eastern and Western, past, present, and emerging) without reducing religion to what is merely familiar to us and without putting a value judgment on one or more religions.

THINKING↔WRITING ACTIVITY 9.11

Defining the Concept *Poverty*

Read the speech "What Is Poverty?" by Jo Goodwin Parker; then write answers to the questions in your journal.

1. How do you respond to Parker's technique of defining by using analogies? Is there one that you find particularly effective?
2. Identify a paragraph in which Parker gives strong, specific physical examples. What effect do these specifics have? Rewrite one sentence, using more general language. Does it seem more, or less, effective than Parker's sentence?
3. Do you think a man might speak or write differently about poverty? What might a father in a similar situation say?

from What Is Poverty?

by Jo Goodwin Parker

You ask me what is poverty? Listen to me. Here I am, dirty, smelly, and with no "proper" underwear on and with the stench of my rotting teeth near you. I will tell you. Listen to me. Listen without pity. I cannot use your pity. Listen with understanding. Put yourself in my dirty, worn out, ill-fitting shoes, and hear me.

Poverty is getting up every morning from a dirt- and illness-stained mattress. The sheets have long since been used for diapers. Poverty is living in a smell that never leaves. This is a smell of urine, sour milk, and spoiling food sometimes joined with the strong smell of long-cooked onions. Onions are cheap. If you have smelled this smell, you did not know how it came. It is the smell of the outdoor privy. It is the smell of young children who cannot walk the long dark way in the night. It is the smell of the mattresses where years of "accidents" have happened. It is the smell of the milk which has gone sour because the refrigerator long has not worked, and it costs money to get it fixed. It is the smell of rotting garbage. I could bury it, but where is the shovel? Shovels cost money.

Poverty is being tired. I have always been tired. They told me at the hospital when the last baby came that I had chronic anemia caused from poor diet, a bad case of worms, and that I needed a corrective operation. I listened politely—the poor are always polite. The poor always listen. They don't say that there is no money for iron pills, or better food, or worm medicine. The idea of an operation is frightening and costs so much that, if I had dared, I would have laughed. Who takes care of my children? Recovery from an operation takes a long time. I have three children. When I left them with "Granny" the last time I had a job, I came home to find the baby covered with fly specks, and a diaper that had not been changed since I left. When the dried diaper came off, bits of my baby's flesh came with it. My other child was playing with a sharp bit of broken glass, and my oldest was playing alone at the edge of a lake. I made twenty-two dollars a week, and a good nursery school costs twenty dollars a week for three children. I quit my job.

Poverty is dirt. You say in your clean clothes coming from your clean house, "Anybody can be clean." Let me explain about housekeeping with no money. For breakfast I give my children grits with no oleo or cornbread without eggs and oleo. This does not use up many dishes. What dishes there are, I wash in cold water and with no soap. Even the cheapest soap has to be saved for the baby's diapers. Look at my hands, so cracked and red. Once I saved for two months to buy a jar of Vaseline for my hands and the baby's diaper rash. When I had saved enough, I went to buy it and the price had gone up two cents. The baby and I suffered on. I have to decide every day if I can bear to put my cracked, sore hands into the cold water and strong soap. But you ask, why not hot water? Fuel costs money. If you have a wood fire it costs money. If you burn electricity, it costs money. Hot water is a luxury. I do not have luxuries. I know you will be surprised when I tell you how young I am. I look so much older. My back has been bent over the wash tubs every day for so long. I cannot remember when I ever did anything else. Every night I wash every stitch my school age child has on and just hope her clothes will be dry by morning.

5   Poverty is staying up all night on cold nights to watch the fire, knowing one spark on the newspaper covering the walls means your sleeping children die in flames. In summer, poverty is watching gnats and flies devour your baby's tears when he cries. The screens are torn and you pay so little rent you know they will never be fixed. Poverty means insects in your food, in your nose, in your eves, and crawling over you when you sleep. Poverty is hoping it never rains because diapers won't dry when it rains and soon you are using newspapers. Poverty is seeing your children forever with runny noses. Paper handkerchiefs cost money and all your rags you need for other things. Even more costly are antihistamines. Poverty is cooking without food and cleaning without soap.

Poverty is asking for help. Have you ever had to ask for help, knowing your children will suffer unless you get it? Think about asking for a loan from a relative, if this is the only way you can imagine asking for help. I will tell you how it feels. You find out where the office is that you are supposed to visit. You circle that block four or five times. Thinking of your children, you go in. Everyone is very busy. Finally, someone comes out and you tell her that you need help. That never is the person you need to see. You go see another person, and after spilling the whole shame of your poverty all over the desk between you, you find that this isn't the right office after all—you must repeat the whole process, and it never is any easier at the next place.

You have asked for help, and after all it has a cost. You are again told to wait. You are told why, but you don't really hear because of the red cloud of shame and the rising black cloud of despair.

Poverty is remembering. It is remembering quitting school in junior high because "nice" children had been so cruel about my clothes and my smell. The attendance officer came. My mother told him I was pregnant. I wasn't, but she thought that I could get a job and help out. I had jobs off and on, but never long enough to learn anything. Mostly I remember being married. I was so young then. I am still young. For a time, we had all the things you have. There was a little house in another town, with hot water and everything. Then my husband lost his job. There was unemployment insurance for a while and what few jobs I could get. Soon, all our nice things were repossessed and we moved back here. I was pregnant then. This house didn't look so bad when we first moved in. Every week it gets worse. Nothing is ever fixed. We now had no money. There were a few odd jobs for my husband, but everything went for food then, as it does now. I don't know how we lived through three years and three babies, but we did. I'll tell you something, after the last baby I destroyed my marriage. It had been a good one, but could you keep on bringing children in this dirt? Did you ever think how much it costs for any kind of birth control? I knew my husband was leaving the day he left, but there were no goodbys between us. I hope he has been able to climb out of this mess somewhere. He never could hope with us to drag him down.

That's when I asked for help. When I got it, you know how much it was? It was, and is, seventy-eight dollars a month for the four of us; that is all I ever can get. Now you know why there is no soap, no needles and thread, no hot water, no aspirin, no worm medicine, no hand cream, no shampoo. None of these things forever and ever and ever. So that you can see clearly, I pay twenty dollars a month rent, and most of the rest goes for food. For grits and cornmeal, and rice and milk and beans. I try my best to use only the minimum electricity. If I use more, there is that much less for food.

10   Poverty is looking into a black future. Your children won't play with my boys. They will turn to other boys who steal to get what they want. I can already see them behind the bars of their prison instead of behind the bars of my poverty. Or they will turn to the freedom of alcohol or drugs, and find themselves enslaved. And my daughter? At best, there is for her a life like mine.

But you say to me, there are schools. Yes, there are schools. My children have no extra books, no magazines, no extra pencils, or crayons, or paper and the most important of all, they do not have health. They have worms, they have infections, they have pink-eye all summer. They do not sleep well on the floor, or with me in my one bed. They do not suffer from hunger, my seventy-eight dollars keeps us alive, but they do suffer from malnutrition. Oh yes, I do remember what I was taught about health in school. It doesn't do much good. In some places there is a surplus commodities program. Not here. The county said it cost too much. There is a school lunch program. But I have two children who will already be damaged by the time they get to school.

But, you say to me, there are health clinics. Yes, there are health clinics and they are in the towns. I live out here eight miles from town. I can walk that far (even if it is sixteen miles both ways), but can my little children? My neighbor will take me when he goes; but he expects to get paid, *one way or another*. I bet you know my neighbor. He is that large man who spends his time at the gas station, the barbershop, and the corner store complaining about the government spending money on the immoral mothers of illegitimate children.

Poverty is an acid that drips on pride until all pride is worn away. Poverty is a chisel that chips on honor until honor is worn away. Some of you say that you would do *something* in my situation, and maybe you would, for the first week or the first month, but for year after year after year?

Even the poor can dream. A dream of a time when there is money. Money for the right kinds of food, for worm medicine, for iron pills, for toothbrushes, for hand cream, for a hammer and nails and a bit of screening, for a shovel, for a bit of paint, for some sheeting, for needles and thread. Money to pay *in money* for a trip to town. And, oh, money for hot water and money for soap. A dream of when asking for help does not eat away the last bit of pride. When the office you visit is as nice as the offices of other governmental agencies, when there are enough workers to help you quickly, when workers do nor quit in defeat and despair. When you have to tell your story to only one person, and that person can send you for other help and you don't have to prove your poverty over and over and over again.

15   I have come out of my despair to tell you this. Remember I did not come from another place or another time. Others like me are all around you. Look at us with an angry heart, anger that will help you help me. Anger that will let you tell of me. The poor are always silent. Can you be silent too?

Writing Thoughtfully to Define Concepts

Writing a full definition, often called an *extended definition,* is among the most important and most difficult of writing activities. Defining terms is a necessary part of college-level writing and speaking. For productive discussions about complex issues, all involved must agree on the meanings of significant terms, so definitions are often required. Difficulties arise because significant terms related to complex issues are usually abstract concepts, with possibilities of different definitions for different people. For example, the common political terms *conservative* and *liberal* often have varied meanings, even to people who identify themselves as one or the other.

No one has much trouble agreeing on definitions of physical objects. A table, a tree, a television set—not many arguments arise about what these objects are. But like *liberal* and *conservative,* concepts such as *religion, love, democracy, femininity,* and *masculinity* can be defined in different ways. If people discussing ideas like these do not establish definitions, their discussions will not be productive. Worse, these discussions probably will lead to disagreements, arguments, and even wars. The readings and Thinking↔Writing Activities in this chapter have been selected and planned to demonstrate the importance of definitions.

Notice how with both simple objects and complex concepts, defining is somewhat easier as long as a single word is being looked at. As soon as modifying and classifying ideas are added, defining becomes more challenging and more significant to critical thinking. A *beautiful* table, a *good* tree to plant in a *small* yard, the *best* television set to buy for *your family room*—now these objects call for fuller definitions. The *kind* of democracy that can work in a country with a *history of despotism,* the *kind* of love that a *parent* might have for an *adult child*—these are the types of concepts that people must define in order to present arguments, to make decisions, to solve problems. These are the kinds of terms that you might want to define in the **Writing Project** in this chapter because they are the kinds that involve judgments; they are important to our lives because they influence our actions.

Clear, satisfying definitions can be as extended as book chapters or articles or entire books; however, a definition often will be developed in a paragraph or two as a vital part of a paper or report. In the **Writing Project** for this chapter, you will write an essay that defines; you will see the need for using a variety of thinking/organizing patterns as you develop it. The principles for writing definitions are not fixed rules; there may be times when you would have good reasons for varying or ignoring some of them. Try to use them, though, unless you have good reason not to.

1. Establish the need for a definition. Do people disagree on the meaning of the concept? Are there multiple meanings? Are earlier definitions no longer satisfactory? Is this a new concept or new terminology?
2. Choose carefully the word or words in which you state the concept. Definitions provide precision, so you need to be sure that you have presented the concept in the words that are most indicative.
3. Deal in some way with two kinds of dictionary definitions: the short one in a regular college dictionary and the historical presentation in the *Oxford English Dictionary*. The terseness of the ordinary definition is usually the reason why an extended definition is needed. Word origins and past meanings can often illuminate the meaning that you want to present.
4. Be sure that you identify the category into which the concept fits.
5. Show comparative thinking. Point out similar concepts, but then make clear how your concept is distinct. Think of analogies that can illuminate the meaning of the concept.
6. Provide specific examples to show what the concept means. Illustrative anecdotes are often effective.
7. Include the meaning of the concept in the thesis statement. Give careful thought to where you state the thesis.
8. Throughout your definition, emphasize that you are establishing the meaning you believe the concept has within the context that you have identified.
9. Address the foregoing principles in separate paragraphs or sections of the definition. Provide each paragraph with a clear topic sentence whenever appropriate.
10. Document any sources that you use. Introduce source material into your definition, explain and comment on it, and cite correctly.

WRITING PROJECT

This chapter has included both readings and **Thinking↔Writing Activities** that encourage you to define concepts that affect your life. Be sure to reread what you wrote for the Activities; you may be able to use some of what you wrote for help in completing this project.

WRITING PROJECT   Defining an Important Concept

Write an essay in which you define a concept that is important to your life now or to your future life in the twenty-first century. Include in your paper explanations of why this concept is significant for you and why it needs defining or redefining. You may want to think of a concept that is expressed in a phrase, rather than in a single word, as discussed above. Include material from two sources in addition to any dictionaries that you consult. Integrate your sources into your essay and document them as your professor directs. After you have drafted your essay, revise it to the best of your ability. Follow instructions given by your professor as to topic limits, length, formats, and so forth.

Begin by considering the key elements in the **Thinking↔Writing Model.**

Purpose

You have a variety of purposes here. You want to think about and formulate a definition that is significant to you as you continue your college studies, or decide on your profession, or enter a new phase in your personal life. Also, you can hone your revision skills by working through the revision questions that follow.

Audience

You have a multilevel audience. *You* are an important audience, for in facing the challenge of defining a complex concept, you can think more clearly about some aspect of your life. Your classmates can learn from your definition and also can be a valuable audience in peer reviews of a draft, reacting as intelligent readers who are not as knowledgeable as you about the concept that pertains to your life. In addition, you should think about and identify people outside your class who would enjoy or profit from reading your definition. Of course, your instructor remains the audience who will judge how well you have planned, drafted, revised, and presented your paper. As a writing teacher, your instructor cares about clear focus, logical organization, solid evidence, accurate documentation of sources, and correctness. Keep these in mind as you revise, edit, and proofread.

Subject

All of us need to be able to define abstract, complex terms that are foundations for our thinking, our decisions, and our actions in life. College courses, family life, spiritual concerns, and romantic relationships all involve concepts that need to be well defined so that we understand what we mean when we speak and write, so that we understand what others mean when they communicate with us, and—most important—so that we can avoid confusion and conflict.

Writer

This project provides you with the opportunity to participate in the "conversation of ideas" that is the lifeblood of thoughtful, reflective people in a society. By defining a rich, complex concept, you are explaining how the concept you have selected has personal meaning for you. Since concepts exist in the world, you are also suggesting to others—your audience—how they might think about your analysis of the concept. The definition you propose may help them understand something in their experience more clearly, or it may provide an added meaning they have not previously considered. The outside sources integrated into your analysis ensure that your definition is grounded in a common understanding that goes beyond your own unique experience.

The Writing Process

The following sections will guide you through the recursive stages of generating, planning, drafting, and revising as you work on an essay in which you define a significant concept. Try to be particularly conscious of both the critical thinking you do as you articulate your definition and the critical thinking and decision making you do when you revise.

Generating Ideas

- Refer back to the responses you wrote for the Thinking↔Writing Activities connected with the readings on gender issues, the exercise about responsibility, and the essay on defining religion. These concepts are important in many people's lives, so perhaps you will write about one of them—or perhaps what you read and wrote will lead you to another concept to define.

- Think about the activities or concerns that are central to your life. Some of these are probably rather serious in nature, as are the subjects discussed in this chapter, but some parts are surely more lighthearted, like sports you play or watch, or television comedies, or thriller movies, or parties. Whatever the level of seriousness, all areas of our lives are based on concepts that we should be able to define.

- Next, think of concepts inherent in some of your activities, such as a satisfying relationship with your girlfriend or boyfriend, or what it means to be a good athlete or college student or member of your religion.

- Now, list the properties of two or three concepts that you have identified. Include specific examples. How should each example be classified?

- Think about why any of these concepts need to be defined or redefined. Do people agree on the meaning? Have you formulated a meaning that is more precise and accurate?

- Share your lists and thinking with classmates and, if you can, with people involved in the area in which the concept is important.

- Use as many thinking patterns as you can to discover ideas about your concept. What is it different from? similar to? analogous to? Describe it; think about what causes it; think about what effects it has.

- Look up the key words in the concept in a good college-level dictionary and also in the *Oxford English Dictionary*. Ask your professor or one of your college librarians to explain the OED to you. See if you can use any of your concept's word history to help with your definition.

- Freewrite for at least five minutes about why the concept is important to your life, why it needs to be defined, and what information needs to be in your definition.

Defining a Focus

- Look at your freewriting and lists to see what main idea you are moving toward in your definition. Write this idea in any way that you can.

- Now draft a thesis statement that gives the key ideas in your definition. Recently a student defining freedom of religion had as her thesis sentence: "To me, freedom of religion means more than simply being able to practice our religions as we believe that we should; it also means that we must understand and respect other people's religions." Another student, working on a definition of today's superwoman, wrote, "The main properties of a superwoman are being capable, tenacious, and independent."

- Be sure that your thesis statement emphasizes the meaning of the concept that you are defining.

Organizing Ideas

Essays emphasizing definition are not easy to organize because there are so many approaches to a clear definition of a complex concept. Because the thesis—the essence of the definition—needs to be placed in a context and explained in a number of ways, the question of where to state the thesis is especially crucial. This is the kind of essay in which it might come at the end. (Reread the "What Is Religion?" essay on pages 352–356 to see how this organizing technique was used.) When you state the thesis at the end, you need to lead up to it or preview it throughout the essay. However, you will want to think of stating the thesis provisionally near the beginning and referring to it as you establish your definition.

Identify the approaches that you have used in your generative writing and early drafts. Where have you used contrast, comparison, analogy, narration, and so on? The material developed by each of these approaches is likely to form a paragraph. The definitions that you have found in your dictionary and in the OED will need a paragraph or two of connection with the definition that you are developing. As you always should do, give careful thought to paragraphing. Try your drafted paragraphs in different orders to discover which order will help your readers understand your definition.

Because it is important readers understand the need for a definition, and explaining that need is an effective way to begin. The significance of this concept in your life might be part of a beginning or a conclusion.

Drafting

Begin with the paragraph easiest to draft. Explaining the concept's significance in your life is likely to be easy, since you are writing about your thoughts and feelings; showing the need for a definition should not be difficult because you are writing about one of your convictions. Therefore, you may want to draft these personal paragraphs first. Then you might feel more comfortable explaining the connection of the word history to your concept and also find it easier to make classifying, comparative, and contrastive explanations.

As you draft, be sure that each paragraph contains real-life examples that pertain to the meaning of the concept, unless for some good reason a specific paragraph does not need examples.

After you draft your paragraphs, make every effort to write topic sentences that focus on how the material in the paragraph helps to establish the *meaning* of your concept.

As you draft the conclusion, be sure that it provides a satisfying ending with some reference to the thesis and emphasis on the meaning of the concept.

Revising

Ideally, at this point, you should put your draft aside for a day or two. If deadlines won't permit you to do that, then at least take a break before you try to revise. When you are ready to "re-see" your writing, begin by reading it through slowly, preferably aloud. If possible, have someone whose opinion you respect read it; ask for feedback. Then work through the hierarchy of revision concerns that follows. Remember that you have at least one and possibly two decisions to make for each question: (1) Is improvement needed? and (2) If improvement is needed, how, exactly, can I make my draft better?

1. **Think big.** Look at your draft as a whole.
- Does it fulfill the assignment in terms of topic and length?
- Have you stated the thesis clearly?
- Do all parts of the draft relate to the thesis?
- Is the organization logical?
- Do you provide enough evidence?
- Is your point of view consistent?
- Is there a discernible flow between your paragraphs?
- Have you documented information from your sources accurately?
- Have you used quotation marks around direct quotes or set the quotes off by indenting?

2. **Think medium.** Look at your draft paragraph by paragraph.
- Will your introduction make your audience want to read on?
- Is the introduction appropriate for the rest of the draft?
- Is your focus stated clearly if you are working with a "visible" structure?
- If you are working with an "invisible structure," is your focus implied?
- Are topic sentences used effectively?
- Does each body paragraph develop a different idea?
- Should any paragraphs be combined or eliminated?
- Is your conclusion effective?

3. **Think small.** Look at your draft sentence by sentence.
- Are any sentences difficult to understand?
- Are any so long that your audience could get lost in them?
- Are sentences with blended quotations (that is, quotations that are integrated into the syntax of the sentence instead of introduced with "He said . . ." or "she said . . .") complete and easy to read?
- Are quotations shortened with ellipsis marks accurate and readable?
- Are there several choppy sentences that can be combined?
- Are any sentences vague?
- Do any sentences need to be corrected for standard English grammar and usage?

4. **Think "picky."** Look at your draft as your fussiest critic might.
- Are any words not clear or not quite right for your meaning?
- Are any words misspelled?
- Are there any punctuation errors?
- Is your format correct?
- Are the pages numbered consecutively?

- Does your paper make a good impression by being neat?
- Is there anything else you could do to improve your draft?

Proofreading

After you prepare a final draft, check again for correct grammar and punctuation. Proofread carefully for omitted words or punctuation marks. Run your spelling checker program, but be aware of its limitations. Proofread carefully for the kinds of errors the computer can't catch.

Student Essays

The following essays show how two students responded to this assignment.

STUDENT WRITING
The Real Teacher
by Mary Kamara

The job of a high school teacher is to impart knowledge to his or her students on the subject being taught. However, from my view, I do not think that imparting knowledge really defines the work of a good teacher. The teacher also has to lead, counsel, and act as a role model. My tenth grade English teacher displayed all those qualities, and I am happy to say today that this teacher served as a model for my life. Memories of her still linger in my mind.

Her name was Mrs. Davies. When I was in her class, she had taught for eighteen years. Besides teaching English, she tried to influence the behavior of her students in a positive direction. In a conversation I had with her once after I graduated, she said that she knew that she had to behave very nicely in front of her students to set the pace for them. She was always very polite and respectful, even when she had to discipline us. She understood the importance of the position of teacher in the African town where we lived.

There were moments in her class when I would do something wrong like talking or not paying attention, and she would set me straight. I used to think that she was mean, but then I realized that she helped me become a person who knows how to behave. I always try to show respect wherever I find myself, and I owe this to her.

In an article in *Phi Delta Kappan,* it says ". . . without guidance and support, students may find themselves excluded from settings where valued knowledge is pursued. Then they are more likely to lose their motivation to attend school, and they may give up on their dreams" (Maddox, Smith 228). I relate to this statement because my nephew, a very bright boy, dropped out of school, partly due to lack of guidance at his school. He did not have a teacher like Mrs. Davies.

Besides the discipline, Mrs. Davies was a motivator and a counselor. She encouraged me and other students to aim high. Yet it was her exemplary behavior that influenced me a lot. According to the *Encyclopedia of Psychology*, "All individuals learn various roles by being trained into them, by imitating them, and by a process of identification with the available role models in a particular situation" (Smith 326). I decided to be a teacher myself, so that I could be a good role model, too.

In conclusion, I want to stress that the job of a high school teacher should be defined as more than just to impart knowledge. Teachers must influence young minds by guiding and by acting as role models.

Works Cited

Davies, Rhonda. Personal conversation. 1979.

Maddox, Anne, and Renee Smith. "Untracking and Students' Futures." *Phi Delta Kappan* Nov. 1995: 227–229.

Smith, P. W. "Role Expectations." *Encyclopedia of Psychology*, 2nd ed.

STUDENT WRITING
Genius
by Tze Wing Chan

Have you ever been called "genius"? I hope you have. When we know someone who has outstanding ability, we say that this person must be a genius. Even though the word genius is used frequently, everybody might not agree on the exact meaning of the word. We might wonder sometimes what a real genius is and why we cannot all be geniuses. Since the meaning of the word "genius" seems questionable, I did some research in order to learn about it.

The word "genius" has changed meaning through history. According to one definition in the *Oxford English Dictionary*, genius means:

> A native intellectual power of an exalted type, such as is attributed to those who are esteemed greatest in any department of art, speculation, or practice; instinctive and extraordinary capacity for imaginative creation, original thought, invention, or discovery.

Perhaps this modern definition is accepted by almost everybody, but it was derived from different meanings as time went by. The very beginning sources are Latin and Greek words that mean to be born. The ancient Romans considered genius as the spirit that protected one's household (Sternberg 483). Greigson and Gibbs-Smith discussed the origin of the word in *Ideas* and said that the term came "to personify one's wishes"; and to mean "the guardian angel"; then later on, by the seventeenth century, it meant talent and innate ability (159). After a long time, the word "genius" acquired the meaning that we know nowadays. According to the *Oxford English Dictionary*, in 1749 in the book *Tom Jones,* the modern meaning is used in the phrase "By the wonderful force of genius only, without the least assistance of learning."

After thinking about these meanings, I decided that childhood life experiences and good fortune are factors that can cause one to develop his or her innate ability. Some of the sources that I found discussed these ideas. Sternberg said that some geniuses, such as some of the Nobel prize winners in literature, suffered from their family situations (486). These geniuses might have had no parents or been discriminated against, which might make them feel and think differently. On the other hand, some geniuses come from families which offered them opportunities to work with their interests from the time that they were children. For example, Mozart and Beethoven came from musical families.

A cause that I found very interesting, discussed in the *Encyclopedia of Human Intelligence* is good fortune. As the author Sternberg stated:

> The difference between being outstandingly able and being considered a genius is akin to the distinction between being one of the numerous soldiers who act bravely in a battle and one of the few who are awarded a medal for heroism (484).

So to be considered as a genius, it is essential that one should have an innate ability in a certain area, but also luck. For instance, a poet who has unbelievable skill for writing poems might never be recognized as a genius if no one around him or her knows how to appreciate the poems. Therefore, a genius is the product of the ability combined with fortune.

Geniuses have existed at all times. Even though we can see some of the factors that cause someone to be a genius, we might still not be exactly sure why it happens. If God created all of us equal, how can one have some powers that others cannot have? Some people might consider this an injustice. However, I think that we need geniuses. How would we communicate if Alexander Graham Bell had not invented the telephone? Geniuses and their creations benefit us all, even if we all do not have "a native intellectual power of an exalted type."

Works Cited

"Genius." *The Encyclopedia Dictionary of Psychology.* 3rd ed. 1986.
"Genius." *The Oxford English Dictionary.* 1933
Griegson, Geoffrey, and Charles H. Gibbs-Smith. "Genius." *Ideas.* 2nd ed. 1957.
Sternberg, Robert J. "Genius." *Encyclopedia of Human Intelligence.* 1994.

PART THREE

Thinking and Writing to Explore Issues and Take Positions

As you have become more aware of your own thinking and writing abilities, and more confident in using them, you may also have become more respectful of the thinking and writing of others. You have observed how not only your academic work but even democracy itself depends on valid analysis of sources of belief and of other people's positions and arguments. You have been learning how to evaluate information in order to solve problems and how to express your own perspective clearly.

In Part 1 of this book, you were focusing on yourself.

In Part 2, your focus was on incorporating the ideas of others. Here in Part 3, the focus will be on presenting both your own ideas and those of others in well-reasoned writing.

The **Writing Projects** at the end of each chapter in Part 3 ask you to integrate ideas from other sources into your own written work. (Those ideas might come from the readings in this book, items you discover in a library, or material from other sources.) As you do so, you will learn effective, responsible ways of introducing, documenting, and commenting on ideas from others. And you will practice using the formats of academic citation. Your instructor and your handbook will provide information on citation methods.

CHAPTER 10

Believing and Knowing—Writing to Analyze

Critical Thinking Focus: Analyzing beliefs and their accuracy

Writing Focus: Evaluating evidence

Reading Theme: The media: shaping our thinking

Writing Project: Analyzing influences on beliefs

Thinking and Writing Critically About Beliefs

Writers write what they believe, and their purposes often include explaining their beliefs and persuading others to adopt them. Yet what exactly are beliefs and how are they constructed? When should they be kept, when should they be modified, and when should they be discarded? What are the differences between believing and knowing, and how do writers handle these differences? How do writers present beliefs they hold with varying degrees of certainty?

In this "information age," we are flooded with data, stories, and pictures from television, radio, newspapers, magazines, books, and computers. Much of this information is accurate, but much is not. We are aware of the "spin doctors" who seek to influence the way we interpret information, trying to persuade us to accept their construction of events. Thus, critical thinkers and thoughtful writers face a continuing challenge to evaluate information they receive and to redefine beliefs accordingly.

Chapter 2 examined the sources of beliefs, especially those related to personal life. This chapter continues that discussion by examining the nature of beliefs, by presenting guidelines for evaluating beliefs, and by drawing distinctions between believing and knowing and between knowledge and truth.

The chapter then analyzes three ways in which writers can present their beliefs: as reports, inferences, and judgments.

The Nature of Beliefs

Throughout our lives, we form beliefs about the world around us to explain why things happen as they do, to predict how things will happen, and to govern the way we decide to act. Consider, for example, the extent to which you believe the following statements.

1. Human beings need to eat in order to stay alive.
2. Smoking marijuana is a harmful activity.
3. Every human life is valuable.
4. Developing your mind is as important as taking care of your body.
5. People should care about other people, not just themselves.

Your responses to these statements reflect certain beliefs you have, beliefs not all people share equally.

So what exactly are "beliefs"? A belief represents an interpretation, evaluation, conclusion, or prediction about the nature of the world. The statement "I believe that the U. S. Constitution's guarantee of 'the right of the people to keep and bear arms' does not prohibit all governmental regulation of firearms" represents an *interpretation* of the Second Amendment. To say "I believe that watching soap operas is unhealthy because they focus almost exclusively on the scamy side of human life" expresses an *evaluation* of soap operas. The statement "I believe that one of the main reasons two out of three people in the world go to bed hungry each night is that industrially advanced nations like the United States have not done a satisfactory job of sharing their knowledge" expresses a *conclusion* about the problem of world hunger. To say, "I believe that if drastic environmental measures are not undertaken to slow the global warming trend, the polar icecaps will melt and the earth will be flooded" is to make a *prediction* about events that will occur in the future.

Besides expressing an interpretation, evaluation, conclusion, or prediction about the world, beliefs also express the speaker's *endorsement* of the accuracy of those beliefs—an indication that the belief is held to be true. This endorsement by the speaker is a necessary dimension of beliefs, and we assume it to be the case even if he or she doesn't directly say, "I believe." The statement "Astrological predictions are meaningless because there is no persuasive evidence that the position of the stars has any effect on human affairs" expresses a belief even though it doesn't specifically include the words *I believe.*

In addition, it is necessary to recognize that beliefs are not static—at least not if we apply a critical approach. We form and re-form our beliefs in an ongoing way throughout much of our lives. This process often follows the following sequence:

1. We *form* beliefs in order to explain what is taking place. (These initial beliefs are often based on our past experiences.)
2. We *test* these beliefs by acting on the basis of them.
3. We *revise* (or re-form) these beliefs if our actions do not achieve our goals.
4. We *re-test* these revised beliefs by using them as a basis for action.

As we actively participate in this ongoing process of forming and re-forming beliefs, we are using our critical thinking abilities to identify and critically examine our beliefs by, in effect, asking the following questions:

- How effectively do these beliefs *explain what is taking place?*
- To what extent are the beliefs *consistent with other beliefs* about the world?
- How effectively do the beliefs help us to *predict what will happen* in the future?
- To what extent are these beliefs *supported by sound reasons and compelling evidence* derived from *reliable sources?*

This process of critical exploration enables us to develop more understanding of various situations in our experience and to exert more control over them.

> **Beliefs:**   interpretations, evaluations, conclusions, or predictions that we endorse as true.

Four Kinds of Beliefs

1. *Interpretation:* The Supreme Court's recent rulings against affirmative action mean that no institution can now make hiring or admissions decisions based on race.
2. *Evaluations:* Children today spend too much time watching television and too little time reading.
3. *Conclusions:* The United States needs to limit legal immigration to decrease competition with native-born workers for jobs.
4. *Predictions:* With the shrinking of the global community, there will be an increasing need in the future for Americans to speak more than one language.

THINKING ↔ WRITING ACTIVITY 10.1

Creating Different Beliefs

In your journal, state in a sentence or two a belief that you have in each of the four categories discussed (interpretation, evaluation, conclusion, prediction).

At least some of these statements should be ones that not everyone would agree with.

1. *Interpretation:* I believe that "X means this."
2. *Evaluation:* I believe that "X is good/bad, harmful/beneficial, and so forth."
3. *Conclusion:* I believe that "X is what exists/should exist."
4. *Prediction:* I believe that "X will happen."

Chapter 2, in its introductory discussion of beliefs, identified four sources of beliefs: persons of authority, recorded references, observed evidence, and personal experience. The last two involve direct experience. Yet how we interpret and understand direct experience—what conclusions we draw from what we perceive—depends to some extent on what we already believe. In offering evidence to support their beliefs, people generally choose those perceptions and experiences that fit with their previous beliefs; contradictory experiences may be ignored or downplayed. In the following pair of readings, two writers offer differing beliefs about the situation of the homeless in the United States, based on differing perceptions of direct experience. L. Christopher Awalt's essay appeared as a "My Turn" column in *Newsweek* magazine. Following that is a chapter from a book about homelessness, "The Allesandros" by Jonathan Kozol, a long-time advocate for the politically and socially disenfranchised.

THINKING ↔ WRITING ACTIVITY 10.2

Thinking Critically About Homelessness

Before you begin to read, write in your journal two or three of your beliefs about homelessness and the homeless. After you have read both pieces, write answers to any two of the following questions.

1. Awalt and Kozol have formed differing beliefs based on direct experience working with the homeless. Awalt states his beliefs directly; Kozol is less direct, but his beliefs are nonetheless clear. Summarize their differing beliefs.
2. Why do you think the experiences the two men describe are so different? Do you think the experiences each writer presents are primarily responsible for his beliefs—or do previously held beliefs seem to have contributed to either writer's perception of direct experience?
3. Are any of your beliefs about homelessness based on direct experience? If so, whose experiences are closer to yours, Awalt's or Kozol's? How do your own beliefs contribute to your response to each essay?
4. Are Awalt's and Kozol's experiences with the homeless equally effective as evidence for each writer's beliefs? Do you feel as though you have enough evidence in general to form your own beliefs about homelessness? Why or why not?

from Brother, Don't Spare a Dime
by L. Christopher Awalt

Homeless people are everywhere—on the street, in public buildings, on the evening news and at the corner parking lot. You can hardly step out of your house these days without meeting some haggard character who asks you for a cigarette or begs for "a little change." The homeless are not just constant symbols of wasted lives and failed social programs— they have become a danger to public safety.

What's the root of the homeless problem? Everyone seems to have a scapegoat: Advocates of the homeless blame government policy; politicians blame the legal system; the courts blame the bureaucratic infrastructure; the Democrats blame the Republicans; the Republicans, the Democrats. The public blames the economy, drugs, the "poverty cycle," and "the breakdown of society." With all this finger-pointing, the group most responsible for the homeless being the way they are receives the least blame. That group is the homeless themselves.

How can I say this? For the past two years I have worked with the homeless, volunteering at the Salvation Army and at a soup kitchen in Austin, Texas. I have led a weekly chapel service, served food, listened, counseled, given time and money, and shared in their struggles. I have seen their response to troubles, and though I'd rather report otherwise, many of them seem to have chosen the lifestyles they lead. They are unwilling to do the things necessary to overcome their circumstances. They must bear the greater part of the blame for their manifold troubles.

Let me qualify what I just said. Not everyone who finds himself out of a job and in the street is there because he wants to be. Some are victims of tragic circumstances. I met many dignified, capable people during my time working with Austin's homeless: the single father struggling to earn his high-school equivalency and to be a role model for his children; the woman who fled a good job in another city to escape an abusive husband; the well-educated young man who had his world turned upside down by divorce and a layoff. These people deserve every effort to help them back on their feet.

5 But they're not the real problem. They are usually off the streets and resuming normal lives within a period of weeks or months. Even while "down on their luck," they are responsible citizens, working in the shelters and applying for jobs. They are homeless, true, but only temporarily, because they are eager to reorganize their lives.

For every person temporarily homeless, though, there are many who are chronically so. Whether because of mental illness, alcoholism, poor education, drug addiction, or simple laziness, these homeless are content to remain as they are. In many cases they choose the streets. They enjoy the freedom and consider begging a minor inconvenience. They know they can always get a job for a day or two for food, cigarettes, and alcohol. The sophisticated among them have learned to use the system for what it's worth and figure that a trip through the welfare line is less trouble than a steady job. In a society that has mastered dodging responsibility, these homeless prefer a life of no responsibility at all.

Waste of time.   One person I worked with is a good example. He is an older man who has been on the streets for about 10 years. The story of his decline from respectability to alcoholism sounded believable and I wanted to help. After buying him toiletries and giving him clothes, I drove him one night to a Veterans Administration hospital, an hour and a half away, and put him into a detoxification program. I wrote him monthly to check on his progress and attempted to line up a job for him when he got out. Four months into his program, he was thinking and speaking clearly and talking about plans he wanted to make. At five months, he expressed concern over the life he was about to lead. During the sixth month, I called and was told that he had checked himself out and returned home. A month later I found him drunk again, back on the streets.

Was "society" to blame for this man? Hardly. It had provided free medical care, counseling, and honest effort. Was it the fault of the economy? No. This man never gave the economy a chance to solve his problems. The only person who can be blamed for his failure to get off the streets is the man himself. To argue otherwise is a waste of time and compassion.

Those who disagree will claim that my experience is merely anecdotal and that one case does not a policy make. Please don't take my word for it. The next time you see someone advertising that he'll work for food, take him up on it. Offer him a hard day's work for an honest wage, and see if he accepts. If he does, tell him you'll pay weekly, so that he will have to work for an entire week before he sees any money. If he still accepts, offer a permanent job, with taxes withheld and the whole shebang. If he accepts again, hire him. You'll have a fine employee and society will have one less homeless person. My guess is that you won't find many takers. The truly homeless won't stay around past the second question.

10   So what are the solutions? I will not pretend to give ultimate answers. But whatever policy we decide upon must include some notion of self-reliance and individual responsibility. Simply giving over our parks, our airports, and our streets to those who cannot and will not take care of themselves is nothing but a retreat from the problem and allows the public property that we designate for their "use" to fall into disarray. Education, drug, and alcohol rehabilitation, treatment for the mentally ill, and job training programs are all worthwhile projects, but without requiring some effort and accountability on the part of the homeless for whom these programs are implemented, all these efforts do is break the taxpayer. Unless the homeless are willing to help them-

selves, there is nothing anyone else can do. Not you. Not me. Not the government. Not anyone.

The Allesandros

by Jonathan Kozol

Far from any zone of safety lives a man named Mr. Allesandro. He's six feet tall and weighs 120 pounds—down 20 pounds from late September. When he came to the hotel a year ago he weighed 165. I first met him in the ballroom before Christmas when I handed him an apple. One bright apple. One week later he does not forget and, when he sees me in the lobby, asks me if I have some time to talk.

His two daughters are asleep. Christopher, his nine-year-old, is lying on the top bunk, fully dressed and wrapped beneath a pile of blankets, but he is awake and vigilant and almost belligerently alert. It's a cold night and the room appears to be unheated. Mr. Allesandro shows me a cracked pane of glass that he has covered over with a sheet of garbage plastic and Scotch tape. The two coils of the hot plate offer a symbolic reassurance ("heat exists") but they do not provide much warmth. He's wearing a coat and woolen hat. His mother, who is seventy-three, lives with them; for some reason, she's not here.

There aren't many men as heads of households in this building; this fact, I think, adds to his feeling of humiliation. His story, quickly told, remains less vivid for me later on than certain details like his trembling hands, the freezing room, the strange sight of his watchful boy, unsleeping on the bed. The boy reminds me of a rabbit staring from a thicket or caught in the headlights of a car.

These, as Mr. Allesandro tells me, are the facts: He was one of several maintenance workers in a high-rise building in Manhattan owned by one of the well-known developers. It was early autumn and his wife, for reasons I don't learn until much later, just picked up one day and disappeared. He tried to keep his job and home by rising early, feeding the children, bringing them to school, then rushing to his job. But his shift required him to be on duty very early. He was reprimanded and, when he explained his problem, was permitted to stay on but cut back to a half-time job. Half-time work was not enough to pay the rent. He was evicted. In the subsequent emergency he had to take leave from his job.

5   "My mother went with me to the EAU. We asked them if we could be placed together. That way, she could get the kids to school and I could keep my job." Instead, they put him in a barracks shelter with the children but would not allow his mother to go with them. As best he understands, this is because she drew a Social Security check and was on a different budget from his own. Eligibility rules are difficult to fathom;

but, even where the consequences are calamitous and costly, they are faithfully observed.

"So I'm alone there in this place with about 200 cots packed side by side. Men and women, children," he says, "all together. No dividers. There's no curtains and no screens. I have to dress my kids with people watching. When my girls go to the toilet I can't take them and they're scared to go alone. A lot of women there are frantic. So I stand and wait outside the door."

He went back to the EAU and begged once more. "In my line of work," he says, "you don't earn much of your money from the salary. The people in the building get to know you and you do them favors and they give you money in return. Christmas is a time you get your tips. They'll hand you an envelope. Twenty dollars. Fifty dollars. Some give you a hundred. These are very wealthy people . . ." So his disappointment was intensified by recognition of the fact that he could not get back his job in time to benefit from the expected generosity of people whom he'd known: "Some of those people knew me well. They liked me." He seems desperate to be assured that he was liked, remembered, missed, by people who had frequently befriended him.

The use of barracks shelters as deterrence to the homeless is not absolute. Assignments are made "on an ad hoc basis," as one social worker states it. But nothing that Mr. Allesandro said could bring the EAU to place his mother with him. His former boss, he says, had told him he would take him back if he could start the day at 5:00 A.M. "There's no way that I could do it. Would you leave your kids alone within a place like that at 5:00 A.M.? I couldn't do it."

The upshot is this: He loses the chance to go back to his job a few weeks before Christmas. Although he's worked for many years, he hasn't been on *this* job long enough to have accumulated pension benefits. Dispossession from his home has left him unemployed; unemployment now will render permanent his homelessness.

10   Having finally lost everything he had, he returns a few weeks later to the EAU. This time having undergone "deterrence" and still being homeless, he is granted "temporary" placement at the Martinique. His mother can join him now. But he is no longer a wage earner; he's an AFDC father, broken in spirit, mourning for those lost tips which he will obsessively recall each time we talk. His job has been assigned to someone else. He loses self-control. He thanks God for his mother. This strikes me as a gruesome and enormously expensive instance of municipal assault upon a man's work ethic and familial integrity at the same time.

How does he feel not working?

"It's a nightmare, I'm Italian. You know—I don't mean this to sound prejudiced"—all of the white people here, I notice, are extremely careful and apologetic on this score—"my people work. My father and grandfather worked. My mother worked. I can do construction, carpentry. I can repair things. I'm somebody who's mechanically inclined. I would make beds, I would clean toilets. I'd do anything if I could have a decent job."

He searches the ads, walks the pavement, rides the subway; but he cannot find a job that pays enough to rent a home and feed three children. His rent allowance is $281. He's seen apartments for $350 and $400. If he takes an apartment over his rent limit he will have to make the difference up by cutting back on food and clothes. His mother's pension is too small to offer them a safety margin. "I wouldn't risk it. I'm afraid to take a chance. Even if I got a job, what if I lost it? I'd be back there with the children in the barracks."

So, like everybody else, he's drowning in the squalor of the Martinique Hotel but dreads the thought of being forced to leave.

15   "My mother helps to make it like a home. She tries. We got the kids a kitten, which is something that is not allowed. I don't like to break the rules, but you have got to give them something to remember that they're children."

Thinking of his hunger, I ask how he feeds the cat.

"We don't need to. We have never bought one can. She eats better than we do—on the mice and rats."

Around midnight I notice that Christopher is wide awake and watching from the bed: blue eyes, pale skin, blondish hair. Mrs. Allesandro cuts the children's hair.

Where is Mrs. Allesandro?

20   Mr. Allesandro calls her "grandma" and he speaks of her as if she were *his* grandmother as well. Grandma fell in the stairwell Friday afternoon. There had been a fire and the stairs were still slick from the water left there by the fire hoses. She's in the hospital for an examination of her hip. He tells me that she has a heart condition. "If anything happens to her [pauses] . . . I'd be dead. She's the one that's holding us together."

Other people in this building speak of Mrs. Allesandro in almost identical words. They count on her perhaps even a little more than on the nurse or on the other people in the crisis center. Unlike the crisis workers she is here around the clock. As short of food and money as the Allesandros are, I am told that she is often in the hallways bringing food to neighbors, to a pregnant woman, a sick child living somewhere on the floor. A man who knows her but does not live on this floor speaks of Mrs. Allesandro in these words: "Here she is, an old Italian lady. Here are all these women. Most of them are Puerto Rican, black . . . You will see them holding onto her, crying to her as if she was their mother."

Mrs. Allesandro, however, is not here tonight. Her son is on his own—a skeleton of hunger, disappointment, fear. I look at him, at the two girls, asleep, and at the boy—awake, alert. The boy's persistent gaze unsettles me. I ask him: "Are you sleepy?" He just shakes his head. His father is too proud to tell me that the boy is hungry. I feel embarrassed that it's taken me so long to ask. At my request he opens the refrigerator door. There is one packaged dinner, smuggled out of the lunch program. "There was something wrong with it," he says. It has a rancid smell. "It's spoiled." There's a gallon tin of peanut butter, two part-empty jars of applesauce, some hardened bread. That's it.

Mr. Allesandro takes the $20 that I hand him to the corner store. Christopher sits up halfway and talks with me. He lists for me the ten largest cities of America. I ask him whether he likes school. He does not give the usual perfunctory affirmative response. "I hate it," Christopher says. I ask him what he does for fun. He plays ball on the sidewalk at the corner of the street across from the hotel.

"Is there room to play ball on the sidewalk?"

25   He explains: "We play against the building of the bank—against the wall."

He falls asleep after I think of giving him a candy bar. His father returns in twenty minutes with a box of Kellogg's Special K, a gallon of juice, half-gallon of milk, a loaf of bread, a dozen eggs, a package of sausages, a roll of toilet paper. He wakes his son. The boy has a bowl of cereal with milk. His father stands before the counter where he placed the food. He looks like a man who has been admitted to an elegant buffet.

Is Mr. Allesandro laden with anxiety? Is Christopher depleted, sick, exhausted? Yes, I suppose both statements are correct. Are they candidates for psychiatric care? Perhaps they are, but I should think a more important observation is that they are starving.

A few months after my evening with the Allesandros, President Reagan meets a group of high school students from New York. Between government help and private charity, he says, "I don't believe there is anyone that is going hungry in America simply by reason of denial. . . ." The president says there is a problem of "people not knowing where or how to get this help." This is what he also says of those who can't find space in public housing that he has stopped building.

His former counselor and now attorney general, Edwin Meese, concedes that people have been turning to soup kitchens but refuses to accept that they are in real need. They go to soup kitchens "because the food is free," he says, and adds, "that's easier than paying for it."

30   Marian Wright Edelman of the Children's Defense Fund makes this interesting calculation: If Defense Secretary Caspar Weinberger were to give up just a single Pentagon budget item, that which pays for him to have a private dining room, one million low-income school children could get back their morning snack—a snack denied them by administration cuts.

Hundreds of miles from Christopher's bedroom in the Martinique, a reporter describes an underground limestone cave near Kansas City: the largest surplus-food repository in the nation. In this cave and in some other large facilities, in the winter of 1986, the government was storing some 2 billion pounds of surplus food. To a child like Christopher, the vision of millions of pounds of milk and cheese and butter secreted in limestone caves might seem beyond belief. Storage of this surplus food costs taxpayers $1 million a day.

Getting surplus food from limestone caves to children's tables calls for modest but essential transportation costs. In an extraordinary action, termed illegal by the General Accounting Office, the president deferred funds allocated by the Congress for transporting food to homeless people. The sum involved, $28 million, is a small amount beside the $365 million spent to store this food in limestone caves and other warehouse areas. The withholding of such funds may possibly make sense to an economist. I do not know whether it would make much sense to Christopher.

November 1986: I'm in New York and visit with the Allesandros. Grandma's back. She says her health is good. But Christopher looks frighteningly thin. Food was scarce before. The situation's worsened since I was here last. Families in the homeless shelters of New York have been cut back on their food-stamp allocations. The White House has decided to consider money paid for rental to the hotel owners as a part of family income. By this standard, families in the Martinique are very rich. "Tightening of eligibility requirements" has an abstract sound in Washington. On the twelfth floor of the Martinique what does it mean?

I study the computerized receipts that Mr. Allesandro has received. In June, his food-stamp allocation was $145. In August, the first stage in government reductions lowered this to $65. In October: $50. As of December it will be $33.

35

Mrs. Allesandro does not speak in ambiguities about the lives of her grandchildren. I ask her what the cuts will mean. "They mean," she says, "that we aren't going to eat." New York announces it will help make up the difference but, at the time I visit, no supplemental restaurant allowances have been received.

Beliefs Based on Indirect Experience

No matter how much we have experienced in our lives, the fact is, of course, that no one person's direct experiences are enough to establish an adequate set of accurate beliefs. We all depend on the experience of other people to provide us with beliefs and also to serve as foundations for those beliefs. For example, does China exist? How do we know? Have we ever been there and seen it with our own eyes? Probably not; nevertheless, we believe in the existence of China and its over one billion inhabitants. Of all the beliefs each one of us has, few are actually based on our direct personal experience. Instead, other people have communicated to us virtually all these beliefs and the evidence for them, in some way or form. As we reach beyond our personal experiences to form and revise beliefs, we find that information is provided by two sources: people of authority and recorded references.

As we have seen in the essays about homelessness by Awalt and Kozol, the beliefs of others cannot be accepted without question. Each of us views the world through unique lenses, which shape and influence the way we select and present information. Comparing different sources helps to make these lenses explicit and highlights the different interests and purposes involved. In fact, reaching to sources may lead us to recognize that there are a variety of competing viewpoints, some fairly similar, some quite contradictory. In critically examining the beliefs of others, it is essential for us to pursue the same goals of accuracy and completeness that we set when examining beliefs based on personal experience. As a result, we focus on the reasons or evidence that support the information others are presenting.

THINKING ↔ WRITING ACTIVITY 10.3

Origins of My Beliefs

Look back at the beliefs you've been writing about for previous activities. To what extent have these beliefs been shaped by indirect sources—by family, friends, teachers, television, magazines, books, radio, the Internet, and so forth? Indicate some specific ways in which your beliefs have been influenced by two or three indirect sources and tell why you considered those sources reliable.

Evaluating Information and Sources

When we depend on information provided by others, there is a key question we must ask: How reliable is the person or other source providing the information?

Most crucial to determining the reliability of information from an indirect source is determining the reliability of the source itself.

How Reliable Is the Source?

We know that some sources—such as advertising—can be very unreliable, whereas other sources, such as *Consumer Reports,* are considered generally reliable. Sometimes, however, the reliability of a source of information is not immediately clear. In those cases, we have to consider a variety of standards or criteria helpful for evaluating a source's reliability, whether the source is written or spoken. Essential questions to ask include the following.

- How knowledgeable or experienced is the source?
- Was the source able to make accurate observations?
- What do we know about the past reliability of the source?

How Knowledgeable or Experienced Is the Source?

When we seek information from indirect sources, we want to locate persons of authority or recorded references that offer a special understanding of the subject. When a car begins making strange noises, we search for someone who knows cars. When we want to know more about a social issue, such as homelessness, we turn to articles and books written by people who have studied the problem.

In seeking information from sources, it is important to distinguish between "lay" sources and "expert" sources who have training, education, and experience in a particular area. It is also important that any expert source's credentials be up-to-date. A book about careers in the computer industry published twenty years ago is not likely to be reliable. Sports and entertainment figures often endorse products in television commercials, but the reliability of their testimony is not very strong if those products have nothing to do with sports or entertainment (and these "experts" may have been paid large sums of money and told exactly what to say). Finally, expert opinion should not be accepted without question or critical examination, even if the experts meet all the criteria that we have been exploring. As noted earlier, each of us sees the world through individual lenses that color the objectivity of his or her observations.

Was the Source of the Information Able to Make Accurate Observations?

You may be familiar with an experiment in which an angry student enters a classroom, argues with the professor, then pulls out a gun and apparently shoots the professor before running out. Students in the class are then quickly informed that the situation has been staged to test their powers of observation and asked to record what happened in as much detail as they can remember. Invariably many "witnesses" are quite mistaken in much of what they remember, while others can recall many fine details exactly. The same is true in any kind of eyewitness accounts: some people have quite sharp memories, while others may "remember" many imagined details. In addition, one's vantage point as a witness may color the reliability of one's testimony. The amount of light, obstructions to one's vision, and other matters can keep one's perceptions from being wholly reliable.

The reliability of indirect sources also depends on the personal viewpoints and beliefs (the lenses) the source brings to a situation. These personal feelings, expectations, and interests often influence what one perceives without one's full awareness of the fact. For example, a group that sponsored an anti-racism rally on a campus might claim a crowd of more than five hundred, while campus security issues a report estimating the rally at about two hundred. We have seen that two different writers can come to very different conclusions after spending time working in a homeless shelter. What further questions could be asked and how might further sources be located to evaluate the reliability of such differing sources?

How Reputable Is the Source?

As we work at evaluating the reliability of sources, it is useful to consider how accurate and reliable their information has been in the past. If someone has consistently given sound information over a period of time, we gradually develop confidence in the accuracy of that person's reports. Police officers and newspaper reporters must continually evaluate the reliability of information sources. Of course, this works the other way as well. When people consistently give inaccurate or incomplete information, others lose confidence in their reliability. Nevertheless, few people are either completely reliable or completely unreliable in the information they offer. You probably realize that your own reliability tends to vary, depending on the situation, the type of information you are providing, and the person to whom you are giving the information. Thus, in trying to evaluate the information offered by others, you have to explore each of the following factors before arriving at a provisional conclusion, which may then be revised in the light of additional information.

Information Evaluation Questions

1. How reliable is the information?
   a. What are the main ideas being presented?
   b. What reasons or evidence support the information?
   c. Is the information accurate? Does anything about it seem false?
   d. Does anything seem to have been left out?

2. How reliable is the source of the information?
   a. What is the source of the information?
   b. What are the interests or purposes of this source?
   c. How may these interests and purposes have affected the information being offered?
   d. How have these interests and purposes influenced the way this information is presented?

THINKING ↔ WRITING ACTIVITY 10.4

Evaluating Sources of My Beliefs

Look back at the beliefs you have been writing about for previous activities in this chapter. You have already identified some sources that helped you establish those beliefs or that have reinforced them. Choose one of your beliefs that is based at least partly on indirect experience (sources such as people of authority and recorded references). Now, on the basis of the criteria just discussed, evaluate one source of your belief in terms of reliability. Does the source seem reliable? How can you tell?

Believing and Knowing

Developing beliefs that are as accurate as possible is important to critical thinkers because the more accurate our beliefs, the better we are able to understand the world around us and to predict what will occur in the future. As the preceding discussion has suggested, however, the beliefs we form can vary tremendously in accuracy.

We use the word *knowing* to distinguish beliefs supported by strong reasons or evidence (such as belief that there is life on earth) from beliefs for which there is less support (such as belief that there is life on other planets) or from beliefs disproved by reasons or evidence to the contrary. The following saying expresses another way to understand the difference between believing and knowing:

"You can believe what is not so, but you cannot know what is not so."

In the following essay, astrophysicist Alan Lightman considers a question that would seem to have an obvious answer. In doing so, he analyzes the difference between believing and knowing.

from Is the Earth Round or Flat?

by Alan Lightman

I propose that there are few of you who have personally verified that the Earth is round. The suggestive globe in the den or the Apollo photographs don't count. These are secondhand pieces of evidence that might be thrown out entirely in court. When you think about it, most of you simply believe what you hear. Round or flat, whatever. It's not a life-or-death matter, unless you happen to live near the edge.

A few years ago I suddenly realized, to my dismay, that I didn't know with certainty if the Earth were round or flat. I have scientific colleagues, geodesists they are called, whose sole business is determining the detailed shape of the Earth by fitting mathematical formulae to someone else's measurements of the precise locations of test stations on the Earth's surface. And I don't think those people really know either.

Aristotle is the first person in recorded history to have given proof that the Earth is round. He used several different arguments, most likely because he wanted to convince others as well as himself. A lot of people believed everything Aristotle said for 19 centuries.

His first proof was that the shadow of the Earth during a lunar eclipse is always curved, a segment of a circle. If the Earth were any shape but spherical, the shadow it casts, in some orientations, would not be circular. (That the normal phases of the moon are crescent-shaped reveals the moon is round.) I find this argument wonderfully appealing. It is simple and direct. What's more, an inquisitive and untrusting person can knock off the experiment alone, without special equipment. From any given spot on the Earth, a lunar eclipse can be seen about once a year. You simply have to look up on the right night and carefully observe what's happening. I've never done it.

5   Aristotle's second proof was that stars rise and set sooner for people in the East than in the West. If the Earth were flat from east to west, stars would rise as soon for Occidentals as for Orientals. With a little scribbling on a piece of paper, you can see that these observations imply a round Earth, regardless of whether it is the Earth that spins around or the stars that revolve around the Earth. Finally, northbound travelers observe previously invisible stars appearing above the northern horizon, showing the Earth is curved from north to south. Of course, you do have to accept the reports of a number of friends in different places or be willing to do some traveling. Aristotle's last argument was purely theoretical and even philosophical. If the Earth had been formed from smaller pieces at some time in the past (or *could* have been so formed), its pieces would fall toward a common center, thus making a sphere. Furthermore, a sphere is clearly the most perfect solid shape. Interestingly, Aristotle placed as much emphasis on this last argument as on the

first two. Those days, before the modern "scientific method," observational check wasn't required for investigating reality. Assuming for the moment that the Earth is round, the first person who measured its circumference accurately was another Greek, Eratosthenes (276–195 B.C.). Eratosthenes noted that on the first day of summer, sunlight struck the bottom of a vertical well in Syene, Egypt, indicating the sun was directly overhead. At the same time in Alexandria, 5,000 stadia distant, the sun made an angle with the vertical equal to 1/50 of a circle. (A stadium equaled about a tenth of a mile.) Since the sun is so far away, its rays arrive almost in parallel. If you draw a circle with two radii extending from the center outward through the perimeter (where they become local verticals), you'll see that a sun ray coming in parallel to one of the radii (at Syene) makes an angle with the other (at Alexandria) equal to the angle between the two radii. Therefore Eratosthenes concluded that the full circumference of the Earth is 50 x 5,000 stadia, or about 25,000 miles. This calculation is within one percent of the best modern value.

For at least 600 years educated people have believed the Earth is round. At nearly any medieval university, the quadrivium was standard fare, consisting of arithmetic, geometry, music, and astronomy. The astronomy portion was based on the *Tractatus de Sphaera*, a popular textbook first published at Ferrara, Italy, in 1472 and written by a 13th century, Oxford-educated astronomer and mathematician, Johannes de Sacrobosco. The *Sphaera* proves its astronomical assertions, in part, by a set of diagrams with movable parts, a graphical demonstration of Aristotle's second method of proof. The round Earth, being the obvious center of the universe, provides a fixed pivot for the assembly. The cutout figures of the sun, the moon, and the stars revolve about the Earth.

By the year 1500, 24 editions of the *Sphaera* had appeared. There is no question that many people *believed* the Earth was round. I wonder how many *knew* this. You would think that Columbus and Magellan might have wanted to ascertain the facts for themselves before waving goodbye. To protect my honor as a scientist, someone who is supposed to take nothing for granted, I set out with my wife on a sailing voyage in the Greek islands. I reasoned that at sea I would be able to calmly observe landmasses disappear over the curve of the Earth and thus convince myself, firsthand, that the Earth is round.

Greece seemed a particularly satisfying place to conduct my experiment. I could sense those great ancient thinkers looking on approvingly, and the layout of the place is perfect. Hydra rises about 2,000 feet above sea level. If the Earth has a radius of 4,000 miles, as they say, then Hydra should sink down to the horizon at a distance of about 50 miles, somewhat less than the distance you were to sail from Hydra to Kea. The theory was sound and comfortable. At the very least, I thought, you would have a pleasant vacation.

As it turned out, that was all you got. Every single day was hazy. Islands faded from view at a distance of only eight miles, when the land was still a couple of degrees above the horizon. I learned how much water vapor was in the air but nothing about the curvature of the Earth.

10   I suspect that there are quite a few items you take on faith, even important things, even things you could verify without much trouble. Is the gas you exhale the same as the gas you inhale? (Do you indeed burn oxygen in your metabolism, as they say?) What is your blood made of? (Does it indeed have red and white "cells"?) These questions could be answered with a balloon, a candle, and a microscope.

When you finally do the experiment, you relish the knowledge. At one time or another, you have all learned something for yourselves, from the ground floor up, taking no one's word for it. There is a special satisfaction and joy in being able to tell somebody something you have pieced together from scratch, something you really know. I think that exhilaration is a big reason why people do science.

Someday soon, I'm going to catch the Earth's shadow in a lunar eclipse, or go to sea in clear air, and find out for sure if the Earth is round or flat. Actually, the Earth is reported to flatten at the poles, because it rotates. But that's another story.

THINKING ↔ WRITING ACTIVITY 10.5

Thinking About Your Beliefs and Knowledge

Look again at the beliefs you have been writing about for previous activities. Could you say of any of them "I know this" rather than merely "I believe this"? Why? Write answers to these questions in your journal.

Knowledge and Truth

Authorities often disagree about the true nature of a given situation or the best course of action. It is not uncommon, for example, for doctors to disagree about a diagnosis; for economists to differ on the state of the economy; or for psychiatrists to disagree on whether a convicted felon is a menace to society or a victim of social forces.

What do we do when experts disagree? As critical thinkers, we must analyze and evaluate all the available information, develop our own well-reasoned beliefs, and recognize when we lack sufficient information to arrive at well-reasoned beliefs. We must realize, too, that such beliefs may evolve over time as we gain information or improve our insight.

Although there are compelling reasons to view knowledge and truth as evolving, some people resist doing so. Either they take refuge in a belief in the absolute, unchanging nature of knowledge and truth, as presented by the appropriate authorities, or they conclude that there is no such thing as knowledge or truth and that trying to seek either is futile.

Understanding Relativism

In this latter view of the world, known as *relativism,* all beliefs are considered "relative" to the person or context in which they arise. For the relativist, all opinions are equal in validity to all others; we are never in a position to say with confidence that one view is right and another one wrong. Although a relativistic view is appropriate in some areas of experience—for example, in matters of taste such as fashion—in many other areas it is not. Knowledge, in the form of well supported beliefs, does exist. Some beliefs are better than others, not because an authority has proclaimed them so but because they can by analyzed in terms of the criteria listed earlier in this chapter.

Understanding Falsifiable Beliefs

Another important criterion for evaluating certain beliefs is that the beliefs be *falsifiable.* This means that it is possible to state conditions—tests—under which the beliefs could be disproved, and that the beliefs then pass those tests. For example, if you believe that you can create ice cubes by placing water-filled trays in a freezer, you can conduct an experiment to determine whether your belief is accurate. If no ice cubes form after you put the trays in the freezer, your theory is disproved. If, however, you believe that your destiny is related to the positions of the planets and stars (as astrologers do), it is not clear how you can conduct an experiment to determine whether your belief is accurate. Since a belief that is not falsifiable can never be proved, such a belief is questionable.

THINKING ↔ WRITING ACTIVITY 10.6

Constructing Knowledge

Read the following passages, which purport to give factual reports about the events that were observed at the Battle of Lexington during the American Revolution.* After analyzing these accounts, develop your own version of what you believe took place on that day. Include such information as the size of the two forces, the sequence of events (for example, who fired the first shot?), and the manner in which the two groups conducted themselves (were they honorable? brave?). In rating the reliability of each source, consider the following:

Account 1 is drawn from a mainstream American history textbook.

Account 2 is taken from a British history book, written by a former prime minister of England.

Account 3 comes from a colonist who participated in this event with the colonial forces. He gave the account thirty years after the battle, in order to qualify for a military pension.

Knowledge and Truth: A critical thinker sees knowledge and truth as ongoing goals that we are striving to achieve through exploration and analysis, not fixed destinations.

Account 4 comes from a British soldier who participated in the event. He gave the account in a deposition while he was a prisoner of war of the colonial forces.

*This exercise was developed by Kevin O'Reilly, creator of the Critical Thinking in History Project.

FOUR ACCOUNTS OF THE BATTLE OF LEXINGTON

In April 1775, General Gage, the military governor of Massachusetts, sent out a body of troops to take possession of military stores at Concord, a short distance from Boston. At Lexington, a handful of "embattled farmers," who had been tipped off by Paul Revere, barred the way. The "rebels" were ordered to disperse. They stood their ground. The English fired a volley of shots that killed eight patriots. It was not long before the swift-riding Paul Revere spread the news of this new atrocity to the neighboring colonies. The patriots of all of New England, although still a handful, were now ready to fight the English. Even in faraway North Carolina, patriots organized to resist them. —Samuel Steinberg, *The United States: Story of a Free People*

At five o'clock in the morning the local militia of Lexington, seventy strong, formed up on the village green. As the sun rose the head of the British column, with three officers riding in front, came into view. The leading officer, brandishing his sword, shouted, "Disperse, you rebels, immediately!" The militia commander ordered his men to disperse. The colonial committees were very anxious not to fire the first shot, and there were strict orders not to provoke open conflict with the British regulars. But in the confusion someone fired. A volley was returned. The ranks of the militia were thinned and there was a general melee. Brushing aside the survivors, the British column marched on to Concord. —Winston Churchill, *History of the English-speaking Peoples*

The British troops approached you rapidly in platoons, with a General officer on horse-back at their head. The officer came up to within about two rods of the centre of the company, where I stood—the first platoon being about three rods distant. They there halted. The officer then swung his sword, and said, "Lay down your arms, you damn'd rebels, or you are all dead men—fire." Some guns were fired by the British at you from the first platoon, but no person was killed or hurt, being probably charged only with powder. Just at this time, Captain Parker ordered every man to take care of himself. The company immediately dispersed; and while the company was dispersing and leaping over the wall, the second platoon of the British fired, and killed some of your men. There was not a gun fired by any of Captain Parker's company within my knowledge. —Sylvanus Wood, *Deposition*

I, John Bateman, belonging to the Fifty-Second Regiment, commanded by Colonel Jones, on Wednesday morning on the nineteenth day of April instant, was in the party marching to Concord, being at Lexington, in the County of Middlesex; being nigh the meeting-house in said Lexington, there was a small party of men gathered together in that place when your Troops marched by, and I testify and declare, that I heard the word of command given to the Troops to fire, and some of said Troops did fire, and I saw one of said small party lay dead on the ground nigh said meeting-house, and I testify that I never heard any of the inhabitants so much as fire one gun on said Troops. —John Bateman, *Testimony*

Media and Truth

We are all aware in a general way that the media shape our beliefs by the information they provide and the interpretations they give to that information. We may not be aware, however, of some of the subtle ways in which this is done or of the profound influences that result. As you read the following essays, consider how your beliefs might be shaped by the sources discussed by these writers.

The following article by Harry Waters originally appeared in *Newsweek*. It reports on studies conducted by a University of Pennsylvania professor, concerning the influence of television on people's beliefs.

from Life According to TV
by Harry Waters

The late Paddy Chayefsky, who created Howard Beale, would have loved George Gerbner. In "Network," Chayefsky marshaled a scathing, fictional assault on the values and methods of the people who control the world's most potent communications instrument. In real life, Gerbner, perhaps the nation's foremost authority on the social impact of television, is quietly using the disciplines of behavioral research to construct an equally devastating indictment of the medium's images and messages. More than any spokesman for a pressure group, Gerbner has become the man that television watches. From his cramped, book-lined office at the University of Pennsylvania springs a steady flow of studies that are raising executive blood pressures at the networks' sleek Manhattan command posts.

George Gerbner's work is uniquely important because it transports the scientific examination of television far beyond familiar children-and-violence arguments. Rather than simply studying the link between violence on the tube and crime in the streets, Gerbner is exploring wider and deeper terrain. He has turned his lens on TV's hidden victims—women, the elderly, blacks, blue-collar workers and other groups—to document the ways in which video-entertainment portrayals subliminally condition how we perceive ourselves and how we view those around us. Gerbner's subjects are not merely the impressionable young; they include all the rest of us. And it is his ominous conclusion that heavy watchers of the prime-time mirror are receiving a grossly distorted picture of the real world that they tend to accept more readily than reality itself.

The 63-year-old Gerbner, who is dean of Penn's Annenberg School of Communications, employs a methodology that meshes scholarly observation with mundane legwork. Over the past 15 years, he and a tireless trio of assistants (Larry Gross, Nancy Signorielli and Michael Morgan) videotaped and exhaustively analyzed 1,600 prime-time programs involving more than 15,000 characters. They then drew up multiple-choice questionnaires that offered correct answers about the world at large along with answers that reflected what Gerbner perceived to be the misrepresentations and biases of the world according to TV. Finally, these questions were posed to large samples of citizens from all socioeconomic strata. In every survey, the Annenberg team discovered that heavy viewers of television (those watching more than four hours a day), who account for more than 30 percent of the population, almost invariably chose the TV-influenced answers, while light viewers (less than two hours a day), selected the answers corresponding more closely to actual life. Some of the dimensions of television's reality warp:

Sex

Male prime-time characters outnumber females by 3 to 1 and, with a few star-turn exceptions, women are portrayed as weak, passive satellites to powerful, effective men. TV's male population also plays a vast variety of roles, while females generally get typecast as either lovers or mothers. Less than 20 percent of TV's married women with children work outside the home—as compared with more than 50 percent in real life. The tube's distorted depictions of women, concludes Gerbner, reinforce stereotypical attitudes and increase sexism. In one Annenberg survey, heavy viewers were far more likely than light ones to agree with the proposition: "Women should take care of running their homes and leave running the country to men."

Age

5 People over 65, too, are grossly underrepresented on television. Correspondingly, heavy-viewing Annenberg respondents believe that the elderly are a vanishing breed, that they make up a smaller proportion of the population today than they did 20 years ago. In fact, they form the nation's most rapidly expanding age group. Heavy viewers also believe that old people are less healthy today than they were two decades ago, when quite the opposite is true. As with women, the portrayals of old people transmit negative impressions. In general, they are cast as silly, stubborn, sexually inactive and eccentric. "They're often shown as feeble grandparents bearing cookies," says Gerbner. "You never see the power that real old people often have. The best and possibly only time to learn about growing old with decency and grace is in youth. And young people are the most susceptible to TV's messages."

Race

The problem with the medium's treatment of blacks is more one of image than of visibility. Though a tiny percentage of black characters come across as "unrealistically romanticized," reports Gerbner, the overwhelming majority of them are employed in subservient, supporting roles—such as the white hero's comic sidekick. "When a black child looks at prime time," he says, "most of the people he sees doing interesting and important things are white." That imbalance, he goes on, tends to teach young blacks to accept minority status as naturally inevitable and even deserved. To assess the impact of such portrayals on the general audience, the Annenberg survey forms included questions like "Should white people have the right to keep blacks out of their neighborhoods?" and "Should there be laws against marriages between blacks and whites?" The more that viewers watched, the more they answered "yes" to each question.

Work

Heavy viewers greatly overestimated the proportion of Americans employed as physicians, lawyers, athletes and entertainers, all of whom inhabit prime-time in hordes. A mere 6 to 10 percent of television characters hold blue-collar or service jobs vs. about 60 percent in the real work force. Gerbner sees two dangers in TV's skewed division of labor. On the one hand, the tube so overrepresents and glamorizes the elite occupations that it sets up unrealistic expectations among those who must deal with them in actuality. At the same time, TV largely neglects portraying the occupations that most youngsters will have to enter. "You almost never see the farmer, the factory worker or the small businessman," he notes. "Thus not only do lawyers and other professionals find they cannot measure up to the image TV projects of them, but children's occupational aspirations are channeled in unrealistic directions." The Gerbner team feels this emphasis on high-powered jobs poses problems for adolescent girls, who are also presented with views of women as homebodies. The two conflicting views, Gerbner says, add to the frustration over choices they have to make as adults.

Health

Although video characters exist almost entirely on junk food and quaff alcohol 15 times more often than water, they manage to remain slim, healthy and beautiful. Frequent TV watchers, the Annenberg investigators found, eat more, drink more, exercise less and possess an almost mystical faith in the curative powers of medical science. Concludes Gerbner: "Television may well be the single most pervasive source of health information. And its overidealized images of medical people, coupled with its complacency about unhealthy life-styles, leaves both patients and doctors vulnerable to disappointment, frustration and even litigation."

Crime

On the small screen, crime rages about 10 times more often than in real life. But while other researchers concentrate on the propensity of TV mayhem to incite aggression, the Annenberg team has studied the hidden side of its imprint: fear of victimization. On television, 55 percent of prime-time characters are involved in violent confrontations once a week; in reality, the figure is less than 1 percent. In all demographic groups in every class of neighborhood, heavy viewers overestimated the statistical chance of violence in their own lives and harbored an exaggerated mistrust of strangers—creating what Gerbner calls a "mean-world syndrome." Forty-six percent of heavy viewers who live in cities rated their fear of crime "very serious" as opposed to 26 percent for light viewers. Such paranoia is especially acute among TV entertainment's most common victims: women, the elderly, nonwhites, foreigners and lower-class citizens.

10   Video violence, proposes Gerbner, is primarily responsible for imparting lessons in social power: it demonstrates who can do what to whom and get away with it. "Television is saying that those at the bottom of the power scale cannot get away with the same things that a white, middle-class American male can," he says. "It potentially conditions people to think of themselves as victims."

At a quick glance, Gerbner's findings seem to contain a cause-and-effect, chicken-or-the-egg question. Does television make heavy viewers view the world the way they do or do heavy viewers come from the poorer, less experienced segment of the populace that regards the world that way to begin with? In other words, does the tube create or simply confirm the unenlightened attitudes of its most loyal audience? Gerbner, however, was savvy enough to construct a methodology largely immune to such criticism. His samples of heavy viewers cut across all ages, incomes, education levels and ethnic backgrounds—and every category displayed the same tube-induced misconceptions of the world outside.

Needless to say, the networks accept all this as enthusiastically as they would a list of news-coverage complaints from the Ayatollah Khomeini. Even so, their responses tend to be tinged with a singular respect for Gerbner's personal and professional credentials. The man is no ivory-tower recluse. During World War II, the Budapest-born Gerbner parachuted into the mountains of Yugoslavia to join the partisans fighting the Germans. After the war, he hunted down and personally arrested scores of high Nazi officials. Nor is Gerbner some videophobic vigilante. A Ph.D. in communications, he readily acknowledges TV's beneficial effects, noting that it has abolished parochialism, reduced isolation and loneliness and provided the poorest members of society with cheap, plug-in exposure to experiences they otherwise would not have. Funding for his research is supported by such prestigious bodies as the National Institute of Mental Health, the surgeon general's office and the American Medical Association, and he is called to testify before congressional committees nearly as often as David Stockman.

Mass Entertainment

When challenging Gerbner, network officials focus less on his findings and methods than on what they regard as his own misconceptions of their industry's function. "He's looking at television from the perspective of a social scientist rather than considering what is mass entertainment," says Alfred Schneider, vice president of standards and practices at ABC. "We strive to balance TV's social effects with what will capture an audience's interests. If you showed strong men being victimized as much as women or the elderly, what would comprise the dramatic conflict? If you did a show truly representative of society's total reality, and nobody watched because it wasn't interesting, what have you achieved?"

CBS senior vice president Gene Mater also believes that Gerbner is implicitly asking for the theoretically impossible. "TV is unique in its problems," says Mater. "Everyone wants a piece of the action. Everyone feels that their racial or ethnic group is underrepresented or should be portrayed as they would like the world to perceive them. No popular entertainment form, including this one, can or should be an accurate reflection of society."

15   On that point, at least, Gerbner is first to agree; he hardly expects television entertainment to serve as a mirror image of absolute truth. But what fascinates him about this communications medium is its marked difference from all others. In other media, customers carefully choose what they want to hear or read: a movie, a magazine, a best seller. In television, notes Gerbner, viewers rarely tune in for a particular program. Instead, most just habitually turn on the set—and watch by the clock rather than for a specific show. "Television viewing fulfills the criteria of a ritual," he says. "It is the only medium that can bring to people things they otherwise would not select." With such unique power, believes Gerbner, comes unique responsibility: "No other medium reaches into every home or has a comparable, cradle-to-grave influence over what a society learns about itself."

THINKING ↔ WRITING ACTIVITY 10.7

Thinking Critically About Television

In your journal, write a one-page response to one of the following questions:

1. According to Harry Waters, George Gerbner believes that "heavy watchers of the prime-time mirror are receiving a grossly distorted picture of the real world that they tend to accept more readily than reality itself." How well does the evidence offered in Waters's article support this belief?

2. This article was written in 1982. Do you think television has changed in the years since then? Do you have any reason to believe that the "prime-time mirror" is a more accurate reflection of reality today? Keep in mind that many of the "realities" the article describes—the growth in population of people over sixty-five, the proportion of various professions in the work force, and so forth—have changed very little.

3. Can you think of any specific beliefs of yours that have much of their basis in your television viewing? To what extent do you think Gerbner's claims may be exaggerated? Do you know anyone you would consider a "heavy watcher"? If so, how realistic do you find that person's beliefs about the world?

Cynthia Crossen is a *Wall Street Journal* reporter. Her book *Tainted Truth: The Manipulation of Fact in America* reports on the many "scientific, objective" studies, published under the guise of objectivity, that actually are conducted to reflect their sponsors' intentions. The following chapter from that book focuses on studies designed to influence beliefs about public policy issues.

from False Truth and the Future of the World
by Cynthia Crossen

Common sense, common knowledge and the gospels of environmentalism held that disposable diapers were bad for the earth. Yet a study, published to great fanfare in the spring of 1990, found that disposable diapers were actually no worse for the environment than reusable cotton ones.

This was good news for many parents. Cotton diapers may have been ecologically correct, but they were also less efficient and less convenient. Some who bought disposable diapers were guilt-ridden, embarrassed to be seen toting a 26-pack around the neighborhood. Now research exonerated them of a crime against nature. They could love the earth *and* throw away a dozen plastic-and-chemical-gel diapers a day.

The study's sponsor? Procter & Gamble, one of the biggest buyers of research in the United States and, of course, the country's largest maker of disposable diapers. The company controls about half the $3.5-billion-a-year U.S. market with its Pampers and Luvs brands. For several years, it had been fighting a public relations battle against environmentalists and the cloth diaper industry. Although the disposable diaper industry, born in the 1960s, was thriving, the Earth Day mentality had made inroads. Between 1988 and 1990, customers for cloth diapers almost doubled. Even more ominous for the disposable makers, more than a dozen state legislatures were considering various bans, taxes and warning labels on disposable diapers.

A few studies later, the campaign against disposables was all but dead. Researchers paid by the disposable diaper industry had produced a new, improved truth about disposable diapers. Disposables, symbol of the throwaway society, were environmentally correct. In fact, they would no longer even be called disposable; henceforth they would be known as "single-use." The media disseminated the studies' contrarian findings widely. "People Claiming Cloth Diapers Are Clearly Superior May Be All Wet," said the *Louisville* (Kentucky) *Courier-Journal.* "Grass Isn't Greener on Green Side, Environmentally Conscious Choices May Be Doing More Harm," said the *Cincinnati Enquirer.* In statehouses around the country, diaper legislation withered away. By early 1992, Gerber Products, the largest supplier of cloth diapers in the country, said it would close three cloth-weaving operations and lay off 900 workers. "In the past year," Alfred A. Piergallini, Gerber's chairman and chief executive, said at the time, "there was a dramatic change in the cloth diaper market caused by reduced environmental concerns about disposable diapers."

5　　Procter & Gamble's diaper study was a landmark example of the public policy study, a form of research that increasingly shapes people's beliefs and decisions on social, political, economic and environmental questions. Political debates of the 1980s and 1990s on issues from homelessness to garbage to the spotted owl have been driven by research. The industry that generates this research has developed an unspoken but almost inviolable rule: Its numbers will anoint the ideology of whoever commissioned the research. The sponsor is rarely surprised or betrayed.

Studies done for public policy debates rank second only to research done for advertising in their disdain for objectivity and fact. While in other arenas researchers would be embarrassed to admit their study was partisan, in public policy they are not. "Who says it has to be neutral?" challenged an aide to U.S. Representative Fortney H. Stark about a distorted cable television questionnaire his office had sent out. Commenting on the same study, the aide later said, "We're proud that it was biased. Our viewpoint is that cable TV should be re-regulated."

The researchers themselves are not evil. They are devoted to their profession, and they genuinely seek to improve its methods. Yet they have let their ethical habits slip to a level more often seen among lobbyists and public relations executives. A Washington economist, who asked not to be named because his former employer is still a member of the House of Representatives, described two studies he did on a hydro-electric dam project planned for the home district. "My boss says, 'Write me the best justification for this project that you can.' So I did this cost-benefit analysis that made the project look like a gold mine. About a month later, he calls me in and says, 'Give me the most objective, independent, comprehensive analysis of this project you can.' I came back to him and said, 'This project is a dog.' He knew how to use me and that's fine. Researchers are for hire."

Exaggeration, hyperbole, creative projections, wild assumptions and hand-waving are the building blocks of public policy research, where people fight for the ear of the people and the good of the world. Anything goes. Most public policy wars are fought on huge plains, where people are counted in the millions, economic impacts in the billions and the very survival of mankind and the earth may be at stake—the very places it is most tempting to justify means with ends. Public policy studies are seldom challenged by either the press or public because they address mammoth and complex questions about which most people have little if any personal experience or knowledge. Nor has the press, by and large, learned to accord research studies the routine skepticism that reporters bring to more obviously self-serving news releases.

The creative manipulation of public policy studies crosses all political, gender, racial, religious and age lines. Whatever your beliefs and politics, your team does it. Organizations from Procter & Gamble, the country's largest advertiser, to the smallest and poorest social action groups sponsor advocacy research. No result is too absurd or self-evident to be peddled to the press.

- "Rental Housing for Poor Still a Problem, Study Says," announced a newspaper headline about a study sponsored by two nonprofit advocacy groups for the poor.

- "Americans Want to Live to 100 Years, Survey Says; Bar Nursing Homes, Losing Independence," reported the nonprofit Alliance for Aging Research, which advocates more investment in scientific research about aging.

- "Life on Streets Dangerous for Homeless Youth," concluded a study sponsored by the Chicago Coalition for the Homeless.

10   Public interest groups are masters of the tactical study. Their motives for their creative numbers are less commercial than industry's, but they can be just as self-centered. Public interest groups thrive on attention from the press because that is how they recruit new members. While business may understate hazards, public interest groups tend to exaggerate them. "Each group convinces itself that its worthy goals justify oversimplification to an 'ignorant' public," wrote Daniel E. Koshland, Jr.

Among life-and-death issues, researchers are not quite so fastidious about creating perfectly neutral questions for their surveys. A mail survey for the environmental guerrilla group Greenpeace asked people's attitudes on several issues. Among the leading questions was this: "Depletion of Earth's protective ozone layer leads to skin cancers and numerous other health and environmental problems. Do you support Greenpeace's demand that DuPont, the world's largest producer of ozone-destroying chemicals, stop making unneeded ozone-destroying chemicals immediately?"

But from industry: "Do you favor setting up an additional Consumer Protection Agency over all the others, or do you favor doing what is necessary to make the agencies we now have more effective in protecting the consumer's interests?" asked a survey commissioned by the Business Roundtable, which was opposing the creation of a federal consumer protection agency. Seventy-five percent of those surveyed said they opposed creating such an agency. The survey was released during the height of congressional debate on the subject.

And from a Connecticut representative to Congress, a body that has become addicted to questionnaires: Would you support universal health care if it would mean the loss of thousands of jobs, particularly in Connecticut?

Legislators know most studies prepared for policy debates are sponsored by a self-interested industry or lobby. What they may not realize is that such research nevertheless influences the course of events. Occasionally a piece of research has a decisive influence on the outcome of the debate—Procter & Gamble's diaper study, for example. But more often, contradictory studies simply paralyze the decision-making process, shelving the resolution of immediate problems. "Someone will produce a study that statistically demonstrates X or Y," said Ray Sentes, a Canadian political science professor who has studied the effects of asbestos on human health. "So the workers have to rush out and get an epidemiologist to do a study for them. And so it goes. For ten years we flash studies at each other. If the practical outcome of a scientific study ends up being delay of any activity, shouldn't the scientist say, 'You don't need this study'?" For issues like the health effects of asbestos, Sentes noted, it would take several studies of thousands of people over dozens of years to come up with meaningful results. "They don't have the time or the money or the data," he said. "So they do these slash-and-burn studies that get plonked into the middle of the public policy process."

15   Strategic research has dominated modern debates over abortion, gun control, family leave, recycling, school choice and the speed limit, just to name a few. Each issue has its dueling polls. The timber industry has its polls showing most people wouldn't sacrifice a single job to protect an endangered species; and nature groups have their poll showing that most people support the Endangered Species Act. Proponents of school choice have surveys showing that people want it, and opponents have their surveys showing people do not. Gun control activists have surveys showing that many people want increased regulation of guns; the National Rifle Association has surveys showing the opposite.

The battle over abortion rights has produced hundreds of surveys showing contrary results. In June 1991, the abortion warrriors—Planned Parenthood and the National Right to Life Committee—each produced survey results showing people's opinions of a recent Supreme Court ruling that the government could prohibit the discussion of abortion in family planning clinics that received federal funding. Planned Parenthood's survey asked this question: "Do you favor or oppose that Supreme Court decision preventing clinic doctors and medical personnel from discussing abortion . . . ?" Sixty-five percent said they opposed the ruling.

The other survey first asked people if they favored or opposed the Supreme Court ruling. The survey described the ruling as "the federal government is not required to use taxpayer funds for family planning programs to perform, counsel or refer for abortion as a method of family planning." The Supreme Court, of course, had said no such thing: the question was whether the government should be permitted, not required, to finance family planning programs where abortion was discussed. No one was talking about abortion as a method of family planning. And the Supreme Court was ruling on whether such clinics could discuss, not perform, abortions. Even so, only 48 percent said they favored the court's decision. Then the survey asked, "If you knew that any government funds not used for family-planning programs that provide abortion will be given to other family-planning programs that provide contraception and other preventive methods of family-planning, would you then favor or oppose the Supreme Court's ruling?" Here the group got the mandate it was seeking, the one they pitched to the press: 69 percent said they favored the decision. In hearings before the House of Representatives, which was considering an amendment that would prevent the regulation from being enforced, the National Right to Life poll was cited. The amendment was defeated.

Since bigger numbers almost always mean bigger allocations or more attention, most of the numbers flying around policy debates exaggerate on the high side. The National Association for Prenatal Addiction Research and Education says as many as 375,000 babies who may have been affected by drugs are born every year; that is, 375,000 babies whose mothers ingested either alcohol or a drug at one point in their pregnancy. In the late 1970s, the American Cancer Society predicted that cancer would claim the lives of at least 8.5 million Americans in the 1980s. In fact, between 1980 and 1990, 4.5 million Americans died of cancer. And while it costs only $3,205 to provide disposable cups, forks, plates, etc., for one school for one year, it costs a staggering $12,413 for reusable material—or so argued a Tennessee school district fighting the mandated use of reusable materials. The disposable figure included the price of buying the materials, the labor of handling them and their waste disposal; the figure for reusables included the cost of the materials, the labor to wash them, the cost of the washing equipment and the water. It did not compare the cost of making the reusables and disposables, nor did it take into account environmental costs. Furthermore, if it is so economical to use disposables, why have they not replaced glass, china and stainless steel in every home in America?

"Even if congressmen discount for biases in the material they are given," wrote James Payne, "this does not solve the problem. When you cut a 50-fold exaggeration in half, you are still left believing a 25-fold exaggeration."

20   The size of the homeless population has been the subject of several studies whose estimates range from 230,000 to 3 million. Homeless advocates have estimated 2 million to 3 million people have been homeless at some time during the previous year. (On any particular night, advocates say, the number of homeless may be closer to half a million to one million.) The advocates' number was derived from estimating the percentage of the population that was homeless—1 percent—and building in a huge margin of error. Martha Burt of the Urban Institute said that the last time 1 percent of the population was homeless was in the heart of the Depression. "Nineteen thirty-three is what 1 percent homeless looks like," she said.

In 1984, the Department of Housing and Urban Development estimated there were between 250,000 and 300,000 homeless. That figure was developed from sixty local experts estimating how many homeless they had in their cities. Their answers were added together and then projected to the nation. In 1987, the Urban Institute estimated 500,000 to 1,000,000 homeless. That number was derived from sampling homeless shelters and soup kitchens in cities with populations of more than 100,000 and then doing elaborate adjustments.

In March 1990, the Census Bureau sent 15,000 census takers out one night—S night, it was called, for streets and shelters—to count the homeless. They found 230,000. Homeless advocates quickly disputed the figure, saying that with a few exceptions the census takers did not go to any city with a population of less than 50,000: they did not count any homeless people they saw in alleyways or streets; and they, like other homeless researchers, had no way of counting the people sleeping on the couch or floor of someone's house who might be looking for shelter the following night. Research built on shelter data is inherently skewed because a huge part of the homeless population—single people who are highly impaired and chronically homeless—tend not to use shelters.

In November 1993, another count of the homeless in two big cities—New York and Philadelphia—was released. This study counted the homeless using computer records of Social Security numbers at city shelters. The study found that 3.3 percent of New York's population had stayed in a shelter sometime over the past five years. The stay could be as short as one day. Should one one-day stay sometime in the past five years define a person as homeless?

It is not possible to count the homeless population precisely; they are transient, wary of authority and sometimes mentally ill or addicted to drugs. Sadly, the issue of counting the homeless long ago overwhelmed the moral debate on what to do about people living in the street, as though without agreeing on the numbers there could be no agreement that homelessness is a problem. A decade after the plight of the homeless appeared on the national agenda, there is still a sizable homeless population. Statistical formulas do not solve our problems any faster or better, and they cannot eliminate politics, as the political scientist Kenneth Prewitt points out. They simply push politics back one stop, to disputes about methods: "Arguments about numerical quotas, availability pools and demographic imbalance become a substitute for democratic discussion of the principles of equity and justice."

25   In public policy debates and deliberations, words like decency, right and wrong, peace, fairness, trust and hope have lost their force. Numbers, which can offer so much illumination and guidance if used professionally and ethically, have become the tools of advocacy. Even if their cause is worthy, people who massage data undermine the power and purity of statistics that may be crucial to future decisions. There are numbers we will never know, and we should admit it. It is essential to understand the homeless before making policy about them. But in this case, as in so many others in public policy, understanding is not the same as counting.

THINKING ↔ WRITING ACTIVITY 10.8

Evaluating "Scientific Studies"

After you have read "False Truth and the Future of the World," respond to any one of these questions in your journal.

1. In the introduction to her book, Crossen states that her own survey found that while 76 percent of her respondents agreed that "you can find a scientific study to prove just about anything you want to prove," 86 percent said that "references to scientific research in a story increased its credibility." Why are scientific studies used so extensively by the media? Do you think such studies increase a news story's credibility?

2. Crossen gives several examples showing that the way a survey question is worded influences the kinds of responses people make to it. Do you think a survey can be conducted in a completely objective way? Why or why not?

3. Crossen suggests that competing, contradictory studies effectively serve to prevent any progress on solving serious social problems, such as homelessness. Is it also true that competing beliefs among politicians and others in power tend to stymie real solutions? Can you imagine any way such competing beliefs could be combined to discover something closer to the "truth"?

Writing Thoughtfully About Beliefs

When you write, you are presenting your beliefs. No matter what its form—letters, college papers, business documents, even stories and poems—your written expression states what you believe. When you write, you present your beliefs in three ways: *reports, inferences, and judgments.* Your choice of words establishes which of the three you are using:

- Report: My bus was late today.
- Inference: My bus will probably be late tomorrow.
- Judgment: The bus system is unreliable.

Now try to identify which of the three is being used in these statements:

1. Each modern nuclear warhead has over one hundred times the explosive power of the bomb dropped on Hiroshima.
2. With all the billions of planets in the universe, the odds are that there are other forms of life in the cosmos.
3. In the long run, the energy needs of the world will best be met by solar energy technology rather than nuclear energy or fossil fuels.

As you examine these various statements, you can see that they provide readers with different *types* of information. For example, the first statement in each list reports aspects of the world that can be verified—that is, checked for accuracy. Appropriate investigation can determine whether the bus was actually late today and whether modern nuclear warheads really have the power attributed to them. When you describe the world in ways that can be verified through investigation, you are *reporting factual information* about the world.

> **Reporting Factual Information:** describing the world in ways that can be verified through investigation.

Looking at the second statement in each list, you can see that each provides a different sort of information from the first one. These statements cannot be verified. There is no way to investigate and determine with certainty whether the bus will indeed be late tomorrow or whether there is in fact life on other planets. Although these conclusions may be based on factual information, they go beyond factual information to make statements about what is not currently known. When you describe the world in ways based on factual information, yet go beyond this information to make statements regarding what is not currently known, you are said to be *inferring* conclusions about the world.

> **Inferring:** describing the world in ways that are based on factual information, yet going beyond this information to make statements about what is not currently known.

Finally, as you examine the third statement in each list, it is apparent that these statements are different from both factual reports and inferences. They describe the world in ways that express the speaker's evaluation—of the bus service and of energy sources. These evaluations are based on certain standards (criteria) that the speaker is using to judge the bus service as unreliable and solar energy as more promising than nuclear energy or fossil fuels. When you describe the world in ways that express your evaluation on the basis of certain criteria, you are said to be *judging*.

> **Judging:** describing the world in ways that express an evaluation based on certain criteria.

You continually use these various ways of describing and organizing your world—reporting, inferring, and judging—to make sense of your experience. In most instances, you are not aware that you are actually performing these activities, nor are you usually aware of the differences among them. Yet these three activities work together to help you see the world as a complete picture.

THINKING ↔ WRITING ACTIVITY 10.9

Distinguishing Reports, Inferences, Judgments

1. Write six sentences: two as reports, two as inferences, and two as judgments.
2. Locate a short article from a newspaper or magazine and identify the reports, inferences, and judgments it contains.

Reporting Factual Information

The statements written as reports express the most accurate beliefs you have about the world. Factual beliefs have earned this distinction because they are verifiable, usually with one or more of the senses. For example, consider the following factual statement: *That young woman is wearing a brown hat in the rain.* This statement about an event in the world is considered factual because it can be verified by your immediate sense experience—what you can (in principle or in theory) see, hear, touch, taste, or smell. It is important to say *in principle or in theory,* because often you do not use all of your relevant senses to check out what you are experiencing. Look again at the example of a factual statement: you would normally be satisfied to see this event, without insisting on touching the hat or giving the person a physical examination. If necessary, however, you could perform these additional actions—in principle or in theory.

You use the same reasoning when you believe other people's factual statements that you are not in a position to check immediately. For instance:

■ The Great Wall of China is more than fifteen hundred miles long.

■ There are large mountains and craters on the moon.

■ Your skin is covered with germs.

You consider these factual statements because even though you cannot verify them with your senses at the moment, you could in principle or in theory verify them with your senses *if* you were flown to China, *if* you were rocketed to the moon, or *if* you were to examine your skin with a powerful microscope. The process of verifying factual statements involves *identifying* the sources of information on which they are based and *evaluating* the reliability of these sources, topics examined in some detail earlier in this chapter.

You communicate factual information to others by means of reports. A report is a description of something that has been experienced, then communicated in as accurate and complete a way as possible. Through reports you can share your sense experiences with other people, and this mutual sharing enables you to learn much more about the world than if you were confined to knowing only what you experience. The recording (making records) of factual reports also makes possible the accumulation of knowledge acquired by previous generations.

Because factual reports play such an important role in the exchange and accumulation of information about the world, it is important that they be as accurate and complete as possible. This brings us to a problem. We have already seen in previous chapters that our perceptions and observations often are not accurate or complete. This means that often when we think we are making true factual reports, the reports actually are inaccurate or incomplete. For instance, consider our earlier "factual statement": *That young woman is wearing a brown hat in the rain.* Here are questions you could ask concerning the accuracy of the statement:

- Is the woman really young, or does she merely look young?
- Is the person really a woman, or a man disguised as a woman?
- Is that really a hat the woman is wearing, or something else (such as a helmet or a paper bag)?

Of course, there are methods you could use to clear up these questions with more detailed observations. Can you describe some of these methods?

Besides difficulties with observations, the "facts" that you see in the world actually depend on more *general beliefs* that you have about how the world operates. Consider this question: *Why did the man's body fall from the top of the building to the sidewalk?* Having had some general science courses, you might say something like "The body was simply obeying the law of gravity," and you would consider this a "factual statement." But how did people account for this sort of event before Newton formulated the law of gravity? Some popular responses might have included the following:

- Things always fall down, not up.
- The spirit in the body wanted to join with the spirit of the earth.

When people made statements like these and others, such as "Humans can't fly," they thought that they were making "factual statements." Increased knowledge and understanding have since shown these "factual beliefs" to be inaccurate, and so they have been replaced by "better" beliefs. These "better beliefs" explain the world in a way that is more accurate and predictable. Will many of the beliefs now considered to be factually accurate also be replaced by beliefs that are more accurate and predictable? If history is any indication, this will most certainly happen. Newton's formulations have already been replaced by Einstein's, based on the latter's theory of relativity. Einstein's have been refined and modified as well and may be replaced someday.

THINKING↔WRITING ACTIVITY 10.10

Evaluating Factual Information

1. Locate and carefully read an article that deals with a major social issue.
2. Summarize the main idea and key points of the article.
3. Describe the factual statements used to support the main idea.
4. Evaluate the accuracy of the factual information.
5. Evaluate the reliability of the sources of the factual information.

Inferring

Imagine yourself in the following situations.

1. It is 2:00 A.M. and your roommate comes crashing into the room. He staggers to his bed and falls across it, dropping (and breaking) a nearly empty whiskey bottle. Startled, you gasp, "What's the matter?" With alcohol fumes blasting from his mouth, he mumbles: "I jus' wanna hadda widdel drink!" What do you conclude?
2. Your roommate has just learned that she passed a math exam for which she had done absolutely no studying. Humming the refrain, "I did it my way," she comes dancing over to you with a huge grin on her face and says, "Let me buy you dinner to celebrate!" What do you conclude about how she is feeling?
3. It is midnight and the library is about to close. As you head for the door, you spy your roommate shuffling along in an awkward waddle. His coat bulges out in front as if he's pregnant. When you ask, "What's going on?" he gives you a glare and hisses, "Shhh!" Just before he reaches the door, a pile of books slides from under his coat and crashes to the floor. What do you conclude?

In these examples, it would be reasonable to make the following conclusions:

1. Your roommate is drunk.
2. Your roommate is happy.
3. Your roommate is stealing library books.

Although these conclusions are reasonable, they are not factual reports; they are *inferences*. You have not directly experienced your roommate's "drunkenness," "happiness," or "stealing." Instead, you have *inferred* it on the basis of your roommate's behavior and the circumstances. What clues in these situations might lead to these conclusions? One way of understanding the inferential nature of these views is to ask yourself the following questions:

1. Have you ever pretended to be drunk when you weren't? Could other people tell?
2. Have you ever pretended to be happy when you weren't? Could other people tell?
3. Have you ever been accused of stealing something when you were perfectly innocent? How did this happen?

From these examples you can see that whereas factual beliefs can in principle be verified by direct observation, *inferential beliefs* go beyond what can be directly observed. For instance, in the examples just given, your observation of certain of your roommate's actions led you to infer things that you were *not* observing directly—"He's drunk," "She's happy," "He's stealing books."

Making such simple inferences is something you do all the time. It is so automatic that usually you are not even aware that you are going beyond your immediate observations, and you may have difficulty drawing a sharp line between what you *observe* and what you *infer*. Making such inferences enables you to see the world as a complete picture, to fill in the blanks and round out the fragmentary sensations being presented to your senses. Presenting your inferences in writing paints a complete picture for your readers, filling in the blanks and presenting them with your beliefs as a complete picture.

Your writing may also include *predictions* of what will be taking place in the near future. Predictions and expectations are also inferences because you attempt to determine what is currently unknown from what is already known.

It is possible that your inferences may be mistaken; in fact, they frequently are. You may infer that the woman sitting next to you is wearing two earrings and then discover that she has only one. You may expect the class to end at noon and find that the teacher lets you go early—or late. In the last section, we concluded that not even factual beliefs are ever absolutely certain. Comparatively speaking, inferential beliefs are a great deal more uncertain than factual beliefs, and it is important to distinguish between the two.

The distinction between what is observed and what is inferred is paid particular attention in courtroom settings, where defense lawyers usually want witnesses to describe *only what they observed*—not what they *inferred* as part of the observation. When a witness includes an inference such as "I saw him steal it," the lawyer may object that the statement represents a "conclusion of the witness" and move to have the observation stricken from the record. For example, imagine that you are a defense attorney listening to the following testimony. At what points would you make the objection: "This is a conclusion of the witness"?

I saw Harvey running down the street, right after he knocked the old lady down. He had her purse in his hand and was trying to escape as fast as he could. He was really scared. I wasn't surprised because Harvey has always taken advantage of others. It's not the first time that he's stolen either, I can tell you that. Just last summer he robbed the poor box at St. Anthony's. He was bragging about it for weeks.

Finally, you should be aware that even though in *theory* facts and inferences can be distinguished, in *practice* it is almost impossible to communicate with others in speech or writing by sticking only to factual observations. A reasonable approach is to state your inference *along with* the observable evidence on which the inference is based (e.g., John *seemed* happy because . . .). Our language has an entire collection of terms (*seems, appears, is likely,* etc.) that signal we are making an inference and not expressing an observable fact, and thoughtful writers use these words carefully and deliberately.

Many of the predictions that you make are inferences based on your past experiences and the information that you presently have. Even when there appear to be sound reasons supporting them, these inferences are often wrong due to incomplete information or unanticipated events. The fact that even people considered by society to be "experts" regularly make inaccurate predictions with absolute certainty should encourage you to exercise caution when presenting your beliefs as inferences. Here are some examples:

"So many centuries after the Creation, it is unlikely that anyone could find hitherto unknown lands of any value." —THE ADVISORY COMMITTEE TO KING FERDINAND AND QUEEN ISABELLA OF SPAIN, BEFORE COLUMBUS'S VOYAGE IN 1492

"What will the soldiers and sailors, what will the common people say to 'George Washington, President of the United States'? They will despise him to all eternity." —JOHN ADAMS, 1789

"What use could the company make of an electrical toy?" —WESTERN UNION'S REJECTION OF THE TELEPHONE IN 1878

"The actual building of roads devoted to motor cars is not for the near future in spite of many rumors to that effect." —A 1902 ARTICLE IN HARPER'S WEEKLY

"You ain't goin' nowhere, son. You ought to go back to driving a truck." —JIM DENNY, GRAND OLE OPRY MANAGER, FIRING ELVIS PRESLEY AFTER ONE PERFORMANCE, 1954

Examine the following list of statements, noting which are *factual beliefs* (based on observations) and which are *inferential beliefs* (conclusions that go beyond observations). For each factual statement, describe how you might go about verifying the information. For each inferential statement, describe a factual observation on which the inference could be based. (*Note:* Some statements may contain *both* factual beliefs and inferential beliefs.)

- When my leg starts to ache, that means snow is on the way.
- The grass is wet—it must have rained last night.
- I think that it's pretty clear from the length of the skid marks that the accident was caused by that person's driving too fast.
- Fifty men lost their lives in the construction of the Queensboro Bridge.
- Nancy said she wasn't feeling well yesterday—I'll bet that she's out sick today.

Now consider the following situations. What inferences might you be inclined to make on the basis of what you are observing? How could you investigate the accuracy of your inference?

- A student in your class is consistently late for class.
- You see a friend of yours driving a new car.
- An instructor asks the same student to stay after class several times.
- You don't receive any birthday cards.

So far, we have been exploring relatively simple inferences. Many of the inferences people make, however, are much more complicated. In fact, much of our knowledge about the world rests on our ability to make complicated inferences in a systematic and logical way. However, just because an inference is more complicated does not mean that it is more accurate; in fact, the opposite is often the case. One of the masters of inference is the legendary Sherlock Holmes. In the following passage, Holmes makes an astonishing number of inferences on meeting Dr. Watson. Study Holmes's conclusions carefully. Are they reasonable? Can you explain how he reaches these conclusions?

"You appeared to be surprised when I told you, on our first meeting, that you had come from Afghanistan."
"You were told, no doubt."

"Nothing of the sort. I knew you came from Afghanistan. From long habit the train of thoughts ran so swiftly through my mind that I arrived at the conclusion without being conscious of intermediate steps. There were such steps, however. The train of reasoning ran, 'Here is a gentleman of a medical type, but with the air of a military man. Clearly an army doctor, then. He is just come from the tropics, for his face is dark, and that is not the natural tint of his skin, for his wrists are fair. He has undergone hardship and sickness, as his haggard face says clearly. His left arm has been injured. He holds it in a stiff and unnatural manner. Where in the tropics could an English army doctor have seen much hardship and got his arm wounded? Clearly in Afghanistan.' The whole train of thought did not occupy a second. I then remarked that you came from Afghanistan, and you were astonished." —Sir Arthur Conan Doyle, *A Study in Scarlet*

THINKING↔WRITING ACTIVITY 10.11

Analyzing an Incorrect Inference

Describe an experience in which you made an incorrect inference that resulted in serious consequences. For example, it might have been a situation in which you mistakenly accused someone, an accident based on a miscalculation, a poor decision based on an inaccurate prediction, or some other event. Analyze that experience by answering the following questions:

1. What was (were) your mistaken inference(s)?
2. What was the factual evidence on which you based your inference(s)?
3. Looking back, what could you have done to avoid the erroneous inference(s)?

THINKING↔WRITING ACTIVITY 10.12

Scientific Inferences

The following essay, "Evolution as Fact and Theory," was written by a geology professor at Harvard University who also writes widely on scientific themes for nonscientific audiences. This essay illustrates the ongoing process by which natural scientists use inferences to discover factual information and to construct theories explaining this factual information. Read the selection carefully, then answer the questions that follow.

1. According to Stephen Jay Gould, author of the essay, evolution is both a scientific "fact" and a scientific "theory" asserting that all life forms are the result of a process of gradual development and differentiation over time, much like the progressive growth of tree branches from the central trunk. In contrast, creationism asserts that all basic forms of life were brought into

being in a sudden act by a supernatural creator. From your reading of the article, explain what you understand about the theory of evolution and about creationism.

2. Gould defines "facts" as the "world's data" and refers to observing an apple fall from the tree as Isaac Newton is alleged to have done. Identify some of the facts Gould presents in his writing as evidence to support the theory of evolution.

3. Gould defines "theories" as "structures of ideas that explain and interpret facts," such as Newton's theory of gravitation introduced to explain facts like falling apples. In addition to facts, Gould states, the theory of evolution is supported by reasonable inferences. Identify the inferences he cites as evidence.

from Evolution As Fact and Theory
by Stephen Jay Gould

Kirtley Mather, who died last year at age 89, was a pillar of both science and the Christian religion in America and one of my dearest friends. The difference of half a century in our ages evaporated before our common interests. The most curious thing we shared was a battle we each fought at the same age. For Kirtley had gone to Tennessee with Clarence Darrow to testify for evolution at the Scopes trial of 1925. When I think that we are enmeshed again in the same struggle for one of the best documented, most compelling and exciting concepts in all of science, I don't know whether to laugh or cry.

According to idealized principles of scientific discourse, the arousal of dormant issues should reflect fresh data that give renewed life to abandoned notions. Those outside the current debate may therefore be excused for suspecting that creationists have come up with something new, or that evolutionists have generated some serious internal trouble. But nothing has changed; the creationists have not a single new fact or argument. Darrow and Bryan were at least more entertaining than we lesser antagonists today. The rise of creationism is politics, pure and simple; it represents one issue (and by no means the major concern) of the resurgent evangelical right. Arguments that seemed kooky just a decade ago have re-entered the mainstream.

Creationism Is Not Science

The basic attack of the creationists falls apart on two general counts before we even reach the supposed factual details of their complaints against evolution. First, they play upon a vernacular misunderstanding of the word "theory" to convey the false impression that we evolutionists are covering up the rotten core of our edifice. Second, they misuse a popular philosophy of science to argue that they are behaving scientifically in attacking evolution. Yet the same philosophy demonstrates that their own belief is not science, and that "scientific creationism" is therefore meaningless and self-contradictory, a superb example of what Orwell called "newspeak."

In the American vernacular, "theory" often means "imperfect fact"— part of a hierarchy of confidence running downhill from fact to theory to hypothesis to guess. Thus the power of the creationist argument: evolution is "only" a theory, and intense debate now rages about many aspects of the theory. If evolution is less than a fact, and scientists can't even make up their minds about the theory, then what confidence can we have in it? Indeed, President Reagan echoed this argument before an evangelical group in Dallas when he said (in what I devoutly hope was campaign rhetoric): "Well, it is a theory. It is a scientific theory only, and it has in recent years been challenged in the world of science—that is, not believed in the scientific community to be as infallible as it once was."

5   Well, evolution *is* a theory. It is also a fact. And facts and theories are different things, not rungs in a hierarchy of increasing certainty. Facts are the world's data. Theories are structures of ideas that explain and interpret facts. Facts do not go away when scientists debate rival theories to explain them. Einstein's theory of gravitation replaced Newton's, but apples did not suspend themselves in mid-air pending the outcome. And human beings evolved from apelike ancestors whether they did so by Darwin's proposed mechanism or by some other, yet to be discovered.

Moreover, "fact" does not mean "absolute certainty." The final proofs of logic and mathematics flow deductively from stated premises and achieve certainty only because they are *not* about the empirical world. Evolutionists make no claim for perpetual truth, though creationists often do (and then attack us for a style of argument that they themselves favor). In science, "fact" can only mean "confirmed to such a degree that it would be perverse to withhold provisional assent." I suppose that apples might start to rise tomorrow, but possibility does not merit equal time in physics classrooms.

Evolutionists have been clear about this distinction between fact and theory from the very beginning, if only because we have always acknowledged how far we are from completely understanding the mechanisms (theory) by which evolution (fact) occurred. Darwin continually emphasized the difference between his two great and separate accomplishments: establishing the fact of evolution, and proposing a theory— natural selection—to explain the mechanism of evolution. He wrote in *The Descent of Man:* "I had two distinct objects in view; firstly, to show that species had not been separately created, and secondly, that natural selection had been the chief agent of change. . . . Hence if I have erred in . . . having exaggerated its [natural selection's] power . . . I have at least, as I hope, done good service in aiding to overthrow the dogma of separate creations."

Thus Darwin acknowledged the provisional nature of natural selection while affirming the fact of evolution. The fruitful theoretical debate that Darwin initiated has never ceased. From the 1940s through the 1960s, Darwin's own theory of natural selection did achieve a temporary hegemony that it never enjoyed in his lifetime. But renewed debate characterizes our decade, and while no biologist questions the importance of natural selection, many now doubt its ubiquity. In particular, many evolutionists argue that substantial amounts of genetic change may not be subject to natural selection and may spread through populations at random. Others are challenging Darwin's linking of natural selection with gradual, imperceptible change through all intermediary degrees; they are arguing that most evolutionary events may occur far more rapidly than Darwin envisioned.

Scientists regard debates on fundamental issues of theory as a sign of intellectual health and a source of excitement. Science is—and how else can I say it?—most fun when it plays with interesting ideas, examines their implications, and recognizes that old information may be explained in surprisingly new ways. Evolutionary theory is now enjoying this uncommon vigor. Yet amidst all this turmoil no biologist has been led to doubt the fact that evolution occurred; we are debating *how* it happened. We are all trying to explain the same thing: the tree of evolutionary descent linking all organisms by ties of genealogy. Creationists pervert and caricature this debate by conveniently neglecting the common conviction that underlies it, and by falsely suggesting that we now doubt the very phenomenon we are struggling to understand.

10   Using another invalid argument, creationists claim that "the dogma of separate creations," as Darwin characterized it a century ago, is a scientific theory meriting equal time with evolution in high school biology curricula. But a prevailing viewpoint among philosophers of science belies this creationist argument. Philosopher Karl Popper has argued for decades that the primary criterion of science is the falsifiability of its theories. We can never prove absolutely, but we can falsify. A set of ideas that cannot, in principle, be falsified is not science.

The entire creationist argument involves little more than a rhetorical attempt to falsify evolution by presenting supposed contradictions among its supporters. Their brand of creationism, they claim, is "scientific" because it follows the Popperian model in trying to demolish evolution. Yet Popper's argument must apply in both directions. One does not become a scientist by the simple act of trying to falsify another scientific system; one has to present an alternative system that also meets Popper's criterion—it too must be falsifiable in principle.

"Scientific creationism" is a self-contradictory, nonsense phrase precisely because it cannot be falsified. I can envision observations and experiments that would disprove any evolutionary theory I know, but I cannot imagine what potential data could lead creationists to abandon their beliefs. Unbeatable systems are dogma, not science. Lest I seem harsh or rhetorical, I quote creationism's leading intellectual, Duane Gish, Ph.D., from his recent (1978) book *Evolution? The Fossils Say No!* "By creation we mean the bringing into being by a supernatural Creator of the basic kinds of plants and animals by the process of sudden, or fiat, creation. We do not know how the Creator created, what processes He used, *for He used processes which are not now operating anywhere in the natural universe* [Gish's italics]. This is why we refer to creation as special creation. We cannot discover by scientific investigations anything about the creative processes used by the Creator." Pray tell, Dr. Gish, in the light of your last sentence, what then is "scientific" creationism?

The Fact of Evolution

Our confidence that evolution occurred centers upon three general arguments. First, we have abundant, direct, observational evidence of evolution in action, from both the field and the laboratory. It ranges from countless experiments on change in nearly everything about fruit flies subjected to artificial selection in the laboratory to the famous British moths that turned black when industrial soot darkened the trees upon which they rest. (The moths gain protection from sharp-sighted bird predators by blending into the background.) Creationists do not deny these observations; how could they? Creationists have tightened their act. They now argue that God only created "basic kinds," and allowed for limited evolutionary meandering within them. Thus toy poodles and Great Danes come from the dog kind and moths can change color, but nature cannot convert a dog to a cat or a monkey to a man.

The second and third arguments for evolution—the case for major changes—do not involve direct observation of evolution in action. They rest upon inference, but are no less secure for that reason. Major evolutionary change requires too much time for direct observation on the scale of recorded human history. All historical sciences rest upon inference, and evolution is no different from geology, cosmology, or human history in this respect. In principle, we cannot observe processes that operated in the past. We must infer them from results that still survive: living and fossil organisms for evolution, documents and artifacts for human history, strata and topography for geology.

15   The second argument—that the imperfection of nature reveals evolution—strikes many people as ironic, for they feel that evolution should be most elegantly displayed in the nearly perfect adaptation ex-

pressed by some organisms—the camber of a gull's wing, or butterflies that cannot be seen in ground litter because they mimic leaves so precisely. But perfection could be imposed by a wise creator or evolved by natural selection. Perfection covers the tracks of past history. And past history—the evidence of descent—is our mark of evolution.

Evolution lies exposed in the *imperfections* that record a history of descent. Why should a rat run, a bat fly, or porpoise swim, and I type this essay with structures built of the same bones unless we all inherited them from a common ancestor? An engineer, starting from scratch, could design better limbs in each case. Why should all the large native mammals of Australia be marsupials, unless they descended from a common ancestor isolated on this island continent? Marsupials are not "better," or ideally suited for Australia; many have been wiped out by placental mammals imported by man from other continents. This principle of imperfection extends to all historical sciences. When we recognize the etymology of September, October, November, and December (seventh, eighth, ninth, and tenth, from the Latin), we know that two additional items (January and February) must have been added to an original calendar of ten months.

The third argument is more direct: transitions are often found in the fossil record. Preserved transitions are not common—and should not be, according to our understanding of evolution . . . —but they are not entirely wanting, as creationists often claim. The lower jaw of reptiles contains several bones, that of mammals only one. The nonmammalian jawbones are reduced, step by step, in mammalian ancestors until they become tiny nubbins located at the back of the jaw. The "hammer" and the "anvil" bones of the mammalian ear are descendants of these nubbins. How could such a transition be accomplished?, the creationists ask. Surely a bone is either entirely in the jaw or in the ear. Yet paleontologists have discovered two transitional lineages of therapsids (the so-called mammal-like reptiles) with a double jaw joint—one composed of the old quadrate and articular bones (soon to become the hammer and anvil), the other of the squamosal and dentary bones (as in modern mammals). For that matter, what better transitional form could we desire than the oldest human, *Australopithecus afarensis*, with its apelike palate, its human upright stance, and a cranial capacity larger than any ape's of the same body size but a full 1,000 cubic centimeters below ours? If God made each of the half dozen human species discovered in ancient rocks, why did he create an unbroken temporal sequence of progressively more modern features—increasing cranial capacity, reduced face and teeth, larger body size? Did he create a mimic evolution and test our faith thereby?

Conclusion

I am both angry at and amused by the creationists; but mostly I am deeply sad. Sad for many reasons. Sad because so many people who respond to creationist appeals are troubled for the right reason, but venting their anger at the wrong target. It is true that scientists have often been dogmatic and elitist. It is true that we have often allowed the white-coated, advertising image to represent us—"Scientists say that Brand X cures bunions ten times faster than. . . ." We have not fought it adequately because we derive benefits from appearing as a new priesthood. It is also true that faceless bureaucratic state power intrudes more and more into our lives and removes choices that should belong to individuals and communities. I can understand that requiring that evolution be taught in the schools might be seen as one more insult on all these grounds. But the culprit is not, and cannot be, evolution or any other fact of the natural world. Identify and fight your legitimate enemies by all means, but we are not among them.

I am sad because the practical result of this brouhaha will not be expanded coverage to include creationism (that would also make me sad), but the reduction or excision of evolution from high school curricula. Evolution is one of the half dozen "great ideas" developed by science. It speaks to the profound issues of genealogy that fascinate all of us— the "roots" phenomenon writ large. Where did we come from? Where did life arise? How did it develop? How are organisms related? It forces us to think, ponder, and wonder. Shall we deprive millions of this knowledge and once again teach biology as a set of dull and unconnected facts, without the thread that weaves diverse material into a supple unity?

20   But most of all I am saddened by a trend I am just beginning to discern among my colleagues. I sense that some now wish to mute the healthy debate about theory that has brought new life to evolutionary biology. It provides grist for creationist mills, they say, even if only by distortion. Perhaps we should lie low and rally around the flag of strict Darwinism, at least for the moment—a kind of old-time religion on our part.

But we should borrow another metaphor and recognize that we too have to tread a straight and narrow path, surrounded by roads to perdition. For if we ever begin to suppress our search to understand nature, to quench our own intellectual excitement in a misguided effort to present a united front where it does not and should not exist, then we are truly lost.

Judging

Identify and write a description of a friend you have, a course you have taken, and the college you attend. Be sure your descriptions are specific and include *what you think* about the friend, the course, and the college.

1. _____ is a friend I have. He/she is . . .
2. _____ is a course I have taken. It was . . .
3. _____ is the college I attend. It is . . .

Now review your writing. Does it include factual descriptions? Note any factual information that can be verified. In addition to factual reports, your writing may contain inferences based on factual information. Can you identify any inferences? In addition to inferences, your writing may also include judgments about the person, the course, and the school—descriptions that express your evaluation based on certain criteria. Facts and inferences are designed to help you figure out what is actually happening (or will happen); the purpose of judgments is to express your evaluation about what is happening (or will happen). For example:

- *My new car has broken down three times in the first six months.* (Factual report)
- *My new car will probably continue to have difficulties.* (Inference)
- *My new car is a lemon.* (Judgment)

When you write that your new car is a "lemon," you are presenting a judgment based on certain criteria you have in mind. For instance, a "lemon" is usually a newly purchased item with which you have repeated problems—generally an automobile. To take another example of judging, consider the following statements:

- *Carla always does her work thoroughly and completes it on time.* (Factual report)
- *Carla will probably continue to do her work in this fashion.* (Inference)
- *Carla is a very responsible person.* (Judgment)

By judging Carla to be responsible, you are evaluating her on the basis of the criteria or standards that you believe indicate a responsible person. One such criterion is completing assigned work on time. Can you identify additional criteria for judging someone to be responsible?

Review your previous descriptions of a friend, a course, and your college. Can you identify any judgments in your description?

1. Judgments about your friend.
2. Judgments about your course.
3. Judgments about your college.

For each judgment you have listed, identify the criteria on which the judgment is based.

1. Criteria for judgments about your friend.
2. Criteria for judgments about your course.
3. Criteria for judgments about your college.

Differences in Judgments

Many of our disagreements with other people focus on differences in judgments. To write thoughtfully, you need to approach such differences in judgments intelligently by following these guidelines:

- *Make explicit the criteria or standards* used as a basis for the judgment.
- *Try to establish the reasons* that justify these criteria.

For instance, if I write "Professor Andrews is an excellent teacher," I am basing my judgment on certain criteria of teaching excellence. Once these standards are made explicit, they can be discussed to see whether they make sense and what justifies them. Of course, my idea of what makes an excellent teacher may be different from someone else's, and I can test my conclusion by comparing my criteria with those of other class members. When disagreements occur, my only hope for resolution is to use the two steps just identified.

In short, not all judgments are equally good or equally poor. The credibility of a judgment depends on the criteria used to make the judgment and on the evidence or reasons that support these criteria. For example, there may be legitimate disagreements about judgments on the following points:

- Who was the greatest United States president?
- Which movie deserves the Oscar this year?
- Which is the best baseball team this year?

However, in these and countless other cases, the quality of judgments depends on presenting the criteria used for the competing judgments and then demonstrating that your candidate best meets those criteria by providing supporting evidence and reasons. With this approach, you can often engage in intelligent discussion and establish which judgments are best supported by the evidence.

THINKING ↔ WRITING ACTIVITY 10.13

Analyzing Judgments

Review the following passages, which illustrate various judgments. For each passage, do the following:

1. Identify the evaluative criteria on which the judgments are based.

2. Describe the reasons or evidence the author uses to support the criteria.
3. Explain whether you agree or disagree with the judgments and give your rationale.

One widely held misconception concerning pizza should be laid to rest. Although it may be characterized as fast food, pizza is not junk food. Especially when it is made with fresh ingredients, pizza fulfills our basic nutritional requirements. The crust provides carbohydrates; from the cheese and meat or fish comes protein; and the tomatoes, herbs, onions, and garlic supply vitamins and minerals. —Louis Philip Salamone, *"Pizza: Fast Food, Not Junk Food"*

Let us return to the question of food. Responsible agronomists report that before the end of the year millions of people if unaided might starve to death. Half a billion deaths by starvation is not an uncommon estimate. Even though the United States has done more than any other nation to feed the hungry, our relative affluence makes us morally vulnerable in the eyes of other nations and in our own eyes. Garrett Hardin, who has argued for a "lifeboat" ethic of survival (if you take all the passengers aboard, everybody drowns), admits that the decision not to feed all the hungry requires of us "a very hard psychological adjustment." Indeed it would. It has been estimated that the 3.5 million tons of fertilizer spread on American golf courses and lawns could provide up to 30 million tons of food in overseas agricultural production. The nightmarish thought intrudes itself. If we as a nation allow people to starve while we could, through some sacrifice, make more food available to them, what hope can any person have for the future of international relations? If we cannot agree on this most basic of values—feed the hungry—what hopes for the future can we entertain? —James R. Kelly, *"The Limits of Reason"*

Distinguishing Reports, Inferences, and Judgments

Although the activities of reporting, inferring, and judging tend to be woven together in your experiences and in your writing, it is important for you to be able to distinguish these activities. Each plays a different role in helping you make sense of your world for yourself and for your readers, and you should be careful not to confuse these roles. For instance, although writers may appear to be reporting factual information, they may actually be expressing personal evaluations, which are not factual. Consider the statement "Los

Angeles is a smog-ridden city drowning in automobiles." Although seeming to be reporting factual information, the writer really is expressing his or her personal judgment. Of course, writers can identify their judgments with such phrases as "in my opinion," "my evaluation is," and so forth.

Sometimes, however, writers do not identify their judgments. In some cases they do not do so because the context within which they are writing (such as a newspaper editorial) makes it clear that the information is judgment rather than fact. In other cases, however, they want their judgments treated as factual information. Confusing the activities of reporting, inferring, and judging, whether accidental or deliberate, can be misleading and even dangerous.

Confusing factual information with judgments can be personally damaging as well. For example, there is a big difference between these two statements:

- *I failed my exam today.* (Factual report)
- *I am a failure.* (Judgment)

Stating the fact "I failed my exam today" describes your situation in a concrete way, enabling you to see it as a problem you can hope to solve through reflection and hard work. If, though, you make the judgment "I am a failure," this sort of general evaluation does not encourage you to explore solutions to the problem or improve your situation.

Finally, another main reason for distinguishing the activities of reporting, inferring, and judging concerns the accuracy of statements. We noted, for instance, that factual statements tend to be reasonably accurate because they are by nature verifiable, whereas inferences are usually much less certain. As a result, it is crucial for you to be aware of whether you are presenting a belief as a report, an inference, or a judgment. If you write the superintendent of your apartment building a note saying "My thermostat is broken," an inference on your part based on the fact that you feel uncomfortably hot, you will feel foolish when you discover that you have a fever and the thermostat is functioning well.

Beliefs and Your Writing

Understanding and evaluating beliefs pertains in three particular ways to your college papers as well as to the writing you will do in other settings. First, as you understand more fully the distinctions among reports, inferences, and judgments, you will be able to present different types of beliefs more accurately. While you may not often use the terms *report, inference,* or *judgment,* you will word your beliefs in precise ways that indicate the level of speculation behind your statements.

Second, a strong relationship exists between the thesis of a paper and your beliefs about the topic. The thesis, most of all, expresses what you believe is the main point of your paper. As you work to clarify your thesis statement, you clarify your beliefs about the issue you are writing about. And when you state the thesis clearly in your paper, you are making your beliefs clear to your readers.

Third, as a college writer and quite possibly as a working professional, you will regularly use source material in your papers. The techniques for evaluating beliefs that are discussed in this chapter will help you judge sources of information. Then, as you present what others have said, in your researched writing, you can comment on those beliefs as you integrate the sources into your papers. The **Writing Project** that follows is designed to help you evaluate beliefs and their sources.

WRITING PROJECT

This chapter has included both readings and **Thinking↔Writing Activities** that encouraged you to think about where your beliefs come from. Be sure to reread what you wrote for the activities, as you may be able to use some of it for help in completing this project.

WRITING PROJECT   Analyzing Influences on Beliefs

Write an essay in which you consider some influences on the development of your beliefs within an academic field that interests you. As much as possible, apply some of the concepts discussed in this chapter. (Cite the chapter as your instructor directs.) Think about the effects of personal experiences and the impact of your teachers and other people of authority.

As a student, you receive much information that influences your beliefs from print and electronic sources. Therefore, a major section of this paper will be an analysis of two specific, up-to-date media sources, such as newspaper, magazine, or journal articles; material from a Web site; a film or a video; a book or book chapters. The two sources you use should be about the same topic unless you have a good reason to use sources about different topics. Use the Information Evaluation Questions presented in this chapter as a guide. Be sure to comment on how these sources agree or differ and on how the sources influence the beliefs which you hold. If you completed the **Writing Project** in Chapter 7, you may want to see how the comparative and analytical techniques used there can apply to this section of this Writing Project. Follow your instructor's directions as to topic limitations, length, format, citation methods, and so forth.

Begin by considering the key elements of the **Thinking↔Writing Model.**

Purpose

Your primary purpose here is to further your own development as a capable college student. You are exploring some of the ways in which you come to accept concepts in an academic field, possibly the field in which you plan to major. In addition, you are sharing your insights with your audience, which always provides another purpose: to write an effective paper.

On a technical level, you are required to take different kinds of information and pull them together to support one or more general points. In fact, such *synthesis* is the central purpose of many kinds of academic and professional writing. Most research papers and case studies, field reports and pro-ject summaries, product proposals and business plans begin with a body of related information that the writer must bring together and organize into a unified whole.

You also have more intellectual purposes. You will look closely and crit-ically at your own ways of defining what you believe and what you think of as true, as well as what you do not believe and what you think of as false. You will also decide how to present your ideas: as reports, inferences, or judg-ments.

Audience

For this essay about the influences on your beliefs, it is best to think of your audience as including a broad spectrum of different kinds of readers. You may write for the other members of your class, but in doing so be sure to imagine that part of your audience will hold beliefs that differ from yours. If you are liberal politically, imagine that you will have more conservative peo-ple among your readers. If you are religious, imagine that your audience will include people of other faiths who might question your religious views. To *write critically* about your beliefs means to write to an audience that does not entirely share them.

Of course, your professor remains the audience who will judge how well you have planned, drafted, and revised. As a writing teacher, your professor cares about clear focus, logical organization, specific examples, and correct-ness. Keep this in mind as you revise, edit, and proofread.

Subject

Examining the sources of beliefs and evaluating evidence are among the most challenging of subjects to think and write about. If you are just beginning your study of the field about which you are writing, you may not have enough background to be very questioning or judgmental. However, you should be aware of criteria that any thoughtful student can see: specific sup-port for a claim; current information if currentness is significant; appropriate-seeming samples and authorities; responsible attribution. Also, you have some understanding of reports, inferences, predictions, and judgments to ap-ply to your analysis.

Writer

For this **Writing Project,** you should let yourself be as open as possible to new ways of thinking about your beliefs. After such critical analysis, many writ-ers are strengthened in their beliefs, or they may realize that some beliefs are based on unreliable information and need to be re-evaluated.

As with the Writing Projects in Part One, you are in a position of author-ity here when you are writing about your own reactions and realizations. At the same time, since you are writing about an academic field rather than about your personal life, you are a writer who is dealing with other people's beliefs in addition to your own. You may want to consider whether you are a more accepting or more skeptical person.

The Writing Process

The following sections will guide you through the stages of planning, drafting, and revising your essay analyzing sources of your beliefs about concepts in an academic field.

Generating Ideas

1. Identify in the **Thinking↔Writing Activities** some ideas you may be able to use. Then write informally about them.
2. Think about teachers, books, films, articles, and Internet and other sources of information in your field that have provided you with information that you believe. Why have they had this effect?
3. Think about any sources that you are reluctant to trust or believe. Why have they had this effect?
4. What concepts in this field do you believe most firmly?
5. Are there some that you question?
6. If you can, talk to a professor or two in the field about how their beliefs have developed. Ask them for guidance in evaluating sources. (Be sure to credit them appropriately in your paper.)
7. Freewrite for five minutes about your ideas for this project.
8. Look at the list of questions for exploring topics in Chapter 1. Which of them can help you generate ideas for this project?

Defining a Focus

There's a challenge in this **Writing Project,** because unlike some of the others in this book, it does not direct your approach. So you must find a focus or a thread that runs through your ideas or an umbrella-idea to cover several points.

1. Focus on a specific concept, such as evolution in biology or parallel processing in computer science. Trace your experience with this idea. What specific sources have contributed to your understanding of it?
2. Focus on your level of belief. How do you determine that a concept is believable? What causes you to question it?
3. Focus on a concept that has changed, such as the significance of uniforms and caps in nursing. What do you believe now? Why?
4. Focus on a common characteristic among the sources of your convictions about the concept.
5. Focus on differences. Does a popular press or television account differ from what your professor or your textbook has said? How do any differences affect your beliefs?

6. Draft a focus sentence or thesis statement that gives direction to the essay.
7. Create a map or web or rough outline so that you can see how ideas might cluster or separate.

Organizing Ideas

Once you have determined your focus and thought about information from your own background and sources you analyzed to support this focus, map out an outline indicating the order in which you will present your main points.

1. If you are exploring the evolution of your beliefs, your organization may be chronological, moving forward in time.
2. If you are looking at level of certainty about beliefs, then your organization may be topical, focusing on one belief at a time.
3. If you are contrasting two differing perspectives on beliefs, your organization may divide into two basic parts, the first focusing on one perspective and the second on the other.
4. You may need to combine or reorganize the approaches suggested in items 1–3.
5. Keep in mind that you may find yourself modifying your outline as you draft.

Drafting

Begin with the part easiest to draft. Is it writing about your teachers, perhaps, or is it dealing with your print or electronic sources?

Perhaps then you should shift to a part that is hard to draft and at least make some notes or get some questions on paper.

Draft a new outline or map, if necessary, as you rethink what you want to say. Look at the preliminary focus sentence that you drafted. Do you need to rework it now or should you wait until after you have drafted more?

Shape the paragraphs that will make up the body of your essay. Draft clear topic sentences; think about where in each paragraph the topic sentence should be placed.

Draft an opening paragraph and a concluding paragraph, understanding that you may want to revise them substantially later.

Revising

Ideally, at this point, you should put your draft aside for a day or two. If deadlines won't permit you to do that, then at least take a break before you try to revise. When you are ready to "re-see" your writing, begin by reading it through slowly, preferably aloud. If possible, have someone whose opinion you respect read it; ask for feedback. Then work through the hierarchy of revision concerns that follows. Remember that you have at least one and possibly two decisions to make for each question: (1) Is improvement needed? and (?) If improvement is needed, how, exactly, can I make my draft better?

1. **Think big.** Look at your draft as a whole.
- Does if fulfill the assignment in terms of topic and length?
- Have you stated the thesis clearly?
- Do all parts of the draft relate to the thesis?
- Is the organization logical?
- Do you provide enough evidence?
- Is your point of view consistent?
- Is there a discernible flow between your paragraphs?
- Have you documented information from your sources accurately?
- Have you used quotation marks around direct quotes or set the quotes off by indenting?

2. **Think medium.** Look at your draft paragraph by paragraph.
- Will your introduction make your audience want to read on?
- Is the introduction appropriate for the rest of the draft?
- Is your focus stated clearly if you are working with a "visible" structure?
- If you are working with an "invisible" structure, is your focus clearly implied?
- Are topic sentences used effectively?
- Does each body paragraph develop a different idea?
- Should any paragraphs be combined or eliminated?
- Is your conclusion effective?

3. **Think small.** Look at your draft sentence by sentence.
- Are any sentences difficult to understand?
- Are any so long that your audience could get lost in them?
- Are sentences with blended quotations (that is, quotations that are integrated into the syntax of the sentence instead of introduced with "He said . . ." or "She said . . .") complete and easy to read?
- Are quotations shortened with ellipsis marks accurate and readable?
- Are there several choppy sentences that can be combined?
- Are any sentences vague?
- Do any sentences need to be corrected for standard English grammar and usage?

4. **Think "picky."** Look at your draft as your fussiest critic might.
- Are any words not clear or not quite right for your meaning?
- Are there any words misspelled?
- Are there any punctuation errors?
- Is your format correct?
- Are the pages numbered consecutively?
- Does your paper make a good impression by being neat?
- Is there anything else you could do to improve your draft?

Proofreading

After you prepare a final draft, check again for correct grammar and punctuation. Proofread carefully for omitted words or punctuation marks. Run your spelling checker program, but be aware of its limitations. Proofread carefully for the kinds of errors the computer can't catch.

Student Essay

Here is how one student responded to an assignment for a course in Criminal Justice. Her professor asked the students to show how media treatments of a current issue helped them to develop opinions about that issue. The essay shows how an instructor might limit the topic to the part of the **Writing Project** that asks for an analysis of sources.

STUDENT WRITING
Dealing with Sex Offenders
by Jessie Lange

In the past few years we have heard much about Megan's Law, which states that people should be made aware of charged sex offenders in their community. While I wholeheartedly believe that people, for the protection of themselves and their children, have the right to know, there is another twist on the issue I hadn't thought about until I heard a story recently on *60 Minutes*. The story involved Stephanie's Law—a new law in place in some states under which sex offenders are kept *after* they have served their time to go through a therapy program in an attempt to "cure" them. The question that this provoked in me was not whether the state should have the right to hold sexual criminals beyond their sentence, but whether they can be cured at all. If not, should they ever be released back into a world where they are likely to do more damage, destroy more lives?

A recent *New York Times* article described a rehabilitation program in Texas whereby prisoners are immersed in religion—taking classes, having discussions, and owning up to their "sins." Interestingly, while there are 79 men convicted of "robbery, drug possession, and murder" participating, those convicted of sexual crimes are not accepted into the program. This is partly because they are "looked down on by other prisoners" and partly because, according to criminologists, "sexual criminals are the most difficult to rehabilitate."

In fact, there is a question as to whether this rehabilitation is even possible. Sexual criminals in particular seem to be under the influence of urges which are out of their control. The *60 Minutes* report said that, while many may have good intentions in being treated through therapy and returning to society, it may be out of their hands. They may say they understand their wrongs, they may feel cured, but if they are released it seems impossible for even the offenders to know if they will be able to control their impulses. If there is such a question, do they deserve a chance at freedom when it means potentially committing another crime?

There is no question in my mind that, while many sex offenders do not repent for what they have done and have no real interest in being cured, there are also many for whom their crimes are almost out of their hands—as disgusting to them as to anyone else. The *New York Times* ran an article entitled "Sex Offender Agrees To Be Castrated." In Illinois, a convicted child sex offender is having himself castrated "in an effort to win a lighter sentence." The offender, in fact, "volunteered to be castrated even before he was convicted" previously of an attack on a young girl. It seems as though the man is making an attempt to control his urges but, according to the article "Experts disagree on whether castration helps" in controlling these urges.

Both the *New York Times* and *60 Minutes* have good reputations as reliable media sources. I read this paper and watch this show regularly. (I'm pleased that my parents introduced me to them.) I think that these reports are as reliable as the popular press can be. If I decide to do research on this subject and write a substantial paper, I will have to use criminal justice and sociology journals and try to interview one or two experts, as well.

I have not had any personal experience with sex offenders, but I have read and heard enough to know that their crimes destroy not only the lives of victims, but the families and friends of the victims and that their crimes can so haunt victims that these fears are never resolved. In addition, victims of sexual crimes may grow up to inflict these crimes on others, continuing the cycle. In my opinion, the damage done by sex offenders and the risk of untreatable urges to commit these crimes, a risk illustrated by the high percentage of repeat offenders, is too great to justify their release. At least not until there is a proven "cure," a sure-fire way to *know* that they are treatable, have been treated, and will not continue to make victims of others.

Through the media, I have come to understand that many may be operating on urges not within their control, but this does not justify their release. At some point the blame has to fall on the individual. If they were to learn that their rehabilitation was an impossibility, I think that those who are truly disgusted by their crimes might even agree that they are too dangerous to be returned to a society where they have already done so much damage.

CHAPTER 11

Solving Problems—Writing to Propose Solutions

Critical Thinking Focus: The problem-solving model

Writing Focus: Proposing solutions

Reading Theme: Solving a social problem

Writing Project: Applying the problem-solving model

Writing to Propose Solutions

Problem solving is one of the most powerful thinking patterns we possess, and writing is the main vehicle used to analyze challenging problems and propose solutions. On a personal level, you very likely have had the experience of writing a letter (or e-mail) in regard to a problem you were dealing with. You might have been trying to figure out how to sustain a romantic relationship while geographically separated, helping a friend resolve a personal crisis, or writing to family members to coordinate a holiday reunion. Academically, you probably have engaged in writing assignments in which you were asked to analyze a social problem and propose possible solutions. In the work arena, memos and position papers aimed at solving problems are an integral part of most careers, from finance to filmmaking.

Although writing to propose solutions is a common form of writing, it is a very challenging form to do *well*. In order to compose an insightful and compelling document, you need to take the following steps.

■ *Define the problem clearly.* Your audience needs to understand that there *is* a problem, one important enough for you to invest mental energy in solving.

- *Analyze the problem systematically.*   Complex problems are often a confusing tangle of needs, ideas, frustrations, goals, and pieces of information. You need to *dis*entangle the issues so that your audience can understand what the core of the problem is and what alternatives are possible.

- *Propose a well-reasoned solution.*   After presenting a lucid analysis of the problem, along with feasible alternatives, you need to reach a conclusion that you support with thoughtful reasons and solid evidence. As part of your proposed solution, you should explain why other alternative solutions are less desirable than the one you selected. You should also address anticipated objections to your solution and explain how these difficulties can be overcome.

In order to master this form of problem-solving *writing*, you first need to master this form of *thinking*. To analyze the problem cogently and articulate your analysis clearly, you must apply the critical and creative thinking abilities that you have been developing. Helping you to assimilate this complex form of thinking and writing is the purpose of this chapter.

Thinking Critically About Solving Problems

Throughout your life, you are continually solving problems. As a student, for example, you are faced with a steady stream of academic assignments, quizzes, exams, papers, homework projects, oral presentations. In order to solve these problems effectively—to do well on an exam, for instance—you need to *define* the problem (what areas will the exam cover, and what will be the format?), identify and evaluate various *alternatives* (what are possible study approaches?), and then put all these factors together to reach a *solution* (what will be your study plan and schedule?). Relatively simple problems like preparing for an exam do not require a systematic or complex analysis. You can solve them with just a little effort and concentration. The difficult and complicated problems in your personal life, such as choosing a college major or terminating a relationship, can be a different story. Because these are such crucial situations, you owe it to yourself to solve each such problem in the best possible way, using all your creative and critical thinking skills.

The problems that exist in society also need the very best thinking of all citizens. Violent crime is far too common, parents feel stressed about their children's safety, illegal drugs continue to destroy lives, and both racism and sexism create conflicts. These problems may seem overwhelming, and it is true that you cannot control them in the way you may be able to control your own life situations. Still, by thinking creatively and critically about them, and by gathering information about them, you can at least develop your own positions on what to do about them. Then you will be in a position to act on these problems and to vote for candidates whose positions are similar to yours.

To help you prepare to meet the challenges of solving both personal and societal problems, this chapter will examine a powerful problem-solving approach, first considering it in relation to personal problems and then in relation to the larger problems of society. We will next consider readings on societal problems, and end with an essay-writing assignment, in which the problem-solving model is applied to one such problem.

The Problem-Solving Model in Detail

Consider the following problem:

> My best friend is addicted to drugs, but he won't admit it. Jack always liked to drink, but I never thought too much about it. After all, a lot of people like to drink socially, get relaxed, and have a good time. But over the last few years he's started using other drugs as well as alcohol, and it's ruining his life. He's stopped taking classes at the college and will soon lose his job if he doesn't change. Last week I told him that I was really worried about him, but he told me that he has no drug problem and that in any case it really isn't any of my business. I just don't know what to do. I've known Jack since we were in grammar school together and he's a wonderful person. It's as if he's in the grip of some terrible force and I'm powerless to help him.

In working through this problem, the student who wrote this description could simply think of one possible course of action and try it. But if he or she chooses instead to approach the problem as a critical thinker, the student will have to think carefully and systematically in order to reach a solution.

In order to think effectively in situations like this, we usually ask ourselves a series of questions, although we may not be aware of this mental process. These are the questions you ask yourself in a five-step problem-solving method.

1. What is the *problem?*
2. What are the *alternatives?*
3. What are the *advantages* and/or *disadvantages* of each alternative?
4. What is the *solution?*
5. How well is the solution *working?*

Let's explore these questions further—and the thinking process that they represent—by applying them to the problem just described. Put yourself in the position of the student whose friend seems to have a serious addiction.

What Is the Problem?

There are a variety of ways to define the problem facing this concerned student. For instance, you might define it as simply as "Jack has a drug dependency." You might view the problem as "Jack has a drug dependency *and he won't admit it.*" You might even define the problem as "Jack has a drug dependency and he won't admit it—*and I want to help him solve this problem.*" Notice that each redefinition of the problem results in a more specific definition, which in turn helps us more clearly understand the essence of the problem and our responsibility with respect to it.

What Are the Alternatives?

In dealing with this problem, you have a wide variety of possible actions to consider before selecting the best choices. Identify some of the alternatives you might consider.

1. Speak to your friend in a candid and forceful way to convince him that he has a serious drug dependency.
2.
3.

What Are the Advantages and Disadvantages of Each Alternative?

Evaluate the strengths and weaknesses of each of the alternatives you identified so you can weigh your choices and decide on the best course of action.

1. Speak to your friend in a candid and forceful way to convince him that he has a serious problem.
   Advantage: He may respond to your direct emotional appeal, acknowledge that he has a problem, and seek help.
   Disadvantage: He may react angrily, further alienating you from him and making it more difficult for you to have any influence on him.
2. _____
   Advantage: _____
   Disadvantage: _____
3. _____
   Advantage: _____
   Disadvantage: _____

What Is the Solution?

After evaluating the various alternatives, select what you think is the most effective alternative for solving the problem and describe the sequence of steps you would take to act on the alternative.

Alternative: _____

Steps: _____

1. _____

2. _____

How Well Is the Solution Working?

The final step in the process comes after you have taken the steps to implement the alternative you have chosen. You review the solution and decide whether it is working well. If it is not, you must modify your solution or perhaps choose an alternate solution you disregarded earlier. In this situation, trying to figure out the best way to assist your friend to recognize his dependency and seek treatment leads to a series of decisions. This is what the thinking process is all about—trying to make sense of what is going on in our world and acting appropriately in response. When we solve problems effectively, our thinking process exhibits a coherent organization. It follows the general approach we have just explored.

If we can understand the way our mind operates when we are thinking effectively, we can apply this understanding to improve our thinking in new, challenging situations. In the remainder of this chapter, we will explore a more sophisticated version of this problem-solving approach and apply it to a variety of complex, difficult problems.

THINKING↔WRITING ACTIVITY 11.1

A Problem Solved

1. Describe in specific detail an important problem you have solved recently.
2. Explain how you went about solving the problem. What were the steps, strategies, and approaches you used to understand the problem and make an informed decision?
3. Analyze your thinking process by completing the five-step problem-solving method we have been exploring.
4. Share your problem with other members of the class and have them try to analyze and solve it. Then explain the solution you arrived at.

Solving Complex Problems

Imagine yourself in the following situation. What would your next move be, and what are your reasons for deciding on it?

You are about to begin your second year of college, following a very successful first year. Until now, you have financed your education through a combination of savings, financial aid, and a part-time job (sixteen hours a week) at a local store. However, you just received a letter from your college reducing your financial aid package by half, due to budgetary problems. The letter concludes, "We hope this aid reduction will not prove to be too great an inconvenience." From your perspective, the loss of aid isn't an inconvenience—it's a disaster! Your budget last year was already tight, and with your job, you had barely enough time to study, participate in a few college activities, and have a modest (but essential) social life. To make matters worse, your mother has been ill, reducing her income and creating financial problems at home. You're feeling panicked—what in the world are you going to do?

We noted earlier that when we first approach a difficult problem, it often seems a confused tangle of information, feelings, alternatives, opinions, considerations, and risks. The problem of the college student just described is a complicated situation that does not seem to have a single simple solution. Without the benefit of a systematic approach, our thoughts might wander through the tangle of issues like this:

I want to stay in school . . . but I'm not going to have enough money. . . . I could work more hours at my job . . . but I might not have enough time to study and get top grades . . . and if all I'm doing is working and studying, what about my social life? . . . and what about Mom and the kids—they might need my help. . . . I could drop out of school for a while . . . but if I don't stay in school what kind of future do I have? . . .

Very often when we are faced with difficult problems like this, we simply do not know where to begin in trying to solve them. Every issue is connected to many others. Frustrated by not knowing where to take the first step, we often give up trying to understand the problem. Instead, we may behave in one of the following ways:

1. *Act impulsively* without thought or consideration (e.g., "I'll just quit school").
2. *Do what someone else suggests* without seriously evaluating the suggestion (e.g., "Tell me what I should do—I'm tired of thinking about this").
3. *Do nothing* as we wait for events to make the decision for us (e.g., "I'll just wait and see what happens before doing anything").

None of these approaches is likely to succeed in the long run, and each one can gradually reduce our confidence in dealing with complex problems. An alternative to these reactions is to *think critically* about the problem, analyzing it with an organized approach based on the five-step method we identified above.

PROBLEM-SOLVING METHOD

Step 1: What is the problem?
- a. What do I know about the situation?
- b. What are the results I am aiming for in this situation?
- c. How can I define the problem?

Step 2: What are the alternatives?
- a. What are the boundaries of the problem situation?
- b. What alternatives are possible within these boundaries?

Step 3: What are the advantages and disadvantages of each alternative?
- a. What are the advantages of each alternative?
- b. What are the disadvantages of each alternative?
- c. What additional information do I need in order to evaluate each alternative?

Step 4: What is the solution?
- a. Which alternative(s) will I pursue?
- b. What steps can I take to act on the alternative(s) chosen?

Step 5: How well is my solution working?
- a. What is my evaluation?
- b. What adjustments are necessary?

Although we will be using an organized method for working through difficult problems and arriving at thoughtful conclusions, the fact is that our minds do not always work in such a logical, step-by-step fashion. Effective problem solvers typically pass through all the steps we will be examining, but not always in the sequence we will be describing. Instead, the best problem solvers have an integrated and flexible approach to the process, an approach in which they deploy a repertoire of problem-solving strategies as needed. Sometimes, exploring the various alternatives helps them to go back and redefine the original problem; similarly, seeking to implement the solution can often suggest new alternatives or a new alternative that combines best points of previous alternatives.

The key point is that although the problem-solving steps are presented in a logical sequence here, you are not locked into following these steps in a mechanical and unimaginative fashion. At the same time, in learning a problem-solving method like this, it is generally not wise to skip steps, because each step deals with an important aspect of the problem. As you become more proficient in using the method, you will find that you can apply its concepts and strategies to problem solving in an increasingly flexible and natural fashion, just as learning the basics of an activity like driving a car gradually develops into a more organic and integrated performance of the skills involved. Before applying a method like the one we have just outlined to your problem, however, you need to ready yourself by *accepting* the problem.

Accepting the Problem

To solve a problem, you must first be willing to *accept* the problem by *acknowledging* that it exists and *committing* yourself to trying to solve it. Sometimes you may have difficulty recognizing there *is* a problem, unless it is pointed out to you. At other times you may actively *resist* acknowledging a problem, even when it is pointed out to you. The person who confidently states, "I don't really have any problems," sometimes has very serious problems—but is simply unwilling to acknowledge them.

However, mere acknowledgment is not enough to solve a problem. Once you have identified a problem, you must commit yourself to trying to solve it. Successful problem solvers are highly motivated and willing to persevere through the many challenges and frustrations of the problem-solving process. How do you find the motivation and commitment that prepare you to enter the problem-solving process? There are not simple answers, but a number of strategies may be useful to you:

- *List the benefits.*   Making a detailed list of the benefits you will derive from successfully dealing with the problem is a good place to begin. Such a process helps you clarify why you might want to tackle the problem, motivates you to get started, and serves as a source of encouragement when you encounter difficulties or lose momentum.

- *Formalize your acceptance.*   When we formalize our acceptance of a problem, we are "going on record," either by preparing a signed declaration or by signing a "contract" with someone else. This formal commitment serves as an explicit statement of our original intentions that we can refer to if our resolve weakens.

- *Accept responsibility for your life.*   Robert F. Kennedy, the former U.S. Attorney General who was assassinated in 1968, once said, "Some people see things as they are, and ask, 'Why?' I see things as they could be, and ask, 'Why not?' " All of us have the potential to control the direction of our own individual lives, but to do so we must accept our freedom to choose and the responsibility that goes with it. As we saw in the last chapter, critical thinkers actively work to take charge of their lives rather than letting themselves be passively controlled by external forces.

- *Create a "worst case" scenario.*   Some problems persist because we are able to ignore their possible implications. When we create a worst-case scenario, we remind ourselves, as graphically as possible, of the potentially disastrous consequences of our actions. For example, using vivid color photographs and research conclusions, we can remind ourselves that excessive smoking, drinking, or eating can lead to myriad health problems and social and psychological difficulties as well as an early and untimely demise.

- *Identify the constraints.*   If we are having difficulty accepting a problem, it is usually because something is holding us back. For example, we might be concerned about the amount of time and effort involved; we might be reluctant to confront the underlying issues the problem represents; we might be worried about finding out unpleasant things about ourselves or others; or we might be inhibited by other problems in our lives, such as a tendency to procrastinate. Whatever the constraints, using this strategy involves identifying and describing all the factors that are preventing us from attacking the problem, and then addressing these factors one at a time.

Step 1: What is the Problem?

The first step in solving a problem is to determine exactly what the central issues of the problem are. Otherwise, our chances of solving it are considerably reduced. We may even spend our time trying to solve the wrong problem. For instance, consider the different formulations of the following problems. How might these formulations lead us in different directions in trying to solve it?

> *"School is boring"* vs. *"I feel bored in school."*
> *"I'm a failure"* vs. *"I just failed an exam."*

In each of these cases, a very general conclusion (first formulation) has been replaced by a more specific characterization of the problem (second formulation).

The general conclusions ("I'm a failure") do not suggest productive ways of resolving the difficulties. They are too absolute, too all-encompassing. On the other hand, the more specific descriptions of the problem situation ("I just failed an exam") *do* permit us to attack the problems with useful strategies. In short, the way we define a problem determines not only *how* we will go about solving it, but whether we feel that the problem can be solved at all. Correct identification of a problem is essential if we are going to be able to perform a successful analysis and reach an appropriate conclusion. If we misidentify the problem, we can find ourselves pursuing an unproductive, even destructive, course of action.

Consider the problem of the college student whose financial aid package was cut in half (page 436), and analyze it using our problem-solving method. (*Note:* As you work through this problem-solving approach, apply the steps and strategies to an unsolved problem in your own life. You will have an opportunity to write up your analysis when you complete *Thinking↔Writing Activity 11.2* on page 451.) Recall that in order to complete the first major step of the problem-solving approach, "What is the problem?" it is necessary to address three component questions:

1. What do I know about the situation?
2. What results am I aiming for in this situation?
3. How can I define the problem?

Step 1A: What do I know about the situation?   Solving a problem begins with determining what you *know* to be the case and what you *think* may be the case. To explore the problem successfully, you need to have a clear idea of the details of your beginning circumstances. Sometimes a situation may appear to be a problem when it really isn't, simply because your information isn't accurate. Suppose you are convinced that someone you are attracted to doesn't reciprocate your interest. If this belief is inaccurate, your "problem" doesn't really exist.

You can identify and organize what you know about the problem situation by using *key questions*. In Chapter 1, we examined six types of questions that can be used to explore situations and issues systematically: *fact, interpretation, analysis, synthesis, evaluation, application*. By asking—and trying to answer—questions of fact, you are establishing a sound foundation for exploring your problem. Imagine that you are the student described earlier who is facing a reduction in financial aid. Answer the following questions of fact—who, what, where, when, how, why—about your problem.

1. *Who* are the people involved in this situation?
   Who will benefit from solving this problem?
   Who can help me solve this problem?
2. *What* are the various parts or dimensions of the problem?
   What are my strengths and resources for solving this problem?
   What additional information do I need in order to solve this problem?
3. *Where* can I find people or additional information to help me solve the problem?
4. *When* did the problem begin?
   When should the problem be resolved?
5. *How* did the problem develop or come into being?
6. *Why* is solving this problem important to me?
   Why is this problem difficult to solve?
7. *Additional questions:*

Step 1B: What results am I aiming for in this situation?   The second part of answering the question "What is the problem?" consists of identifying the specific *results* or objectives you are trying to achieve. The results will eliminate the problem if you are able to achieve them. Whereas the first part of Step 1 oriented you in terms of the history of the problem and the current situation, this part encourages you to look to the future. To identify results, you need to ask yourself the question "What are the objectives that, once achieved, will solve this problem?" For instance, one of the results or objectives in the sample problem might be having enough money to pay for college. Describe additional results you might be trying to achieve in this situation.

1. Having enough money to pay for college.
2. _____
3. _____
4. _____

Step 1C: How can I define the problem?   After exploring what you know about the problem and the results you want to achieve, you need to conclude Step 1 by defining the problem as clearly and specifically as possible. Defining the problem is a crucial task in the problem-solving process because this definition will determine the direction of your analysis. To define the problem, you need to identify its central issue(s). Sometimes defining the problem is relatively straightforward, such as "Trying to find enough time to exercise."

Often, however, identifying the central issue of a problem is a much more complex process. For example, the statement "My problem is relating to other people" suggests a complicated situation with many interacting variables that resists simple definition. In fact, you may not begin to develop a clear idea of the problem until you engage in the process of trying to solve it. Or you might begin by believing that your problem is, say, not having the *ability* to succeed, but end by concluding that the problem is really a *fear* of success.

As you will see, the same insights apply to societal problems as well. To take one example, the problem of high school dropouts might initially be defined in terms of problems in the school system, whereas later formulations might identify drug use or social pressure as the core of the problem.

Although there are no simple formulas for defining challenging problems, you can pursue several strategies in identifying the central issue most effectively:

- *View the problem from different perspectives.*   As you saw in Chapter 2, perspective-taking is a key ingredient of thinking critically, and it can help you to zero in on many problems as well. When you describe how various individuals might view a given problem—such as the high school dropout rate—the essential ingredients of the problem being to emerge. In our sample student financial-aid problem, how would you describe the *student's perspective? the college's perspective? the student's mother's perspective?*

- *Identify component problems.*   Larger problems are often composed of component problems. To define the larger problem, it is often necessary to identify and describe the subproblems that make it up. Poor performance at school, for instance, might result from a number of factors like ineffective study habits, inefficient time management, and preoccupation with a personal problem. Defining, and dealing effectively with, the larger problem means defining and dealing with the subproblems first. Can you identify two possible subproblems in the financial-aid problem?

■ *State the problem clearly and specifically.* A third defining strategy is to state the problem as clearly and specifically as possible, on the basis of an examination of the problem's objectives. This sort of clear and specific description of the problem is an important step in solving it. If you state the problem in *very general* terms, you won't have a clear idea of how best to proceed in dealing with it. If you can describe your problem in *specific* terms, your description will begin to suggest actions you can take to solve the problem. Examine the differences between the statements of the following problem:

General: "My problem is money."
More specific: "My problem is budgeting my money so that I won't always run out near the end of the month."
Most specific: "My problem is developing the habit and the discipline to budget my money so that I won't always run out near the end of the month."

Review your analysis of the student's financial-aid problem; then state the problem in writing as clearly and specifically as you can.

Step 2: What Are the Alternatives?

Once you have identified a problem clearly and specifically, your next move is to examine each possible action that might help you to solve it. Before you list the alternatives, however, it makes sense to determine which actions are possible and which are not. You can do this by exploring the *boundaries* of the problem situation.

Step 2A: What are the boundaries of the problem situation? Boundaries are limits that you simply cannot change. They are part of the problem, and they must be accepted and dealt with. For example, in our sample situation, involving loss of financial aid, the fact that a day has only twenty-four hours must be accepted as part of the problem situation. There is no point in developing alternatives that ignore this fact. At the same time, you must be careful not to identify as boundaries circumstances that can be changed. For instance, you might assume that your problem must be solved in your current location, without realizing that relocating to a less expensive college is one of your options. Identify additional boundaries that might be part of this sample situation and some of the questions you would want to answer regarding these boundaries.

Step 2B: What alternatives are possible within these boundaries? After you have established a general idea of the boundaries of the problem situation, you can proceed to identify the possible courses of action that can take place within these boundaries. Of course, identifying all the possible alternatives is not always easy; in fact, it may be part of your problem. Often we do not see a way out of a problem because our thinking is set in certain ruts,

Generating Alternatives: The best approach to solving problems involves generating many different possible alternatives instead of just a few.

fixed in certain perspectives. We are blind to other approaches, either because we reject them before seriously considering them ("That will never work!") or because they simply do not occur to us. You can use several strategies to overcome these obstacles:

■ *Discuss the problem with other people.* Discussing possible alternatives with others uses a number of the aspects of critical thinking you explored in Chapter 2. As you saw then, thinking critically involves being open to seeing situations from different viewpoints and discussing your ideas with others in an organized way. Both of these abilities are important in solving problems. As critical thinkers we live—and solve problems—in a community, not simply by ourselves. Other people can often suggest alternatives we haven't thought of, since these people are outside the situation and thus have a more objective perspective, and since they naturally view the world differently than we do, because of their past experiences and their personalities. In addition, discussions are often creative experiences that generate ideas the participants would not have come up with on their own. The dynamics of these interactions lead to products that are greater than the individual "sum" of those involved.

■ *Brainstorm ideas.* Brainstorming, a method introduced by Alex Osborn, builds on the strengths of working with other people to generate ideas and solve problems. In a typical brainstorming session, a group of people work together to generate as many ideas as possible in a specific period of time. As ideas are produced, they are not judged or evaluated, as this tends to inhibit the free flow of ideas and discourages people from making suggestions. Evaluation is deferred until a later stage. People are encouraged to build on to the ideas of others, since the most creative ideas are often generated through the constructive interplay of various minds.

■ *Change your location.* Your perspectives on a problem are often tied into the circumstances in which the problem exists. For example, a problem you may be having in school is tied into your daily experiences and habitual reactions to these experiences. Sometimes you need a fresh perspective, getting away from the problem situation so that you can view it with more clarity and in a different light. Using these strategies, as well as your own reflections, identify as many alternatives to help solve our sample problem that you can think of.

1. Attend school part-time
2. _____
3. _____
4. _____

Step 3: What Are the Advantages and Disadvantages of Each Alternative?

Once you have identified the various alternatives, your next step is to *evaluate* them. Each possible course of action has certain advantages in the sense that if you select that alternative, there will be some positive results. At the same time, each of the possible courses of action probably has disadvantages as well, in the sense that if you select that alternative, there may be a cost involved or a risk of some negative results. Determine how helpful each course of action would or would not be in solving the problem.

Step 3A: What are the advantages of each alternative? The alternative we listed in Step 2 for the sample problem ("Attend college part-time") might include the following advantages.

ALTERNATIVES	ADVANTAGES
1. Attend college part-time	This would remove some of the immediate time and money pressures I am experiencing while still allowing me to prepare for the future. I would have more time to focus on the courses that I am taking and to work additional hours.

Identify the advantages of each of the alternatives that you listed in Step 2. Be sure that your responses are thoughtful and specific. For example, how many additional hours could your work? How much additional income would that generate?

Step 3B: What are the disadvantages of each alternative?   The alternative we listed in Step 2 for the sample problem might include the following disadvantages.

ALTERNATIVES	DISADVANTAGES
1. Attend college part-time	It would take me much longer to complete my schooling, thus delaying my progress toward my goals. Also, I might lose motivation and drop out before completing school because the process would be taking so long. Being a part-time student might threaten my eligibility for financial aid.

Now identify the disadvantages of each of the alternatives that you listed for Step 2. Make sure that your responses are thoughtful and specific. For example, how much longer would it take to get your degree?

Step 3C: What additional information do I need to evaluate each alternative?   The next part of Step 3 consists in determining what you must know (*information needed*) to best evaluate and compare the alternatives. For each alternative there are questions that must be answered if you are to establish which alternatives make sense and which do not. In addition, you need to figure out where best to get this information (*sources*).

One useful way to identify the information you need is to ask the question *"What if* I select this alternative?" For instance, one alternative in our sample problem was to "attend college part-time." When you ask yourself *"What if* I attend college part-time?" you are trying to predict what will occur if you select this course of action. To make these predictions, you must answer certain questions and find the information to answer them.

■   How long will it take me to complete my schooling?

■   How long can I continue in school without losing interest and dropping out?

■   Will I threaten my eligibility for financial aid if I become a part-time student?

The information—and the sources of it—that must be located for the first alternative in our sample problem might include the following.

ALTERNATIVE	INFORMATION NEEDED AND SOURCES
1. Attend college part-time	*Information:* How long will it take me to complete my schooling? How long can

I continue in school without losing interest and dropping out? Will I threaten
my eligibility for financial aid if I become a part-time student?
Sources: Myself, other part-time students,
school counselors, financial aid office.

Identify the information needed and the sources of this information for each
of the alternatives that you identified on page 445. Be sure that your responses are thoughtful and specific.

Step 4: What Is the Solution?

The purpose of Steps 1 to 3 is to analyze your problem in a systematic and detailed fashion—to work through the problem in order to become thoroughly
familiar with it and the possible solutions to it. After breaking down the problem in this way, your final step should be to try to put the pieces back together—that is, to decide on a thoughtful course of action based on your
increased understanding. Even though this sort of problem analysis does not
guarantee finding a specific solution to the problem, it should *deepen your understanding* of exactly what the problem is about. And in locating and evaluating the alternatives, it should give you some very good ideas about the general
direction you should move in and the immediate steps you should take.

Step 4A: What alternative(s) will I pursue?   There is no simple formula or
recipe to tell you which alternatives to select. As you work through the different
courses of action that are possible, you may find that you can immediately rule
some out. In the sample problem, for example, you may know with certainty
that you do not want to attend college part-time (alternative 1) because you will
forfeit your remaining financial aid. However, if may not be so simple to select
which of the other alternatives you wish to pursue. How do you decide?

The decisions we make usually depend on what we believe to be most
important to us. These beliefs regarding what is most important to us are
known as *values*. Our values are the starting points of our actions and
strongly influence our decisions. For example, if we value staying alive (as
most of us do), we will make many decisions each day that express this
value—eating proper meals, not walking in front of moving traffic, and so on.

Our values help us *set priorities* in life—that is, decide what aspects of our
lives are most important to us. We might decide that for the present, going to
school is more important than having an active social life. In this case, going to
school has higher priority than having an active social life. Unfortunately, our
values are not always consistent with each other—we may have to choose *either* to go to school *or* to have an active social life. Both activities may be important to us; they are simply not compatible with each other. Very often the
conflicts between our values constitute the problem. Let's examine some strategies for selecting alternatives that might help to solve the sample problem.

- *Evaluate and compare alternatives.*   Although each alternative may have certain advantages and disadvantages, not all advantages are equally desirable or potentially effective. For example, giving up on college entirely would certainly solve some aspects of the sample problem, but its obvious disadvantages would rule out this solution for most people. Thus, it makes sense to try to evaluate and rank the various alternatives on the basis of how effective they are likely to be and how they match up with your value system. A good place to begin is at the "Results" stage, Step 1B. Examine each of the alternatives and evaluate how well it will contribute to achieving the results you are aiming for in the situation. You may want to rank the alternatives or develop your own rating system to assess their relative effectiveness.

  After evaluating the alternatives in terms of their anticipated *effectiveness*, the next step is to evaluate them in terms of their *desirability*, relative to your needs, interests, and value systems. Again, you can use either a ranking or a rating system to assess their relative desirability. After completing these two separate evaluations, you can select whatever alternatives seem most appropriate. Review the alternatives you identified in the sample problem; then rank or rate them according to their potential effectiveness and desirability, assuming that this problem is your own.

- *Synthesize a new alternative.*   After reviewing and evaluating the alternatives you generated, you may develop a new alternative that combines the best qualities of several options while avoiding the disadvantages some of them have if chosen exclusively. In the sample problem, you might combine attending college part-time during the academic year with attending school during the summer session, so that progress toward your degree won't be impeded. Examine the alternatives you identified and develop a new option that combines the best elements of several of them.

- *Try out each alternative—in your imagination.*   Focus on each alternative and try to imagine, as concretely as possible, what it would be like if you actually selected it. Visualize what impact your choice would have on your problem and what the implications would be for your life as a whole. By trying out the alternative in your imagination, you can sometimes avoid unpleasant results or unexpected consequences. As a variation of this strategy, you can sometimes test alternatives on a very limited basis in a practice situation. Suppose you are trying to overcome your fear of speaking out in groups; you can practice various speaking techniques with your friends or family until you find an approach that works for you.

After trying out these strategies on the sample problem, select the alternative(s) you think would be most effective and desirable from your standpoint.

Step 4B: What steps can I take to act on the alternative(s) chosen?   Once you have decided on an alternative to pursue, your next move is to plan what steps to take in acting on it. Planning the specific steps you will take is extremely important. Although thinking carefully about your problem is necessary, it is not enough if you hope to solve the problem. You have to *take action*. In the same problem, for example, imagine that one of the alternatives you have selected is "Find additional sources of income that will enable me to work part-time, go to school full-time." The specific steps you would want to take might include these:

1. Contact the financial aid office at the college to learn what other forms of financial aid are available and how to apply for them.
2. Contact some of the local banks to find out what sort of student loans are available.
3. Look for a higher-paying job so that I can earn more money without working additional hours.
4. Discuss the problem with students in similar circumstances in order to generate new ideas.

Identify the steps you would have to take in pursuing the alternative(s) you identified on page 443.

Plans, of course, do not implement themselves. Once you know what actions you have to take, you need to make a commitment to taking the necessary steps. This is where many people stumble in the problem-solving process; they remain paralyzed by inertia or fear. Sometimes, to overcome such blocks and inhibitions, you need to re-examine your original acceptance of the problem, perhaps making use of some of the strategies you explored on pages 437–438. Once you get started, the rewards of actively attacking your problem are often enough incentive to keep you focused and motivated.

Step 5: How Well Is the Solution Working?

As you work toward reaching a reasonable and informed conclusion, be wary of falling into the trap of thinking there is only one "right" decision and if you do not figure out what it is and carry it out, all is lost. You should remind yourself that any analysis of problem situations, no matter how careful and systematic, is ultimately limited. You simply cannot anticipate or predict everything that is going to happen in the future. As a result, every decision you make is provisional, in the sense that your ongoing experience will inform you if your decisions are working out or if they need to be modified. As you saw in Chapter 2, this is precisely the attitude of the critical thinker— someone who is *receptive* to new ideas and experiences and flexible enough to change or modify beliefs on the basis of new information. Critical thinking is not a compulsion to find the "right" answer or make the "correct" decision; it is a continuing process of exploration and discovery.

Step 5A: What is my evaluation?   In many cases the relative effectiveness of your efforts will be apparent. In other cases you will find it helpful to pursue a more systematic evaluation, along the lines suggested in the following strategies.

■ *Compare the results with the goals.*   The essence of evaluation is comparing the results of your efforts with the initial goals you are trying to achieve. For example, the goals of your sample problem are embodied in the results you specified on page 439. Compare the anticipated results of the alternative(s) you selected. To what extent will your choice meet these goals? Are any goals not likely to be met by your alternative(s)? If so, which ones? Could they be addressed by other alternatives? Asking these questions and others will help you to clarify the success of your efforts and will provide a foundation for future decisions.

■ *Get other perspectives.*   As you have seen throughout the problem-solving process, getting the opinions of others is a productive strategy at virtually every stage, and this is certainly true for evaluation. Other people often can provide perspectives that are both different and more objective than ours. Naturally, the evaluations of others are not always better or more accurate than your own, but even when they are not, reflecting on these different views usually deepens your understanding of the situation. It is not always easy to receive the evaluations of others, but open-mindedness to outside opinions is a very valuable attitude to cultivate, for it will stimulate and guide you to produce your best efforts.

   To receive specific, practical feedback, you need to ask specific, practical questions that will elicit such information. General questions ("What do you think of this?") typically result in overly general, unhelpful responses ("It sounds okay to me"). Be focused in soliciting feedback and remember that you do have the right to ask people to be *constructive* in their comments; that is, to provide suggestions for improvement rather than just say what they think is wrong. For example, you can say, "What do you know about me that you think will help me maintain my motivation to stay in school—even if it takes two years longer than I planned?" Or you can ask, "Do you have any ideas about how I can cut my expenses by 10 percent each month?"

Step 5B: What adjustments are necessary?   As a result of your review, you may discover that the alternative you selected is not feasible or is not leading to satisfactory results. Suppose that in the sample problem, you cannot find additional sources of income that will allow you to work part-time instead of full-time. In that case, you simply have to go back and review the other alternatives to identify another possible course of action. At other times, you may find that the alternative you selected is succeeding fairly well but requires some adjustments as you continue to work toward your desired outcomes. In fact, this is a typical situation that you should expect to occur. Even when things initially appear to be working reasonably well, an active thinker continues to ask questions such as "What might I have overlooked?" and "How could I have done this differently?" Of course, asking—and trying to answer—questions like this is even more essential if solutions are hard to come by (as they usually are in real-world problems) and if you are to retain the flexibility and optimism you need to tackle a new option.

THINKING ↔ WRITING ACTIVITY 11.2

Analyzing A Problem in Your Life

As you worked your way through this section, it was suggested that you apply the problem-solving method to an important *unsolved* problem in your own life. If you have not done so, this Thinking↔Writing Activity provides you with the opportunity to do it now. Select from your own life a problem that you are currently grappling with and have not been able to solve. After selecting one, strengthen your acceptance of the problem by using one or more of the strategies described on page 439 and describing your efforts. Discuss your problem with other class members to generate fresh perspectives and unusual alternatives that might not have occurred to you.

In your journal, write each of the questions that make up the problem-solving method: then write specific responses to the questions. Although you may not reach a "guaranteed" solution to your problem, you will deepen your understanding of the problem and develop a concrete plan of action that will help you move in the right direction. Implement your plan of action and monitor the results.

Described below are common problems other students have described. Your instructor may have you work in a group with other class members to analyze one of these problems as a way of preparing you to analyze one of your own.

Problem 1: My Major
The most important unsolved problem that exists for me is the inability to make that crucial decision of what to major in. I want to be secure with respect to both money and happiness when I make a career for myself, and I don't want to make a mistake in choosing a field of study. I want to make this decision before beginning the next semester so that I can start immediately in my career. I've been thinking about managerial studies. However, I often wonder if I have the capacity to make executive decisions when I can't even decide on what I want to do with my life.

Problem 2: Taking Tests

One of my problems is my difficulty in taking tests. It's not that I don't study. What happens is that when I get the test I become nervous and my mind goes blank. For example, in my social science class, the teacher told the class on Tuesday that there would be a test on Thursday. That afternoon I went home and began studying for the test. By Thursday I knew most of the work, but when the test was handed out, I got nervous and my mind went blank. For a long time I just stared at the test, and I ended up failing it.

Problem 3: Smoking

My problem is "the weed." I have been smoking cigarettes for over five years. At first I did it because I liked the image and most of my friends were smoking as well. Gradually, I got hooked. It's such a part of my life now, I don't know if I can quit. Having a cup of coffee, studying, talking to people—it just seems natural to have a cigarette in my hand. I know there are a lot of good reasons for me to stop. I've even tried a few times, but I always ended up bumming cigarettes from friends and then giving up entirely. I don't want my health to go up in smoke, but I don't know what to do.

Problem 4: Learning English

One of the serious problems in my life is learning English as a second language. It is not so easy to learn a second language, especially when you live in an environment where only your native language is spoken. When I came to this country three years ago, I could speak almost no English. I have learned a lot, but my lack of fluency is getting in the way of my studies and my social relationships.

Problem 5: Drinking

This is my first year of college. One disturbing thing I have encountered is the amount of drinking that students engage in when they socialize. Although I enjoy drinking in moderation, most students drink much more than "in moderation" at parties. They want to "get drunk," "lose control," "get wasted." And the parties aren't just on weekends—they're every night of the week! The problem is that there is a lot of pressure for me to join in the drinking and partying. Most of the people you enjoy being with are joining in, and I don't want to be left out of the social life of the college. But it's impossible to party so much and still keep up to date with my course work. And all that drinking certainly isn't good for me physically. But on the other hand, I don't want to be excluded from the social life, and when I try to explain that I don't enjoy heavy drinking, my friends make me feel immature and a little silly. What should I do?

Solving Social Problems

The problems we have analyzed up until this point are "personal" problems in the sense that they represent individual challenges we encounter as we live our lives. Problems are not only of a personal nature, however. We also face problems as members of a community, society, and the world. As with personal problems, we need to approach these kinds of problems in an organized and thoughtful way in order to explore the issues, develop a clear understanding, and decide on an informed plan of action. For example, racism and prejudice directed toward African Americans, Hispanics, Asians, Jews, homosexuals, and other minority groups seems to be on the rise at many college campuses. There has been an increase of overt racist incidents at colleges and universities during the past several years, which is particularly disturbing given the lofty egalitarian ideals of higher education. Experts from different fields have offered a variety of explanations to account for this behavior. Consider why you believe these racial and ethnic incidents are occurring with increasing frequency.

Making sense of a complex, challenging situation like this is not a simple process. Although the problem-solving method we have been using in this chapter is a powerful approach, its successful application depends on having sufficient information about the situation we are trying to solve. Therefore it is often necessary for us to research articles and other sources of information to develop informed opinions about the problem we are investigating.

The famous newspaperman H. L. Mencken once said, "To every complex question there is a simple answer—and it's wrong!" We have seen in this chapter that complex problems do not have simple solutions, whether or not they are personal problems or larger social problems like racial prejudice or world hunger. We have also seen that by working through these complex problems thoughtfully and systematically, we can achieve a deeper understanding of their many interacting elements, as well as develop and implement strategies for solving them.

Becoming an effective problem solver does not mean merely applying a problem-solving method in a mechanical fashion, any more than becoming a mature critical thinker involves mastering a set of thinking skills. Rather, solving problems, like thinking critically, reflects a total approach to making sense of experience. When we think like problem solvers, we approach the world in a distinctive way. Instead of avoiding difficult problems, we have the courage to meet them head-on and the determination to work them through. Instead of acting impulsively or relying exclusively on the advice of others, we are able to make sense of complex problems in an organized way and develop practical solutions and initiatives.

A sophisticated problem solver employs all the critical thinking abilities we have examined in this book. And while we might agree with Mencken's evaluation of simple answers to complex questions, we might endorse a rephrased version: "To many complex questions there are complex answers—and these are well worth pursuing."

Thinking Passages

The next section of this chapter presents two articles dealing with significant social problems. The first, "Young Hate," by David Shenk, examines the problem of intolerance on college campuses. The information provides a foundation for thoughtful analysis of this troubling problem and perhaps for productive solutions. The second article, "When Is It Rape?", by Nancy Gibbs, addresses another current and complicated problem on college campuses.

THINKING ↔ WRITING ACTIVITY 11.3

Analyzing a Social Problem

Work with one of the articles—either the one that interests you more or the one you are assigned. After reading the article carefully, identify and analyze the problem being discussed, using the problem-solving method developed in this chapter. Write answers to the questions on pages 437–438.

from Young Hate
by David Shenk

Death to gays. Here is the relevant sequence of events: On Monday night Jerry Mattioli leads a candlelight vigil for lesbian and gay rights. *Gays are trash.* On Tuesday his name is in the school paper and he can hear whispers and feel more, colder stares than usual. On Wednesday morning a walking bridge in the middle of the Michigan State campus is found to be covered with violent epithets warning campus homosexuals to *be afraid, very afraid,* promising to *abolish faggots from existence,* and including messages specifically directed at Mattioli. Beginning Friday morning fifteen of the perpetrators, all known to Mattioli by name and face, are rounded up and quietly disciplined by the university. *Go home faggots.* On Friday afternoon Mattioli is asked by university officials to leave campus for the weekend, for his own safety. He does, and a few hours later receives a phone call from a friend who tells him that his dormitory room has been torched. MSU's second annual "Cross-Cultural Week" is over.

"Everything was ruined," Mattioli says. "What wasn't burned was ruined by smoke and heat and by the water. On Saturday I sat with the fire investigator all day, and we went through the room, literally ash by ash. . . . The answering machine had melted. The receiver of the telephone on the wall had stretched to about three feet long. That's how intense the heat was."

"Good news!" says Peter Jennings. A recent *Washington Post*/ABC News poll shows that integration is up and racial tension is down in America, as compared with eight years ago. Of course, in any trend there are fluctuations, exceptions. At the University of Massachusetts at Amherst, an estimated two thousand whites chase twenty blacks in a clash after a 1986 World Series game, race riots break out in Miami in 1988 and in Virginia Beach in 1989; and on college campuses across the country, our nation's young elite experience an entire decade's aberration from the poll's findings: incidents of ethnic, religious, and gender-related harassment surge throughout the eighties.

Greatest hits include Randy Bowman, a black student at the University of Texas, having to respectfully decline a request by two young men wearing Ronald Reagan masks and wielding a pistol to exit his eighth-floor dorm room through the window; homemade T-shirts, *Thank God for AIDS* and *Aryan by the Grace of God*, among others, worn proudly on campus; Jewish student centers shot at, stoned, and defaced at Memphis State, University of Kansas, Rutgers (*Six million, why not*), and elsewhere; the black chairperson of United Minorities Council at U Penn getting a dose of hi-tech hate via answering machine: *We're going to lynch you, nigger shit. We are going to lynch you.*

5   The big picture is less graphic, but just as dreadful: reports of campus harassment have increased as much as 400 percent since 1985. Dropout rates for black students in predominantly white colleges are as much as five times higher than white dropout rates at the same schools and black dropout rates at black schools. The Anti-Defamation League reports a sixfold increase in anti-Semitic episodes on campuses between 1985 and 1988. Meanwhile, Howard J. Ehrlich of the National Institute Against Prejudice and Violence reminds us that "up to 80 percent of harassed students don't report the harassment." Clearly, the barrage of news reports reveals only the tip of a thoroughly sour iceberg.

Colleges have responded to incidents of intolerance—and the subsequent demands of minority rights groups—with the mandatory ethnic culture classes and restrictions on verbal harassment. But what price tranquility? Libertarian and conservative student groups, faculty, and political advisors lash out over limitations on free speech and the improper embrace of liberal political agendas. "Progressive academic administrations," writes University of Pennsylvania professor Alan Charles Kors in the *Wall Street Journal*, "are determined to enlighten their morally benighted students and protect the community from political sin."

Kors and kind bristle at the language of compromise being attached to official university policy. The preamble to the University of Michigan's new policy on discriminatory behavior reads, in part, "Because there is tension between freedom of speech, the right of individuals to be free from injury caused by discrimination, and the University's duty to protect the educational process . . . it may be necessary to have varying standards depending on the locus of regulated conduct." The policy tried to "strike a balance" by applying different sets of restrictions to academic centers, open areas, and living quarters, but in so doing, hit a wall. Before the policy could go into effect, it was struck down in a Michigan court as being too vague. At least a dozen schools in the process of formulating their own policies scurried in retreat as buoyant free-speech advocates went on the offensive. Tufts University president Jean Mayer voluntarily dismissed his school's "Freedom of Speech versus Freedom from Harassment" policy after a particularly inventive demonstration by late-night protesters who used chalk, tape, and poster board to divide the campus into designated free speech, limited speech, and non-free speech zones. "We're not working for a right to offensive speech," says admitted chalker Andrew Zappia, co-editor of the conservative campus paper, *The Primary Source*. "This is about protecting free speech, in general, and allowing the community to set its own standards about what is appropriate. . . .

"The purpose of the Tufts policy was to prosecute people for what the university described as 'gray area'—meaning unintentional—harassment." Zappia gives a hypothetical example: "I'm a Catholic living in a dorm, and I put up a poster in my room [consistent with my faith] saying that homosexuality is bad. If I have a gay roommate or one who doesn't agree with me, he could have me prosecuted, not because I hung it there to offend him, but because it's gray area harassment. . . . The policy was well intended, but it was dangerously vague. They used words like *stigmatizing, offensive, harassing*—words that are very difficult to define."

Detroit lawyer Walter B. Connolly, Jr., disagrees. He insists that it's quite proper for schools to act to protect the victims of discrimination as long as the restrictions stay out of the classroom. "Defamation, child pornography, fighting words, inappropriate comments on the radio—there are all sorts of areas where the First Amendment isn't the preeminent burning omnipotence in the sky. . . . Whenever you have competing interests of a federal statute [and] the Constitution, you end up balancing."

10   If you want to see a liberal who follows this issue flinch, whisper into his or her ear the name Shelby Steele. Liberals don't like Steele, an (African American) English professor at California's San Jose State; they try to dismiss him as having no professional experience in the study of racial discrimination. But he's heavily into the subject, and his analyses are both lucid and disturbing. Steele doesn't favor restrictions on speech, largely because they don't deal with what he sees as the problem. "You don't gain very much by trying to legislate the problem away, curtailing everyone's rights in the process," he says. In a forum in which almost everyone roars against a shadowy, usually nameless contingent

of racist thugs, Steele deviates, choosing instead to accuse the accusers. He blames not the racists, but the weak-kneed liberal administrators and power-hungry victims' advocates for the mess on campuses today.

"Racial tension on campus is the result more of racial equality than inequality," says Steele. "On campuses today, as throughout society, blacks enjoy equality under the law—a profound social advancement. . . . What has emerged in recent years . . . in a sense as a result of progress . . . is *a politics of difference,* a troubling, volatile politics in which each group justifies itself, its sense of worth and its pursuit of power, through difference alone." On nearly every campus, says Steele, groups representing blacks, Hispanics, Asians, gays, women, Jews, and any combinations therein solicit special resources. Asked for—often demanded, in intense demonstrations—are funds for African-American (Hispanic . . .) cultural centers, separate (face it, segregated) housing, ethnic studies programs, and even individual academic incentives—at Penn State, minority students are given $275 per semester if they earn a C average, twice that if they do better than 2.75.

These entitlements, however, do not just appear *deus ex machina.* Part two of Steele's thesis addresses what he calls the "capitulation" of campus presidents. To avoid feelings of guilt stemming from past discrimination against minority groups, Steele says, "[campus administrators have] tended to go along with whatever blacks put on the table, rather than work with them to assess their real needs. . . . Administrators would never give white students a theme house where they could be 'more comfortable with people of their own kind,' yet more and more universities are doing this for black students." Steele sees white frustration as the inevitable result.

"White students are not invited to the negotiating table from which they see blacks and others walk away with concessions," he says. "The presumption is that they do not deserve to be there, because they are white. So they can only be defensive, and the less mature among them will be aggressive."

Course, some folks see it another way. The students fighting for minority rights aren't wicked political corrupters, but champions of a cause far too long suppressed by the white male hegemony. Responsive administrators are engaged not in capitulation, but in progress. And one shouldn't look for the cause of this mess on any campus, because he doesn't live on one. His address used to be the White House, but then he moved to 666 St. Cloud Road. Ronald Reagan, come on down.

15   *Dr. Manning Marble, University of Colorado:* "The shattering assault against the economic, social, and political status of the black American community as a whole [is symbolized by] the Reagan Administration in the 1980s. The Civil Rights Commission was gutted; affirmative action became a 'dead letter'; social welfare, health care, employment training, and educational loans were all severely reduced. This had a disproportionately more negative impact upon black youth."

The "perception is already widespread that the society at large is more permissive toward discriminatory attitudes and behaviors, and less committed to equal opportunity and affirmative action," concluded a 1988 conference at Northern Illinois University. John Wiener, writing in *The Nation,* attacks long-standing institutions of bigotry, asserting, for example, that "racism is endemic to the fraternity subculture," and praises the efforts of some schools to double the number of minority faculty and increase minority fellowships. On behalf of progressives across the land, Wiener writes off Shelby Steele as someone who is content to "blame the victim."

So the machine has melted, the phone has stretched to where it is useless. This is how intense the heat is. Liberals, who largely control the administration, faculty, and students' rights groups of leading academic institutions, have, with virtually no intensive intellectual debate, inculcated schools with their answers to the problem of bigotry. Conservatives, with a long history of insensitivity to minority concerns, have been all but shut out of the debate, and now want back in. Their intensive pursuit of the true nature of bigotry and the proper response to it—working to assess the "real needs" of campuses rather than simply bowing to pressure—deserves to be embraced by all concerned parties, and probably would have been by now but for two small items: (a) Reagan, their fearless leader, clearly *was* insensitive to ethnic/feminist concerns (even Steele agrees with this); and (b) some of the more coherent conservative pundits *still* show a blatant apathy to the problems of bigotry in this country. This has been sufficient ammunition for liberals who are continually looking for an excuse to keep conservatives out of the dialogue. So now we have clashes rather than debates: on how much one can say, on how much one should have to hear. Two negatives: one side wants to crack down on expression, the other on awareness. The machine has melted, and it's going to take some consensus to build a new one. Intellectual provincialism will have to end before young hate ever will.

A Month in the Life of Campus Bigotry

April 1.
Vandals spray-paint "Jewhaters will pay" and other slogans on the office walls of *The Michigan Daily* (University of Michigan) in response to editorials condemning Israel for policies regarding the Palestinians. Pro-Israeli and pro-Palestinian shanties defaced; one is burned.

U of M: Fliers circulated over the weekend announce "White Pride Month."

20   Southern Connecticut State University reportedly suspends five fraternity officers after racial brawl.

April 2.
Several gay men of the University of Connecticut are taunted by two students, who yell "faggot" at them.

April 3.
The University of Michigan faculty meet to discuss a proposal to require students to take a course on ethnicity and racism.

April 4.
Students at the University of California at Santa Barbara suspend hunger strike after university agrees to negotiate on demands for minority faculty hiring and the changed status of certain required courses.

April 5.
The NCAA releases results of survey on black student athletes, reporting that 51 percent of black football and basketball players at predominantly white schools express feelings of being different; 51 percent report feelings of racial isolation; 33 percent report having experienced at least six incidents of individual racial discrimination.

25   The *New York Times* prints three op-ed pieces by students on the subject of racial tension on campus.

Charges filed against a former student of Penn State for racial harassment of a black woman.

April 6.
University of Michigan: Hundreds of law students wear arm bands, boycott classes to protest lack of women and minority professors.

Michigan State University announces broad plan for increasing the number of minority students, faculty, and staff; the appointment of a senior advisor for minority affairs; and the expansion of multicultural conferences. "It's not our responsibility just to mirror society or respond to mandates," President John DiBioggio tells reporters, "but to set the tone."

April 7.
Wayne State University (Detroit, Michigan) student newspaper runs retraction of cartoon considered offensive following protest earlier in the week.

30   Controversy develops at the State University of New York at Stony Brook, where a white woman charges a popular black basketball player with rape. Player denies charges. Charges are dismissed. Protests of racial and sexual assault commence.

April 12.
Twelve-day sit-in begins at Wayne State University (Michigan) over conditions for black students on campus.

April 14.
Racial brawl at Arizona State.

April 20.
Demonstrations at several universities across the country (Harvard, Duke, Wayne State, Wooster College, Penn State, etc.) for improvements in black student life.

    Separate escort service for blacks started at Penn State out of distrust of the regular service.

April 21.
35   200-student sit-in ends at Arizona State University when administrators agree to all thirteen demands.

April 24.
Proposed tuition increase at City Universities of New York turns into racial controversy.

April 25.
After eighteen months in office, Robert Collin, Florida Atlantic University's first black dean, reveals he has filed a federal discrimination complaint against the school.

    Two leaders of Columbia University's Gay and Lesbian Alliance receive death threat. "Dear Jeff, I will kill you butt fucking faggots. Death to COLA!"

April 26.
A black Smith College (Massachusetts) student finds note slipped under door, ". . . African monkey do you want some bananas? Go back to the jungle. . . ."

40   "I don't think we should have to constantly relive our ancestors' mistakes," a white student at the University of North Carolina at Greensboro tells a reporter. "I didn't oppress anybody. Blacks are now equal. You don't see any racial problems anymore."

    White Student Union is reported to have been formed at Temple University in Philadelphia, "City of Brotherly Love."

April 28.
Note found in Brown University (Rhode Island) dorm. "Once upon a time, Brown was a place where a white man could go to class without having to look at little black faces, or little yellow faces or little brown faces, except when he went to take his meals. Things have been going downhill since the kitchen help moved into the classroom. Keep white supremecy [sic] alive!!! Join the Brown chapter of the KKK today." Note is part of series that began in the middle of the month with "Die Homos." University officials beef up security, hold forum.

April 29.
Controversy reported over proposed ban on verbal harassment at Arizona State.

April 30.
Anti-apartheid shanty at University of Maryland, Baltimore County, is defaced. Signs read "Apartheid now," and "Trump Plaza."

45   University of California at Berkeley: Resolution is passed requiring an ethnic studies course for all students.

University of Connecticut: Code is revised to provide specific penalties for acts of racial intolerance.

from When Is It Rape?

by Nancy Gibbs

Be careful of strangers and hurry home, says a mother to her daughter, knowing that the world is a frightful place but not wishing to swaddle a child in fear. Girls grow up scarred by caution and enter adulthood eager to shake free of their parents' worst nightmares. They still know to be wary of strangers. What they don't know is whether they have more to fear from their friends.

Most women who get raped are raped by people they already know—like the boy in biology class, or the guy in the office down the hall, or their friend's brother. The familiarity is enough to make them let down their guard, sometimes even enough to make them wonder afterward whether they were "really raped." What people think of as "real rape"—the assault by a monstrous stranger in the shadows—accounts for only one out of five attacks.

So the phrase "acquaintance rape" was coined to describe the rest, all the cases of forced sex between people who already knew each other, however casually. But that was too clinical for headline writers, and so the popular term is the narrower "date rape," which suggests an ugly ending to a raucous night on the town.

These are not idle distinctions. Behind the search for labels is the central mythology about rape; that rapists are always strangers, and victims are women who ask for it. The mythology is hard to dispel because the crime is so rarely exposed. The experts guess—that's all they can do under the circumstances—that while one in four women will be raped in her lifetime, less than 10 percent will report the assault, and less than 5 percent of the rapists will go to jail.

5   Women charge that date rape is the hidden crime; men complain it is hard to prevent a crime they can't define. Women say it isn't taken seriously; men say it is a concept invented by women who like to tease but not take the consequences. Women say the date-rape debate is the first time the nation has talked frankly about sex; men say it is women's un-

conscious reaction to the excesses of the sexual revolution. Meanwhile, men and women argue among themselves about the "gray area" that surrounds the whole murky arena of sexual relations, and there is no consensus in sight.

In court, on campus, in conversation, the issue turns on the elasticity of the word *rape,* one of the few words in the language with the power to summon a shared image of a horrible crime.

At one extreme are those who argue that for the word to retain its impact, it must be strictly defined as forced sexual intercourse: a gang of thugs jumping a jogger in Central Park, a psychopath preying on old women in a housing complex, a man with an ice pick in a side street. To stretch the definition of the word risks stripping away its power. In this view, if it happened on a date, it wasn't rape. A romantic encounter is a context in which sex *could* occur, and so what omniscient judge will decide whether there was genuine mutual consent?

Others are willing to concede that date rape sometimes occurs, that sometimes a man goes too far on a date without a woman's consent. But this infraction, they say, is not as ghastly a crime as street rape, and it should not be taken as seriously. The New York *Post,* alarmed by the Willy Smith case, wrote in a recent editorial, "if the sexual encounter, *forced or not,* has been preceded by a series of consensual activities— drinking, a trip to the man's home, a walk on a deserted beach at three in the morning—the charge that's leveled against the alleged offender should, it seems to us, be different than the one filed against, say, the youths who raped and beat the jogger."

This attitude sparks rage among women who carry scars received at the hands of men they knew. It makes no difference if the victim shared a drink or a moonlit walk or even a passionate kiss, they protest, if the encounter ended with her being thrown to the ground and forcibly violated. Date rape is not about a misunderstanding, they say. It is not a communications problem. It is not about a woman's having regrets in the morning for a decision she made the night before. It is not about a "decision" at all. Rape is rape, and any form of forced sex—even between neighbors, coworkers, classmates and casual friends—is a crime.

10   A more extreme form of that view comes from activists who see rape as a metaphor, its definition swelling to cover any kind of oppression of women. Rape, seen in this light, can occur not only on a date but also in a marriage, not only by violent assault but also by psychological pressure. A Swarthmore College training pamphlet once explained that acquaintance rape "spans a spectrum of incidents and behaviors, ranging from crimes legally defined as rape to verbal harassment and inappropriate innuendo." No wonder, then, that the battles become so heated. When innuendo qualifies as rape, the definitions have become so slippery that the entire subject sinks into a political swamp. The only way to capture the hard reality is to tell the story.

A 32-year-old woman was on business in Tampa last year for the Florida supreme court. Stranded at the courthouse, she accepted a lift from a lawyer involved in her project. As they chatted on the ride home, she recalls, "he was saying all the right things, so I started to trust him." She agreed to have dinner, and afterward, at her hotel door, he convinced her to let him come in to talk. "I went through the whole thing about being old-fashioned," she says. "I was a virgin until I was twenty-one. So I told him talk was all we were going to do."

But as they sat on the couch, she found herself falling asleep. "By now, I'm comfortable with him, and I put my head on his shoulder. He's not tried anything all evening, after all." Which is when the rape came. "I woke up to find him on top of me, forcing himself on me. I didn't scream or run. All I could think about was my business contacts and what if they saw me run out of my room screaming rape."

"I thought it was my fault. I felt so filthy, I washed myself over and over in hot water. Did he rape me? I kept asking myself. I didn't consent. But who's gonna believe me? I had a man in my hotel room after midnight." More than a year later, she still can't tell the story without a visible struggle to maintain her composure. Police referred the case to the state attorney's office in Tampa, but without more evidence it decided not to prosecute. Although her attacker has admitted that he heard her say no, maintains the woman, "he says he didn't know that I meant no. He didn't feel he'd raped me, and he wanted to see me again."

Her story is typical in many ways. The victim herself may not be sure right away that she has been raped, that she had said no and been physically forced into having sex anyway. And the rapist commonly hears but does not heed the protest. "A date rapist will follow through no matter what the woman wants because his agenda is to get laid," says Claire Walsh, a Florida-based consultant on sexual assaults. "First comes the dinner, then a dance, then a drink, then the coercion begins." Gentle persuasion gives way to physical intimidation with alcohol as the ubiquitous lubricant. "When that fails, force is used," she says. "Real men don't take no for an answer."

15   The Palm Beach case serves to remind women that if they go ahead and press charges, they can expect to go on trial along with their attacker, if not in a courtroom then in the court of public opinion. The New York *Times* caused an uproar on its own staff not only for publishing the victim's name but also for laying out in detail her background, her high-school grades, her driving record, along with an unattributed quote from a school official about her "little wild streak." A freshman at Carleton College in Minnesota, who says she was repeatedly raped for four hours by a fellow student, claims that she was asked at an administrative hearing if she performed oral sex on dates. In 1989 a man charged with raping at knife point a woman he knew was acquitted in Florida because his victim had been wearing lace shorts and no underwear.

From a purely legal point of view, if she wants to put her attacker in jail, the survivor had better be beaten as well as raped, since bruises become a badge of credibility. She had better have reported the crime right away, before taking the hours-long shower that she craves, before burning her clothes, before curling up with the blinds down. And she would do well to be a woman of shining character. Otherwise the strict constructionist definitions of rape will prevail in court. "Juries don't have a great deal of sympathy for the victim if she's a willing participant up to the nonconsensual sexual intercourse," says Norman Kinne, a prosecutor in Dallas. "They feel that many times the victim has placed herself in the situation." Absent eyewitnesses or broken bones, a case comes down to her word against his, and the mythology of rape rarely lends her the benefit of the doubt.

She should also hope for an all-male jury, preferably composed of fathers with daughters. Prosecutors have found that women tend to be harsh judges of one another—perhaps because to find a defendant guilty is to entertain two grim realities: that anyone might be a rapist, and that every woman could find herself a victim. It may be easier to believe, the experts muse, that at some level the victim asked for it. "But just because a woman makes a bad judgment, does that give the guy a moral right to rape her?" asks Dean Kilpatrick, director of the Crime Victim Research and Treatment Center at the Medical University of South Carolina. "The bottom line is, Why does a woman's having a drink give a man the right to rape her?"

Last week the Supreme Court waded into the debate with a 7-to-2 ruling that protects victims from being harassed on the witness stand with questions about their sexual history. The Justices, in their first decision on "rape shield laws," said an accused rapist could not present evidence about a previous sexual relationship with the victim unless he notified the court ahead of time. In her decision, Justice Sandra Day O'Connor wrote that "rape victims deserve heightened protection against surprise, harassment, and unnecessary invasions of privacy."

That was welcome news to prosecutors who understand the reluctance of victims to come forward. But there are other impediments to justice as well. An internal investigation of the Oakland police department found that officers ignored a quarter of all reports of sexual assaults or attempts, though 90 percent actually warranted investigation. Departments are getting better at educating officers in handling rape cases, but the courts remain behind. A New York City task force on women in the courts charged that judges and lawyers were routinely less inclined to believe a woman's testimony than a man's.

20   The present debate over degrees of rape is nothing new; all through history, rapes have been divided between those that mattered and those that did not. For the first few thousand years, the only rape that was punished was the defiling of a virgin, and that was viewed as a prop-

erty crime. A girl's virtue was a marketable asset, and so a rapist was often ordered to pay the victim's father the equivalent of her price on the marriage market. In early Babylonian and Hebrew societies, a married woman who was raped suffered the same fate as an adulteress—death by stoning or drowning. Under William the Conqueror, the penalty for raping a virgin was castration and loss of both eyes—unless the violated woman agreed to marry her attacker, as she was often pressured to do. "Stealing an heiress" became a perfectly conventional means of taking—literally—a wife.

It may be easier to prove a rape case now, but not much. Until the 1960s it was virtually impossible without an eyewitness; judges were often required to instruct jurors that "rape is a charge easily made and hard to defend against; so examine the testimony of this witness with caution." But sometimes a rape was taken very seriously, particularly if it involved a black man attacking a white woman—a crime for which black men were often executed or lynched.

Susan Estrich, author of *Real Rape,* considers herself a lucky victim. This is not just because she survived an attack 17 years ago by a stranger with an ice pick, one day before her graduation from Wellesley. It's because police, and her friends, believed her. "The first thing the Boston police asked was whether it was a black guy," recalls Estrich, now a University of Southern California law professor. When she said yes and gave the details of the attack, their reaction was, "So you were really raped." It was an instructive lesson, she says, in understanding how racism and sexism are factored into perceptions of the crime.

A new twist in society's perception came in 1975, when Susan Brownmiller published her book *Against Our Will. Men, Women and Rape.* In it she attacked the concept that rape was a sex crime, arguing instead that it was a crime of violence and power over women. Throughout history, she wrote, rape has played a critical function. "It is nothing more or less than a conscious process of intimidation, by which *all men* keep *all women* in a state of fear."

Out of this contention was born a set of arguments that have become politically correct wisdom on campus and in academic circles. This view holds that rape is a symbol of women's vulnerability to male institutions and attitudes. "It's sociopolitical," insists Gina Rayfield, a New Jersey psychologist. "In our culture men hold the power, politically, economically. They're socialized not to see women as equals."

25   This line of reasoning has led some women, especially radicalized victims, to justify flinging around the term rape as a political weapon, referring to everything from violent sexual assaults to inappropriate innuendoes. Ginny, a college senior who was really raped when she was sixteen, suggests that false accusations of rape can serve a useful purpose. "Penetration is not the only form of violation," she explains. In her view, rape is a subjective term, one that women must use to draw attention to

other, nonviolent, even nonsexual forms of oppression. "If a woman did falsely accuse a man of rape, she may have had reasons to," Ginny says. "Maybe she wasn't raped, but he clearly violated her in some way."

Catherine Comins, assistant dean of student life at Vassar, also sees some value in this loose use of "rape." She says angry victims of various forms of sexual intimidation cry rape to regain their sense of power. "To use the word carefully would be to be careful for the sake of the violator, and the survivors don't care a hoot about him." Comins argues that men who are unjustly accused can sometimes gain from the experience. "They have a lot of pain, but it is not a pain that I would necessarily have spared them. I think it ideally initiates a process of self-exploration. 'How do I see women?' 'If I didn't violate her, could I have?' 'Do I have the potential to do to her what they say I did?' Those are good questions."

Taken to extremes, there is an ugly element of vengeance at work here. Rape is an abuse of power. But so are false accusations of rape, and to suggest that men whose reputations are destroyed might benefit because it will make them more sensitive is an attitude that is sure to backfire on women who are seeking justice for all victims. On campuses where the issue is most inflamed, male students are outraged that their names can be scrawled on a bathroom-wall list of rapists and they have no chance to tell their side of the story.

"Rape is what you read about in the New York *Post* about seventeen little boys raping a jogger in Central Park," says a male freshman at a liberal-arts college, who learned that he had been branded a rapist after a one-night stand with a friend. He acknowledges that they were both very drunk when she started kissing him at a party and ended up back in his room. Even through his haze, he had some qualms about sleeping with her: "I'm fighting against my hormonal instincts, and my moral instincts are saying, 'This is my friend and if I were sober, I wouldn't be doing this.'" But he went ahead anyway. "When you're drunk, and there are all sorts of ambiguity, and the woman says 'Please, please' and then she says no sometime later, even in the middle of the act, there still may very well be some kind of violation, but it's not the same thing. It's not rape. If you don't hear her say no, if she doesn't say it, if she's playing around with you—oh, I could get squashed for saying it—there is an element of say no, mean yes."

The morning after their encounter, he recalls, both students woke up hung over and eager to put the memory behind them. Only months later did he learn that she had told a friend that he had torn her clothing and raped her. At this point in the story, the accused man starts using the language of rape. "I felt violated," he says, "I felt like she was taking advantage of me when she was very drunk. I never heard her say 'No!,' 'Stop!,' anything." He is angry and hurt at the charges, worried that they will get around, shatter his reputation and force him to leave the small campus.

30   So here, of course, is the heart of the debate. If rape is sex without consent, how exactly should consent be defined and communicated, when and by whom? Those who view rape through a political lens tend to place all responsibility on men to make sure that their partners are consenting at every point of a sexual encounter. At the extreme, sexual relations come to resemble major surgery, requiring a signed consent form. Clinical psychologist Mary P. Koss of the University of Arizona in Tucson, who is a leading scholar on the issue, puts it rather bluntly: "It's the man's penis that is doing the raping, and ultimately he's responsible for where he puts it."

Historically, of course, this has never been the case, and there are some who argue that it shouldn't be—that women too must take responsibility for their behavior, and that the whole realm of intimate encounters defies regulation from on high. Anthropologist Lionel Tiger has little patience for trendy sexual politics that make no reference to biology. Since the dawn of time, he argues, men and women have always gone to bed with different goals. In the effort to keep one's genes in the gene pool, "it is to the male advantage to fertilize as many females as possible, as quickly as possible and as efficiently as possible." For the female, however, who looks at the large investment she will have to make in the offspring, the opposite is true. Her concern is to "select" who "will provide the best set-up for their offspring." So, in general, "the pressure is on the male to be aggressive and on the female to be coy."

No one defends the use of physical force, but when the coercion involved is purely psychological, it becomes hard to assign blame after the fact. Journalist Stephanie Gutmann is an ardent foe of what she calls the date-rape dogmatists. "How can you make sex completely politically correct and completely safe?" she asks. "What a horribly bland, unerotic thing that would be! Sex is, by nature, a risky endeavor, emotionally. And desire is a violent emotion. These people in the date-rape movement have erected so many rules and regulations that I don't know how people can have erotic or desire-driven sex."

Nonsense, retorts Cornell professor Andrea Parrot, co-author of *Acquaintance Rape: The Hidden Crime.* Seduction should not be about lies, manipulation, game playing or coercion of any kind, she says. "Too bad that people think that the only way you can have passion and excitement and sex is if there are miscommunications, and one person is forced to do something he or she doesn't want to do." The very pleasures of sexual encounters should lie in the fact of mutual comfort and consent: "You can hang from the ceiling, you can use fruit, you can go crazy and have really wonderful sensual erotic sex, if both parties are consenting."

It would be easy to accuse feminists of being too quick to classify sex as rape, but feminists are to be found on all sides of the debate, and many protest the idea that all the onus is on the man. It demeans women to suggest that they are so vulnerable to coercion or emotional manipulation that they must always be escorted by the strong arm of the law. "You can't solve society's ills by making everything a crime," says Albuquerque attorney Nancy Hollander. "That comes out of the sense of overprotection of women, and in the long run that is going to be harmful to us."

What is lost in the ideological debate over date rape is the fact that men and women, especially when they are young, and drunk, and aroused, are not very good at communicating. "In many cases," says Estrich, "the man thought it was sex, and the woman thought it was rape, and they are both telling the truth." The man may envision a celluloid seduction, in which he is being commanding, she is being coy. A woman may experience the same event as a degrading violation of her will. That some men do not believe a woman's protests is scarcely surprising in a society so drenched with messages that women have rape fantasies and a desire to be overpowered.

By the time they reach college, men and women are loaded with cultural baggage, drawn from movies, television, music videos and "bodice ripper" romance novels. Over the years they have watched Rhett sweep Scarlett up the stairs in *Gone With the Wind*; or Errol Flynn, who was charged twice with statutory rape, overpower a protesting heroine who then melts in his arms; or Stanley rape his sister-in-law Blanche du Bois while his wife is in the hospital giving birth to a child in *A Streetcar Named Desire*. Higher up the cultural food chain, young people can read of date rape in Homer or Jane Austen, watch it in *Don Giovanni* or *Rigoletto*.

The messages come early and often, and nothing in the feminist revolution has been able to counter them. A recent survey of sixth- to ninth-graders in Rhode Island found that a fourth of the boys and a sixth of the girls said it was acceptable for a man to force a woman to kiss him or have sex if he has spent money on her. A third of the children said it would not be wrong for a man to rape a woman who had had previous sexual experiences.

Certainly cases like Palm Beach, movies like *The Accused* and novels like Avery Corman's *Prized Possessions* may force young people to reexamine assumptions they have inherited. The use of new terms, like acquaintance rape and date rape, while controversial, has given men and women the vocabulary they need to express their experiences with both force and precision. This dialogue would be useful if it helps strip away some of the dogmas, old and new, surrounding the issue. Those who hope to raise society's sensitivity to the problem of date rape would do well to concede that it is not precisely the same sort of crime as street rape, that there may be very murky issues of intent and degree involved.

On the other hand, those who downplay the problem should come to realize that date rape is a crime of uniquely intimate cruelty. While the body is violated, the spirit is maimed. How long will it take, once the wounds have healed, before it is possible to share a walk on a beach, a drive home from work or an evening's conversation without always listening for a quiet alarm to start ringing deep in the back of the memory of a terrible crime?

Writing Thoughtfully About Solving Problems

The purpose of this chapter is to help you *think* more like a problem solver, an ability that will enhance every area of your life. It will help you solve personal problems, such as the student facing a reduction in financial aid that we considered earlier in the chapter. It will help you analyze complex social problems, such as those described in the previous articles on racism and date rape. And it will also help you in your writing, an area that will be the focus of the rest of this chapter.

Problem solving provides you with a framework that you can use in much of your writing. Using a problem-solving approach will assist you in organizing your ideas as well as generating information to write about. In some academic situations you may sometimes worry about making the essay "long enough," and using a problem-solving approach will often help you in this regard. In fact, now you may have so much to say that you can't imagine how to get it all into a short essay. This closely parallels a "real-life" work situation where you have gathered information or conducted a study over a long period of time and find yourself facing mountains of data.

When you base your writing on a problem-solving approach, you are likely to find that you know much more about the problem you are writing about and its alternative solutions than any of your readers, including your professor.

That is not usually the case when you write an analysis of a poem for your literature professor or an explanation of the causes of inflation for your economics professor. Academic writing often feels uncomfortable because you, the writer, know that your professor, the audience, almost certainly already knows as much as you do and probably more. So you are left with the uncomfortable feeling of "Why am I telling this person what he/she already knows?"

So using a problem-solving approach in your writing takes care of some difficulties for you, but creates others. Just because your audience knows so little about the subject, your problem, you need to provide enough background information and history of the problem for your discussion of the alternative solutions to make sense to your audience. The following principles for writing about problem solving are not etched in stone; you may have good reason for not following some of them. Yet in general, they should help you convert your answers to the questions in the problem-solving model into a clear, correct, and concise essay.

1. *Be acutely aware of the needs of your audience.*   You may have lived with the problem under consideration for so long, or researched it so thoroughly, that you almost cannot remember a time when the details were not familiar to you. However, your readers need specific details of background, history, special circumstances, and so forth, and they need this information presented in an order that they can understand. So unless you have some pressing reason not to do so, begin with this information in the clearest order you can devise. As you write your essay, continually ask yourself, "Does my audience have all the necessary information to understand the point I am trying to make?"

2. *Present all the information your audience needs in order to understand the problem before you begin to discuss alternative solutions.*

3. *Include a thesis statement indicating that you are going to discuss alternative solutions.*

4. *Discuss each alternative solution by explaining what it would involve and presenting its advantages and disadvantages.*   Provide enough specific information to allow your audience to "see" the advantages and disadvantages; don't just say, "This job would pay less." Instead, say, "This job would pay $2.00 per hour, or $40.00 per week, less than my present job, so I would not be able to meet my fixed monthly expenses."

5. *Present the alternative solutions in the order that will most help the audience understand them and understand why you would choose the one you do.*

6. *Conclude your essay by choosing one solution, or some combination of solutions, and explain clearly why you chose it.* If you have had time to implement the solution, tell whether it is working or not. If you have not yet implemented it, explain how you will judge whether it is working or not.

WRITING PROJECT

This chapter has included both readings and Thinking↔Writing Activities that encouraged you to become familiar with the problem-solving model and the steps required for implementing it. Be sure to reread what you wrote for those activities, as you may be able to use some of it for help in completing this project.

> **WRITING PROJECT**   Analyzing a Problem
>
> Write an essay in which you apply the five-step problem-solving method to a major local, national, or international problem in need of solution. Locate articles that provide background information and analysis of the problem. Be sure to document these sources honestly and correctly. After you have drafted your essay, revise it to the best of your ability. Follow instructions given by your professor as to length, format, and so forth.

Begin by considering the key elements in the Thinking↔Writing Model.

Purpose

You have a variety of purposes here. You can use this opportunity to learn about a major problem in order to arrive at the best possible solution—and thus become a better-informed citizen. In doing so, you will be practicing the creative and critical thinking involved in the problem-solving model. Also, you can sharpen your revision skills by carefully working through the revision questions presented on pages 472–473.

Audience

Something interesting occurs with audience here: while working through the problem-solving model, you are your own audience, for in describing the problem and working through the alternative solutions, you may find yourself actually choosing the solution to the problem. As you begin to shape the answers to the questions in the model into an essay, your audience becomes readers other than yourself, and their needs begin to take over your attention.

Your classmates can be a valuable audience for peer review of a draft, reacting as intelligent readers who do not know as much as you about the problem and its possible solutions, but who become interested as they read your description of it and your evaluation of the possible solutions. Finally, your professor remains the audience who will judge how well you have planned, drafted, and revised. As a writing teacher, he or she cares about a clear focus, logical organization, specific details and examples, and correctness. Keep these in mind as you revise, edit, and proofread.

Subject

Problems are problems precisely because they are difficult to think about and to solve. Sometimes this is true because we don't have enough accurate information to arrive at an intelligent solution, and sometimes this is true because we think we know what the solution is, but for some reason are reluctant to take action. Therefore, we often tend to put off making a choice and taking action for as long as possible. It may be helpful to consider that *not* choosing and acting is choosing to do nothing. Doing nothing actually is one choice that can be included in the problem-solving method. Evaluating the advantages and disadvantages of doing nothing can help us to determine whether or not it will produce a solution to the problem.

Writer

This assignment affords you the opportunity to present an *informed* analysis of an important social issue, based on your research and analysis. Many people have opinions on a wide variety of issues, but most of these opinions are *uninformed,* lacking the support of thoughtful reasons or compelling evidence. As a critical thinker and thoughtful writer, it is necessary for you to develop the habit of explaining your opinions in a careful, organized, well-supported fashion.

The Writing Process

The following sections will guide you through the stages of generating, planning, drafting, and revising as you work on an essay about solving an important problem. Try to be particularly conscious of both the critical thinking you do when working through the problem-solving model, and the critical thinking and decision making you do when you revise.

Generating Ideas

You may find yourself in one of three situations:

1. If your professor's instructions specify a particular local, national, or international problem for you to write on, you must begin there. You might begin by working through the problem-solving model and writing down answers to each question, based on what you know now. Then you will be able to see what you need to know and thus what to look for as you research the problem.
2. If your professor's instructions allow you to choose any important local, national, or international problem, you might begin by brainstorming a list of each of these types of problems. Then you can select the one that seems most important, or the one in which you are most interested, or the one about which you already know the most.

3. If your professor's instructions allow you to write on a personal problem, you might begin by brainstorming a list of problems you now face. It might help to make three columns: school problems, work problems, and personal problems. Then you can pick one, preferably one that needs to be solved soon and for which you need to gather information, to work on.

Whichever situation you found yourself in, once you have worked through the problem-solving model, you will almost certainly spot gaps in your information. Think about how much additional information you would need in order to evaluate each of the alternative solutions. Locate that information, asking for assistance from a librarian if necessary. Once you have filled in all the gaps and decided on which solution to choose—and how you will know if it is working—you are ready to switch your attention to presenting your information to your audience.

Defining a Focus

Write a thesis statement that will make clear to your audience that you are going to explore a problem-solving situation. You might decide to write something like "After thinking about the problem carefully, I realize that I have only two possible choices." Or you might decide to name the possible choices: "America's possible solutions to its budget problem include raising more revenue, cutting the budget, or some combination of the two." You may even decide to announce your chosen solution in your thesis statement: "After carefully weighing the alternatives, raising more revenue while continuing to cut the budget appears to be the best choice."

Organizing Ideas

The five-step method for solving problems fits well with essay structure. Your description of the problem together with necessary history and other background information will give you a working introduction, to end with your thesis statement. Each of the alternative solutions, explained in as much detail as possible, along with its advantages and disadvantages, will provide one section of the body (one or more paragraphs). Your decision on the best solution and how it could be monitored will provide a conclusion.

Drafting

Begin with the paragraph easiest to draft. Keep your written answers to each part of the problem-solving model in front of you.

Remember to begin each section of the body with a topic sentence that names the alternative solution being discussed. If you are discussing advantages or disadvantages in separate paragraphs, draft topic sentences that prepare your readers for that information—sentences such as "Unfortunately, cutting the budget further has serious disadvantages for many Americans." Then provide the audience with as much information as necessary.

You will, of course, have to decide on the best order for the sections. Experiment until you discover the one that seems most helpful to your audience. Switch the sections around on your word processor; even cut up a printout and tape it together in different kinds of order until you discover one that seems smooth and logical.

In your conclusion, name the solution you have chosen. You may want to explain why, if you think that will not be obvious to your audience. Remember to explain how you will monitor the results of your solution.

Revising

Ideally, at this point, you should put your draft aside for a day or two. If deadlines won't permit you to do that, then at least take a break before you try to revise. When you are ready to "re-see" your writing, begin by reading it through slowly, preferably aloud. If possible, have someone whose opinion you respect read it; ask for feedback. Then work through the hierarchy of revision concerns that follows. Remember that you have at least one and possibly two decisions to make for each question: (1) Is improvement needed? and (2) If improvement is needed, how, exactly, can I make my draft better?

1. **Think big.** Look at your draft as a whole.
   - Does it fulfill the assignment in terms of topic and length?
   - Have you stated the thesis clearly?
   - Do all parts of the draft relate to the thesis?
   - Is the organization logical?
   - Do you provide enough evidence?
   - Is your point of view consistent?
   - Is there a discernible flow between your paragraphs?
   - Have you documented information from your sources accurately?
   - Have you used quotation marks around direct quotes or set the quotes off by indenting?

2. **Think medium.** Look at your draft paragraph by paragraph.
   - Will your introduction make your audience want to read on?
   - Is the introduction appropriate for the rest of the draft?
   - Is your focus stated clearly if you are working with a "visible" structure?
   - If you are working with an "invisible" structure, is your focus clearly implied?
   - Are topic sentences used effectively?
   - Does each body paragraph develop a different idea?
   - Should any paragraphs be combined or eliminated?
   - Is your conclusion effective?

3. **Think small.** Look at your draft sentence by sentence.
   - Are any sentences difficult to understand?
   - Are any so long that your audience could get lost in them?

- Are sentences with blended quotations (that is, quotations that are integrated into the syntax of the sentence instead of introduced with "He said . . ." or "she said . . .", complete and easy to read?
- Are quotations shortened with ellipsis marks accurate and readable?
- Are there several choppy sentences that can be combined?
- Are any sentences vague?
- Do any sentences need to be corrected for standard English grammar and usage?

4. **Think "picky."** Look at your draft as your fussiest critic might.
- Are any words not clear or not quite right for your meaning?
- Are any words misspelled?
- Are there any punctuation errors?
- Is your format correct?
- Are the pages numbered consecutively?
- Does your paper make a good impression by being neat?
- Is there anything else you could do to improve your draft?

Proofreading

After you prepare a final draft, check again for correct grammar and punctuation. Proofread carefully for omitted words or punctuation marks. Run your spelling checker program, but be aware of its limitations. Proofread carefully for the kinds of errors the computer can't catch.

Student Essays

The following essays show how two students responded to this assignment—one student writing about a personal problem and citing informally, the other writing about a social problem and citing according to Modern Language Association (MLA) format.

STUDENT WRITING
Problem Solving Made Easy
by Jana Riggle

Life is full of problems; some are easier to solve than others, and some never get solved. I have had a problem for the last two years that, so far, I have not been able to solve. My problem is that my mother and my boyfriend do not get along. This problem has always seemed too overwhelming to deal with. I didn't know where to start, until I read *Thinking Critically,* by John Chaffee. This book shows its readers how to break their problems into steps in order to reach solutions. It gave me a place to start, and I will now try to solve my problem, using the book's five-step problem solving process.

Thinking Critically says, "The first step in solving problems is to determine exactly what the central issues of the problems are." In my problem the central issue is that my mother, due to her dislike of my boyfriend, refuses to acknowledge him, which in turn hurts me. I want my mother to not mind being in the same room with my boyfriend for more than five minutes. Most of all, I want my mother to stop fighting with him.

The second step to solving a problem according to *Thinking Critically* is to "examine each of the possible actions that might help solve the problem." It also helps, the book says, to determine the actions which are impossible or the boundaries of the problem. The boundary of my problem is that I will not leave my boyfriend in order for my mother to stop fighting with him. This leaves me with the alternatives of going on with the situation as it is, having my mother and my boyfriend sit down and try to talk out their differences, or not having my boyfriend around my house.

The third step in *Thinking Critically* is to determine the advantages and disadvantages of each alternative. The first alternative of letting the problem continue and hope it will solve itself presents me with the disadvantage that I have to continue to put up with the problem and it may never be solved. The advantage is that maybe, just maybe, it will solve itself without any interference from me. My second alternative of having my boyfriend and my mother sit down and try to talk out their differences has the disadvantage that she may decide she dislikes him more. The advantage is that she may start to see in him what I do and start to get along with him. The last alternative of not having him near my house has the advantage of not having to listen to her put him down, but the disadvantage that the problem will not really be solved.

The fourth step, the book says, is to find a solution by pursuing an alternative and acting on it. The alternative that looks best to me is to try to have my mother and my boyfriend sit down and have a civil conversation. I think they will agree to it if I tell them how much it means to me, that I love them both, and that I just want her to learn to tolerate him.

The fifth step of this process is to determine how well the solution is working and what adjustments to the original solution might have to be made. Since I have not yet tried out my solution, I cannot evaluate it.

I believe that these five steps really work and that they can simplify even the most confusing problems. The steps offer specific ways to move towards solving a problem, which can turn an overwhelming problem into something that a person can deal with.

STUDENT WRITING
Critical Thinking about Uncritical Drinking
by Joshua Bartlett

There is widespread agreement that excessive student drinking is a serious problem on many college campuses. However, there are different views on the causes of this problem and on the best solutions for it. In this paper I will present some perspectives on the problem of student drinking and conclude with suggestions on how to deal with this serious threat to student health and success.

Why do college students drink to excess? According to many experts, it is mainly due to the influence of the people around them. When most students enter college, they do not have a drinking problem. However, although few realize it, they are entering a culture in which alcohol is often the drug of choice, one that can easily destroy their lives. According to some estimates, 80 to 90 percent of the students on many campuses drink alcohol, and many of them are heavy drinkers (Engs 543). One study found that nearly 30 percent of university students consume more than 15 alcoholic drinks a week (Gerson A43). An additional study found that among those who drink at least once a week, 92 percent of the men and 82 percent of the women consume at least five drinks in a row, and half said they wanted to get drunk (Rosenberg 81).

The results of all this drinking are predictably deadly. Virtually all college administrators agree that alcohol is the most widely used drug among college students and that its abuse is directly related to emotional problems and violent behavior, ranging from date rape to death (Dodge "Campus Crime" A33+; Leatherman A33). For example, at one university, a 20-year-old woman became drunk at a fraternity party and fell to her death from the third floor ("Clemson" A3). At another university, two students were killed in a drunk-driving accident after drinking alcohol at an off-campus fraternity house; the families of both students have filed lawsuits against the fraternity (Dodge "Beer Kegs Banned" A28). When students enter a college or university, they often become socialized into the alcohol-sodden culture of "higher education," at both formal and informal parties. The influence of peer pressure is enormous. Students often find it difficult to resist the pressures from their friends and fellow students to drink.

However, some observers of young people believe that, although peer pressure is certainly a factor in excessive college drinking, it is only one of a number of factors. They point out that the misuse of alcohol is a problem for all youth in our society, not just college students. For example, a recent study by the surgeon general's office shows that 1 in 3 teenagers consumes alcohol every week. This abuse leads to traffic deaths, academic difficulties, and acts of violence

(Elson 64). Another study based on a large, nationally representative sample indicates that although college students are more likely to use alcohol, they tend to drink less per drinking day than nonstudents of the same age (Crowley 14); in other words, most college students who drink are more social drinkers than problem drinkers. One survey of undergraduate students found that college drinking is not as widespread as many people think (O'Hare 540). The conclusion from this data is that even though drinking certainly takes place on college campuses, it is no greater a problem than in the population at large.

Whatever the extent, the misuse of alcohol by college students is a serious situation with a number of probable causes. Certainly the influence of friends, whether in college or out, plays a role, as I've already discussed. But it is not the only factor. To begin with, there is evidence that family history is related to alcohol abuse. For example, one survey of college students found more problem drinking among students whose parents or grandparents had been diagnosed with alcoholism (Perkins and Berkowitz 237–240). Another study found that college students who come from families with high degrees of conflict display a greater potential for alcoholism (Pardeck 342–343).

Another important factor to consider in the misuse of alcohol by young people is advertising. A recent article entitled "It Isn't Miller Time Yet, and This Bud's Not for You" underscores the influence advertisers exert on the behavior of youth (Siler 52). By portraying beer drinkers as healthy, fun-loving, attractive young people, they create role models that many youths imitate. In the same way that cigarette advertisers used to encourage smoking among our youth—without regard to the health hazards—so alcohol advertisers try to sell as much booze as they can to whoever will buy it—no matter what the consequences.

A final factor in the abuse of alcohol is the people themselves. Although young people are subject to a huge number of influences, in the final analysis, they are free to choose what they want to do. They don't have to drink, no matter what the social pressures. In fact, many students resist these pressures and choose not to drink excessively or at all. In short, some students choose to think critically, while others choose to drink uncritically.

In order to encourage good judgment by more students and to minimize the causes of excessive drinking, I think that the following strategies could help solve the college alcohol problem. Only the last one has any disadvantages to be considered.

(1) Colleges should have orientation and educational programs aimed at preventing alcohol abuse, and colleges should give top priority to campaigns against underage and excessive drinking.

(2) Advertising and promotion of alcoholic beverages on college campuses and in college publications should be banned. Liquor distributors should not sponsor campus events. In addition, alcoholic beverage companies should be petitioned not to target young people in their ads.

(3) Depending on the campus culture, colleges should ban or restrict alcohol use on campus and include stiff penalties for students who violate the rules.

(4) Students at residential colleges should be able to live in substance-free housing, offering them a voluntary haven from alcohol, other drugs, tobacco, and peer pressure.

(5) Colleges should create attractive alcohol-free clubs or pubs.

(6) Colleges should ban the use of beer kegs, a symbol of cheap and easy availability of alcohol.

(7) Fraternities should eliminate all alcohol-based contexts or hazing torments.

(8) Where possible, the on-campus drinking age should be reduced to 18, so that students won't be forced to move parties off-campus. At off-campus parties, there is no college control, and as a result students tend to drink greater quantities and more dangerous concoctions.

Of course, this suggestion has the disadvantages of being in conflict with laws in many states or counties and also of seeming to encourage drinking by connecting it even more extensively with social events. But it has the advantages of control and of eliminating the attraction of what's forbidden.

In conclusion, alcohol abuse on college campuses is an extremely serious problem that is threatening the health and college careers of many students. As challenging as this problem is, I believe that it can be solved if students, teachers, and college officials work together in harmony and with determination to implement the suggestions made in this paper.

Works Cited

"Clemson Issues Ban on Parties Using Alcohol." *Chronicle of Higher Education* 31 Jan. (1990 : A3.)

Crowley, Joan E. "Educational Status and Drinking Patterns: How Representative Are College Students." *Journal of Studies on Alcohol* 52.1 (1991) : 10–16.

Dodge, Susan. "Campus Crime Linked to Students' Use of Drugs and Alcohol." *Chronicle of Higher Education* 17 Jan. 1990 : A33+.

———. "Use of Beer Kegs Banned by Some Colleges and National Fraternities." *Chronicle of Higher Education* 12 June 1991 : A27–28.

Elson, John. "Drink Until You Finally Drop." *Time* 16 Dec. 1991 : 64.

Engs, Ruth C. "Family Background of Alcohol Abuse and Its Relationship to Alcohol Consumption among College Students: An Unexpected Finding." *Journal of Studies on Alcohol* 51.6 (1990) : 542–547.

Gerson, Mark. "30 Pct. of Ontario's Students Called 'Heavy Drinkers.'" *Chronicle of Higher Education* 12 April 1989 : A43.

Leatherman, Courtney. "College Officials Are Split on Alcohol Policies; Some Seek to End Underage Drinking; Others Try to Encourage 'Responsible' Use." *Chronicle of Higher Education* 31 Jan. 1990 : A33–35.

O'Hare, Thomas M. "Drinking in College: Consumption Patterns, Problems, Sex Differences and Legal Drinking Age." *Journal of Studies on Alcohol* 51.6 (1990) : 536–541.

Pardeck, John T. "A Multiple Regression Analysis of Family Factors Affecting the Potential for Alcoholism in College Students." *Adolescence* 26.102 (1991) : 341–347.

Perkins, H. Wesley, and Alan D. Berkowitz. "Collegiate COAs and Alcohol Abuse: Problem Drinking in Relation to Assessment of Parent and Grand-parent Alcoholism." *Journal of Counseling and Development* 69.3 (1991) : 237–240.

Rosenberg, Debra. "Bad Times at Hangover U." *Newsweek* 19 Nov. 1990 : 81.

Siler, Julie Flynn. "It Isn't Miller Time Yet, and This Bud's Not For You." *Business Week* 24 June 1991 : 52.

CHAPTER 12

Constructing Arguments—Writing to Establish Agreement

Critical Thinking Focus: Using reasons, evidence, and logic

Writing Focus: Convincing an audience

Reading Theme: Arguments about important issues

Writing Project: Arguing a position on a significant issue

An Introduction to the Principles of Argument

People who study communication, argument, and rhetoric believe that much of what we say and write can be defined as argument because most statements seek listeners' or readers' agreement with the ideas being presented. Unless someone is just saying "Hmmmm" or "Hello" or is asking a question only to obtain information, the purpose of his or her statement usually is to make a point and to convince the audience of its validity. Essays, letters, stories, poems, movies—and even paintings and clothes—can be arguments or have argumentative purposes. However, a separate chapter devoted to argument is necessary, even though most of your previous writing has had argumentative characteristics. Some writing is supposed to be predominantly argumentative, and you need to know how to produce it and how to analyze it. Arguing effectively is essential to academic and professional success; and since politicians and, especially, advertisers use argumentative techniques on us, we need to increase our understanding of both valid and fallacious arguments.

Classical Concepts

The concepts that guide logical argument are central to Western culture. Articulated by the philosophers and rhetoricians of ancient Greece and Rome, they have been studied and applied for more than 2,000 years. Even though emotions, gut reactions, and intuition cannot be brushed aside—because they are so human—logical thinking and the resulting structured arguments are expected in business, government, and scholarship. Therefore, as a college composition student, you have both practical and historical reasons for giving attention to principles of argument or rhetoric.

The Greek philosopher Aristotle, in his famous work the *Rhetoric* and in other writings on logic, is the source of many concepts basic to our ideas of argument. But even Aristotle, more than three hundred years B.C., was responding to earlier works on rhetoric; and to this day, those who have followed him have modified and redefined his ideas and those of other classical rhetoricians. Some of these concepts are *ethos,* the character of the speaker/writer; *pathos,* the effect on the audience; and *logos,* the logic and substance of the argument. Other centuries-old concepts are techniques for *generation* or discovery of ideas; *arrangement* of sections of an argument; the thinking methods of *deduction* and *induction;* techniques for *refutation;* and moral concerns about the use of rhetorical power for honorable ends.

Links to the Thinking↔Writing Model

The classical rhetoricians were concerned with spoken arguments; print was not a medium for them. Speech is, of course, still essential to human communication, both person to person and via electronic media. This book concentrates on writing, but the ancient concepts have never gone out of use, and they function well to promote effective writing. The topics in the Thinking↔Writing Model that is the foundation for this book show a contemporary application of many of those principles.

Notice how *subject, purpose, audience,* and *writer* connect in multiple ways with the concepts of *logos, pathos,* and *ethos.* If *logos* means both content and the logic of its presentation, *logos* connects with the Model's topics of *subject, defining a focus,* and *organizing ideas,* as well as with *thinking critically. Pathos* connects, of course, with the Model's *audience* and *purpose; ethos,* with *writer* and also with the editing and proofreading stages of *revising,* since a well-finished paper gives a good impression of its writer.

The classical concepts of *discovery* and *arrangement* are clearly connected to the Model's *thinking creatively, generating ideas, organizing ideas,* and *drafting.*

Establishing Agreement

Today, the words *argument* and *rhetoric* are regularly used in conversation and in the media differently from the ways they are used in this chapter. Popularly, *argument* often means a quarrel, and *rhetoric* is often used to mean insubstantial or misleading language (which is connected to the classical concerns about the use of rhetorical power for honorable ends.) In this chapter, **argument** means "speaking or writing in which reasons or evidence support claims or conclusions," and **rhetoric** means "the use of the best means of persuasion."

Some people believe that the purpose of argument is to coerce or to "win." As we have seen in this book, though, critical thinkers strive to develop the most informed understanding, which involves trying to fully appreciate other perspectives. Instead of attempting to prove others wrong, a more desirable purpose is to bring agreement or consensus about the issue being discussed. Sometimes people are so far apart in their convictions that agreement cannot be reached and an impasse (or worse) occurs. Sometimes people "agree to disagree" and work around their differences; but if agreement comes, good feelings can result in progress or problem solving or other desired achievements. By thinking critically, you can inspire others to think critically as well, so that all parties are working *together* to achieve the clearest understanding rather than splintering into adversarial factions.

Among the argumentative techniques that lead to mutual understanding are clarifying common principles, identifying differences to see which are important and which are trivial, using sound evidence, speaking or writing in a reasonable tone, acknowledging other points of view, conceding points that cannot be upheld, and looking for acceptable compromise positions.

This chapter will introduce concepts related to argument, provide readings and **Thinking↔Writing Activities** to help you grasp them, and conclude with a **Writing Project** that asks you to write a logical, well-organized argument for a position that is important to you, an argument addressed to an audience that you hope will agree with your claims. The chapter will be exploring ways to construct effective arguments and ways to evaluate arguments.

Thinking Critically About Argument

Consider the following dialogue about whether marijuana should be legalized. Have you participated in such exchanges? In what ways do dialogues like this differ from written argument? How do such dialogues provide a starting point for written arguments?

Dennis: Have you read about the medical uses of marijuana—that people who have cancer, AIDS, and some other diseases might be helped by smoking? I think some doctors are prescribing it and some states are maybe changing their laws. Maybe this will change people's thinking more than all those discussions of unenforced laws, unjust punishments, and victimless crimes that have been going on since my uncles were in college.

Caroline: Well, I agree that we need to think about drug laws. But I hope you agree that we have to be careful. Drugs pose a serious threat to the young people of our country. Look at all the people who are addicted to drugs, who have their lives ruined, and who often die at an early age of overdoses. And think of all the crimes people commit to support their drug habits. So I don't know if anything that's illegal now should be legalized . . . and the laws should be enforced.

Dennis: That's ridiculous. Smoking marijuana is nothing like using drugs such as heroin or even cocaine. It follows that smoking marijuana should not be against the law if it's harmless and maybe even helpful to some sick people.

Caroline: I don't agree. Although marijuana may not be as dangerous as some other drugs, it does affect things like a driver's ability to judge distances. And smoking it surely isn't good for you. And I don't think that anything that is a threat to your health should be legal.

Dennis: What about cigarettes and alcohol? We know that they are dangerous. Medical research has linked smoking cigarettes to lung cancer, emphysema, and heart disease. Alcohol damages the liver and also the brain. Has anyone ever proved that marijuana is a threat to our health? And even if it does turn out to be somewhat unhealthy, it's certainly not as dangerous as cigarettes and alcohol.

Caroline: That's a good point. But to tell you the truth, I'm not so sure that cigarettes and alcohol should be legal. And in any case, they are legal. The fact that cigarettes and alcohol are bad for your health is not reason to legalize another drug that can cause health problems.

Dennis: Look—life is full of risks. We take chances every time we cross the street or climb into our cars. In fact, with all the irresponsible drivers on the road, driving could be a lot more hazardous to our health than any of the drugs around. Many of the foods we eat can kill. For example, red meat contributes to heart disease, and artificial sweeteners can cause cancer. The point is, if people want to take chances with their health, that's up to them. And many people in our society like to mellow out with marijuana. I read somewhere that over 70 percent of the people in the United States think that marijuana should be legalized.

Caroline: There's a big difference between letting people drive cars and letting them use dangerous drugs. Society has a responsibility to protect people from themselves. People often do things that are foolish if they are encouraged to or given the opportunity. Legalizing something like marijuana encourages people to use it, especially young people. It follows that many more people would use marijuana if it were legalized. It's like society saying "This is all right—go ahead and use it."

Dennis: I still maintain that marijuana isn't dangerous. It's not addictive—like heroin is—and there is no evidence that it harms you. Consequently, anything that is harmless should be legal.

Caroline: Marijuana may not be physically addictive like heroin, but I think that it can be psychologically addictive, because people tend to use more and more of it over time. I know a number of people who spend a lot of their time getting high. What about Carl? All he does is lie around and get high. This shows that smoking it over a period of time definitely affects your mind. Think about the people you know who smoke a lot—don't they seem to be floating in a dream world? How are they ever going to make anything of their lives? As far as I'm concerned, a pothead is like a zombie—living but dead.

Dennis: Since you have had so little experience with marijuana, I don't think that you can offer an informed opinion on the subject. And anyway, if you do too much of anything, it can hurt you. Even something as healthy as exercise can cause problems if you do too much of it. But I sure don't see anything wrong with toking up with some friends at a party or even getting into a relaxed state by yourself. In fact, I find that I can even concentrate better on my school work after taking a little smoke.

Caroline: If you believe that, then marijuana really has damaged your brain. You're just trying to rationalize your drug habit. Smoking marijuana doesn't help you concentrate—it takes you away from reality. And I don't think that people can control it. Either you smoke and surrender control of your life, or you don't smoke because you want to retain control. There's nothing in between.

Dennis: Let me point out something to you. Because marijuana is illegal, organized crime controls its distribution and makes all the money out of it. If marijuana were legalized, the government could tax the sale of it—like cigarettes and alcohol—and use the money for some worthwhile purpose. For example, many states have legalized gambling and use the money to support education. In fact, the major tobacco companies have already copyrighted names for different marijuana brands—like "Acapulco Gold." Obviously they believe that marijuana will soon become legal.

Caroline: The fact that the government can make money out of something doesn't mean that they should legalize it. We could also legalize prostitution or muggings and then tax the proceeds. Also, even if the cigarette companies are prepared to sell marijuana, that doesn't mean that selling it makes sense. After all, they're the ones who are selling us cigarettes. . . .

Can you think of other views on the subject of legalizing marijuana? Can you think of other subjects on which dialogues are taking place now?

Recognizing Arguments

The preceding discussion is an illustration of two people's engaging in dialogue, the systematic exchange of ideas. Participating in this sort of dialogue with others is one of the keys to thinking critically. It stimulates you to develop your mind by carefully examining the way you make sense of the world. Discussing issues with others encourages you to be mentally active, to ask questions, to view issues from different perspectives, to develop reasons that support conclusions, and to write convincingly.

This chapter focuses on that last quality of thinking critically—supporting conclusions with reasons—because when we offer reasons to support a conclusion, we are presenting an argument, the essence of most college and business writing.

> **Argument:**   a form of thinking in which certain statements
>   (reasons or evidence) are offered in support of another
>   statement (a conclusion or a claim).

In the dialogue, Dennis presents the following argument for legalizing marijuana:

Reason: Marijuana might help some people who have serious diseases.
Reason: Marijuana isn't dangerous like heroin and cocaine.
Reason: Governments could tax the sale of marijuana the way they do cigarettes and alcohol.
Conclusion: Marijuana should be legalized.

Expanding the definition of *argument* given in the box, we can define the main ideas that make up an argument:

> **Reasons or Evidence:**   statements that support another statement
>   (a conclusion, claim, or thesis), justify it, or make it more
>   probable.

> **Conclusion, Claim, or Thesis:**   a statement that explains, asserts,
>   or predicts on the basis of statements (known as reasons) that
>   are offered as evidence for it.

The type of thinking that uses argument—reasons in support of conclusions— is known as *reasoning,* and it is a type of thinking explained throughout this book. We are continually trying to explain, justify, and predict through the process of reasoning, and often we must present our thinking in writing.

Of course, our reasoning—and that of others—is not always correct. The reasons someone offers may not really support the conclusion they are supposed to, or a conclusion may not really follow from the reasons stated, or the reasons may be questionable or wrong. These difficulties are illustrated in a number of arguments contained in the discussion on marijuana.

Nevertheless, whenever we accept a conclusion as likely or true on the basis of certain reasons, or whenever we offer reasons to support a conclusion, we are using arguments—even if our reasoning is weak or faulty and needs to be improved.

Let us return to the discussion about marijuana. After Dennis presents one argument, Caroline presents another, giving reasons that lead to a conclusion that conflicts with the one Dennis has arrived at:

Reason: Drugs pose a very serious threat to the young people of our country.
Reason: Many crimes are committed to support drug habits.
Conclusion: As a result, society has to have drug laws and enforce them to convince people of the seriousness of the situation.

Which of Dennis's or Caroline's arguments do you see as reasonable? Which seem weak or faulty?

Cue Words for Arguments

English, like other languages, provides guidance in our efforts to identify reasons and conclusions. Certain key words, or cue words, signal that a reason is being offered in support of a conclusion or that a conclusion is being announced on the basis of certain reasons. After you read the following list, go back to the dialogue and see how and when Dennis and Caroline used these words.

Here are some commonly used cue words for reasons and conclusions:

CUE WORDS SIGNALING REASONS

since	in view of
for	first, second
because	in the first (second) place
as shown by	may be inferred from
as indicated by	may be deduced from
given that	may be derived from
assuming that	for the reason that

CUE WORDS SIGNALING CONCLUSIONS

therefore	then
thus	it follows that
hence	thereby showing
so	demonstrates that
(which) shows that	allows us to infer that
(which) proves that	suggests very strongly that
implies that	you see that
points to	leads me to believe that
as a result	allows us to deduce that
consequently	

Of course, identifying reasons, conclusions, and arguments involves more than looking for cue words. The words and phrases just listed do not always signal reasons and conclusions, and in many cases arguments are made without the use of cue words. Cue words, however, do alert us that an argument is being offered. Careful use of cue words helps us to write effective arguments.

THINKING↔WRITING ACTIVITY 12.1

Thinking About Arguments

Write responses in your journal. If you have the chance, discuss your responses with your classmates and note where agreements and disagreements occur.

1. Review the discussion on marijuana and underline cue words signaling that Dennis and Caroline are giving reasons or announcing conclusions.
2. Identify one argument you find convincing and one you find unconvincing. Write your reasons for your opinions, referring to specific places in the dialogue.

THINKING↔WRITING ACTIVITY 12.2

Analyzing Extended Arguments About Legalizing Drugs

The following two essays discuss the issue of whether drugs should be legalized. The first passage, "Drugs," is by essayist and novelist Gore Vidal. The second, "The Case for Slavery," is by *New York Times* editor and columnist A. M. Rosenthal. After carefully reading the essays, answer these questions:

1. Try to state in one sentence the thesis, conclusion, or claim of each essay. Where did each writer make his thesis clear? Did you find the placement effective? Why or why not?
2. Identify two or three specific reasons that each writer gives for his thesis.
3. What impression does each essay give of its writer? Why?
4. Do you agree with either writer's position? Explain. What shapes your identity as an audience for these arguments?
5. Can you connect these questions with *ethos, logos,* and *pathos* as defined on page 482?

Drugs

by Gore Vidal

It is possible to stop most drug addiction in the United States within a very short time. Simply make all drugs available and sell them at cost. Label each drug with a precise description of what effect—good and bad—the drug will have on the taker. This will require heroic honesty. Don't say the marijuana is addictive or dangerous when it is neither, as millions of people know—unlike "speed," which kills most unpleasantly, or heroin, which is addictive and difficult to kick.

For the record, I have tried—once—almost every drug and liked none, disproving the popular Fu Manchu theory that a single whiff of opium will enslave the mind. Nevertheless many drugs are bad for certain people to take and they should be told why in a sensible way.

Along with exhortation and warning, it might be good for our citizens to recall (or learn for the first time) that the United States was the creation of men who believed that each man has the right to do what he wants with his own life as long as he does not interfere with his neighbor's pursuit of happiness. (That his neighbor's idea of happiness is persecuting others does confuse matters a bit.)

5

This is a startling notion to the current generation of Americans. They reflect a system of public education which has made the Bill of Rights, literally, unacceptable to a majority of high school graduates who now form the "silent majority"—a phrase which that underestimated wit Richard Nixon took from Homer who used it to describe the dead.

Now one can hear the warning rumble begin: If everyone is allowed to take drugs everyone will and the GNP will decrease, the Commies will stop us from making everyone free, and we shall end up a race of zombies, passively murmuring "groovy" to one another. Alarming thought. Yet it seems most unlikely that any reasonably sane person will become a drug addict if he knows in advance what addiction is going to be like.

Is everyone reasonably sane? No. Some people will always become drug addicts just as some people will always become alcoholics, and it is just too bad. Every man, however, has the power (and should have the legal right) to kill himself if he chooses. But since most men don't, they won't be mainliners either. Nevertheless, forbidding people things they like or think they might enjoy only makes them want those things all the more. This psychological insight is, for some mysterious reason, perennially denied by our governors.

It is a lucky thing for the American moralist that our country has always existed in a kind of time-vacuum: We have no public memory of anything that happening before last Tuesday. No one in Washington today recalls what happened during the years alcohol was forbidden to the people by a Congress that thought it had a divine mission to stamp out Demon Rum—launching, in the process, the greatest crime wave in the country's history, causing thousands of deaths from bad alcohol, and creating a general (and persisting) contempt among the citizenry for the laws of the United States.

The same thing is happened today. But the government has learned nothing from past attempts at prohibition, not to mention repression.

Last year when the supply of Mexican marijuana was slightly curtailed by the Feds, the pushers got the kids hooked on heroin and deaths increased dramatically, particularly in New York. Whose fault? Evil men like the Mafiosi? Permissive Dr. Spock? Wild-eyed Dr. Leary? No.

10   The Government of the United States was responsible for those deaths. The bureaucratic machine has a vested interest in playing cops and robbers. Both the Bureau of Narcotics and the Mafia want strong laws against the sale and use of drugs because if drugs are sold at cost there would be no money in it for anyone.

If there was no money in it for the Mafia, there would be no friendly playground pushers, and addicts would not commit crimes to pay for the next fix. Finally, if there was no money in it, the Bureau of Narcotics would wither away, something they are not about to do without a struggle.

Will anything sensible be done? Of course not. The American people are as devoted to the idea of sin and its punishment as they are to making money—and fighting drugs is nearly as big a business as pushing them. Since the combination of sin and money is irresistible (particularly to the professional politician), the situation will only grow worse.

The Case for Slavery

by A. M. Rosenthal

Across the country, a scattered but influential collection of intellectuals is intensely engaged in making the case for slavery.

With considerable passion, these Americans are repeatedly expounding the benefits of not only tolerating slavery but legalizing it:

It would make life less dangerous for the free. It would save a great deal of money. And since the economies could be used to improve the lot of the slaves, in the end they would be better off.

The new antiabolitionists, like their predecessors in the nineteenth century, concede that those now in bondage do not themselves see the benefits of legalizing their status.

5   But in time they will, we are assured, because the beautiful part of legalization is that slavery would be designed so as to keep slaves pacified with the very thing that enslaves them!

The form of slavery under discussion is drug addiction. It does not have every characteristic of more traditional forms of bondage. But they have enough in common to make the comparison morally valid—and the campaign for drug legalization morally disgusting.

Like the plantation slavery that was a foundation of American society for so long, drug addiction largely involves specifiable groups of people. Most of the enchained are children and adolescents of all colors and black and Hispanic adults.

Like plantation slavery, drug addiction is passed on from generation to generation. And this may be the most important similarity: Like plantation slavery, addiction can destroy among its victims the social resources most valuable to free people for their own betterment—family life, family traditions, family values.

In plantation-time America, mothers were taken from their children. In drug-time America, mothers abandon their children. Do the children suffer less, or the mothers?

10 Antiabolitionists argue that legalization would make drugs so cheap and available that the profit for crime would be removed. Well-supplied addicts would be peaceful addicts. We would not waste billions for jails and could spend some of the savings helping the addicted become drug-free.

That would happen at the very time that new millions of Americans were being enticed into addiction by legalization—somehow.

Are we really foolish enough to believe that tens of thousands of drug gang members would meekly steal away, foiled by the marvels of the free market?

Not likely. The pushers would cut prices, making more money than ever from the ever-growing mass market. They would immediately increase the potency and variety beyond anything available at any Government-approved narcotics counters.

Crime would increase. Crack produces paranoid violence. More permissiveness equals more use equals more violence.

15 And what will legalization do to the brains of Americans drawn into drug slavery by easy availability?

Earlier this year, an expert drug pediatrician told me that after only a few months babies born with crack addiction seemed to recover. Now we learn that stultifying behavioral effects last at least through early childhood. Will they last forever?

How long will crack affect neurological patterns in the brain of adult crack users? Dr. Gabriel G. Nahas of Columbia University argues in his new book, *Cocaine: The Great White Plague,* that the damage may be irreversible. Would it not be an act of simple intelligence to drop the legalization campaign until we find out?

Then why do a number of writers and academicians, left to right, support it? I have discussed this with antidrug leaders like Jesse Jackson, Dr. Mitchell Rosenthal of Phoenix House, and William J. Bennett, who search for answers themselves.

Perhaps the answer is that the legalizers are not dealing with reality in America. I think the reason has to do with class.

20   Crack is beginning to move into the white middle and upper classes. That is a tragedy for those addicted.

However, it has not yet destroyed the communities around which their lives revolve, not taken over every street and doorway. It has not passed generation to generation among them, killing the continuity of family.

But in ghetto communities poverty and drugs come together in a catalytic reaction that is reducing them to social rubble.

The antiabolitionists, virtually all white and well-to-do, do not see or do not care. Either way they show symptoms of the callousness of class. That can be a particularly dangerous social disorder.

Arguments as Inferences

When you construct arguments, you are constructing views of the world by means of your ability to infer. As you saw in Chapter 10, inferring is a thinking process used to reason from what one already knows (or believes to be the case) to new knowledge or beliefs. This is usually what you do when you construct arguments: work from reasons you know or believe in to conclusions based on them.

Just as you can use inferences to make sense of different types of situations, you can also construct arguments for different purposes. We have already noted that some people believe in using arguments to coerce or to "win" and we saw how a more desirable goal is to clarify issues, develop mutual understanding, and if possible, bring about agreement or consensus on the issue being discussed. Notice how you can work toward agreement when you construct arguments to do any of the following:

- Decide
- Explain
- Predict
- Persuade

An example of each of these different types of arguments follows. After examining each example, construct an argument of the same type related to issues in your own life. Identify an audience for each argument.

Constructing Arguments to Decide

Reason: Throughout my life, I've always been interested in all different kinds of electricity.
Reason: There are many attractive job opportunities in the field of electrical engineering.
Conclusion: Electrical engineering would be a good major for me.
Audience: Myself, my parents, my academic adviser, the scholarship office.

An argument to decide
Reason:
Reason:
Conclusion:
Audience:

Constructing Arguments to Explain

Reason: I was delayed leaving my house because my dog needed emergency walking.
Reason: There was an unexpected traffic jam caused by motorists slowing down to view an overturned chicken truck.
Conclusion: Therefore, I couldn't help being late for our appointment.
Audience: The person waiting for me.

An argument to explain
Reason:
Reason:
Conclusion:
Audience:

Constructing Arguments to Predict

Reason: Some people will always drive faster than the speed limit allows, no matter whether the limit is 55 or 65 mph.
Reason: Car accidents are more likely at higher speeds.
Conclusion: It follows that a reinstated 65 mph limit will result in more accidents.
Audience: Legislators, voters, drivers.

An argument to predict
Reason:
Reason:
Conclusion:
Audience:

Constructing Arguments to Persuade

Reason: Chewing tobacco can lead to cancer of the mouth and throat.
Reason: Young people sometimes begin chewing tobacco because they see ads that feature sports heroes they admire.
Conclusion: Therefore, ads for chewing tobacco should be banned.
Audience: Parents, voters, legislators, advertising agencies, media executives.

An argument to persuade
Reason:
Reason:
Conclusion:
Audience:

Evaluating Arguments

To construct good arguments, you must be skilled in evaluating the effectiveness, or soundness, of arguments already constructed. You must investigate the aspects of each argument independently to determine the soundness of the argument as a whole:

1. How true are the reasons being offered to support the conclusion?
2. To what extent do the reasons support the conclusion, claim, or thesis—or to what extent does the conclusion follow from the reasons offered?

Truth: How True Are the Supporting Reasons?

The first aspect of an argument that you must evaluate is the truth of the reasons being used to support a conclusion. Ask yourself these questions: Does each reason make sense? What evidence is the writer offering as part of each reason? Are any reasons consistent with my own experience? Are reasons based on sources that can be trusted?

You use these questions and others like them to analyze the reasons offered and to determine how true they are. As you saw in Chapter 10, *Believing and Knowing,* evaluating the kinds of beliefs usually found as reasons in arguments is a complex and ongoing challenge.

Validity: Do the Reasons Support the Claim or Conclusion?

In addition to determining whether the reasons are true, evaluating arguments involves investigating the relationship between the reasons and the claim or the conclusion (which becomes the thesis of a piece of writing that argues a position on an issue).

When the reasons support the conclusion in such a way that the conclusion follows from the reasons being offered, the argument is valid. (In formal logic, the term *validity* is reserved for deductively valid arguments in which the conclusions follow necessarily from the premises.) If, however, the reasons do not support the conclusion, if the conclusion does not follow from the reasons being offered, the argument is invalid. Remember that *valid* and *true* do not have the same meaning; as has just been pointed out, you must first evaluate the truth of a reason, then determine validity.

> **Valid Argument:**   an argument in which the reasons support the conclusion in such a way that the conclusion follows from the reasons offered.

> **Invalid Argument:**   an argument in which the reasons do not support the conclusion; the conclusion does not follow from the reasons offered.

One way to focus on the concept of *validity* is to assume that all the reasons in the argument are true, then try to determine how probable they make the conclusion. The following is an example of one type of valid argument:

Reason: Anything that is a threat to our health should not be legal.
Reason: Marijuana is a threat to our health.
Conclusion: Therefore, marijuana should not be legal.

This is a valid argument because if we assume that the reasons are true, its conclusion does necessarily follow. Of course, we may not agree that either or both of the reasons are true; in that case, we will not agree with the conclusion. Nevertheless, the structure of the argument is *valid*. This particular form of thinking is known as *deduction,* and we will examine deductive reasoning more closely in the pages ahead.

Following is a different type of argument:

Reason: As part of a project in my social science class, we selected 100 students in the school to be interviewed. We took special steps to ensure that these students were representative of the student body as a whole (total students: 4,386). We asked the selected students whether they thought the United States should actively try to overthrow foreign governments that the United States disapproves of. Of the 100 students interviewed, 88 students said the United States should definitely not be involved in such activities.
Conclusion: We can conclude that most students in this school believe the United States should not be engaged in attempts to actively overthrow foreign governments that the United States disapproves of.

This is a persuasive argument because if we assume that the reason is true, that reason provides strong support for the conclusion. In this case, the key part of the reason is the statement that the 100 students selected were representative of the entire 4,386 students at the school. To evaluate the truth of the reason, we might want to investigate the procedure used to select the 100 students in order to determine whether this sample was in fact representative of all the students. (Notice that the conclusion carefully said "in this school." It did not say imprecisely "most students.")

This particular form of thinking is an example of *induction,* and we will explore inductive reasoning more fully in the pages ahead.

The Soundness of Arguments

When an argument includes both true reasons and a valid structure, the argument is considered sound. When an argument has either false reasons or an invalid structure, however, the argument is considered unsound.

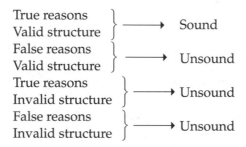

True reasons
Valid structure ⟶ Sound

False reasons
Valid structure ⟶ Unsound

True reasons
Invalid structure ⟶ Unsound

False reasons
Invalid structure ⟶ Unsound

From this chart, we are reminded that in terms of arguments, *truth* and *validity* are not identical concepts. An argument can have true reasons and an invalid structure, or false reasons and a valid structure. In both cases the argument is unsound. Consider the following argument:

Reason: Professor Davis believes that megadoses of vitamins can cure colds.
Reason: Davis is a professor of computer science
Conclusion: Megadoses of vitamins can cure colds.

This argument is obviously not valid: even if we assume that the reasons are true, the conclusion does not follow. Professor Davis's expertise with computers does not provide her with special knowledge in nutrition and medicine. This invalid thinking is neither structurally nor factually acceptable. It is clearly not a sound argument.

Now, *consider* this argument:

Reason: For a democracy to function most effectively, the citizens should be able to think critically about the major social and political issues.
Reason: Education plays a key role in developing critical thinking abilities.
Conclusion: Therefore education plays a key role in ensuring that a democracy is functioning most effectively.

A good case could be made for the soundness of this argument because the reasons are persuasive and the argument structure is valid. Of course, someone might contend that one or both of the reasons are not completely true, which illustrates an important point about the arguments we construct and evaluate. Many of the arguments we encounter in life fall somewhere between complete soundness and complete unsoundness because often we are not sure if our reasons are completely true. Throughout this book, we have found that developing accurate beliefs is an ongoing process and that our beliefs are subject to clarification and revision. As a result, the conclusion of any argument can be only as certain as the reasons supporting the conclusion.

To sum up, evaluating arguments effectively involves both the truth of the reasons and the validity of the argument structure. The degree of soundness an argument has depends on how accurate the reasons turn out to be and how valid the argument's structure is.

THINKING ↔ WRITING ACTIVITY 12.3

Analyzing Extended Arguments About an AIDS Vaccine

Read the following articles about a vaccine for AIDS and write answers to these questions in your journal.

1. What is the claim or thesis of each article?
2. Identify two or three reasons that each writer gives for his claim.
3. Evaluate, or explain how you would proceed in evaluating, one reason in each article.
4. Which argument seems more convincing to you, and why?
5. What impression do you receive of these writers from these articles? How do you characterize their tones of voice?

from For a National Effort to Develop a Vaccine to Counteract AIDS

by Robert E. Pollack

The time has come for the Government to underwrite a nationwide effort to produce an effective vaccine against HTLV III, the virus that causes AIDS. Though a frightening new disease, AIDS is no longer so novel that such an effort would be premature.

Samples of the virus have been isolated and their entire sets of genes decoded. The human populations for testing and eventual inoculation with a vaccine exist and are ready to volunteer. Yet the communities of physicians, and of public and corporate researchers, seem unable to organize the process. Why is the nation unwilling or unable to expend the effort and money to launch an applied-biology and bioengineering effort to develop and test a vaccine?

Let's examine what is known about viruses. Most viruses cannot "find" just any human cell; they have to attach to a cell's surface, and the attachment has to be a specific match between a portion of the cell's surface membrane and a portion of the virus's coat. HTLV III is ordinary in its habits much like other viruses. It is remarkable only for the fastidious way in which it chooses the cell it will attach to, enter and take over.

HTLV III must find and attach to a particular kind of white blood cell. This sort of cell is the very one everyone's body needs in order to recognize and reject a multiplicity of micro-organisms, fungi, parasites, yeasts and bacteria. That is the reason AIDS patients suffer from so many different diseases. As the virus takes over these cells, the body loses its defenses and eventually succumbs to one or many of a host of infectious agents.

5   Two scientific reasons are given for the reluctance to begin a national effort to develop a vaccine. One is that AIDS might be caused by a family of closely related variants of the same virus and that therefore no vaccine could be effective. The other is that there are no animals suitable for initial testing of a vaccine and thus no way to be sure a vaccine is safe for testing in people.

It seems to me and to some colleagues that these objections, though sound, are not conclusive. The exquisite specificity of HTLV III's recognition of certain white blood cells suggests that all variants of the virus will have in common at least one part of their outer coat—the region that finds and binds to this specific kind of cell.

Gene-splicing is the answer to the second objection and the key to making a vaccine. HTLV III is a new virus, but its known properties so far suggest that it is not so exotic as to be beyond the grasp of recombinant DNA techniques. All the genes of more than one AIDS virus have been isolated and chemically identified. This knowledge should permit scientists to put genes from an AIDS virus into a bacterium. Once they are there, the bacterium, grown in large quantities, can be the source of material for testing as a vaccine. And vaccines produced this way would be totally incapable of causing AIDS.

In the absence of an animal model for AIDS, such vaccines could not now be tested in volunteers, because Government regulations require that new vaccines be first tested in an animal. These rules no longer make sense for vaccines produced by recombinant techniques.

There is at least one other reason for our nation's inability to act: irrational fear and hostility directed at a minority. The population at risk and ready to volunteer for testing is largely homosexual. Our political leaders apparently do not wish to be involved with this minority. As a result, the clock runs out on thousands of victims without even the beginning of an effort to develop the vaccine that might prevent new cases from occurring. This is a social disaster.

10   Consider what we could be doing. We have a population of homosexuals available for prospective study of such vaccines. These men,

like the estimated million or so Americans who already have antibodies to HTLV III, are highly motivated to participate in the large-scale studies necessary to develop an optimal vaccine.

We have as well a population of perhaps 100,000 [This figure represents the estimate in 1985. In 1990, estimates of persons with AIDS-related complex in the United States ranged as high as 1 million (Editor's note).] people with what is known medically as "AIDS-related complex"—a syndrome in which a person has an AIDS virus in his blood but does not show the full set of symptoms characteristic of AIDS. In addition, there are perhaps 10,000 people with AIDS whose white cells are drastically reduced. These 10,000 have a currently irreversible disease, and many have repeatedly offered themselves for any experimental treatments.

A vaccine for any virus-caused cancer will have to be made by recombinant techniques in order to separate the gene for the vaccine from all cancer-causing genes in the virus. Therefore, if we proceed immediately to organize biotechnology for the production and testing of recombinant AIDS vaccines, we gain time on the eventual production of vaccines for leukemias, lymphomas and other human tumors that are likely to be caused by viruses.

All physicians have taken an oath to do no harm. But in fact they do harm by sitting quietly by, or referring AIDS victims to another physician or hoping the disease will quietly go away after it destroys a few thousand homosexual men and narcotics addicts. It is not enough to offer succor and solace. Physicians and scientists should lobby actively for a nationwide effort to develop an AIDS vaccine.

from Why an AIDS Vaccine?

by Charles Krauthammer

The reviews are in on President Clinton's dramatic declaration pledging the United States to finding an AIDS vaccine, moonshotlike, within 10 years. Apart from AIDS activists who complain that the president did not commit serious moonshot money to the enterprise ("cheap talk"—Larry Kramer), the reaction was mostly favorable. Who, after all, can be against a vaccine against anything?

No one seems to want to raise the obvious, if indelicate, question: Why embark on a huge national venture to create a vaccine for a disease that is already extraordinarily preventable?

Unlike most communicable diseases, AIDS is not contracted casually. Unlike TB, it is not contracted by being coughed on in the subway. Unlike dysentery, it is not contracted by drinking the wrong water. To get AIDS you must, in all but the rarest cases, engage in very complicated consensual social behavior, namely unsafe sex or intravenous drug abuse.

It would be nice to live in a world where one could engage in such behaviors while enjoying vaccine-induced immunity. But is that really a top national priority? Would any president propose as a top national priority an anti-lung-cancer vaccine so that people who smoke—48 million Americans do—could do so with immunity?

5   Nor do presidents call for a 10-year campaign to produce a vaccine against cirrhosis of the liver. Why? Not because we want to stigmatize people who drink or smoke. But for a very practical reason: These behaviors being voluntary and preventable, it makes a lot more sense to spend the scarce intellectual, scientific and financial resources of the country trying to give people immunity from diseases that they cannot otherwise protect themselves against.

The classic case is polio. When FDR contracted it in 1921, we had not a clue how people got it. By the '50s, frightened parents kept their children away from swimming pools and movie theaters and even crowds. They lived in terror not knowing what they might be doing that was contributing to their kids' chances of getting polio.

With no obvious behavioral cause, polio was the classic case of a disease crying out for a vaccine. Meningitis, cervical cancer and multiple sclerosis occupy a similar position today. But AIDS?

Moreover, Clinton is calling for a huge technological innovation (which many in the field doubt is a reasonable prospect anyway) to prevent the spread of AIDS. Yet at the same time, the traditional way of controlling the spread of communicable diseases has been largely abandoned in the case of AIDS. And uniquely in the case of AIDS.

We fight just about every epidemic—tuberculosis, syphilis, gonorrhea—by identifying carriers and warning their contacts. The usual epidemiological tracing has not been done for AIDS. Gay activists and civil libertarians have vociferously opposed it. And the politicians have caved.

10   The story of this travesty—"the effective suspension of traditional public health procedures for AIDS"—is laid out in damning detail by Chandler Burr in the current *Atlantic Monthly* ("The AIDS Exception: Privacy vs. Public Health").

"AIDS has been so thoroughly exempted from traditional public health approaches," writes Burr, "that civil libertarians have defeated in court attempts by health authorities to notify the spouses of people who have died of AIDS that their husbands or wives were HIV-infected."

In 1985, in fact, gay activists brought suit to prevent the use of the first test for HIV, unless assured the tests would not be used for widespread screening of gays. Even today they oppose mandatory HIV screening for pregnant women, even though we know that early treatment of the mothers would reduce by 50 to 75 percent the number of kids who are born with HIV.

"Traditional public health is absolutely effective at controlling infectious disease," says Dr. Lee Reichman, who works with tuberculosis and AIDS patients. "It should have been applied to AIDS from the start, and it wasn't. Long before there was AIDS, there were other sexually transmitted diseases, and you had partner notification and testing and reporting. This was routine public health at its finest and this is the way STDs were controlled."

Marcia Angell, executive editor of the *New England Journal of Medicine,* is blunter than most: "I have no doubt . . . that if, for example, we screened all expectant mothers, we could prevent AIDS in many cases. And if we traced partners, we would prevent AIDS in many cases. And if we routinely tested in hospitals, we would prevent AIDS in many cases."

15   And if we had a president with guts, he would be demanding these elementary measures to save people from getting AIDS today—instead of waving a wand and telling scientists to produce for him a magic vaccine 10 years from now.

Forms of Argument

Arguments occur in many forms, but two major thinking methods provide the foundations for most arguments and also influence the forms in which arguments are organized. These methods are (1) *deduction* and (2) *induction.* They can be seen as (1) moving from general principles to specific applications and (2) moving from specific instances to general conclusions. Deduction and induction are seldom used in "pure" or textbook ways in real-life arguments. Instead, they often are compressed or combined, so seeing and analyzing their uses can sometimes be difficult. In fact, some teachers and students feel that studying them separately is more an exercise than a practical activity.

However, as a critical thinker, a writer of arguments, and an analyst of arguments, you need to understand the principles of deduction and induction. This chapter presents them so that you can see how they function and interrelate. Then you should be able to see how you and others use them, both consciously and unconsciously, in trying to convince audiences.

Deductive Reasoning

The deductive argument is the one most commonly associated with the study of logic. Though it has a variety of valid forms, they share one characteristic: if you accept the supporting reasons (also called premises) as true, you must necessarily accept the conclusion as true.

> **Deductive Argument:**   an argument form in which one reasons from premises that are known or assumed to be true to a conclusion that follows necessarily from these premises.

For example, consider the following famous deductive argument:

Reason/Premise: All persons are mortal.
Reason/Premise: Socrates is a person.
Conclusion: Therefore, Socrates is mortal.

In this example of deductive thinking, accepting the premises of the argument as true means that the conclusion necessarily follows; it cannot be false. Many deductive arguments, like the one just given, are structured as syllogisms, an argument form that consists of two supporting premises and a conclusion. There are also, however, a large number of invalid deductive forms, one of which is illustrated in the following defective syllogism:

Reason/Premise: All persons are mortal.
Reason/Premise: Socrates is a person.
Conclusion: Therefore all persons are Socrates.

This example is deliberately absurd, but people do shift terms in such ways and think such things as that all tall people should play basketball, just because basketball players are usually tall. Despite the variety of invalid deductive structures, once you become aware of the concept of validity, you should be able to detect invalidity. In the next several pages, we will briefly examine some common valid deductive forms.

One is the *application of a general rule.* Whenever we reason with the form illustrated by the valid Socrates syllogism, we are using the following argument structure:

Premise: All A (people) are B (mortal).
Premise: S is an A (Socrates is a person).
Conclusion: Therefore, S is B (Socrates is mortal).

This basic argument form is valid no matter what terms are included. For example:

Premise: All politicians are untrustworthy.
Premise: Bill White is a politician.
Conclusion: Therefore, Bill White is untrustworthy.

Notice again that, with any valid deductive form, if we assume that the premises are true, we must accept the conclusion. Of course, in this case there is considerable or complete doubt that the first premise is true.

Although we are not always aware of it, we use this basic type of reasoning whenever we apply a general rule In the form "All A is B." For instance:

Premise: All children eight years old should be in bed by 9:30 P.M.
Premise: You are an eight-year-old child.
Conclusion: Therefore, you should be in bed by 9:30 P.M.

Often we present this kind of reasoning in an abbreviated form called an *enthymeme*, which assumes the first premise: You should be in bed by 9:30 because you're an eight-year-old child; Bill White is a politician, so he's untrustworthy.

Describe an example from your own experience in which you use this deductive form, both as a syllogism and as an enthymeme.

Other Deductive Forms

Deductive arguments, or syllogisms and enthymemes, come in many other forms, most of which have names given by logicians. At some time while you are in college, you should consider taking a course in critical thinking or logic and learn about as many kinds of reasoning as you can. This chapter provides only an introduction.

Affirming the antecedent
Premise: If I have prepared thoroughly for the final exam, I will do well.
Premise: I prepared thoroughly for the exam.
Conclusion: Therefore, I will do well on the exam.

When we reason like this, we are using the following argument structure:

Premise: If A (I have prepared thoroughly), then B (I will do well).
Premise: A (I have prepared thoroughly).
Conclusion: Therefore, B (I will do well).

Like all valid deductive forms, this form is valid no matter what specific terms are included. For example:

Premise: If the Democrats register 20 million new voters, they will win the presidential election.
Premise: The Democrats registered more than 20 million new voters.
Conclusion: Therefore, the Democrats will win the presidential election.

As with other valid argument forms, the conclusion will be true if the reasons are true. Although the second premise in this argument expresses information that can be verified, the first premise would be more difficult to establish.

Denying the consequent
Premise: If Michael were a really good friend, he would lend me his car for the weekend.
Premise: Michael refuses to lend me his car for the weekend.
Conclusion: Therefore, Michael is not a really good friend.

When we reason in this fashion, we are using the following argument structure:

Premise: If A (Michael is a really good friend), then B (He will lend me his car).
Premise: Not B (He won't lend me his car).
Conclusion: Therefore, not A (He's not a really good friend).

Again, like other valid reasoning forms, this form is valid no matter what subject is being considered. As always, the truth of the premises must be evaluated.

Disjunctive syllogism
Premise: Either I left my wallet on my dresser or I have lost it.
Premise: The wallet is not on my dresser.
Conclusion: Therefore, I must have lost it.

When we reason in this way, we are using the following argument structure:

Premise: Either A (I left my wallet on my dresser) or B (I have lost it).
Premise: Not A (I didn't leave it on my dresser).
Conclusion: Therefore, B (I have lost it).

This valid reasoning form can be applied to any number of situations and still yield valid results. For example:

Premise: Either your stomach trouble is caused by what you are eating or it is caused by nervous tension.
Premise: You can tell me that you have been taking special care with your diet.
Conclusion: Therefore, your stomach trouble is caused by nervous tension.

To determine the accuracy of the conclusion, we must determine the accuracy of the premises. If they are true, the conclusion must be true.

All the foregoing basic argument forms are found not only in informal everyday conversations but also at more formal levels of thinking. They appear in academic disciplines, in scientific inquiry, in debates on social issues, and so on. Many other argument forms—both deductive and inductive—also constitute human reasoning. By sharpening your understanding of these ways of thinking, you will be better able to make sense of the world by constructing and evaluating effective arguments.

THINKING ↔ WRITING ACTIVITY 12.4

Evaluating Deductive Arguments

Analyze the following arguments by completing these steps.

1. Summarize the reasons and conclusions given.
2. Identify which, if any, deductive argument forms are used.
3. Evaluate the truth of the reasons that support the conclusion.

The state is by nature clearly prior to the family and to the individual, since the whole is of necessity prior to the part. —Aristotle, *Politics*

The extreme vulnerability of a complex industrial society to intelligent, targeted terrorism by a very small number of people may prove the fatal challenge to which Western states have no adequate response. Counterforce alone will never suffice. The real challenge of the true terrorist is to the basic values of a society. If there is no commitment to shared values in Western society—and if none are imparted in our amoral institutions of higher learning—no increase in police and burglar alarms will suffice to preserve our society from the specter that haunts us—not a bomb from above but a gun from within. —James Billington, *"The Gun Within"*

To fully believe in something, to truly understand something, one must be intimately acquainted with its opposite. One should not adopt a creed by default, because no alternative is known. Education should prepare students for the "real world" not be segregating them from evil but by urging full confrontation to test and modify the validity of the good. —Robert Baron, *"In Defense of Teaching Racism, Sexism, and Fascism"*

The inescapable conclusion is that society secretly wants crime, needs crime, and gains definite satisfactions from the present mishandling of it! We condemn crime; we punish offenders for it; but we need it. The crime and punishment ritual is a part of our lives. We need crimes to wonder at, to enjoy vicariously, to discuss and speculate about, and to publicly deplore. We need criminals to identify ourselves with, to envy secretly, and to punish stoutly. They do for us the forbidden, illegal things we wish to do and, like scapegoats of old, they bear the burdens of our displaced guilt and punishment—"the iniquities of us all." —Karl Menninger, *"The Crime of Punishment"*

Inductive Reasoning

The preceding section has focused on *de*ductive reasoning, an argument form in which one reasons from premises that are known or assumed to be true to a conclusion that follows necessarily from the premises. This section introduces *inductive reasoning*, an argument form in which one reasons from premises or instances that are known or assumed to be true to a conclusion that is supported by the premises but does not follow necessarily from them.

> **Inductive Reasoning:**   an argument form in which one reasons from premises, instances, or data that are known or assumed to be true to a conclusion that is supported by the premises but does not follow necessarily from them.

When you reason inductively, your premises, instances, or data provide evidence that makes it more or less probable (but not certain) that the conclusion is true. The following statements are examples of conclusions reached through inductive reasoning. As you read them, think about how the data might have been obtained and what arguments could be based on each statement.

1. A recent Gallup poll reported that 74 percent of the American public believes that abortion should remain legal.
2. On the average, a person with a college degree will earn over $830,000 more in his or her lifetime than a person with just a high school diploma.
3. The outbreak of food poisoning at the end-of-year school party was probably caused by the squid salad.
4. The devastating disease AIDS is caused by a particularly complex virus that may not be curable.
5. The solar system is probably the result of an enormous explosion—a "big bang"—that occurred billions of years ago.

Each of the first two statements is an example of inductive reasoning known as **empirical generalization,** a general statement about an entire group made on the basis of observing some members of the group. The final three statements are examples of **causal reasoning,** a form of inductive reasoning in which it is claimed that an event (or events) is the result of the occurrence of another event (or events).

Causal Reasoning and the Scientific Method

You were introduced to causal reasoning in Chapter 8 and also to the fallacies that can result if causes are not analyzed logically. Review pages 287–294 as a reminder of the characteristics of this pattern of induction.

Causal reasoning is the backbone of the natural and the social sciences. It is central to the *scientific method,* which works on the assumption that the world is constructed in a complex web of causal relationships that can be discovered through systematic investigation. You work with the scientific method in your science courses.

Empirical Generalization

An important tool used by both natural and social scientists is empirical generalization. Have you ever wondered how the major television and radio networks can accurately predict election results hours before the polls close? These predictions are made possible by the power of empirical generalization, which is defined as reasoning from a limited sample to a general conclusion based on this sample. Arguments are often based on such generalizations.

> **Empirical Generalization:**   a form of inductive reasoning in which a general statement is made about an entire group (the "target population") based on observing some members of the group (the "sample population").

Network election predictions, as well as public opinion polls that occur throughout a political campaign, are based on interviews with a select number of people. Ideally, pollsters would interview everyone in the target population (in this case, voters), but this, of course, is hardly practical. Instead, they select a relatively small group of individuals from the target population, known as a sample, who they have determined will adequately represent the group as a whole. Pollsters believe that they can then generalize the opinions of this smaller group to the target population. And the results are accurate, with a few notable exceptions (such as in the 1948 presidential election, when New York Governor Thomas Dewey went to bed believing he had been elected president and woke up a loser to Harry Truman).

There are three key criteria for evaluating inductive arguments:

- Is the sample known?
- Is the sample sufficient?
- Is the sample representative?

Is the Sample Known?

An inductive argument is only as strong as the sample on which it is based. For example, sample populations described in vague and unclear terms— such as "highly placed sources" or "many young people interviewed"—

provide a treacherously weak foundation for generalizing to larger populations. In order for an inductive argument to be persuasive, the sample population should be explicitly *known* and clearly identified. Natural and social scientists take great care in selecting the members in the sample groups. Information on members of the sample groups is available to outside investigators who may wish to evaluate and verify the results.

Is the Sample Sufficient?

The second criterion for evaluating inductive reasoning is to consider the *size* of the sample. It should be large enough to give an accurate sense of the group as a whole. In the polling example discussed earlier, we would be concerned if only a few registered voters were interviewed and the results of these interviews were generalized to a much larger population. Overall, the larger the sample, the more reliable the inductive conclusions. Natural and social scientists have developed precise guidelines for determining the size of the sample needed to achieve reliable results. For example, poll results are often accompanied by a qualification such as "These results are subject to an error factor of ± 3 percentage points." This means that if the sample reveals that 47 percent of those interviewed prefer candidate X, we can reliably state that 44 to 50 percent of the target population prefer candidate X. Because a sample is usually a small portion of the target population, we can rarely state that the two match each other exactly—there must always be some room for variation. The exceptions to this are situations in which the target population is completely homogeneous. For instance, tasting one cookie from a bag of cookies is usually enough to tell us whether or not the entire bag is stale.

Is the Sample Representative?

The third crucial element in effective inductive reasoning is the *representativeness* of the sample. If we are to generalize with confidence from the sample to the target population, we have to be sure the sample is similar in all relevant aspects to the larger group from which it is drawn. For instance, in the polling example, the sample population should reflect the same percentage of men and women, of Democrats and Republicans, of young and old, and so on, as the target population. It is obvious that many characteristics, such as hair color, favorite food, and shoe size are not relevant to the comparison. The better the sample reflects the target population in terms of *relevant* qualities, however, the better the accuracy of the generalizations. On the other hand, when the sample is *not* representative of the target population— for example, if the election pollsters interviewed only females between the ages of thirty and thirty-five—the sample is termed *biased,* and any generalizations about the target population will be highly suspect.

How do we ensure that the sample is representative of the target population? One important device is *random selection,* a selection strategy in which every member of the target population has an equal chance of being included in the sample. For example, the various techniques used to select winning lottery tickets are supposed to be random—each ticket is supposed to have an equal chance of winning. In complex cases of inductive reasoning—such as polling—random selection is often combined with the confirmation that all the important categories in the population are adequately represented. For example, an election pollster would want to be certain that all significant geographical areas are included, and then would randomly select individuals from within those areas to compose the sample.

Understanding the principles of empirical generalization is of crucial importance to effective thinking because we are continually challenged to evaluate this form of inductive thinking in our lives. In addition, if we are writing about political or social issues, we often use the results of inductive investigations.

THINKING ↔ WRITING ACTIVITY 12.5

Analyzing Inductive Reasoning

Review the following examples of inductive reasoning. Select two and evaluate the quality of the thinking by answering the following questions.

1. Is the sample known?
2. Is the sample sufficient?
3. Is the sample representative?
4. Do you believe that the conclusions are likely to be accurate? Why or why not?
5. What are some arguments that might be based on examples that you chose?

In a study of a possible relationship between pornography and antisocial behavior, questionnaires went out to 7,500 psychiatrists and psychoanalysts whose listing in the directory of the American Psychological Association indicated clinical experience. Over 3,400 of these professionals responded. The result: 7.4 percent of the psychiatrists and psychologists had cases in which they were convinced that pornography was a causal factor in antisocial behavior; an additional 9.4 percent were suspicious; 3.2 percent did not commit themselves; and 80 percent said they had no cases in which a causal connection was suspected.

A survey by the Sleep Disorder Clinic of the VA hospital in La Jolla, California (involving more than one million people), revealed that people who sleep more than ten hours a night have a death rate 80 percent higher than those who sleep only seven or eight hours. Men who sleep less than four hours a night have a death rate 180 percent higher, and women with less (than four hours) sleep have a rate 40 percent higher. This might be taken as indicating that too much and too little sleep cause death.

In a recent survey, twice as many doctors interviewed stated that if they were stranded on a desert island, they would prefer X Aspirin to Extra Strength Y.

Being a general practitioner in a rural area has tremendous drawbacks—being on virtul 24-hour call 365 days a year; patients without financial means or insurance; low fees in the first place; inadequate facilities and assistance. Nevertheless, America's small-town G.P.s seem fairly content with their lot. According to a survey taken by Country Doctor, fully 50 percent wrote back that they "basically like being a rural G.P." Only 1 in 15 regretted that he or she had not specialized. Only 2 out of 20 rural general practitioners would trade places with their urban counterparts, given the chance. And only 1 in 30 would "choose some other line of work altogether."

THINKING ↔ WRITING ACTIVITY 12.6

Designing a Polling Project

Select an issue that you would like to poll a group of people about—a group such as the population of your school or your neighborhood. Describe in specific terms how you would go about constructing a sample both large enough and representative enough for you to generalize the results to the target population accurately. Then decide how you might use this information in a paper in which you present an argument. Which college sources might ask for such research? In what community activities could this kind of information gathering be valuable? Write your answers in your journal.

Fallacies: Forms of False Reasoning

Certain forms of reasoning are not logical. These types of pseudoreasoning (false reasoning) are often termed *fallacies:* arguments that are not sound because of various errors in reasoning. Fallacious reasoning is sometimes used to influence others. It seeks to persuade not on the basis of sound arguments and critical thinking, but on the basis of emotional and illogical factors. Sometimes fallacious reasoning is used inadvertently. However, it is always dangerous, so it is important to recognize it as well as to avoid its use. Detecting fallacious reasoning can be a significant factor in evaluating sources of beliefs, the concept discussed in Chapter 10.

> **Fallacies:** unsound arguments that are often persuasive because they can appear to be logical, because they usually appeal to our emotions and prejudices, and because they can support conclusions that we want to believe are accurate.

In Chapter 9, Forming Concepts, we explored the way that we form concepts through the interactive process of *generalizing* (identifying the common qualities that define the boundaries of the concept) and *interpreting* (identifying examples of the concept). This generalizing and interpreting process is similar to the process involved in constructing empirical generalizations, as we seek to reach a general conclusion based on a limited number of examples and then apply this conclusion to other examples. Although generalizing and interpreting are useful in forming concepts, they also can give rise to fallacious ways of thinking, including the following:

- Hasty generalization
- Sweeping generalization
- False dilemma

Hasty Generalization

Consider the following examples of reasoning. Do you think the arguments are sound? Why or why not?

- My boyfriends have never shown any real concern for my feelings. My conclusion is that men are insensitive, selfish, and emotionally superficial.
- My mother always gets upset over insignificant things. This leads me to believe that women are very emotional.

In both of these cases, a general conclusion has been reached that is based on a very small sample. As a result, the reasons provide very weak support for the conclusions that are being developed. It just does not make good sense to generalize from a few individuals to all men or all women. The conclusion is *hasty* because the sample is not large enough or not representative enough to provide adequate justification for the generalization.

Sweeping Generalization

Whereas the fallacy of hasty generalization deals with errors in the process of generalizing, the fallacy of *sweeping generalization* focuses on difficulties in the process of interpreting. Consider the following examples of reasoning. Do you consider the arguments sound? Why or why not?

- Vigorous exercise contributes to overall good health. Therefore, vigorous exercise should be practiced by recent heart attack victims, people who are out of shape, and women in the last month of pregnancy.

- People should be allowed to make their own decisions, providing that their actions do not harm other people. Therefore, people who are trying to commit suicide should be left alone to do what they want.

In both of these cases, generalizations that are true in most cases have been deliberately applied to instances that are clearly intended to be exceptions to the generalizations because of special features that the exceptions possess. Of course, the use of a sweeping generalization stimulates us to clarify the generalization, rephrasing it to exclude instances, like those given here, that have special features. For example, the first generalization could be reformulated as "Vigorous exercise contributes to overall good health, *except* for recent heart attack victims, people out of shape, and women who are about to give birth." Sweeping generalizations become dangerous when they are accepted without critical analysis and reformulation.

Examine the following examples of sweeping generalizations, and in each case (a) explain *why* it is a sweeping generalization, and (b) reformulate the statement to make it a legitimate generalization.

1. A college education stimulates you to develop as a person and prepares you for many professions. Therefore, all persons should attend college, no matter what career they are interested in.
2. Drugs such as heroin and morphine are addictive and therefore qualify as dangerous drugs. This means that they should never be used, even as painkillers in medical situations.
3. Once criminals have served time for the crimes they have committed, they have paid their debt to society and should be permitted to work at any job they choose.

False Dilemma

The fallacy of the *false dilemma*—also known as the *either/or* fallacy or the *black-or-white* fallacy—occurs when one is being asked to choose between two extreme alternatives without being able to consider additional options. For example, we may say, "You're either for me or against me," meaning that a choice has to be made between these alternatives. Sometimes giving people only two choices on an issue makes sense ("If you decide to swim the English Channel, you'll either make it or you won't"). At other times, however, viewing situations in such extreme terms may be a serious oversimplification—for it would mean viewing a complicated situation in terms that are too simple.

The following statements are examples of false dilemmas. After analyzing the fallacy in each case, suggest different alternatives than those being presented. **Example:** "Everyone in Germany is a National Socialist—the few outside the party are either lunatics or idiots." (Adolf Hitler, quoted by the *New York Times*, April 5, 1938)

Analysis: Hitler was saying that Germans who were not Nazis were lunatics or idiots. By limiting the population to these groups, Hitler was simply ignoring all the people who did not qualify as Nazis, lunatics, or idiots.

1. "America—love it or leave it!"
2. "She loves me; she loves me not."
3. "Live free or die."
4. "If you're not part of the solution, then you're part of the problem."
5. "If you know about BMW, you either own one or you want to."

Fallacies of Relevance

Many fallacious arguments appeal for support to factors that have little or nothing to do with the argument being offered. In these cases, false appeals substitute for sound reasoning and a critical examination of the issues. Such appeals, known as fallacies of relevance, include the following kinds of fallacious thinking:

- Appeal to authority
- Appeal to pity
- Appeal to fear
- Appeal to ignorance
- Appeal to personal attack

Appeal to Authority

In Chapters 2 and 10, we explored the ways in which we sometimes use various authorities to establish our beliefs or prove our points. At that time, we noted that to serve as a basis for beliefs, authorities must have legitimate expertise in the area in which they are advising—like an experienced mechanic diagnosing a problem with your car. However, people occasionally appeal to authorities who are not qualified to give an expert opinion. Consider the reasoning in the following advertisements. Do you think the arguments are sound? Why or why not?

- Hi. You've probably seen me out on the football field. After a hard day's work crushing halfbacks and sacking quarterbacks, I like to settle down with a cold, smooth Maltz beer.

- SONY. Ask anyone.
- Over 11 million women will read this ad. Only 16 will own the coat.

Each of these arguments is intended to persuade us of the value of a product through the appeal to various authorities. In the first case, the authority is a well-known sports figure; in the second, the authority is large numbers of people; and in the third, the authority is a select few, appealing to our desire to be exclusive ("snob appeal"). Unfortunately, none of these authorities offers legitimate expertise about the product. Football players are not beer experts; large numbers of people are often misled; and exclusive groups of people are frequently mistaken in their beliefs. To evaluate authorities properly, we have to ask:

- What are the professional credentials on which the authorities' expertise is based?
- Is their expertise in the area they are commenting on?

Appeal to Pity

Consider the reasoning in the following arguments. Do you think the arguments are sound? Why or why not?

- I know that I haven't completed my term paper, but I really think that I should be excused. This has been a very difficult semester for me. I caught every kind of flu that came around. In addition, my brother has a drinking problem, and this has been very upsetting to me. Also, my dog died.
- I admit that my client embezzled money from the company, Your Honor. However, I would like to bring several facts to your attention. He is a family man with a wonderful wife and two terrific children. He is an important member of the community. He is active in the church, coaches a Little League baseball team, and has worked very hard to be a good person who cares about people. I think that you should take these things into consideration in handing down your sentence.

In each of these arguments, the reasons offered to support the conclusions may indeed be true. Yet they are not relevant to the conclusion. Instead of providing evidence that supports the conclusion, the reasons are designed to make us feel sorry for the person involved and therefore to agree with the conclusion out of sympathy. Although these appeals are often effective, the arguments are not sound. The probability of a conclusion can be established only by reasons that support and are relevant to the conclusion.

Appeal to Fear

Consider the reasoning in the following arguments. Do you consider the arguments sound? Why or why not?

- I'm afraid I don't think you deserve a raise. After all, there are many people who would be happy to have your job at the salary you are currently receiving. I would be happy to interview some of these people if you really think that you are underpaid.

- If you continue to disagree with my interpretation of *The Catcher in the Rye*, I'm afraid you won't get a very good grade on your paper.

In both of these arguments, the conclusions being suggested are supported by an appeal to fear, not by reasons that provide evidence for the conclusions. In the first case, the threat is that if you do not forgo your salary demands, your job may be in jeopardy. In the second case, the threat is that if you do not agree with the teacher's interpretation, you will receive a low grade. In neither instance are the real issues—Is a salary increase deserved? Is the student's interpretation legitimate?—being discussed. People who appeal to fear to support their conclusions are interested only in prevailing, regardless of which position might be more justified.

Appeal to Ignorance

Consider the reasoning in the following arguments. Do you find the arguments sound? Why or why not?

- You say that you don't believe in God. But can you prove that an omnipotent spirit doesn't exist? If not, then you have to accept the conclusion that it does in fact exist.

- Greco Tires are the best. No others have been proved better.

When this argument form is used, the person offering the conclusion is asking his or her opponent to *disprove* the conclusion. If the opponent is unable to do so, the conclusion is asserted to be true. This argument form is not valid because it is the job of the person proposing the argument to prove the conclusion. The fact that an opponent cannot disprove the conclusion offers no evidence that the conclusion is justified.

Appeal to Personal Attack

Consider the reasoning in the following arguments. Do you think the arguments are valid? Why or why not?

- Senator Smith's opinion about a tax cut is wrong. It's impossible to believe anything he says since he left his wife for that model.

- How can you have an intelligent opinion about abortion? You're not a woman, so this is a decision that you'll never have to make.

This argument form has been one of the fallacies most frequently used through the ages. Its effectiveness results from ignoring the issues of the argument and focusing instead on the personal qualities of the person offering the argument. Trying to discredit the other person is an effort to discredit the argument—no matter what reasons are offered. This fallacy is also referred to as the *ad hominem* argument, which means "to the man" rather than to the issue, and as *poisoning the well,* as we are trying to ensure that any water drawn from the opponent's well will be treated as undrinkable.

The effort to discredit can take two forms, as illustrated in the preceding examples. The fallacy can be *abusive* in the sense of directly attacking the credibility of an opponent. In addition, the fallacy can be *circumstantial* in the sense of claiming that a person's circumstances, not character, render his or her opinion so biased or uninformed that it cannot be treated seriously (as in the second example). Other examples of the circumstantial form of the fallacy would include disregarding the views on nuclear-plant safety given by an owner of a nuclear plant.

THINKING ↔ WRITING ACTIVITY 12.7

Analyzing Fallacies

1. Find in advertisements, political statements, or other arguments that you have encountered, examples of two or three false appeals. Write a brief explanation of why you think the appeal is not warranted. Look for the following fallacies:

   - Appeal to authority
   - Appeal to pity
   - Appeal to fear
   - Appeal to ignorance
   - Appeal to personal attack

2. Write a few sentences explaining how you can avoid fallacies in your own writing.

THINKING ↔ WRITING ACTIVITY 12.8

Analyzing well-known arguments to see how they use deduction, induction, evidence *(logos), ethos, pathos,* appeals—and perhaps fallacious reasoning— is a challenging activity and one that can help you with your own arguments. Read *The Declaration of Independence,* and the "Declaration of Sentiments and Resolutions" in this chapter, and "I Have a Dream" (pages 170–173 in Chapter 5). Then write answers to the following questions in your journal.

1. What is the thesis of each of these arguments? Where is it stated in each?
2. How does *The Declaration of Independence* use deduction and induction? Identify the premises and the conclusion in the second paragraph. Comment on the instances that are listed beginning in the third paragraph. Comment on the effectiveness of this deliberate use of these basic reasoning methods.
3. How does "I Have a Dream" use induction?
4. In your library or on the Internet, locate a copy of King's "Letter from Birmingham Jail." What differences in approach do you see between it and "I Have a Dream"? What about the tone or *ethos*?
5. These political arguments address major human questions. What in them could be applicable to arguments that you might write about academic or business issues? What might not be applicable?

The Declaration of Independence

In Congress, July 4, 1776
The unanimous declaration of the thirteen
United States of America

When in the course of human events, it becomes necessary for one people to dissolve the political bands which have connected them with another, and to assume among the powers of the earth, the separate and equal station to which the Laws of Nature and of Nature's God entitle them, a decent respect to the opinions of mankind requires that they should declare the causes which impel them to the separation.

We hold these truths to be self-evident, that all men are created equal, that they are endowed by their Creator with certain unalienable rights, that among these are life, liberty and the pursuit of happiness. That to secure these rights, governments are instituted among men, deriving their just powers from the consent of the governed. That whenever any form of government becomes destructive of these ends, it is the right of the people to alter or to abolish it, and to institute new government, laying its foundation on such principles and organizing its powers in such form, as to them shall seem most likely to effect their safety and happiness. Prudence, indeed, will dictate that governments long established should not be changed for light and transient causes; and accordingly all experience hath shown, that mankind are more disposed to suffer, while evils are sufferable, than to right themselves by abolishing the forms to which they are accustomed. But when a long train of abuses and usurpations, pursuing invariably the same object evinces a design to reduce them under absolute despotism, it is their right, it is their duty, to throw off such government, and to provide new guards for their future security. Such has been the patient sufferance of these Colonies; and such is now the necessity which constrains them to alter their former systems of government. The history of the present King of Great Britain is a history of repeated injuries and usurpations, all having in direct object the establishment of an absolute tyranny over these States. To prove this, let facts be submitted to a candid world.

He has refused his assent to laws, the most wholesome and necessary for the public good.

He has forbidden his Governors to pass laws of immediate and pressing importance, unless suspended in their operation till his assent should be obtained; and when so suspended, he has utterly neglected to attend to them.

5   He has refused to pass other laws for the accommodation of large districts of people, unless those people would relinquish the right of representation in the Legislature, a right inestimable to them and formidable to tyrants only.

He has called together legislative bodies at places unusual, uncomfortable, and distant from the depository of their public records, for the sole purpose of fatiguing them into compliance with his measures.

He has dissolved representative houses repeatedly, for opposing with manly firmness his invasions on the rights of the people.

He has refused for a long time, after such dissolutions, to cause others to be elected; whereby the legislative powers, incapable of annihilation, have returned to the people at large for their exercise; the State remaining in the meantime exposed to all the dangers of invasion from without and convulsions within.

He has endeavoured to prevent the population of these States; for that purpose obstructing the laws of naturalization of foreigners; refusing to pass others to encourage their migration hither, and raising the conditions of new appropriations of lands.

10   He has obstructed the administration of justice, by refusing his assent to laws for establishing judiciary powers.

He has made judges dependent on his will alone, for the tenure of their offices, and the amount and payment of their salaries.

He has erected a multitude of new offices, and sent hither swarms of officers to harass our people, and eat out their substance.

He has kept among us, in times of peace, standing armies without the consent of our legislatures.

He has affected to render the military independent of and superior to the civil power.

15   He has combined with others to subject us to a jurisdiction foreign to our constitution, and unacknowledged by our laws; giving his assent to their acts of pretended legislation:

For quartering large bodies of armed troops among us:

For protecting them, by a mock trial, from punishment for any murders which they should commit on the inhabitants of these States:

For cutting off our trade with all parts of the world:

For imposing taxes on us without our consent:

20   For depriving us, in many cases, of the benefits of trial by jury:

For transporting us beyond seas to be tried for pretended offences:

For abolishing the free system of English laws in a neighbouring Province, establishing therein an arbitrary government, and enlarging its boundaries so as to render it at once an example and fit instrument for introducing the same absolute rule into these Colonies:

For taking away our Charters, abolishing our most valuable laws, and altering fundamentally the forms of our governments:

For suspending our own Legislatures, and declaring themselves invested with power to legislate for us in all cases whatsoever.

25   He has abdicated government here, by declaring us out of his protection and waging war against us.

He has plundered our seas, ravaged our coasts, burnt our towns, and destroyed the lives of our people.

He is at this time transporting large armies of foreign mercenaries to complete the works of death, desolation and tyranny, already begun with circumstances of cruelty and perfidy scarcely paralleled in the most barbarous ages, and totally unworthy the head of a civilized nation.

He has constrained our fellow citizens taken captive on the high seas to bear arms against their country, to become the executioners of their friends and brethren, or to fall themselves by their hands.

He has excited domestic insurrections amongst us, and has endeavoured to bring on the inhabitants of our frontiers, the merciless Indian savages, whose known rule of warfare, is an undistinguished destruction of all ages, sexes, and conditions.

30   In every stage of these oppressions we have petitioned for redress in the most humble terms: our repeated petitions have been answered only by repeated injury. A prince whose character is thus marked by every act which may define a tyrant is unfit to be the ruler of a free people.

Nor have we been wanting in attention to our British brethren. We have warned them from time to time of attempts by their legislature to extend an unwarrantable jurisdiction over us. We have reminded them of the circumstances of our emigration and settlement here. We have appealed to their native justice and magnanimity, and we have conjured them by the ties of our common kindred to disavow these usurpations, which would inevitably interrupt our connections and correspondence. They too have been deaf to the voice of justice and of consanguinity. We must, therefore, acquiesce in the necessity, which denounces our separation, and hold them, as we hold the rest of mankind, enemies in war, in peace friends.

We, therefore, the Representatives of the United States of America, in General Congress assembled, appealing to the Supreme Judge of the world for the rectitude of our intentions, do, in the name, and by the authority of the good people of these Colonies, solemnly publish and declare, That these United Colonies are, and of right ought to be Free and Independent States; that they are absolved from all allegiance to the British Crown, and that all political connection between them and the State of Great Britain, is and ought to be totally dissolved; and that as Free and Independent States, they have full power to levy war, conclude peace, contract alliances, establish commerce, and to do all other acts and things which Independent States may of right do. And for the support of this declaration, with a firm reliance on the protection of Divine Providence, we mutually pledge to each other our lives, our fortunes, and our sacred honor.

from Declaration of Sentiments and Resolutions, Seneca Falls
by Elizabeth Cady Stanton

When, in the course of human events, it becomes necessary for one person of the family of man to assume among the people of the earth a position different from that which they have hitherto occupied, but one to which the laws of nature and nature's God entitle them, a decent respect to the opinions of mankind requires that they should declare the causes that impel them to such a course.

We hold these truths to be self-evident: that all men and women are created equal; that they are endowed by their Creator with certain inalienable rights; that among these are life, liberty, and the pursuit of happiness; that to secure these rights governments are instituted, deriving their just powers from the consent of the governed. Whenever any form of government becomes destructive of these ends, it is the right of those who suffer from it to refuse allegiance to it, and to insist upon the institution of a new government, laying its foundation on such principles, and organizing its powers in such form, as to them shall seem most likely to effect their safety and happiness. Prudence, indeed, will dictate that governments long established should not be changed for light and transient causes; and accordingly all experience hath shown that mankind are more disposed to suffer, while evils are sufferable, than to right themselves by abolishing the forms to which they were accustomed. But when a long train of abuses and usurpations, pursuing invariably the same object evinces a design to reduce them under absolute despotism, it is their duty to throw off such government, and to provide new guards for their future security. Such has been the patient sufferance of the women under this government, and such is now the necessity which constrains them to demand the equal station to which they are entitled.

The history of mankind is a history of repeated injuries and usurpations on the part of man toward woman, having in direct object the establishment of an absolute tyranny over her. To prove this, let facts be submitted to a candid world.

He has never permitted her to exercise her inalienable right to the elective franchise.

He has compelled her to submit to laws, in the formation of which she had no voice.

He has withheld from her rights which are given to the most ignorant and degraded men—both natives and foreigners.

Having deprived her of this first right of a citizen, the elective franchise, thereby leaving her without representation in the halls of legislation, he has oppressed her on all sides.

He has made her, if married, in the eye of the law, civilly dead.

He has taken from her all right in property, even to the wages she earns.

He has made her, morally, an irresponsible being, as she can commit many crimes with impunity, provided they be done in the presence of her husband. In the covenant of marriage, she is compelled to promise obedience to her husband, he becoming, to all intents and purposes, her master—the law giving him power to deprive her of her liberty, and to administer chastisement.

He has so framed the laws of divorce, as to what shall be the proper causes, and in case of separation, to whom the guardianship of the children shall be given, as to be wholly regardless of the happiness of women—the law, in all cases, going upon a false supposition of the supremacy of man, and giving all power into his hands.

After depriving her of all rights as a married woman, if single, and the owner of property, he has taxed her to support a government which recognizes her only when her property can be made profitable to it.

He has monopolized nearly all the profitable employments, and from those she is permitted to follow, she receives but a scanty remuneration. He closes against her all the avenues to wealth and distinction which he considers most honorable to himself. As a teacher of theology, medicine, or law, she is not known.

He has denied her the facilities for obtaining a thorough education, all colleges being closed against her.

He allows her in Church, as well as State, but a subordinate position, claiming Apostolic authority for her exclusion from the ministry, and, with some exceptions, from any public participation in the affairs of the Church.

He has created a false public sentiment by giving to the world a different code of morals for men and women, by which moral delinquencies which exclude women from society are not only tolerated, but deemed of little account in man.

He has usurped the prerogative of Jehovah himself, claiming it as his right to assign for her a sphere of action, when that belongs to her conscience and to her God.

He has endeavored, in every way that he could, to destroy her confidence in her own powers, to lessen her self-respect, and to make her willing to lead a dependent and abject life.

Now, in view of this entire disfranchisement of one-half the people of this country, their social and religious degradation—in view of the unjust laws above mentioned, and because women do feel themselves aggrieved, oppressed, and fraudulently deprived of their most sacred rights, we insist that they have immediate admission to all the rights and privileges which belong to them as citizens of the United States.

20 In entering upon the great work before us, we anticipate no small amount of misconception, misrepresentation, and ridicule; but we shall use every instrumentality within our power to effect our object. We shall employ agents, circulate tracts, petition the State and National legislatures, and endeavor to enlist the pulpit and the press in our behalf. We hope this Convention will be followed by a series of Conventions embracing every part of the country.

Resolutions

WHEREAS, The great precept of nature is conceded to be, that "man shall pursue his own true and substantial happiness." Blackstone in his Commentaries remarks, that this law of Nature being coeval with mankind, and dictated by God himself, is of course superior in obligation to any other. It is binding over all the globe, in all countries and at all times; no human laws are of any validity if contrary to this, and such of them as are valid, derive all their force and all their validity, and all their authority, mediately and immediately, from this original; therefore,

Resolved, That such laws as conflict, in any way, with the true and substantial happiness of woman, are contrary to the great precept of nature and of no validity, for this is "superior in obligation to any other."

Resolved, That all laws which prevent woman from occupying such a station in society as her conscience shall dictate, or which place her in a position inferior to that of man, are contrary to the great precept of nature, and therefore of no force or authority.

Resolved, That woman is man's equal—was intended to be so by the Creator, and the highest good of the race demands that she should be recognized as such.

Resolved, That the women of this country ought to be enlightened in regard to the laws under which they live, that they may no longer publish their degradation by declaring themselves satisfied with their present position, nor their ignorance, by asserting that they have all the rights they want.

Resolved, That inasmuch as man, while claiming for himself intellectual superiority, does accord to woman moral superiority for it is preeminently his duty to encourage her to speak and teach, as she has an opportunity, in all religious assemblies.

Resolved, That the same amount of virtue, delicacy, and refinement of behavior that is required of woman in the social state, should also be required of man, and the same transgressions should be visited with equal severity on both man and woman.

Resolved, That the objection of indelicacy and impropriety, which is so often brought against woman when she addresses a public audience, comes with a very ill-grace from those who encourage, by their attendance, her appearance on the stage, in the concert, or in feats of the circus.

Resolved, That woman has too long rested satisfied in the circumscribed limits which corrupt customs and a perverted application of the Scriptures have marked out for her, and that it is time she should move in the enlarged sphere which her great Creator has assigned her.

Resolved, That it is the duty of the women of this country to secure to themselves their sacred right to the elective franchise.

Resolved, That the equality of human rights results necessarily from the fact of the identity of the race in capabilities and responsibilities.

Resolved, therefore, That, being invested by the Creator with the same capabilities, and the same consciousness of responsibility for their exercise, it is demonstrably the right and duty of woman, equally with man, to promote every righteous cause by every righteous means; and especially in regard to the great subjects of morals and religion, it is self-evidently her right to participate with her brother in teaching them, both in private and in public, by writing and by speaking, by any instrumentalities proper to be used, and in any assemblies proper to be held; and this being a self-evident truth growing out of the divinely implanted principles of human nature, any custom or authority adverse to it, whether modern or wearing the hoary sanction of antiquity, is to be regarded as a self-evident falsehood, and at war with mankind.

[At the last session Lucretia Mott offered and spoke to the following resolution:]

Resolved, That the speedy success of our cause depends upon the zealous and untiring efforts of both men and women, for the overthrow of the monopoly of the pulpit, and for the securing to women an equal participation with men in the various trades, professions and commerce.

Deductive and Inductive Reasoning in Writing

As pointed out earlier in this chapter, writers and speakers seldom use deductive or inductive reasoning solely or purely. In their arguments, conclusions reached by induction become premises for deductions; statements that are premises are given but not demonstrated, as in the opening sentences of *The Declaration of Independence*. Deductively developed paragraphs interact with inductively developed ones, as in Gould's "Evolution as Fact and

Theory" (see the sections "Creationism Is Not Science" and "The Fact of Evolution").

However, deduction is used obviously when a definition or principle is established by the writer, and the point of the paper or paragraph is to claim that the item being discussed fits the definition or demonstrates the principle. If the readers agree with the definition and also agree that the item fits it, the claim is proved for whatever purpose the writer has. Political science, literature, philosophy, theology, psychology, and law are among the many fields that employ deductive arguments in this way.

Inductive reasoning is reflected in two ways in writing. One is structural. When a writer chooses to present instances of evidence first, leading readers to the claim given as a conclusion, the paragraph or paper is organized inductively. Composition instructors tend to steer students away from using this technique to structure entire papers, since great skill is needed to keep readers with the argument. The sections "Organizing Ideas" and "Revising" in the Writing Projects in this book have asked you to think carefully about where you state your thesis or claim, for this reason. It is usually more effective to use deductively based structure.

A reflection of inductive reasoning that is used often in writing occurs when the writer makes a claim in a topic sentence or thesis statement, then simply exemplifies it. The writer is asking the readers to re-enact the inductive process that led the writer to make the claim. Notice how the list of evils alleged to have been committed by the British government functions this way in *The Declaration of Independence*. Notice how regularly you use this technique, and how often much of what you read uses it, too.

In addition, deduction often appears in the abbreviated form of the *enthymeme* (see page 501), and induction through the small sample of the example, the inference, and the anecdote. This practice is neither wrong nor fallacious. Writers cannot take the time or the space to state all the premises of every deduction or to give multiple instances to support each idea. However, critical thinkers need to understand these reductions so that claims and evidence can be evaluated. Deduction and induction, the basic reasoning methods, are at work in various ways in what we write and read.

Writing Thoughtful Arguments

This chapter has emphasized the importance of basic concepts and terminology connected with argument because reasoned argument, leading to agreement, is the foundation of a democratic society and also is often the key to success in personal, academic, and business activities.

Because so much college and professional writing is argumentative, this **Writing Project** asks you to concentrate on the two central elements of

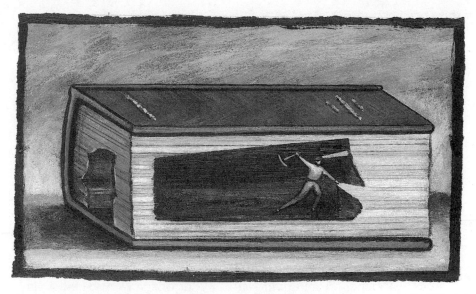

Argumentative Papers: Composing informed argumentative papers involves researching relevant information from authoritative sources and integrating this information into the paper in appropriate ways.

argument: establishing a clear thesis and providing sound evidence for it. In addition, you will be particularly conscious of being logical, of avoiding fallacious statements, of considering your audience, and of presenting yourself as a reasonable, well-informed proponent of your claims.

WRITING PROJECT

WRITING PROJECT   Arguing a Position on a
                   Significant Issue

Write an essay in which you argue logically for a position on an issue that you consider significant. Use several print sources, any electronic sources that your instructor has specified, and—if possible—an interview to support your claims. Follow directions given by your instructor as to the number and range of sources, length of the paper, and academic format for citation of sources. Be sure to follow exactly the model in your handbook when you complete your paper in MLA, APA, or another currently accepted format chosen by your instructor.

On a page separate from your paper, identify the audience to whom you are addressing your argument and explain why that audience will benefit from understanding your position. Also, either in the argument or as an accompanying note, explain why this issue is important to you, so that your classmates and your instructor, as they help you revise your drafts, can see where your expertise and possible biases have had their origins.

The following principles for writing responsible arguments are fundamental to the Western tradition of logical structured argument. Always be sure to follow them as well as you can.

1. Formulate the thesis statement carefully; place it purposefully. Use deductive and inductive approaches as appropriate to develop and support the thesis.
2. Provide a context for the thesis; give reasons for its importance.
3. Provide sound evidence. Present evidence clearly and specifically.
4. Acknowledge and show understanding of other points of view. Grant validity to any when it is justified. Refute courteously those with which you disagree, to strengthen your argument.
5. Use the thinking/organizing patterns in Part 2. Arguments often rely on definitions. Causes for a situation and the effects of a proposal are often vital to an argument. Narratives and chronologies are often effective. Contrast, comparisons, and analogies illuminate your points.
6. Avoid fallacious reasoning.
7. Be aware of your tone. You want to sound reasonable, thoughtful, and polite as you argue your points.
8. Remember that the conclusion to an argument is extremely important. Restate the thesis and/or end with a suggestion, a call for action, decision, or further thought.

This chapter has included both readings and **Thinking↔Writing Activities** that encouraged you to think about argument. Be sure to reread what you wrote for those activities; you may be able to use some of it for help in completing this **Writing Project.**

Begin by considering the key elements in the **Thinking↔Writing Model.**

Purpose

Your primary purpose is to write an argument that will bring your intended audience into agreement with your claim or thesis. As you work toward that goal, you will have to think critically about something that you care about and clarify or modify your view, which is another useful purpose.

Audience

The audience is a major concern in any argument. Two things that a successful writer understands are the characteristics and attitudes of the audience. When you create an argument, you must have a specific audience in mind. While pandering dishonorably to the audience by distorting evidence or by flattery is bad rhetoric, an arguer needs to accommodate the needs and the make-up of the audience. Some factors to consider are knowledge—an expert audience needs less background than a less informed one; age—younger and older people often have different points of view; roles—we all have different roles and respond differently as they change; relationships—an audience of peers can be approached differently than an audience of another status; the emotional level of the issue and situation—a highly charged situation needs a different approach from a calm one.

Your classmates, as always, will be a good audience for this assignment, first as expert reviewers of your drafts and, if you are dealing with an issue at your college or one pertaining to students, as an involved audience.

Finally, your instructor remains the audience who will judge how well you have planned, drafted, and revised. As a writing teacher, your instructor cares about a well-formulated thesis, logic, evidence, good organization, and correctness. Keep these in mind as you revise, edit, and proofread.

Subject

Whenever you argue for a position about which you are concerned, you are addressing an important subject. In addition, the techniques of argument themselves constitute a subject that merits much attention because argument has such importance in our lives.

Writer

As you work on this **Writing Project,** you should feel excited about the subject, since you selected something that you consider important. Also, if you have been using sources in other projects, you should be comfortable incorporating other people's ideas into your writing and documenting it appropriately. A new role for you may be that of the good rhetorician, the responsible arguer; but if you use your developing critical thinking abilities, you will manage that role well.

The Writing Process

The following sections will guide you through the stages of generating, planning, drafting, and revising as you work on your argument.

Generating Ideas

- You may be involved with some issue because of your sex or ethnicity, because of your field of study, or through some organization in which you participate; or you may be concerned about a problem at your college, in your community, in your country, or elsewhere in the world. If so, you should have no difficulty deciding what to write about. Perhaps you have so many concerns that you will have to select among them.

- If no issue comes quickly to you, look around your campus and your community to see what problems exist or what changes might be made.

- Watch the news, read the local paper and national publications such as the *New York Times,* the *Wall Street Journal, Newsweek,* and *Time.* Talk with friends, family members, and professors about significant issues.

- Think about questions in your fields of interest: your favorite college subjects, sports, entertainment, food, cars, parks, houses. Some of these questions will pertain to serious issues; some might be more light-hearted; many will merit a reasoned argument.

- Freewrite about one or two of your concerns. See how many issues or positions you come up with in five minutes.

Defining a Focus

After selecting the issue to write about, draft a thesis statement that describes the position for which you will argue. Be sure that the statement covers your points fully; it may be a complex sentence. Share it with classmates to profit from their responses. Revise it on the basis of their feedback.

Organizing Ideas

Your argument should probably be set up in the traditional "no-fail" structure: introduction, thesis, evidence, handling of other views, summing up, conclusion/recommendation for action. However, you may be able to use some other arrangement effectively.

Notice how your material adapts itself to various thinking patterns. Use them firmly to clarify your points.

Select and place material from your sources carefully. Connect this material smoothly with your ideas by introducing and commenting on it.

Drafting

Begin with the part easiest to write, which for this paper might be the beginning, since you have thought so much about your thesis and its context.

However, never get stymied trying to work out a beginning. Draft other sections in any order that works for you. You might want to draft the paragraphs that present your evidence, then consider inductive or deductive methods that you should use.

Be sure to keep track of publication information for all sources. Note abbreviated titles, authors, and pages in your draft. Then, when you revise, you can cite in the required format. Be sure to use quotation marks or indenting in your draft whenever you quote.

Revising

Ideally, at this point, you should put your draft aside for a day or two. If deadlines won't permit you to do that, then at least take a break before you try to revise. When you are ready to "re-see" your writing, begin by reading it through slowly, preferably aloud. If possible, have someone whose opinion you respect read it; ask for feedback. Then work through the hierarchy of revision concerns that follows. Remember that you have at least one and possibly two decisions to make for each question: (1) Is improvement needed? and (2) If improvement is needed, how, exactly, can I make my draft better?

1. **Think big.** Look at your draft as a whole.
- Does it fulfill the assignment in terms of topic and length?
- Have you stated the thesis clearly?
- Do all parts of the draft relate to the thesis?
- Is the organization logical?
- Do you provide enough evidence?
- Is your point of view consistent?
- Is there a discernible flow between your paragraphs?
- Have you documented information from your sources accurately?
- Have you used quotation marks around direct quotes or set the quotes off by indenting?
2. **Think medium.** Look at your draft paragraph by paragraph.
- Will your introduction make your audience want to read on?
- Is the introduction appropriate for the rest of the draft?
- Is your focus stated clearly if you are working with a "visible" structure?
- If you are working with an "invisible" structure, is your focus clearly implied?
- Are topic sentences used effectively?
- Does each body paragraph develop a different idea?
- Should any paragraphs be combined or eliminated?
- Is your conclusion effective?

3. **Think small.** Look at your draft sentence by sentence.
- Are any sentences difficult to understand?
- Are any so long that your audience could get lost in them?
- Are sentences with blended quotations (that is, quotations that are integrated into the syntax of the sentence instead of introduced with "He said . . ." or "she said . . .") complete and easy to read?
- Are quotations shortened with ellipsis marks accurate and readable?
- Are there several choppy sentences that can be combined?
- Are any sentences vague?
- Do any sentences need to be corrected for standard English grammar and usage?
4. **Think "picky."** Look at your draft as your fussiest critic might.
- Are any words not clear or not quite right for your meaning?
- Are any words misspelled?
- Are there any punctuation errors?
- Is your format correct?
- Are the pages numbered consecutively?
- Does your paper make a good impression by being neat?
- Is there anything else you could do to improve your draft?

Proofreading

After you prepare a final draft, check again for correct grammar and punctuation. Proofread carefully for omitted words or punctuation marks. Run your spelling checker program, but be aware of its limitations. Proofread carefully for the kinds of errors the computer can't catch.

Student Essay

The following essay shows how one student responded to the assignment of arguing a position on a significant issue.

STUDENT WRITING

Teach Them, Guide Them . . .

by Monica Ericsson

In America today, there are far more cases of murder and other violent crimes committed by teenagers than ever before. While the overall crime rate has dropped, the amount of juvenile offenses have increased over the past few years. We ask ourselves: What can we do in order to stop this terrifying wave of raging teenagers? Should we punish them? Should we punish their parents? Well, since there have been few cases where punishments have actually turned a bad citizen into a good citizen, we must presume that violence cannot be treated by more violence. We must realize that these teenagers may not—and most often do not—have the luxury of a nice, stable family, good friends, and a role model to show them what is right and what is wrong. These unfortunate souls are acting to protect themselves, the way they know how. It is up to us—the more fortunate ones—to guide them, teach them, and give them a reason to believe in themselves. We should grab the problem by the root, that is, deal with young criminals after their first or second offense—not the fifth or sixth. We need to create a program to rehabilitate first to third time juvenile offenders. This program should include education, the chance to play sports, and, just as importantly, friendship.

The level of juvenile crimes in America today is alarmingly high. According to Paul J. McNulty, who in 1995 wrote the article "Natural Born Killers," even where the national rate of homicide has dropped substantially from 1985 to 1995, homicides committed by 15- to 19-year-old boys has jumped up 154% (84). The juvenile arrest rate for murder has risen 93% (84). The 1995 *FBI Uniform Crime Report* states that 2,269 of all murder offenders in 1995 were under eighteen years of age (United States 233). In addition, teenagers are involved in other violent acts: From 1985 to 1991, McNulty says, the juvenile arrest rate for violent crimes rose 96% (84). The FBI reports that in 1995, 96,292 teenagers from 15- to 19-years of age were arrested for violent crimes (United States 233).

In order to reduce these numbers, we should create a program that includes education, sports, and friendship to rehabilitate first to third time juvenile offenders in our country. To begin with, the program would include education. The juveniles will, just as in regular schools, have a schedule of classes, they will be working for a grade, and they will be required to show up on time, stay until class is over, and do homework assignments. Now, one might wonder how this could possibly work. Why would these teenagers follow all these rules when they would not in regular school? The answer is simple. By receiving more attention and positive feedback than what is possible in regular schools, they will stay motivated to study. We all feel positively about being praised for having done something good. It keeps us going. Well, these troubled teenagers are not different. They are just like you and me, only they did not have the stability they deserved, growing up. Furthermore, the program would include sports. The juveniles would get an opportunity to join, for example, a basketball team, where they can get an outlet for their energy in a positive way, enjoy themselves, and learn to interact with other teenagers without the use of violence. The program would also include building friendships between delinquents and nondelinquents, where the latter, even without any kind of education in drug-abuse or violence, will positively influence the teenagers with their lifestyles, listen to them when they need someone to talk to, and care about them.

By creating this program, we will make them believe in a positive future for themselves, hence, make them realize that committing crimes will not be a part of a successful future. According to Ed Earnest, author of *Youth Day Treatment Program Works for Alabama,* a similar program, the Community Intensive Treatment for Youth (CITY) Program of Alabama, where they focus on education, has already been in effect for over a decade, and it has shown positive results: A 16-year-old juvenile was enrolled in CITY in 1988. After eight months, he passed the GED exam. "In 1989, [he] enrolled in a state university and earned his bachelor's degree in mathematics with a 3.85 grade point average. He is [as of August 1996] working toward a second degree in engineering. In addition to these accomplishments, he has had no encounters with the law since joining the CITY program" (70–72).

Moreover, a basketball program involving 16 neighborhood teams in Washington, D.C. has kept a substantial number of teenagers off the streets, and taught them to interact with each other in a nonviolent manner, according to Avis Thomas-Lester, a staff-writer for the *Washington Post* and author of *Basketball Program on the Rebound.* Thomas-Lester quotes one of the participants who was at risk of becoming a juvenile, 17-year-old Carey Coates: "Coming to the game really helped keep me off the street" (B, 6:1). Also quoted is Inspector Winston Robinson, police commander in the 7th Police District: "It gives them a chance to meet each other and challenge each other in a team sport and not in a violent way" (B, 6:1). Officer James McNeill, also of the 7th District, is a certified referee who volunteers to keep this possible. He states that the teenagers have no problems with the prohibition of swearing, fighting or arguing with the decisions made by the referees. As a matter of fact, there are only positive attitudes toward the rule (B, 6:1).

Furthermore, research done by *Public/Private Ventures,* according to John J. Dilulio, Jr. author of *How to Defuse the Youth Crime Bomb,* reveals that "Delinquents that had friendships with nondelinquents were 46 percent less likely than a comparison group to initiate drug use, 27 percent less likely to start drinking, one third less likely to commit assaults, and half as likely to be [absent] from school" (23).

One of the most important factors that would make this proposal possible is the fact that the cost for this kind of program is much lower than the cost for a juvenile institution. According to Earnest, "The cost per person per day for the 240 CITY program slots in the eight program locations [in the state of Alabama] is $43.83, while the cost per bed per day in the juvenile institution is estimated to be more than $120" (141).

Given that the three separate approaches to deal with juvenile offenders that have been illustrated in this proposal (education, sports, and friendships) have all had positive results, there is no reason why combining them into one program should not work. We all need to understand why the young criminal offenders think the way they do. We need to get close to them, show them that we care, and make them believe in a future for themselves. By creating this program, we would plug in those empty holes of education, sports, and friendships, which is what these teenagers need to develop in the right direction. By putting this in effect at an early stage, we will teach them how to interact with other people without the use of violence. As a result, we have created a better future for these unfortunate, misguided young people—and for us, who are at the receiving end of the youth crime wave.

Works Cited

Dilulio, Jr., John J. "How to Defuse the Youth Crime Bomb." *Weekly Standard* 10 March 1997: 20–23.

Earnest, Ed. "Youth Day Treatment Program Works for Alabama." *Corrections Today* Aug. 1996: 70–73+.

McNulty, Paul J. "Natural Born Killers." *Police Review* Winter 1995: 84–87.

Thomas-Lester, Avis. "Basketball Program on the Rebound." *Washington Post* 14 June 1996: B, 6:1.

United States Department of Justice. "The FBI Uniform Crime Reports." *Crime in the United States.* Oct. 1995.

Text Credits

Chapter 2: Page 35: From *The Autobiography of Malcolm X,* by Malcolm X with the assistance of Alex Haley. Copyright © 1964 by Alex Haley and Malcolm X. Copyright © 1965 by Alex Haley and Betty Shabazz. Reprinted by permission of Random House, Inc.; page 37: Excerpt from *An American Childhood* by Annie Dillard. Copyright © 1987 by Annie Dillard. Reprinted by permission of HarperCollins Publishers, Inc.; page 39: N. Scott Momaday, "The End of My Childhood" from *Names: A Memoir*, Harper & Row, 1976. © N. Scott Momaday. Reprinted with permission of the author; page 41: "Open Admissions and the Inward I" by Peter J. Rondinone. Reprinted by permission of the author.

Chapter 3: Page 68: Excerpt from *Pizza Tiger* by Tom Monaghan with Robert Anderson, pp. 241–243, 1986, Random House. Reprinted by permission of Domino's Pizza, Inc.; page 70: "Perfecting Our Strategy" by Pauli Murray from *Song in a Weary Throat: An American Pilgrimage*. Reprinted by permission of Charlotte Sheedy Literary Agency; page 72: Reprinted by permission of Open Court Publishing Company, a division of Carus Publishing Company, Peru, IL from *Unended Quest* by Karl Popper; page 76: "Original Spin," by Lesley Dormen and Peter Edidin, *Psychology Today* July/August 1989. Reprinted with permission from Psychology Today Magazine. Copyright © 1989 (Sussex Publishers, Inc.).

Chapter 4: Page 96: Reprinted by permission of G. P. Putnam's Sons, a division of Penguin Putnam Inc. from *The Joy Luck Club* by Amy Tan. © 1989 by Amy Tan; page 109: From: *The Poetry of Robert Frost*, edited by Edward Connery Latham, © 1944 by Robert Frost. Copyright 1916, 1969 by Henry Holt & Company. Reprinted by permission of Henry Holt and Company, Inc.; page 113: Donald M. Murray, "The Maker's Eye" Revising Your Own Manuscripts." Reprinted by permission of the author; page 116: William Zinsser, "Writing with a Word Processor" excerpted from "The Act of Writing: One Man's Method" from *Writing with a Word Processor*, Harper & Row, 1983. Copyright © 1983 by William K. Zinsser. Reprinted by permission of the author; page 122: "How to Say Nothing in Five Hundred Words" from *Understanding English* by Paul Roberts. Copyright © 1958 by Paul Roberts. Reprinted by permission of Addison Wesley Educational Publishers Inc.

Chapter 5: Page 158: From *Blue Highways: A Journey into America* by William Least Heat Moon. Copyright © 1982 by William Least Heat Moon. By permission of Little, Brown and Company; page 166: "An Account of Avianca Flight 52," *The New York Times*, January 30, 1990. Copyright © 1990 by The New York Times. Reprinted by permission; page 170: "I Have a Dream," by Martin Luther King, Jr. Copyright 1963 by Martin Luther King, Jr., copyright renewed 1991 by Coretta Scott King; page 179: "Sex, Lies and Conversation," by Deborah Tannen, *The Washington Post*, June 24,

1990, copyright Deborah Tannen. Reprinted by permission. The material in this article is based in part on the author's book *You Just Don't Understand* (Ballantine, 1990); page 186: "Separation Anxiety" from *The New York Times,* January 19, 1996. Copyright © 1996 by The New York Times. Reprinted by permission; page 190: "On Racist Speech," by Charles R. Lawrence III, *The Chronicle of Higher Education,* October 25, 1989. Charles Lawrence teaches constitutional law at the Georgetown University Law Center. He is co-author of *Words That Wound: Critical Race Theory, Assaultive Speech and the First Amendment;* and *We Won't Go Back: Making The Case For Affirmative Action;* page 194: "Free Speech on the Campus," by Nat Hentoff, *The Progressive,* May 1989. Nat Hentoff—columnist for *The Washington Post* and *Village Voice.* Reprinted by permission of the author; page 204: "Equal to a Pebble" by Roberto Obregon from *Word Up!* Hope for Youth Poetry. Reprinted by permission of El Centro De La Raza, Seattle, WA.

Chapter 6: Page 214: Excerpt from *The Way to Rainy Mountain* by N. Scott Momaday, University of New Mexico Press. Copyright © 1969. Reprinted by permission of the University of New Mexico Press; page 218: "Back, But Not Home," by Maria Muniz, *The New York Times,* July 13, 1979. Copyright © 1979 by The New York Times. Reprinted by permission; page 222: "We Are Breaking the Silence About Death," by Daniel Goleman from *Psychology Today,* September 1976. Reprinted with permission from Psychology Today Magazine. Copyright © 1976 (Sussex Publishers, Inc.).

Chapter 7: Page 242: First three paragraphs on the assassination of Malcolm X, *The New York Times,* February 22, 1965. Copyright © 1965 by The New York Times. Reprinted by permission; page 242: "Death of Malcolm X," *Life,* March 5, 1965. Life Magazine/Copyright Time Inc. Reprinted with permission; page 243: Excerpt from "I Saw Malcolm Die," *New York Post,* February 22, 1965. Reprinted with permission from the *New York Post.* 1965 Copyright, NYP Holdings, Inc. Paragraph on the assassination of Malcolm X, Associated Press, February 22, 1965. Reprinted by permission of the Associated Press; page 244: Excerpt from the *Amsterdam News* February 27, 1965. Reprinted by permission of New York Amsterdam News; page 245: Accounts of Events at Tiananmen Square, 1989, *The New York Times,* June 4, 1989. Copyright © 1989 by The New York Times. Reprinted by permission; page 263: Excerpts from Anne Wilson Schaef, Women's Reality: An Emerging Female System in a White Male Society. Copyright © 1981 by Anne Wilson Schaef. Reprinted by permission of HarperCollins Publishers, Inc.; page 237 © John Jonik from cartoonbank.com. All rights reserved. page 266: From *America Revised* by Frances Fitzgerald. Copyright © 1979 by Frances Fitzgerald. By permission of Little, Brown and Company.

Chapter 8: Page 293: "Holy Water" from *The White Album* by Joan Didion. Copyright © 1979 by Joan Didion. Reprinted by permission of Farrar, Straus, & Giroux, Inc. Last stanza of "California Winter," pp. 262–3 of *Collected Poems* 1940–1978, Random House 1978. © 1964, 1987 Karl Shapiro by arrangement with Wiesner & Wiesner, Inc.; Page 298: Reprinted courtesy of *Sports Illustrated* September 18, 1995.Copyright © 1995, Time, Inc. "The Last Days of Florida Bay" by Carl Hiasson. All Rights reserved; page 299: Coastal Alert by Dwight Holing is published by Island Press, Washington, D.C. Reprinted by permission; page 302: Excerpts from *This Land* *is Your Land* by John Naar and Alex J. Naar. Copyright © 1993 by John Naar and Alex J. Naar. Illustrations copyright © 1993 by Alex J. Naar. Reprinted by permission of HarperCollins Publishers, Inc.

Chapter 9: Page 333: "Prologue" reprinted with the permission of Simon & Schuster from *Femininity* by Susan Brownmiller. Copyright © 1993 by Susan Brownmiller; page 337: Michael Norman, "Standing His Ground," *New York Times Magazine,* April 1, 1984. Copyright © 1984 by The New York Times. Reprinted by permission; page 340: Ain't I a Woman? By Sojourner Truth; page 341: Richard Cohen, " Men and Their Hidden Feelings." © 1983, Washington Post Writer's Group. Reprinted with permission; page 343: Carol Tavris, "How Friendship was 'Feminized,'" *The New York Times*, May 28, 1997. Copyright © 1997 by the New York Times. Reprinted with permission; page 350: *Ways of Being Religious: Readings for a New Approach to Religion* by Streng, Frederick J., © 1973. Reprinted by permission of Prentice-Hall, Inc. Upper Saddle River, NJ; page 355: Jo Goodwin Parker, "What is Poverty?" from *America's Other Children*, George Henderson, ed., 1971, University of Oklahoma Press. Reprinted by permission.

Chapter 10: Page 374: "Brother, Don't Spare a Dime", *Newsweek,* by Christopher Awalt, October 21, 1991. page 376: From *Rachel and Her Children* by Jonathan Kozol. Copyright © 1988 by Jonathan Kozol. Reprinted by permission of Crown Publishers, Inc; page 385: Is the Earth Round or Flat? by Alvin Lightman; page 391: Life According to TV by Harry Walters, from *Newsweek*, December 6, 1982, Newsweek, Inc. All rights reserved. Reprinted by permission; page 396: "False Truth and the Future of the World" reprinted with the permission of Simon & Schuster from *Tainted Truth* by Cynthia Crossen. Copyright © 1994 by Cynthia Crossen; page 412: "Evolution as Fact and Theory" by Stephen Jay Gould, *Discover* magazine, 1981. Reprinted by permission of the author.

Chapter 11: Page 452: Young Hate by David Shenk. David Shenk (dshenk@bigfoot.com) is a writer living in Brooklyn. This article originally appeared in the February 1990 issue of CV MAGAZINE; page 459: "When Is It Rape?" by Nancy Gibbs from *Time*, June 3, 1991. © 1991 Time Inc. Reprinted by permission.

Chapter 12: Page 487: From *Homage to Daniel Shays* by Gore Vidal. Copyright © 1970 by Gore Vidal. Reprinted by permission of Random House, Inc.; page 488: "The Case for Slavery," by A.M. Rosenthal, *The New York Times*, September 26, 1989. Copyright © 1989 by The New York Times. Reprinted by permission; page 495: "For a National Effort to Develop a Vaccine to Counteract Aids, " by Robert E. Pollack, *The New York Times*, November 27, 1985 by The New York Times. Reprinted by permission; page 497: Charles Krauthammer, "Why an Aids Vaccine?" *The Washington Post*, May 30, © 1997, Washington Post Writers Group. Reprinted by permission.

Illustration Credits

Pages 14, 24, 61, 93, 157, 209, 273, 287, 389, 442, 523 : Illustrations by Warren Gebert.

INDEX